17 9a

AUTOMATIC DATA-PROCESSING SYSTEMS

Principles and Procedures

AUTOMATIC
DATA-PROCESSING
SYSTEMS

Principles and Procedures

ROBERT H. GREGORY

RICHARD L. VAN HORN

WADSWORTH PUBLISHING COMPANY, INC.
SAN FRANCISCO

In 1956 the Army Ordnance Corps initiated an automatic data-processing systems (ADPS) career program for education of top management, training in needed skills, and career development. One urgent requirement in this program was a comprehensive textbook; to fill that need, this ADPS textbook was developed and written under contract with the Massachusetts Institute of Technology.

Automatic Data-Processing Systems: Principles and Procedures deals with business-data processing. It is introductory, requiring no previous knowledge of electronic computing systems. Computer programming and systems analysis are covered in detail. More important, a blending of theoretical and practical approaches to data processing explains *why*, as well as *what*, and *how*. Some new concepts in management information are developed, and management tools and techniques are included.

The Ordnance Corps pioneered in the development of electronic computers and sponsored the first high-speed electronic digital computer. The ENIAC—Electronic Numerical Integrator and Calculator—was designed and constructed at the University of Pennsylvania for the Ballistics Research Laboratories, Aberdeen Proving Ground, and was installed in 1947. Within twelve years there were more than six thousand electronic computers in use for business, engineering, and scientific purposes.

In technology as in pure science, the practical and effective use of new discoveries always lags behind the discoveries themselves. As this text makes clear, the amazing ability of electronic computers has not yet made business management a "push-button" process, nor will it do so in the near future. The successful application of automatic data-processing systems to business problems will continue to require imaginative and analytical thinkers at all levels—operating, programming, systems analysis and design, and management. Only human brain power can control the capacity of these systems to produce information; and unless that control is effective, management runs the risk of becoming lost in a morass of detail.

PREFACE

At the heart of this book is a distinction between data and information: data are the raw material from which management must distill information. The concept is simple, but the problems of putting it to work are often complex. Information must be defined and measured before a system can be designed which will automatically increase the information content of reports. And in designing such a system, technical virtuosity is not enough to insure its success; economic factors are crucial in the long run. The cost of getting more accurate processing must be compared to the value of having the improved information it can produce.

This book is intended for readers with various interests, and it can be used in several ways. The detailed summaries following each chapter are probably the best quick guide to individual chapter coverage.

Those who may be beginning their training in systems analysis will profit most by reading all the chapters in sequence.

Readers familiar with equipment and programming can profitably begin with Part Four (Principles of Processing Systems).

Management personnel might well begin with Parts Six (Equipment Acquisition and Utilization), Four, and Five (Systems Design), in that order; these sections provide sufficient information for making informed decisions on proposed applications, equipment selection, and systems design.

Systems analysts experienced in other processing methods may want to start with Part Four; they may then find the earlier sections on equipment and processing more useful. Parts Five and Six are especially appropriate for analysts because they deal with the effect of new processing techniques on systems analysis.

At least one of the three appendices should be of interest to most readers. Appendix I is a brief history of earlier methods of processing data—calculating devices, typewriters, punched-card machines, and computers; it can help place current developments in a proper perspective. Appendix II contains questions and problems (graduated according to difficulty) designed to emphasize certain points in the chapters and to encourage methodical thinking about data-processing problems. Appendix III is a glossary of terms common to the field of electronic data processing; it includes all terms given a new meaning in this book.

Andrew J. Allott, Director, Electronic Computing Systems, Office, Chief of Ordnance, framed the idea of this text for Ordnance Corps educational purposes. Francis C. Crotty, Chief, Civilian Training, Office of Manpower, furnished guidance on training and policy and offered comments and suggestions. Howard C. Holland, Assistant Chief, Data Processing Systems Branch, Ordnance Comptroller, as Technical Project Officer, assisted in organization of the material for systems analysis and management studies. He also served as our unflagging mentor and friendly critic.

Dr. C. V. L. Smith, Martin H. Weik, Michael Romanelli, and George W. Reitwiesner of Ballistics Research Laboratories, Aberdeen Proving Ground, Maryland, made valuable suggestions for correction and improvement. Ernest Casale and others at Frankford Arsenal, Pennsylvania, contributed material on equipment components, characteristics, and operation.

Several people at the Massachusetts Institute of Technology participated in the writing of this book, and we are happy to acknowledge their contributions to it. David W. Dailey selected and edited entries for the glossary. J. Craig Molsberry and Michael J. Erdei formulated the two chapters on programming. Howard Krasnow wrote the chapter on available equipment and Herbert Bryer (of Sylvania Electric Products, Inc.) updated it. Bruce MacDonald covered equipment components and sorting, and Harvey Wagner (now of Stanford University) made valuable suggestions about the content of Chapters 10 and 18.

Finally, we are indebted to Mrs. Martha Thompson, who cheerfully typed innumerable versions and revisions of the manuscript.

CONTENTS

PART ONE

ORIENTATION

CHAPTER ONE

INTRODUCTION

Substantial changes in business activity during recent years have encouraged the creation of new data-processing systems. Conversely, changes in data-processing equipment and methods are suggesting new methods of doing business. Electronic data processing, operations research, and other new scientific and engineering developments are fast becoming a part of common business practice. And it is probable that data-processing and management-control methods will change more rapidly during the next ten years than they did in the 1950's.

This progress will not make manual data processing and conventional control techniques obsolete; but it will make knowledge of automatic data processing invaluable for business managers, data-processing personnel, and systems and procedures analysts. All people who rely on facts for performing or managing business operations—people who need facts for answering questions and making reports—have a vital interest in the origination and processing of data.

Attention is focused in this book on data processing for business applications; namely, finance, accounting, inventory control, production control, and personnel. Scientific and engineering computing are not covered. This chapter is a brief and general introduction to data processing. It tells why and how data are processed, describes processing facilities, explains and illustrates the application of an automatic data-processing system, and cites managerial implications of newer methods for dealing with data. Your attention is called to Appendix I, which gives a brief history of equipment—calculators, typewriters, punched cards, and electronic computers—that preceded automatic data processors, in order to give some perspective to our understanding of recent developments (Chapin, 1957).* This chapter, as an introduction, is not complete and self-contained; many passing references in it will be amplified later.

---

*Annotated references, included at the end of each chapter, are referred to within the text by author or title and year of publication.

WHY DATA ARE PROCESSED

Data about business events are gathered, stored, processed, and reported for various reasons. Some of the more important reasons are these: to keep detailed facts about individual transactions; to produce routine operating documents, such as pay-checks and purchase orders; to summarize masses of facts into useful, informative reports, such as reports on sales in given areas and on costs of production; and to make analyses of business problems, such as finding locations for factories and warehouses which will give minimum transportation costs.

Data Availability

Facts are the raw material of data processing. The facts that are initially obtained may be restricted to the minimum facts required immediately. Frequently, supplemental facts are obtained at first in an attempt to meet probable or possible demands for facts at a later date.

Often it is necessary to postpone solution of a problem until the specific facts required are obtained. An efficient scheme for obtaining facts depends on balancing the cost of having facts available—either too many or too few—against the benefits that can be derived from having the necessary facts when they are wanted. The point is that it is probably impossible to obtain just the right set of facts about events "today." Your choices are to try to reconstruct facts about yesterday or to wait for "tomorrow" in order to gather the necessary facts about events as they occur.

Document Production

The preparation of readable documents is an important phase of data processing. Documents are still a common means of communication between most companies, and they are widely used within companies that have manual data-processing systems. Much effort, often called "paper work simplification," goes into improving document standardization, preparation, and flow, partly because the handling of documents can be improved without making radical changes in either equipment or organization.

It is usually taken for granted, where data collection is done by people and the output from processing goes to people, that readable documents are required. The need for documents that are readable by people is reduced, or even eliminated, when equipment is used for gathering and processing data. The output of machines at one stage—whether punched tape, cards, or machine-readable printed characters—can be used as input at the next stage of processing, in either the same or a different company. The use of readable documents is sometimes restricted to small-volume operations where mechanization at the next stage is not feasible. Among the readable documents that will continue to be used for many years are bills to customers and reports to managers.

Management Information

An important reason for developing elaborate schemes for processing data is to supply company management with the critical facts needed to control operations. The word "data" might be used to cover all the facts that are obtained. Another word, such as "information," is needed to cover the particular facts that management wants to know.

Although information is derived from data, information has some qualities that can serve as a guide in processing data. A manager in a company is interested in securing facts about operations for which he is responsible. He wants these facts to be accurate, of recent origin, and related to problems he can solve by his decisions. Further, a manager is more interested in learning about unpredictable rather than predictable developments. He has no need to be told repeatedly something he already knows. Thus, the idea follows that information should have an element of newness or novelty about it; it should deal with the unexpected.

Some examples will help distinguish "data" from "information." Newspapers are bought for information; one who already knows the paper's contents, either because so little is happening or because editions are published too frequently, will not buy it. The Loch Ness monster is said to be a summertime phenomenon created to stimulate interest in Scottish newspapers. Reporting unexpected or little-known facts, such as the costs of jobs that exceed a standard, is an example of selecting and emphasizing items to increase the readers' attention. The facts that are on standard may be included for completeness or omitted for brevity, according to the readers' interests.

The difference between a mass of facts and a few critical facts is illustrated by the plight of a business man who furnished 1,350 pounds of records to a tax collector. He was brought to court by the collector, who wanted five additional books, weighing only 10 or 20 pounds, that he considered critical. Every day business men are given pounds of reports when they want only a few critical facts. Managers do not really care about source reports, documents, and data, although these are useful elsewhere in the organization.

The nature of information can be described, but it is difficult to measure information itself as a quantity. Whether a new system will produce better information than the old system did is difficult to determine, even after the new system is introduced. Information production (as opposed to routine data processing) and the related areas of management control, including automatic decision making, are challenging and profitable areas of study.

HOW DATA ARE PROCESSED

The basic functions of processing data are not new. People responsible for operating any enterprise—business, government, or otherwise—have long processed data to obtain facts about operations and information for their control.

The basic operations involved in processing data with any kind of facilities are these: to originate data; to manipulate, according to some plan, the new data and files prepared in an earlier cycle; and to report results. These three operations include elements related as follows:

1. Obtaining new data inputs to the system.
2. Manipulating data according to a prescribed plan. This requires:
    (a) a storage unit to hold data and processing instructions.
    (b) an operating unit to perform arithmetical and logical operations.
    (c) a control unit to manage operations.
3. Producing output documents, reports, or instructions for action.

Origination of Data

The origination of data includes the three stages—collection, conversion, and verification—required to get facts into a form suitable for processing.

Data Collection. "Data collection" captures facts when they are available; they may be processed later, when needed. For example, the time an employee starts or stops work on a particular job may be recorded in writing by a timekeeper, stamped in numerals by a time clock, or punched into a card. A storekeeper identifies and counts any material received in the stock room in order to prepare a receiving report. Requisitions for material, on the other hand, specify the desired quantity and serve as the original record of the transactions by which such quantities are issued. Employees of utility companies indicate customer meter readings by marking cards which are later run through equipment that "senses" the marks and punches them.

Data collection often starts with the manual operation of keyboards that punch cards or paper tape or that record on magnetic tape. New input data may be only a small part of the total data handled at each cycle; the inventory file, for example, is used repeatedly to introduce necessary changes for receipts, issues, and price changes, as well as to introduce and delete items. Data already in files are much easier to handle than new data, because "master" cards or tapes may be selectively duplicated for use as new input data. The date, batch number or transaction serial number, and fixed data can be entered automatically during the data collection operation.

Several devices recently developed for business use are capable of automatically collecting data in machine-processable form. One class of automatic devices yields data in a machine-processable form that is not readable by people. Examples of such devices are point-of-sale recorders, transaction recorders, and time clocks that punch tape or cards. Another class of automatic data collection devices produces numerals and letters on paper or cards in a form readable by both machines and people. Character-reading machines "read" the characters and convert them to a form suitable for automatic processing. Great improvements have been made in character-recognition equipment in recent years; some equipment is now capable of reading even handprinted numerals and letters.

The manual operations of reading and writing, typing, or key punching are widely used for data collection. Other important techniques are pre-preparation of constant data, by-product preparation as part of other operations, and duplication from card, plastic, or metal plates. A simple time clock records the basic facts for a transaction; a more complex clock might record all the facts—worker, time, job involved, and units produced—and thereby deserve the name, "automatic transaction recorder."

Data Conversion. The medium that is most efficient for the original collection of data—paper, cards, tape—must often be converted to a different medium for further use. Some companies, for example, initially record inventory counts on audio tape recorders; conversion is thus required for further processing. People are able to work with oral, handwritten, or typed data; but equipment usually requires that data be recorded in a carefully prescribed form. Data from handwritten documents may be manually punched into cards or tape or written on magnetic tape for input to automatic processors. In some cases, punched tape or cards are prepared manually and then converted automatically to magnetic tape for input.

Machines are used to read typed, printed, or even handwritten characters and to convert them to a form suitable for machine processing. Enough research has been done to indicate the feasibility of audio-recognition devices for automatically converting the spoken word into a form suitable for further processing.

The form in which data are originally captured and the nature of subsequent conversion depend on several things: the volume of data involved, the number of points of origination, the permissible financial investment at each point of origination, transmission requirements, conversion costs, and the most efficient form for use in subsequent stages. Large volumes of data originating at a few points warrant large investments in elaborate collection and conversion facilities.

Data Verification. Data are verified to obtain a desired degree of accuracy. The standard "a desired degree" does not imply perfection. Some inaccuracies, a slight misspelling of a name, for example, are trivial; but other inaccuracies, say, crediting the wrong customer for a collection on account, may be intolerable. Verification includes checking data to determine whether they are complete, plausible, and acceptable.

In general, a complete transaction involves four elements: (1) parties to the transaction (one of which is the firm itself), (2) identification of what is involved, (3) quantity involved, and (4) the date of the transaction. A receipt of material, for example, involves identification of the vendor and receiving clerk, description or stock number of the item, the number of units, and the time received. A receiving report that omits any of these is incomplete—a fact that can be verified immediately after origination.

Implausible mistakes are those serious enough to halt processing until they are corrected; although they may be set aside so that other operations can continue. An alphabetic character in a numerical statement of an amount is an implausible mistake because it defies further processing: an alphabetic quantity cannot be multiplied by unit price to find value.

A mistake that is plausible, as an incorrect numeral in numerical expressions of quantity, will not prevent further processing; but it will be unacceptable because all further calculations based on it will be inaccurate. An example of this type of mistake would be the reporting of 180 hours worked by an employee in one week. This figure is obviously incorrect; it is plausible because the quantity 180 consists of numerals only and could be multiplied by the wage rate, but unacceptable because the result is certain to be incorrect.

A mistake that is plausible but probably intolerable arises when the data, though processable, are outside of normal range. It is logically possible, for example, that an employee could work 80 hours in a week, but it is improbable even with a two-shift operation. Processing may be continued and the data flagged or noted to be verified subsequently.

To summarize: the point at which input data are verified and the method of verification depend upon what other facts are needed to detect a mistake and on the consequences of not correcting it at the earliest possible stage.

Manipulation of Data

Manipulation includes the operations of rearranging and processing data, with the word "processing" narrowly defined.

Rearranging. The rearrangement of data involves changing the sequence and introducing or extracting items without affecting their content through computations. The need for rearrangement of data arises in several ways. Data may be initially mixed or jumbled, as when two or more kinds of transactions originate together but may require separate handling thereafter. Data about, say, payroll, inventory, and sales, received over a wire circuit, are usually classified or sorted by type because processing procedures and files are designed to cope with one class of transactions at a time. The task of sorting transactions by type is minimized by specializing the organizational arrangement so that only one or a limited number of types of transactions originate together. Such specialization also facilitates enforcing control over who can originate certain kinds of transactions, such as issuing material, authorizing payment of bills, or inquiring about the contents of restricted files.

2 A second kind of rearrangement of data arises when each type of transaction is used to produce several outputs. Depending upon the kind of output desired and the file arrangement, the transactions may have to be arranged in different sequences for efficient processing. Consider the steps involved in processing orders received from customers. Orders are the basis for sales analysis, customer accounting, inventory and production control, and salesmen's compensation. Data on sales might be summarized by geographical area or by product class without sorting into any sequence. If efficient processing methods require that the customer or inventory file be kept in a certain order, then transactions are sorted into that sequence before updating a particular file. Sorting into a new sequence may be required before the transactions can be processed against another file organized in a different sequence. Two sets of sorted data already in the same sequence may be merged to obtain one over-all sequence most efficiently. For example, inventory transactions for the first four days in a week can be sorted into sequence according to stock identification number, and transactions for the fifth day can be sorted separately. Merging the two sequences into one reduces the work load after the end of the week and gets results sooner.

Closely related to the need for arranging transactions in the same sequence as the file before processing them is the problem of keeping the file itself in a specified sequence and eliminating inactive records. File maintenance for customers' accounts, for instance, may involve inserting records for new customers in alphabetic sequence and deleting inactive records. Files kept on magnetic tape are often arranged in alphabetic or numerical sequence and are most efficiently processed in the same sequence.

Random-access equipment is designed to handle transactions without regard for file or transaction sequence. In such a case, a file containing records arranged in one sequence and transactions in a different, perhaps a random sequence may be processed together satisfactorily. If facilities are available for random-sequence processing, then changes introduced into the file need not be in any particular sequence and rearrangement of the whole file could be avoided. In cases where random-sequence processing cannot handle occasional items, these items can be processed with new input—in which case the carry-over items and new transactions may be arranged in the same sequence for more efficient processing.

③ A third example of rearrangement occurs when the elements of data in an item are in one sequence but are wanted in a different sequence. Rearrangement within an item may be handled during either the input conversion or the output printing operation.

Processing.   The term "data processing" encompasses the whole range of operations from input of data to output of results. The word "processing" alone is usually restricted to those operations not included in data origination, rearrangement, and output. Processing thus involves the following kinds of operations: updating files for inventory receipts and issues; computing gross and net pay; making decisions based on quantitative criteria, such as allowing a customer further credit if the amount and age of his balance are within credit limits; estimating sales based on predictions of market behavior, advertising expenditure, and economic forecasts; converting sales estimates into material requirements, labor estimates, and production schedules; summarizing numerous individual transactions into a few numbers; recognizing and dealing with exceptional cases; looking up table values, such as prices or discounts applicable for various quantities; and compiling and recording desired output.

Ancillary to these processing operations are some others used to insure accurate results: verifying data by comparison with facts already in files; controlling input data to guard against losing a valid transaction or introducing a spurious transaction; checking arithmetical accuracy by repeating operations or by performing them in parallel through separate channels, as in having two bookkeepers in a bank post the same depositor's account on separate machines to reduce the risk of inaccurate results; and determining that prescribed procedures are actually used. When precautions to insure accuracy are required to facilitate processing, they are incorporated in the main stream of processing. On the other hand, some precautionary measures are used primarily to keep interested parties—management and auditors—informed; such measures are used in addition to, rather than included in, the main stream of processing.

Some operations are often considered non-productive because they merely facilitate performance of operations that are directly related to the desired output. This classification corresponds to the indirect-direct labor classification in factory operations. Actually, all essential operations are productive because work done at one stage facilitates work at another. Consider the consequences resulting at a later stage because of plausible but unacceptable mistakes in data collection. An issue of materials charged against an incorrect number may later cause the creation of a new account with a negative balance, go to the wrong account, be set aside for investigation, or halt processing until the mistake is corrected. Verifying identification numbers against a master list at an early stage of processing may improve overall efficiency. Keeping file maintenance (insertion and deletion of records) separate from file processing (updating records in the file) may be more efficient than trying to do both at one time.

Output

Output preparation follows the origination and manipulation of data. Processed results are seldom in precisely the form desired, so it is often necessary to select what is wanted and to present it in acceptable form. Job manufacturing costs are examples of output reports on what has happened. A manufacturing schedule is a forecast of what is supposed to happen. A simple example of an action document is a bill for a customer to pay. The content, frequency, and format of output are determined jointly by the people who use the output and those responsible for processing it.

Methods of output preparation depend on whether demands are scheduled over a period of time, the length of time available for meeting the demands, and the ability to forecast what will be demanded. Some examples will show how these factors bear on output preparation. It would be simple to prepare an annual report of fixed assets within one month after the end of the year if the assets are classified by number of years owned (less than one year, one to five years, and so forth). If the data about fixed assets are available and activity was low during the year, there would be ample opportunity to plan procedures, and the permissible one-month delay in processing would allow fairly smooth scheduling of work.

Output preparation would be more difficult, however, in cases where the number of transactions is high and the reporting interval and permissible delay in processing are short. Buyers (merchandise managers) in a department store might want weekly reports of receipts, sales, and inventory for each item by the following Monday afternoon. This demand would put heavy loads on the system, but the work of output preparation would be several times greater if buyers wanted daily reports at 10 a.m. every morning. Entirely different file-processing methods might be required, however, if buyers wanted up-to-the-minute reports of sales activity or an inventory about any one item. Furnishing quick answers to questions about current status involves continual updating of files and complex interrogation equipment.

Outputs not anticipated in advance may pose extremely difficult problems; novel output requirements involve new output-preparation methods, and they are likely to require new processing techniques to get desired results. Still worse, unexpected output requirements may demand the use of data that are not readily available, if at all. Or data may be available in a raw form that is not economically feasible to process. An equally perplexing situation may result from an immediate need for data which, although once collected, have been discarded. In some cases, it may be possible to reconstruct data, but in others it is necessary to start afresh. For a simple example, an oil company may ask, "Do service stations on the right-hand side of a street leading out from the center of town sell more gasoline than those on the left?" Answering this may require obtaining, for the first time, data about station location to be used in conjunction with sales data already available. The question, "Do left-handed employees sell more than right-handed ones?" may not be answerable either because data are not available or because the turnover of employees makes it impossible to reconstruct the data. It is impossible to answer this disarmingly simple question until enough time elapses to permit gathering new data. Often, even incomplete statistics cannot be reconstructed, so that unanticipated questions pertaining to the past are not answerable. The most open-ended output requirement, and probably the most difficult to deal with, springs from the question: "Look, we have these kinds of facts on file; what types of useful reports can we prepare from them?"

In summary, data processing involves (1) collecting data for new transactions; (2) manipulating new inputs and data already in files according to prescribed plans; and (3) producing output documents, reports, and instructions for various purposes.

PROCESSING FACILITIES

In order to reduce the "how" of processing data from general to concrete terms, it is necessary to consider the facilities that are used. The facilities must be capable of receiving input data, manipulating data according to some plan, and producing output. Manipulation, which is a critical element, demands facilities capable of (a) controlling operations to follow the prescribed plan, (b) storing data and processing instructions, and (c) performing arithmetical and logical operations. Many kinds of facilities are used to process data; in the broadest sense, they range from people working without benefit of equipment to equipment operating with little aid from people.

People

Mechanistically considered, a human being was the earliest form of data processor. A person receives input data chiefly by seeing or hearing them and stores them in his brain, which also serves as an operating and control unit. Outputs are oral or written reports and various physical actions.

A human being is a remarkable data processor because he operates with an internally stored program. That is to say, the brain contains instructions and data, controls the execution of instructions, and modifies them to suit the situation. Consider the simple problem of computing inventory value from the following facts:

Quantity	Price	Amount
32	1.30	
67,000	.40 per C	
1.480	—	
BCDA	9.23	

An experienced clerk or a calculator operator has enough instructions in his head, or in equipment operating booklets or company manuals, to find computing procedures. An answer of $41.60 for the first item seems correct, although the money unit is not stated. The "per C" in the second item probably means "per hundred," and raises the question whether quantity and price are in comparable or different units, for by one interpretation the amount is $268.00 and by the other, $26,800. The third item raises two questions: Is 1.480 actually 1.480 or a mistake in writing 1,480? Where can the price for the third item be obtained? The fourth item poses the problem of multiplying BCDA, which might mean 2341, or some other quantity in code, by 9.23; this is so absurd that the clerk may stop and appeal for clarification. What appears at first to be a simple problem—to multiply quantity by price to get amount of inventory value—turns out to be quite intricate on close examination.

The human mind can perform, or at least control, the performance of many different operations: starting work, getting instructions and data, adding, subtracting, multiplying, dividing, remembering results, moving or "indexing" from one set of data to the next, comparing two items and modifying instructions to follow a different path depending upon the outcome of the comparison, putting out results, and, of course, stopping when completed. The ability to select the subsequent processing path dependent upon the outcome at any stage is invaluable for modifying operations as they are being performed. In calculating gross-to-net pay, the rule for making deductions may be to stop if net pay falls below a certain amount, say, $15.00. A person computing pay would unconsciously apply this rule if gross pay appeared large enough to cover all possible deductions. More care would be exercised and deductions would be applied one at a time, if net pay approached this criterion. Any remaining deductions would be skipped for that employee, but the original procedure would, of course, be applied for calculating the next employee's net pay.

The human mind is a very adaptable processor, but it is sometimes unreliable. The mind is slow in performing arithmetical operations and erratic in applying logical rules. Where judgment is required, people are indispensable because some operations of data processing and decision making are inseparable. Even the most elaborate data-processing systems, as will be shown later, require people to make decisions at some stages because of the extreme difficulty of planning to handle every eventuality. A person unaided by other facilities is an efficient processor for small, relatively simple situations and is a vital element of every data-processing system.

Oral communication is widely used when no documentary record is required. It is not always desirable because of the noise in transmission and the requirement that both speaker and listener must be available and functioning on-line in order to communicate.

Records

Records were the earliest aid developed for processing data. Consisting first of pictures and marks, writing now relies on "alphabets" of letters and numerals. Business alphabets consist of ten numerals, twenty-six letters, and other symbols, called "alphanumerals," that allow compact storage of huge quantities of facts. The alphabets are often represented as A through Z; 0 through 9; #, ., &, /, $; and, perhaps, a through z. Characters are also represented by punched holes in cards or paper tape and by positive and negative charges in magnetizable material. The familiar shape of A, B, C and so on is often altered in favor of other schemes that are more efficient for processing purposes, although not readily usable by people.

Records, viewed in the broadest sense, increase tremendously the size and reliability of data storage, which would otherwise be restricted to what people can remember. Schemes for representing characters also provide a simple way to transmit data. People remain responsible for data input, control, and output, unless aided by other processing facilities.

Limited-purpose Office Machines

The development of modern calculating devices in the seventeenth century and of the typewriter in the nineteenth provided important aids for calculating and recording.

Calculating machines perform simple arithmetical operations quickly and accurately and some of them print results on paper. Since people are slow and inaccurate at arithmetical operations, the invention and improvement of calculating devices to add, subtract, multiply, and divide was an important step forward.

Manual writing speeds, sometimes as slow as ten words a minute, were increased to sixty words a minute by the typewriter. More important, legibility was improved and the preparation of multiple copies with carbon paper and duplicating devices became possible.

The functions of the calculator and the typewriter were combined to create bookkeeping and accounting machines, which have control bars to aid the operator in performing such multiple operations as preparing statements, ledgers, and journals. It is interesting to note in passing that an accounting machine intended for business purposes was used without modification in 1931 to compute nautical tables by the difference method (described in the history of computing in Appendix I). The use of an accounting machine as a "difference engine" for scientific calculations exemplifies the fact that users often apply machines to problems not foreseen by the designers.

Limited-purpose office machines electrically powered for punching and reading paper tape are widely used to reduce data to a mechanically processable form and may do so as a by-product of other operations. Electric typewriters are used to print limited volumes of reports.

Punched-card Machines

The basic operations of punched-card machines are punching, sorting, calculating, and printing. Early versions of punched-card machines required manual effort in punching data in cards, handling cards individually during the sorting operation, and counting the sorted cards. Since 1890 machines have become more automatic, so that less manual effort is required to originate data, sort cards, make calculations, and copy results from tabulators. People handle cards in bulk and start, feed, tend, and stop machines. Present-day punched-card machines and electronic calculators, with people handling cards between stages, can receive punched input data, perform about a dozen different arithmetical and logical operations at the rate of 15,000 a minute, and produce printed reports or punched cards for further processing. The substitution of punched-card for manual processing may lead to important changes in procedures (Spinning, 1953).

Electronic Digital Computers

The most recent development in data-processing facilities is the electronic digital computer. The unique feature of an electronic computer, also called an "internally stored program computer," is the fact that operating instructions are stored in the same way and the same place as the data that are to be processed. Instructions stored in the computer memory can be manipulated exactly as if they were data. The capacity to change instructions as operations are being executed increases the applicability of instructions to a wide, although not unlimited, variety of situations that arise in processing.

Electronic digital computers have been designed to execute a variety of instructions, both arithmetical and logical, ranging in number from about a dozen to two hundred at speeds of a few hundred to a hundred thousand operations a second. High-speed execution of instructions is an important feature of electronic computers. For example, a company that spent 3 man-months calculating the critical shaft speed for a steam generator found that the same problem could be solved in 40 hours with punched-card machines, in 1 hour on an early model electronic computer, in 15 minutes on a later version, and in 15 seconds on a still newer model computer. The ratio of computer to manual time needed to solve the problem was 1:115,000.

Automatic Data-processing Systems

An automatic data-processing system performs standard data-handling operations with minimum manual help. Its chief feature is that it increases the ratio of equipment to labor used in processing data; but it is not entirely automatic (Montalbano, 1956).

The equipment used in an automatic system includes an electronic digital computer with appropriate peripheral equipment for data collection, conversion, input, and output. High-speed computing requires comparable speeds for input and output to achieve efficiently balanced operations.

An automatic data-processing system consists of the following components:

1. An electronic data processor—digital computer.
2. Peripheral equipment associated with the computer, such as data-preparation devices, input and output devices, and sorting devices.
3. Procedures that tell what data are needed and when, how obtained, and how used.
4. Instruction routines for the computer to follow.
5. Personnel to operate and maintain equipment, analyze and set up procedures, prepare instructions, provide input data, utilize reports, review results, and supervise the entire operation.

The data processor is a critical part of an automatic data-processing system. Use of an automatic processor permits important changes in methods of processing data.

An automatic system consisting of suitable equipment and supporting personnel can:

1. Bring specially prepared data into the storage element.

2. Perform a required sequence of operations on the data:
    (a) logical—sorting, file maintenance, file reference, file search.
    (b) arithmetical—addition, subtraction, multiplication, division.
3. Make decisions to perform appropriate operations as dictated by changes in the data or intermediate results.
4. Issue complete or selective reports after completing processing operations.

The alphabet for data, files, and reports for business is alpha-numerical, that is, it includes both alphabetic and numerical characters. Large volumes of data are processed in conjunction with files to update the files and produce documents and reports. File contents are analyzed to find relationships and searched to answer simple inquiries. Business-data processing involves repetitive cycles and tight time schedules for producing results that are intimately related to company operations (Martin, 1954).

Scientific and engineering computation generally deals with numerals only. Small volumes of data, which may be drawn from the business file or from facts about current operations, are intensively processed to answer specific questions, to prepare tables, or to control processes. The distinction between business and engineering computations is not radical, and the use of equipment for one purpose may justify its use for the other.

Comparison of Automatic and Punched-card Facilities

A brief comparison of some features of automatic and punched-card facilities is useful since they are often competitors for business use. The capabilities of punched-card and automatic data processors are compared in Table 1-1.

Automatic processing has an interesting and little-noticed feature. It is, in some ways, more similar to manual than to punched-card methods. Both people and automatic equipment use lengthy, involved operating routines to select and deal with desired items picked from a large number of items. Instruction routines are repeated, modified, or discontinued as required by the facts of a situation or by the intermediate results computed during processing.

Troublesome Aspects

Two aspects, preparation of input data and use of output, have caused difficulty in the past and appear more deficient when automatic processing methods are used. Input data need to be in a suitable form and sufficiently accurate for efficient processing. The most common medium is paper containing handwritten or typed data. Collecting data on paper documents appears, at first glance, to be economical because

TABLE 1-1. *Comparison of Punched-card and Automatic Data-processor Equipment*

Character-istics	Punched-card Processor	Automatic Data Processor
Bulk stor-age of data	Stores data on punched cards	Stores data on magnetic tape drums or disks
Manual handling of data after pre-paration	Requires people to handle cards fre-quently—at each minor and major stage in processing	Requires people to handle magnetic tape at major stages of process-ing only
Data input and output rate	Handles 100 to 1,000 cards a minute for a maximum rate of 1,300 characters a second	Handles input and out-put at rates of 10,000 to 100,000 and more charac-ters a second
Computation speed	Performs a few opera-tions a second	Performs thousands of arithmetical and logical operations a second
Number of operations on each pass of data	Performs one or a few operations	Performs a long sequence of operations
Access to data for computa-tions	At any one time can refer to data on one or a few cards	Can select one item of data out of hundreds or thousands
Versatility	Follows a limited preset pattern of operations on each pass of data	Changes pattern of op-erations, within broad limits, depending on data received or results pro-duced

anyone can do the work and little equipment is required, so that data can be gathered on the spot. Actually, it is difficult to instruct pro-perly all the people involved and furnish suitable working conditions. Paper documents have the deficiency that the data on them need to be converted to a machine-processable medium—punched tape, punched cards or magnetic tape—for efficient processing in the next stage. Some types of manually prepared media—marks in certain locations and even carefully written characters—can be converted automatically to machine-processable form, although this is being done only on a limited scale at present.

Data need to be accurate enough to meet the standards of accuracy imposed by output requirements. It is also important that input data be accurate enough to be processed economically, considering the methods and equipment that are used. An example will help clarify these points about accuracy and economical processing. An important problem in magazine publishing is subscription fulfillment. A subscriber, Howard R. Jones, 420 Spring Ave., Austin, Minn., may try to renew his subscription by sending money and one of the following facts about himself:

1. Howard R. Jones, 420 Spring Ave., Austin, Minn.
2. Jones Howard, 420 Spring Ave., Austin. Mi.
3. H. R. Jones, 420C Spring Ave., Austin
4. H. R. Jones
5. Nothing to identify himself

Discrepancies may exist in inversion, transposition, abbreviation, omission or addition; in fact, ten per cent or so of the renewals received by a magazine publisher have one or more discrepancies.

Input data corresponding exactly to the file are most economically processable by any method. The second type of input data—names reversed and state abbreviated more than typically—causes some difficulty because it is necessary to decide, by looking at either the renewal application or the record in the file, whether Jones or Howard is the surname and whether "Mi." corresponds to "Minn." In the third case the letter "C" may designate an apartment not previously indicated in the file record, but omission of the state may cause some difficulty in deciding which of six cities named "Austin" in the United States was intended. The fourth case is more difficult to process because it may be necessary to search the file for all H. R. Joneses as well as Joneses whose names might have the initials "H. R.," and try to isolate one. A search of this type is difficult to perform with any data-processing system where only a few items in the file are available for examination at one time. The fifth case is not processable by any system using either manual, automatic, or other techniques; in time, Jones will probably complain and properly identify himself.

Clerks preparing input data make mistakes too—"H. R. Jones" may become "H. R. James" in the manual input operation.

Systems built around manual operations create mistakes but, somehow, seem to keep functioning. Automatic equipment is likely to have more difficulty dealing with erroneous input data. Data are rejected and processing operations hang up. However, some ingenious processing schemes have been developed to have the data processor edit the data and do a better job of file searching than people ordinarily do. For example, a name can be searched against several variations of the name—with and without initials, first and second names interchanged—if the input data as received does not match a record in the file.

A second general problem in business-data processing is finding the most efficient use of information for decision making. In order to utilize a report, a person must find the item or items of interest, correctly interpret the meaning of what he reads, obtain available related facts, apply proper rules of decision making, arrive at a decision, and carry out the decision. Some of these operations might be performed by the data-processing system, instead of by a manager relying on reports and his abilities.

The first step in decision making, finding the items of interest, can, to some extent, be handled by a data-processing system reporting off-standard or unexpected items—"exception reporting." It is possible to carry this idea further and process only those data pertinent to decisions. In order to do this, the program must provide for measuring pertinence at an early stage and follow an appropriate path thereafter.

For some applications, all the processing steps—from finding items of interest to carrying out decisions—might be handled by the equipment. In some mass-production industries, such as auto manufacture, the data-processing system may be directly connected to the factory to control the assembly of engines, bodies, trim, upholstery, and color into automobiles.

When the cost of processing data is reduced, the preparation of input and utilization of output become relatively more expensive than before unless their costs are also cut. The problems of input preparation and output use seem more acute merely because they have not been improved as much as the processing operations handled by the computer itself.

AN EXAMPLE OF BUSINESS-DATA PROCESSING

The problem of sales analysis for the General Appliance Company—which involves accumulating, analyzing, summarizing, and reporting sales and inventory data to managers in charge of marketing—is used to illustrate processing by manual methods and by automatic equipment (*The General Electric Company Sales Analysis Application*, 1957). The company has four decentralized departments, each making a major home appliance: stoves, refrigerators, washers, and air conditioners. Distribution is handled through company branches (dealing in appliances only), company supply houses (handling appliances and other products of the company), and independent firms.

Figure 1-1 is the general scheme for using manual processing of inventory in doing sales analysis. Data available at the central office are shipments from a warehouse to a distributor (which are used as receipts for a distributor after an appropriate time delay), distributor reports of sales, and the sales file resulting from processing the prior week's sales. A clerk processes the shipment (receipts) and sales to update the file and prepare the transaction lists. The general scheme of manual processing is similar to the computer run shown later.

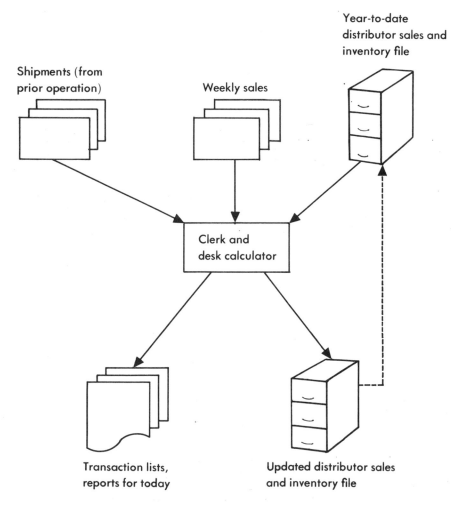

FIGURE 1-1. *Manual processing of distributor sales and inventory*

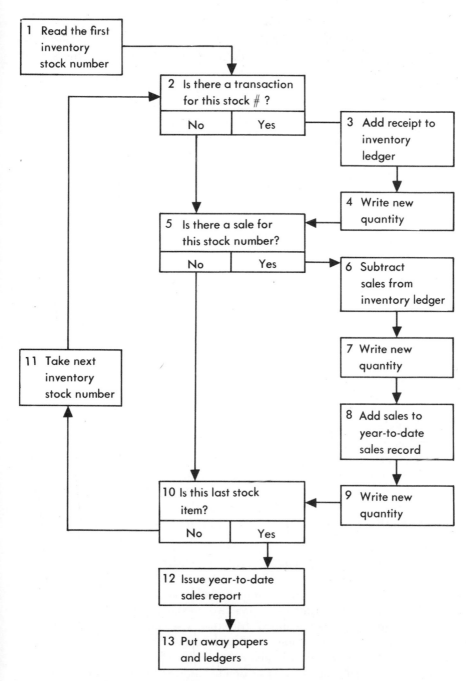

FIGURE 1-2. *Steps involved in processing distributor sales and inventory*

Figure 1-2 shows the steps involved in a manual processing of distributor sales and inventory. This flow chart includes start and input (step 1), input (11), arithmetical functions (3, 6, and 8), logical functions (2, 5, and 10), output (4, 7, 9, 12), and stop (13). Simplified flow charts of this type are made more detailed and elaborate during actual systems analysis and computer programming.

For many years the marketing section of each department had maintained a punched-card system to process manually prepared data. The requirements overtaxed the methods used, because facts were not available from which all departments could project requirements for material purchases, warehouse storage, advertising expenditures in selected areas, and other needs. Analysis indicated that with complete, current marketing data covering sales activity in the field, each department's marketing section could determine nationwide sales trends, forecast future sales, and better regulate production in the factory.

To compute distributor inventory, the new system, built around an automatic data processor, relies on weekly reports of sales by products at company branches, supply houses, and independent firms, and on monthly reports of warehouse shipments to each distributor. The basic model file, listing the model number of all appliances produced in each department, is the foundation of the sales analysis plan. The basic model file contains data on standard cost, federal excise tax, average transportation cost, allowances for complaint, and replacement costs. This file is maintained by adding new models and deleting discontinued models. Other data are changed as new estimates are calculated.

Distributor inventory of each model is computed from warehouse-reported shipments and distributor-reported sales. Weekly sales and inventory statistics are projected into monthly and year-to-date accumulations. Marketing managers use these sales reports to analyze retail trade, to study the sales of each model, and to divert shipments to understocked distributors. Monthly and year-to-date quotas for each distributor are compiled and entered on the report at the close of the fiscal month. Other reports prepared automatically, and their content, are these:

1. *Distributor gross margin report*—by distributor, to show each appliance model, the number of units, and dollar sales for month and year-to-date with gross margin in dollars and as a percentage of sales.
2. *Transaction register*—by appliance, to show all transactions between factory warehouses and distributors. Used to make simple analyses and to answer questions not deserving automatic processing.
3. *Warehouse shipments report*—monthly extract from transaction register used in accounting section to adjust or reconcile book inventory for each warehouse.

4. *Journal entry*—summary of all transactions during month used to integrate statistical data with general accounting.

Basically, this sales analysis application consists of a series of weekly and monthly computer runs. The process chart in Figure 1-3 shows the fundamental idea of a computer run. Valid warehouse shipments to distributors and sales by distributors are processed with the master file of distributor sales and inventory; this produces a distributor sales and inventory tape. The valid shipments tape was produced in a prior run, and weekly sales are converted from card to tape prior to starting the run illustrated.

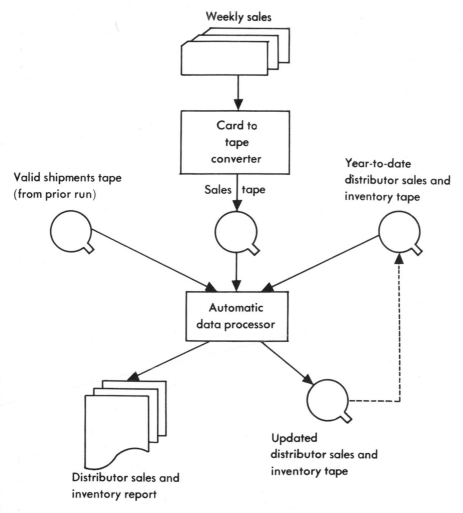

FIGURE 1-3. *Automatic processing of distributor sales and inventory*

TABLE 1-2. *Sales Analysis Runs and Output From Computer*

Run Number, Name, and Frequency	Input	Processing	Output	
			Tape for Run	Report
1. Transaction (weekly)	Weekly transactions-shipments tape Basic model file tape	Check model number of transaction against file number Sort and edit transactions by distributor and product line	Valid warehouse shipments tape 2	Weekly transactions register
2. Distributor sales and inventory (weekly)	1 Valid warehouse shipments tape (2) Inventory and year-to-date sales and distributor quota tape	Compile weekly, monthly, and year-to-date sales by distributors Compute inventory of each distributor Add weekly sales of distributor to year-to-date distributor sales and inventory tape	Inventory and year-to-date sales and distributor quota tape (2)	Updated year-to-date distributor sales and inventory report
3. Cost computation (monthly)	Weekly transaction tapes for month Basic model file tape	Merge weekly transactions by product line, model, and distributor Compute, for each transaction, standard cost, federal excise tax, transportation cost, and replacement cost	Monthly transactions tape 4 Year-to-date distributor gross margin tape 5	
4. Warehouse shipments (monthly)	3 Monthly transactions tape	Sort monthly transactions by warehouse number Extract and edit data for warehouse shipments reports		Warehouse shipment report
5. Gross margin (monthly)	3 Year-to-date distributor gross margin tape (5) Monthly gross margin tape	Compute factory gross margin for each distributor Add current month's gross margin to year-to-date total	Updated year-to-date distributor gross margin tape (5)	Distributor gross margin report
6. Transaction (monthly)	3 Monthly transactions tape	Summarize monthly transactions by distributor type Extract and edit data for monthly transaction register	Summarized monthly transactions tape 7	Monthly transactions report
7. Accounting (monthly)	6 Summarized monthly transactions tape	Prepare trial balance or journal entry for month's transactions Duplicate trial balance on four departmental accounting tapes	Departmental general accounting tapes X	Sales journal entries

Table 1-2 shows seven runs involved in sales analysis. The second run, distributor sales and inventory, is essentially the same as that already illustrated. Tracing each of the runs from input through processing to output will reveal that output is often used in a succeeding run; for example, in run 1, the output, "valid warehouse shipments tape 2," is used in run number 2, distributor sales and inventory. In some cases the output is used in the next cycle of the same run, as indicated by a number in parentheses; for example, tape output of run 2, "inventory and year-to-date sales and distributor quota tape (2)," is used as input for run 2 in the next cycle.

The automatic system of sales reporting makes it possible to have current facts from two levels of distribution—factory warehouse and wholesale distributor. It is also valuable for enabling management to do the following things:

1. Know sales activity in the field.
2. Analyze seasonal sales patterns.
3. Compare activity of wholesale distributors.
4. Regulate factory production and employment.
5. Forecast future sales trends.
6. Study customer reaction to products.
7. Complete general accounting and cost accounting.
8. Plan advertising campaigns.

For the General Appliance Company, the most important benefit of using a computer for sales analysis is the fact that weekly reports can be obtained easily, while under the manual system they were not practical because of the time required to produce a comprehensive analysis. Other advantages are shorter processing time, increased accuracy, and reduced clerical costs. Centralized processing of shipments to distributors and of sales by them makes it possible to determine in advance what appliances will be needed to replenish depleted distributor stocks.

IMPLICATIONS FOR MANAGEMENT

The introduction of automatic data-processing systems into business has many implications for management. Manpower, space for processing and storage of data, and costs per unit of data processed may be reduced. On the other hand, if the work load increases greatly, total costs may increase. The total work load frequently increases when unit costs are reduced because it is practicable to collect and process data that were previously ignored.

Another advantage lies in the production of more accurate and recent information. Often the processing delay—the time between occurrence of reported events and the availability of reports—can be greatly reduced. A shorter delay in processing may make more frequent reporting practicable. In some cases the use of more equipment may increase the delay in getting certain results even though the average delay is shortened considering all output as a whole. This corresponds to the situation in mass-production industries where elaborate tooling is used for quick production of many units although a few units or a special model might be completed sooner by hand. Decreased manual handling increases accuracy by eliminating certain types of mistakes. Two major areas where mistakes occur—preparation of input data and interpretation of reports—require special attention for improvement.

Some benefit may be gained from overcoming inertia. Almost everyone in an organization knows how operations can be improved; but often, changes are not made for various reasons. Either no one is available to plan changes, or someone might be offended by them. The enthusiasm and effort generated by a study for a proposed automatic data-processing system are useful for making long-overdue changes. Some observers say that the fear of change is a greater obstacle to adoption of new methods than is inertia. But it appears that introduction of new equipment facilitates the immediate adoption of many changes that can be refined later for more efficiency (Gregory, 1955). This viewpoint reflects the belief that people are often more willing to use new equipment than to accept novel ideas.

Present and future developments in data processing will impinge on four fields of management: (1) decision making, (2) human relations and supervision, (3) planning and operations, and (4) company or agency growth.

Decision making will become more efficient because a manager will spend less time making routine decisions than at present. Today, many problems go to top management because simple facts that lead to unique answers are not available. In the future, decisions will follow a course based more on facts and less on intuition, although judgment will still be required for decision making (Adams, 1956). In still more advanced schemes, when sufficient facts are available, the system will be programmed to make many decisions that are now handled by managers. Managers will continue to be most valuable for using broad experience to make decisions when some facts are missing or objectives are not explicit. Improvements in data processing will enable them to make better decisions by having more useful facts available; but managers will continue to deal with uncertainties that cannot be eliminated.

Human relations in business will change because equipment will do more of the work now done by people. But an increased demand for more facts may require a larger work force. Improved processing methods will enable a manager to get more work from the same number of people because they are aided by more equipment. A manager frequently needs subordinates to collect and screen out control information and to implement decisions; a data processor can do much of the work of data selection, so that a manager can focus his attention on the best plan of action. New ideas about the span of control will be necessary. Improved information and control schemes will eliminate many routine problems constantly brought to a manager's attention. The entire structure of an organization may be simplified and control of it decentralized because better data processing will furnish less-experienced people with a better basis for action. A highly skilled data-processing group will assist management by doing much of the routine record work previously associated with each administrative area of the business. Each new development in data-processing methods promises to replace people, but actual results to date are often different, for present-day systems still require many people. In fact, the trend to more mechanized systems creates challenging opportunities for managers, systems analysts, programmers, and even clerks. People are needed to direct, review, and maintain operations of the most automatic systems now considered feasible. The main result of progress will be increased output per person.

Planning and operating a business will be different because an organization can respond faster to changed conditions. An entirely new operating program may be put into operation in a few minutes by giving the data processor a new set of objectives. As pointed out above, occasionally a company now connects the data system directly to the factory to control its operations, and it appears that this practice will spread. Management will be able to take preventive control action rather than having to rely upon corrective action after the fact.

Company growth will be faster, if growth has been slow because of deficient information to control operations and plan for the future. Since larger equipment processes more data at a lower cost per unit handled, although at a higher investment in equipment and procedures, some competitive advantage may be gained by a company's obtaining the largest-size equipment practicable for it.

Business management must deal with selecting and developing data-processing and control systems that are to be adopted and used two or more years in the future. A long time and a huge amount of effort are involved in designing a new data-processing system. Whether an automatic system is desirable and how it can be applied most advantageously are questions to be answered by carefully planned and conducted studies. Systems studies involve selecting the objectives for the system, cataloguing all major data-processing areas, determining whether automatic techniques have merit, and investigating possible systems that appear to have merit. Following a systems study that leads to a positive recommendation, there exist the problems of obtaining and installing equipment; of training people; of designing the system required to go with the equipment selected; of testing, parallel running, and cutting over from the old to a new system; and of evaluating results from the new system to revise it as required.

The benefits derived from a resourceful, carefully planned approach to a new system are large. The cost of a serious mistake, either from the wrong action or from inaction, can be severe. Automatic systems are not an answer to all data-processing problems, but they can be highly effective for applications proved suitable by careful planning.

SUMMARY

Rapid changes, which may amount to an "office revolution," are occurring in the techniques of processing data. Changes in equipment occur first and are followed by improvements in the system designed around such new equipment in order to exploit it fully.

Data are gathered, stored, processed, and reported in order to have facts available, produce routine documents, develop informative reports, and analyze business problems. The raw facts about events might be thought of as "data," and "information" can be used to cover the selective facts that management wants to know.

The elements in processing data are:

1. Obtaining new data inputs to the system.
2. Manipulating data according to a prescribed plan. This requires:
   (a) a storage unit to hold data and processing instructions.
   (b) an operating unit to perform arithmetical and logical operations.
   (c) a control unit to manage operation.
3. Producing output documents, reports, or instructions for action.

The "facilities," broadly defined, that are used for processing data include people, records, office machines, punched-card machines, electronic computers, and automatic data processors. Automatic data-processing systems can:

1. Bring specially prepared data into the storage element.
2. Perform a required sequence of operations on the data:
   (a) logical—sorting, file maintenance, file reference, file search.
   (b) arithmetical—addition, subtraction, multiplication, division.
3. Make decisions to perform appropriate operations as dictated by changes in the data or intermediate results.
4. Issue complete or selective reports after completing processing operations.

More than equipment alone is needed for an efficient system, personnel for planning and operations, instruction routines for equipment, and processing procedures are required.

An automatic data-processing system consists of the following components: (1) an electronic data processor—digital computer; (2) peripheral equipment associated with the computer, such as data-preparation devices, input and output devices, and sorting devices; (3) procedures that tell what data are needed and when, how obtained, and how used; (4) instruction routines for the computer to follow; and (5) personnel to operate and maintain equipment, analyze and set up procedures, prepare instructions, provide input data, utilize reports, review results, and supervise the entire operation.

A comparison of punched-card and automatic data processing indicates the higher storage, handling, computation speed, and versatility of the latter.

An example of the procedures followed by an appliance manufacturer shows the salient features of manual and automatic processing for inventory and sales analysis. The automatic system of sales reporting furnishes the company with current facts at two levels of distribution—factory warehouse and wholesale distributors. Such increased knowledge enables the manufacturer to analyze sales and distribution patterns, regulate factory production, forecast and plan sales activities, and perform general and cost accounting.

Automatic data-processing systems have important implications for management in two areas: reduced costs of processing, and improved accuracy and timeliness of information. Present and future developments in data processing will impinge on four fields of management: decision making, human relations and supervision, planning and operations, and company growth.

The benefits from a resourceful, carefully planned approach to a new system are large; but the cost of a serious mistake, either from the wrong action or inaction, can be severe.

REFERENCES AND SUPPLEMENTAL READINGS

Adams, Charles W. "Processing Business Data," *Control Engineering*, vol. 3: 105-112 (June 1956). Business-data systems, or more aptly, "management information systems," have three principal functions: to perform routine record-keeping, computation, and decision-making programs based on precise policies and procedures; to accumulate, as a by-product of routine work, a collection of statistical medians, means, extremes, and other measures of effectiveness; and to serve as a computational tool in arriving at a valid basis for formulating and modifying company policies and procedures. Judgment is still required for decision making. Four data-processing problems present in every sizable business are payroll, accounts payable, accounts receivable, and inventory. Payroll and inventory are interesting because of processing requirements, although inventory control is more important for business management.

Chapin, Ned. *An Introduction to Automatic Computers*, Princeton, New Jersey, D. Van Nostrand Co., Inc., 1957, 525 pp. Chapter 12, "Computer Fundamentals," contains a history of computing devices from the notched sticks and knotted strings of pre-history to the commercially available automatic computers with variable blocks and variable field-lengths of 1955.

The General Electric Company Sales Analysis Application, New York, Remington Rand Univac, 1957, 24 pp. Describes the sales analysis system using a Univac computer devised for the General Electric Company Appliance and Television Receiver Division. (Used as the basis for the "General Appliance Company" case in Chapter 1.)

Gregory, Robert H. "Computers and Accounting Systems," *Accounting Research*, vol. 6: 38-48 (January 1955). Accountants have been responsible for processing data longer than any other group in business. They have tried to meet business requirements for certain kinds of facts by using available techniques, although a time lag exists between invention and widespread acceptance of a new technique. Limited-capacity facilities restrict processing to an application-by-application approach, whereas data and information requirements are actually business-wide. The belief in 1954, when the article was written, was that intensive systems analysis preparatory to introduction of electronic computers would result in a comprehensive system for a business to replace the individualistic approach to each application.

Martin, William L. "A Merchandise Control System," pp. 184-191 in *Proceedings of the Western Joint Computer Conference: Trends in Computers—Automatic Control and Data Processing*, New York, American Institute of Electrical Engineers, 1954. This article discusses the application of general-purpose, stored-program computers to the problems of inventory control, order filling, and customer invoicing. It covers a typical mail-order operation of fairly good size which processes ten customer orders per second. Treatment of the problem is general and does not give details on computer programming or comparisons between available equipment. Some attention is given to economy and the broad advantages of faster and more accurate methods of handling normal clerical operations.

Montalbano, Michael. "Elements in Data-Processing System Design," presented at the tenth national meeting of the Operations Research Society of America, November 16, 1956. This article is a general discussion of data processing ("handling of business information") in industry. Montalbano points out that (a) no data processing is automatic, (b) effective data-processing system design involves operations research techniques, and (c) a qualitative description of a system (in words and pictures) is useful in preparing a quantitative one (in numbers and measurements). Most of the article deals with qualitative description and its application to some frequent problems in using business data-processing systems. The author comments on a number of factors that he feels are not adequately explained by conventional treatments. Important ideas of "loop" and "feedback" in data processing and management are stressed.

Spinning, H. M. "Calculation of Crude-Oil Run Tickets by Electronics," *The Oil and Gas Journal*, vol. 51: 70-71 + (February 1953). Describes two methods of processing crude-oil runs from gaugers' tickets to royalty payments. The manual method relied on look-up in tables prepared for each tank to convert height at quarter-inch intervals into volume. The introduction of punched-card methods changed the approach to a combination of table look-up for the volume up to the point where the diameter changed and calculation of volume within that interval. Correction for temperature, impurities, and gravity were basically the same by both methods.

CHAPTER TWO

PROCESSING DATA
BY MACHINE

The ability to obtain and store data for later use is invaluable to technical and cultural progress. The efficient storage and use of data depend on the combination of symbols, media, writer, and reader. Symbols used to represent data include the Arabic numerals (0 through 9), the English alphabet (A through Z), notes on a musical scale, and many others. In other centuries and countries different alphabets and numerals have been used: Sanskrit in Indo-Europe, cuneiform in Assyria, hieroglyphs in Egypt, notched sticks in England, and Roman numerals in the Roman Empire. Some alphabets are represented by symbols that, although useful for their intended purposes, are difficult or impossible for people to read: dots and dashes for telegraphic transmission, holes in player piano rolls, punched cards and paper tape, and magnetized spots on a suitable surface.

Media upon which data have been recorded are numerous and varied: clay, stone, wax, sticks, papyrus, paper, cardboard, photographic plates, plastic, and metal. Examples of plastic media are identification charge-plates with embossed characters and magnetic tapes (plastic coated with iron oxide).

The "writer" for recording data includes an instrument and an operating or controlling element, although the two appear inseparable at first glance. Writing instruments have included the brush, pencil, knife, hammer and chisel, seal, movable type, typewriter, punch, and magnetic recorder. The operating or controlling element is commonly a person, either working alone or with the aid of electric or mechanical power.

The "reader" for data can be a person, a punched-card or punched-tape reader, or a magnetic-tape reader. The reader may even be equipment in the factory; for example, weaving machines read cards or tape with instructions for weaving a desired pattern in cloth or lace, and milling machines are controlled by data stored on punched or magnetic tape.

Every known storage method imposes some restrictions on data-processing techniques. The compatible combinations of alphabet, storage medium, writer, and reader are limited. People can easily read an alphabet of letters and numerals cut into stone, but the inscribing is possible only by slow work with a hammer and chisel or abrasives. Magnetic tapes will hold only certain coded representations of letters and numerals and then require the use of special electrically operated writing and reading devices. Written paper records, which have been widely used for only a few hundred years, demand certain processing skills—sight, writing ability, and some intelligence. People are trained from childhood to recognize letters and numerals singly and collectively as words, records, and files. Several versions of character-recognition equipment now translate characters printed in ordinary or special ink in a type style that people can also read. Equipment to read handwriting—numerals and letters printed with some care—has been developed and may become widely used.

MACHINE-PROCESSABLE DATA

Methods for recording business data in machine-processable form have been in use for about seventy years. Some knowledge of the principles and methods involved in representing data in machine-processable form is vital to a study of automatic data processing. Widely used methods are punched holes in cards and tape, marks in specified locations, specially shaped printed characters, and magnetic conditions in a magnetizable material (Haskins and Sells, 1957).

Punched Cards

Holes punched in cards represent a basic way of storing data for mechanized processing. Herman Hollerith invented the punched card and some electric processing equipment while working at the Census Bureau in 1886. The early versions of punched-card equipment developed for census enumeration had space for punching 240 holes, each hole representing the presence or absence of a single fact in "yes-no" form. A person's age could be represented by punching one of 85 holes. Fewer holes would serve, however, if they were to represent age groups (one hole for ages 1 through 5, one for ages 81 through 85, and so on). Cards were inserted manually into a reading station to be read electrically. The reading operation caused a cover on a pocket to open so that the card could be laid manually into the correct sorting pocket. Card counting was also a manual operation.

The limit of 240 permissible holes, each used to represent one fact, restricted the data content of a card. This content was increased by using smaller holes and punching more of them in a card, by adopting a numerical scheme for the holes in a column (0 through 9), and by using two or more columns together to represent larger numbers. In this way, three columns containing a total of 30 positions could provide for any number between 000 and 999. If each position were used to represent a single fact, then 1,000 positions would be required. This need led to the development of a numerical scheme for punching numbers.

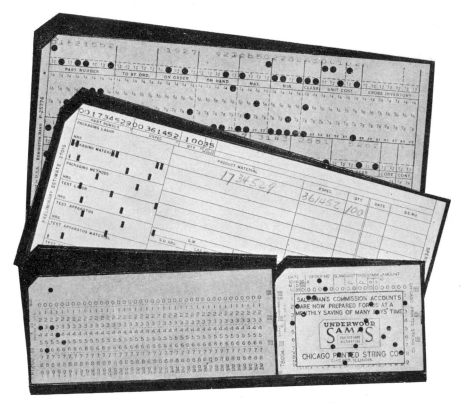

FIGURE 2-1. *Punched cards with numerical data*

Figure 2-1 shows numerals in 80- and 90-column cards and on smaller cards with a similar coding. The standard 80-column card has ten punching positions (0 through 9) in each vertical column; only one hole is punched for each numeral to be represented. Compare the punched with the printed numerals in the number "1734529." Although this number has seven digits, nine horizontally ranged spaces are allotted to it on the card, the first two spaces being punched with zeros so that the digits in the extreme right margin are vertically aligned. Filling out a field of spaces with non-significant zeros at the left of the desired number helps in detecting skipped or double-punched columns, because every column is then supposed to have one and only one punch for numerals.

The data on the 90-column card are arranged in two banks of 45 columns each. The rows in each bank are treated as 0, 1_2, 3_4, 5_6, 7_8, 9, although 0 and 9 are not marked. Zero and odd digits are punched by a single hole representing 0, 1, 3, 5, 7, or 9. Even digits are represented by punching the holes marked 2, 4, 6, or 8 (and also the 9) to distinguish them from the odd numerals in the same rows.

The method of representing zero to nine in either the upper or the lower half of a 90-column card is as follows:

Card Row				Numerals						
	0	1	2	3	4	5	6	7	8	9
0	●									
1_2		●	●							
3_4				●	●					
5_6						●	●			
7_8								●	●	
9			●		●		●		●	●

The use of one of five holes to represent 0, 1, 3, 5, 7 and one of these five with a second hole in the 9 position to get the even-value digits is essentially a qui-binary, or five-two code. Of course, only one key stroke is required to punch the hole or holes used to represent one digit. This code is more compact than the simple decimal code (0 through 9), for it requires only six punching positions. This card can store 90 digits instead of 80, and wider tolerances are permissible during punching and processing because the holes are larger.

The accepted qui-binary or five-two code scheme looks like a minor variation of the code described above. Use of one hole for 0 or 1; 2 or 3; 4 or 5; 6 or 7; 8 or 9 with a second hole to select the odd or even digit has an interesting feature: each digit is represented by one hole in each of two specified areas. The failure to punch one of the two holes or the punching of an extra hole can be determined either by visual inspection or by features built into the equipment.

Light Values					
0 5	O ●	● O	● O	O ●	● O
0	O	O	●	●	O
1	●	O	O	O	O
2	O	O	O	O	O
3	O	●	O	O	O
4	O	O	O	O	●
Number	6	3	0	5	4

Some computer designers use a bi-quinary or two-five code scheme to display numbers on the computer control panel for operators to read for checking purposes. The arrangement for displaying the number 63054 in neon lights, for example, is shown above.

It is possible, although wasteful, to use two columns for each letter by a scheme of 01 for A, 02 for B, 12 for K, and so on. Another important development in punched-card data storage was the coding of letters and special symbols by two or three holes in the same column to increase the capacity for alphabetic data. Multiple punches consist of a zone punch to indicate the portion of the alphabet and a numerical punch to indicate a particular letter within that portion. Figure 2-2 shows cards with two kinds of codes for alphanumerical symbols.

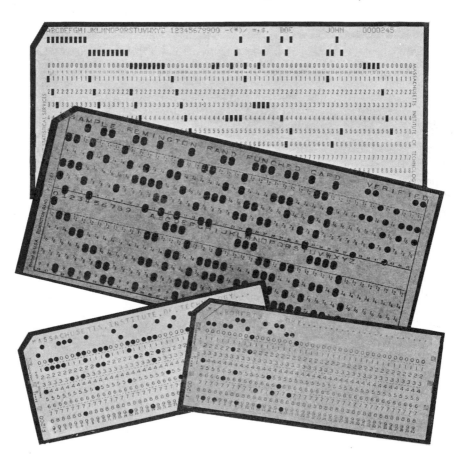

FIGURE 2-2. *Punched cards with alphanumerical codes*

Punched cards are important because data stored on them can be processed electro-mechanically. This requires that people follow instructions for handling cards and employ suitable programs in the form of wired plugboards inserted in the machines. A punched card is processed by being passed over a sensing device (electric brushes or feeler pins) which reads the holes; the machine senses one or more holes and takes appropriate action. Simple calculations and sorting (arranging according to kind, class, or numerical sequence), collating or merging (combining two individually sorted decks into one sequence) are done at speeds of one hundred to one thousand cards a minute. Most card readers use electric brushes or mechanical pins, but some readers direct a light beam at the card and use a photoelectric cell to sense the existence of holes. Punched cards are widely used for data collection and processing within a business. Examples of business uses are time cards, personnel records, inventory control records, and cost accounts. A punched card, perhaps of reduced size, can be attached to identify any item while it is in inventory. When the item is used or sold, the card can be detached for processing, either directly or after conversion to a card better suited to machine handling. Punched cards are also used for documents—checks, bills, airplane tickets, toll road tickets, and even purchase orders—which pass between companies and people.

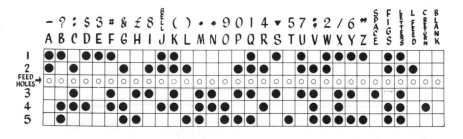

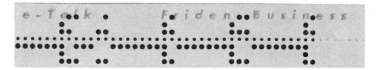

FIGURE 2-3. *Punched tape and five-channel code*

Punched Tape

A common type of punched paper tape has ten columns per inch and can store an alphanumerical character in each column. Paper tape stores data more compactly than punched cards, being narrower— about 11/16″ or 1″ wide—and thinner. Although the basic code for punched tape has five channels that yield 32 possible combinations ($2^5 = 32$), two combinations are used for shifting to the figures or letters mode, corresponding to upper and lower case on a typewriter, so that 52 alphanumerical and special characters are possible. (See Figure 2-3.) The fact that 52 characters are obtained does not violate the rule that the maximum number of combinations using 5 holes is 32. To indicate mode and character two columns of holes are, in effect, used together, so that the possible number is increased from 32 to 60. The general rule for the number of characters possible for n channels where M carriage shifts are used to change modes and C characters are common to all modes, is:

$$(2^n - M - C) \times M + C$$

The number of characters possible with two modes using two-mode shifts is $(2^5 - 2) \times 2$, which is 60. But 4 characters (space, feed, return, and blank) are the same in both modes, so that the net number is 56.

Wider tape will hold more channels, thus allowing the use of more possible characters. The characters possible with six-channel tape are basically the same as with five-channel, except that they include both upper and lower case letters. Seven-channel code is the same as a six-channel code with a checking channel. Eight-channel code permits inclusion of field designation, which indicates where data should be placed on a form.

Paper tape was developed to speed up transmission over telegraph lines. Punched cards may be converted to tape for wire transmission or mailing. Cards can also be transmitted directly over wire by using special card-reading and card-punching equipment.

Recent work called "integrated data processing" has aimed at developing a system of completely mechanized handling, from the original collection of data to the preparation of final documents and reports. An important facet of some integrated systems is the use of punched tape as a common language between many kinds of office equipment that punch or read the five-channel code. The language is "common" because it provides communication between equipment as diverse as cash registers and punched cards. Five-channel code is not restricted to tape; it can be punched along the edges of ordinary or continuous-form cards used for filing purposes, or even on standard-size cards that are punched in standard fashion. Although commonly made of paper for single or infrequent use, tape may be laminated from paper and mylar or paper and metal to withstand repeated use.

Limitations of Punched-hole Equipment

Although punched-card equipment is an important advance over manual methods, it has some serious drawbacks. The mechanical problems of punching, reading, and card handling reduce operating speeds. Since plugboards in which wires are inserted to select and sequence operations hold a limited number of fixed instructions, processing flexibility is limited for each pass of the cards. Simple arithmetical calculations can be made efficiently; but extensive, complex calculations can be made only inefficiently, if at all.

The data density of cards is low because of the hole-size required, the alphanumerical codes used, the thickness of cards, and the fixed-field-length requirement (the number of columns assigned to a field must cover the longest item that may occur). More data for ready reference by people (up to 25 lines) can be typed or printed on a card than can be punched into the same card. Punched-tape strips are compact but are clumsy to file for later use. The difficulty of altering data punched in cards or tape is a desirable feature for cards used as evidence, but it restricts work cards to a one-time use. Paper or plastic file cards, on the other hand, may be used repeatedly. Cards are bulky to send by mail, and transmission over a telegraph line is limited to 5 cards a minute with one receiving-sending unit, and to 44 cards a minute over a telephone line using four sending-receiving units.

The serial nature of punched tape (each character follows the other in a word although the holes for a character are in parallel) and its indefinite length speed up reading and, perhaps calculating and tabulating, but it may make sorting more difficult. It should be observed that several cleverly designed sorters for punched paper tape have been devised and are used by telephone companies in automatically accounting for telephone message charges. Widespread acceptance of punched-card and tape processing equipment, despite its deficiencies, has stimulated the development of more efficient means of storing data for machine processing.

Magnetic Recording

Magnetic recording of digital data corresponds to audio recording methods except that signals are recorded separately instead of continuously. More care is also required, for the loss of even a few digits may be worse than losing part of a voice recording.

Magnetic spots are recorded in iron oxide or other metal, which is coated on plastic, aluminum or some other non-magnetic metal, or even on cardboard. The iron-oxide-coated material is used in the form of reels of tape, drums, disks, or cards. Magnetic cores are small doughnuts of magnetizable material strung on wires. Magnetic recording media are shown in Figure 2-4.

The operations in magnetic recording are (1) erasing prior contents, (2) recording desired data, and (3) reading whenever wanted. Two heads—one for erasing unwanted contents and another for recording and reading—are close to but usually not in contact with the iron oxide surface. The magnetic spots can be erased and the material

DRUM

CORE

TAPE

FIGURE 2-4. *Magnetic recording media*

re-used almost indefinitely; but when the data on a magnetic tape
are to be used for evidence or an audit, they can be made permanent.

Characters are often written in a seven-channel code on tape ½ in.
or ¾ in. wide at densities ranging from 100 to 500 characters an inch.
The 80 alphanumerical characters that can be punched in a card can be
recorded on .16 in. to .8 in. of tape. Recording density on drums is
usually lower—not more than 100 characters an inch on each track
around the drum. There are eight or so tracks per inch along the drum
in the direction parallel to the axis. Tapes are moved past the read-
write at speeds ranging from 75 to 200 inches a second, and the drums
rotate at speeds between 1 and 20 thousand revolutions a minute. The
read-write process is controlled electrically; it is extremely fast, being
done while the tape or drum is in motion. Tape-reading or writing
speeds range from 10 to 60 thousand alphanumerical characters a
second.

Magnetic cores are strung on stationary wires and are not moved.
Electricity is sent through the wires to write or read the magnetic state
of any desired core. Data can be written in or read out of magnetic
cores in a few millionths of a second.

Character Representation

At various points in a data-processing system many different
methods can be used for representing data: handwriting; punched
holes; the positions of wheels, gears, and levers, as in a desk calculator;
electric pulses; and magnetic states. Selection of a method for representing data depends on whether people, machines, or both will use
the data. Various methods are suitable for different applications. If
one method were used throughout, efficiency would be reduced; ordinarily, several methods are used and conversion is required between
them.

Many different sizes and shapes of holes, spots, or electric pulses
might be used to represent alphanumerical data—just as many different
frequencies, shapes, and amplitudes of audio signals are used to record
music. Few components would be needed to handle digital data represented in this way, but the components would be very complex. Another approach is to have simpler components and use more of them.
Automatic processing equipment is designed with many components
that are stable in either one of two states. Two stable states may be
represented in various ways: by a punched hole or no hole; by a magnetic spot with north-south or the opposite polarity; by a relay open
or closed; by an electric pulse or no pulse; or by a dot or dash. The
"yes-no," "on-off," or "0-1" scheme is widely used. It is popular because it is easier to design equipment that can be put in one of two
stable states and make it stay there than it is to provide for many stable
states. A light switch is a simple example of a two-state, "on-off" de-

vice. Combinations of the two symbols 0-1, called "binary digits" or "bits," are used to represent numerals, letters, and other symbols. Many ingenious schemes exist.

NUMBER SYSTEMS

The various number systems in use are treated in enough detail here to show the relationship between number systems that people like to use and those preferred by computer designers. Number systems are treated intensively by Richards (1955).

People like the decimal number system because it seems natural; they learned to count on their fingers. In Yucatan the Maya civilization used a system of numerals based upon a scale containing elements of both 5 and 20 ("Numerals" and "Numeral Systems," 1957). Many other number bases are widely used, although we tend to think of them as merely counting schemes. Examples are 12 for dozen, 16 for ounces in a pound, 3 for feet in a yard, and 5280 for feet in a mile. Non-decimal fractions are widely used; for example, 1/8 for security prices and 1/16 for fractions of an inch. People even find the British monetary system of mixed radices (4 farthings to a penny, 12 pennies to a shilling, 20 shillings to a pound, and decimal thereafter) comprehensible although far more complex than a single radix scheme. Facetiously, one might hypothesize that if people were closer to the octopus than to the monkey, they would think the octal system (with the base 8) quite natural and probably would not use the decimal system at all.

The base or radix of a number system need only be greater than 1 and is usually, but not always, an integer. The radix in the decimal system is 10, in counting by the dozen it is 12, and for counting by pairs it is 2. The number of marks in a number system is equal to the radix used. The decimal system has ten marks or digits—0 through 9. The binary system has two digits, 0 and 1. The octal system has eight symbols, 0 through 7.

When counting beyond the radix in one position, the digit in the next position to the left is increased by 1 and counting is resumed at 0. In short, large numbers make use of the same digits, 0 to 9, by adding 1 in the next position to the left and continuing counting. Counting beyond the radix in the decimal system seems easy because of constant practice; it seems natural that 10 and 11 should follow 9, and so on.

The concept of a value being associated with each digit facilitates number representation. By way of contrast, consider that in using the ten Roman numerals—I, V, X, L, C, D, M, $\overline{X}$, $\overline{C}$, and $\overline{M}$—the value of a number depends on the characters used and their sequence (if they are different), but not on their individual positions. For example, III is 3, IV is 4, VI is 6, both XC and LXXXX are 90, and $\overline{M}$MCLXVI is

operations hold a limited number of fixed instructions, processing flexibility is limited for each pass of the cards. Simple arithmetical calculations can be made efficiently; but extensive, complex calculations can be made only inefficiently, if at all.

The data density of cards is low because of the hole-size required, the alphanumerical codes used, the thickness of cards, and the fixed-field-length requirement (the number of columns assigned to a field must cover the longest item that may occur). More data for ready reference by people (up to 25 lines) can be typed or printed on a card than can be punched into the same card. Punched-tape strips are compact but are clumsy to file for later use. The difficulty of altering data punched in cards or tape is a desirable feature for cards used as evidence, but it restricts work cards to a one-time use. Paper or plastic file cards, on the other hand, may be used repeatedly. Cards are bulky to send by mail, and transmission over a telegraph line is limited to 5 cards a minute with one receiving-sending unit, and to 44 cards a minute over a telephone line using four sending-receiving units.

The serial nature of punched tape (each character follows the other in a word although the holes for a character are in parallel) and its indefinite length speed up reading and, perhaps calculating and tabulating, but it may make sorting more difficult. It should be observed that several cleverly designed sorters for punched paper tape have been devised and are used by telephone companies in automatically accounting for telephone message charges. Widespread acceptance of punched-card and tape processing equipment, despite its deficiencies, has stimulated the development of more efficient means of storing data for machine processing.

Magnetic Recording

Magnetic recording of digital data corresponds to audio recording methods except that signals are recorded separately instead of continuously. More care is also required, for the loss of even a few digits may be worse than losing part of a voice recording.

Magnetic spots are recorded in iron oxide or other metal, which is coated on plastic, aluminum or some other non-magnetic metal, or even on cardboard. The iron-oxide-coated material is used in the form of reels of tape, drums, disks, or cards. Magnetic cores are small doughnuts of magnetizable material strung on wires. Magnetic recording media are shown in Figure 2-4.

The operations in magnetic recording are (1) erasing prior contents, (2) recording desired data, and (3) reading whenever wanted. Two heads—one for erasing unwanted contents and another for recording and reading—are close to but usually not in contact with the iron oxide surface. The magnetic spots can be erased and the material

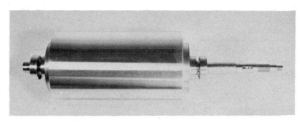

DRUM

CORE

TAPE

FIGURE 2-4. *Magnetic recording media*

1,001,166; but IVXLCM$\overline{\text{M}}$ is gibberish because it violates the rules for arranging the characters in sequence for addition and subtraction.

The concept of positional value is fundamental to simple, straight-forward number systems. A digit has its individual value whenever it is written and is independent of the digits to its left or right. But— and this is the important point in modern number systems—the effective value of a digit is increased by the number base raised to the power of the digit position occupied. The digit positions are counted to left and right from a decimal point, as follows:

$$+n, \ldots, +4, +3, +2, +1, 0, -1, -2, -3, \ldots, -n$$

The digits in the number 675.42, treated as a decimal number, have the values:

$$(6 \times 10^2) + (7 \times 10^1) + (5 \times 10^0) + (4 \times 10^{-1}) + (2 \times 10^{-2})$$
$$\text{or}$$
$$600 + 75 + 5 + .4 + .02$$

If the same number 675.42 is treated as an octal number, the digits have the value:

$$(6 \times 8^2) + (7 \times 8^1) + (5 \times 8^0) + (4 \times 8^{-1}) + (2 \times 8^{-2})$$

The meaning of the positional value concept will become clearer as several number systems are studied.

Decimal

In a decimal number, the first digit to the left of the decimal point is multiplied by 10^0, which is equal to 1, so that the first digit is counted at face value. The second or tens digit is multiplied by 10^1, which is 10. The hundreds digit is multiplied by 10^2 or 100, and so on.

Digits to the right of the decimal point are divided by 10, 100, 1000 (or multiplied by 1/10, 1/100, 1/1000), which are powers of 10— 10^1, 10^2, 10^3—corresponding to each digit position to the right of the decimal point.

The complete number is the sum of all the weighted digits. For example, the digits 5, 4, 9, 7, 6, 5, 8 written as a number, 5497.658, mean:

$$
\begin{aligned}
5 \times 10^3 &= 5000. \\
4 \times 10^2 &= 400. \\
9 \times 10^1 &= 90. \\
7 \times 10^0 &= 7. \\
6 \times 10^{-1} &= .6 \\
5 \times 10^{-2} &= .05 \\
8 \times 10^{-3} &= \underline{.008} \\
&\ 5497.658
\end{aligned}
$$

Powers of 10 are used to find positional values because there are 10 symbols. The largest digit is 9, but it is possible to represent 10 by assigning a magnified value to the smallest non-zero digit, 1, and attaching 0.

Long familiarity has led people to think that the decimal system is objectively "natural." It is easy for us to forget how difficult it once was to learn the sums and products of two decimal digits. The decimal addition and multiplication tables are difficult to learn because each table for even single digit numbers has a hundred entries.

Binary

An equipment designer worries little about what people think is natural; he concentrates on designing a system that will simplify equipment design, reduce construction cost, and operate efficiently. Data can be translated automatically from the decimal system to any number system designed into equipment (Lerner, 1955). The fact that it is easiest to design and build equipment with two stable states (that might be thought of as yes-no, on-off, or 0-1) makes the binary system desirable. The 0 and 1 are the only two binary digits—often referred to as "bits."

The bits in a binary number have weighted position values of 2^0, 2^1, 2^2 to 2^n, which are equal to 1, 2, 4 and so on. This is similar to the weighting scheme of 10^0, 10^1, 10^2, etc., for digit positions. Counting in decimal and binary shows the similarities:

Decimal	Binary
0	0
1	1
2	10
3	11
4	100
5	101
6	110
7	111
8	1000
9	1001
10	1010
11	1011
12	1100
50	110010
100	1100100
512	1000000000

To the right of the binary point, each bit is divided by 2, 4, 8, and so on. Examples of fractions in one number system also show how some numbers may be difficult to express in the other:

Decimal	Binary
.5	.1
.25	.01
.125	.001
.0625	.0001
.375	.011
.33333 . . .	.01010101 . . .

Converting numbers larger than 1 from the decimal system to another system can be done by successively dividing by the base of the new system and keeping the remainder each time. For the simple case of converting 11_{10} (meaning 11 to the base 10) to binary:

Decimal Division	Remainder	Binary Value		Positional Value		Decimal Equivalent
$11 \div 2 = 5$	1	1	x	1	=	1
$5 \div 2 = 2$	1	1	x	2	=	2
$2 \div 2 = 1$	0	0	x	4	=	0
$1 \div 2 = 0$	1	1	x	8	=	8
						11

The binary value reading upward, 1011_2, is equal to 11_{10}. As another example, 5497_{10} converted to binary is 1010101111001_2.

Decimal Division	Remainder Binary Value	Decimal Equivalent of Binary	
$5497 \div 2 = 2748$	1	$1 \times 2^0 =$	1
$2748 \div 2 = 1374$	0	$0 \times 2^1 =$	0
$1374 \div 2 = 687$	0	$0 \times 2^2 =$	0
$687 \div 2 = 343$	1	$1 \times 2^3 =$	8
$343 \div 2 = 171$	1	$1 \times 2^4 =$	16
$171 \div 2 = 85$	1	$1 \times 2^5 =$	32
$85 \div 2 = 42$	1	$1 \times 2^6 =$	64
$42 \div 2 = 21$	0	$0 \times 2^7 =$	0
$21 \div 2 = 10$	1	$1 \times 2^8 =$	256
$10 \div 2 = 5$	0	$0 \times 2^9 =$	0
$5 \div 2 = 2$	1	$1 \times 2^{10} =$	1024
$2 \div 2 = 1$	0	$0 \times 2^{11} =$	0
$1 \div 2 = 0$	1	$1 \times 2^{12} =$	4096
			5497

Decimal fractions are converted to binary by successively multiplying by two and saving either the 1 or 0 that develops at the left of the decimal point. Conversion of $.658_{10}$, for example, gives $.101010001_2$.

Binary Value   Decimal Multiplication

$$.658 \times 2 = \underline{1.316}$$ Save the 1 and multiply .316 by 2, etc.

1	$.316 \times 2 = .632$
0	$.632 \times 2 = 1.264$
1	$.264 \times 2$
0	$.528 \times 2$
1	$.056 \times 2$
0	$.112 \times 2$
0	$.224 \times 2$
0	$.448 \times 2$
0	$.996 \times 2$
1	$.992 \times 2$
	and so on

The binary fraction continues indefinitely in this case, but it is rounded in the ninth position to cut it off. Putting together the parts to the left and right of the decimal point, as calculated above, 5497.658_{10} is equivalent to $1010101111001.101010001_2$.

Octal

The octal system has a radix of 8 and uses the digits 0 and 1 through 7, so that octal numbers look like decimal numbers except that the numbers are longer and the digits 8 and 9 are not used. The left-hand part of the decimal number 5497.658_{10}, is $12571._8$, calculated by dividing by 8 and keeping the remainder.

Decimal Division	Remainder (Octal Value)	Decimal Equivalent of Octal
$5497 \div 8 = 687$	1	$1 \times 1 = 1$
$687 \div 8 = 85$	7	$7 \times 8^1 = 56$
$85 \div 8 = 10$	5	$5 \times 8^2 = 320$
$10 \div 8 = 1$	2	$2 \times 8^3 = 1024$
$1 \div 8 = 0$	1	$1 \times 8^4 = \underline{4096}$
		5497

The right-hand part of the decimal number $.658_{10}$ is equal to $.5207_8$, calculated by multiplying by 8 and keeping the whole digit.

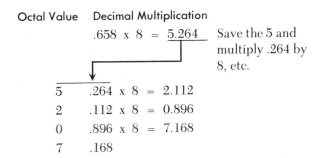

Octal Value   Decimal Multiplication

.658 x 8 = 5.264   Save the 5 and
                    multiply .264 by
                    8, etc.

5   .264 x 8 = 2.112
2   .112 x 8 = 0.896
0   .896 x 8 = 7.168
7   .168

The whole number 5497.658_{10} is equal to 12571.521_8 rounded in the last place. An octal number is easily converted to or from a binary number on a digit-by-digit basis:

Octal	1	2	5	7	1	.	5	2	0	7
Binary	001	010	101	111	001		.101	010	000	111

The binary number obtained by converting from decimal to octal to binary is, of course, the same as was obtained earlier by directly converting from decimal to binary. A reverse process of grouping three bits into one octal numeral ($101010_2 = 52_8$, for example) is often used to facilitate reading binary numbers.

Codes Based on Binary

Users and designers of data-processing equipment have different viewpoints about the ideal number system to use. Business users prefer a decimal number system because input data and output are typically decimal. Computer designers, on the other hand, prefer a binary system because it is easier to design and build equipment with components expected to maintain two stable states rather than ten. There are two ways to reach a compromise on the number system conflict. One way is to retain decimal numbers for input and output, and design the machine to operate with pure binary numbers. Using two number systems requires converting input from decimal to binary and output back to decimal. The task of manual conversion is so onerous for people, as indicated by the examples given earlier, that the computer is programmed to handle it. Converting a decimal number to a binary number may be done during a card-reading cycle. If magnetic-tape input is used, the conversion operation may impede processing enough to be impractical. Conversion may be undesirable for business applications that involve a small amount of processing in relation to input-output volumes.

Another way to reconcile the decimal-binary conflict is to represent each decimal digit in a binary code and avoid the task of converting the number as a whole into binary. The conversion of a decimal number into a binary-coded decimal, as discussed below, is simpler than its conversion into binary. But this greater ease of conversion is gained at the cost of longer numbers, since binary-coded decimal numbers are longer than the corresponding binary numbers. Manipulating binary-coded decimal numbers also involves either more circuitry or slower processing. Business applications are generally thought to be handled more efficiently by a processor using a binary-coded decimal scheme than by one using binary.

Three bits will represent an octal digit, but four are required to represent the ten possible decimal digits. The potential number of combinations of bits are:

2 bits:	00,	01,	10,	11			
3 bits:	000,	001,	010,	011,	100,	101,	110,	111
4 bits:	0000,	0001,	0010,	0011,	0100,	0101,	0110,	0111
	1000,	1001,	1010,	1011,	1100,	1101,	1110,	1111

Four bits give sixteen possible combinations ($2^4 = 16$), but only ten are needed for a binary coding of the decimal digits 0 through 9. The remaining six combinations are not used for decimal numerals but can be used for other symbols. The fact that six out of sixteen possible combinations are not used for binary-coded decimal is one reason why a binary equivalent, being more compact, is often preferred. Only 3.3 bits in binary are needed to represent one decimal digit, whereas binary-coded decimal requires four bits per decimal digit.

There are many binary-coded decimal schemes. One, called "8421," derives from the value assigned each bit position. Four bits are used to represent each decimal digit as follows:

Decimal	5	4	9	7	.	6	5	8
Binary-coded decimal	0101	0100	1001	0111	.	0110	0101	1000

The binary number equal to 5497.658_{10} was previously shown to be $1010101111001.101010001_2$, which contains twenty-two bits; the binary-coded decimal equivalent contains twenty-eight. The 8-4-2-1 code is a weighted four-bit code, and the weight of each bit position must be used to convert to the decimal digit. It is important that converting decimal to binary-coded decimal can be done either by people or by equipment, and without multiplication or division.

Weighting each bit position is not an essential feature of a numerical code; several non-weighted codes are used in computers. The most widely used non-weighted code is called "excess 3." The binary equivalent of decimal 3 (0011) is added to the binary value of each decimal digit in the 8-4-2-1 code. For example, the value of decimal 5 in 8-4-2-1, which is 0101, is increased by 0011 to get 1000 in excess 3 code.

	Decimal	Binary-coded Decimal
5	=	0101
+3	=	+ 0011
5 in excess 3 code		1000

Addition in binary involves the rule $0+0=0$, $1+0=1$, $0+1=1$, $1+1=0$ and carry 1.

The excess 3 code is useful because it makes some arithmetical operations easier. The 9's complement of a number is obtained in excess 3 code merely by converting each 1 to 0 and each 0 to 1. For example, 5 is 1000 in excess 3 code and is complemented to 0111 by converting each 1 to 0 and each 0 to 1. The complement 0111 is in excess 3 code and has a value of 4 in binary-coded decimal when the excess 3 is removed $-0111-0011=0100$. Subtraction operations are often done by means of complementing the amount to be subtracted and adding the complement. Subtraction by complements is discussed in the chapter on arithmetic and control units.

Codes with five, six, or more bits per decimal digit are often used. The increase in the number of bits above the 3.3 bits required in pure binary to represent a decimal digit may be offset by other advantages. The bi-quinary code is a 7-bit weighted code with positional values of 5, 0 (bi) and 4, 3, 2, 1, 0 (quinary). A decimal numeral represented in this code contains one "bi" bit and one "quinary" bit. The existence of any combination other than one bit from each group indicates a malfunction in the computer.

Numerical coding system values for 0 to 9 are shown in Table 2-1. Many other codes exist, some of which are used for computers. Equipment designers select the code that is best for a given application. Business applications involve a higher ratio of input-output operations to computations than do engineering and mathematical applications. Therefore, equipment intended for business applications is designed with a machine code, such as binary-coded decimal, that is easily converted from (or to) a code suitable for use by other machines and people. Economical conversion operations are desirable even though computing costs are increased by using a code not so well suited for internal operations as the binary code.

TABLE 2-1. *Numerical Coding Systems*

Decimal Digit	Binary	Octal	Binary-coded Decimal Representation			
			8421	Excess 3	7421	Bi-quinary 50 43210
0	0	0	0000	0011	0000	01 00001
1	1	1	0001	0100	0001	01 00010
2	10	2	0010	0101	0010	01 00100
3	11	3	0011	0110	0011	01 01000
4	100	4	0100	0111	0100	01 10000
5	101	5	0101	1000	0101	10 00001
6	110	6	0110	1001	0110	10 00010
7	111	7	0111	1010	1000	10 00100
8	1000	10	1000	1011	1001	10 01000
9	1001	11	1001	1100	1010	10 10000

ALPHANUMERICAL SYSTEMS

Alphabetic characters are more difficult to represent than numerals since they are more varied—26 letters and 10 or so special characters instead of 10 numerals. Furthermore, alphabetic characters are not convertible into binary numbers by the usual scheme of division. The name John Jones cannot be represented in binary in any easy way.

Six-bit Code

The binary-coded decimal scheme using four bits to handle 16 characters can be extended to six bits to represent 64 characters, six bits yielding 2^6 or 64 possible combinations. Using six bits for each character makes it possible to represent the English alphabet A to Z in upper case characters, Arabic numerals 0 to 9, and 28 other characters in what might be called a binary-coded alphanumerical scheme.

Examples of special symbols, numerals (in excess 3 code), and letters in binary-coded alphanumerical are:

(	00 0010
)	00 0011
/	01 0010
0	01 0011
1	01 0100
7	01 1010
C	10 0010
D	10 0011
S	11 0010
T	11 0011

Notice that (, /, C, and S have the same four right-hand bits but differ in the two left-hand bits. In some ways this is comparable to the two top row or zone punches—X and Y— on a standard 80-column punched card that are used with punches for 0 to 9 to represent alphabetical characters. The four right-hand bits which yield 16 combinations are used with two left-hand bits yielding 4 combinations for a a total of 64. This range of characters serves for many purposes but does not provide for both lower (a, b, c...z) and upper case characters. An important point easily overlooked is that the combination of bits "10 0010" does not mean "C" to a computer, but is merely assigned that value by people using the equipment. The bits 10 0010 can just as easily stand for any letter in any alphabet that does not use more than 64 characters; the desired letter is placed on keyboards used for preparing input and on printers for output.

Parity-bit

An extra binary digit, called the "parity-bit," is often attached to each character solely to detect whether the equipment is malfunctioning by dropping or gaining a bit. If the equipment designer chooses to use an odd-parity-bit rule, an odd number of bits is used to represent each character. The gain or loss of one bit results in an even number of bits and violates the odd-bit rule. For example, the character "B" may be represented as 100001, with an odd parity-bit attached in the parity channel to give 1 100001. The loss of one bit gives 2 bits or the gain of one bit gives 4, and both of these violate the odd-parity-bit rule.

Channel		Character				
Name	Number	)	*	8	B	X
Parity-bit channel	7	0	0	1	1	0
Zone channels	6	0	0	0	1	1
	5	0	0	1	0	1
	4	0	1	1	0	0
	3	1	1	0	0	1
Numerical channels	2	0	0	1	0	1
	1	0	1	1	1	1
Number of bits		1	3	5	3	5

The even-parity-bit rule—add a bit, if required, to make the number of bits in a character even—gives essentially the same result as the odd-bit rule. One reason for using the odd-bit rule is to guard against the loss of all bits, resulting in zero bits, which might be accepted as passing the even-bit rule. Interestingly, an equipment manufacturer may use an odd parity-bit for recording on magnetic tape and an even parity-bit for punched paper tape.

There are other ways of detecting the complete loss of a character, such as counting the number of characters each time they are handled or using a parity-bit for each channel along tape. The lengthwise, or longitudinal parity-bit scheme is useful for detecting the loss of a bit in a channel. In conjunction with the vertical parity-bit, the longitudinal bit can be used to detect and correct an equipment malfunction of one bit. The message "213786 425 390 JOHN DOE" (with < and > for start message and end message, and ● for item separator) might be recorded on tape with a parity-bit for each character in Channel 7 and for each channel in the position marked p.

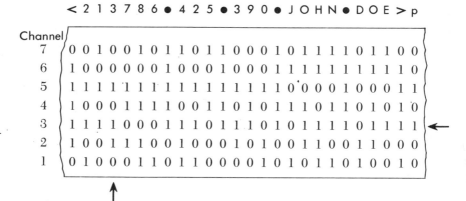

If a bit were lost so that the first 3, for example, was recorded as 0010010 with only two bits, the odd-parity-bit rule would be violated in both the column and the row marked with arrows. With only one bit lost (or gained), correction could be made by complementing whatever exists at the intersection of lines drawn from the two arrows. The complementing of 0 to 1 or 1 to 0 would correct the malfunction of the recording equipment. More elaborate parity-bit schemes, especially longitudinal ones, are used to detect and correct more severe malfunctions. A six-bit code with parity-bit added is commonly used to detect the loss of bits in alphanumerical codes on magnetic tape. When data are transferred into the computer, the parity-bit scheme may be dropped because the risk of losing a bit during computation is far less than during tape reading or writing.

An example of a six-bit code with parity-bit at the left of the character is shown in Figure 2-5. This code is arranged in the collating or sorting sequence, which means that data in this code could be arranged in numerical and alphabetic sequence. The five messages,

< 4357 ● DOE, JOHN > , < 2476 ● ROE, RICHARD > , < 1289 ●
BAKER, CHARLEY > , < 2476 ● ROE, JOHN > , and < 7365 ●
BAKER, ABLE > , could be sorted into two different sequences by
using either the whole message or only the second item (and following
items, if desired) as a key to identify the message.

CHARACTER DESCRIPTION	SYMBOL	P*	2^5	2^4	2^3	2^2	2^1	2^0	OCTAL EQUIVALENT
Blank		1	0	0	0	0	0	0	00
Space	—	0	0	0	0	0	0	1	01
Cross	‡	0	0	0	0	0	1	0	02
Open Parenthesis	(	1	0	0	0	0	1	1	03
Close Parenthesis	)	0	0	0	0	1	0	0	04
Quotes	"	1	0	0	0	1	0	1	05
Colon	:	1	0	0	0	1	1	0	06
Dollars	$	0	0	0	0	1	1	1	07
Percent	%	0	0	0	1	0	0	0	10
Semicolon	;	1	0	0	1	0	0	1	11
Ampersand	&	1	0	0	1	0	1	0	12
Apostrophe	'	0	0	0	1	0	1	1	13
Minus	⊖	1	0	0	1	1	0	0	14
Asterisk	*	0	0	0	1	1	0	1	15
Period	.	0	0	0	1	1	1	0	16
Carriage Shift (CS)		1	0	0	1	1	1	1	17
Page Change (PC)		0	0	1	0	0	0	0	20
Line Shift (LS)		1	0	1	0	0	0	1	21
Slant	/	1	0	1	0	0	1	0	22
Zero (Numeric)	0	0	0	1	0	0	1	1	23
One	1	1	0	1	0	1	0	0	24
Two	2	0	0	1	0	1	0	1	25
Three	3	0	0	1	0	1	1	0	26
Four	4	1	0	1	0	1	1	1	27
Five	5	1	0	1	1	0	0	0	30
Six	6	0	0	1	1	0	0	1	31
Seven	7	0	0	1	1	0	1	0	32
Eight	8	1	0	1	1	0	1	1	33
Nine	9	0	0	1	1	1	0	0	34
Comma	,	1	0	1	1	1	0	1	35
Number	#	1	0	1	1	1	1	0	36
Carriage Normal		0	0	1	1	1	1	1	37
A	A	0	1	0	0	0	0	0	40
B	B	1	1	0	0	0	0	1	41
C	C	1	1	0	0	0	1	0	42
D	D	0	1	0	0	0	1	1	43
E	E	1	1	0	0	1	0	0	44
F	F	0	1	0	0	1	0	1	45
G	G	0	1	0	0	1	1	0	46
H	H	1	1	0	0	1	1	1	47
I	I	1	1	0	1	0	0	0	50
J	J	0	1	0	1	0	0	1	51
K	K	0	1	0	1	0	1	0	52
L	L	1	1	0	1	0	1	1	53
M	M	0	1	0	1	1	0	0	54
N	N	1	1	0	1	1	0	1	55
O	O	1	1	0	1	1	1	0	56
P	P	0	1	0	1	1	1	1	57
Q	Q	1	1	1	0	0	0	0	60
R	R	0	1	1	0	0	0	1	61
S	S	0	1	1	0	0	1	0	62
T	T	1	1	1	0	0	1	1	63
U	U	0	1	1	0	1	0	0	64
V	V	1	1	1	0	1	0	1	65
W	W	1	1	1	0	1	1	0	66
X	X	0	1	1	0	1	1	1	67
Y	Y	0	1	1	1	0	0	0	70
Z	Z	1	1	1	1	0	0	1	71
End File (FF)		1	1	1	1	0	1	0	72
End Data (ED)		0	1	1	1	0	1	1	73
Item Separator (ISS)	●	1	1	1	1	1	0	0	74
End Message (EM)	>	0	1	1	1	1	0	1	75
Start Message (SM)	<	0	1	1	1	1	1	0	76
		1	1	1	1	1	1	1	77†

* The parity bit (P) is shown as it appears on magnetic tape (odd parity); on paper tape, parity is even.

† 77 with odd parity (1111111) is a legitimate octal number on magnetic tape. On paper tape, 77 is a legitimate octal number only when there is no punch in the seventh (P) channel (even parity). The Paper Tape Reader ignores a row in which all seven channels are punched, interpreting this as a corrective measure.

FIGURE 2-5. *The RCA 501 code, with odd parity-bit*

The sequence using the whole message as the sorting key would
be correct numerically, although not necessarily correct alphabetically.

1289	BAKER, CHARLEY
2476	ROE, JOHN
2476	ROE, RICHARD
4357	DOE, JOHN
7365	BAKER, ABLE

The sequence using the second item as the sorting key would be
correct alphabetically, but not numerically.

7365	BAKER, ABLE
1289	BAKER, CHARLEY
4357	DOE, JOHN
2476	ROE, JOHN
2476	ROE, RICHARD

Each of these sequences is in ascending order according to the key used and the values in the collation table. When keys contain both alphabetic and numerical characters, the resulting sorted sequence depends on whether numerals precede letters (as is true for the code shown above) or vice versa.

Multi-mode Codes

The fact that four bits are enough for a numerical code whereas six are required for an alphanumerical code poses a dilemma. If a four-bit code is used for recording numerals, then an alphabetic character might be represented by a two-digit number; this means that eight bits must be used to do the work of six. For example, "A" might first be given the decimal number 01 and then coded as 0011 0100 in binary-coded decimal, excess 3. The two-for-one scheme is more efficient for numerals than for alphabetic characters, but is acceptable where alphabetic data are small in volume and letters are printed as letters and not as two-decimal digits that people must convert into letters.

A variation of the two-for-one scheme is the three-for-two, which uses the twelve bits of three numerals for directly representing two alphanumerical characters. This scheme is carried further in some equipment so that 24 bits treated as a word may be used as 8 octal, 6 decimal, or 4 alphanumerical characters. These modes are alternatives to using the 24 bits as one binary number. One parity-bit can serve for the 24 bits. Longer words of 36 and 48 bits, which are multiples of 3, 4, and 6, may also be used in similar fashion by specifying the mode and by grouping the bits.

Twenty-four bits	101001110100101101100100
Groups of three bits	
Octal numbers	5 1 6 4 5 5 4 4
Groups of four bits	
Binary-coded decimal	
(excess 3)	7 4 1 8 3 1
Groups of six bits	
Alphanumerical	J U N E
One group of twenty-four bits	
Binary	10963812

Some equipment manufacturers, on the other hand, use a two-for-three scheme by putting three numerals into the 12 bits available for two alphabetic characters. For example, three words of 10 numerals each in 6-bit alphanumerical code can be condensed one-third; this can be done by dropping the 00 zone bits of the numerals and writing the 4-bit code on magnetic tape in the space allotted to two alphanumerical words. The condensed numbers are returned to ordinary 6-bit form for internal storage and processing.

The selection of an efficient code for representing data depends on whether alphabetic or numerical data are involved, as well as on the amount of processing to be done each time the data are handled. If numbers are predominant in the data, a numerical code—either pure binary or binary-coded decimal—offers more compact storage than an alphanumerical code, although at the cost of clumsy methods for handling letters. Conversely, alphabetic data can be handled directly by alphanumerical codes which are not efficient for handling numerals (six bits must be used for a numeral where $3\frac{1}{3}$ would suffice). Processing inside the computer is more efficient for numbers represented in binary, but such processing requires a conversion to decimal or alphabetic form that people can use. Frequent conversion between alphanumerical and binary offsets some of the benefits derived from more efficient internal processing. Newer machines, as pointed out above, are being designed to handle data in binary, octal, decimal, or alphabetic modes.

ORGANIZATION OF DATA

Data-processing equipment senses, stores, and manipulates a wide variety of characters. Individual characters must be grouped together in a way that is practical for use by people and machines.

The organization of data can be illustrated by the Jameson Knitting Company's scheme for keeping track of customers' orders. An order record is prepared on paper (see Figure 2-6) for each order received from a customer; it identifies the customer, lists the items ordered, and posts the quantity shipped or back-ordered. Each numeral, letter, punctuation mark, or symbol is a *character*. Characters are grouped into *items* to specify a particular unit of information—order number, date, alphabetic name, street address, stock number, and quantity. A *line* consists of one or more items of data placed on the same horizontal level—order number and date are two items in one line.

The data kept about a customer's order originate from several sources in the form of *messages*. Examples of messages in this case are the customer's order and the shipping department's report of the quantity of each stock number shipped or back-ordered. The messages are processed to make up a *record*. These records comprise the back order *file*. The organization of data on paper, from the smallest to the largest unit, is by character, item, line, message, record, and file.

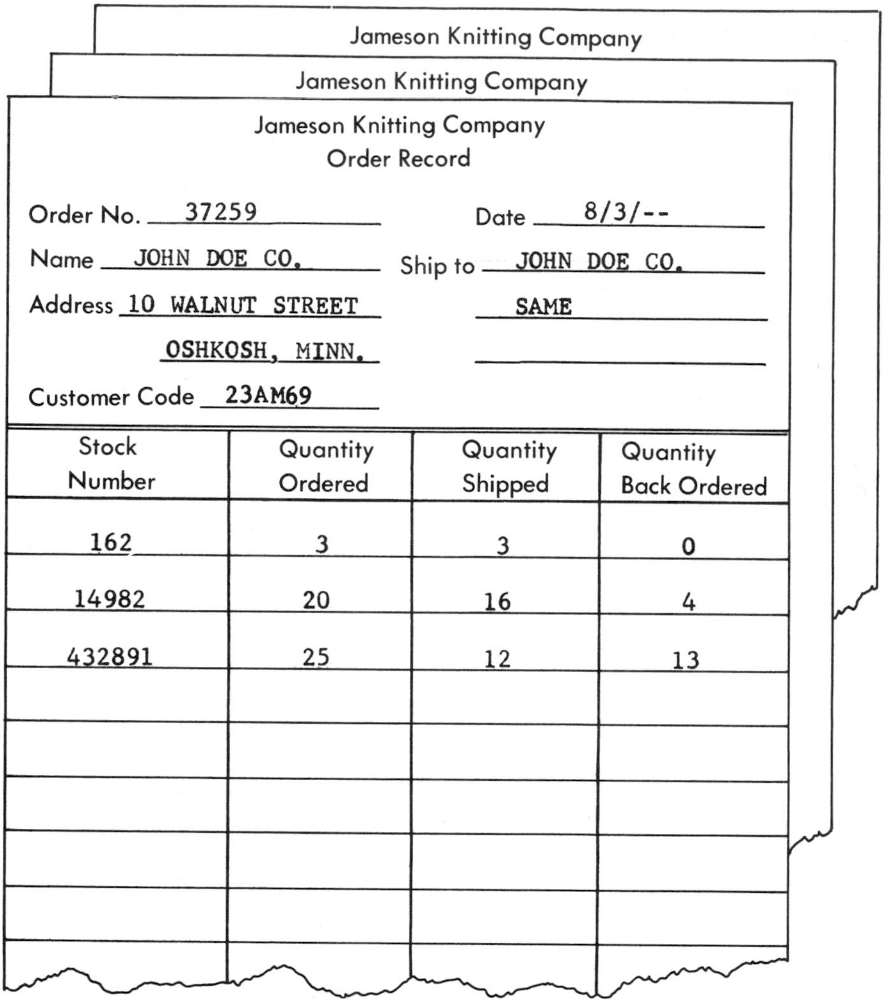

Jameson Knitting Company

Jameson Knitting Company

Jameson Knitting Company
Order Record

Order No. ___37259___   Date ___8/3/--___

Name ___JOHN DOE CO.___   Ship to ___JOHN DOE CO.___

Address _10 WALNUT STREET_   _SAME_

_____OSHKOSH, MINN._____   _____

Customer Code __23AM69__

Stock Number	Quantity Ordered	Quantity Shipped	Quantity Back Ordered
162	3	3	0
14982	20	16	4
432891	25	12	13

FIGURE 2-6. *Customer order record, paper*

Fixed-variable Length Items

A customer order file kept on paper records illustrates the use of fixed-variable length items. The maximum number of characters needed for any item is anticipated and provided for in printing the form. The length provided for each item can be fixed individually, so that a long space can be provided for customer name (which is not controllable and may take 30 or 40 characters). Stock numbers, on the other hand, can be established as desired and restricted to a few digits, although 10 or 20 digits are often used for unique identifications in large inventory systems. Since space on paper records is inexpensive, field lengths can be set generously to handle the longest item likely to occur. And, of course, people are clever enough to modify the length of an item by writing in the margin, if necessary, to process the records satisfactorily.

Punched cards pose a more difficult problem for fixing item length. Since the total number of columns available in a card is usually 80 or 90, their use must be economized to prevent some records from carrying over to several cards. Once a field—the number of columns— is assigned to an item, the maximum length is fixed for punched-card processing. If the longest stock number is 20 characters, then a field of 20 columns is assigned for use with both long and short numbers. For example, the numbers 387-A4295725-9291 and B7070 would be punched into a 20-column field as 000387-A4295725-9291 and 000000000000000B7070. The quantities of items, on the other hand, might range from 1 to 9999 and require only four columns. An entirely different arrangement of data might be used for name and address cards and for each stock number ordered by a customer.

In short, the term "fixed-variable" means that the amount of space allotted to an item in a certain record is variable until a certain amount is assigned. Thereafter, the amount of space for that item is fixed so that shorter items are filled out and longer items cannot be fitted into the space assigned.

Variable-length Items

The facilities used for processing data may be able to deal equally well with long and short items without special regard for the longest case that may occur (*RCA Electronic Data Processing System 501,* 1958). If so, it is only necessary to identify the item and use the number of characters that are needed. Blank paper, without any designation of items, is a simple example of a variable-length item record. On blank paper a record might contain explicit identification and items in sequence without regard for format or spacing.

> Order No. 37259 Date 8/3/—Name John Doe Co. Ship to John Doe Co. Address 10 Walnut St. Same Oshkosh, Minn. Same Customer code 23AM69 Stock number Quantity ordered Quantity shipped Quantity back-ordered 162 3 3 0 14982 20 16 4 432891 25 12 13

The order record written in variable-length items occupies less space on blank paper than variable-fixed length items on a printed form. More skill is required to associate headings—stock number, quantity ordered, shipped, and back-ordered—with the related items. The loss of one item might cause the others to be misinterpreted.

The name of each item need not be listed explicitly but can be implied from the sequence of the items by following a specified sequence and separating the items. The order for John Doe can be compressed where ● is an item separator and < indicates start of record and > indicates end of record.

> < 37259 ● 8/3/— ● John Doe Co. ● John Doe Co. ● 10 Walnut St. ● Same ● Oshkosh, Minn. ● Same ● 23AM69 ● 162 ● 3 ● 3 ● 0 ● 14982 ● 20 ● 16 ● 4 ● 432891 ● 25 ● 12 ● 13 >

The item following the second item separator is expected to be the customer's name so that, if the date is omitted, the separators are included for counting purposes: < 37259 ●● John Doe Co. ● . . . . When records are organized in this manner, a repetitive pattern develops—stock number, quantity ordered, shipped, and back-ordered—so that the 10th, 14th, or 18th item is always the stock number. Computers that handle variable-length items (see Figure 2-7) can store and process data recorded in this fashion on magnetic tape.

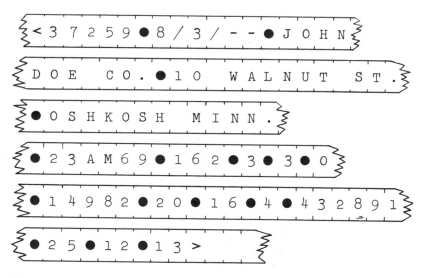

FIGURE 2-7. *Customer order record, magnetic tape, variable-length field*

Fixed Word and Block

"Word" is often defined as a fixed number of characters or character locations that are treated as a unit. Word length is fixed by the computer designer and incorporated in the circuitry. Common word lengths are 10 or 12 alphanumerical characters and 24, 36, or 48 bits. Every computer word must contain the specified number of characters or bits. Excess positions in computer words can be filled with spaces where the original items of data are short. Figure 2-8 shows the layout for a customer order on magnetic tape with fixed word length.

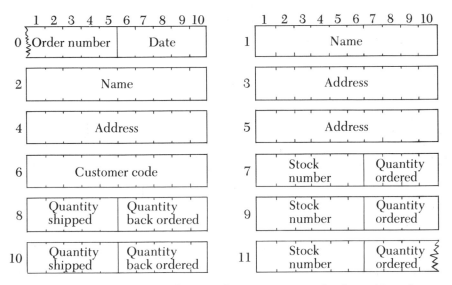

FIGURE 2-8. *Customer order record, magnetic tape, fixed word length*

Longer items occurring in the data can be handled by using two or more computer words together to represent one item. Fixed-word equipment uses extra storage space, if words are filled out with spaces. If two or more items of data are packed into one word, extra steps are required to separate or unpack the items for individual processing. An opposite situation arises when an item is longer than a computer word so that two words are used to store an item. Both words must be treated together when making comparisons during sorting or when performing arithmetical operations.

"Block" means a fixed number of words treated as a unit on a magnetic tape and in computer storage. Data on magnetic tape can be read only while the tape is moving at speeds of approximately 100 inches a second. Inter-record gaps or blank spaces of about one-half inch on tape are required for starting and stopping tape movement. If the tape-packing density is 200 characters an inch, ten characters in a word occupy one-twentieth inch of tape. Tapes written with individual words would have ten times as much start-stop space as data space. In order to conserve space on tape, data are handled as fixed-length blocks of characters; for example, 720 characters consisting of 60 words of 12 characters each. A computer designed to handle variable-length fields may handle blocks as short as eight characters with no upper limit for length. In the conversion of data from punched cards to tape, the block length is limited to the 80 characters in a card. Short blocks may be consolidated into longer blocks during the first processing run to reduce tape length and cut read-write time in subsequent passes.

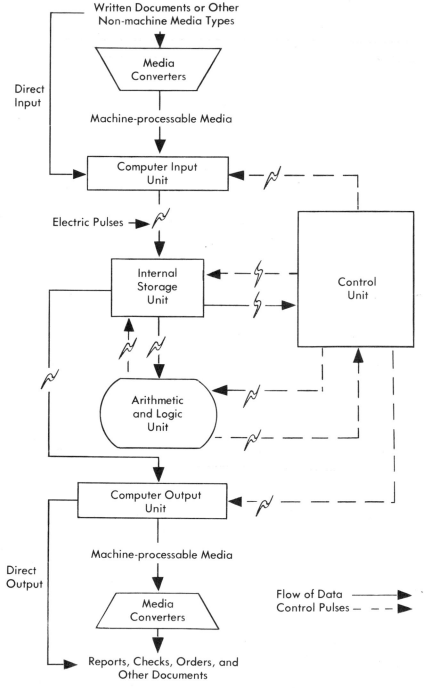

FIGURE 2-9. *Schematic outline of automatic data-processing system*

CENTRAL PROCESSING UNIT

A key feature of automatic data processing is the storage of data for electronic manipulation according to instructions stored with the data. Efficient processing involves media converters and input units, which get the data and instructions into storage for processing. Similarly, output units and converters are used to unload the processor and get results into a usable form.

Figure 2-9 is a schematic diagram of the major elements of an automatic data-processing system. Input units are magnetic-tape, paper-tape, and punched-card readers. Electric typewriters are used for small-volume input and modification of instructions. Output units are magnetic-tape-recording units, card and tape punches, high-speed printers, and electric typewriters.

The central processing unit has three components: (1) internal storage unit to receive input data, supply data and instructions during processing, and furnish results to the output unit; (2) arithmetic and logic section to perform calculations and make comparisons; (3) unit to control operations of the storage and arithmetic-logic units.

The internal storage element, made of magnetic cores or a magnetic drum, forms an integral part of the computer and is directly controlled by it. Internal storage is compartmentalized into thousands of individual locations that can store data or instructions. Each location has an address that is unique, so that it can be located by its number or by description—as we would locate a house from the instruction, "1627 Ann Arbor Avenue," or "3 blocks beyond the house where the Browns live." The first addressing scheme, which uses the street number, is called "absolute;" the second is called "relative," since it describes one location by referring to another one. Some interesting features of the relative addressing scheme will be discussed later.

Computers with internally stored programs have operating instructions stored internally with the data. Although similar to data, instructions are distinguished by their use. Instructions are executed by the control unit, to operate on the data or to modify other instructions to fit new conditions that arise during processing. Computers with externally stored programs, on the other hand, get their operating instructions from wired plugboards. Some computers utilize both internally and externally stored programs, since each type has desirable features.

The arithmetic and logic unit might be called an electronic adding machine, for it performs adding and subtracting operations. Multiplication involves repeated additions and shifts, and division involves subtractions and shifts. An electronic arithmetic and logic unit can execute thousands of arithmetical operations a second compared to the addition of several ten-digit numbers a minute by an experienced desk-calculator operator.

The arithmetic and logic unit is used to make simple decisions that involve choosing between alternatives. If numbers are involved, a decision is an extension of addition or subtraction operations. The arithmetic unit distinguishes between positive and negative numbers. Depending on whether the remainder obtained from subtracting one number from another is positive or negative, the appropriate sequence of instructions is selected next. For example, a 5 per cent discount may be allowed on sales of $50.00 and over. It is easy to determine whether the amount of sale is $50.00 or more by subtracting $49.99 from the sales price and checking the remainder. If the remainder is positive, the steps for calculating discount are used. No discount is allowed, of course, if the remainder is zero or negative, so the discount calculation steps are skipped.

Items of data involving letters are compared in order to find which item is earlier or later in the collation table of values assigned to alphanumerical characters. For letters, collation table values are in alphabetic sequence. The binary value for B is higher than for A, that for C higher than the one for B, and Z has the highest binary value of the letters. Logical comparison of the name entries, "Jones, John" with "James, John" will indicate that "Jones, John" has a higher collation table value. In a sorting run using names as the sorting keys, "James" would be put ahead of "Jones" to get an alphabetic sequence. Numerical keys—stock numbers and invoice numbers—are used for sorting items into numerical sequence. Comparison is preferable to subtraction to find whether one item is smaller or larger than another, for the comparison operation does not disturb the two numbers in the same way that subtraction does.

The control unit of an electronic data processor is comparable to a telephone exchange. It sets switches and directs the operations and flow of data through the system.

Somewhat simplified, the operating procedure of a typical computer is as follows:

1. The control unit *reads* an instruction contained in a particular storage location.
2. The control unit *decodes* the pulses received from storage. Each sequence of pulses causes the control unit to carry out a specific operation, such as comparing, adding, or storing data. Pulses also indicate the location of the data involved in the operation.
3. The control unit reads the next instruction in sequence or goes to another place, as directed, to find the next instruction to execute.

Instructions and data in computer storage are distinguished solely by the routing of pulses from internal storage. Pulses routed to the control unit are interpreted as instructions; those routed to the arithmetic unit are treated as data. Frequently, it is desirable to send an instruction to the arithmetic unit so that it can be treated as data and modified. For example, an instruction written as "ADD 276" means "add the contents of storage address 276 to the contents of the accumulator." This instruction, which is stored internally as a number, can be altered by placing it in the accumulator and adding to it the contents of some storage address that contains 1 to get, in effect, "ADD 277." When this modified instruction is placed back in storage and used in a later cycle, the content of address 277 is added. The ability to operate on and change an instruction during processing is an extremely important feature of electronic processors.

On the other hand, data misdirected to the control unit are treated as an instruction. Since data are seldom in the correct form to be treated as instructions, an error indicator flashes and the computer stops.

DATA FLOW

The flow of data through a business involves pre-input, input, comparisons and computations, and output.

The first stage, pre-input, involves collection of data in a suitable form. Handwritten or typed documents, oral orders, clock and meter readings, and physical counts are transferred to punched cards, punched tape, or magnetic tape by various means. Data converted into machine-processable forms from time cards, material receipts and issues, and other sources need not be handled manually again. Cards and punched tapes may be converted to magnetic tape for high-speed input.

The desired data medium—magnetic tape, punched cards, or punched tape—is placed in an input unit that is electrically connected to the computer. Instructions to the control unit turn on the input unit and read some data. Electrical signals representing data on the input medium are converted to computer code and sent to a specified internal storage location. The read-in may be regulated by a buffer unit that compensates for the differences between the reading speed of a punched-card unit and the much higher rate at which the computer can receive data. Simultaneous operations of reading while computing and writing, called "read while compute while write," are used to speed up operations.

The third stage in data flow consists of the logical and arithmetical operations: to arrange data in sequence, if required; to maintain files for insertion and deletion of changes; to update files for transactions; to issue reports and answer questions; to prepare production schedules and material requirements; and to compute answers to non-routine problems, such as finding the best location for a new warehouse in view of plant and customer locations.

Output of results is the fourth stage in the flow of data. An output instruction going to the control unit causes the transfer of the contents of one or more storage addresses to an output unit. Electric pulses in storage are decoded to create a corresponding record on an output unit that handles magnetic tape, printed paper copy, punched cards, or paper tape. Huge differences exist between the speeds of internal data transfer and "writing" on an output medium. This difference may be adjusted by output buffers that can receive results from the computer at high speeds and then store the results until a lower speed output unit is ready to unload the buffer. After loading the buffer, the computer can continue other operations, so that computing and writing are done almost simultaneously, with only short interruptions of the computer. The output unit may be designed to request a transfer of results whenever it is ready to receive them; this simplifies the operating instructions required for the computer.

A common solution to the problem of a printing unit's slowing down computer output is to use off-line printing. Results are transferred from internal storage to magnetic tape at speeds ranging from 10,000 to 100,000 characters a second. The computer is then free to perform other operations while the magnetic tape is run through a high-speed printer handling from 1,000 to 5,000 lines a minute. At 120 characters per line, this is 2,000 to 10,000 characters a second.

Television-like data display tubes can receive computer output about as fast as magnetic tape and serve as on-line output under direction of the control unit of the computer. Photographs of the display tube face are the readable copy.

SUMMARY

Many methods are used to represent, store, and operate on data. The efficient storage and use of data depend on the symbols, media, writer, and reader. Each combination of these factors imposes some restrictions on data-processing techniques, for all factors must operate compatibly.

Punched cards and punched paper tape have been widely used for storing business data. The codes, as originally developed, tended to be limited to numerals alone, but were expanded to include alphabetical characters fairly recently. Cards and tape both involve the mechanical operations of punching holes in paper. The width, length, and thickness of cards and tape influence the alphabet used, data density, and processing methods.

Magnetic recording media are similar to cards and paper tape in some respects, but have the highly desirable features that fewer mechanical operations are involved and the media can be re-used for other data.

Number systems owe much to the historical context in which they originated and developed. Various number systems—decimal, duo-decimal, hexadecimal, octal and binary, which you would recognize as counting by 10, 12, 16, 8 and 2, respectively—are widely used today, although we tend to overemphasize the decimal system. Computer designers prefer the binary system of data representation because two-state devices are easier to build and operate than multi-state devices. People, however, much prefer other systems so that some conversion from one system to another is required and is usually performed by equipment.

Four-bit codes, with sixteen possible combinations, are often used for numerals. Six-bit codes are used to represent numerals, letters and special characters but are, of course, limited to a total of 64 characters ($2^6 = 64$). Alphanumerical codes usually have an additional parity-bit to detect the gain or loss of a bit that would change the desired character to an illegal character. A total of seven bits—six bits for the character plus a parity-bit—could represent 128 characters ($2^7 = 128$); but only half of the possible characters are considered legal. The adoption of the odd (or even) parity-bit scheme, according to the computer designer's choice, makes illegal all the characters that have an even (or odd) number of bits. The "loss" resulting from ruling out half of the possible number of characters that can be formed with any specified number of bits when one is designated as a parity-bit, is widely considered a fair price to pay for the increased ability to detect errors. The general idea of parity-bits need not be limited to one bit for a character—transverse parity. One or more additional parity-bits may be used for several characters—longitudinal parity. Both transverse and longitudinal parity are sometimes used to increase the ability to detect and even correct errors in data recorded on tape.

Multi-mode schemes are used to represent letters in codes that are basically numeric. The eight bits designated for two numerals can be used for one letter—two-for-one scheme—or the twelve bits designated for three numerals can be used for two letters—three-for-two scheme. Some computers are designed to treat the bits of a word in any one of several ways at the programmer's option: binary, alphanumerical, or octal, to maximize the density of data storage for the particular kind of data involved.

Data are organized in the following ways for processing:

1. Character—numeral, letter, punctuation, or other symbol.
2. Item—characters grouped to specify a particular unit of information: order number, date, alphabetic name.

3. Line—one or more items of data on the same level, for example, stock number, name, quantity and price.
4. Message—two or more lines of data that relate to the same transaction.
5. Record—organized and processed messages.
6. File—a collection of related records.

There are several schemes for organizing items for processing in view of the fact that their length may vary greatly. The "fixed-variable" scheme allows you to choose any length that you wish for an item, say, the stock number. But, once chosen, all stock numbers must be the same length at the expense of filling out short numbers with zeros or blanks.

The "variable-length" scheme permits any item to be any length, without any restraints. An item separator is used between every two items. An item is not identified by its location but is identified by its sequence in relation to other items. This plan, in order to keep the item count correct, requires indication of any items omitted.

The "fixed-word-and-block" scheme specifies the number of characters that are treated as a word and the number of words handled as a block. The word and block length are designed into the equipment by the manufacturer and the user must adhere to these restrictions.

The flow of data through a business involves the following phases:

1. Pre-input—collect data in a suitable form.
2. Input—transfer or read-in data to the processing unit.
3. Logical and arithmetic operations—maintain and process files, develop reports, and obtain answers to questions.
4. Output—prepare and issue reports and answers in a form suitable for the user's requirements.

REFERENCES AND SUPPLEMENTAL READINGS

Haskins & Sells. *Introduction to Data Processing*, New York, Haskins & Sells, 1957, 107 pp. This book relates the principal methods and devices used in data processing to the basic operations they perform. The first chapter provides a general survey of the needs for data, sources of data, and processing methods. The second chapter outlines and discusses the basic data-processing operations of (a) classifying, (b) sorting, (c) calculating, (d) summarizing, (e) recording, and (f) communicating. Specific methods and devices for performing these operations are considered in the third chapter. The fourth chapter is devoted to punched-card methods and discusses (a) representation of data on cards and (b) methods of operation and functions performed by basic punched-card equipment. The discussion of electronic data processing in the fifth chapter touches on (a) code forms (for both punched-card and electronic systems), (b) basic abilities, (c) principal components, (d) auxiliary equipment, and (e) programming. The principles and problems in the areas of integrated data processing, and the organization and control of data-processing activities are considered in the last two chapters. Numerous diagrams illustrating equipment, equipment operation, and methods of representing data on media are included in the book.

Lerner, Irwin S. "Digital Computers Need Orderly Number Systems," *Control Engineering*, vol. 2: 82-89 (November 1955). Only a few of the available number systems are well suited to machine methods. This article deals with systems for counting and forming numbers in decimal, binary, and octal. Several methods of coding decimal digits in binary form are shown to simplify computer design yet give results in decimal form for people to use. A code may be extended to provide a check against computer malfunction. Some codes require the addition of a checking digit.

"Numerals" and "Numeral Systems." *Encyclopaedia Britannica*, vol. 16: 610-15 (1957). Treats the development of numerals from the early Hindu, through cuneiform to the Greek and Roman. These systems had special symbols for larger numerals and used the add-subtract process to form numbers. For example, in Roman numerals LIX means $50 + (-1 + 10)$.

Cuneiform inscriptions show some appreciation of the place value concept. The Mayans developed a base 20 number system and attached place value to each position with values of 360, 20, and 1 in the first three positions.

The zero, which is an important feature of number systems using place value, was known in India by the close of the eighth century.

The pair system, used by New Guinea tribes, has numerals for "one" and "two" only and forms other numerals by addition to the pair: $5 = 2 + 2 + 1$. Two forms of the decimal system are the quinary decimal, which forms 6 through 9 as $5 + 1$, $5 + 2$, and so forth, and the pure decimal consisting of 0 through 9.

RCA Electronic Data Processing System 501, Programmers' Reference Manual, Camden, New Jersey, Radio Corporation of America, 1958, 81 pp. This programmers' reference manual is similar to the manuals furnished by the equipment manufacturer for each computer manufactured. It includes descriptions of the general system, on-line peripheral equipment, the computer, and the instruction code. The merits of completely variable organization of data on tape which the 501 computer employs are contrasted with fixed-variable and fixed word-length organization of data.

Richards, R. K. *Arithmetic Operations in Digital Computers*, New York, D. Van Nostrand Co., Inc., 1955, 384 pp. This text was prepared in answer to the question, "How does a digital computer work?" from the logical or internal-design viewpoint. A complete treatment of number systems is presented along with the basic theorems of Boolean Algebra. Various techniques in current use for addition and multiplication are demonstrated both for binary systems and for the binary-coded decimal machines. Chapters are included on computer organization and control, and on programming.

CHAPTER THREE

BASIC COMPUTER PROGRAMMING

Programming a computer involves analyzing the problem to be solved and devising a plan to solve it. The list of instructions for carrying out a sequence of desired operations and solving a problem is called a "routine." Problem analysis, which is almost independent of the methods used to process data, is covered in a later chapter. Instruction routines, on the other hand, are closely related to the equipment and processing methods used. A desirable way to learn how to prepare instruction routines is to study a specific computer and its related equipment. The hypothetical computer discussed in this chapter has typical, although simplified, features; studying it will reveal basic principles applicable to programming many computers. Except when otherwise stated, the comments in this chapter pertain to the hypothetical computer, although they may apply to actual computers. A manufacturer's programming manual is, of course, the best source of facts about a particular computer, and it should be consulted by anyone learning to program that computer (*IBM 650 Magnetic Drum Data-Processing Machine Manual of Operations*, 1957, and *Univac II Data Automation System*, 1957).

This chapter covers basic techniques of programming. Some features of advanced programming are described in Chapter 8. Chapters 4 through 7 cover input-output equipment, storage, arithmetic and control units, and available automatic processing equipment. Only passing reference is made in this chapter to equipment components; Chapters 4 through 7 should be consulted for a more detailed discussion of them. (The beginning student may find it useful to study these four chapters and then review this chapter on basic programming before continuing with advanced programming techniques.) Some textbooks concentrating on programming are: Andree (1958); McCracken (1957); and McCracken, Weiss, and Lee (1959). Thomas (1953) has a short, intensive coverage of programming.

INTRODUCTION

Many simplifications are made in devising the hypothetical computer discussed here. Questions and problems at the end of the chapter develop some points in more detail. Practice in answering questions and solving problems is invaluable in learning the fundamentals of programming.

All stored-program computers (those handling instruction routines stored with data) have the four main units shown in Figure 3-1. Solid lines indicate paths for data flow and broken lines show paths for control pulses.

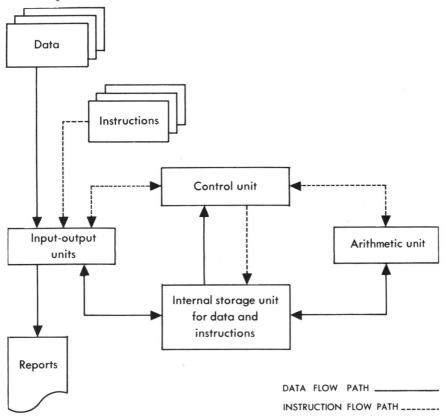

FIGURE 3-1. *Simple block diagram of a computer*

Input-Output

Input and output units bring in data and give out results in the form of reports, summaries, or files for later use. The input and output units available for the hypothetical computer discussed here are several combination card reader-punches and some magnetic-tape-handling units.

Internal Storage

The internal storage unit, where data and instructions must be placed before they can be used, has 1,000 locations or addresses numbered 000 to 999. Reference to data or instructions is made by means of the storage location numbers, for example, "237" or "652," where the data or instructions are contained.

Each storage location can hold a "word" of 7 alphanumerical characters and a plus or minus sign. The sign is stored at the left end of all words but is not significant for alphabetic words, such as + JOHN D., or – MAIN ST. A word in high-speed storage is treated as part of the instruction routine, if it is sent along control pulse paths to direct operation of the computer. A word sent along data flow paths is treated as data. Whether a word is treated as data or an instruction depends on how it is used, for the two look alike in storage. As will be shown later, an instruction can be treated in the same fashion as data to modify it for later use. The ability to modify instructions during processing is a central feature of stored-program computers.

Arithmetic and Control

The arithmetic unit performs the four arithmetical operations: adding, subtracting, multiplying, and dividing. This unit also handles logical operations, such as determining whether an inventory balance is below the re-order point. The control unit sets up computer circuits to decode and execute the instruction routine, as explained in Chapter 2.

OPERATIONS

An instruction can be put in any storage location that can hold a sign and 7 alphanumerical characters. A short word length of 7 characters and sign is used here for brevity. The unique number 7 is useful to avoid thinking of the hypothetical computer as being real, for few, if any, computers have a word of this length.

Instruction Format

The composition of an instruction in the hypothetical computer includes the following elements:

1. An instruction operation code of three characters, which instructs the computer to read, write, compare, add, subtract, and so forth.
2. Three characters for identifying (1) the location of data to be operated on, (2) the location to store a result, or (3) the location of an instruction. These characters may also be a special constant.
3. Designation, by a single character, of a special unit of the machine, such as an "A" for index register A.

The format of an instruction written on programming sheets, punched in cards, or stored in internal storage is as follows:

Sign	1	2	3	4	5	6	7
+	R	C	2		0	2	3

Positive sign for instructions — Operation code — Refers to an index register — Address or special constant

The precise arrangement of letters and numerals in an instruction is important because it is possible to operate arithmetically on an instruction by adding, say, 4 in the right end to change the instruction illustrated from +RC2 023 to +RC2 027.

The instruction "+RC2 023" means "read the next card in card reader number 2 and store the data from that card in the necessary number of words in high-speed storage starting at location 023." Instruction codes and other alphabetic data are written in capital letters because the code scheme used in the hypothetical computer cannot handle both capital and lower-case letters. The lower-case letters used to explain how instructions work are for the programmer's benefit and do not go into the computer.

Sequence of Execution

Instructions are performed in the order of the addresses at which they are placed in high-speed storage, unless the machine is specifically instructed to change the sequence by skipping either forward or backward. The control unit has an instruction counter that keeps track of the storage location of the current instruction. The sequence can be changed by an instruction that resets the counter to the location of the instruction that should be executed next. The instruction counter is, in a sense, a guide for finding the instruction to execute. The instruction register contains the instruction itself.

Instruction Cycle

The computer described here operates in a cyclical manner. The computer cycle for performing one instruction consists of five steps:

1. The control unit takes the address of the next instruction from the instruction counter and copies the instruction into the instruction register.
2. The control unit decodes the instruction in the instruction register.
3. If the operation requires data from storage, the word specified by the address part of the instruction is transferred to the appropriate operating unit.
4. The appropriate unit performs the required operations, such as adding, subtracting, or placing results in storage.

5. The address in the instruction counter is increased by one, or, if the regular sequence of instructions is being broken, it is reset to the desired address to start the next cycle.

The control unit returns to step 1, unless the instruction program calls for the machine to halt operations.

INPUT-OUTPUT OPERATIONS

Certain types of input-output operations are basic to all stored-program computers. Punched cards and magnetic tape are the input and output media provided for the hypothetical computer discussed in this chapter. It is assumed that any data needed were previously punched in cards or recorded on tape. Output from the computer is punched in cards or written on tape. Any printed copy desired will be prepared later by an off-line printer. In an actual operation, the programmer must specify complete details for data input and output format and operating instructions for people.

Punched Cards

Two punched-card units are connected to the computer for on-line operation. Reading and punching are completely independent operations: data cannot be read from and punched into the same card. Program instructions for the read-punch units select the desired unit, number 1 or 2, and either read or punch a card. Reading data into storage destroys what was already there; but punching data into cards or tape leaves the contents of storage unchanged. The instructions for reading and punching cards are as follows:

Code		Explanation
RCn	x	Read the next card in card unit n where n is 1 or 2. Place the data from the card into ten consecutive storage locations starting with address x, where x is a three-digit number 000 through 999.
PCn	x	Punch the next card in card unit n (1 or 2) with ten words from ten consecutive storage locations starting with address x.

The small letters "n" and "x" are used solely for identifying elements of an instruction and are not interpreted by the computer. You will recall that the computer can handle only upper-case letters.

A routine can be developed from these two instructions for reading one or more cards into storage and punching the data into other cards. The cards will merely be duplicated, which is a trivial operation on punched-card equipment, but the idea of an instruction routine is introduced. The program will read data from six cards in card reader number 2 and punch the data in six cards in card punch unit number 1.

The program itself can be placed anywhere in high-speed storage, but it is assumed, for simplicity, that someone has already read it into locations with addresses 000 to 011 to simplify operations here. Data are read into storage locations 100 through 159 and remain there after punching is completed.

Location	Content		Explanation
000	RC2	100	Ten words on the first card in card unit 2 are read and placed in storage locations 100 through 109.
001	RC2	110	Ten words on the second card in unit 2 are read into storage locations 110 through 119.
002	RC2	120	Similar to first two read operations: next card is used
003	RC2	130	and storage locations are advanced by 10.
004	RC2	140	
005	RC2	150	
006	PC1	100	Ten words in storage locations 100 through 109 are punched in the first card in card unit 1.
007	PC1	110	Similar to first punch operation: next card is punched
008	PC1	120	and storage locations are advanced by 10.
009	PC1	130	
010	PC1	140	
011	PC1	150	

Layout in Storage

It is important to note that the *twelve* instructions are stored in locations 000 through 011. When 000 is the location of the first instruction, the second is stored in location 001. Care is necessary to avoid the error of counting from 1 instead of from 0. Drawing a chart of storage and indicating the contents of selected locations, as in Figure 3-2, is useful.

Magnetic Tape

Magnetic tapes are also used for data input and output. Data can be read from or written on any tape, but in the computer discussed here reading and writing cannot both be done at the same time. The ten tape-handling units are numbered 0 through 9 for selection purposes; the reel of magnetic tape placed on tape-handling unit number 3, for instance, is available when tape unit 3 is selected for use. A file number can be recorded on magnetic tape for identification; but when the tape is placed on a tape-handling unit, it is identified by the number assigned that tape-handling unit.

Transfers of data from and to cards and tape are much slower than high-speed storage transfers. Special devices called "buffers" are used exclusively between input-output units and high-speed storage. Data

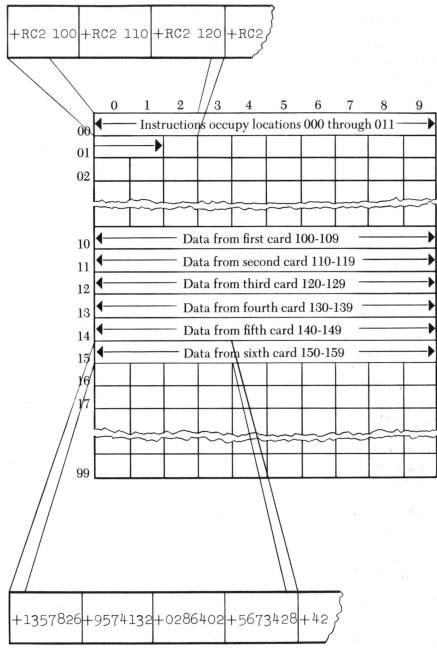

FIGURE 3-2.   *Layout of instructions and data in storage*

are handled in groups of words called "blocks" to facilitate movement between buffers and either input-output units or high-speed storage. A block of words for punched-card input-output is 10 words and for magnetic-tape input-output, 60 words.

In handling one block of data, a tape-handling unit operates as follows: accelerates tape up to rated speed, reads or writes 60 words, decelerates, and stops tape motion. Records are not written continuously on tape, but gaps are left between records to permit acceleration and deceleration of tape. Special instructions are used to move blocks of words (1) between tape units and the buffer and (2) between the buffer and high-speed storage. Magnetic tape can be read while moving in only one direction (from beginning to end) in the computer discussed here, although some computers read data from tape moving in either direction.

The instructions to transfer data from high-speed storage to the output buffer and to write on tape are as follows:

Code		Explanation
BOn	x	Block transfer out a block of data from 60 consecutive locations starting with address x to the buffer storage of tape unit n where n designates tape unit 0 through 9.
WTn	x	Write on tape the block of data in the buffer of tape unit n onto the tape in that unit. Data in the buffer remain unchanged but prior contents of tape are lost.

A simple program, similar to that shown for reading 6 cards and punching them, shows how cards are read into storage, transferred to a magnetic-tape buffer, and written on tape.

Location	Content		Explanation
000	RC2	100	Read ten words on the first card in card input unit 2
001	RC2	110	and place in storage locations 100 through 109. Re-
002	RC2	120	peat for next five cards placing in succeeding loca-
003	RC2	130	tions 10 words later.
004	RC2	140	
005	RC2	150	
006	B09	100	Sixty words in storage locations 100 through 159 are transferred to the buffer storage of tape unit 9.
007	WT9	---	The sixty-word block of data in the buffer storage of tape unit 9 is written on the tape.

This hypothetical instruction routine merely illustrates input-output operations. The reading and writing operations would also be used with other instructions (discussed later) to process data.

To complete the input-output operation, instructions are needed for (1) reading the tape, (2) transferring a block, and (3) rewinding the tape.

Code		Explanation
RTn	- - -	Read the next block of data on tape unit number n, where n is from 0 to 9, and place the data in buffer storage for that tape unit. Data on tape are unchanged.
BIn	x	Block transfer in a block of data from the buffer of tape unit number n into 60 consecutive locations in high-speed storage starting with address x.
RWn	- - -	Rewind the tape on tape unit n. No change occurs in data on tape or in buffer storage.

These three instructions and four defined and illustrated earlier—RCn   x, PCn   x, BOn   x, WTn   x—will handle input and output of data for both punched cards and magnetic tapes. Other instructions are used to simplify the input-output operations, perform computations, and make decisions.

CYCLES

The input-output routines illustrated above are inefficient as far as programming time and the use of storage for instructions are concerned; but they are efficient as far as computing time is concerned. Too many instructions are used to read data from cards into storage or to punch stored data into cards. If each card contained fewer words, perhaps only two, a block of sixty words would take thirty cards and would require thirty reading instructions.

Some repetitious instructions are only slightly different each time they are used, as, RC2 100, RC2 110, RC2 120. Their use can be simplified greatly by setting up the instruction RC2 only once, and modifying the address part from 100 to 110, 120, and so on, as it is used. Index registers are used to modify the instruction address during each cycle.

Index Registers

An index register is a counter that can be set to 000 or any desired number. The number in an index register is used in conjunction with a computer instruction in order to get an "effective address" that is used in executing the desired instruction. Neither index content nor instruction address alone is used, but both are taken together to form the effective address for the purpose of executing the instruction. Neither the index nor the instruction is changed by the effective address scheme; this means that the index register can be used with as many different instructions as desired to get an effective address for each. For example, if an index register containing the number 10 is used with the order RC2 127, then the effective address is $127 + 10$ or 137. Contents of the next card in reader number 2 will be put in storage locations starting at 137 (not 127); but the instruction RC2 127 remains unchanged. The index register content can be increased from 10 to 20 before it is used in the next cycle, so that the effective location for storing contents of the next card will be $127 + 20$ or 147.

The computer described here has three index registers identified as A, B, and C. Each index register contains a three-digit number from 000 to 999 which can be set or increased, as desired, and used in association with addresses of instruction when they are executed to form effective addresses. The number in an index register can be compared to the contents of any desired storage location. This affords a criterion for determining whether the instruction loop has been repeated enough times to complete the cycle—which must be done before other operations can be performed.

General Scheme of Indexing

The three parts of indexed operations are the set-up, the loop, and the exit. In the set-up or initial steps, select an index register and set its contents at zero or some other value. A criterion, which is a number used to test the content of the index register by comparison during each loop, is placed in a storage location. The criterion is often equal to $i + (n \times L)$ where i is the initial value of the index, n is the increment or spacing between operands, and L is the number of loops to be performed. The criterion may be by other schemes for indexing: $i + (n \times L) - 1$; 0, or n.

The loop consists of three functions. The first of these is to execute the operations desired in the main program by using the effective address (the address in the instruction plus the number in the index register). The second is to increase the number in the index register by the "spacing" of the operands (words to be operated on), which may be in consecutive locations, two words apart, or any distance apart. In organized records, the spacing between operands is equal to record length, as illustrated below. The third function is to test the index register number against the criterion to find whether the loop has been repeated enough times. If the cycle is incomplete—shown by the fact that the index number is not equal to the criterion—the loop continues to execute the desired operations. If testing the index register against the criterion indicates that the cycle is complete—because the index register number is equal to the criterion—the computer exits from the loop and continues with the main program.

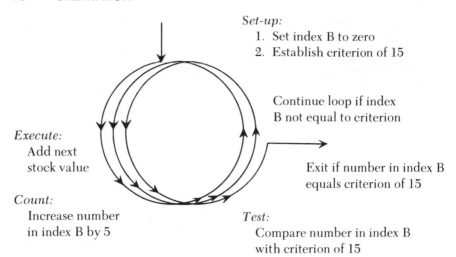

Set-up:
1. Set index B to zero
2. Establish criterion of 15

Continue loop if index
B not equal to criterion

Execute:
Add next
stock value

Exit if number in index B
equals criterion of 15

Count:
Increase number
in index B by 5

Test:
Compare number in index B
with criterion of 15

| Effective Address | Index B | | Criterion | Result of Test |
	Increase	Content		
Set-up		0	15	
Loop 1 103 + 0 = 103	5	5	15	Not equal, repeat
Loop 2 103 + 5 = 108	5	10	15	Not equal, repeat
Loop 3 103 + 10 = 113	5	15	15	Equal, exit to
				continue program

FIGURE 3-3. *Fundamentals of operations involving an index*

Forgetting for a moment the necessary instruction, consider the indexing operations for the simple case of adding the value of inventory on hand. Figure 3-3 shows the indexing of three stock items that have five-word records in storage locations 100 through 114. The records are organized as follows, with the operands of interest indicated by arrows:

100	101	102	103	104	105	106	107
Stock number	Quan	Price	Value	Bin	Stock number	Quan	Price

Spacing 5

108	109	110	111	112	113	114
Value	Bin	Stock number	Quan	Price	Value	Bin

Spacing 5

Three loops are required for three items with a spacing of 5, so the criterion is set at 3 x 5 or 15. Assume that the loop contains an ADD

B103, which has an effective address of 103 in the first loop when index B is zero. In the second loop the effective address is 108 when index B contains 5, and 113 when index B contains 10. After the addition operation is executed in the third loop, the number in index B is increased to 15, which equals the criterion of 15 set up earlier, and when the test is made, results in the computer's making an exit from the loop and continuing with the main program.

Indexing Instructions

The instructions to set, increase, and test index registers are as follows:

Code		Explanation
SIS y	x	Set *index* register y (where y designates index A, B, or C) from *s*torage. The three right-hand digits from the storage location with address x are put into the index. The content of storage location is not disturbed. The sign of the word in the storage position is irrelevant since an index is not signed.
INC y	n	*Inc*rease the content of register y by the number n, where n is the increment—not a storage location. "n" is a three-digit number from 000 through 999 inclusive. 999 increased by 1 is 000.
CIS y	x	*C*ompare content of *index* register y to the criterion in the right-hand three digits in *s*torage location x without regard for the other four characters. If the index register content is not equal to the criterion, take the next instruction in sequence. If they are equal, skip one instruction and continue—that is, advance the instruction counter by 2 instead of by 1 and execute the instruction in that location. Contents of the index register and storage location remain unchanged.

The format of an instruction involving an index register is shown below. The character in the fourth position identifies the index; the numerals in positions 5 through 7 indicate an address in the instruction for setting or comparing an index register. Character positions 5 through 7 indicate a number in instructions used for increasing the content of an index register.

Sign	1	2	3	4	5	6	7
+	S	I	S	y	0	2	0

Positive sign for instructions — Operation code — Identifies register A, B, C — Address or special constant

Effective Addresses

One useful feature of an index register is its ability to modify the basic address of any indexable instruction to get an effective address when the instruction is executed. For example, the instruction RTn y x, when an index is indicated in the "y" position by the letter A, B, or C, is executed with the effective address of x plus the number in index A, B, or C. The effective address concept of location x plus content of an index register will be stated, for brevity, as "location x, indexed." An instruction that can be indexed when it is executed is said to be "indexable." A blank in the "y" character in an instruction means that no index is used and the effective address is merely equal to x.

All instructions that contain the letter y to identify an index are indexable except the three that are used to set, increase, and compare an index register: SIS y x, INC y n, and CIS y x. These three instructions are called "indexing" instructions.

It is important to understand that the effective address scheme changes neither the instruction being executed nor the index register involved. The use of indexes for effective addressing is similar to catalysts in chemical operations: they make the operations possible but are not, themselves, affected.

Sequence Interruption

One more instruction is required to return to the start of the loop in order to repeat it. The execution of instructions in a straightforward sequence as stored is interrupted and the loop repeated from the beginning.

Code	Explanation
JMP y x	The content of the instruction counter is changed to x. The effect of this is to *jump* unconditionally to take the next instruction from storage location x, indexable.

If the instruction is JMP A120 and index register A contains the number 555, the next instruction will be taken from storage location 675. It is possible to jump to a lower-numbered storage location even though index registers contain only positive numbers and their contents are used to increment the specified address to get the effective address. For example, JMP A450 with index register A containing 700 would give an effective address of 150. The sum of $450 + 700 = 1150$ is treated as 150, because the highest storage location is numbered 999 so that an address of 1000 is considered to be 000. If no index is indicated, as in JMP 267, the next instruction is taken from storage location 267.

Indexed Read-in

The instructions for setting, using, modifying, and testing index registers can be illustrated on the read-write program given earlier to show the efficiency of indexing the reading instructions. Assume that only the first 2 words on 30 cards are wanted on the output tape, although all 10 words on each input card must be read at one time. The 10 words from the first card are read into storage locations 100 to 109. The 10 words from the next card are read into locations 102 to 111 to cover all but the first 2 words from the first card. The read-in operation is performed 30 times after which high-speed storage contains 2 words from each of the first 29 cards in locations 100 to 157, and the 10 words from card number 30 in locations 158 to 167. The contents of 30 cards, in effect, are shingled in locations 100 to 167 with only the desired first two words remaining in locations 100 to 159. The 8 words that are not wanted in locations 160 to 167 will be ignored when writing only 60 words on tape and, therefore, discarded. A program to read 30 cards, store the first 2 words from each card, and write the 60 words on tape is:

Location	Content	Explanation
000	0000060	Criterion of spacing interval of 2, times the number of loops (30).
001	0000000	Zero used to set index initially.
002	SIS A001	Set index A to 0.
003	RC2 A100	Read the next card in reader number 2 and store in ten consecutive locations beginning at effective address of 100 plus content of index A. Index A contains 0 on first cycle, 2 on second, and so forth, to 58 on thirtieth.
004	INC A002	Increase content of index register A by 2: from 0 to 2 on first cycle, 2 to 4 on second, and so forth.
005	CIS A000	Compare contents of index register A and storage location 000 which contains 060 in the three right-hand digits. If contents are unequal, take next instruction in sequence—006; if equal, skip one instruction to address 007. The criterion of 60 is used to cover 30 loops and a spacing of 2 each cycle: 30 x 2 = 60.
006	JMP 003	Arrival at this point from the preceding comparison instruction means that the cycle count is not yet complete; therefore, jump to storage location 003 to read another card until 30 cards are read and stored in shingled fashion.
007	B09 100	Arrival at this point from the instruction in 005 means that the loop count of 60 is equal to the criterion of

060 in location 000 and the cycle is complete. Therefore, transfer the block of words from locations 100
through 159 into buffer of tape unit number 9.

008   WT9   --- Write block of data from buffer storage to tape on
unit number 9.

009   JMP   002 Jump to location 002 to reset index register A to 000
and repeat the reading cycle 30 more times. This will
continue until the card reader is emptied or tape is
filled and the machine stops.

It is useful to visualize how 30 reading operations and one writing
operation are performed by means of a loop consisting of 8 instructions and 2 constants. The flow diagram is in Figure 3-4.

The values in index register A and the effective address used for
storing card contents during each loop are traced in Table 3-1. After
the loop is completed 30 times, index register A contains 060 so that
the program jumps to address 007 on the comparison instruction. The
60 words are transferred to buffer and written on tape. A jump returns
the program to location 002 to set index register A to 000 and restart
the cycle through the loop 30 times. The use of index registers is intricate enough that the routine and trace of operations should be examined carefully. The critical points are the first and last loops in each
cycle, because it is easy to lose or gain a cycle by careless programming.

TABLE 3-1. *Trace of Operations in Read-write Loop*
Using an Index Register

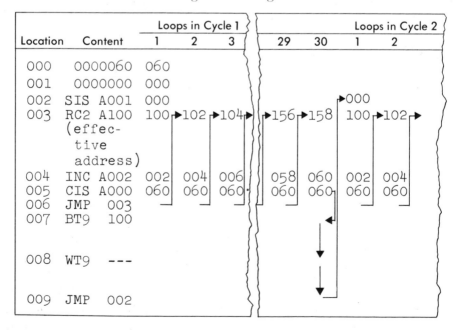

Location	Content	Loops in Cycle 1			Loops in Cycle 2			
		1	2	3	29	30	1	2
000	0000060	060						
001	0000000	000						
002	SIS A001	000					000	
003	RC2 A100 (effective address)	100	102	104	156	158	100	102
004	INC A002	002	004	006	058	060	002	004
005	CIS A000	060	060	060	060	060	060	060
006	JMP 003							
007	BT9 100							
008	WT9 ---							
009	JMP 002							

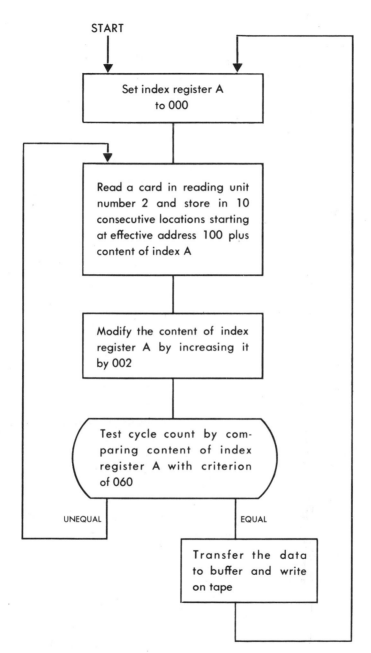

FIGURE 3-4. *Flow diagram of read-write loop using an index*

Consecutive Word Selection

The program for taking the first 2 words from a series of cards and writing them on tape is relatively simple because the other 8 words can be discarded merely by storing words from the next card over them. If some other words, say, numbers 4 through 9 from each of 10 cards are wanted, several instructions are required to discard the first 3 words on each card yet keep the desired words after the read-in operation. The steps involved, which are illustrated in Figure 3-5 for the first, second, and tenth cards, can be described as follows:

1. Read the 10 words from a card into an area in storage reserved for working on data.

2. Block transfer 60 words, starting with word number 4 from the new card, to a buffer unit serving as temporary storage. The fact that words 4 through 10 from the next card and 53 other words are picked up by the instruction to transfer out a block causes no difficulty.

3. Block transfer in 60 words (card words 4 through 10 and 53 others) from buffer storage to a second working area in high-speed storage. The unwanted tenth word from each card will be destroyed when data from the next card are stored over it.

4. The 6 desired words from each of 10 cards in the second working storage area are transferred to a tape unit buffer and then written on tape.

Saving 6 words from the center part of a card shows how two working areas in storage are useful to select, rearrange, and discard data. The two-stage transfer of 60 words into and out of buffer storage in order to get the words desired is indirect. An instruction to move one (or more) words from one location in high-speed storage to another would be more direct and is provided in some computers.

The illustration above will handle the selection of one or several consecutive words from any part of a card. Desired words can be selected merely by discarding unwanted words at either or both ends of the ten words read from a card. More complexities arise if words separated on each card are wanted—the first, third, and eighth words, for instance. After the data on a card are read into storage, individual words can be selected and stored wherever desired by means of two new instructions involving a special register called the "accumulator." For the purpose of moving data about in storage, the accumulator is a one-word special storage location that can be loaded from or unloaded into any other location in high-speed storage. This special register is called "accumulator" because it is used in arithmetical operations, as described later. The instructions for loading the accumulator and storing its contents are:

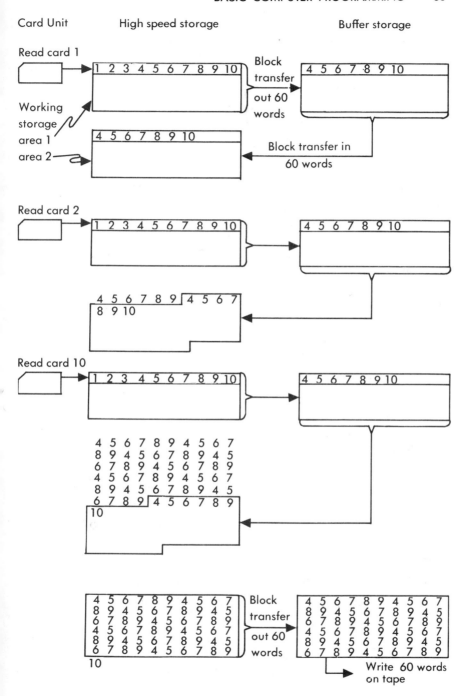

FIGURE 3-5. *Use of buffer storage to isolate words 4 through 9 from each of 10 cards*

Code			Explanation
CAA y	x		Clear *accumulator* content to zero and *add* the content of storage location x, indexable. The accumulator will have the same content as the storage location which is not disturbed by this operation.
STA y	x		*Store* the content of the *accumulator* in the storage location x, indexable. The accumulator content remains unchanged, but the prior content of the storage location involved is destroyed.

Individual Word Selection

Consider an example involving reading data from cards, selecting desired words, and writing them on tape. The first and fourth words from cards are to be put on one tape, with the first words in the first 30 words in a tape block and the fourth words in the second half of the block: 1,1,1,1 . . . 4,4,4,4 . . . . The first and ninth words from each card are to be stored in alternate fashion 1,9,1,9 . . . on another tape.

The program to read data cards, select desired words, and write them on tape in the specified sequence is:

Location	Content	Explanation
000	0000030	Criterion for testing cycle count.
001	0000000	Constant for setting indexes.
002	SIS A001	Set indexes A and B to 0.
003	SIS B001	
004	RC2 050	Read ten words from a card in card reader number 2 into storage locations 050 to 059.
005	CAA 050	Clear accumulator and add first word from card.
006	STA A100	Store in locations 100 and 200 on first cycle, in 101
007	STA B200	and 202 on second cycle, and so forth.
008	CAA 053	Store fourth word from card in location 130 on first
009	STA A130	cycle, 131 on second cycle, and so forth.
010	CAA 058	Store ninth word in location 201 on first cycle, 203
011	STA B201	on second cycle, and so forth.
012	INC A001	Increase index register A by 1 and B by 2.
013	INC B002	
014	CIS A000	Compare content of index register A with criterion
015	JMP 004	030 in location 000 to determine whether 30 cards were read. If index register A is less than 30, jump to location 004 to read next card. If index register A is equal to 30, cycle is complete. Go to location 016 for next instruction.

016	B07	100	Load buffer of tape unit 7 with 60 words from loca-
017	WT7	---	tions 100 to 159 and write on tape number 7.
018	B08	200	Load buffer and write tape number 8.
019	WT8	---	
020	JMP	002	Return to beginning of program to reset indexes and restart cycle if there are more cards and tape; otherwise, machine stops.

COMPARISONS

The program illustrated above for selecting 2 words from each card and writing them in blocks of 60 words on tape keeps the words in the same order as the cards. If the input cards are in sequence, then the output will be in the same sequence. Two choices exist if data must be in sequence for efficient processing. The first is to sort the cards and check their sequence during the computer input operation. The second is to leave the cards unsorted, but to sort the data into the desired sequence by using the computer to select the next item in sequence and using magnetic tapes for storing items between sorting passes, if high-speed storage cannot cope with all the data. The procedures for sorting with a computer are discussed at some length in Chapter 9.

Comparisons and the Three-way Exit

The simple task of checking the sequence of data in a computer requires an instruction that can compare the contents of two storage locations. When the contents of two locations, one of which is the accumulator and the other is in high-speed storage, are compared, there are three possible results: (1) the content of the accumulator is smaller than storage location content, (2) the contents are equal, and (3) the content of the accumulator is larger. The flow-chart block for this instruction is:

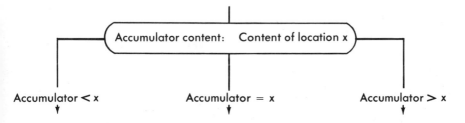

| Accumulator < x | Accumulator = x | Accumulator > x |

Following the comparison instruction, one jump instruction is required to handle the "less than" condition. A second jump instruction after the comparison is required when accumulator content is equal to x. The third case, when accumulator content is greater than x, can be handled as a continuation of the main stream of the program so that no jump is required. The compare and jump instructions are used in programs as follows:

082	CMP	x	Compare contents of accumulator and location x.
083	JMP	027	Content of accumulator < content of x, go to 027.
084	JMP	144	Content of accumulator = content of x, go to 144.
085	RC2	210	Content of accumulator > content of x, continue
086	CAA	---	main stream of program.

The phrase "less than" makes sense with numerals but should be interpreted as "earlier than" for alphabetic and special characters. "Earlier than" is determined according to the values assigned by the computer designer to numerals, letters, and special symbols, such as those shown in the code table in Chapter 2. The ascending order in that table is 0 through 9 followed by letters A through Z, with special characters fitted in at various places. That code table is assumed to be used here. Since code table values are used for sorting operations, it is also called "collation table."

The instruction for comparison and a halt instruction required to stop operations at a desired point are defined as follows:

Code		Explanation
CMP y	x	*Compare* content of accumulator with content of storage location x, indexable. Take next instruction, if content of accumulator < content of location (x + y). Take second following instruction, if content of accumulator = content of (x + y). Take third following instruction, if content of accumulator > content of (x + y). Content of accumulator is unchanged.
HLT	x	Unconditional *halt.* Computer halts after this instruction with instruction counter set to address specified in x. If x is blank, instruction counter is set to 000. Other contents of computer remain unchanged.

File Sequence Checking

Use of the compare instruction will be illustrated by checking the sequence of a file of names that are supposed to be in order. The names below are a maximum of fourteen characters long, stored in two words with this format: last name, space, first name, space, middle name or initial, and spaces.

S	1	2	3	4	5	6	7	S	1	2	3	4	5	6	7
+	S	M	I	T	H		J	+	O	H	N		P		
+	S	M	I	T	H	E		+	J	A	M	E	S		C
+	S	M	I	T	H	F	I	+	E	L	D		E	D	

The program, written in segments or blocks to facilitate each part of the processing, is as follows: First, read in the file of names from a tape mounted on tape unit number 1. Second, write out on tape unit number 3 the names from storage locations 500 through 559 that are in order. Third, write out on tape unit number 2 the names from storage locations 400 through 459 that are not in order.

Instructions are included to stop the computer when the last item in the file is handled. The word after the last name in the file contains 7 "Z's" as an end-of-file tag. When this word is reached in the input file, it is written on both write-out tapes. The tapes are rewound and can be used in further processing or removed for storing in the tape library. The program, when finished, will halt the computer's operations. The organization of data and programs in high-speed storage is shown in Figure 3-6.

The program for checking the sequence of names in a file stored on tape is shown as a flow diagram in Figure 3-7, and can be described as follows:

Location	Content	Explanation
290	+0000000	Constants to set indexes, test the cycle count, and
291	+0000060	test for the end of file.
292	+ZZZZZZZ	
298	+0000000	Initially contains 0; used for temporary storage of
299	+0000000	each name found to be in order.

The first series of program steps checks the first computer word of the name for end-of-file tag, then for sequence. New blocks of data are read in from tape number 1 as needed. Jumps to other parts of the program are made as required. The program starts in location 912, which is near the end of the block, in order to save an extra instruction.

Location	Content		Explanation
900	CAA	A300	The first word of the name in location 300 is loaded into the accumulator in the first cycle, 302 in the second cycle, and so forth.
901	CMP	292	The first word of the name in the accumulator is compared to the end-of-file tag, ZZZZZZZ.

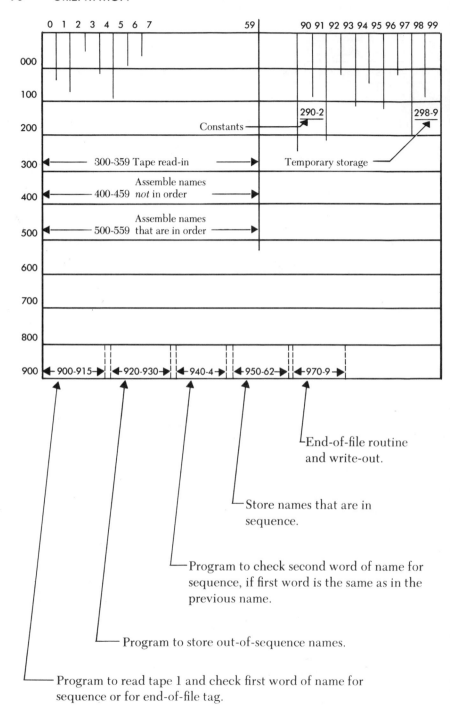

FIGURE 3-6. *Organization of data and program in high-speed storage*

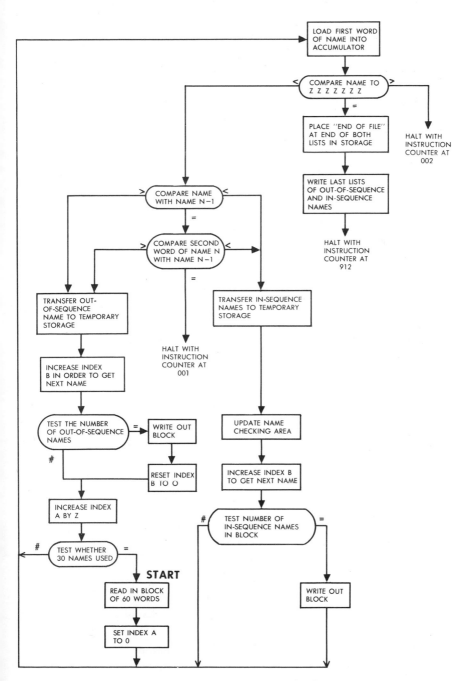

FIGURE 3-7. *Flow diagram of sequence checking for names*

902	JMP	905	First word of name is earlier than end-of-file tag in collation table; jump to name comparison routine.
903	JMP	970	First word of name = end-of-file tag indicates end of file, jump to end-of-file routine.
904	HLT	002	Reaching this point indicates an inexplicable mistake, for it implies that word in name is greater than ZZZZZZZ. Setting the instruction counter to 002 before halt tells the operator the nature of the halt.
905	CMP	298	Compare first word of name in the accumulator with prior first word of name which was placed in temporary storage.
906	JMP	920	Current first word of name in the accumulator is less than prior first word in temporary storage and is out of order. Go to routine for out-of-order names.
907	JMP	940	Two first words of names are identical. Go to program to check second words of names.
908	JMP	950	First word of current name is greater than first word of prior name which was in sequence, so that current name is in sequence. Go to routine for names that are in sequence.
909	INC	A002	When other sections of the program are completed, the instruction counter is jumped to 909 and index register A is increased by 2, which is the spacing of the first words of the names in input data.
910	CIS	A291	Compare index register A to 060 contained in storage location 291.
911	JMP	900	If cycle not performed 30 times (if index A does not contain 060), go to 900 to start cycle for next name. If cycle is complete, go to location 912.
912	RT1	---	Read in a block of 60 words of data from tape
913	BI1	300	on tape unit number 1 and store in locations 300 to 359 inclusive.
914	SIS	A290	Set index A with content of storage location 290, which is 0.
915	JMP	900	Go to location 900 to check next name in file.

The following series of program steps stores names that are not in sequence and writes them on tape number 2. This segment of the program is reached because a name was found to be out of sequence when testing either the first or second word. Since the accumulator contents are different in each case, the first step is to put the first word of the name in the accumulator. The word being considered is indicated by the content of index A. Index B is used to keep track of the block of words that are out of sequence.

920	CAA A300	The two words of the current name, which is
921	STA B400	out of sequence, are placed in the write-out
922	CAA A301	block.
923	STA B401	

| 924 | INC B002 | Increase index B by 2 to get the spacing for the next two words to be put in the block. |

| 925 | CIS B291 | If the block of names out of sequence is not |
| 926 | JMP 909 | full, go to 909 to check another name. If the block is full, continue with instruction 927. |

| 927 | B02 400 | Transfer block of 60 words to buffer number 2 |
| 928 | WT2 --- | and write on tape. |

| 929 | SIS B290 | Reset index B to 0 and go to 909 to check an- |
| 930 | JMP 909 | other name. |

The third series of program steps checks the second word of the name, if the first word matched the previous name which was in order. If both words are the same, the two names are identical and the program halts. In this case "001" is placed in the instruction counter so the operator will know the cause of the halt. The program could, if desired, be arranged to punch this name out on a card or write it out on a separate tape.

| 940 | CAA A301 | The second word of the current name is placed in the accumulator. |

941	CMP 299	The second word of the current name is com-
942	JMP 920	pared with the second word of the previous
943	HLT 001	name which was in order. If the current name is
944	JMP 950	ahead of the prior name, the program jumps to the out-of-order routine. If both names are the same, the program halts and sets the instruction counter at 001. If the current name is in sequence, the program jumps to the in-order routine.

The next series of program steps stores and writes the names that are in order. These steps are similar to those in locations 220 through 230. The only difference is that the name in locations 298 and 299 is updated, so that the next comparison will be with the now-current name. (This is not done when the name is out of order.)

950	CAA	A300	The two words of a name are written in the in-
951	STA	C500	order block, and the checking locations in tem-
952	STA	298	porary storage are updated.
953	CAA	A301	
954	STA	C501	
955	STA	299	

956	INC	C002	Similar to instructions in addresses 924 through
957	CIS	C291	930.
958	JMP	909	
959	B03	500	
960	WT3	---	
961	SIS	C290	
962	JMP	909	

The next, and final, group of instructions is the routine followed at the end of the file. The end-of-file tag is put on the end of the two write-out tapes, all tapes are rewound, and the computer stops.

970	STA	B400	The end-of-file tag, which is already in the ac-
971	STA	C500	cumulator, is placed at the end of both groups
			of output names.

972	B02	400	The last blocks (which may be incomplete) are
973	WT2	---	written on the output tapes, and all tapes are
974	RW2	---	rewound.
975	B03	500	
976	WT3	---	
977	RW3	---	
978	RW1	---	

| 979 | HLT | 912 | The computer stops with instruction counter set to 912 and will continue operating from that point, if restarted. |

The halt order should always be used at the end of a program where it is possible for the instruction counter to continue. Otherwise, some stray word in the next storage location may be interpreted as an instruction.

Test Negative and Two-way Exit

The comparison instruction involves the contents of the accumulator and a storage location; it results in a three-way branch for the <, =, and > conditions. A simpler instruction is the "jump if negative," which involves only the sign of the accumulator and results in a two-way branch for the negative and non-negative conditions. Designed primarily for use with arithmetical operations (to be described later), the jump-if-negative instruction is useful for determining the end of a file of positive items by attaching one more item with a negative sign, such as:

–	E	N	D	F	I	L	E

The word "ENDFILE" can be printed to assure that the end of the file was actually reached and that a negative sign within the data was not used incorrectly. In a numerical file containing both positive and negative signs, the alphabetic tag will follow numerical words in the sorting sequence. More important, the negative sign will cause the –ENDFILE tag to differ from alphabetic files that have a plus sign for each word.

The jump-if-negative instruction is a conditional jump; it is executed if and only if the sign of the accumulator is negative when this instruction is reached in the program.

Code	Explanation
JIN y x	Jump, if content of accumulator is negative, to effective address of x plus content of index y (A, B, or C, or blank) for next instruction; otherwise, continue regular sequence of instructions. Accumulator content is unchanged.

SHIFTING

Thus far in the discussion of programming, the instructions used have handled whole words without changing the individual characters within a word. It is often desirable to shift the position of characters in a word to "unpack" or separate two or more items that are stored in one computer word to save space. There are many cases in which an item of data is less than 7 characters long, so that unused character positions may be used to store other information. Packing two or more items into one word often saves time as well as space, because fewer words need to be read into high-speed storage than if each short item occupies a word that is filled out with blanks.

One method used to unpack data is called "shifting." Shifting involves the accumulator and another part of the arithmetic unit called the M-Q (for multiplier-quotient) register. Shifting does not involve the sign position, indicated by s, in either the accumulator or the M-Q. For purposes of shifting data, the M-Q register can be considered simply as a continuation of the right-hand end of the accumulator, as follows:

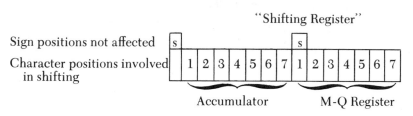

"Shifting Register"

Sign positions not affected

Character positions involved in shifting

Accumulator   M-Q Register

If a word in the accumulator is shifted 7 positions to the right, it will be completely in the M-Q register. If the word is then shifted 7 positions to the left, it will be back in the accumulator. Any characters shifted off either the left end of the accumulator or the right end of the M-Q are discarded, and there is no indication of discarded digits. The open positions originating in the left of the accumulator from a right shift are filled with zeros. Similarly, open positions originating at the right of the M-Q from a left shift are filled with zeros. Following are some examples of shifting alphabetic characters to isolate a desired item:

		Accumulator								M-Q Register						
Character positions	s	1	2	3	4	5	6	7	s/1	2	3	4	5	6	7
Original contents	+	S	M	I	T	H			+/J	O	H	N		P	
Shift right three positions	+	0	0	0	S	M	I	T	+/H		J	O	H	N	
Shift left eight positions	+		J	O	H	N		0	+/0	0	0	0	0	0	0
Shift right four positions	+	0	0	0	0		J	O	+/H	N		0	0	0	0

Instructions used in shifting words between the accumulator and M-Q registers and for loading and storing the M-Q are:

Code		Explanation
SHL	n	*Sh*ift *l*eft the contents of combined accumulator and M-Q register n places where n is a number from 1 through 13, inclusive. Sign positions of accumulator and M-Q are not affected. Any characters shifted off the left end of accumulator are lost. Spaces vacated on the right are filled with zeros. ("n" is written as a three-digit number on the right side of the instruction word, for example: SHL 005.)
SHR	n	*Sh*ift *r*ight the contents of combined accumulator and M-Q register n places to the right where n is a number from 1 through 13. Sign positions of the accumulator and M-Q are not affected. Any characters shifted off the right end of M-Q are lost. Spaces vacated on the left are filled with zeros.
CAM y	x	*C*lear the contents of both accumulator and M-Q to zero and *a*dd to *M*-Q the content of location x, indexable. The sign of the accumulator is the same as the sign of the word in M-Q. Content of the storage location x, indexed, is not changed.
STM y	x	*St*ore the content of the *M*-Q register in location x, indexable. The content of the M-Q is not changed. Original content of storage location x, indexed by y, is lost.

DATA READ-IN

In the interests of a simplified discussion of programming, it has been assumed that a program was already in the computer when wanted. Actually, the first step in processing data with a computer is to get the program into storage, where it is available for processing by the computer. The first step in loading instructions and data into a computer is to get enough instructions into the computer by manual means so that those instructions can bring in as many more instructions as desired. A few instructions are used to "bootstrap" in more instructions.

General Scheme

There are four stages in loading a program already punched in cards into the hypothetical computer discussed here. The steps, which are discussed more fully later, can be outlined as follows:

1. Use the console to load the first card in the program load routine into high-speed storage.
2. The first card bootstraps the second card into high-speed storage.

3. The load routine on the first two cards will read in an indefinite number of program cards.

4. The last program card makes a transfer to the start of the program which includes data read-in and execution of the program itself.

The bootstrap load cards, the program cards (in skeleton), and transfer card for a program to be discussed later, are shown together in Figure 3-8.

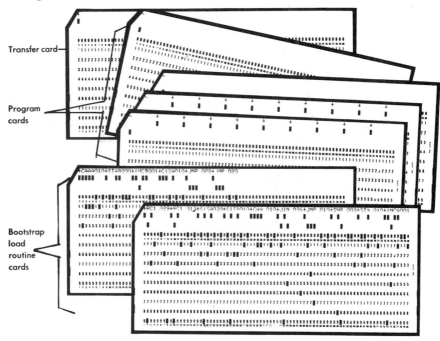

FIGURE 3-8. *Bootstrap load, program, and transfer cards*

The program cards are discussed first because their format affects the bootstrap load routine. Each program card (which has only the – and + signs to indicate the location of instruction words) will have from two to ten words on it. The first word on each card, which might be called the "word-count and location," indicates the number of words to be stored and where they are to be stored. The word-count and location word on each program card, which is used solely for storing the other words and is only temporarily stored, has the following format:

s	1	2	3	4	5	6	7
–	0	0	0	w	x	x	x

The word-count "w" indicates the number of words on the card that are to be stored; this number ranges from 1 through 9, depending on whether the card is partially or completely filled with instruction words. The location part of the first word, xxx, indicates where the second word on the card (which is the first program word on that card) should be stored. Other words are stored in sequence.

The last card to be loaded, called a "transfer card," has only one word with the following format:

s	1	2	3	4	5	6	7
+	J	M	P		x	x	x

A plus sign, instead of a minus as on the other program cards, distinguishes the transfer card from them so that it is executed as an instruction instead of merely directing other words into storage. Execution of the JMP xxx instruction transfers control to xxx where the main program starts.

Bootstrap Load Routine

The load routine makes use of the fact that one card can be read into the computer by means of control switches on the console. The console switches are set to read the first card into the locations specified in the first card, say 019 through 028 in this case, and then to jump to get the next instruction from location 019. The instruction in location 019 causes the computer to read one more card which contains the rest of the bootstrap load routine. A load routine of 16 words punched into two cards can read in an indefinite number of other program or data cards and can start execution of the program. Loading a program and starting its execution is similar to a chain reaction. If everything is ready, then a small event can trigger the whole operation.

The load routine, punched into the first two cards illustrated in Figure 3-8, is listed under "card content" below, with the location and explanation added for clarity:

Location	Card Content		Explanation
			Assume that the console switches were used to read the first card in the reader into ten locations starting at 019. The console transfers control to the first instruction and continues the load routine.
019	+RC1	029	Read the second card in the load routine into locations 029 through 038. The instruction in 019 will not be needed again and will be destroyed when the main program cards are read into locations 010 through 019.
020	+RC1	010	Read a main program card into locations 010 through 019 for temporary storage while examining

the first word to determine what to do with the other words.

021   +SIS A030   Set index register A with the three right-hand digits of location 030 which are 000. The 000 is taken from another instruction word to avoid using a separate word as a constant.

022   +SIS B010   Set index B with the right-hand three digits of the first word of a card—the word location digits.

023   + CAA   010   Clear accumulator and add the first word from a card in order to get its sign.

024   +JIN   026   If sign of accumulator is negative, the accumulator contains a count and location word for the other words on the card.

025   +JMP   010   If sign of accumulator is positive, then the word in location 010 is the transfer word to the first program instruction to be executed. Two jumps are made, one to location 010 and a second to the location specified there.

026   +SHR   003   The word-count and location word wxxx loaded in accumulator by the CAA   010 operation above is shifted right three places to put the w in the right-hand position. The location digits were set in index B by the SIS B010 operation above and need not be retained in storage location 010 any longer. They are discarded by the shift operation.

027   +STA   010   The word-count w which was shifted to the number 7 (right-hand) position in the accumulator by the SHR 003 operation is stored in the right-hand position of the word-count, as follows: –000000w.

028   +INC A001   Increase index register A by 1 to count the words handled from the program card being stored.

029   +CAA A010   Clear accumulator and add the word in the effective address (contents of location 010 and index register) 011 on first loop, 012 on second, and to 019 on ninth loop, if there are 9 words to be stored from the card, when the cycle is completed.

030   +STA B000   Store the accumulator content in the effective address of 000 plus the content of index register B which was set in operation 022 with the desired location for the first word to be stored.

031   +INC B001   Increase index register B by 1 to load program

words into consecutive storage locations when repeating loop.

032   +CIS A010   Compare the words-stored count in index register
A with the number of words to be stored, which is
in location 010.

033   +JMP 028   Contents of index register A and location 010 are
not equal; therefore, return to location 028 to re-
peat loop for storing a word.

034   +JMP 020   Contents of index register A and location 010 are
equal; therefore, go to location 020 to read the
next card.

Use of the load routine illustrated above precludes storing any
part of the main program in locations 010 through 034, except for
the temporary storage of each card in locations 010 through 019 while
it is being transferred to desired locations. Anything else stored in locations 010 through 034 will either destroy the load routine or be destroyed when the next card is read. Another similar load routine can
be stored somewhere else, if these locations are required for the main
program. As soon as the main program is read in, the space occupied
by the load routine can be used for other purposes. The point is that
storage must be allocated among load routine, main program, and data
so that they do not interfere with each other.

Locations 000 to 009 were not used in the load routine because
they are often reserved for jump instructions to start the program running again after a halt occurs. Certain halt instructions (HLT   x)
throughout the program may specify a storage location from 000 to 009
for setting the instruction counter when the computer halts. A JMP   x
instruction stored in that location transfers control to an error-correc-
tion routine, when the computer is restarted. Used in this way, the
jump instruction serves to connect the program halt and the error-
correction routine with a temporary stop, at location 003, for instance.
The fact that the program arrives at location 003 gives some indication
of the nature of the halt that was encountered.

PACKING AND UNPACKING DATA

The load routine given above contained a simple example of unpacking two words stored in one word. The first word on each card in
the main program contained the word-count w and location word xxx.
Unpacking for separate use was simple. The xxx was loaded in an index
register. By shifting the original word three positions to the right, the
word-count w was obtained in position 7 so that it could be used as a
criterion for cycle counting.

Packing several items into one word to economize data read-in time and storage space is done often enough that the related procedures for unpacking the items for separate processing deserve treatment here. A water utility uses a word with the following format for meter readings:

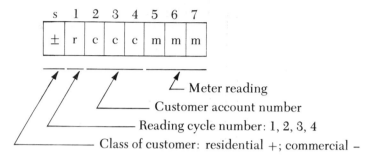

Only one word of new input, along with the master file record, is required to compute a bill for a customer. The meter-reading cards punched with the data shown are sorted into sequence by cycle and customer account number on digits 1 to 4 before being read into the computer. After read-in, the sequence is checked by the program using the whole word to avoid the trouble of extracting the reading cycle and account number from the whole word, including meter reading. Since the computer compares the word as a whole from left to right, the meter reading in the low-order position is, in effect, ignored. The + in sign position indicates residential customer and the –, commercial customer.

Residential customer meter readings are as stated (for example, 038 equals 38 cu. ft.), but commercial customer readings are in hundreds of cubic feet (for example, 167 equals 16,700 cu. ft.). The two classes are interspersed in the master file because it is organized in the same sequence as meter readers follow on their routes.

The program for processing meter readings is designed to operate with the items unpacked and placed in storage as follows:

Location	Content
060	Meter-reading cycle number in character position 7 preceded by at least two zeros to avoid interference with indexing; but the sign is immaterial here.
061	Customer account number in positions 5 through 7 and correct sign for word; but content of the rest of word is immaterial.
062	Meter reading, in actual cubic feet, in positions 5 through 7 for residential and 3 through 7 for commercial customers; other positions must be zero and sign plus.

Index register A will be used to keep track of the location of the meter-reading word to be unpacked next. The program is to be written in appropriate form for loading, which means that the first word on each card contains the word-count and location assigned to the second word. Unpacking instructions are stored in locations 670 through 682 and include a jump to another routine starting at location 600 to compute the bill after unpacking is complete. The unpacking routine punched into cards is listed in the third column:

Store in Location	Card and Word Number	Content	Explanation
Tempo-rary only	1-1	-0009670	Word count 9 and location 670 for storing second word on first card.
670	1-2	+CAM 670	Clear M-Q register and add something to get a plus sign. This instruction adds itself, which method is as suitable as any other.
671	1-3	+CAA A000	Clear accumulator and add a meter-reading word. Index A is assumed to indicate its location. Accumulator gets the sign of the word added.
672	1-4	+SHR 006	Shift accumulator and M-Q contents right 6 positions so that reading cycle number is in position 7 of accumulator.
673	1-5	+STA 060	Store reading cycle number.
674	1-6	+SHL 003	Shift accumulator and M-Q contents so that customer account number occupies positions 5 through 7 in accumulator.
675	1-7	+STA 061	Store customer account number in 061.
676	1-8	+SHL 007	Shift left 7 places to discard all digits except meter reading and shift right 11 places to get into positions 5 through 7 of M-Q.
677	1-9	+SHR 011	
678	1-10	+JIN 681	If accumulator is negative, indicating commercial customer, jump to shift instruction.
Tempo-rary only	2-1	-0004679	Word-count 4 and location 679 for storing second word on second card.

679	2-2	+STM	062	Reaching this point indicates residential customer; store cubic feet in 062.
680	2-3	+JMP	600	Exit from the unpacking routine to location 600 to start bill computation.
681	2-4	+SHL	002	Reaching this point indicates commercial customer; shift M-Q content left 2 positions to multiply meter reading by 100.
682	2-5	+JMP	679	Jump to instruction to store content of M-Q.

The 13 instructions given above (the word-count and location words are not instructions) are required to unpack each meter-reading card and set up the quantity for bill calculation. It is useful to trace the contents of the "shifting register" throughout the routine to deal with a meter reading of –1352964 previously read into storage.

		Contents of "Shifting Register"															
Location	Operation	Accumulator							M-Q							
		s	1	2	3	4	5	6	7	s	1	2	3	4	5	6	7
		±	C	A	N	B	E	A	N	±	Y	T	H	I	N	G	X
670	+ CAM 670	+	0	0	0	0	0	0	0	+	C	A	M	-	6	7	0
	+ CAA A000	-	1	3	5	2	9	6	4	+	C	A	M	-	6	7	0
	+ SHR 006	-	0	0	0	0	0	0	1	+	3	5	2	9	6	4	C
	+ STA 060	-	0	0	0	0	0	0	1	+	3	5	2	9	6	4	C
	+ SHL 003	-	0	0	0	1	3	5	2	+	9	6	4	C	0	0	0
	+ STA 061	-	0	0	0	1	3	5	2	+	9	6	4	C	0	0	0
	+ SHL 007	-	9	6	4	C	0	0	0	+	0	0	0	0	0	0	0
	+ SHR 011	-	0	0	0	0	0	0	0	+	0	0	0	9	6	4	
	+ JIN 681	-	0	0	0	0	0	0	0	+	0	0	0	0	9	6	4
679	+ STM 062	-	0	0	0	0	0	0	0	+	0	0	9	6	4	0	0
	+ JMP 600	-	0	0	0	0	0	0	0	+	0	0	9	6	4	0	0
681	+ SHL 002	-	0	0	0	0	0	0	0	+	0	0	9	6	4	0	0
	+ JMP 679	-	0	0	0	0	0	0	0	+	0	0	9	6	4	0	0

Only three locations, 670, 679, and 681, are identified above because the others are immaterial. Note that the operation in location 679 is reached *after* the left shift of 2 positions (in location 681) for commercial customers, but this shift is omitted for residential customers. The bootstrap load routine, unpacking routine (calculation routine omitted), and transfer cards are in Figure 3-9.

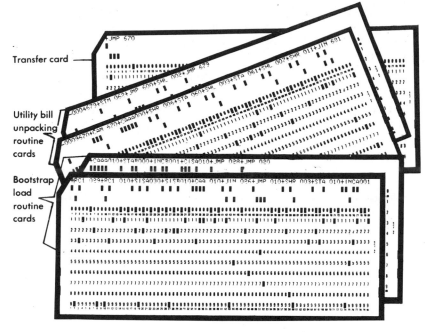

Transfer card

Utility bill
unpacking
routine
cards

Bootstrap
load
routine
cards

FIGURE 3-9. *Bootstrap load, utility bill unpacking routine,
and transfer card*

ARITHMETICAL OPERATIONS

The computer instructions discussed thus far have been limited to input and output, and the instructions to index, compare, shift, jump, store, clear and add, compare, and halt. These types of operations constitute a large part of the business-data-processing routines which move data about without changing them.

The arithmetical operations of adding, subtracting, multiplying, and dividing are required to calculate bills, inventories, sales forecasts, and production schedules. Arithmetical operations will be explained briefly here and their use in a program illustrated.

Addition and Subtraction

Addition and subtraction operations are designed into the hypothetical computer as follows:

Code	Explanation
ADD y x	*Add* content of storage location x, indexable, to content of accumulator. Accumulator contains new sum but storage location is unchanged.
SUB y x	*Sub*tract content of storage location x, indexable, from content of accumulator. Accumulator contains remainder.

Addition of a series of numbers is started with a CAA y x order to clear accumulator and add the first number, followed by an ADD y x order for each succeeding number, and, finally, an STA y x order to store the total.

Operations involved in subtracting a series of numbers are essentially the same as for addition except that the accumulator may contain a starting number or be set to zero by an initial CAA y x order. An SUB y x order is used for each number to be subtracted. The repetitive orders of ADD y x and SUB y x can, of course, be indexed for use as many times as desired even though written only once in the program.

Assume the following numbers are in storage locations identified as W, X, Y, and Z:

$$W = +0003472$$
$$X = +0012350$$
$$Y = -0000013$$
$$Z = -0000480$$

The rules of algebraic addition and subtraction can be illustrated as follows, ignoring insignificant zeros:

CAA	W	+	3472	CAA	W	+	3472
ADD	X	+	12350	SUB	X	+	12350
		+	15822			-	8878
CAA	W	+	3472	CAA	W	+	3472
ADD	Y	-	13	SUB	Y	-	13
		+	3459			+	3485
CAA	Z	-	480	CAA	Z	-	480
ADD	W	+	3472	SUB	W	+	3472
		+	2992			-	3952
CAA	Y	-	13	CAA	Y	-	13
ADD	Z	-	480	SUB	Z	-	480
		-	493			+	467

A program to add and subtract numbers that are stored on magnetic tape will illustrate how the addition and subtraction instructions are used. Numbers to be added are read from tape unit 1 into storage locations 100 through 159. Numbers to be subtracted are read from tape unit 2 into storage locations 200 through 259. One number will be added and one subtracted until 6 blocks of each are used. The one-word answer will be punched in a card in card unit number 2.

The program punched in cards ready for loading is as follows, with "location" listed for reference purposes only:

Card	(Location)	Word	Explanation
1	019 to 028		Bootstrap load routine, which is identical to the one shown earlier, is punched in two cards and read into storage locations 019 through 034.
2	029 to 034		
3	---	− 0004550	Word-count and location word.
	550	+ 0000000	
	551	+ 0000060	Constants. Word in block criterion.
	552	+ 0000006	Block count criterion.
	553	+ 0000009	Zero fill-in.
4	---	− 0009600	Word-count and location word.
	600	+ CAA 550	Clear accumulator to plus zero.
	601	+ SIS B550	Set index B to zero and use to count number of blocks read.
	602	+ SIS A550	Set index A to zero and use to keep track of data word in blocks.
	603	+ RT1 ---	Read a block from tape 1 and store at locations 100 through 159.
	604	+ BI1 100	
	605	+ RT2 ---	Read a block from tape 2 and store at locations 200 through 259.
	606	+ BI2 200	
	607	+ ADD A100	Add contents of location 100, indexed.
	608	+ SUB A200	Subtract contents of location 200, indexed.
5	---	− 0009609	Word-count and location word.
	609	+ INC A001	Increase index A by 1. If not 60, return to location 607 to add next number. If 60, go to location 612.
	610	+ CIS A551	
	611	+ JMP 607	
	612	+ INC B001	Increase index B by 1. If not 6, return to location 602 to read in next block. If 6, go to location 615.
	613	+ CIS B552	
	614	+ JMP 602	
	615	+ STA 400	Store answer in location 400.
	616	+ SIS A550	Set index A to zero and clear accumulator to plus zero.
	617	+ CAA 550	
6	---	+ 0006618	Word-count and location word.
	618	+ STA A401	Store zeros in locations 401 through 409 so that a card punched with contents of locations 400 through 409 will contain the answer and 9 words of zeros.
	619	+ INC A001	
	620	+ CIS A553	
	621	+ JMP 618	

| 622 | + PC2 400 | Punch 10 words in card: answer in word 1 and zeros in words 2 through 10. |
| 623 | + HLT --- | |

7   010   + JMP 600   Transfer card read into locations 010 through 019 and executed to start program at location 600.

Instructions Used in Program

The program to read in, add, and subtract six blocks of 60 numbers each and to punch the one-word net answer in a card has 45 instructions; these instructions can be roughly classified as follows to show how many times they are used in executing the program.

	Number of Instructions	Set-up	Tape Read-in	Number Manipulation	Output Preparation	Card Output
Program load routine	16	202				
Constants	4	4				
Data input	4		4			
Indexing						
Set	3	3				
Increase	3		1	1	1	
Compare	3		1	1	1	
Jump	4	1	1	1	1	
Arithmetic						
Clear and add	2	1				1
Add	1			1		
Subtract	1			1		
Store accumulator	2				1	1
Punch a card	1					1
Halt	1					1
Number of instructions	45	211	7	5	4	4
Number of times performed to handle 6 blocks of 60 numbers each		1	6	360	9	1
Effective use of instructions		211	42	1800	36	4
Effective total						2683

While the add and the subtract operations appear only once in the program to add 360 numbers, each is used 360 times. If the time required to perform each instruction is known, the total running time for the program can be calculated. Machine speeds and program running time are discussed in Chapters 7 and 8.

Overflow

Continued addition or subtraction of numbers may result in an answer containing too many digits to be put into storage locations that can hold only 7 digits. For example, adding +6,000,000 and +7,000,000 gives an eight-digit total of +13,000,000 in the accumulator, which is called an "overflow" condition.

Since the overflow may occur without the programmer's realizing it, the computer designer may extend the accumulator by one position to indicate the occurrence of overflow. One bit is enough to indicate overflow in a yes-no fashion. Whenever the possibility of overflow is likely to occur, the programmer should test for overflow and, if it has occurred, go to a correction routine before repeating the operations that caused overflow. The computer will halt automatically and a console light will indicate overflow if an instruction causing overflow is not followed immediately by the test "jump on overflow."

A schematic diagram of the accumulator including an overflow bit is:

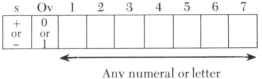

Contents   Any numeral or letter

The overflow position (Ov) contains the binary number 1 whenever overflow occurs; otherwise, it contains 0. The overflow bit is available only for testing and is not affected by shifting or other non-arithmetical operations. The overflow position is available to the machine for a decimal digit when doing multiplication and division, but this does not concern the programmer. Overflow testing is done by the jump-on-overflow instruction defined as follows:

Code		Explanation
JOV	x	Jump on *overflow*, if one occurs, to take next instruction from storage location x. Continue regular sequence of operations, if no overflow.

Occurrence of overflow in the main program and correction by means of a subroutine illustrates the nature of the problem. The main program is in locations 1 to 99, some numbers being added are in 100 and 101 (location 100 contains +9,000,000 and 101, +8,000,000), and the correction routine is in 936 to 944.

Location and Content		Accumulator s OV 1234567		Explanation
023 + CAA	100	+ 0	9000000	Addition of two numbers causes overflow and jump-to-correction routine.
024 + ADD	101	+ 1	NONSENSE	
025 + JOV	936			
936 + CAA	100	+ 0	9000000	Shift first number one position right and store in original location.
937 + SHR	001	+ 0	0900000	
938 + STA	100	+ 0	0900000	
939 + CAA	101	+ 0	8000000	Shift second number one position to right and store.
940 + SHR	001	+ 0	0800000	
941 + STA	101	+ 0	0800000	
942 + CAA	000	+ 0	0000001	Get an overflow indicator of 1 from storage location 000 and store in location 945.
943 + STA	945	+ 0	0000001	
944 + JMP	023	+ 0	0000001	Return to main program to repeat addition operation.
945 +			0000000	Initially zero; use to store overflow indicator, 0 or 1.

After the overflow correction and return (JMP   023) to the main program, the instructions in locations 023 and following are repeated and overflow will not occur. The overflow condition indicator of 1 in location 945 is used for locating the decimal point in the answer.

Multiplication

The multiplication operation is interesting because the product of two seven-digit numbers is thirteen or fourteen digits, although many of the left-hand digits may be zero. Consider two examples of multiplication, using, for brevity, only four-digit numbers.

Multiplicand	6789	0021
Multiplier	x 2345	0003
	33945	0063
	27156	0000
	20367	0000
	13578	0000
Product	15920205 = 8 digits	0000063 = 7 digits

Since the number of digits in the product is equal to the sum (or the sum minus one) of the number of digits in both operands, the accumulator and M-Q registers are used together for multiplication in much the same way that they were used in the shifting operations described earlier. The operations in multiplication are:

1. Clear accumulator and M-Q registers and place the multiplier in the M-Q register by the CAM y   x instruction.
2. The multiplicand is obtained from a specified storage location by the MLT y x instruction.
3. Store the product (which is in the M-Q register only if the product is 7 digits or less but extends into the accumulator if more than 7 digits) by means of STM y   x and STA y   x orders.

The multiplication order is defined as follows:

Code	Explanation
MLT y x	*Mul*tiply content of location x, indexable, by the content of the M-Q. Product low-order digits are at the right in M-Q register and high-order digits at the left in accumulator, if more than 7 digits. Storage location content is unchanged.

Algebraic rules are followed in multiplication:

$$(+)x(+)=(+), (-)x(+)=(-), (+)x(-)=(-), (-)x(-)=(+)$$

A simple example of multiplication is to multiply the quantity of an item by its price to find its value. Quantity, 1547 units, is in storage location 100 and price, $2.3613 each, in 101.

Location and Content		Accumulator s OV 1 2 3 4 5 6 7	M-Q s 1 2 3 4 5 6 7	Explanation
600	+CAM	100 + 0 0000000	+0001547	Load multiplier.
601	+MLT	101 + 0 0000003	+6529311	Multiply.
602	+SHL	003 + 0 3652	+9311000	Separate the dollars.
603	+STA	102 + 0 3652	+9311000	Store dollar answer.

Responsibility for keeping track of the decimal point in the product 36529311 rests with the programmer. A left shift of 3 positions puts the product in whole dollars in the accumulator. A right shift of 4 places would arrange it in the M-Q register. The dollar product can be stored from the appropriate register. The answer $ .9311 in the M-Q register, as illustrated above, is discarded so that the dollar product stored, $3652, should be $3653, if rounded.

In order to round the amount 36529311 to the nearest dollar the operation in location 602 should be SHL   004 to put 36529 in accumulator followed by the addition of 5 in the seventh position to get 36534. SHR   001 leaves 3653, which is the correctly rounded product, in the accumulator where it can be stored. M-Q contents are, as before, discarded. Some computers have a multiply-round instruction which gives a correctly rounded product after multiplication.

Division

The fourth arithmetical instruction is to divide. Steps involved in the division operation are:

1. Clear the accumulator and M-Q registers by a CAM y x instruction where location x contains + zero.
2. Place the dividend in the accumulator by a CAA y x instruction.
3. Divide the dividend by a divisor by use of the DIV y x instruction. The quotient is formed in the M-Q register with the correct algebraic sign, following rules similar to those for multiplication. The remainder, with the sign of the dividend, is left in the accumulator.
4. The quotient can be stored by STM y x and the remainder, if wanted, by STA y x.

The division instruction is defined as follows:

Code	Explanation
DIV y x	Divide the dividend in accumulator by divisor in location x, indexable. Quotient is formed in M-Q register and remainder is left in accumulator. Content of original location unchanged.

A special rule is involved for the division operation. The divisor "as stored" (without regard for sign and decimal point) must be larger than the dividend to avoid stopping the machine in a "divide halt" condition. For example, an attempt to divide +0000080 by +0000040 will stop the computer. Shifting the dividend one place to the right before starting division to get +0000008 in the accumulator makes the divisor as stored +0000040 larger than the dividend. Having the divisor "as stored" larger than the dividend is a relative matter, so that the dividend can be shifted right or the divisor shifted left as is more convenient, apart from the problem of losing significant digits. Right-hand digits of the dividend shift out of the accumulator into the M-Q register so that they are not lost.

The division operation is performed automatically by shifting the accumulator content (and also M-Q content, although it may contain zero) one position to the left, subtracting the divisor as many times as possible, and storing the count in the right-hand position of the M-Q. In this case +0000040 can be subtracted from +0000080 two times, so 2 is stored in the right end of the M-Q. The accumulator and M-Q contents are again shifted left and the subtraction operation attempted six more times. The M-Q contains +2000000 at the end of the division operation. Where the dividend and divisor are both whole numbers with decimal points at the right, decimal point correction for machine shifting is required only during the division operation. In dividing +0000080 by +0000040, decimal point location requires a right shift of 7 positions (which is the number of positions formed in the quotient) *minus* the number of right-hand shifts originally made in the dividend (1 in this case) to avoid a divide-halt condition. A right shift of 6 for the M-Q content of +2000000 gives a quotient of +0000002 for 80 ÷ 40.

The programmer is responsible for anticipating the relative sizes of the dividend and divisor and for making adjustments to avoid a divide-halt condition during division. After the quotient has been obtained in the M-Q register, it can be stored by an STM y   x instruction. The remainder, which is in the accumulator, can be stored by an STA y   x instruction.

SPECIAL OPERATIONS

Two kinds of special operations are of interest here. One type involves the ability to address selected elements of the computer in performing instructions. The other type involves arithmetical operations on alphabetic data.

Special Addresses

In many of the instructions described in this chapter the accumulator or M-Q registers were explicitly named, for example, CAA y   x or STM y   x. In other instructions the use of these registers was implicit, for example, the SHR   n and ADD y   x.

It is sometimes useful to be able to address directly the accumulator, M-Q register, and console switches. Since all the possible three-digit numbers 000 through 999 are used for addresses of storage locations, letters are used in the hypothetical computer:

> ACC   Accumulator
> MQR   M-Q register
> CNS   Console switches

The computer operator can use the computer console switches to introduce data by manually setting the switches. The internal units can "read" these data but cannot physically change the position of the switches and, therefore, cannot store data in them. Instructions such as STA yCNS and STM yCNS are not valid instructions to store data.

On the other hand, an index register may be set with the content of any of these three special addresses. Instructions such as SIS ACNS and CIS   BMQR are perfectly valid, for data are merely being read from the M-Q register.

Interesting arithmetical operations can be performed between the accumulator and M-Q register by instructions such as these:

ADD MQR   Add contents of M-Q register to accumulator.

SUB MQR   Subtract contents of M-Q register from accumulator.

CMP MQR   Compare contents of M-Q register with accumulator
and take three-way branch on outcome: MQR < ACC,
MQR = ACC, and MQR > ACC.

On the other hand, there are limitations on the use of these special addresses. The address "ACC" cannot be used in an operation involving the accumulator, for that would involve trying to address the accumulator while it is being used. The address "MQR" is similarly restricted for operations involving the M-Q register. None of these addresses may be referred to as the location of an instruction—JMP ACC, for example—because there is no way to find the address of the next instruction. Input and output operations are restricted to addressing high-speed storage. These addresses cannot be put in an index, nor can an instruction such as CAA ACNS be used because the content of index A would be irrelevant.

Arithmetic and the Alphabet

Performance of arithmetical operations on alphabetic data is useful for modifying instructions by changing addresses of storage locations or numbers that refer to tape or card units. Special rules apply to arithmetical operations on words containing non-numerals. The addition of two letters—A + B, for example—is possible in some computers and may be useful in isolated cases, but it does not have a generally accepted meaning. Multiplication or division of words containing non-numerals is usually meaningless.

Addition or subtraction of words containing non-numerals is not possible and will stop the hypothetical computer. On the other hand, numerical words may be added to or subtracted from the numerical parts of alphanumerical words; but carries to and borrows from non-numerals are lost. Some examples are:

$$
\begin{array}{llll}
+\text{ABZ3583} & +\text{CAA } 167 & +\text{CAA } 160 & +\text{B12 } 160 \\
+\underline{2126814} & +\underline{0000001} & +\underline{0001900} & +\underline{0010000} \\
+\text{ABZ0397} & +\text{CAA } 168 & +\text{CAA } 060 & +\text{B13 } 160
\end{array}
$$

Three of these examples show how an instruction can be modified by arithmetical operations. CAA   167 increased to CAA   168 and stored back in the original location will cause the program to get a new data word in the next loop. This scheme for modifying instructions is comparable to indexing and is used for computers that do not have index registers.

The character "blank" is non-numerical so that it overrides zeros in addition. This property makes it possible to use a word containing blanks and zeros as a mask for extracting characters that are wanted and discarding others. For example, the format of the water utility meter-reading card described earlier in this chapter was (s)rcccmmm. The customer number "c" was unpacked by shifting first one direction and then the other to discard unwanted digits. An easier method to isolate the customer number is this:

CAA	Masking word	bOOObbb (where "b" indicates blank)
ADD	Meter-reading	
	word	(s)rcccmmm
	Sum	(s)bcccbbb

Data words to be operated on arithmetically in the computer should have a zero or some other digit in every character position. The word +0000001 is valid for arithmetical operations; but the word of blanks and numerals, " +   1," is not valid.

SUMMARY

The fundamental point about internally stored program computers is that data and the program are stored in exactly the same fashion. Whether computer contents are used as data or as instruction is a matter of choice for the programmer. Usually each type is used in the way originally intended, but instructions are treated as data in order to modify them before using them again. When programs go awry, data may be mistakenly "executed" as instructions and give nonsensical results.

The precise instruction format devised by engineers must, of course, be adhered to by programmers. The format specifies the use of each character position for operation code, index register, and address or special constant.

A program to read the data from one deck of cards or a tape and punch another deck of cards or write on tape is trivially simple; but it shows the need for address modification to make cycles efficient and cut the number of program steps. Index registers are special counters that can be set, increased or decreased with desired constants, and tested to determine their content during each loop in a cycle. Content of an indexed register is used in conjunction with indexable instructions to execute operations on "effective" addresses instead of the originally specified addresses. The indexing scheme is invaluable for performing repetitive operations on data that are stored in some organized fashion.

Comparison orders are at the heart of the decision-making process. Various comparisons are made to determine, for example, whether an inventory balance is larger or smaller than the re-order point, whether one item belongs ahead of another when sorting, and whether a data processing loop has been performed the desired number of times.

Jump orders are used following comparison instructions to transfer to that part of the program which will perform the routine appropriate for each condition tested.

Shifting operations are used to line up characters before comparison or addition operations and to isolate desired characters.

Instructions for addition, subtraction, multiplication, and division are usually included to perform arithmetical operations, although some computer designers omit the divide operation for economy in view of its infrequent use in business-data processing. In fact, arithmetical operations compose only a small fraction of the operations in business programs. The programmer still has many responsibilities in arithmetical operations. He must keep track of the decimal point by scaling when working in fixed point. Floating point computers manage the decimal point; but the programmer must worry about the numbers themselves and the possibility that the resulting precision is more apparent than real. Table 3-2 lists and describes each instruction "built-in" the hypothetical computer covered here.

The instructions and operations for a hypothetical computer may serve as a general guide to computers with internally stored programs. Some specific examples of other types of instructions are given in the questions and problems for this chapter. Chapter 8 covers some advanced programming techniques which can simplify the programmer's work; the use of these techniques demands a thorough understanding of the basic principles presented in this chapter.

TABLE 3-2. *Instructions for the Hypothetical Computer*

Input and Output

RCn	y	x	Read a card in card unit n and store in location x and following, indexable.
PCn	y	x	Punch a card in card unit n with ten words from storage at location x and following, indexable.
BOn	y	x	Block transfer out to tape n buffer storage a block of 60 words from location x and following, indexable.
WTn	– – –		Write on tape n a block of data in its buffer storage.
RTn	– – –		Read 60 words from tape on tape unit n and place in buffer storage for that tape unit.
BIn	y	x	Block transfer in 60 words from buffer of tape unit n into storage location x and following, indexable.

RWn   — — —   Rewind tape on tape unit n.

Index

SIS y   x   Set index y from storage location x (not indexable).

INC y   n   Increase index y by the number n (not indexable).

CIS y   x   Compare index y to storage location (not indexable). Next two instructions are used for "not equal" and "equal" exits.

Tests

JMP y   x   Unconditional jump to location x, indexable.

CMP y   x   Compare contents of accumulator and content of location x, indexable. Next three instructions are used for content of accumulator $<$, $=$, and $>$ location x.

JIN y   x   Jump, if accumulator negative, to x, indexable.

JOV   x   Jump on overflow condition in accumulator to location x.

Load and Store Accumulator and M-Q

CAA y   x   Clear accumulator and add content of location x, indexable.

STA y   x   Store content of accumulator in location x, indexable.

CAM y   x   Clear accumulator and M-Q registers and add content of location x into M-Q, indexable.

STM y   x   Store content of M-Q register in location x, indexable.

Arithmetic

ADD y   x   Add content of location x to accumulator, indexable.

SUB y   x   Subtract content of location x from accumulator, indexable.

MLT y   x   Multiply content of location x, indexable, by content of M-Q register.

DIV y   x   Divide the dividend in accumulator by divisor in location x, indexable.

Miscellaneous

HLT   x   Unconditional halt; with instruction counter set to x (or 000 if blank).

SHL   n   Shift combined contents of accumulator and M-Q registers n places to the left.

SHR   n   Shift combined contents of accumulator and M-Q registers n places to the right.

REFERENCES AND SUPPLEMENTAL READINGS

Andree, Richard V. *Programming the IBM 650 Magnetic Drum Computer and Data-Processing Machine*, New York, Henry Holt and Co., Inc., 1958, 109 pp. This book is an introduction to the IBM 650 Computer. These notes, according to Andree, provide a text with suitable problems, and are not intended as a reference manual. The first 4 chapters are self-contained; but chapters 5 to 9 lean on published IBM manuals which the student is encouraged to consult. Chapter 6 emphasizes over-all principles, 7 discusses interpretive systems using the Bell Interpretive System as an example, and 8 covers compilers with emphasis on IT and FOR TRANSIT.

IBM 650 Magnetic Drum Data-Processing Machine Manual of Operations, New York, International Business Machines Corporation, 1957, 111 pp. This manual of operations covers the characteristics of the type 650 drum processor: input-output unit, operation codes and programming, console operation, optimum programming, and special operating devices.

McCracken, Daniel D. *Digital Computer Programming*, New York, John Wiley & Sons, Inc., 1957, 253 pp. This book is directed toward people without previous knowledge of computing and also toward those whose work requires some general knowledge of how problems are solved on a computer. A hypothetical computer called TYDAC is used to illustrate the basic principles involved in programming, without regard for particular computers. In addition to the usual topics, the book includes a chapter each on floating decimal methods, program check-out, interpretive programming, and double-precision arithmetic.

McCracken, Daniel D., Harold Weiss, Tsai-Hwa Lee, *Programming Business Computers*, New York, John Wiley & Sons, Inc., 1959, 510 pp. This book was, according to the authors, written for the person involved in the day-to-day application of computers to business data-processing problems. The first part covers the nature of the data-processing problems, the central concept of the file, flow charting, and the general characteristics of electronic computers. The second part (Chapters 5-12) deals with coding, including arithmetic operations, jumps, address computations, loops and index registers, subroutines, input and output devices and programs, and verifying program accuracy.

Thomas, Walker H. "Fundamentals of Digital Computer Programming," *Proceedings of the I.R.E.*, vol. 41: 1245-49 (October 1953). A simplified stored-program digital computer with only eight instructions is used to demonstrate the fundamentals of computer programming. A number of basic techniques, including the computer's capacity to alter its own program, are illustrated by means of programs that perform elementary arithmetic and logical computations.

Univac II Data Automation System, The, New York, Remington Rand Univac, 1957, 196 pp. Emphasizing programming for the Univac II, this manual covers process charting, flow charting, and coding; methods for processing items from internal and external storage; input and output; and system design. Practice programming exercises and solutions are a useful adjunct to the text.

PART TWO

AUTOMATIC
EQUIPMENT

CHAPTER FOUR

INPUT-OUTPUT
EQUIPMENT

Business-data-processing systems must handle a large volume of data that may originate in various forms and in widely separated locations. Although relatively simple arithmetical operations are performed, the processing may be complex, and the results of it put to a number of different uses. Input devices must bring data together quickly enough to take advantage of high-speed processing; expensive computers should not be kept waiting for lack of data. Output devices must handle results rapidly to keep up with the speed of other components and furnish output in various forms to meet the requirements of different end-uses.

Suitable input and output equipment is essential for an efficient system. Widely scattered operations rely heavily on communication networks for data input and output, and important costs are involved. This chapter covers the nature and characteristics of input and output devices and of communication equipment.

INPUT DEVICES

The input operation is frequently inefficient and may even be a bottleneck in business-data systems. The usual scheme is to convert source data to some machine-processable medium—punched card, paper tape, or magnetic tape—for further handling.

Operators at manual keyboards convert typed or written copy to a desired medium. Manual conversion is slow, and the error ratio is high enough that duplicate operations, calculations, and editorial checking are often used to detect mistakes and increase accuracy. The manual work in key punching can be reduced and accuracy increased by gang punching or otherwise mass producing the facts that are common to many items. Character recognition devices "read" typed or printed documents to prepare a suitable medium. Data punched in cards during this or a prior operation are often converted to magnetic tape for faster read-in to a computer.

Pre-input

"Pre-input" devices, which might also be called "off-line" devices, are used for preparing and converting data. The devices are "off-line" because they are not connected to the computer when the data are first prepared. At a later stage, and perhaps after a conversion operation, the data are introduced into the computer. Pre-input devices, which capture data in various kinds of media, can be classified according to the media produced. Error-checking schemes, which are used to get accurate output, and several special devices that eliminate most of the manual work in data preparation are discussed separately.

Paper-tape Punches. Many kinds of paper-tape punches are available. Simple devices merely punch tape, while more elaborate devices produce readable copy, duplicate other tapes, or control the content and format of the copy. Source data can be converted to punched paper tape with electric typewriters. Manual keyboard operation produces a paper tape and a readable page ("hard copy") at the same time. The electric typewriter also "reads" paper tape and types hard copy or punches a second tape, or both, as desired.

The hard copy produced when the tape is punched can be read against the original data as one way of verifying accuracy. A better verification plan, in terms of increased accuracy of output, involves another operator making a second tape from the original copy. Both punched tapes are run through a comparing device to produce a third tape. If both input tapes agree, the third tape is punched automatically. If the two input tapes disagree, the machine locks, so that the operator must determine what is correct, punch the output tape, and restart the comparison.

Another verification plan is a compromise between the two described above. The original tape is used as input to a tape-punching typewriter and, if the second typing agrees with the first, a second output tape is produced automatically. If the first tape and second operation disagree, the operator chooses and correctly punches the output tape.

By-product Paper-tape Punches. Source data are frequently punched in paper tape as a by-product of another operation. Many kinds of office equipment produce five-channel paper tape and some produce six-, seven-, or eight-channel tape (Taylor, 1955).

In typing a sales order, for example, a suitable typewriter can also punch paper tape containing either the same data or only a selected part of the data. The by-product tape eliminates the duplicate work that would be involved in punching the tape later. The sales order, which can be produced in multiple copies for ordinary purposes, is useful for checking tape accuracy since the hard copy and tape must agree. The degree of accuracy achieved depends on the skill and care used in typing and verifying plus the skill of subsequent users in detecting mistakes. The tape can be used for input to the computer or for processing on any tape-reading machine.

FIGURE 4-1. *Flexowriter with punched tape and hard copy output*

The Flexowriter shown in Figure 4-1 is widely used for punching five-, six-, seven-, or eight-channel tape and for preparing hard copy. Some models of electric typewriters can also produce five- or eight-channel edge-punched cards while typing a printed page. They can read tape and retype a page without change or with desired modifications. Accounting, adding, calculating, and other office machines—examples of which are shown in Figure 4-2—produce paper tape as a by-product of normal office operations.

Card Punches. Punched cards are a common medium for getting data into machine-processable form. Striking a key on a punch, shown in Figure 4-3, punches the hole or holes in a column to represent one character. A printing punch also prints the characters along the top of the card above the corresponding punched column.

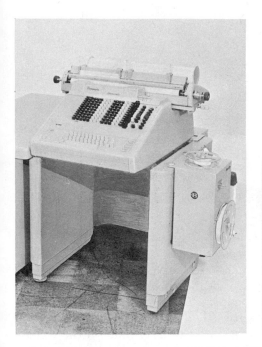

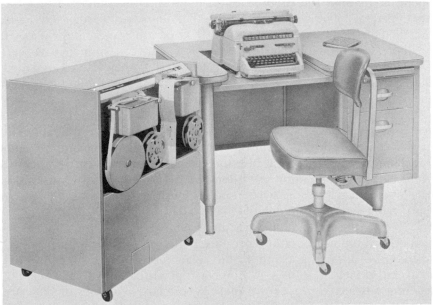

FIGURE 4-2. *Tape-punching office equipment*

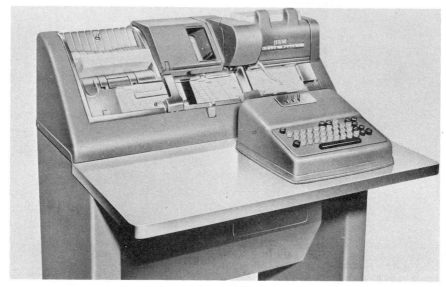

FIGURE 4-3. *Card key-punch*

The original data and punched cards may be given to a second operator for complete or partial verification. Numerical data may be verified but alphabetic data skipped, since a lower margin of accuracy is sometimes more tolerable for letters than for numerals. Since a verifier senses holes but does not punch, verification continues if the second operator, reading the original data, depresses the same keys as the first operator. The verifier stops if the depressed verifier key and punched character are different, and the operator determines whether he depressed the wrong verifier key or the card was punched wrong. Cards are usually punched to indicate whether they passed or failed the verification test; a new card can be produced by repunching only the part that failed verification and by duplicating the rest.

Manual key-punching work, which is done at about the same speed as typewriting, can be reduced by automatic duplication of master copies or decks of constant or repetitive data. Some input is in a machine-processable form because it originates from card-punching time clocks or transaction recorders, as described below. Marking a card in specified locations with a special sensitized pencil permits automatic mark-sensing to punch the marked data.

Typewriters are adapted for direct connection to card punches so that normal typing operations produce punched cards as a by-product. Accounting, adding, and other office machines can also be connected to a card punch. Figure 4-4 shows a typewriter and a bookkeeping machine connected to a card punch. Where large volumes of data are involved, the data on cards may be converted to magnetic tape before input to a computer.

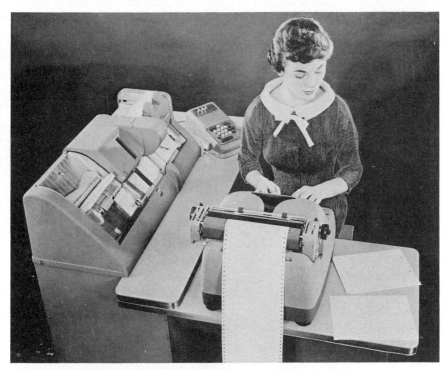

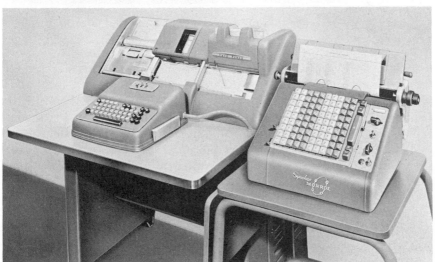

FIGURE 4-4. *Typewriter and an office machine connected to card punches*

Magnetic-tape Writers. A manually operated keyboard device is used for recording data on magnetic tape directly from source data. The device in Figure 4-5 records data on magnetic tape and produces a typed copy for the record and for checking purposes.

FIGURE 4-5. *Keyboard to prepare magnetic tape and page copy*

The typical verification schemes of scanning copy or of duplicating key-stroke operations and comparing the two results can be used with magnetic-tape writers. Duplicate operations cost more than scanning but give more accurate results. The input tape is put in the verifier and the original data retyped. The verifier stops if the second typing is not identical with the data already on tape. The mistake can be "erased" from the magnetic tape and the correct character substituted. In some cases, where the accuracy of input data is vital, three, four, or even five tapes have been prepared independently and then compared after read-in to the computer in order to isolate discrepancies and try to get perfectly accurate input.

Advance Preparation. The input methods described above use data on typed or handwritten documents that are not machine processable. Manual conversion of individual documents, character by character, to get data into suitable form is expensive and may be inaccurate. The idea of "advance preparation" of input data means that output from one stage serves as data input at the next stage of processing. One example of advance preparation is use of the master file produced in one run as input in the next run or cycle.

Another example of advance preparation of input data is the punched-card bill which is prepared and sent to a customer and which he is supposed to return with his payment. When this is done, a cashier gets a customer's bill card to identify the collection. The collected bill card is then used as data input for crediting a customer's account, so that manual conversion of input data is eliminated. Mass preparation of data at one stage can minimize manual conversion at the next stage.

Advance preparation of data can be widely used within an organization, for there is almost complete freedom over the media used internally. On the other hand, there are usually many constraints over the kind of media that can be used to communicate with customers, employees, and other organizations. The fact that they may be unwilling or unable to accept a certain medium—an individual cannot cope with a bill on magnetic tape—limits the variety of media that can be realistically considered.

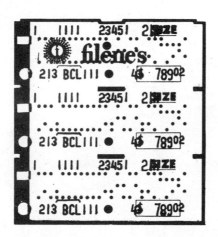

FIGURE 4-6. *Merchandise inventory tag*

Tag Readers. Inventory control is facilitated by mass producing punched cards or other machine media at the time of purchase or manufacture. Special devices print and punch tags with the item name, number, size, manufacturer, and other desired facts. Figure 4-6 shows an example of a merchandise inventory tag that is mass produced when inventory is received.

When an item in stock is used or sold, one part of the tag is detached. A machine reads the detached part of each tag and converts the data to a medium suitable for further processing. Some kinds of tags originally attached to the item may be used for further processing without any conversion.

Transaction Recorder. A section of an inventory tag may be detached and placed in a transaction recorder at the point of sale. A recorder that also serves as a cash register is shown in Figure 4-7. The recorder automatically reads holes in a tag and produces a continuous punched tape, which also includes the variable data that the operator manually enters on a keyboard. Whenever desired (daily or less frequently), the tapes can be converted to punched cards or fed directly into a computer for processing. Direct wire transfer of data from transaction recorders to a computer is useful for quickly updating account balances and interrogating them.

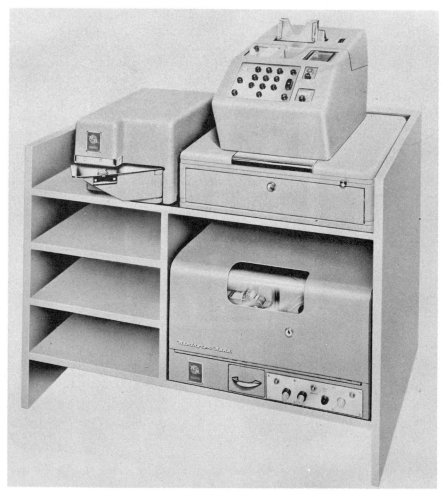

FIGURE 4-7. *Point-o-Sale Recorder*

A factory production recorder, another type of transaction recorder, punches a card with start-stop time and numbers for workers, jobs, and machines. A transacter *(transaction transmitter)* located at any number of remote stations accepts punched cards or tags containing pre-recorded data. In addition, the transacter identifies its operator and location together with the specific item or machine operation covered by its report. Pertinent variable data are set on a dial by the operator, and a transaction code is designated by a selector on the panel. The data are sent from the transacter to a central compiler that adds the following to each message: shift, date, time, end-message code, and processing instructions. Once the complete data for a transaction are captured, they can be stored, transmitted, and processed as desired.

A device called FLIDEN *(flight data entry)* is used for quick, accurate input of aircraft flight control data to a computer. The operator sees the whole message displayed on a television-like tube while he enters the data. He can read the message, backspace as many characters as he wishes to delete mistakes, and then enter the correct characters. When satisfied with the accuracy of the message as set up and displayed for checking, the operator can transfer it to the computer. The idea is that the immediate feedback to the operator coupled with his ability to correct the message will increase both accuracy and speed of input. This concept is applicable, of course, to entering other kinds of data.

Character Readers.   Another data-input system reads characters printed on original paper documents (Harrell, 1959). Character-recognition devices convert visually readable characters into machine-processable form. The Stanford Research Institute designed the first magnetic-ink character reader for sorting and accounting for paper checks. Since then other companies have also developed data-processing systems for handling checks printed with magnetizable ink. Inks containing ferrites are printed on paper by any wet printing process; electric typewriters and some kinds of adding machines can use a special ribbon for printing characters that can be magnetized for reading.

Documents printed with magnetizable ink are passed through a permanent magnet which polarizes the ink in the printed characters (0 to 9 and four letters) and then through a reader at 150 inches a second. At 8 characters an inch, the reading rate is 1,200 characters a second. The output signal obtained from vertically scanning the character is examined to identify the character. Specially shaped characters, as shown in Figure 4-8, are used to improve reliability of reading and the system is said to be secure against most common types of defacement.

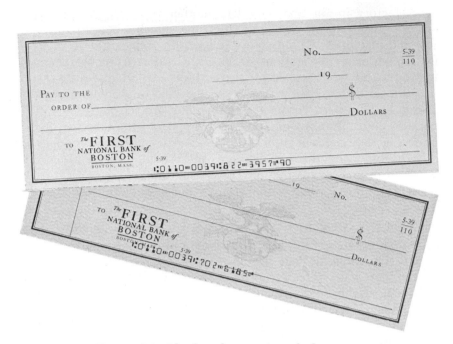

FIGURE 4-8. *Check with magnetic-ink characters*

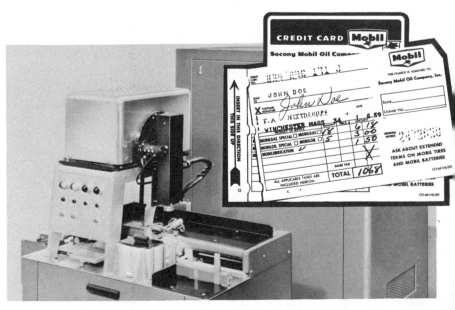

FIGURE 4-9. *Credit card, sales ticket, and Scandex character-sensing equipment*

The Intelligent Machines Research Corporation has built many machines for reading characters printed in ordinary ink and standard type styles (Tersoff, 1958). One machine of this type, called Scandex (shown in Figure 4-9), was built for converting customers' numbers from readable to punched form. When a retail gasoline station makes a sale, for instance, the customer's name and account number are imprinted from a plastic plate to an unpunched card. The item involved and amount of the sale are recorded manually. The cards, with imprinting and writing, are sent to a central location where a Scandex unit reads the customer's number and punches it in the same card. Optical equipment vertically and horizontally scans each numeral, and a logical network decodes the scan pattern into a character. The amount of sale is manually key punched in the card. Cards containing basic data—customer's number and amount of sale—are then used for billing customers and in any other ways desired.

Equipment has been developed to read handwritten characters (Dimond, 1958). It is based on the ingenious idea that a grid can be set up so that each character written will cross a different combination of grid lines. Dots printed at the intersections of the grid lines encourage people to print carefully, around the dots, so that machines can read the characters:

Section of Grid   Numerals Written on Grid

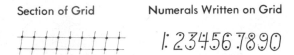

The machine reads by determining which grid lines are crossed and decoding the pattern into a numeral. More guide dots and grid lines are used for alphabetic characters than for numerals. Machines to read handwriting have the interesting incidental feature of forcing people to write legibly—something that people have not been able to teach each other to do in hundreds of years. The fact that banks, oil companies, telephone companies, and postal departments have become very much interested in buying character-reading machines indicates that they may be widely used in the future.

Input Converters

Some computers are designed to accept data on magnetic tape only, because of its high read-in rate. Furthermore, magnetic tape is often preferred even though punched cards or paper tape can be used. Automatic converters transfer data from one medium to another. The methods of recording (punched hole or magnetic spot) and of number system representation (decimal, binary, binary-coded decimal, and five- through eight-channel code) are ordinarily changed during conversion. Efficient converters increase the compatibility and flexibility of different types of equipment, so that each unit of equipment can be selected on its own merits, with less regard to whether all use the same medium.

Punched Cards to Magnetic Tape.   Many data processors include punched-card to magnetic-tape converters. Converters are vital, if punched cards are used in the pre-input stage and magnetic tape is used as on-line computer input. A card to tape converter is shown in Figure 4-10. Converter control is independent of the computer and it operates off-line. Wired plugboard panels are used for editing operations during conversion. Card reading and magnetic-tape writing are usually checked for accuracy.

FIGURE 4-10. *Punched-card to magnetic-tape converter*

Most converters operate at speeds of 240 to 400 cards a minute (320 to 533 characters per second). Newer converters operate at about 1,000 cards per minute, which is 1,333 characters a second.

Paper to Magnetic Tape.   Paper to magnetic-tape converters are included in several systems. Paper-tape readers can usually handle five- through eight-channel code. The paper-tape unit of one computer system reads only seven-bit computer code and requires special devices for punching this code in tape. The converter is simpler and less expensive, although inflexible, for it does not deal with six-channel tape code. Some converters do a limited amount of editing. Most converters operate at about 200 characters a second; but newer equipment reads 1,000 characters a second and there are indications that higher speeds will be reached soon.

Paper Tape to Punched Cards. Paper-tape to punched-card converters are important for large-scale data processors, since paper-tape to magnetic-tape converters are rare. Data converted into cards can be read into the computer; but if faster read-in is required, cards can be converted off-line to magnetic tape. The converter shown in Figure 4-11 reads paper tape and punches cards at the rate of 20 characters a second. Conversion of paper tape to punched cards or some other form is important for integrated data-processing systems based on paper tape.

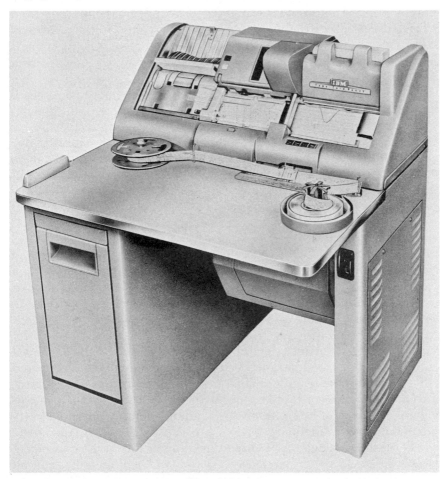

FIGURE 4-11. *Paper-tape to punched-card converter*

On-line Input

On-line input devices are connected to the computer for direct read-in. Selection of a device depends on data volumes, equipment speeds, and the permissible processing time. Magnetic-tape read-write units are used for mass data input, whereas punched-card or punched paper-tape readers are widely used for intermediate volumes. Keyboard devices read in limited amounts of data, program corrections, and file interrogations. The computer-console switches may be used to read in some data or fragments of a program, especially the initial steps required to start program read-in.

Magnetic-tape Units. A magnetic-tape transport unit is used for on-line read-in and write-out of huge volumes of data. Figure 4-12 shows a schematic diagram of the arrangement for reading tape data into computer storage or for writing data on tape. One read-write head is located at each of the seven data channels across the tape to read or write data on the tape in a suitable pattern. The end of the tape is determined either by a photocell or electric contacts which sense a metallic strip attached near the end of the tape, or by rubber "bumpers" attached to the tape to activate a switch. Erasing heads electrically erase any data previously recorded on tape—which might interfere with the recording of new data. Loops of tape between tape reels and read-write heads take up differences in starting and stopping speeds. High speed read-in of data is likely to fill the portion of main storage allotted to data read-in faster than data can be cleared out of it. When this happens, reading must be interrupted until the processor is ready to receive more data. Steady, high-speed movement of tape past the reading head generates a magnetic field for each bit recorded on tape. Reading consists of sensing the magnetic fields. Data are recorded on tape with spaces or gaps which permit starting and stopping without losing any data. The computer manufacturer specifies whether a block of data consists of a fixed or variable number of characters. An inter-record gap is placed between successive blocks to permit stopping during processing. Reading can continue without stopping in each gap if the computer can handle data as fast as received. The need for inter-record gaps growing out of the technical features of high-speed magnetic-tape reading should be contrasted with the paper-tape reading techniques described below. Users must, of course, design records in keeping with the features that the manufacturer builds into the equipment, including the arrangement of records and read-write methods.

Parity-bit schemes, as described in Chapter 2, are used to detect read-write malfunctions in most tape units. Dual recording of all seven data channels is used in some systems. Data that pass the parity-bit test, in one or several attempts to read, are accepted. A similar plan of checking data after writing on tape (echo checking or proofreading) is used in some computers. Many magnetic-tape units operate at read-write rates of 10,000 to 60,000 characters a second obtained from tape speeds of 75 to 112 inches a second and at densities of 100 to 500 characters an inch. Some newer units reach speeds of 100,000 or more characters a second, primarily through higher-density recording. Data written on magnetic tape by means of key-operated devices and card to tape converters are in short records (120 or 80 characters) and at low densities (50 or 128 characters an inch). Longer records and higher densities are achieved on tapes written by the computer.

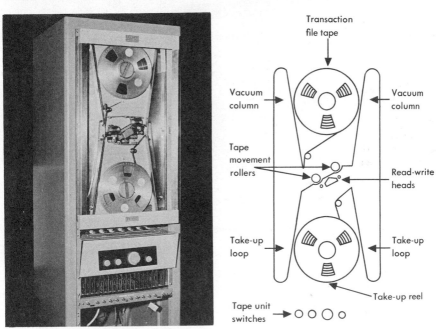

FIGURE 4-12. *Magnetic-tape unit*

Punched-card Readers. On-line punched-card readers, as shown in Figure 4-13, are used with many business processors. The computer controls the card reader and starts and stops reading operations as required. Punched-card readers have wired plugboard panels for editing operations, which include checking for double punches, blank columns, and field consistency (no alphabetic characters in a numerical field and vice versa). Contents of columns can be omitted, altered, or rearranged for transfer into storage. Card readers usually verify operational accuracy by reading each card twice, and contents are accepted only if the two readings are identical. Conversion between the punched-card code and the code used in the computer is handled either by the read-in equipment or by a computer program.

Typical reading speeds are 125 to 250 cards a minute (167 to 333 characters per second). One card reader operates at 1,000 cards a minute (1,333 characters per second) and equipment to read 2,000 and even 3,000 cards a minute has been developed.

FIGURE 4-13. *Punched-card reader*

Paper-tape Readers. Paper-tape readers are often used with small data processors, and sometimes with large ones. Paper-tape readers are especially valuable where data are received over wire circuits. Readers handle five- through eight-channel code under control of the computer.

Limited editing operations may be performed during read-in. Most readers operate at 200 to 500 characters a second. Equipment with speeds of 1,000 characters a second is available and higher speeds will be reached. Paper-tape reading equipment can stop tape movement between any two adjacent characters, the regular spacing of which is ten characters an inch; this means that any one character can be read into the computer and examined and the tape movement stopped before the next character comes into reading position. Thus, no special inter-record gap is required because the space between any two characters serves as a start-stop gap. There is a further difference in reading paper and magnetic tape. Paper tape is read by photoelectric cells (or electromechanical feeler pins in slower readers) which sense the presence or absence of holes in each character position; this method allows tape to be read as slowly as desired.

Keyboards.   A keyboard device may be used to enter data directly into computer storage. Keyboards are used for program testing, program alteration, procedures, and file interrogation. Manually operated keyboards are rarely used for mass input because people can type no more than a few hundred characters a minute. People make too many mistakes to permit direct, unverified entry of data into a computer.

Multiplexed Input.   Keyboard input may be desirable even though limited by manual operating speeds. A large number of keyboards connected to the computer at one time—multiplexed input—effectively increases input speed. Keyboard data are first read into buffer storage and the computer is notified when the transfer to buffer is completed. Data are then copied from the buffer to main storage.

Data from each keyboard are accepted in turn; but priority may be given to some keyboards to accept their input ahead of others. A computer can handle a large number of keyboard inputs in this manner without excessive waiting time. A "program interrupt" feature in some computers permits a read-in unit filled with data to take the initiative and interrupt the program just long enough to start the transfer of data. Processing of other data continues during the read-in of new data.

The American Airlines Reservisor System has many inquiry sets directly connected to a computer. Data are entered in an inquiry set in two ways: (1) on coded plates containing fixed data; (2) on a manual keyboard which enters variable data.

Each inquiry set at a ticket sales office is connected directly to a computer that maintains inventory records on flights. An agent inserts the coded plate into the inquiry set shown in Figure 4-14 to select legs of flights from one point to another. Date, flight leg, and number of seats desired are entered manually in the keyboard, and lights on the inquiry set indicate whether the desired space is available. If the space is available and the customer buys a ticket, the agent pulls the "sell" switch. The computer subtracts the number of seats sold to update the available balance for that flight.

Buffer Storage.   The computer can accept and record data in storage faster than input units can supply it. Buffer storage is used to compensate for this difference in operating speeds. A buffer may be a small intermediate storage unit between the input unit and computer

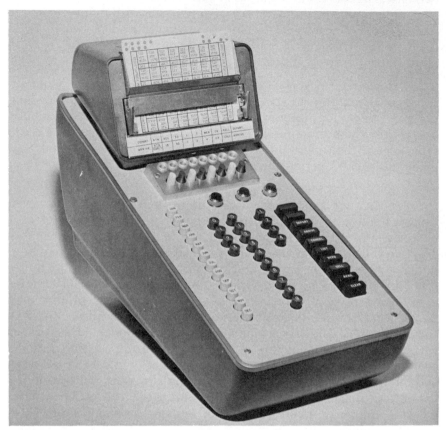

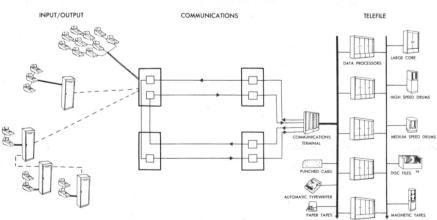

FIGURE 4-14. *Inquiry set and coded plate;*
schematic of Reservisor system

storage and connected to them; in other cases, part of the main storage is used for buffering, for program storage, or for data storage.

The computer directs the input unit to read data into buffer storage and continues with other operations until the read-in operation is completed. The computer transfers data from buffer storage into main internal storage at a high speed, without limitation for the speed at which the buffer was filled. Buffering does not, of course, increase the speed of data read-in above the rated capacity of a card or tape unit. But buffering does have the virtue of minimizing interruptions of the computer while data are being read in so that more processing can be done per unit of time.

Some computers continue processing throughout the whole read-in cycle. Concurrent operations of this type are called "read-while-compute" and neither the computer nor the read-in unit is delayed by waiting for the other. Read-while-compute increases the efficiency of data-processing operations but does not permit exceeding the rated speed of read-in units. Data-processing operations can still be "read-in limited," if data are wanted faster than they are read in. Operations are "computer limited," if the processing cycle is longer than the read-in cycle. Rarely are the processing and read-in cycles exactly the same length; but focusing attention on the longer one will often bring the two into closer balance.

OUTPUT DEVICES

Processed results may go directly to an on-line printer, if output is needed quickly. Ordinarily, results are recorded in machine-processable form for off-line printing and later processing as required. Off-line printing is desirable if slow printers operating on-line will hinder the computer.

On-line Media Producers

On-line devices convert computer output directly to magnetic tape, punched cards, paper tape, printed reports, or visual displays in television-like tubes. Magnetic tape is frequently used for large volumes, whereas typewriters are adequate for answers to a limited number of file interrogations.

Magnetic-tape Units. A magnetic-tape unit used for data read-in is also used interchangeably for data write-out. A magnetic-tape unit is efficient for write-out because it accepts data much faster than a punched-card or paper-tape device. Read-out rates of 10,000 to 60,000 characters a second are common, and some units operate at 100,000 or more characters a second.

Some computers do not buffer input or output to magnetic tape, so that computations stop during data read-in or write-out. Other manufacturers provide for concurrent operations of read-in, computing, and write-out. Some manufacturers design for only two concurrent computer operations—read-in and computing, for instance. One computer is designed so that the user can select any two concurrent operations—read-compute, compute-write, or read-write.

Card Punches. A card punch is often connected to and controlled by the computer for on-line output. Buffers take up speed differences between computer output and card-punching rates. Results are first read from internal storage into buffer storage; the computer then directs the card punch to take data from buffer storage. During the punching cycle, other operations continue. Some processors are designed so that the card punch retains the initiative to call for data when it is ready to accept data. This program-interrupting feature simplifies programming because the computer program need not keep asking the card punch if it is ready to accept more data.

Plugboard panels control some editing operations during read-out and punch. Data punched into a card are reread or checked by other schemes to verify the accuracy of punching. Most card punches operate at speeds between 100 and 250 cards a minute.

Paper-tape Punches. Several computers have directly connected paper-tape punches. Punches usually produce one code, but they can be readily converted to punch any code from five to eight channels.

Buffer storage is used between computer storage and paper-tape punches, and some punches perform limited editing during read-out. Paper punches operate at speeds of 20 to 500 characters a second.

Output Converters

Many computers have output facilities for only one or two media so that converters are used to transfer the data to other media. A wide choice of output methods from the computer may be available, although all of these are not necessarily efficient in practice. One efficient scheme is to use magnetic tape for fast write-out from the computer and to convert from tape to other media while the computer continues other operations.

Magnetic Tape to Punched Cards. Many business systems have equipment to convert data from magnetic tape to punched cards. Tape to card converters operate off-line (independently of the main computer). Control panels are wired for editing during conversion, and accuracy checking for both magnetic-tape reading and card punching is customary. Magnetic-tape to punched-card converters operate at speeds of 100 to 250 cards a minute.

Some applications require both printing and punching on the same card. Elaborate processing schemes are used to (1) print cards on continuous forms, (2) burst them apart, (3) punch desired data into the cards and, finally (4) verify that the corresponding data are printed and punched on the same card.

Magnetic Tape to Paper Tape.   Some business processors convert data from magnetic tape to paper tape. In one system, paper-tape code is identical with magnetic-tape code. Generally, data can be punched in any one of several code schemes and the converter may perform limited editing operations during conversion. Remington Rand manufactures a magnetic to perforated-tape (MTP) converter for reading Univac tape and punching the data in a five-level, six-level, or seven-level, 64-character communication code. The converter automatically punches teletypewriter function codes (Figs., Ltrs., CR, and LF) in the paper tape. Any other special codes required for the operation of the communication system must be inserted in proper order by the device that generates the magnetic tape.

A direct conversion can be made from the Univac C-10 code to a selected, five-level communication code. It is possible to delete selected computer codes or to use them for starting and stopping the paper-tape punch. Illegal computer codes (ones without an equivalent in communication code), unless deleted, will stop conversion and indicate an error. Control codes, unused teletypewriter codes, and illegal computer codes are not punched on the paper tape. The translator and control unit of the converter checks the seven-level code and adds the necessary teletypewriter function codes to the paper tape. The operating speed, which is limited by mechanical problems involved in punching tape, is 60 characters a second.

Punched Cards to Paper Tape.   Card to paper-tape converters may be used with large-scale systems to go from magnetic tape to paper tape. In two stages, magnetic-tape data can be converted to punched cards, and cards then converted to paper tape. Conversion from punched cards to the desired number of channels on paper tape is common in integrated data-processing systems. Two-stage conversion may have the disadvantages of requiring more equipment and taking longer to perform than direct conversion. Converters sense 15 characters a second and punch paper tape.

Multiple Converters.   An approach to the conversion problem that is adopted by some companies is to build multiple or universal converters which can convert from any one medium to any other. The Electronic Engineering Company, for example, has developed a computer language translator for an off-line conversion of media, code, and format which does not interfere with normal computer operations.

Media can be converted to or from digital computers, magnetic tape, electric typewriters, card readers, paper-tape punches, teletype lines, manual keyboards, and card punches.

Several types of code conversion are available, depending on the input-output devices to be combined into a single system: any four-level code to any four-level code (excess three to binary-coded decimal, and so forth); single-character six-bit alphanumerical to other single-character alphanumerical; two-character numerical to single-character numerical; binary to octal; binary to binary-coded decimal; and binary-coded decimal to binary.

Data format on magnetic tape varies from one computer manufacturer to another and sometimes between models made by one manufacturer. A universal converter is expected, therefore, to translate data from one magnetic-tape format to another. It must, of course, translate between the formats used for punched cards and paper tape (including teletype), as well as magnetic tape.

Accuracy in the translation of media, code, and format is assured by means of internal parity checking—both laterally across a character and longitudinally along the tape—if originally used on the tape. Output from the buffer memory is checked for both lateral and longitudinal parity during the tape rewind. The translator can be programmed to stop automatically, if a parity malfunction is detected at any of the checkpoints, to allow analysis by the operator.

Mechanical Printers

Page printers work from most forms of data media—magnetic tape, punched cards, and paper tape. Fast printers connected on-line to the computer save an intermediate step.

The traditional method of typing business documents is well-known (Hosken, 1953). It consists of holding paper against a platen, placing an ink-bearing ribbon over the paper, and striking the ribbon with a metal type slug of the desired character. Numerous variations of this plan are used to increase printing speed. Commonly used mechanical printers can be classified as:

1. Single-character—type and matrix
2. Line-at-a-time—type stick, type wheel, and matrix

Single-character. A single-character device, such as an electric typewriter, types one character at a time and can produce five lines of 120 characters in a minute. Typing speeds of 600 characters a minute may be fast enough for a punched-card or punched paper-tape system. An electric typewriter is often used on-line with the computer for typing out a log of machine operations and giving instructions to the computer operator.

A matrix printer is different from the usual type-face printer in having no type slug or type face. A matrix of wires is used at each printing position to form a character. A matrix of 35 wires arranged in a 5 x 7 rectangle is common. To print an "A" the wires that form it are pushed out slightly by means of a notched push rod and a hammer strikes the paper against the matrix to print. The matrix scheme eliminates the problem of moving a type slug into and out of position but a matrix printer requires careful adjustment of the push rods to give an even impression.

One style of matrix printer uses only one row of wires and repeats impressions from selected wires to form a character. Five wires at each printing position across the print line can, with paper moving vertically, print characters down the paper. In another version of the matrix printer, seven pins are used for each printing line with the paper moving in the same direction as the line of print. This plan is useful for printing a fixed number of lines on magazine labels. Each five- or seven-pin head can print 24,000 characters a minute.

Line-at-a-time.   A medium-speed line printer, shown in Figure 4-15, uses either type bars or type wheels to print a whole line of characters at one time. Each printing position has a complete set of alphanumerical and special symbols on movable type bars. Each bar is raised until the desired symbol is in printing position and hammers strike the type bars to print in all positions at one time. A type-bar printer produces up to 90 lines of 100 characters each in a minute.

Figure 4-15. *Line printer*

A type-wheel printer has a wheel instead of a type bar at each printing position. Numerical and alphabetic type faces are arranged around the rim of each wheel and desired characters are rotated into position. The print wheels move forward to strike the paper and produce a printed line. A wheel printer produces 150 lines of 120 characters each in a minute.

Matrix line printers that use 35 wires at each printing position across a line can print as many as 1,000 lines of 120 characters each a minute.

A higher-speed printer, shown in Figure 4-16, consists of a cylinder of print wheels, arranged side by side, that rotate continuously. Raised characters are arranged in bands around the rim of the cylinder. Every character to be used, and there are usually 50 or 60, is located in each band which provides one printing position. A fast-acting hammer opposite each band of characters presses the paper against the desired character at the correct time while the paper is stopped at each print line. Printing speeds of 1,000 lines a minute of 160 alphabetic characters each, or 2,000 lines of numerical characters, are almost commonplace.

FIGURE 4-16. *High-speed printer and output*

Electron-optical Printers

A mechanical printer which strikes the paper with a hard metal surface and moves the paper with a high start-stop speed may tend to tear the paper. Electron-optical printers rely on entirely different principles and do not physically strike the paper. They are extremely fast output devices because high-speed mechanical parts are virtually eliminated.

Cathode-ray.   A cathode-ray output device receives data either directly from the computer or from magnetic tape. The desired data are displayed in suitable form on a cathode-ray tube similar to a television tube.

A photograph of data images on the tube face is used as output copy. One plan is to use 35 mm film to photograph successive displays of data. Later, the film is developed and printed. Any preprinted form can be introduced by means of a glass plate containing the desired form—purchase order, invoice, or whatever—between the tube face and camera.

Electrostatic.   The Charactron shaped-beam tube developed by Stromberg-Carlson displays data at the rate of 10,000 to 20,000 characters a second. This permits printing 5,000 lines of 120 characters each a minute by means of the xerographic process, which can be explained briefly, as follows: Images on the tube face are directed onto a light-sensitive selenium printing drum revolving at high speed. The exposed section of the revolving drum is dusted with a fine, electrically charged powder, carrying a black thermoplastic material called the "toner," to form the image. The powder and toner are electrostatically transferred to any type of blank or preprinted paper, and the toner, acting as an ink, is fixed by heat. When the printing cycle is completed, the drum surface is cleaned and recharged for the next printing.

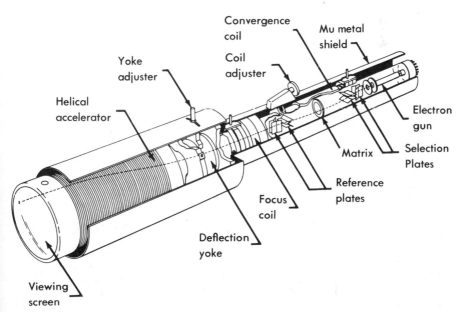

FIGURE 4-17. *High-speed printer shaped-beam tube*

The shaped-beam tube is similar to a television tube in some ways, except that the tube throat contains a matrix plate with desired letters and numerals cut through it. An electron beam is shot through a pre-selected character aperture where it is instantly shaped to the form of the selected character. The shaped beam is then directed to the desired location on the tube face where it is projected to the sensitized surface of the revolving drum of the xerographic printer. The general scheme of the Charactron printer is shown in Figure 4-17. A Charactron printer using the cathode-ray and xerographic principle will print from 10 to 10,000 words a minute, which is equal to 500 lines of 120 characters each.

Ferromagnetographic.   An experimental model of a device based on magnetic principles has been developed. A latent magnetic image of the data is recorded on a magnetizable surface, after which ink containing iron is sprayed on the surface and adheres to the magnetized areas. When the surface is rolled against paper, the inked images are printed on the paper. The drum surface can, of course, be re-used.

Preparing output in a useful form involves editing data, rearranging words and fields, suppressing leading zeros, computing subtotals and totals, and separating items by class—part number, area, and date. The work of output preparation may be divided between the computer and the printer; this minimizes the programming required for the computer and simplifies the wiring board required to control the printer.

Printers can produce an original and one or several carbon copies. More copies can be prepared by first printing some master form and running as many copies as desired. Continuous paper forms of various widths and lengths are used in printers; data can be placed anywhere on these forms, whether they are blank or preprinted. Line printers pose an interesting problem in printing format. Effective printing speeds are highest when each line contains the maximum number of characters and the entire report has a minimum number of lines. But people dislike long lines of solid printing and insist on some spacing between items, which results in more lines of print for the same number of characters and, therefore, increased printing loads.

COMMUNICATION FACILITIES AND EQUIPMENT

The efficiency of the input-output facilities of a widespread organization depends heavily on communication channels and transmitting devices (Fitzgerald, 1956). Mail, air mail, or messengers are often satisfactory. Telegraph and telephone circuits are used for intermediate-speed transmission; if time is critical, faster facilities may be used for high-speed transmission. Microwave radio and closed-circuit television may be used in future data-processing systems. Various transmitting devices can be used for different communication loads.

Communication Channels

Many services exist for transmitting data over telegraph and telephone circuits. Regular commercial telegraph, TWX, Telemeter, and private wire service have features to meet various needs.

Telegraph and Telephone Service. Regular commercial telegraph service is used for transmitting limited amounts of data which are sent to the telegraph office. If volume is sufficient, a tie line and a small transmitter unit provide for facsimile transmission to and from a local office. Pricing is based on message length and the distance sent. Transmission speeds are 60, 75, or 100 words a minute, depending on the quality of service obtained.

A carrier telegraph system manufactured by the Collins Radio Company provides 18 channels for transmitting teletypewriter, supervisory control, or other binary data over wires that are rated as a single voice-band transmission facility. Eighteen duplex channels may be derived on a four-wire circuit or nine channels on a two-wire circuit. Carrier tones separated by 170 cycles per second in the audio range (centered at 425, 595, etc., to 3,315 cycles per second) are used to transmit marks and spaces. Frequency of the carrier tone is shifted 42.5 cycles a second above and below the nominal frequency to represent mark and space. This scheme provides freedom from errors caused by variations in the level of signal received and much of the noise that arises. Each of the eighteen or nine channels may be operated at signaling rates corresponding to teletypewriter speeds of 60, 75, or 100 words a minute.

TWX Service. Teletypewriter Exchange Service, called "TWX Service," provides direct connection between manually or tape-operated typewriters at several points. A message charge includes an initial period of three minutes and a surcharge for each additional minute. Transmitting and receiving equipment at each station is rented on a monthly basis. Maximum transmission speed of TWX is 360 characters a minute. If service is used an hour or more a day between two points, a private wire connection may be more economical. For some users, regular teletypewriter and TWX service may not be suitable as the chief means of data transmission because they do not provide automatic error detection.

Telemeter Service. Telemeter service provides a direct connection between two or more points. The maximum speed of Telemeter service is 390 characters a minute; but the average rate may be lower because of joint participation by patrons in one assigned channel.

A per-word charge applies to the first 15,000 words transmitted each month; additional messages are sent free. Transmission in excess of 50,000 words a month may be handled more economically by private wire. Transmitting and receiving equipment at each station is rented for a fixed monthly fee.

Private Wire Service.   An economical plan to transmit a large volume of data may be to lease a private telegraph or telephone wire. Charges depend on miles of wire leased and time of day or night used. Transmitting and receiving equipment for private wire service is rented on a monthly basis.

Transmitting Devices

Transmitting and receiving equipment can handle paper tape, punched cards, and magnetic tape over telegraph and telephone circuits.

Paper Tape.   Five-channel tape is standard for use with telegraph equipment. Tape data can be transmitted directly over telegraph wires. The Teletypewriter, Figure 4-18, accepts and automatically transmits

FIGURE 4-18. *Teletypewriter*

five-channel tape and produces a typed copy of data transmitted, if desired. The keyboard can be operated manually for direct, although slow, transmission. Data are prepunched in tape for higher-speed transmission. Receiving equipment either prints messages or re-perforates them into paper tape, or both. Transmission speed is 100 characters a minute.

Friden, Inc., makes a device called Teledata which transmits, receives, and checks data coded in five- through eight-channel punched paper tape. As data in punched paper tape are transmitted through the reader they are simultaneously re-perforated and checked on the punch of the Teledata unit located at a distant point. For five-channel tape, parity checking is made by words or groups of characters between space codes. Six- and eight-channel tape permits single and double parity checking. The equipment operates in full duplex mode (transmitting and receiving simultaneously) or half duplex mode (transmitting in either direction but not at the same time). Transmission speeds are 261 to 600 codes a minute depending on the commercial telegraph channel grade (60, 75, and 100 words a minute) that is used.

Punched Cards. Data on punched cards can be transmitted and received directly over telegraph or telephone wires by Transceivers, manufactured by the International Business Machines Corporation.

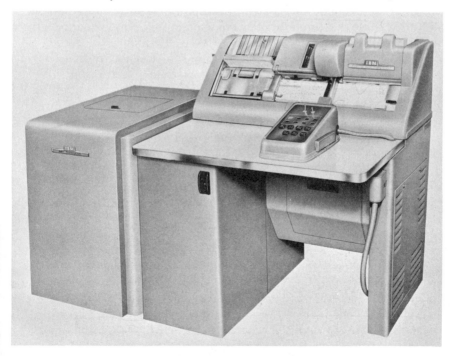

FIGURE 4-19. *Transceiver*

A Transceiver (see Figure 4-19) operating over telegraph circuits transmits 3 to 5 fully punched cards a minute. Operating over telephone circuits, a Transceiver can send 11 fully punched cards a minute. One telephone circuit can handle four units at the same time so that 44 fully punched cards can be transmitted every minute. Card output is increased proportionately if fewer columns are punched in each card. The Transceiver has self-checking features for malfunction detection to assure the degree of accuracy necessary for accounting and computing.

The Collins Radio Company makes a Kinecard Converter for reproducing and transmitting data in standard punched cards at a rate of 100 cards a minute. Used in conjunction with a card-reader-punch unit, the converter translates the pulses and applies them to the eight channels in the transmitting terminal equipment. Pulses from the eight channels are stored in a converter at the receiving terminal until sufficient data are available to supply to the card-punch unit. Malfunctions in data assembly and transmission are detected by odd and even parity checks on each card, and defective cards are isolated by offset stacking.

Magnetic Tape.   Remington Rand has developed a Transrecorder for transmitting data recorded on magnetic tape. It reads data from magnetic tape, transmits the data over telephone wires, and records the data on magnetic tape at the destination. The transmission speed is 6,000 characters a minute over commercial telephone channels rated at 3,000 cycles per second.

The Collins Kineplex magnetic-tape transmission system converts data recorded on magnetic tape into audiotones for transmission over voice-quality telephone circuits. Receiving equipment reproduces a duplicate of the original tape, and tapes may be transmitted in either direction. Transmission is over four tone channels—935, 1,375, 1,815, and 2,255 cycles per second—and each tone is encoded with data from two channels to get eight data-transmission channels. Each of the eight channels handles 300 bits a second for a total rate of 2,400 bits a second or about 21,000 characters of 7 bits each per minute.

Two units are used for handling tape and for translating digital data into audio tones for telephonic transmission. The system operates at tape speeds of 1.5 or 3 inches a second for IBM magnetic tape and 2, 3, or 4 inches a second for Univac magnetic tape. Fast forward and reverse tape speeds for editing and rewinding of tape are provided. Automatic error checking and correction are obtained via lateral and longitudinal parity-bits. The longitudinal parity-bit (along the channel) which is generated before data are transmitted (if it is not already on tape) adds just enough repetitive data, called "redundancy" for short, to reproduce data at an error rate of 1 every 10^5 bits; these errors are caused by interference on the voice circuits. Transmission errors are detected and the record containing the error is automatically re-transmitted. After three attempts, the machine halts, if still unsuccessful, to enable the operator to decide what to do.

A telephone handset is associated with the Kineplex signaling equipment in order to supervise the communication system when data are not being transmitted. The handset has buttons for signaling the remote terminal, for monitoring the audio signal, and for selecting either the data-transmission or voice mode of operation.

If transmitted data are needed in readable form only (as in reports, checks, or statements) a printer may be directly connected to the transmission facility.

SELECTION OF INPUT-OUTPUT SYSTEM

Many characteristics of the input-output system—scope of business applications, type of processing, rate of change, time schedules, geographical origination, report requirements, and accuracy required for output—influence the types and combinations of input-output equipment that should be selected for efficient operations (Gibbons, 1957). Figure 4-20 summarizes the relationship between various kinds of available input-output equipment, only a few of which would be used in any particular system. Some of the more important considerations in developing an efficient input-output system deserve discussion at this point.

The *scope* of business systems covers many activities and functions. Data may originate in various forms. Punched cards may be best suited for collecting data at one point, while paper tape is best for another. Specialized equipment may be efficient for handling large volumes of repetitive data that originate on one medium and which can be brought to one point for mass processing.

The *type of processing* involved influences selection of input-output equipment. Engineering and scientific calculations often involve relatively small amounts of input data. The computer performs complicated and time-consuming operations with them, so that relatively slow input and output equipment may be adequate. Most business-data-processing applications, on the other hand, involve large amounts of input and output data; computation as such being less important, efficient use of the computer requires high-speed input and output facilities. The processing of business data can be done efficiently with input and output facilities of higher speed than would be necessary or desirable for handling engineering and scientific problems.

Preliminary processing outside the computer is often justified, and input system design should exploit this possibility. Sorting a large amount of data may be done more economically on punched cards than

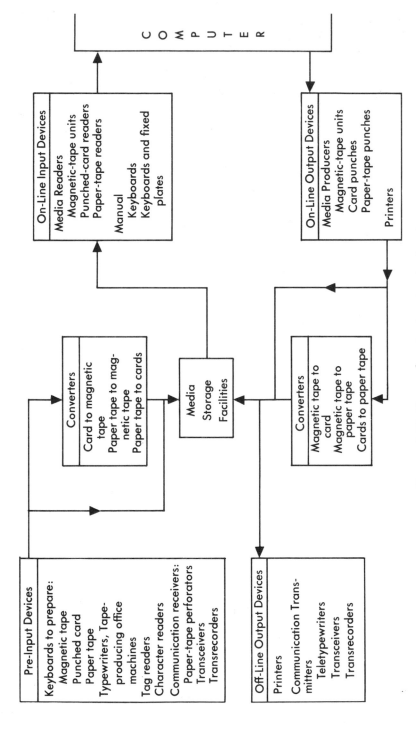

FIGURE 4-20. *Comprehensive input-output system*

on magnetic tape. The cards can be sorted and read in either directly or after conversion to magnetic tape. This is not to say that data already on tape should be converted to cards for sorting, returned to the computer, and processed further. Some factors other than economy of sorting are important. Sorting data with computers is often quicker than with punched-card equipment. The experience of some computer users shows that computer sorting is both more accurate and less expensive than punched-card sorting.

Furthermore, computers do a better job than punched-card equipment at editing input data for accuracy and plausibility. Faulty data can be screened out before they enter the main processing stream. Over-all efficiency can be improved by isolating mistakes in the early stages of processing.

The *rate of change*—the activity of items in files—may vary from a very small percentage to a large one each time a file is processed. Examples of highly active files are payrolls, which must be completely updated each pay period, and checking accounts at banks, which are updated daily with perhaps half of the accounts showing new transactions. At the other extreme, some files are essentially dead—a cemetery, for example, adds to its list of patrons names that are never eliminated.

Some systems involve processing a small number of transactions against large files of data. If files are kept on magnetic tape, the nature of the input-output equipment is fixed. A relatively large amount of new data may be processed against small files. If so, lower-speed files may serve, although magnetic tapes are commonly used.

Time schedules may be loose enough that off-line input and output are adequate. On the other hand, current information may be so critical for successful operations that on-line input and output are imperative. Timely information can often be traded off against other factors to improve operating efficiency. In some cases, the value of getting immediate information can be overemphasized. Other fruitful methods for improving operations should be considered before adopting equipment which will require people to "hurry up and wait."

The *geographical distribution* of operations and data-processing activities should affect the choice of communication facilities. Widespread operations and centralized data processing may require a large communication network for the mass flow of data. If time schedules permit, mail may work as well as an elaborate wire transmission system. The point is often overlooked that high rates of data transmission can be achieved by messenger, air mail, or surface mail.

Requirements for reports vary greatly: the volume needed ranges from small to large; the number of copies may be few or many; the content and format may be strictly repetitive or wholly unpredictable.

Routine reports and documents may require a great amount of off-line printing. Although work scheduling is relatively easy, deadlines are supposed to be met.

The questions to be answered by reports may be unpredictable either because of timing or contents. Intermittent questions to be answered by interrogating the file may be accumulated until the next processing run and the answers obtained routinely. If quicker answers are necessary, on-line keyboard devices may be used to interrogate files. Questions that were not anticipated when designing the data system may require analyzing the data in some new fashion before answers are possible. Many questions not originally anticipated cannot be answered at a reasonable cost, if at all. Such questions often place greater demands on processing procedures than they do on input-output facilities.

It is generally thought that perfectly *accurate output*—no discrepancy between the results obtained and the true results—should be obtainable. Accuracy can be increased by providing enough capacity to handle both the message and the mistakes that arise—erroneous characters, dropped digits, lost messages, and transpositions. If a system with sufficient capacity is efficiently used, it is possible to detect and even to correct mistakes in data origination, transmission, calculation, and output. Increased capacity for accurate data processing can be obtained using more sophisticated codes, more elaborate equipment, and better channels. In the final analysis, the quesion of what degree of accuracy is warranted must be answered by balancing the cost of achieving greater accuracy against the cost of using inaccurate results.

The problems involved in achieving a high degree of *accuracy in communication* deserve some elaboration here. Various methods are used to try to assure that the message received is identical to the one transmitted. The idea of transverse and longitudinal parity-bits or check sums may be extended to include duplicate transmission of part or all of a message. For example, numbers may be repeated after the body of the message, as is done for commercial telegrams. Numbers may be given in numerals and also spelled out, as in bank checks—"270.30" and "two hundred seventy dollars and thirty cents." Each of these schemes attempts to overcome "noise" in the communication channel by including enough redundancy or repetition in the message so that it can be understood even though some of the message is garbled. A check that is written "230.70", "two hundred seventy dollars and thirty cents" is valid and will be paid according to rules that specify the precedence of letters over numerals in case of discrepancy.

Some communication schemes increase redundancy still further by means of duplicate transmission in opposite directions. Point A transmits to point B which then re-transmits to point A, where the messages making the round trip are compared for discrepancies. This is an example of the "transponder" scheme for assuring accurate transmission by means of an immediate response from the receiver. Quick detection of mistakes in transmission, as reflected by discrepancies, increases the effective amount of data transmitted (the number of characters received that have a high probability of being correct), for equipment and line malfunctions are detected as soon as they occur. Transmission is repeated if the trouble is only temporary. If repeated transmission does not give two messages that check as identical, the equipment or lines need servicing. The transponder scheme, like other plans for trying to get accurate transmission, has certain costs associated with it. Here a return circuit is used as much as the forward circuit, if the transmission speeds are the same in both directions and the response includes the whole message.

Two general points are worth considering. The first is that every scheme for trying to improve the accuracy of data transmission increases costs, because more capacity (through use of elaborate codes, better equipment and lines) is required to accommodate noise while still transmitting the message. A second point is that there is never complete assurance that the message received is identical to the message as it originated; there are only varying degrees of probability that the input and output messages are identical. In other words, perfectly accurate transmission probably costs an infinite amount of money. The optimum degree of accuracy to achieve in data transmission is reached when the costs incurred in raising the level of accuracy increase faster than the benefits derived from greater accuracy. The cost and value of accuracy are discussed more fully in Chapter 10.

It is clear that many factors affect the selection of input and output facilities. A mixture of facilities, rather than one type, is often useful. Detailed and complete knowledge about the data to be used and the information needed from them should precede system design.

SUMMARY

Automatic data-processing systems require well-designed input, output, and communication facilities.

Input devices supply machines with data in a form suitable for processing. The pre-input stage bridges the gap between visually readable and machine-processable data. Often, people operate keyboards to punch cards and paper tape or "write" on magnetic tape. Machine-processable data may be a by-product of typing hard copy. Accuracy in pre-input operations is obtained by reading back against copy or by duplicating the operations and comparing the results. Data-preparation costs can be reduced and accuracy increased by preparing data in advance so that they will serve as output at one stage and as input at a later stage. Tag readers, transaction recorders, and character readers mechanize pre-input operations, reducing the manual work and improving the quality of data.

On-line input devices read in the data which have been prepared. Magnetic-tape units have the highest read-in speeds, although the slower punched-tape and punched-card units are widely used. Manual keyboards are used for limited input and for on-line interrogation. Also, keyboards used in parallel speed up data input and file interrogation. Notched plates may be used to supply fixed data.

Output equipment and operations are similar to those involved in input. High-speed devices—magnetic tape and some printers—may be operated on-line. Lower-speed devices are often operated off-line with magnetic tape used as intermediate storage. On-line electric typewriters print the computer operating log and instructions for the console operator.

Input and output converters change media from one form to another. Conversion from magnetic tape to punched cards and then paper tape may be useful in some situations.

Mechanical printers can be classified as single-character and line-at-a-time devices. Typewriters are useful for limited output. Line-at-a-time printers operate in the range of 100 to 1,000 lines a minute. Electron-optical printers deliver output at rates of 10,000 to 20,000 characters a second. Images on the tube face may be photographed and printed later or printed immediately by xerographic methods.

Communication facilities are necessary to link together a widespread organization. Telegraph and telephone lines are available at either per-message or leased-wire rates. Commercial or short-wave radio may be used. Station equipment handles data at speeds of hundreds to thousands of characters a minute. Transmitting devices include paper-tape, punched-card, and magnetic-tape senders and receivers.

Selection of an efficient input-output system depends on the characteristics of the application as well as on the equipment that is available or can be designed to meet special requirements. The operating speeds given in this chapter are merely indicative of what is available and will increase as new equipment is developed. Factors to consider in setting up a processing system are the scope and type of processing, file activity, time schedules, geographical spread, reporting requirements, and accuracy required for output data.

REFERENCES AND SUPPLEMENTAL READINGS

Dimond, T. L. "Devices for Reading Handwritten Characters," pp. 232-37 in *Proceedings of the Eastern Joint Computer Conference: Computers with Deadlines to Meet*, New York, The Institute of Radio Engineers, 1958. This article describes the development of a scheme for encouraging people to write numerals and letters with enough care to permit machine reading. A device called "Stylator" can be used to "read" a character while it is being written. The output from reading handwritten material can be used for processing in any form desired.

Fitzgerald, E. L. "Computers With Remote Data Input," pp. 69-75 in *Proceedings of the Eastern Joint Computer Conference*, New York, The Institute of Radio Engineers, 1956. Fitzgerald deals with the status in 1955 of remote input for commercial data-processing installations. The areas considered are (a) electromechanical recording of data on a storage medium at a remote geographical location, (b) transmission of data to a central location, and (c) conversion of transmitted information to a form suitable for computer input. Applications fall into one of three categories: (a) high time value of input, (b) economy brought about by central processing despite transmission costs, and (c) uniform cutoff dates allowed by remote input applications despite geographical separations. Order and sales statistics, engineering calculations, and construction-site payroll applications are discussed. Equipment involved includes devices for transmitting punched paper tape over private or common carrier wires, and punched cards over teletype or full-voice frequency telephone lines. Other equipment will convert from punched paper to magnetic tape, and vice versa. Magnetic-tape transmission over telephone circuits, with validity checking, should be available soon. Accurate transmission is difficult to achieve, but additional work is being done to improve accuracy. Remote programming is feasible and will become more attractive if noun and verb pseudo-codes are developed.

Gibbons, James. "How Input/Output Units Affect Data-Processor Performance," *Control Engineering*, vol. 4: 97-102 (July 1957). The relationship of input-output devices to the over-all performance of a system is discussed in this article. Considered first are devices for (a) recording data onto machine-processable media, (b) converting data from one medium to another, (c) reading data from media into the computer, and (d) recording data from the computer onto media or in a printed form. Tables are presented indicating such factors as (a) maximum number of on-line units, (b) reading and recording speeds, and (c) checking features for punched-card and magnetic-tape input-output devices used with presently available computers. A case study of the IBM 650, which has grown from a "moderate performance" to a "powerful" unit by recent changes in its input-output devices, is presented. An examination of several small-scale systems reveals that they can be distinguished from medium-size computers by limited input-output facilities even though they may have nearly comparable computing ability. To illustrate the compatibility problems involved with some input-output equipment, the punched-card input-output system for the Datatron is examined in detail. Problems of converting from punched-card to computer code, of organizing card data into computer words, and of developing checking schemes are considered.

Harrell, R. L. "The Role of Character-Recognition Devices in Data-Processing Systems," pp. 54-68 in *Proceedings of the Fifth Annual Computer Applications Symposium*, Chicago, Armour Research Foundation, 1959. This article describes several systems using coded marks (Stanomatic, Heidinger, Hofgaard, and Broido) and some using "readable" characters (RCA, ABA, and IMR). The merits of magnetic and optical scanning are discussed. *Reader's Digest* Book Club's use of a character reader for reading typed data and punching selected coded data in the same card is described.

Hosken, J. C. "Survey of Mechanical Printers," pp. 106-12 in *Proceedings of the Eastern Joint Computer Conference: Review of Input and Output Equipment*, New York, American Institute of Electrical Engineers, 1953. This is a short summary of available mechanical printers and a preview of some new ideas that should be implemented shortly. Five general categories existing in output printers are discussed: (a) single action, one character at a time, like the Flexowriter; (b) line-at-a-time printers, like printing calculators or punched-card tabulators; (c) "on-the-fly" machines using revolving type wheels and synchronized hammers, like the synchroprinter by Anelex; (d) machines forming characters from a matrix of dot-producing hammers, like the Burroughs printer; and (e) bar and helix machines used in facsimile devices. Hosken points out that until recently one of the significant bottlenecks in data-processing systems was slow output equipment. The equipment now available is sufficiently fast, but it is expensive to buy and use. The problem for the engineers to solve is to find cheaper ways to print at high speeds.

Taylor, J. C. "Data Collection as a By-Product of Normal Business Machine Operation," pp. 34-41 in the *Proceedings of the Western Joint Computer Conference*, New York, The Institute of Radio Engineers, 1955. This paper sets forth an explanation of an automatic system for collecting data on punched paper tape as a by-product of normal machine operation. The example used is the recording of data pertaining to merchandise sales in a department store. Cash registers can be equipped (a) to read garment tags previously punched to show style, size, season, price, and so forth; and (b) to transfer this information to punched paper tape. The information recorded on punched paper tape at the point of sale can be used later for processing as desired. The scheme described by Taylor is one proposal for getting information into a mechanically processable form at the first possible moment, the point when the transaction occurs, and for eliminating any need for manual copying.

Tersoff, Abraham I. "Automatic Registration in High-Speed Character Sensing Equipment," pp. 238-42 in *Proceedings of the Eastern Joint Computer Conference: Computers with Deadlines to Meet,* New York, The Institute of Radio Engineers, 1958. This article describes high-speed character sensing by means of a two-dimensional photo scanning system, as successfully used in many analyzing readers. Emphasis is placed on the problem of automatic registration to cope with the variability of typing on mail for automatic reading and sorting.

CHAPTER FIVE

STORAGE

People use various methods to store data: their memories, "little black books," notebooks, organized lists of transactions (journals), summaries by items (accounts), files, and libraries. Wide ranges of data capacity, organization, waiting time, retention period, and cost exist for storage systems. A perfectly ideal storage system should provide: unlimited volume, all methods of organization, zero waiting time, indefinite availability, and no cost. Such storage is obviously in the "blue-sky" class.

Some storage methods possess several features of an ideal system. The human mind seems to involve almost no waiting time, although people often take time to recollect. The mind performs prodigious feats of organizing facts and does so at little or no cost. But capacity and retention time are limited and people often forget critical facts. Libraries, on the other hand, provide for indefinite storage of huge quantities of data; but the organization is inflexible and the waiting time often annoys users. The cost of storing each unit seems low; but the total costs are big enough to disturb librarians.

The point is that a great variety of storage methods is available. No one method is ideal; but a mixture of methods may be used to fill a particular need. A compromise is usually made between the high cost of an ideal system and the amount of money available to buy storage facilities. Small amounts of high unit cost and large amounts of low unit cost storage may be used together to fill a need. Similar comments about data-storage facilities apply to business-data systems. Numerous storage methods are available, but none is ideal. A compromise is reached between what is desirable and what is economical. Furthermore, storage capabilities must be in balance with the processing ability of other equipment components.

The topics discussed in this chapter are the characteristics of data storage, storage devices, and the selection of storage methods.

CHARACTERISTICS OF DATA STORAGE

The characteristics of data storage include the ways that data are represented, methods of getting at stored data, and features of storage units—waiting time, cost, capacity, erasability, and duration of the storage period.

Data Representation

Most storage units use the binary scheme for storing data. Numerical computers use 4 bits for one decimal digit. Many alphanumerical computers designed primarily for business applications use 6 bits for a letter, numeral, or other symbol. The 6 bits allotted to an alphanumerical character are partly wasted when used to store a numeral, because a decimal digit requires only 3.3 bits in the binary mode.

Some numerical computers combine the 8 bits of 2 numerals to store one letter; but this "two-for-one" scheme wastes storage. Another scheme, called "three-for-two," is to store 2 letters in the 12 bits that could represent 3 numerals. Some newer computers represent numbers in the binary mode but use groups of 6 bits for alphabetic data; in this way, a binary word represents a number without wasting any bits but can still be used for an alphabetic character as efficiently as a machine with six-bit binary-coded alphanumerical mode. The compactness of the binary scheme for numbers usually requires the conversion of numbers from decimal to binary when they are first handled. After the numbers are converted, the binary form may be retained throughout all processing until the final output stage, when a conversion from binary to alphanumerical mode is required. All of the schemes for tightly packing either numerals or letters into the same storage space involve special operations at some point.

Addressability

A storage unit may be designed so that numerals and letters can be stored at identifiable locations. Storage locations must be known if their contents are to be found quickly. If storage locations are not specified, some type of scanning or searching through a file is required. In some cases, a combination of specified locations and searching or scanning is used to find the contents of storage.

Each location in certain kinds of storage is assigned an "address." Computer programming must deal with the problems of putting data into storage and obtaining data from storage. Automatic programming schemes use the computer to assist the programmer in keeping track of the storage locations assigned to program instructions and to data. In fact, the programmer can use symbols, such as "NAME" and "ADDRESS," in his program to refer to the storage locations that contain the name and address items in a record. Symbols used to refer to storage locations are called "symbolic addresses." The computer, following a program written especially for the purpose, can replace symbolic addresses with absolute addresses (numbers like 020, 021, 022); this makes it possible to execute a program originally prepared with symbolic addresses. In this way a programmer can refer to an item in storage by an explicit symbol even though he does not know where it is. He need not worry about where an item is located in storage so long as it is actually there, and he knows how to get it. The idea of symbolic addressing is not new; banks that encourage banking-by-mail claim that they are as near as your mailbox, and, for many purposes, you can act as though they were located at the mailbox. Small children may be certain that milk comes from bottles and not from cows. The mail box and the milk bottle are, in a sense, symbolic addresses for the real addresses of the bank and the cow.

The number of characters referred to with an address is different for fixed and variable field-length computers. Computers designed with a fixed word-length would use one address to refer to a word of 8, 10, or 12 characters. Computers designed with a variable field-length feature, on the other hand, use an address to refer to one character. Every character could be addressed, if desired. Either the first or last character of a field is usually addressed, according to the equipment design, and the other end of the field is indicated by a special mark. The special mark may be a separate character or may be combined with the extreme character in the field. Even in variable field-length computers, instructions are likely to have a fixed length of five or six characters and so resemble fixed word-length storage.

Mode of Operation

"Mode of operation" refers to the way—either serial or parallel—that bits, characters, and words are read in or out of storage. In the serial mode, data (bits, characters, and words) are read one after another in a time sequence. In the parallel mode, the bits are read simultaneously.

A combination of the two modes may be used. On magnetic tape the bits in a character are usually read in parallel, and characters that make up a word are read serially—this combination of modes is called "parallel by bits and serial by character." If storage and arithmetic unit modes are different, data go through a buffer for modification as required.

It is interesting to observe the mode of operation of several devices. An office typewriter produces characters serially and is limited to a few hundred *characters* a minute. A Stenotype machine used by court reporters for typing words and even phrases at one time (the characters are typed in parallel) has speeds of several hundred *words* a minute. Telegraphic transmission is usually serial by bit (as dot follows dash) and by word; but some telegraph systems were built with 26 lines, so that the whole alphabet could be transmitted in parallel if the sender and receiver could handle the higher speed. Telegraphic transmission had a higher potential speed by parallel transmission in the early days than it does at present with serial transmission. The efficiency of transmission—measured in terms of actual use of potential capacity—is higher for the serial scheme.

The problem of serial versus parallel operations is, like most others, resolved in terms of economics. The question is whether the increased speed achieved at a particular stage by using more equipment to get parallel operations is worth the cost of the additional equipment.

Features of Storage Units

Capacity, access time, cost, erasability, and volatility are important features of storage units. These features must be considered when trying to match equipment to the applications required of it.

Capacity. The capacity of a storage device is expressed as the number of bits, decimal digits, characters, words, or fields it can store at one time. Each of these units is used under varying conditions. Conversion from one unit to another is necessary in comparing storage capacities.

Effective capacity for storage with a fixed word-length is often less than stated capacity, because short words in the data waste some of the space allotted to a storage word as designed by the engineer. On the other hand, packing two short words of data into one storage word saves space, but may increase processing time. Long data words may occupy part or all of two storage words. The loss of storage is small if storage is used mainly to hold program instructions that are essentially the same length, each of which just fits into one word.

A variable field-length computer, on the other hand, uses minimum space to store each item of data, but raises some problems of how to keep track of where each field is stored.

Access. Access time is the length of time between a call for data from storage and completion of delivery. Some computers with magnetic core storage have access times as short as three microseconds; most are in the range of six to twenty microseconds. Access time for any data in a magnetic core storage unit is constant. Such high speeds are obtained because data in core storage are directly addressable; no mechanical movement, which is much slower than electric switching, is involved.

In other kinds of storage units the elements move serially past read-write heads until the desired address or item is found. One method is to count timing pulses to find a storage location. Magnetic drums and disks use this plan. Average access time, as described below, for data on drums ranges from a few to fifty milliseconds. Average access for data in disk storage runs from 100 to 800 milliseconds.

Another method for getting access to an item involves scanning the data because there is no specified address. The data on magnetic and paper tape, for example, are scanned until a desired item is found.

Minimum access time is the length of time required to get data from the storage location that is most quickly available. Maximum access time applies to the least readily available storage location. The range from minimum to maximum may have an important effect on programs to operate on data in storage that are arranged and searched serially.

The average of the minimum and maximum access times is a better indicator of real access time. If a high fraction of the operating program involves obtaining data from or placing results in storage, short access time is desirable. Frequently used data should, if feasible, be placed in minimum-access locations.

Cost, Capacity, and Access. The three factors of cost, capacity, and access are closely inter-related. A storage device with a short access time costs more per unit of storage to build than a device with a long access time. Most systems, therefore, have a limited amount of quick-access storage. A large-capacity storage device at reasonable cost is associated with longer access time.

Erasability and Volatility. "Erasable" means that stored data can be removed and replaced by new data. All magnetic and electronic storage devices have the erasability feature.

"Volatility" in this instance means that stored data are lost when power is stopped; but this feature need not be critical. Ordinarily, lost data may be recomputed at low cost from original data, or intermediate results can be stored as a precaution. Most of the newer storage devices are non-volatile. Interestingly, some computers designed for military purposes are required to have volatile storage for security purposes. The contents of storage can be destroyed whenever advisable.

STORAGE DEVICES

Two or more levels of storage are used in every data processor to try to achieve an efficient balance between access, cost, and capacity. Storage with quick access costs more per unit than storage with slow access. Most computers are, therefore, designed with larger capacity, slow access storage.

For large-scale data-processing equipment with three levels of storage, the terms "internal," "secondary," and "external" are widely used. These names would be more consistent if modified slightly to "internal primary," "internal secondary," and "external" storage; but the original forms are too widely accepted to change them here. The distinction is often vague and has some aspects of "now-you-see-it, now-you-don't" because a larger processor may have a device classified as "secondary" storage that would rank as the primary storage if used for a medium processor. Furthermore, storage devices are downgraded as new devices are invented. If you prefer some other set of names to the three—internal, secondary, and external—used here to cover the hierarchy of storage devices, you are free to substitute them.

Internal high-speed storage holds the program and data currently in use within the computer. Secondary storage provides a relatively large volume of data for the computer at moderate access speeds. External storage holds data that are in a form suitable for processing but that are not being actively processed. Similarities and differences of these three classes of storage are shown in Table 5-1.

TABLE 5-1. *Classes of Storage Devices*

Type of Storage	Integral Physical Part of Computer	Connected to and Controlled by Computer	Holds Information in Form Prescribed for Computer	Examples
Internal	Yes	Yes	Yes	Magnetic core, drum
Secondary	No	Yes	Yes	Magnetic drum, disk, tape, tape bin
External	No	No	Yes	Magnetic tape, wire, punched card, paper tape

Internal Storage

Internal storage facilities form an integral part of the data processor circuit-wise, although the storage unit may be physically separated from the processor and located in another unit. Internal storage is directly controlled by the processing unit and includes the total storage that is accessible automatically to the computer.

Internal storage holds the program that is being used and the data involved in processing. The storage locations are addressable either by word or by field, which may be as short as one character. The data are read directly from internal storage to the arithmetic and control unit for processing.

The access time for internal storage is short, but capacity is limited because internal storage to hold one bit costs about half a dollar. Magnetic cores and magnetic drums are common internal storage devices. The acoustical delay lines and electrostatic tubes used in early computers are no longer being designed into new computers.

Magnetic Core. A magnetic core is a tiny, doughnut-shaped ring of ferrite capable of retaining either one of two magnetic states. Magnetic cores are placed where "write" wires cross to form a grid. A magnetic-core memory plane is shown in Figure 5-1. Electric current passed through a horizontal and a vertical wire goes through each core, but only one core at the junction of the two wires gets sufficient electricity to change its magnetic state. Other cores along each one of the two wires remain unchanged. A current passed in one direction through the wires magnetizes the core; a current sent in the opposite direction along the wires reverses the core's magnetic state. One state represents a 1, the other a 0 (Fowler, 1956).

FIGURE 5-1. *Magnetic-core storage plane and assembly*

A third "feeler" wire that passes through every core reads the magnetic state of a core when current is sent along both "write" wires in the core that is to be read. The attempt to read causes the core to assume the 0 state. If the core is already in magnetic state 0, no current is induced in the feeler wire. But if the core is storing 1, its state will be reversed by the current passing through the write wires, and a signal will be induced in the feeler wire. The magnetic state of the core is, in effect, "read." Since reading changes the magnetic state of a core, its prior state must be regenerated by an appropriate write signal. The destructive read-out scheme, which requires regeneration of the original state of the core, is inefficient. It is comparable to using a pile driver on a tack: the mechanism will work, but it requires straightening out the tack after the destructive blow.

Each core in a plane holds one bit. A plane may have 32, 64, or some other number of bits in each direction for a total of 1,024, 4,096, or some other number. Many core planes, say 37 or 48, make up a storage unit. The bits that make up a word are often placed in the same x and y position on each plane and read in parallel. Thus a word of 37 bits may be stored in the cores located in row 9 and column 53 of every one of the 37 planes. The 37 bits may be used to store a 36-bit binary number and sign, 6 alphabetic characters, or 9 decimal numerals in binary-coded decimal form and sign.

The basic storage capacity of 1,024, 4,096, or perhaps 8,192 words in a single set of core planes may be increased by using several storage units for one computer. One manufacturer offers from one to seven of the 4,096-word packages for a maximum of 28,672 words with one computer; another offers from one to four of the 8,192-word packages. Modular construction of storage units allows the user to order and "plug-in" one or more units to meet his storage requirements. Magnetic-core access time is in the range of a few to 200 microseconds (0.000005 to 0.000200 seconds) and is the fastest internal storage device in general use. Also, core storage is the most commonly used internal storage device in large computers.

Magnetic-core storage is both erasable and non-volatile. Magnetic cores are individually inexpensive but the electronic circuits required to use them make them more expensive per bit stored than a magnetic drum.

Twistor Grids.   Recent work by the Bell Telephone Laboratories shows that the ferrite core placed at the intersection of the wires in magnetic-core memory can be omitted. Twisted magnetic wire in one direction and plain copper in the other can be used to make a grid. A bit can be stored at each junction of the two kinds of wire. A bit is "written" by current along two wires that cross to make a magnet at the junction. A bit is "read" by sending current along a copper wire and measuring the output of a desired magnetic wire. Output depends on whether it was previously magnetized.

Magnetic wires as small as one-thousandth of an inch in diameter are feasible. At least 10 bits per inch can be stored on each magnetic wire. The fact that the magnetic wires are twisted eliminates the need for a magnetic core at each junction. The Twistor grid has access and density comparable to magnetic-core planes.

Magnetic Drum.   A magnetic drum is a metal cylinder coated with magnetic material. Heads for writing on or reading from the drum are mounted in the drum housing and the drum rotates past the read-write heads.   "Bands" or groups of recording tracks are available around the drum for storing data, as shown in Figure 5-2. Heads are located close together so there are several bands to the inch across the drum.

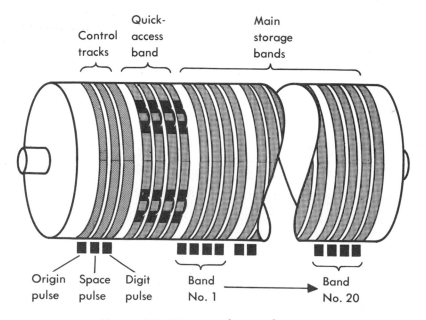

FIGURE 5-2. *Magnetic drum, schematic*

Each band around the drum is divided into many unit areas per inch, each of which stores a bit. A magnetized area represents a 1; an area magnetized in the opposite direction, or perhaps left unmagnetized, represents a 0.

A bit is written in or read from a particular unit area as it rotates under the read-write head. Access time to data stored on a drum depends on rotational speed and the location of desired data. The maximum access time of a full revolution arises when data that are wanted have just passed a reading head. The minimum access is near zero for data just coming into reading position when wanted. The average access time is equal to one-half of a drum revolution. Average access time can be reduced or "optimized" by storing program instructions and data on the drum so that a desired location becomes available just as it is needed.

A read-write head is usually located at one point for a data band. Data written on the band come into the reading position one revolution later. Separate writing and reading heads can be built and placed at short intervals around one band. A writing head records data on the drum and, a fraction of a revolution later, when the data move under the reading head, they are used in processing or returned to the prior writing head. The combination of a writing head, a short space on the drum, and a reading head connected back to the writing head makes a "revolver loop." Several revolver loops may be used on one band around a drum, as shown in Figure 5-3. Revolver loops take more electric circuits than one read-write head and waste that part of the band which is between two loops; but access time is shorter for data kept in loops. Several other versions of the revolver-loop concept are used to speed up access to drum storage locations.

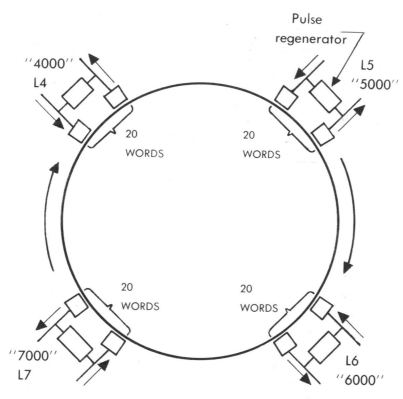

FIGURE 5-3. *Revolver loop on a magnetic drum*

Magnetic drums in use today vary greatly in capacity and operating speeds. Internal storage drums range from 4 to 12 inches in diameter and rotate at speeds of 3,000 to 17,000 revolutions a minute to give average access times of two to ten milliseconds. Capacities range from 10,000 to 60,000 numerical characters. It costs less to store a bit on a magnetic drum than on other devices used for internal storage; the data are erasable but non-volatile.

Magnetic drums are frequently utilized for internal storage in medium-size computers; but slow access rules them out for internal primary storage in large computers. The use of "mass storage," slow-access drums to provide secondary storage for computers will be discussed later.

Delay Line.   A delay line stores data in the form of pulses that travel at low speed through some medium. A tube filled with mercury is often used as a delay line. A crystal at one end converts electric signals into sound pulses representing 1 and 0, and a crystal at the other end of the tube converts the sound pulses back to electric signals. Data wanted for processing are read out of storage, while unwanted data are recirculated through the tube until needed.

The addresses given to data circulating in delay lines are not physically fixed, since the data continue to circulate. A timing pulse is circulated in the system as a reference for finding a desired "address." Input-output gates remain closed until the desired "address" reaches the end of the tube, when the gates open and data can be written or read.

Quartz delay lines also use sound pulses. Other delay lines use electric or magnetic pulses—a nickel wire delay line, for instance. A mercury delay line tube is about 30 inches long and holds about 180 alphanumerical characters. Several delay lines may be used together to get a capacity of 10,000 numerical characters. Since a pulse takes 150 to 350 microseconds to travel through a tube, the average access time is 75 to 175 microseconds. Delay line storage, being volatile and relatively expensive, is not used in recently designed American equipment, although Ferranti, Ltd., in England uses nickel delay lines in some of its computers.

Combinations.   The description of internal storage devices—core, twistor, drum, and delay line—implies that each type is used by itself. Actually, internal storage includes the total storage automatically accessible to the computer. Magnetic drums may augment cores in large systems. On the other hand, small amounts of core storage may be used with a drum to increase the operating speed of medium-sized systems.

Secondary Storage

Secondary storage facilities are not an integral part of the data processor, but they are directly connected to the processor and controlled by it. Although secondary storage, which supplements internal storage, is addressable, data are read into internal storage for processing. It has larger capacity and slower access than internal storage.

Some secondary storage is called "random access," which, carefully defined, means access to storage under conditions in which the next storage location from which data are to be obtained does not depend on the location of the previously obtained data. In other words, it takes the same time to get where you want to go without regard to where you are now. The name, "random access," is often loosely used to mean a relatively low access time to a large volume of data. Some form of random access is imperative for on-line data flow where processing is done with minimal delay. On-line data flow and two other data-flow schemes—in-line and off-line—are discussed in Chapter 9.

Secondary storage is important for holding large master files for processing transactions that occur in random sequence. Secondary storage devices are:

1. Magnetic drum
2. Magnetic disk
3. Magnetic tape
4. Tape bin

Large Magnetic Drum. Mass storage drums supplement the high-speed storage unit in the Univac File-Computer (Welsh, 1957). File storage drums, arranged in pairs, hold six million characters. A total of 10 pairs holding sixty million characters can be connected. Instead of the usual plan of one read-write head for each data track, one set of read-write heads may be moved back or forth for use with all tracks on a drum. This scheme reduces the amount of equipment at the expense of mechanical movement and slower operating speeds.

Figure 5-4. *Magnetic disk*

Magnetic Disk.   A metal disk with magnetic coating is also used for secondary storage. The IBM 650 RAMAC (Random Access Memory Accounting Computer) has a disk storage unit. Disks are mounted on a rotating vertical shaft as shown in Figure 5-4. Each disk has data tracks on both sides. One of three access arms moves vertically to a desired disk and straddles it to write on or read from a specified track on either side of the disk (Lesser, 1957).

Disk storage was first designed to operate with 100 concentric tracks holding 600 numerical digits. One disk would hold 120,000 digits so that 50 disks in a unit would hold six million. Up to four RAMAC units could be attached to one computer to provide 24 million digits of storage. Double density disks have twice as much capacity, so that four units store forty-eight million digits. The random-access time is 500 milliseconds from disk to disk, but only 222 milliseconds between tracks on the same disk. Similar disk storage holding five million alphanumerical characters is used with the IBM 305 and other computers intended for business use.

Magnetic Tape.   Magnetic tape is a tape or ribbon coated with magnetic material. Data can be stored on it as magnetic spots. The tape base is Mylar, some non-magnetic metal, or acetate. Since the iron-oxide coating must be free from defects for reliable recording, the tapes are checked by recording and reading a test pattern of data. Some types of tape readers are able to skip defects, which are indicated by punched holes or in other fashion. Other types will not skip defects so that defective tape is rejected or cut into shorter pieces. Manufacturers usually guarantee new tape to be defect-free.

Seven-channel tape is usually ½ in. wide. Ordinarily, a tape unit is designed to handle reels holding 1,500 to 3,600 ft. of tape. Shorter lengths are used for data preparation on keyboard devices and can be used on the tape readers, if desired. Recording density commonly ranges from 100 to more than 500 characters an inch. A 2,400 ft. roll can store about three to sixteen million characters. The effective storage density is less than the apparent maximum because each inter-record gap may be as short as ½ in. or as long as 2½ inches. The start-stop time enables the tape transport to bring tape up to the rated speed before starting reading or writing. A 2,400 ft. tape with 200 characters an inch holds as many data as twenty-five thousand eighty-column cards.

Tape-reading speed is generally about seventy-five to one hundred and twenty-five inches a second. Effective data-transfer speeds depend on tape speed and data density; but transfer rates of 10,000 to 30,000 characters a second are common. Some tape systems are rated to read or write 90,000 characters a second on one tape. Some computers can simultaneously read or write on two or even more tapes, so that data transfer rates are several times as high as for a single tape.

Reading a 2,400-ft. tape at maximum speed takes about four and one-half minutes. The time to rewind a tape when it reaches its end ranges from one to three minutes. This time must be counted when calculating processing time, because rewinding and demounting tapes, which takes another minute, may impede processing. Many tape changes are done with little interruption of processing by using an alternate tape transport. The next tape will be mounted before it is needed so that only a tape "swap" is made to the next reel when the end of a reel is reached.

Effective reading speed is increased in some systems by reading tape while moving in either the forward or backward direction. For example, in sorting data stored on tape by means of the merging scheme to consolidate two or more sequences of data stored on tapes, as described in Chapter 9, output tapes from one pass can be read backwards on the next pass. In this way the merging operation is continued with no interruption for tape rewinding.

Many business-data processors have about ten tape read-write units, and some can handle several dozen. The mounted tapes are secondary storage, according to the definition used here. The unmounted tape files are external storage, as described below. Tapes are mounted for processing as required and returned to the tape library for storage after processing or for re-use, if the data are no longer wanted.

Tight processing schedules may require that all tape files be ready for processing. Stock management and related operations at Ordnance Tank-Automotive Command have rigid time specifications. The Bizmac processing equipment has about 200 tape stations so that all stock records on tapes remain mounted on tape transports for immediate processing.

Magnetic tape is durable under ordinary operating conditions, for some tapes have been read satisfactorily up to fifty thousand times; data on a worn tape can be transferred to a new tape. Maximum tape performance involves some precautions in handling. Temperature and humidity variations cause magnetic oxide surfaces to crack, dust on tape may cause a reading head to miss a signal, and manual handling of tape leaves oil and moisture, which catches dust and impairs reading. Metal tape resists temperature variations and extreme heat better than plastic tape. A computer may provide for automatic backspacing and rereading of a tape that does not pass the parity test. If the malfunction is caused by dust or some other transient reason, then a second or third reading will probably be satisfactory. Repeated failure to read warrants engineering service for the computer. While the rereading feature is automatic in some computers, it must be programmed for others. Safeguards against exposure to strong magnetic fields, which can erase all the data on tape, are necessary.

A 2,400-ft. reel of magnetic tape costs about $70 while equal card storage costs about $27.50. Tape costs less in the long run for temporary storage because tape is re-usable.

Tape Bin. A tape-bin storage unit consists of magnetic-tape strips arranged so that a read-write device can move directly to a desired strip. The reading head then scans that strip to find a record. Access is faster than for an ordinary reel of tape, which may require a complete search to find a record. An example of a tape bin is a Datafile that includes 50 strips of tape, each of which is 250 ft. long (MacDonald, 1957). The tapes are draped over a guide rod as in Figure 5-5, and tape ends fall into partitioned bins. Each tape contains 40,000 ten-character words recorded in 2 lanes. Fifty tapes in a file store twenty million digits, and up to 10 Datafiles can be connected to a Datatron computer. Two recording heads are automatically positioned under a desired tape. The average access time depends upon the number of (a) tape files connected, (b) tape lanes used, (c) records per Datafile, and (d) characters per record. The average access time ranges from five to fifteen seconds.

FIGURE 5-5. *Datafile*

External Storage

External storage facilities are divorced from the data processor itself; they hold large amounts of data at low cost in forms prescribed for processing. Magnetic tape, punched cards, and paper tape are external storage media. The storage media are put into a suitable handling unit for processing. They rank as secondary storage when connected to and controlled by the computer for reading or writing. The contents of secondary storage are transferred to internal storage before processing.

Magnetic Tape. Magnetic-tape output is obtained from many business processors (the features of magnetic-tape storage are covered in the section on secondary storage). Active tape records mounted on tape read-write units are classified as secondary storage. Inactive tape records taken from the tape read-write units and stored are considered external storage. They are divorced from the computer itself, but hold data in the form prescribed for the computer.

Economic problems are involved in allocating tapes to secondary and external storage. A common solution is to obtain about ten read-write units so that ten tapes, including program and output, can be connected to the computer. Tight processing schedules may demand that more tapes be connected for immediate processing. If so, more tape units may be necessary in order to disperse output data onto as many tapes as desired during big processing runs. On the other hand, if too few tapes are available, short files of mixed output may be written on one tape and additional runs used to disperse the mixed output onto separate tapes. Equipment called a "tape data selector" simplifies the problem of selecting from mixed data stored on one tape when printing reports. This scheme increases the effective number of connected tape units available in a run.

Punched Cards. Punched-card external storage is used for equipment that does not handle tape. Punched cards may be the sole external storage for medium-sized computers; but large systems restrict the use of punched cards to peripheral equipment, which converts data from cards to tape or vice versa.

A record that exceeds the capacity of one card takes two or more cards, and the cross referencing between cards may take one-third of each card. Records split over two or more cards have several deficiencies: data density is reduced, file maintenance is cumbersome, and processing is inefficient. A large file of punched cards can store millions of characters. Although manual selection of file cards appears to be quick, it is slow compared to access to data in secondary storage; still, manual selection from huge files of cards may be economical in view of the higher cost of secondary storage.

Punched cards have some good features for manual use. People can read data printed on the card. A card is a unit record rearrangeable by machine or by hand into any desired order and is durable enough to be processed a few dozen times. The difficulty of altering the data punched and printed on a card makes it useful as evidence; but this feature increases the cost of correction, since the whole card must be repunched. Punched cards are, of course, not erasable and re-usable.

Paper Tape. Paper tape is used for external storage in integrated data-processing systems, as well as for input and output. Paper-tape speed is comparable to punched-card, but much slower than magnetic-tape reading speed. This speed is fast enough for use with small computers, but it limits the usefulness of tape for high-speed computers.

Tape is non-erasable and fairly durable. Short lengths of it can be filed for quick manual reference. A 1,000-ft. reel of tape costs about a dollar. Tape "sandwiches" of some combination of paper, Mylar, and metal that are made for greater durability cost much more.

SELECTION OF STORAGE METHODS

The types and amounts of storage required for an automatic data processor depend on the nature of the application. Some applications require internal storage alone; others rely heavily on secondary storage; still others need large secondary storage as well as external storage. Some factors affecting storage requirements are outlined below.

The *type of processing performed* varies greatly. Scientific or engineering problems involving extensive calculations can utilize large internal storage. Lengthy instructions and many numbers are involved in calculations. Processing is faster if all instructions and data are contained in internal memory. If internal storage is exceeded, instructions and data must be segmented for handling in several runs.

Business applications usually involve limited computations on huge files that are affected by numerous transactions. Transaction and master file data usually exceed internal memory capacity. Programmers have several schemes for handling such situations. One plan is to read in one or more transactions and file records, update these files, write them out, and repeat the cycle. Another plan is to read in many transactions, read in one file record, update that file, write it out, and repeat the cycle.

One plan deserves consideration for processing files where activity is low. It consists of processing the transactions against the master file tape which produces a change tape while leaving the master file tape unchanged. In subsequent cycles, the change tape is updated until it becomes large enough to warrant merging it with the master file by rewriting it completely. The computer time required to rewrite a huge master file on tape is long enough to make any processing scheme that saves tape rewrite time worthy of consideration.

Similar results for files with low activity are obtained by the extract-merge scheme using a file processor. A file processor *extracts* from a main file the records for items that are active and writes them on a separate tape. The data processor is used to process transactions against this selected file, which is 100 per cent active, to update the records. Subsequently, the file processor *merges* the updated records into the main file. A file processor can merge previously updated records into a main file during the same pass that it extracts active records for updating during the next cycle.

Business applications often involve long instruction programs as well as the huge files of records and numerous transactions already mentioned. Instructions alone may exceed the internal storage capacity that is available at any reasonable price. Clearly, some scheme for segmenting instructions, transactions, and files becomes necessary for efficient processing.

The *time limit* between the occurrence of an event and the need for information about that event is a factor in selecting storage equipment. Reliance on external storage may be suitable, if the permissible elapsed time limits are not too stringent. Transactions accumulated over a period of time can be sorted and processed in batches against a master file, on magnetic tape, for instance. External storage and batch processing may be an economical plan for huge master files.

On the other hand, tight time schedules may require that files be available for frequent updating. The ideal arrangement for tight processing and reporting schedules is to have all files available for processing at all times. If transactions must be handled immediately, the master file is usually kept in secondary storage for on-line processing. For example, all inventory tape files can be kept mounted on tape units to avoid manual handling. Faster storage—core, drum, disk, or short tapes—is used for quick processing of transactions in random sequence.

Fast-access storage costs more per unit than slow-access storage. System design involving huge amounts of internal and secondary storage should be examined with care. Equipment and operating cost involved in meeting extremely short time limits may exceed the value of the information obtained.

Information requirements are reflected in the frequency and nature of reports prepared and the references made to files. The nature of the information needed affects the selection of storage methods.

A need for scheduled, formal *reports* may be met efficiently from files kept in external storage, if time limits are not too short. Scheduled processing at reasonable time intervals may be an efficient plan for updating huge files. Part of a file—one-fifth or one-twentieth—may be updated each day to complete the cycle over a period of a week or month. Current reports covering a part of the file can be prepared when that part is updated. If reports are needed immediately after events occur, quick-access internal or secondary storage is required.

Examples of unscheduled reports are *references* to the file and interrogations—questions requiring quick answers. An event may trigger the need for information even though the event is part of the stream of regular transactions. A withdrawal below inventory re-order point, for example, triggers a replenishment order. A need to know the quantity of stock on hand involves an interrogation of the file. Frequent interrogation of files demands storage devices suited to the need. Quick answers require quick-access storage.

Interrogation of current files poses critical problems. Many solutions are proposed, and special equipment exists to cope with file inquiry problems. The point is often overlooked, but interrogation of inactive files becomes more difficult as the volume of file grows. External storage appears to be mandatory for historical files because of their huge volumes. Infrequent reference and loose time limits may make external storage useful for most purposes. In fact, the high unit cost of internal storage precludes its use for mass storage.

The feature of re-usability of storage is valuable for historical reference purposes. Some items in a record are useful only for a short period of time. Data about individual receipts and issues of inventory may be vital for the current and past quarter. Monthly data pertaining to the third and fourth quarters in the past may be necessary. Quarterly summaries may suffice after one year and annual totals after three years, so that file volume can be reduced by condensing unwanted data. In summarizing data some details will be lost unless they are available elsewhere. Condensing records on a re-usable storage medium and discarding the parts no longer wanted corresponds to the transfer of paper or card records to inactive storage. Whereas paper records must either be put in inactive storage as whole documents or destroyed, records on magnetic tape can be selectively condensed in order to discard only those characters or words that are no longer wanted. Re-usable storage that is released by condensing or discarding unwanted records can, of course, be used for other purposes.

Data volume is an important factor in selecting efficient storage methods. Huge volumes restrict system design to some method with low unit cost in order to keep total costs in bounds. Wider choices of methods exist for moderate volumes of data. Business applications involve large volumes of data and varied processing methods so that the use of two or more storage methods is likely to be more efficient than the use of a single method.

Audit requirements also influence selection of storage methods. Company and independent auditors examine data-processing systems for several reasons. They want to determine whether operations meet specified rules and procedures. Also, auditors determine whether records and reports accurately reflect transactions and condition. An operating report covers an interval of time—the month of January, or the year ending June 30. A condition or status report pertains to a point in time—June 30 or August 10. Auditing involves, among other things, examining source data, methods of processing, and content of final reports (Toan, 1955).

Each transaction leaves an "audit trail." Some form of record is necessary for an auditor to trace this trail. For many purposes, an auditor may prefer records in readable rather than machine-processable form, for he is more at home with readable records. Tape contents may be printed and retained for historical reference and for use by auditors. If print-outs are too bulky, they may be reduced to microfilm.

Auditors will utilize new equipment and systems in making audits and will study flow charts and programs to find the rules followed in processing. Machine-operating logs show what programs and data were used in processing, and problems can be devised to test the logic of programs and application to various conditions. Programmers often design safeguards in programs to assure control over data during processing, and auditors can study such features in appraising the internal control plan.

Understanding the available data and methods of storage is important for auditors, but it is only part of the over-all audit problem. Accurate auditing also requires an understanding of equipment, programs, and processing methods; these will be covered in later chapters.

SUMMARY

The ideal storage system is characterized by infinite volume, all methods of organization, no waiting time, indefinite availability, and no cost. It is easy to specify an ideal system; it is impossible to build it.

Actual storage equipment represents a compromise between the desired ideal and what the available amount of money will buy—given the present state of the art of computer design and construction. Most storage systems are a limited mixture of different types of equipment. Small quantities of high unit cost storage and large quantities of low unit cost storage may work together for many applications.

Stored data are represented by bits. Four-bit, six-bit, and other codes are used for numerals, letters, and symbols. The use of an address facilitates finding a desired piece of data. The word "address" refers to the storage location of a word in equipment designed with fixed word-length. "Address" also refers to a field which may be as short as one character in variable field-length equipment. An address scheme is used for internal storage. Some storage systems, notably the tape and card varieties, do not use addresses to designate the locations of data; in these systems, scanning or searching is necessary to find an item.

Important features of storage units are capacity, access time, and erasability. Capacity is the quantity of data that can be put into a storage unit. Access time is the length of time between a call for data from storage and completion of delivery. "Erasability" means that stored data can be replaced by new data.

Storage is classified here as internal, secondary, and external. Internal storage, which is an integral physical part of a data processor, is directly controlled and automatically accessible; some internal storage devices are the magnetic core, magnetic drum, and delay line. Secondary storage is not an integral part of the data processor, but it is directly connected and controlled; examples of secondary storage are the magnetic drum, disk, and several forms of tape. External storage is divorced from the data processor, but it holds data in the form required for processing; examples of it are magnetic tapes, paper tapes, and punched cards.

Three classes of storage are used with most business processors to get an efficient balance between storage volume and unit cost of storage; but since the equipment manufacturer decides what kinds of storage units he will offer, he thereby limits the user's choice.

Factors involved in selecting storage methods are the time limits on processing, information requirements, volume of data, and audit requirements. Time limits—the elapsed time between an event and required reports—are important. Short time limits demand quick-access storage units. If report preparation can be scheduled, files may be kept in lower-cost, external storage. References and interrogations that must be handled immediately after being triggered by events may require that files be kept in secondary or internal storage to reduce the access time.

Audit requirements have some influence on the methods, quantity, and duration of storage. Auditors may prefer or even demand that data are kept in readable form. Auditors will, in time, develop ways of following non-readable audit trails of transactions and thereby exploit the capabilities of new equipment and methods. Safeguards designed into a program by programmers to fulfill their operating requirements will meet part of the auditor's demand for control over data during processing.

REFERENCES AND SUPPLEMENTAL READINGS

Fowler, Franklin, Jr. "The Computer's Memory," *Control Engineering*, vol. 3: 93-101 (May 1956). The six characteristics of a storage system are: (a) it contains elementary locations, each capable of storing a bit, (b) the elementary locations are combined into small groups called words, (c) the words are assigned numbers known as addresses, (d) there is a method of storing data in a desired location, (e) a method for reading data from the desired location, and (f) there is a means of communicating between the storage and the rest of the computer. The commonly used storage systems are grouped and discussed according to the method used to gain access to their data. Magnetic cores, Williams tubes, and ferro-electric storage are the main parallel-access systems considered. Cyclic-access systems discussed include magnetic drums, magnetic-tape loops, disks, tape drums, and acoustic delay lines. Classified as progressive-access systems are punched cards, punched paper tape, and magnetic tape. Most extensive consideration is given to magnetic-drum and magnetic-core storage, but the manner in which a storage device stores a bit of information and the technique for recording on and reading from storage locations are indicated for most of the devices.

Lesser, M. L., and J. W. Haanstra. "The RAMAC Data-Processing Machine: System Organization of the IBM 305," pp. 139-146 in *Proceedings of the Eastern Joint Computer Conference: New Developments in Computers*, New York, American Institute of Electrical Engineers, 1957. This paper describes a new automatic data-processing machine for business applications utilizing a random-access memory system. Unlike the usual batch method of machine processing business transactions, the technique used permits data transfers between any two points in the system and makes multi-choice decisions according to the current status of the data. Employing punched-card input and output, the IBM 305 is designed to handle 10,000 line transactions per day.

MacDonald, D. N. "Datafile—a New Tool for Extensive File Storage," pp. 124-128 in *Proceedings of the Eastern Joint Computer Conference: New Developments in Computers*, New York, American Institute of Electrical Engineers, 1957. This paper discusses the design and application of an advanced magnetic-tape storage system with facilities for automatic access to files as large as two hundred million characters with average access in the five to twenty second range. Employing standard magnetic tape and recording techniques, it also provides an economical solution to the many medium-speed random-access problems and avoids tape handling as such.

Toan, A. B., Jr. "Auditing, Control and Electronics," *Journal of Accountancy*, vol. 99: 40-45 (May 1955). The author discusses the interaction between auditing and electronics, resultant problems, and means for resolving some of the problems. The three areas considered are: (a) determining that original data and subsequent processing are accurate and authentic, (b) controlling approved input material so that all of it and nothing else will enter the records, and (c) providing records that are satisfactory in terms of form and supporting evidence. Electronic systems introduce new kinds of problems because (a) records are no longer in written form, (b) many intermediate records are eliminated, and (c) only a few individuals are responsible for the system. Since auditing depends largely upon comparison of data to establish validity, the computer may help by taking over part of the auditing job. Toan suggests that increasing mechanization may drastically change some techniques of audit and control, but most objectives will remain largely unaffected.

Welsh, H. F., and V. J. Porter. "A Large Drum-File Memory System," pp. 136-139 in *Proceedings of the Eastern Joint Computer Conference: New Developments in Computers*, New York, American Institute of Electrical Engineers, 1957. The magnetic drum-file memory system described in this paper was designed for the Univac-Larc computing system as storage intermediate in speed and capacity between Uniservo magnetic tapes and magnetic-core memory. Drum-file memory may be used for any type of systematic data processing where extremely short access time is not required but economy is important. Economy is achieved through the use of a single flying head that can move parallel to the axis of the drum and perform the read-write operations for the entire drum. The drum-file may also be used as a random-access device where a delay of a second or two is not critical, as, for example, in checking a particular item of an inventory.

CHAPTER SIX

ARITHMETIC AND CONTROL UNITS

The arithmetic and control units are at the heart of an automatic data processor; they are responsible for on-line data transfers and operations throughout the system.

Both the arithmetic and the control units are located in the main frame of the equipment. The arithmetic unit is that part of the circuitry which performs arithmetical operations. The control unit includes the circuitry that performs the following functions:

1. Gets each instruction in the proper sequence
2. Interprets each instruction
3. Applies proper signals that cause the arithmetic unit and other parts of the computer to operate in accordance with an instruction

Data and instructions are read in from input units and placed in specified locations in internal storage under guidance of the control unit. The control unit calls for instructions in storage and interprets them. Data to be processed go from storage to the arithmetic unit, where, under the guidance of the control unit, arithmetical and certain logical operations are carried out. The processed results are returned to storage or written out, again under guidance of the control unit. In short, the control unit guides the input, output, storage, and arithmetic units by coordinating their operation in carrying out an instruction routine.

Arithmetical operations include adding, subtracting, multiplying, and dividing. These operations are basic for processing data, and variations of them give increased flexibility. For example: the accumulator may be cleared and an operation started in a combined clear-and-add or clear-and-subtract operation; numbers can then be divided or multiplied and the result rounded in a combined operation.

Discussion of the arithmetic unit is covered in two parts. In the first, components are discussed and illustrated; in the second, the operations performed and the problems encountered are described at length.

ARITHMETIC UNIT COMPONENTS

Circuits and devices used in an arithmetic unit vary widely from one type of equipment to another, but they are essentially similar from the programmer's viewpoint and in the way that he uses them.

Registers

An arithmetic unit usually has several registers. A register stores a word temporarily, until it is used or while it is being used. Registers may consist of dynamic pulse circuits that have storage with zero access time. Each circuit is a small assembly of vacuum tubes, resistors, capacitors, and diodes that operate as a unit to represent one bit.

The number of registers in the arithmetic unit varies for different computers. An accumulator register and an M-Q register are commonly used. Several other registers may be used to hold other operands involved in an operation.

Accumulator. Sums and other arithmetical results are formed in the accumulator. An accumulator might be used for adding two numbers, as in Figure 6-1. For performing this addition, the control unit instructs the equipment to proceed as follows:

1. Copy the first number from storage into the accumulator.
2. Get the second number from storage and add to (or subtract from) the number in the accumulator.
3. Continue to add (or subtract) other numbers or copy accumulator content into storage.

The accumulator is as long as a computer word. It also has provision for an overflow bit and a plus or minus sign. An accumulator is necessary for single-address equipment that handles one operand at a time. An "operand" is any one of the quantities that enters an operation (the content of a storage location to be operated on), or that arises from an operation. Examples of operands are inventory quantity and unit cost which can be multiplied to get inventory value.

Two-address and three-address computers can bring up both operands simultaneously and add them in circuitry called "adders" instead of in an accumulator. Addition and subtraction of seven-digit operands, for instance, can be handled by an eight-digit accumulator, as described for the hypothetical accumulator in Chapter 3. Seven digits are for the answer—the eighth digit being for overflow, to indicate when an answer outgrows the seven-digit space.

M-Q Register. Multiplication of two seven-digit numbers gives a thirteen-digit or fourteen-digit product. The accumulator deals with the first, or high-order, six or seven digits; but more register space is needed for the other seven digits. The "M-Q" or multiplier-quotient register augments the accumulator for multiplication and division by holding the right-hand seven digits of a fourteen-digit product.

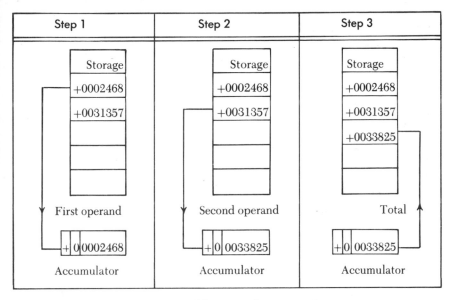

Step 1	Step 2	Step 3

FIGURE 6-1. *Addition in the accumulator*

All thirteen or fourteen digits of the accumulator and M-Q registers are available for storage, if the degree of precision—the number of digits in the answer—warrants. Otherwise, the right-hand seven digits of a product can be dropped and the effect of rounding carried over to the next digit in the accumulator. In division operations, the quotient ends up in the M-Q register and the remainder is in the accumulator.

Adder

An adder is the nucleus of an arithmetic unit and forms the sum of two operands. A half-adder handles one bit each from the addend and augend. The rules for output of a half-adder follow the rules for binary addition:

Input		Output	
Addend A	Augend B	Carry C	Sum S
0	0	0	0
0	1	0	1
1	0	0	1
1	1	1	0

A type of adder called a "coincidence adder" is widely used. It is built up from a number of logical circuits called ("gates,") which are electric circuits with an output signal dependent on the input signals. The basic types of gates, which have two or more input signals and one output signal, are:

1. ["And" gate that transmits an output signal if and only if there is a signal on *all* input lines
2. "Or" gate that transmits an output signal if there is a signal on *any* input line

Closely related to the "and" and "or" gates is an "inverter," which is a device for changing a signal from a given state to the opposite or alternative state—0 to 1 or 1 to 0.

The simplest operation is the addition of two binary numbers of one bit each. The addition of 1 + 1 in binary gives a carry digit of 1 and sum digit of 0, as shown in Figure 6-2, where a 1 indicates a pulse and 0 indicates no pulse. Actually, an adder must be able to handle three input bits—addend, augend, and any carry from the right. A two-input adder is an arrangement of two half-adders to handle three pulses in two steps. A three-input adder handles three pulses in one operation.

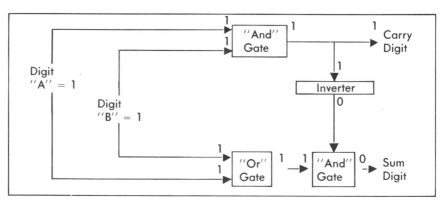

FIGURE 6-2. *Block diagram of a half-adder*

ARITHMETICAL OPERATIONS

A set of adders and other devices can perform addition, subtraction, multiplication, and division operations on operands.

Addition
The operations involved in decimal, binary, and binary-coded decimal addition will be described. (See Richards, 1956, for a longer description.)

Decimal. Brief discussion of addition of decimal numbers with an ordinary desk calculator illustrates some of the features of any method of addition. Consider the problem of adding five numbers:

47154
832961
2466285
6590628
62971

Assume that the desk calculator has a keyboard seven digits wide, a lower dial, and an upper dial. The lower dial (accumulator) has seven digits for a total and an eighth digit to indicate overflow. The upper dial holds seven digits and counts the number of cycles.

Contents of the keyboard and both dials after each operation are shown in Table 6-1. The lower dial contains 09999999 after completing the fifth cycle. The overflow digit is 0, which means that no overflow occurred, so that the correct sum is 9999999. If a sixth number, say 0000005, is added, the lower dial will show 10000004. The 1 means that overflow occurred; the total appears to be 0000004, but that is erroneous.

TABLE 6-1. *Addition on a Desk Calculator*

Operation	Keyboard	Lower Dial (Accumulator)	Upper Dial (Cycle Counter)
Before operations start, the keyboard and dials may contain anything.			
1. Clear	0000000	00000000	0000000
2. Set up first operand	0047154	00000000	0000000
3. Add first operand	0000000	00047154	0000001
4. Set up second operand	0832961	00047154	0000001
5. Add second operand	0000000	00880115	0000002
6. Set up third operand	2466285	00880115	0000002
7. Add third operand	0000000	03346400	0000003
8. Set up fourth operand	6590628	03346400	0000003
9. Add fourth operand	0000000	09937028	0000004
10. Set up fifth operand	0062971	09937028	0000004
11. Add fifth operand	0000000	09999999	0000005

There are several remedies for handling the situation when overflow occurs. One remedy is to return to an earlier step in the program, shift each number one place to the right, and repeat the addition. The right-hand digit is lost and a rounded total may be obtained or the digit just dropped. A left shift is made later to offset the right shift and get the correct decimal place in the result. Another remedy for handling overflow is to split each number into two parts. The split numbers are added as two separate series and their totals combined later. This scheme is a simple example of "double precision" addition. The degree of precision in the total is greater than the capacity in either the accumulator or in individual storage locations.

In the preceding example (Table 6-1), the upper dial shows 0000005, which means that 5 addition operations or cycles were performed. The upper dial holds the multiplier or quotient in other operations. This simple example of addition on a desk calculator shows the clear-and-add instructions, accumulation of running total, cycles, and overflow.

Binary. Addition is simple in machines using binary numbers. A three-input adder that handles only four-bit numbers can add 2 binary numbers in serial fashion, as shown in Figure 6-3.

	Binary Numbers	Decimal Equivalents
Addend A	0101	5
Augend B	1001	9
Sum	1110	14

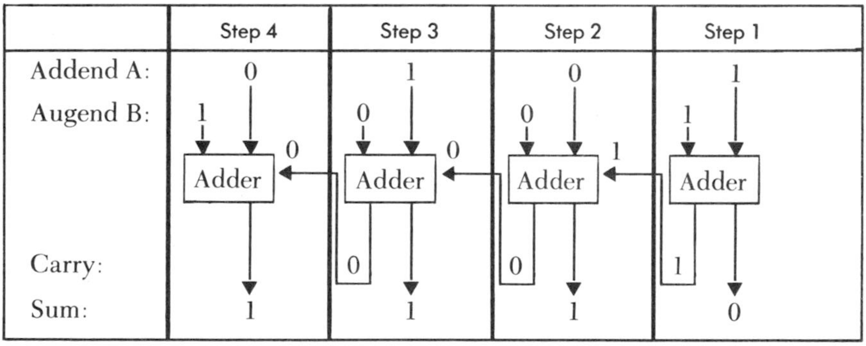

FIGURE 6-3. *Three-input adder*

Binary-coded Decimal. Addition of binary-coded decimal numbers involves rules for generating the carry which are different from those for binary. The 8421 binary-coded decimal scheme uses only 10 of the 16 possible combinations of four bits. Six combinations are skipped, and it is necessary to adjust for this skip each time a decimal carry occurs. If the sum of 2 binary-coded decimal numbers exceeds 0000,1001, then 0110 (binary 6) is added to get the correct total. The following example illustrates the procedure:

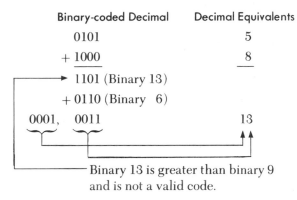

Binary-coded Decimal   Decimal Equivalents

        0101   5

    $+$ 1000   8

        1101 (Binary 13)

    $+$ 0110 (Binary 6)

0001,   0011   13

Binary 13 is greater than binary 9
and is not a valid code.

Somewhat similar corrections are required to correct the carries in other binary-coded decimal schemes, such as excess three.

Subtraction

Subtraction might be handled as the opposite of addition, if special "subtracter" circuits were available. As a matter of fact, fewer extra circuits are required if subtraction is done in three stages by using circuits that are already available. For example, to compute A minus B: (1) form the complement of B; (2) add the complement of B to A; (3) make any adjustment required because a complement was used. Forming the complement of a number looks like a subtraction operation. But it is actually much easier to form a complement because the number to be complemented is subtracted from a string of 9's or 1's in decimal and binary, respectively. The complement of a number is obtained by subtracting it from some power of the number base as in the example given in the next section.

Decimal. The "tens complement" of a number is formed by (1) subtracting it from 10^n minus 1, (2) adding 1 to the least-significant digit, and (3) performing all carries. If the accumulator holds 7 digits, n is 7 and a number to be complemented is subtracted from 9999999. The effect of adding 1 in the second step is to get the tens complement. To compute 428 minus 325 by means of complements in a seven-digit accumulator, the procedure is as follows:

1.	Find the nines complement	9999999
		$-$ 325
		9999674
2.	Add 1 to the right-hand digit	$+$ 1
	The tens complement	9999675
3.	Then add 9999675 to 428	$+$ 428
		10000103

The result is 103. The 1 carried to the eighth or overflow position is discarded because it is not wanted when the tens complement is used.

It is easier to use the nines complement than the tens complement for subtraction because the nines complement of a number is formed by subtracting every digit from 9. The fact that 10^n minus 1 is used, and 1 is *not* added back in the second operation above, is offset later by adding the overflow digit, if one occurs, to the right-hand digit in the remainder. The operation of adding the overflow digit to the right-hand position is called "end-around carry."

The example of 428 minus 325 can be shown by means of the nines complement scheme.

1. Take the nines complement

$$
\begin{array}{r}
9999999 \\
-\quad 325 \\
\hline
9999674
\end{array}
$$

2. Add 9999674 to 428

$$
\begin{array}{r}
9999674 \\
+\quad 428 \\
\hline
10000102
\end{array}
$$

3. The overflow 1 in the eight position is end-around carried to the first position, when the nines complement is used

$$
\begin{array}{r}
10000102 \\
1 \\
\hline
103
\end{array}
$$

If the remainder is negative, no overflow occurs, and therefore an end-around carry is not made. The negative result that arises from adding a complement is itself complemented to get the correct remainder. For example, 333−555 is computed as follows:

1. Take the nines complement

$$
\begin{array}{r}
9999999 \\
-\quad 555 \\
\hline
9999444
\end{array}
$$

2. Add 9999444 to 333

$$
\begin{array}{r}
9999444 \\
+\quad 333 \\
\hline
9999777
\end{array}
$$

3. No end-around carry occurs; therefore, the remainder is negative. Find the complement of 9999777 to get the remainder in its ordinary form

$$
\begin{array}{r}
9999999 \\
-9999777 \\
\hline
222
\end{array}
$$

4. Attach a minus sign to get the remainder

$$-222$$

Binary.   Complements of numbers in decimal and binary systems are useful for subtraction in the same way. The *twos* binary complement is like the *tens* decimal complement; the twos complement of 10010 is 01110. It is obtained by subtracting from 2^n minus 1 (which is 11111 for five bit positions) and adding 1, as follows:

$$
\begin{array}{r}
11111 \\
-10010 \\
\hline
01101 \\
+\quad\quad 1 \\
\hline
01110
\end{array}
$$

The *ones* binary complement is similar to the *nines* decimal complement; the ones complement of 10010 is 01101, which is obtained as follows:

$$
\begin{array}{r}
11111 \\
-10010 \\
\hline
01101
\end{array}
$$

Complementing a binary number is simplicity itself: the ones binary complement can be formed by inversion, which changes each 1 to 0 and each 0 to 1.

Binary-coded Decimal.   Numbers in the excess three code described earlier can be complemented in much the same way as binary numbers are complemented. The nines complement of an excess three code number is formed by simply changing each 1 to 0 and each 0 to 1, as follows:

	Excess 3 Code	Decimal
Original number	0101	2
Ones complement	1010	
Nines complement		7

To subtract a number by adding its ones complement requires an end-around carry, in the same way as before, if an overflow 1 occurs at the left. To find 9 minus 2:

1. Find the ones complement of 2 in excess 3 code.

    0101 = 2 in excess 3 code
    1010 = complement of 2

2. Add the complement to 9.

$$
\begin{array}{r}
1100 = 9 \text{ in excess 3 code} \\
+\quad 1010 = \text{complement of 2} \\
\hline
1\,0110 \\
1 \leftarrow \text{end-around carry} \\
\hline
0111 = 7 \text{ in binary} \\
0011 \quad \text{To return to excess 3 code, add 3.} \\
\hline
1010 = 7 \text{ in excess 3 code}
\end{array}
$$

The nines complement of numbers is typically used for subtraction in the binary or excess three coded decimal modes.

Multiplication

A brief review of manual and desk-calculator multiplication is useful as a refresher before considering multiplication in computers. It is even useful for you to try multiplying some numbers just to get the feel of it.

Longhand. Multiplication by longhand can be illustrated by multiplying two seven-digit numbers: 6598765 times 3401234.

Multiplicand	6598765
Multiplier	3401234
Partial products	26395060
	19796295
	13197530
	6598765
	0000000
	26395060
	19796295
Product	22443943876010

Longhand multiplication uses one-digit multiplication tables (1 times 1, 2, 3 and so on through 9 times 7, 8, and 9) to get partial products which are added to obtain the final answer. The product of 2 seven-digit numbers contains 13 or 14 digits. All of the digits can be saved by splitting the numbers into two parts and placing 7 in each (or, perhaps, only 6 in one) of two storage locations. If less precision is needed, the right-hand 7 digits can be discarded after rounding the next digit to the left, which is the rightmost digit that is saved. The rounding procedure generally used is: add 5 in the highest position that is to be discarded; make the carry, if any; and discard all unwanted digits. The product obtained above can be rounded as follows:

Product as first obtained	2244394	3876010
Add 5 in the highest position to be discarded		5
New sum—no carry in this case	2244394	8876010
Product to be stored	2244394	
Digits discarded		8876010

In using this rounding scheme, you must guard against the upward bias that can result from adding 5 to the highest-order position to be dropped. Furthermore, the product can disappear completely or a spurious answer arise. Consider two cases, as follows:

	Case 1	Case 2
Multiply	12000	13000
	x 400	x 400
	4800000	5200000
Add 5 in seventh position	5	5
	9800000	10200000
Product to be stored	0	1
(six zeros omitted)		
Digits discarded	9800000	0200000

Rounded products of 0 and 1 are obtained by multiplying 12000 and 13000, respectively, by 400. Obviously, the most significant digits, 48 and 52, should be retained. The point involved here is that willy-nilly application of a rule may give entirely unexpected results.

Desk Calculator.   Multiplication of 2 seven-digit numbers with a desk calculator shows how a partial product is accumulated at each step, with the final product available directly after the last multiplier digit is used. On a desk calculator, the multiplicand is ordinarily set up in the keyboard. Repeated operations of adding and shifting end up with the multiplier in the upper dial and the product in the lower dial. The upper dials count the number of cycles—how many times the multiplicand is added—in each digit position.

TABLE 6-2. *Multiplication on a Desk Calculator*
(Modified Scheme)

Operation	Lower Dial	Upper Dial
1. Clear	000000000000000	0000000
2. Set up multiplier in upper dial	000000000000000	3401234
3. Set up multiplicand 6598765 in keyboard	000000000000000	3401234
4. Add multiplicand 4 times	26395060:0000000	3401234
5. Shift	026395060:000000	0340123
6. Add 3 times	224358010:000000	0340123
7. Shift	0224358010:00000	0034012
8. Add 2 times	1544111010:00000	0034012
9. Shift	01544111010:0000	0003401
10. Add 1 time	08142876010:0000	0003401
11. Shift	008142876010:000	0000340
12. Add 0 time	008142876010:000	0000340
13. Shift	0008142876010:00	0000034
14. Add 4 times	2647648876010:00	0000034
15. Shift	02647648876010:0	0000003
16. Add 3 times	22443943876010:0	0000003
17. Shift	022443943876010	0000000

Assume that one change is made in the standard operation of a desk calculator. *Initially*, set the multiplier in the upper dial. Then count downward toward zero in the right-hand digit as the multiplier is used to add the multiplicand to the partial product the specified number of times. The right-hand digit in the upper dial becomes zero as the multiplicand is added. Shift the partial product and multiplier to the right one digit and repeat the operation. The reason for counting from the multiplier down to zero instead of from zero up to the multiplier will be explained shortly.

Multiplication of 6598765 times 3401234 on a calculator with a fifteen-digit accumulator is shown in Table 6-2. The desk-calculator multiplication example shows that only 15 positions in both the lower and the upper dials are used at one time. As the product fills the lower dial, the used digits in the multiplier are shifted out of the upper dial.

TABLE 6-3.   *Multiplication on Desk Calculator With Combined Upper and Lower Dials*

Operation	Lower and Upper Dials
1. Clear	000000000000000
2. Set up multiplier in upper dial	00000000:3401234
3. Set up multiplicand 6598765 in keyboard	00000000:3401234
4. Add multiplicand 4 times	26395060:3401234
5. Shift	026395060:340123
6. Add 3 times	224358010:340123
7. Shift	0224358010:34012
8. Add 2 times	1544111010:34012
9. Shift	01544111010:3401
10. Add 1 time	08142876010:3401
11. Shift	008142876010:340
12. Add 0 time	008142876010:340
13. Shift	0008142876010:34
14. Add 4 times	2647648876010:34
15. Shift	02647648876010:3
16. Add 3 times	22443943876010:3
17. Shift	022443943876010

If the lower and upper dials can operate as a unit, then 15 positions hold both the product digits and the unused multiplier digits. Multiplication of 6598765 times 3401234 by means of combined lower and upper dials is shown in Table 6-3. The partial products are separated by "`:`" from the unused digits of the multiplier. The scheme of joint lower and upper dials is similar to the preceding example, but it shows how desk-calculator capacity is saved by making the upper and lower dials more versatile, for they hold either the multiplier digits or the product digits as required. The left eight digits of the combined dials correspond to an accumulator; the right seven digits are like an M-Q register; and the keyboard corresponds to a special register, which holds the multiplicand. Considering this correspondence, Table 6-3 illustrates the essence of one way multiplication can be performed by a computer.

Computers multiply numbers by using one of the following plans: repeated addition, add and shift, or multiplication tables.

Repeated Addition.   An obvious but inefficient way to multiply numbers is to add the multiplicand as many times as are specified in the whole multiplier. To compute 14 times 12 by repeated addition:

$$
\begin{array}{lr}
(1) & 14 \\
(2) & 14 \\
(3) & 14 \\
& \cdot \\
& \cdot \\
& \cdot \\
(12) & \underline{14} \\
& 168
\end{array}
$$

Add and Shift.   Another multiplication method is called "add and shift." It involves adding the multiplicand the number of times specified by a digit in the multiplier, shifting, and then repeating the operation.

Repeat Add and Shift

14 multiplicand
x 12 multiplier

$\left. \begin{array}{l} 14 \\ \underline{14} \end{array} \right\}$ add 2 times

28 partial product

28 shift the partial product
<u>14</u> add one time

168 final product

The right digit in the multiplier is placed in a counter that counts downward to zero and the multiplicand is added to the partial product as many times as are indicated by the multiplier digit in the counter. Each digit in the multiplier is used in turn, from right to left. The partial product is shifted after each addition operation so that the multiplicand is added to the appropriate positions in the partial product. This scheme is similar to the method described for performing multiplication on a desk calculator. The accumulator and M-Q registers together hold both the product and the multiplier. Repeated add and shift operations put the 6 or 7 left-hand digits in the accumulator. The 7 right-hand digits are in the M-Q register.

Although extra circuitry is required for a computer to multiply by the scheme of adding and shifting, it is widely used in data processors. A counter, provision for shifting the multiplicand, and control circuits are needed. Operation time required is related to the sum of the individual digits in the multiplier. It takes much longer to perform a multiplication operation with a multiplier of 9999999 than 1111111; accordingly, time can be saved by using the operand with the smaller digits as the multiplier.

Multiplication Table. A computer may use a "product generator" to generate multiples of 0 through 9 times the multiplicand. The multiplication table can also be formed by adding a number to itself a given number of times and storing each total. Multiples corresponding to the multiplier are selected, aligned properly, and added to get the product. To multiply 486 by 93, generate multiples of 0 through 9 times 486, or add 486 1 through 9 times, and store the totals:

Multiplication	Addition
0 x 486 = 0	0 = 0
1 x 486 = 486	+ 486 = 486
2 x 486 = 972	+ 486 = 972
3 x 486 = 1,458	+ 486 = 1,458
4 x 486 = 1,944	+ 486 = 1,944
5 x 486 = 2,430	+ 486 = 2,430
6 x 486 = 2,916	+ 486 = 2,916
7 x 486 = 3,402	+ 486 = 3,402
8 x 486 = 3,888	+ 486 = 3,888
9 x 486 = 4,374	+ 486 = 4,374

Next, select multiples of 486 for 3 and 9, align properly, and add.

$$3 \times 486 = 1458$$
$$\underline{9 \ \times 486 = 4374\ }$$
$$93 \times 486 = 45198$$

Another multiplication table approach is to form a digit-by-digit partial product without carries. In multiplying 3 by 6 to get 18, for example, the 1 is a carry digit and the 8 is a mark digit. Carry digits are handled separately and then added to the sum of the mark digits to get the product, as follows:

Left-hand Carry Digits	Right-hand Mark Digits
	486
	93
121	248
375	624
3871	6488
	3871
	45198

By considering each digit individually, the left-hand carry and right-hand mark digits arise as follows for 486 times 3:

$$
\begin{array}{r}
486 \\
\text{x} \quad 3 \\
\hline
18 \\
24 \\
12
\end{array}
$$

The carry digits are the 1, 2, and 1 out of the 18, 24, and 12, whereas the mark digits are the 8, 4, and 2.

Equipment required for the multiplication table approach is more elaborate than that required for repeated addition; but this scheme is faster than either the repeated addition method or the add-and-shift method.

Binary. Multiplication is simple for binary machines, because the binary multiplication table has only four entries.

Multiplicand		Multiplier		Product
0	times	0	=	0
1	times	0	=	0
0	times	1	–	0
1	times	1	=	1

Binary multiplication is essentially the add-and-shift operation described earlier. If the multiplier digit is 1, the partial product is the same as the multiplicand. The partial product is zero for 0 in the multiplier. For example, in 110 times 101:

Multiplicand	110
Multiplier	101
Partial products	110
	000
	110
	11110

Division

The division operation can be performed in machines by subtracting and shifting in a manner similar to the usual procedure in non-automatic desk calculators. The number of subtractions must, of course, be counted. A *1* is added to the appropriate position in the quotient each time the divisor is subtracted from the dividend and the remainder does not switch from one side of zero to the other— positive to negative, or vice versa. When a negative remainder arises (after starting with a positive dividend), the divisor is added back and the remainder shifted one position to the left. Dividing 70455 by 305 illustrates the division operation carried out by repeated subtracting and shifting.

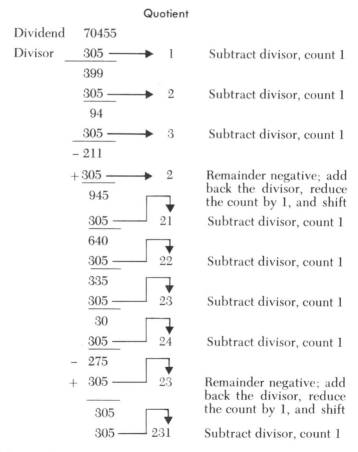

Table 6-4 shows a computer procedure for dividing 2244394 by 6598765. The dividend is placed in the accumulator and the divisor is set up in a special register. By shifting and subtracting, the quotient is formed in the M-Q register. The remainder is separated by ":" from the quotient to facilitate reading. The quotient is .3401233. The remainder of 2722755 is meaningless in this case, since the initial dividend was only seven digits. Earlier, in multiplying 6598765 by 3401234, it was shown that the product was 22443943876010. The fact that only the 7 left-hand digits are used in the division example causes the right-hand digit of the quotient to be 3 instead of 4. If more precision is desired, the right-hand digits 3876010 should be placed in the M-Q register along with the 2244394 in the accumulator before starting the division. Dividing 22443943876010 (in the combined accumulator and M-Q registers) by 6598765 gives the quotient of 3401234 and a remainder of 0. This is a simplified example of double precision division, for the dividend is double length—14 digits—even though the divisor is single length.

TABLE 6-4. *Division in Accumulator and M-Q Registers*

Operation	Accumulator	M-Q Register
1. Clear	00000000	0000000
2. Set up dividend 2244394	02244394	0000000
3. Set up divisor 6598765 in memory register	02244394	0000000
4. Shift the dividend	22443940	000000:0
5. Subtract 3 times	02647645	000000:3
6. Shift	26476450	00000:30
7. Subtract 4 times	00081390	00000:34
8. Shift	00813900	0000:340
9. Subtract 0 time	00813900	0000:340
10. Shift	08139000	000:3400
11. Subtract 1 time	01540235	000:3401
12. Shift	15402350	00:34010
13. Subtract 2 times	02204820	00:34012
14. Shift	22048200	0:340120
15. Subtract 3 times	02251905	0:340123
16. Shift	22519050	:3401230
17. Subtract 3 times	02722755	:3401233

Meaningful remainders arising from the division operation may be stored. The right-hand digit of the quotient can be rounded, if desired, but rounding is more intricate here than it was for multiplication. For example, 6 divided by 7 gives the seven-digit quotient of 8571428 and a remainder of 4. To decide *how* to round the right-hand digit in the quotient, it is first necessary to continue the division operation to get at least one more digit in the quotient. That is, divide the remainder, 4, by 7 to get 57 which, in effect, extends the quotient two more places.

Since 57 is larger than 50, the right-hand digit in the quotient, 8, is rounded to 9; this gives a rounded quotient of 8571429. It is necessary to have additional digits for the quotient when rounding; it is not correct to look merely at the first digit in the remainder.

The division operation can be performed in a binary machine in a similar fashion. Some data processors are not designed to carry out a division instruction—on the grounds that the division operation occurs so infrequently in typical problems that it does not justify the special circuitry required to handle it. Division can be programmed by obtaining the reciprocal of the divisor and multiplying by the dividend; a reciprocal can be generated by a simple formula involving adding and multiplying.

Serial and Parallel Operation

Both the serial and the parallel operating modes are used in computers. "Serial" means that the digits in a number are handled separately. Longhand addition, for example, is done serially.

$$385$$
$$\underline{67}$$
$$452$$

First, the 5 and 7 in the right column are added to get the 2. Next, a carry of 1 is made to the second column and added to the 8 and 6. The carry is added to the 3. Add and carry is continued from right to left, until every column is added.

Serial Adders. The operation of a serial adder is shown in Figure 6-4. The right-hand digits of two operands are added to make one digit in the sum. Any carry is delayed and added in the next step. The operands are shifted one digit to the right after each step so that the next digits are obtained from the same positions as before. The sum is also shifted one position to the right after each step, and the new digit is introduced at the same point each time. Seven steps are necessary to add 2 seven-digit numbers, although steps 4 to 6 are omitted from the illustration. The sum will, at the end of the operation, be positioned just as the operands were.

A detailed study shows that the sum occupies positions just like those vacated by shifting the operands. Computer design can be simplified by putting the sum into the vacant positions where one of the operands was. In the serial mode, the digits from the first column are added during one time interval. Any carry is added with digits from the second column during the next time interval. The operation time depends on the number of digit positions involved. Only one adder is required for the serial mode, regardless of the number of digits in the numbers.

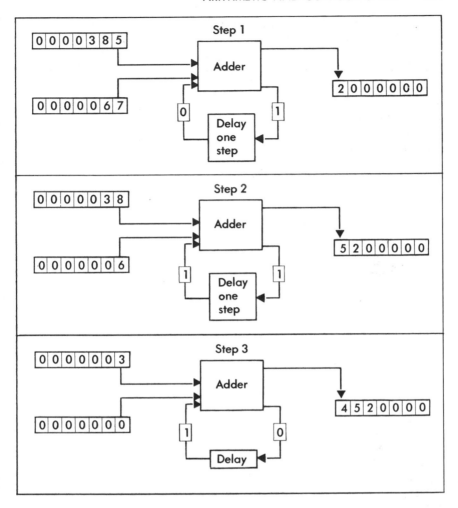

Skip steps 4 to 6

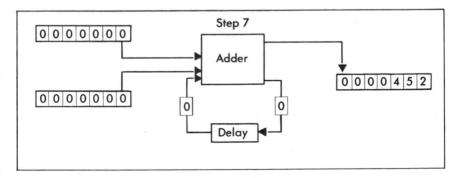

FIGURE 6-4. *Block diagram of a serial adder*

Parallel Adders. All digits of a number are handled at one time in the parallel mode of operation because an adder is provided for each digit position of a number, as is the case for a desk calculator or an adding machine. Digits in all positions are added at the same time. The operation is completed in one time interval plus any time required to handle the carries. The faster speed of the parallel mode of operation is obtained at the expense of more components and ingenious circuitry.

The illustration of addition in the serial mode given earlier used decimal numbers for simplicity. Actually, numbers are represented in binary or binary-coded decimal inside the computer. Binary numbers are longer than decimal numbers so that more adders are involved than the illustration suggests.

LOGICAL OPERATIONS

Arithmetical operations involve all the digits in a number. Each digit in a total may be affected by carries, and each digit in a remainder may be affected by borrows for positions to its right.

The *comparison operation* is one type of operation that is useful for dealing with one or more individual character positions with the effect of carries or borrows ruled out. A word containing letters cannot be subtracted from another word to find which is smaller or, more correctly, which comes first in the alphabetic sequence. Computers may "hang up" when they attempt to subtract letters, for letter codes do not fit the rules for addition and subtraction operations. On the other hand, letters can be compared to find which is earlier in alphabetic sequence. A small code value is given to A and a high code value to Z. The table of code values assigned to letters, numerals, and other symbols make up a collation table, as described in Chapter 2. The essence of alphabetic sorting is to arrange words in the collation table sequence of values by comparing them. A comparison instruction in a program may have three possible results—less than, equal to, and greater than—as explained in Chapter 3.

Extraction is another logical operation. To "extract" means to remove from a set of items all the items that meet some arbitrary criterion. It is also used to mean replacing specific parts of one quantity (as indicated by some other quantity called an extractor) by the contents of specific parts of another quantity. Extraction, in this narrow, detailed sense, is used to get one or more selected characters out of or into a word in the following way. A word consisting of 0's and 1's—or of any "even" and "odd" characters—is placed in a memory register to serve as the extractor. The content of any storage location can be extracted into the accumulator by means of an odd-character extract order. The accumulator content is replaced by the content of the specified storage location in only those character positions where the extractor contains 1's. Other positions in the accumulator remain unchanged. Assume the following conditions:

Storage location 379	$---.--
Accumulator	0684029
Extractor	1000100

The extract *odd*-character order, EXO 379, will replace the characters in the accumulator with characters from location 379 that have *positions* corresponding to the odd-value characters—the 1's—in the extractor, without changing anything else. The result of an EXO 379 order, which is written in the format of the instructions for the hypothetical computer in Chapter 3, is as follows:

Accumulator	$684.29

Another version, the extract *even*-character order, replaces the content of the accumulator with characters that have *positions* corresponding to the even-value characters in the extractor. Furthermore, the new content of the accumulator is transferred to the storage location involved. Consider the following situation:

Storage location 379	$---.--
Accumulator	0591043
Extractor	2333233

The extract even-character order EXE 379—using the 2's as even characters in this case—will give the following result without changing the extractor:

Accumulator	$591.43
Storage location 379	$591.43

The content of the storage location involved in the extract order, 379 in these examples, is immaterial except for the characters that are extracted. The blanks could just as readily be any other characters.

The *shift instruction* is another logical operation. Shifting involves moving a word columnwise to the right or left, that is, each character in a word is moved from one column to the next. An important use of shifting is to align words containing letters before comparing them or to align words containing numerals before adding them. Continued shifting in one direction causes characters to drop off at that end of a word; zeros occupy spaces arising at the other end. Sometimes the computer designer may devise a shift order so that characters shifted out of one end are returned to the other end of the word in a circular fashion. This method is called logical, non-arithmetical, or circular shifting. A circulate order may handle the content of the arithmetic register alone or the combined contents of the arithmetic and M-Q registers; but the operation may be restricted to left-hand shifts— counterclockwise, so to speak. The circulate order is different from arithmetical shifting, which loses digits that drop off the end.

A requirement of logical operations is that the value in a given position of the result depends on a value in only one position of each of the words involved; that is, there are no carries or borrows. The name "logical" operation does not mean that other operations are illogical. Logical operations might be thought of as a special kind of arithmetic; they are sometimes called "non-arithmetical," but the name "logical" is often used.

CONTROL UNIT COMPONENTS AND OPERATION

A control unit for internally stored program computers contains registers, counters, and decoders.

An *instruction register* holds the program instruction that the machine is currently performing. A *decoder* translates the operation part of an instruction by setting up the arithmetic unit circuits to perform the operation specified in the instruction. An *address register* holds the address of the operand required to execute the instruction.

A counter is a storage unit that adds or subtracts some number when a signal is received. The *instruction counter* is used in the control unit of some computers to indicate the address of the instruction that is being executed. The instruction counter increases during each instruction execution cycle to indicate the address of the next instruction. If instructions in storage are being executed in sequence, the counter increases by one in each cycle. The counter can be reset to zero or to any desired instruction by a "jump" instruction.

Control Unit Operation

The operation of the control unit for a single-address computer is shown in Figure 6-5. "Single address" means that each instruction specifies one operand: the instruction "ADD 268" that is stored in storage location 062 means "Add the contents of storage location 268 to the contents of the accumulator."

Assume that computations are in process and we look in on one operating cycle just after an instruction is put in the instruction register. The instruction register contains an instruction, such as "ADD 268" copied from location 062. The operating cycle can be described as consisting of 7 steps (some of which can be combined for description) that are repeated as many times as are required to execute a program.

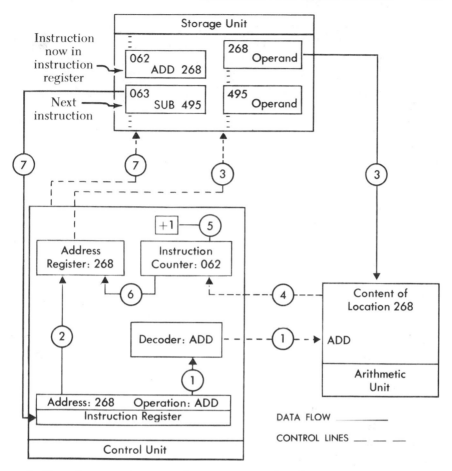

1. Transfer operation part of instruction to decoder: ADD.
2. Transfer address part of instruction: 268.
3. Transfer operand to arithmetic unit.
4. Execute instruction: ADD 268.
5. Increase number in instruction counter by 1:063.
6. Transfer instruction count to address register: 063.
7. Get instruction "SUB 495" and put in instruction register.

FIGURE 6-5. *Operation of control unit in a single-address computer*

The numbers correspond to those in Figure 6-5 showing data flow and control lines, assuming that an instruction is about to be executed:

1. Transfer the operation part of the instruction, ADD, from the instruction register to the decoder.
2. Transfer the address part of the instruction, 268, from the instruction register to the address register.

3. Copy into the arithmetic unit the operand (which may be either data or an instruction) located at address 268.

4. Execute the required operation, ADD, in the arithmetic unit. Notify the control unit when the operation is executed.

5. Increase the number 062 in the instruction counter by 1, to 063, to indicate the address of the next instruction.

6. Transfer the number 063 from the instruction counter to the address register.

7. Get the instruction, "SUB 495," located at address 063 and put it into the instruction register.

Control Console

An operator and the machine communicate with each other through the machine console, several examples of which are shown in Figure 6-6. Man-machine communication is necessary for several reasons. An operator starts processing by placing the first program instruction in the instruction register or by setting its location in the location counter. The control console can be used for detecting program mistakes—often called "debugging." The console is also useful for locating machine malfunctions. The console has neon lights or some other means of displaying the contents of desired storage locations or registers. Switch settings enable an operator to stop operations, read the content of a storage location, observe an instruction, or examine the arithmetic unit after each instruction. A console usually shows why a machine stops because of input, overflow, or program mistake. An operator may trace the mistake by repeating the program step by step.

A console may be used to enter small amounts of data when the computer is stopped. Tracing a routine by means of the console may be inefficient because it is much slower than normal operations. There are special debugging programs, to be described in Chapter 8, that will print out, for *each* instruction executed, the contents of the instruction counter, instruction register, accumulator, M-Q register, and each index. A post-mortem routine can be used by the programmer to locate mistakes without tying up the computer.

The control console is also used to interrogate a file stored on a drum or disk. Any record desired is indicated on the console keyboard and the record itself is typed out on the console typewriter.

Some manufacturers offer an auxiliary unit, called a file reference unit, for referring to or interrogating any magnetic tape. Since search time is longer than for a drum or disk, the file reference unit is separate to avoid disturbing the rest of the system. The reference unit controls a particular magnetic-tape unit from which it is desired to extract specific information, such as details for a stock item. The desired part of the record is printed out by a self-contained printer.

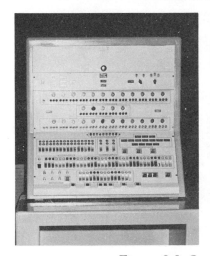
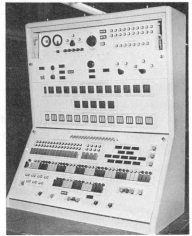

FIGURE 6-6. *Operating consoles*

CONTROL UNIT INSTRUCTION ROUTINES

A control unit causes other components to carry out the necessary operations. A list of coded instructions for the computer to follow is called a "routine." A routine or program tells the control unit:

1. What operations to perform
2. Which data to use
3. Where to place the results

Instruction routines are supplied to data processors in several ways. One way to supply a routine is to design it into the equipment. The routine, existing as a fixed electric circuit in the machine, is limited to use in a narrow class of applications.

The use of a wiring board is a second way to supply an instruction routine to a processor. Wires are inserted in a plugboard to select, in their proper sequence, the operations desired. Spare wiring boards are set up with other routines and used when wanted. A plugboard serves a similar purpose in some computers. A change in the nature of a particular problem involves rewiring or replugging its board.

A third way to supply a routine is to put instructions in internal storage just as though they were data, as described in Chapter 3. Processors that store instructions in the same way as data are called "internally stored program equipment." An instruction routine on tape or cards is read in through input devices and put in storage. The equipment can be given a new or modified instruction routine by reading in another tape or set of cards. An important feature of internally stored programs is the fact that they can be modified by manipulating them just as though they were data.

Some equipment uses a combination of internal storage and plugboards to set up routines and makes the best use of each scheme for controlling operations.

Special-purpose Equipment

A computer with instruction routines designed into the circuits and wires is called "special-purpose" equipment. Such equipment often proves efficient for a single application—such as inventory control or demand analysis—that keeps it fully loaded. On-line operations requiring many interrogation stations are often handled by special-purpose equipment.

It should be pointed out that some factors offset the advantages of efficient, specialized operations. Special-purpose equipment may have higher research and development cost per unit than general-purpose equipment, since fewer copies of a particular design may be made. In some cases, poor systems analysis results in equipment being designed to solve the wrong problem. Furthermore, equipment inflexibility exposes it to the risk of being discarded whenever the application changes.

Externally Stored Routine

Several models of small computers have instruction routines stored in a wiring board or plugboard. Wires or pins in a board inserted in the machine call up operations in their proper sequence. Each application requires the use of a separate board.

An instruction board is unwieldy for a lengthy routine, for a different instruction board is needed for each major phase of processing. Wired instruction routines are not alterable while the machine is running, although they can make some decisions and choose different processing paths. The instruction boards are flexible enough for most problems handled by small computers. Equipment with wired instruction boards is more flexible than special-purpose equipment; but it is less readily adaptable to new applications than is internally stored program equipment. Wired-instruction equipment may be much less expensive than other types.

Internally Stored Routine

As pointed out earlier, instruction routines can be stored internally along with data. The highest-speed storage in the computer holds the instructions and data while they are in use. Each instruction, which must be in a form that the computer can interpret, orders it to perform an operation. A control unit handles instructions in a particular format which may contain 1, 2, 3, or 4 "addresses" that identify a storage location, register, or device in which data or instructions are stored. Each instruction format will be considered briefly.

Single Address.   A single-address instruction, in its simplest form, has two parts:

1. The code for the operation, such as addition or subtraction
2. The address of an operand specifying the location of data to be used or the location in which to store an answer

Three single-address instructions are required to add 2 numbers and store the total. Many instructions do not involve arithmetical operations. Numerous instructions are required for data input, result output, jumps in program execution sequence, shift of accumulator content, and index count to keep track of number of loops completed. An input-output instruction identifies which unit and storage locations are involved in data transfer. A jump instruction states the "jump-to" point in the instruction routine. A shift instruction specifies whether the shift is to the left or right and the number of places. Index-counting instructions specify the particular index counter to use, the initial setting, the amount of increase or decrease during each operating loop, and the location to which the program proceeds.

The instruction counter of a single-address computer automatically increases by one after each operation is executed to indicate where to obtain the next instruction. Instructions are stored in sequentially numbered addresses; but a jump instruction can change the sequence of execution by resetting the instruction counter when a certain specified condition arises—such as completing the desired number of loops or encountering a negative number. Operations start at the new address, but instructions are again executed in sequence.

One and One-half Address. A variation of the single-address instruction scheme is the one and a half address scheme. For example, "ADD 268, 063" may mean: "Add the content of location 268 to the amount in the accumulator and get the next instruction from location 063." An instruction counter is not necessary because each instruction specifies where to get the next instruction. This scheme is reminiscent of a treasure hunt where each "treasure" contains directions on where to find the next one.

The plan of one and a half addresses is useful only if instructions are placed in storage at intervals, instead of in sequence. Instructions are spaced out (interlaced) in magnetic-drum storage to save access time. The "half" address of each instruction can be used to minimize access to the next instruction.

Two Addresses. A two-address instruction may contain an operation and two addresses, both of which may refer to operands. An instruction, "CAD 437, 438," might mean: "Clear the accumulator and add the contents of storage locations 437 and 438."

Three Addresses. A three-address instruction specifies three operands. Two addresses indicate the operands involved and the third specifies where to store the results. "ADD 102, 252, 402" may mean: "Add contents of locations 102 and 252 and store the total in location 402." Instructions are executed in sequence and a control counter keeps track of the instruction being executed. A variation of the three-address system uses one address to indicate the location of the next instruction, in which case the instruction counter can be omitted.

Four Addresses. A four-address scheme has been used in a few computers. Two addresses indicate the locations of the operands, the third indicates where to store the results, and the fourth indicates where to get the next instruction.

Comparison of Address Systems. Each address scheme has some advantages. Multiple-address equipment may be easier to program than single-address equipment, but multiple-address equipment also requires more electric circuits and components.

The efficiency of an address scheme is affected by the types of operations involved. If many complex operations are involved, a three-address or four-address system may be preferable to a single-address computer. On the other hand, some operations may be inefficient because of the required instruction format. Three-address addition instructions may require storing each sum even though a long series of additions is involved. Single-address instructions might be faster for the simple operations involved in summing a series of numbers. A one and one-half address scheme may be used to minimize access for a computer that uses a drum for internal storage; if so, an instruction counter is not needed.

ACCURACY OF ARITHMETIC AND CONTROL OPERATIONS

It is usually demanded of computers that they never give inaccurate results, either because of arithmetic or control operations. Operations are considered satisfactory only if possible equipment malfunctions can be reported so that remedial action can be taken. Reliability may be measured in terms of whether malfunctions are reported, instead of how many malfunctions occur. In fact, computer users often claim that "Our equipment has never made an undetected error." To which one might reply: "Of course not, for if an error is not detected you are not aware of its existence."

More seriously, in order for a computer to be highly reliable there must be a method, first, for detecting errors that are made and, second, for correcting these errors. There are a number of ways to detect and correct computer errors (Mauchly, 1954):

1. The computer checks each arithmetical operation or transfer in a way that is likely to catch almost all errors. When an error is detected, the computer repairs itself and continues operations.
2. The computer automatically detects almost all errors, then repeats operations if erroneous results are detected, and continues.
3. Automatic error-detection circuits cause the computer to stop so that the operator can take appropriate action.
4. Every problem is run at least twice and results are compared. Diagnostic tests run at intervals verify that the computer is operating correctly at that time. Maintenance and problem-result correction are taken, if a malfunction is detected.
5. No automatic checking is included; but complete reliance is placed upon programmed checking to insure correct results. Diagnostic tests, which include marginal testing, are used to indicate correct operation of the computer.

The third scheme—stopping operations upon detection of a malfunction—is used in Univac and involves an addition of about 25 to 30 per cent to the cost of the central computer. The increase in cost of the entire system is, of course, far less. The fourth scheme is widely used for punched-card equipment and is sometimes advocated for computers. The fifth scheme—complete reliance on programmed checking—depends upon the nature of the application. Mathematical applications may be ingeniously checked for less than a 30 per cent increase in programming cost and running time. Business applications, on the other hand, may require much more extensive checking that increases programming and operating costs by two-thirds. Furthermore, some applications may not be amenable to programmed checking so that the merits of programmed checking and built-in checking are not directly comparable.

SUMMARY

The arithmetic unit performs the arithmetical operations of addition, subtraction, multiplication, and division. Variations of these operations give increased flexibility. The control unit carries out instructions in the proper sequence, interprets each instruction, and applies proper signals to the arithmetic unit and other parts in keeping with an instruction.

An arithmetic unit has "registers" for storing words while they are being used. The accumulator which is long enough to hold a computer word, overflow bit, and sign, forms the sums and other arithmetical results. The M-Q register holds the multiplier when the multiplication starts but holds the right-hand digits of the product after multiplication is completed. The left-hand digits of a product reside in the accumulator.

An adder accepts two or more input signals, adds them, and puts out an appropriate signal. "And" gates, "or" gates, inverters, and delay circuits make up an adder. Reviewing the arithmetical operations on a desk calculator sheds some light on how computers operate. For addition, the lower dial on a desk calculator corresponds to the accumulator. The upper dial is like a cycle counter in a computer. Addition on a desk calculator illustrates performance of the operations for clearing and adding, accumulating a running total, and counting the loops in a cycle. Overflow can, of course, result from continued addition.

Addition of binary numbers follows the rules for binary arithmetic; but binary-coded decimal, such as the 8421 code, involves special rules for carries because 6 of the 16 possible numbers are skipped. Subtraction is easier for the computer by means of complementing and adding operations than by straight subtraction. A programmer simply considers the combined operations to be a straight subtraction. A nines complement is formed by subtracting a decimal number from 9999999. A binary number appears to be "subtracted" from 1111111 to get its ones complement, but actually, each 0 is merely changed to 1 and each 1 to 0. Complements of binary-coded 8421 decimal numbers are formed in the same way. Later, the end-around carry operation adds to the right-hand digit any overflow that occurs while adding a complement. This practice compensates for the 1 originally omitted from the ones or nines complement in the right-hand position.

Numbers can be multiplied by repeated addition, by adding and shifting, or by using multiplication tables. Longhand and desk-calculator multiplication operations indicate many features of computer methods. The accumulator and M-Q registers are used together in multiplication. In the add-and-shift method the M-Q register holds the multiplier at the start. The multiplicand is added in the accumulator as many times as are specified by the right-hand digit of the multiplier. After each addition, the contents of both the accumulator and the M-Q register are shifted right one position. The next digit to the left in the multiplier is used for adding the multiplicand the proper number of times to the shifted partial product. When the operation is finished, the left-hand digits in the product are in the accumulator and the right-hand digits are in the M-Q register. The whole product can be put in two storage words, if such precision is wanted. In many cases, the product has so few digits that it can be stored in one word. But if the product digits wanted lie in both the accumulator and the M-Q register, a shift operation is necessary to get the desired digits in either the accumulator or the M-Q register before storing them.

Both the required circuits and operating speed are related to the multiplication and division methods used. The objective is to get an economical balance between equipment and operating cost. Division is started by clearing the accumulator and M-Q registers, putting the dividend in the accumulator, and placing the divisor in a special register. The dividend is shifted one position to the left and the number of times that the divisor can be subtracted from the dividend is entered at the right end of the M-Q register. Contents of the accumulator (remainder) and M-Q register (partial quotient) are shifted left one position, and the operation is repeated.

Serial-mode operation handles one digit at a time. The parallel mode handles all digits in one operation and is faster than the serial mode, although at the expense of more equipment components.

Logical operations, which are a special kind of arithmetical operation, include comparison, extraction, and shifting.

A control unit usually contains an instruction register, address register, instruction counter, and decoder. These elements hold the instruction and the addresses of the operand and the next instruction to execute. The control unit also sets up circuits for executing the instruction.

An operator communicates with the equipment via the control console, which is used to start operations, monitor processing, read some data in and out of storage, and detect certain kinds of mistakes.

Instruction routines are furnished by internal circuits and wires for special-purpose equipment. External wiring or plugboards give some flexibility to equipment. General-purpose equipment operates with internally stored programs that are read in like data to make the equipment highly versatile.

Internally stored program equipment uses various instruction formats. A single-address instruction specifies an operation and one operand. A two-address instruction specifies one operation and either two operands or one operand and the location of the next instruction. Three-address and four-address instructions are also used. Each instruction format is best suited to certain applications.

A high degree of computer reliability in arithmetic and control units is achieved by permitting the equipment to make few errors, detecting most of those that do occur, and correcting those that are detected. The merits of programmed and built-in checking are never quite settled to everyone's satisfaction.

REFERENCES AND SUPPLEMENTAL READINGS

Mauchly, John W. "The Advantages of Built-in Checking," pp. 99-101 in *Proceedings of the Eastern Joint Computer Conference*, New York, The Institute of Radio Engineers, 1954. The user's desire for perfection—a system that never breaks down and never makes errors—cannot be achieved; but improvement is possible by measuring the deviation and using the result to improve performance. Schemes include error detection and self-repair, repeat, or halt; comparison of results from two or more runs; and complete reliance upon programmed checking. Built-in checking features increase the cost of the computer, whereas programmed checking increases the user's programming and operating costs. The two approaches are not wholly comparable, and their relative merits depend upon the applications intended for them.

Richards, R. K. *Arithmetical Operations in Digital Computers*, New York, D. Van Nostrand Co., Inc., 1956, 384 pp. This book contains five chapters of interest on arithmetical operation and controls. Chapter 4 covers binary addition and subtraction; Chapter 5 covers binary multiplication and division. There are two corresponding chapters, 8 and 9, for decimal operations. Chapter 11 deals with computer organization and control.

CHAPTER SEVEN

AUTOMATIC
PROCESSING
EQUIPMENT

Automatic data-processing equipment has been treated in separate chapters as though it consisted of individual components: input and output equipment, storage devices, and arithmetic and control units. In this chapter the components are "assembled" into sets of equipment—often called systems—that are available for use; these systems show what equipment manufacturers have designed for data-processing applications. The tabulated details presented in the Tables may be useful as an initial guide for selecting equipment for further consideration.

This chapter is a synopsis of the characteristics of automatic processing systems: speed, storage, instruction repertoires, tapes and peripheral equipment. In a sense, it is a general model of comparative facts. The Tables, however, should not be used as a check list for accepting or rejecting a particular set of equipment, because many factors that cannot be readily tabulated must be considered. Furthermore, a tabulated list may be incorrect because published specifications are sometimes difficult to interpret.

An index of how suitable a particular set of equipment is for a particular application would, of course, be invaluable. Consider a situation involving large files, many inputs originating at scattered points, random references, and a tight time schedule. A single index for measuring the important features of the application requirement and the equipment available would simplify equipment selection. An index might be constructed by combining the various attributes and assigning to them appropriate weights. But a single, simple index is hardly suitable, for many other attributes must be considered: price, reliability, and service, to name a few.

FEATURES OF DATA PROCESSING EQUIPMENT

The equipment discussed here is usually classified as large scale or medium scale. The classification is somewhat arbitrary, however, since several features—storage, speed, and input-output—are involved. In general, large systems have higher computing speeds and larger internal storage than medium-scale systems. Large data processors usually handle alphabetic and numerical data. Medium systems, on the other hand, are usually built as numerical machines and require modification to handle alphabetic data. The list of equipment compared in the Tables is representative of large and medium computers, but it is not meant to be exhaustive—omission of a particular computer should not be interpreted as having any especial significance.

Components of large- and medium-scale automatic data-processing equipment are covered first. Next, some consideration is given to the dimensions of storage, speed, and versatility.

Internal Storage

The facts concerning internal storage, compiled in Table 7-1, cover type, basic size, expansion factor, access time, transfer mode, and parity check. Magnetic-core internal storage is common in large computers, and magnetic-drum storage is common in medium-size computers. Occasionally both a small amount of core, for speed, and a large drum, for volume, are used in a medium-size computer.

Basic storage size is stated in decimal digits, alphanumerical characters, binary bits, or a combination of these, depending upon the methods available for representing data. Machines that represent numbers in binary fashion appear to have the largest capacity. The binary capacity must, of course, be converted to decimal or alphanumerical characters in order to relate machine capacity to the data to be stored. The number of decimal digits and alphanumerical characters that can be stored are the same except where a machine uses a two-for-one or three-for-two scheme to store alphanumerical characters. In one case the sign position is not needed for alphanumerical characters so that more letters than numerals can be stored.

Storage capacities for binary computers are here converted to decimal and alphanumeric capacities corresponding to magnetic tape codes (6 bits equal 1 character, usually). However, if binary numerical representation is used, the capacity may be greater than indicated in the Tables. For example, the largest number that 36 bits can represent alphanumerically is 999,999. The same 36 bits used as a binary number can represent a number as large as 68,719,476,735 which is $2^{36} - 1$.

The instruction capacity is the number of instructions that can be stored in the basic storage. The number of addresses contained in each instruction is commonly 1 or 3.

TABLE 7-1 Internal Storage

Computer	Type	Basic Size — Decimal Digits	Alpha-numeric Characters	Binary Data Bits	Instruction Capacity	Expansion Factor	Access Time Microseconds	Transfer Mode Parallel in Groups of	Storage Parity Check
Bendix G-15	Drum	15,232	7,888	63,104	2,160	1	540 per word fast stor. 14,500/word genl. stor.	1 bit	None
Control Data 1604	Core	20,000	65,536	393,216	16,384	4	4.8 per word average	1 word	None
Datatron 220	Core	90,112	10,000	N.A.	2,000	5	10 per word	1 word	None
Honeywell 800	Core	49,152	32,768	196,608	4,096	4	6 per word	1 word	In + out
IBM 650	Core Drum	600 20,000	300 10,000	N.A. N.A.	60 2,000	1	96 per word avg. 480 per word avg.		None
IBM 705 III	Core	40,000	40,000	N.A.	8,000	2	9 per 5 char.	5 char.	In + out by character
IBM 7070	Core	50,000	25,000	N.A.	5,000	2	6 per word	1 word	2 bit count in + out
IBM 709	Core	24,576	24,576	143,360	4,096	8	12 per word	1 word	None
LARC	Core	120,000	60,000	N.A.	10,000	9.75	4 per word (up to 7 segments can be accessed in 4 μs)	1 word	In + out by decimal digit
			(Also 99 words or 1199 characters very high speed core)						
LGP 30	Drum	36,864	20,480	131,072	4,096	1	8,000 per word	1 word	None
MOBIDIC	Core	24,576	24,576	147,456	4,096	?	8 per word	1 word	Out
NCR 304	Core	24,000	24,000	N.A.	1,000	2	60 per word	1 word	In + out by character
RCA 502	Core	16,384	16,384	N.A.	2,048	1	15 per tetrad (4 char.)	4 char.	In + out by character
RCA 503	Core	16,384	16,384	N.A.	2,048	16	15 per tetrad	4 char.	In + out by character
RCA 504	Core	16,384	16,384	N.A.	2,048	16	15 per tetrad	4 char.	In + out by character
Transac S-2000	Core	49,152	32,768	192,512	8,192	8	6 per word	1 word	In + out
Univac File Computer Model 1	Core Drum	240 11,640	240 11,640	N.A. N.A.	970 max. plus 48 plug board steps	1	861 per word 3,087 per word		In + out by character
Univac II	Core	22,000	24,000	N.A.	4,000	5	40 per word		In + out by character
Univac 1105	Core	24,576	24,576	147,456	4,096	3	8 per word	1 word	None
USS 80/90 Tape	Drum	50,000	50,000	N.A.	5,000	1	425 per word fast stor. 1,700 per word general storage	1 word	In + out by character

The expansion factor indicates the ratio of increase for the basic storage. A factor of 8 means that the largest storage for that computer can be eight times as large as the basic storage.

Access time is the length of time required to obtain either a word or a specified number of characters from storage, with the transfer, of course, being made in a corresponding mode. A parity check is usually made on transfer of data into storage or out of storage, but in some cases it is omitted completely.

Table 7-2 shows the word content in terms of whether parity-bits are used with each word. Also of interest are the number of decimal digits, alphanumerical characters, and binary bits that can be stored per word. The number of instructions per word—1, 2, or $\frac{1}{2}$—indicates the relationship between word and instruction storage.

Several computers have no index registers, but others have from 3 to 8 with 3 or 4 as the most common number. An index register, you will recall, is used in conjunction with the address contained in an indexable instruction to get an "effective" address during the execution of the instruction. An index register content is not affected by execution of the instruction, but it is increased or decreased at some point during each loop, so that the desired effective address will be obtained during the next execution. Furthermore, the index register is used to keep count of the number of loops performed and, when the desired number is completed, to cause a transfer to another part of the program. In some cases indexing time is zero, but in one case it is 90 μs (microseconds) per addition. One machine features a modification of the index register, wherein a group of special storage locations may be addressed within an instruction to cause the address of the instruction to be increased or decreased. The net effect is to develop an effective address, although neither the indexing word nor the instruction is altered by the process.

Special internal checking ranges from none at all, in most cases, to dual arithmetic circuitry and data regeneration via "orthotronic" control. The idea underlying orthotronic control is that if the usual ratio of 1 parity-bit to 6 data-bits is increased enough, then a higher fraction of mistakes can be detected and corrected by means of the parity-bit relationship.

Secondary Storage

The kinds of secondary storage, shown in Table 7-3, are drum, disk, and a tape data file. Secondary storage is not an integral part of the computer but is directly linked to and controlled by it. The basic size of secondary storage is usually much larger than that of internal storage, and the expansion factor tends to be higher.

Access times to secondary storage are 8 to 192 ms (milliseconds) for drums, Disk access time, involving the movement of mechanical

TABLE 7-2 Word Content and Indexes

Computer	Word Content					Characters Per Instruction	Addresses Per Instruction	Index Registers or Address Modification	Modification Time, μs	Special Internal Checking
	Parity Bit	Decimal Digits	Alpha-numeric Characters	Binary Bits	Instruction					
Bendix G-15	None	Sign + 7	3.5	Sign + 28	1	1 word	2	None	N.A.	Check sum for block of information determined by single command
Control Data 1604	None	Sign + 11	8	48	2	24 bits	1	6	0	
Datatron 220	None	Sign + 10	5	N.A.	1	1 word	1	1	0	Illegal char. code
Honeywell 800	6 check bits	Sign + 11 or 12	8	Sign + 44 or 48	1	1 word	3	to 64	6	Data regeneration orthotronic control
IBM 650	None	Sign + 10	5	N.A.	1	1 word	1	3	0	Char. validity checking in arithmetic unit and on transfers to drum
IBM 705 III		Variable				5	1	Indirect addressing	13	
IBM 7070	None	Sign + 10	5	N.A.	1	1 word	1	99 words	24-36	Instruction and char. validity check
IBM 709	None	6	6	Sign + 35	1	1 word	1	3	0	Parity check transfers. Arithmetic check by recomputing parity bits. Automatic correction for intermittent errors.
LARC	1 per decimal digit	Sign + 11	6	N.A.	1	12 digits	1 + 2 (1 main memory, 1 accumulator, 1 index register)	99 max.	0	
LGP 30	None	Sign + 9	5	32	1	16 bits	1	None	N.A.	Optional memory signal checking circuit available
MOBIDIC	1	Sign + 6	6	Sign + 36	1	1 word	1 or 2	4 or 7	0	Instruction validity and consistency
NCR 304	6 check bits or 1 char.	Sign + 10	10	60	1/2	Majority 20	3	10	60	Character parity + word parity
RCA 502			Variable			8	2	4 static 3 dynamic	90	N.A.
RCA 503			Variable			8	2	4 static 3 dynamic	90	Dual arithmetic circuitry using complements
RCA 504			Variable			8	2	4 static 3 dynamic	90	Dual arithmetic circuitry using complements
Transac S-2000	None	12	8	Sign + 47	2	24 bits	1	8, 16, or 32	0	Instruction validity check
Univac File Computer Model I	None	Sign + 11	12	N.A.	1	1 word	3	None	N.A.	Dual arithmetic operation
Univac II	None	Sign + 11	12	N.A.	2	1/2 word	1	None	N.A.	Dual arithmetic operation
Univac 1105	None	6	6	36	1	1 word	2	None	N.A.	Indication of an error on a 72 command. Instruction validity check
USS 80/90 Tape	None	Sign + 10	10	N.A.	1	1 word	1	3	N.A.	Program checks

TABLE 7-3 Secondary Storage

Computer	Type	Basic Size			Expansion Factor	Access		Transfer	
		Decimal Digits	Alpha-numeric Characters	Binary Data Bits		Time	Per	Time	Per
Bendix G-15	None	N.A.	N.A.	N.A.	N.A.	N.A.	N.A.	N.A.	N.A.
Control Data 1604	Disk	6,000,000 12,000,000	3,000,000 6,000,000	N.A.	4	850 ms maximum 105-235 ms track 70 ms corresponding track other disk side			
Datatron 220	Tape Data File	50,000,000	25,000,000	N.A.	10	27 sec. full file 9 sec. avg. .111 sec. min.		Tape speed 25,000 dec. digits per second	N.A.
Honeywell 800	None	N.A.	N.A.	N.A.	N.A.	N.A.	N.A.	N.A.	N.A.
IBM 650	Disk	6,000,000 12,000,000	3,000,000 6,000,000	N.A.	N.A.	850 ms maximum 105-235 ms track 70 ms corresponding track other disk side			
IBM 705 III	Drum	60,000	60,000	N.A.	9	Avg. 8 ms	Reference	40 µs	Char.
IBM 7070	Disk	6,000,000 12,000,000	3,000,000 6,000,000	N.A.	4	850 ms maximum 105-235 ms track 70 ms corresponding track other disk side			
IBM 709	Drum	49,152	49,152	286,720	2	Avg. 35 ms	Reference	96 µs	Word
LARC	Drum	3,000,000	1,500,000	N.A.	24	1.36 ms	2,500 words	3 µs	Char.
LGP 30	None	N.A.	N.A.	N.A.	N.A.	N.A.	N.A.	N.A.	N.A.
MOBIDIC	Disk	6,250,000	6,250,000	37,500,000	8	85 ms	Reference	240 µs	Word
NCR 304	None	N.A.	N.A.	N.A.	N.A.	N.A.	N.A.	N.A.	N.A.
RCA 502	Drum	1,500,000	1,500,000	N.A.	72	192 ms	Reference	46.9 µs	Char.
RCA 503	Drum	1,500,000	1,500,000	N.A.	756	192 ms	Reference	46.9 µs	Char.
RCA 504	Drum	1,500,000	1,500,000	N.A.	756	192 ms	Reference	46.9 µs	Char.
Transac S-2000	Drum	393,216	262,144	1,572,864	32	Avg. 17 ms	Reference	16 µs	Word
Univac File Computer Model I	Drum	180,000 10,000,000	180,000 10,000,000	N.A.	10	Avg. 17 ms	Word	650 µs to read and transfer	Word
Univac II	None	N.A.	N.A.	N.A.	N.A.	N.A.	N.A.	N.A.	N.A.
Univac 1105	Drum	196,608	196,608	1,179,648	1	17 ms	Word	32 µs	Word
USS 80/90 Tape	None	N.A.	N.A.	N.A.	N.A.	N.A.	N.A.	N.A.	N.A.

parts, ranges from a small fraction of a second for data on adjacent tracks to about a second for data on a different disk. Tape data-file access runs into seconds, but transfers are then made at tape speeds. Transfer time runs from 16 to 96 μs per character for drums, which is at the rate of 10,000 to 62,000 characters a second.

Operating Speed

Operating speed, as shown in Table 7-4, is indicated by the storage access time, arithmetical mode, addition and multiplication time, and availability of floating-point arithmetical operations.

Access times range from 8 to 960 μs. Arithmetical modes are parallel—all characters in a word are handled at one time—or serial on a character-by-character basis.

Addition time is stated in terms of synthetic three-address operations—add A to B and store in C—to try to get comparability even though the computer's instruction format is either one-address or two-address. The synthetic three-address addition time ranges from 24 to 15,648 μs. In several serial machines the addition time is much longer for operands of 10-decimal digits than it is for those of 5-decimal digits.

Similar comments apply to multiplication times, which are stated in terms of the synthetic three-address mode. Times are shown for multiplying 4 digits by 5 digits and 4 digits by 10 digits. A longer operand may not increase the multiplication time, but in some cases it doubles or triples it. In general, multiplication takes from two to twenty times as long as addition operations.

Built-in floating-point operations (in which the computer keeps track of the decimal point) are faster than programmed floating-point operations.

Instructions

Instruction repertoires available in large computers range from several dozen to approximately two hundred distinct commands. Since all computers have comparable basic instructions, attention is directed in Table 7-5 toward selected instructions that may be of especial interest in data-processing applications.

The add-to-storage instruction performs the equivalent of adding the content of the accumulator to the content of a specified storage location and placing the sum in that location. This instruction is useful for summarizing items to accumulate numerous totals.

The intra-storage transfer instruction (often called "memory-to-memory") is used for transferring words from one storage location to another location. It may be the only instruction that will transfer the content of an addressable register, other than the accumulator, directly to storage. A modification of the intra-storage transfer order permits the transfer to take place between dispersed storage locations and a

TABLE 7-4 Operating Speed in Microseconds

Computer	Storage Access	Arithmetic Mode	3 Address ADD Time 5 Dec. Digits	3 Address ADD Time 10 Dec. Digits	3 Address MULTIPLY Time 4 Dig. x 5 Dig.	3 Address MULTIPLY Time 4 Dig. x 10 Dig.	Floating ADD Time Fixed Word	Floating MULTIPLY Time Fixed Wd. Size
Bendix G-15	540 14,500	Serial	1,620	3,240	12,040	12,040	28,000	28,000
Control Data 1604	4.8 avg.	Parallel	21.6	21.6	58.8	58.8	33.2	50.4
Datatron 220	10	Serial by char. Parallel by bit	185	555	230	3,430	315	1,545
Honeywell 800	6	Parallel	24	24	150	150	66 avg.	156 avg.
IBM 650	480 avg.	Serial	Drum 15,648 Core 1,440	Drum 15,648 Core 1,440	Drum avg. 23,166 Core avg. 3,072	Drum avg. 23,166 Core avg. 3,072	Drum avg. 6,736 Core avg. 1,792	Drum avg. 6,436 Core avg. 960
IBM 705 III	9	Serial	180 or 271	281 or 461	676	963	N.A.	N.A.
IBM 7070	6	Serial	180	144	624	600	348-480	1,128-1,176
IBM 709	12	Parallel	72	72	72-288	72-288	132-252	252
LARC	4	Parallel	12	12	24	24	12	24
LGP 30	8,000	Serial	6,750	6,750	24,000	24,000	150,000	206,000
MOBIDIC	8	Parallel	48	48	118	118	50	104
NCR 304	60	Serial by char. Parallel by bit	600	600	2,760 avg.	2,760 avg.	N.A.	N.A.
RCA 502	15	Serial by tetrad Parallel by bit	360	585	5,730	9,330	N.A.	N.A.
RCA 503	15	Serial by tetrad Parallel by bit	360	585	5,730	9,330	N.A.	N.A.
RCA 504	15	Serial by tetrad Parallel by bit	360	585	5,730	9,330	N.A.	N.A.
Transac S-2000	10 and 2	Parallel	46	46	85.3	85.3	50.6	76.1 (with 10 μs storage)
Univac File Computer Model 1	960	Serial	1890	1890	34,300	34,300	N.A.	N.A.
Univac II	40	Serial	440	440	1,920	1,920	N.A.	N.A.
Univac 1105	8	Parallel	78 (two address)	78	146 (two address)	146	188 (two address)	202
USS 80/90 Tape	425 1,700	Serial	255	255	105	180	N.A.	N.A.

TABLE 7-5 *Selected Instructions*

Computer	Add to Storage	Storage to Storage Transfer	Dispersed Location Data Transfer	Repeat	Effective Addressing	Partial Word Addressing	Table Look-up	Program Interrupt	Sense for Tape Availability	End of File
Bendix G-15	No	Yes	No	No	No	No	No	Yes	Yes	Yes
Control Data 1604	Yes	No	No	No	Yes	No	Yes	Yes	Yes	Causes program interrupt or may be sensed
Datatron 220	Yes	Yes	No	No	No	Yes	No	No	No	No
Honeywell 800	As 3 address instruction	As 3 address instruction	Yes	No	Yes	Yes	Yes	Yes	Yes	Causes program interrupt
IBM 650	No	No	No	No	No	No	Yes	No	No	Yes
IBM 705 III	Yes	Yes	No	No	Yes	Yes	No	No	No	Yes
IBM 7070	Yes	Yes	Independently or as part of read/write	No	No	Yes	Yes	Magnetic tape	Yes	Causes program interrupt
IBM 709	No	No	No	No	Yes	No	No	Yes	Yes	Yes
LARC	Yes	Yes	No	No	Yes	No	No	Yes	Yes	Yes
LGP 30	No	No	No	No	Yes	Yes	No	No	N.A.	N.A.
MOBIDIC	No	As 3 address inst.	As part of read or write	Yes	No	No	By means of REPEAT-COMPARE	Real time or magnetic tape	Yes	Causes program interrupt
NCR 304	As 3 address inst. Also summarize inst.	As 3 address inst.	No	No	No	Yes	SIFT locates first item greater than key	No	Yes	Yes
RCA 502	Yes	Yes	Independently or as part of write	Yes	Yes	Yes	Locate nth symbol	Yes	Yes	Yes
RCA 503	Yes	Yes	Independently or as part of write	Yes	Yes	Yes	Locate nth symbol	Yes	Yes	Yes
RCA 504	Yes	Yes	Independently or as part of write	Yes	Yes	Yes	Locate nth symbol	Yes	Yes	Yes
Transac S-2000	Yes	No	No	Yes	No	No	By means of REPEAT-COMPARE	Real time or magnetic tape	Yes	Yes
Univac File Computer Model 1	As 3 address inst.	Yes	No	No	No	Yes	Yes	Yes	Yes	Yes
Univac II	Yes	Yes	No	No	No	Yes	No	No	No	No
Univac 1105	Yes	Yes	No	Yes	No	No	No	External equipment or control panel	Yes (automatic tape control)	Yes
USS 80/90 Tape	Yes	Yes	No	No	No	Yes	No	No	No	No

block of contiguous locations. This transfer of data from dispersed locations may be performed independently or as part of an order to read or write on tape. The instruction refers to a stored table which specifies the addresses of the dispersed memory locations to be used.

The repeat instruction causes the instruction following it to be repeated a specified number of times with the address part of the instruction modified before each execution. This order is useful in the repeat-move combination to block transfer an arbitrary number of words from one part of storage to another. It is also useful in the table look-up operation, described below.

Partial word addressing confines operations to a selected portion of a data word. The instruction specifies which characters are to be operated upon, and instruction execution time is a function of the number of these characters.

Table look-up, which is available in four computers, utilizes a table consisting of a series of arguments (reference facts) arranged in a sequence of ascending absolute values. One or more functions (results within the table) are associated with each argument. Arguments and functions can be stored in the same word or a fixed number of words apart. The known argument is compared against the stored arguments to find the address of the equal argument, or the next higher one, if no equal is present. The address of the argument is used to calculate the data address of the function which can then be inserted into an instruction.

The program-interrupt feature in one computer allows control to be transferred to memory location 0, if bit position 40 of the word contained in the real-time input register contains a 1, which must be supplied by the device that supplies data. The regular program is then interrupted and the address of the last instruction executed is stored where it can later be retrieved after the incoming data are stored and the regular program is to be resumed.

The instruction to sense tape for availability provides for a transfer of program control based on the status of an individual tape transport, for some machines, or a tape coordinator or controller for others. This order is useful in avoiding delays in the main program caused by execution of a tape command involving a busy transport or controller.

The status of an input-output unit can be indicated by an "input-output" indicator which is turned on when the unit reaches an end-of-file or end-of-tape condition and remains on until turned off by the program or by a manual operation. When the end-of-file indicator is turned on, a transfer can be made to an instruction location specified by the transfer-on-signal instruction. The end-of-file subroutine or branch program may provide for the console typewriter to notify the operator to change tape or to alternate automatically between tapes and continue operations. Magnetic tape interrupt characters or conditions may be end-of-file, end-of-tape, or other designated control characters.

Magnetic Tape

Magnetic tapes are widely used for file storage and for high-speed read-in and write-out. Features of magnetic tape that are of interest here are data form and density, block size and tape length, tape operations, and data conversion and tape checks.

Data Format and Density. The format and density of data on magnetic tape are shown in Table 7-6. The way that data are arranged across the tape is the lateral-tape format. The most common lateral-tape format is 6 data-bits and 1 parity-bit recorded across the tape to make one data channel. Two manufacturers use 12 data-bits and 2 parity-bits for two channels of data. Usually 6 bits are used to represent one alphanumerical character or one decimal digit, although in one case $1\frac{1}{2}$ decimal digits can be recorded in the space of one alphanumerical character by using a two-for-three code scheme.

The density of data along each channel ranges from 139 to 556 bits per inch. For those computers able to handle individual bits, the density is also stated in data-bits per inch. Thus, for 6 data-bits across the tape, a linear density of 300 bits per inch would give 1,800 data-bits per inch. The number of alphanumerical characters per inch is the same as the linear density except when two or more character channels are recorded across tape.

The tape speed, ranging from 75 to 150 inches a second, multiplied by the number of characters per inch, gives the maximum number of decimal digits, ranging from 10,000 to about 100,000, that can be transferred per second. Some computers are designed to operate with both low-speed and high-speed tape, although perhaps not completely interchangeably. In actual use, the transfer rates must be reduced because of the time required to pass the inter-record gap even when running continuously.

Block Size and Tape Length. Data-block size, running characteristics, and tape length are shown in Table 7-7. Some computers have fixed-size data blocks ranging from 120 to 1,024 alphanumerical characters. Others are able to handle variable-length fields that may have both a lower and an upper length limit, for example, 50 to 500 characters. The lower limit of field length may be one character and the upper limit may be either the capacity of computer storage or the tape itself.

The inter-block gap for tape acceleration and deceleration, when reading or writing individual blocks on tape, ranges from about .3 inches to 1.5 inches. The inter-block starting or stopping time ranges from a few to about fifty milliseconds. In some cases the starting and

TABLE 7-6 *Magnetic Tape Data Format and Density*

Computer	Lateral Tape Format				Density, Per Inch				Speed Inch/Sec.	Maximum Transfer Rate Thousand Decimal Characters Per Sec.
	Data Bits	Parity	Alpha-numeric Characters	Decimal Digits	Linear Density Bits	Binary Data Bits	Alpha-numeric Chars.	Decimal Digits		
Bendix G-15	4	—	.5	1	60	240	120	240	7.5 read/write 45 search	.43
Control Data 1604	6	1	1	.5	200	1,200	200	300	150	45
Datatron 220	In each of two independent channels									
	4	1	.5	1	208	N.A.	104	208	120	24.9
Honeywell 800	8	1	1.33	2	400	3,200	533	800	120	96
IBM 650	6	1	1	1	200	N.A.	200	200	75	15
IBM 705 III	6	1	1	1	200 556	N.A.	200 556	200 556	75 or 112.5 75 or 112.5	15 or 22.5 41.7 or 62.5
IBM 7070	6	1	1	1	200 556	N.A.	200 556	200 556	75 112.5	15 62.5
IBM 709	6	1	1	1	200	1,200	200	200	75	15
LARC	6	1	1	1	250	N.A.	250	250	100	25
LGP 30	N.A.									
MOBIDIC	12	2	2	3	300	3,600	600	600	150	90
NCR 304	6	1	1	1 or 1.5	200	N.A.	200	200 or 300	150	30
RCA 502	6	1	1	1	222 333	N.A.	222 333	222 333	100	33.3
RCA 503	6	1	1	1	333	N.A.	333	333	100	33.3
RCA 504	6	1	1	1	666	N.A.	666	666	100	66.6
Transac S-2000	12	2	2	3	375	3,600	750	112.5	150	135
Univac File Computer Model I	6	1	1	1	139	N.A.	139	139	75	10.4
Univac II	6	1	1	1	250	N.A.	250	250	100	25
Univac 1105	6	1	1	1	250	1,500	250	250	100	25
USS 80/90 Tape	6	1	1	1	250	N.A.	250	250	100	25

TABLE 7-7 *Block Size and Tape Length*

Computer	Alphanumeric Block Size	Inter-block Gap, inches	Average Inter-block Start or Stop Time, ms	Read Reverse	Rewind In./Sec.	Rewind Time, min.	Tape Length, feet	Independent Tape Search
Bendix G-15	Variable to 378 char.	.2	5	No	45	16	3,600	No
Control Data 1604	Var. to tape limit	.75	2.5	Yes	150 225	3.3 3	2,500 3,600	No
Datatron 220	Var. 10-100 words or 50-500 A/inch	.38	5	No	120	5.8	3,500	Yes
Honeywell 800	Var. to tape limit	.67	4	Yes	360	1.3	2,500	Yes
IBM 650	Var. to 300 alphanumerical char. or 600 numerical char.	.75	10.8	No	75 500	1.2	2,400	No
IBM 705 III	Var. to storage limit	.75	10.8 7.3	No	75 500	1.2	2,400	No
IBM 7070	Var. to storage limit	.75	10.8 7.3	No	75 500	1.2 0.9	2,400	No
IBM 709	Var. to tape limit	.75	10.8	No	75 500	1.2	2,400	No
LARC	Variable	1.05 at 250 cpi 2.4 at 125 cpi	12.02	Yes	100	4.8	2,400 Mylar 1,500 Metallic	Yes
LGP 30	N.A.							
MOBIDIC	Variable to 3,066 char. std. longer at programmer's option	1.5	6	Yes	225	3	3,600	No
NCR 304	Var. 10-100 words	None—head repositioning after operation averages 11.5 milliseconds	5 plus head reposition time	No	225	3	3,600	(Data) Yes
RCA 502	Var. to storage limit	.34	3.5	Yes	200	2.4	2,400	No
RCA 503	Var. to storage limit	.34	3.5	Yes	200	2.4	2,400	No
RCA 504	Var. to storage limit	1.13	7.5	Yes	200	2.4	2,400	No
Transac S-2000	Fixed 1,024 char.	.9	5	Yes	225	3	3,600	No
Univac File Computer Model I	Fixed 120	.5	7	Yes	75	6.5 9.5	2,400 3,600	Yes
Univac II	Fixed 720	1	15	Yes	100	4.8	2,400	No
Univac 1105	Var. to 720 char. Unlimited in by-pass mode	1.2	Start 17 or 29 Stop 8.5	Yes	100	4.8	2,400	No
USS 80/90 Tape	Fixed	1.05 at 250 cpi 2.4 at 125 cpi	12.02	Yes	100	4.8	2,400 Mylar 1,500 Metallic	Yes

stopping times between blocks are different, and they are also different for the reading and writing operations. These times differ when two separate heads are used; one for reading and one for writing. Since the reading head always follows (in terms of tape movement) the writing head, the starting time for reading will always be longer. This time will vary from execution to execution because of current variations in the drive mechanism as well as slight differences in the point where the tape came to rest after the prior tape movement. Accordingly, the tape times shown are average.

The read-reverse feature permits a tape to be read while moving in the reverse of the direction in which it is written. It is invaluable for tape merge-sorting operations because the output tape from one pass can be used as the input tape on the next pass without waiting to rewind the tape. Of course, it may be possible to "overlap" tape rewinding with other operations and thereby reduce the preparatory time for the next pass. Rewinding speeds, which influence the amount of time required to change tapes that are in the forward position, vary from 75 to 500 inches a second so that the rewind time ranges from 1 to 10 minutes. Tape lengths are customarily 2,400 or 3,600 ft., although some tapes are shorter.

The independent tape-search feature permits tapes to be scanned for selected records. The search is initiated by the central processor, but proceeds independently, freeing the processor for other work. The search key or criterion will be located in a predetermined portion of each record; but the size and possible location of this key varies among the different machines.

Tape Operations.   Tape operations, as covered in Table 7-8, can be described in terms of the number of tapes that can be controlled by the computer at one time and the ability to perform simultaneous operations. The maximum number of tapes that can be handled by one tape controller ranges from 1 to 16 and the maximum number of controllers in a computer ranges from 1 to 8. The maximum number of tapes that can be controlled by a computer ranges from 6 to 64.

Simultaneous-operation capability—the ability to perform some combination of reading, computing, and writing at the same time—ranges from nil in some computers to all three in others. In some cases simultaneous operation may be restricted to reading and writing while computing. Where simultaneous reading or writing, or reading and writing, with computing is not available, tape searching may be carried on simultaneously with internal processing. At the upper end of the scale, some computers are designed to execute several programs concurrently (by interlacing time-wise) while performing read-write simultaneously. The maximum data-transfer rate, with a sufficient number of tape controllers, ranges from 12,000 characters to 1,536,000 decimal

TABLE 7-8 *Tape Operations*

Computer	Maximum Number Tapes	Maximum Number Tapes Per Controller	Maximum Number Controllers or Converters	Types Possible	Magnetic Tape Operations Performed While Computing			
					With 1 Controller	With 2 Controllers	With 3 Controllers	With Maximum Controllers
Bendix G-15	4	1	None required	Read, write, or search	N.A.	N.A.	N.A.	N.A.
Control Data 1604	24	4	6	R+W (Read and write)	R/W	2(R/W)	3(R/W)	3(R+W)
Datatron 220	10	10	1	S/S (Search or Scan)	S/S			S/S
Honeywell 800	64	8	8	R+W (Read or write)	R+W	2(R+W)	3(R+W)	8(R+W)
IBM 650	6	6	1	R/W (Read or write)				R/W
IBM 705 III	729 I-30 729 III-20	5 5	6 4	R/W	R/W	2(R/W)	3(R/W)	6(R/W) 4(R/W)
IBM 7070	12	12	1	R/W	2(R/W)	2(R/W)		2(R/W)
IBM 709	48	16	3	R/W	2(R/W)	4(R/W)	6(R/W)	6(R/W)
LARC	40	10	4	R+W Rewind with check Tape search	R+W	2(R+W)	3(R+W)	4(R+W)
LGP 30	N.A.							
MOBIDIC	63	Any 1	4	R/W	R/W	2(R/W)	3(R/W)	4(R/W)
NCR 304	64	8	8	C/S (Tape copy or search)	C/S	2(C/S)	3(C/S)	8(C/S)
RCA 502	6	6	1	R/W	N.A.	N.A.	N.A.	N.A.
RCA 503	63	8	8	R/W	R/W	R/W	R/W	R/W
RCA 504	63	8	8	R/W	R/W	R/W	R/W	R/W
Transac S-2000	256	16	16	R/W	4(R/W)			4(R/W)
Univac File Computer Model I	10	N.A.	None	Computer In/Out (10) Gen. storage	Computer In/Out (10) Gen. storage	Computer In/Out (10) Gen. storage	Computer In/Out (10) Gen. storage	Computer In/Out (10) Gen. storage
Univac II	16	N.A.	None	R+W	R/W	2(R/W)		R+W
Univac 1105	20	10	2	R/W	R/W	2(R/W)	R+W	2(R/W)
USS 80/90 Tape	10	None	N.A.	R+W	R+W	R+W	R+W	R+W

digits a second. Processing speeds are likely to be slowed when several operations are done simultaneously.

Magnetic Tape Input Times and Tape Checks. The magnetic tape reading times for different record configurations and tape checking features are shown in Table 7-9. The card-to-tape format specifies the data configuration on magnetic tape resulting from off-line card-to-tape conversion. The times shown in all cases are for 1,000 records of the nature illustrated: 80 character cards, 500 character and 1,000 character records. In order to minimize the machine time used to pass inter-block gaps, more than one record may be included or "blocked" into one block on tape, as specified.

Special checks for tape operation are dual-head rereading, dual-level sensing, two-way parity, and several others. Only a few computers have the dual-head rereading feature that automatically reads and checks all data that are written. The dual-level signal-sensing capability offers different advantages for reading and for writing. Two energy levels are employed to read data into two registers, high and low. On the reading operation, if the parity check fails for one register, the contents of the other register are used to correct the error. For writing, the two registers are filled and compared by means of the automatic reread from the second head. The high register will be in error if signal strength is weak, whereas the low register will be distorted due to excess noise. The longitudinal parity feature is included in many computers (in addition to the transverse parity-bit) to give two-way parity protection and to reduce further the possibility of undetected errors in reading.

Additional checking features for tape include character counting, dual-parallel recording, and orthotronic control.

Buffers and Printers

The way that data are organized for read-in, as listed in Table 7-10, affects computing speed because an interruption is required to store data.

Buffer capacity is commonly one word or a small number of characters, although in some computers it is 60 or 120 words. Each transfer from buffer to memory causes a memory interruption for the time specified—which ranges from 6 to 15 microseconds in faster computers but is several milliseconds in slower computers.

Printer speeds range from 150 to 1,800 lines a minute. Many are provided with plugboard format control, whereas others require programming control of copy format. The number of character positions per line is typically 120, although some printers have 80, 130, or 160 positions per line and can produce a specified number of carbons. Some printers are restricted in the sense that they operate solely as either on-line or off-line devices.

TABLE 7-9 *Magnetic Tape Input Times for 1,000 Records Read Into One-half Basic Storage and Tape Checks*

Computer	Records Prepared Off-line On Card-to-tape Converter		500 Alphanumeric Character Records		1,000 Alphanumeric Character Records		Special Tape Checks		
	Blocking No. of Characters Between Gaps	Time in Seconds	Blocking Records Per Block	Time in Seconds	Blocking Records Per Block	Time in Seconds	Re-read (Dual-head)	Vertical Parity	Other
Bendix G-15	N.A.	N.A.	2 +	Less than 4	3 +	Less than 6	None	None	Programmed checks
Control Data 1604	N.A.		Variable	16.7	Variable	33.3	Read back or write	No	Short/long block check
Datatron 220	N.A.		1	43.9	.5	87.8	No	No	Digit and word count
Honeywell 800	80	6.7	6	13.3	.3	21.2	No	Yes	Orthotronic control
IBM 650	80	26.9	.6	69.3	.3	148.5	No	Yes	
IBM 705 III	80	15.3	40	33.8 8.3	20	67.6 16.5	Yes	Yes	Dual level sense
IBM 7070	80	15.3	25	34.1 8.5	12	68.4 17	Yes	Yes	Dual level sense
IBM 709	80	15.4	24	34.2	12	68.4	Yes	Yes	Dual level sense
LARC	6 120 char. blockettes	29.9	1.4	31.3	.7	62.6	No	No	Rewind with parity and digit count
LGP 30	N.A.								
MOBIDIC	3 x 80 = 240	4.2	6	7.3	3	14.5	Yes	No	
NCR 304	100	.04	20 per read (no gap)	17.4	10 per read (no gap)	35.0	Yes	Yes	Diagonal parity
RCA 502	80	5.8	16	18.4	8	33.3	Yes	Yes	Dual recording (parallel) on tape
RCA 503	80	5.8	16	18.4	8	33.3	Yes	Yes	Dual recording (parallel) on tape
RCA 504	80	5.8	16	18.4	8	33.3	Yes	Yes	Dual recording (parallel) on tape
Transac S-2000	12 x 80 = 960	1.4	2	8.8	1	17.6	Yes	Yes	Automatic reread blocks on error. Horizontal parity. Block word count
Univac File Computer Model 1	N.A.		.24	128.5	.12	248.1	No	No	120 char. count per block
Univac II	6 120 char. blockettes (1" gap)	29.9	1.4	31.3	.7	62.6	No	No	720 char. count per block
Univac 1105	6 120 char. blockettes (1" gap)	31.7	1.4	44.2	.7	88.6	No	No	Parity error. 720 char. count per fixed block
USS 80/90 Tape	1000 char. + 100 signs (USS Mode) 720 char. (Univac Mode)	N.A.	1.4 2	31.3 33.6	.7 1	62.6 ms 67.2	No	No	<720 (<1100) >720 (>1100) >739 (>1121)

TABLE 7-10 *Word Buffers and Line Printers*

Computer	Buffer or Tape Control Capacity	Buffer to Storage Parallel by	Main Storage Interrupt Each	For	Speed Lines Per Minute	Plugboard Format Control	Number of Print Positions	Number of Carbons	Printer Available
Bendix G-15	None	N.A.	N.A.		100	Yes	120	4	On-line Off-line
Control Data 1604	1 word	Word	Word	4.8 us	150	No	120	5	On-line Off-line
Datatron 220	14 char.	Char.	Full execution time		A.N. 1225 / Num. 1500	Yes	120	5	On-line Off-line
Honeywell 800	4 words	Word	Word	6 us	600 900	No	120		On-line Off-line
IBM 650	60 words of core storage serves dual function		Buffer is addressable by word					5	On-line Off-line
IBM 705 III	10 char.	5 char.	5 char.	9 us	500 1000	Yes	120	5	On-line Off-line
IBM 7070	2 signs + 2 words	Word	Word	6 us	150	Yes	80 ch. in 120 pos.		On-line only
IBM 709	36 bits	Word	Word	12 us	150	Yes	120	5	On-line Off-line
LARC	Direct storage access from all input-output devices. Segmented storage allows simultaneous access to all input-output devices				600 (Univac H.S. printer) or Electronic page printer at 10 pages per second of 12,000 char. per page	Yes No	130 120	5	On-line Off-line
LGP-30	N.A.								
MOBIDIC	1 word	Word	Word	8 us	600-900	Yes	120-190	4	On-line Off-line
NCR 304		Word	Full time or 333 microseconds/word		A.N. 600 850 / Num. 750 1200	Yes	120	5	On-line Off-line
RCA 502	8 char. in 8 char. out	Tetrad	Tetrad	15 us	600-900	Off-line only	120	3	On-line Off-line
RCA 503	8 char. in 8 char. out	Tetrad	Tetrad	15 us	600-900	Off-line only	120	3	On-line Off-line
RCA 504	8 char. in 8 char. out	Tetrad	Tetrad	15 us	600-900	Off-line only	120	3	On-line Off-line
Transac S-2-000	1 word	Word	Word	10 or 2 us	900	No	120 or 160	5	On-line Off-line
Univac File Computer Model I	120 char.	Char.	10 words	5 ms	400 or 600	Yes	130	5	On-line Off-line
Univac II	60 words in 60 words out	6 char.	60 words	3.5 ms	600	Yes	130	5	On-line Off-line
Univac 1105	2 of 120 words	Word	120 words	2 ms read 2.4 ms write	600	Yes	130	4	Off-line only
USS 80/90 Tape	100 words + sign (USS Mode) 72 words + sign (Univac Mode)	Block			600	No	130	5	On-line

TABLE 7-11 *Card and Tape Devices*

Computer	Card			Plugboard Format Control	Number of Devices	Paper Tape		
	No. of Dev.	Read Speed	Punch Speed			Read Speed	Punch Speed	Channel Variety
Bendix G-15	To 3	100 cpm	100 cpm	Yes	To 7	250 ch/s 400 ch/s	17 ch/s 60 ch/s	5, 6, 7, 8
Control Data 1604	3 read 3 punch	250 cpm	100 cpm	No	1 read 1 punch	350 ch/s	60 ch/s	5, 7, 8
Datatron 220	1 cardatron controls 7 devices	240 cpm	100 cpm	Internal electronic band format control	10 read 10 punch	1000 ch/s	60 ch/s	7
Honeywell 800	8	240 cpm 650 cpm 900 cpm	100 cpm 200 cpm	Reader only	8	200 ch/s 1000 ch/s	60 ch/s	5, 6, 7, 8
IBM 650	1 3	250 cpm 200 cpm	250 cpm 100 cpm	Yes Yes	To 3 read	150 ch/s	N.A.	5, 8
IBM 705 III	Any practical number	250 cpm	100 cpm	Yes	None	N.A.	N.A.	N.A.
IBM 7070	3 read 3 punch	500 cpm	250 cpm	Yes	None	N.A.	N.A.	N.A.
IBM 709	3 read 3 punch	250 cpm	100 cpm	Yes	None	N.A.	N.A.	N.A.
LARC	1	450 cpm	N.A.	No	1	10 ch/s	10 ch/s	5, 6, 7, 8
LGP 30	4 read	60 cpm	N.A.	No	6	200 ch/s	200 ch/s	5, 6, 7, 8
MOBIDIC	To 63	250 cpm	250 cpm	Yes	To 63	270 ch/s	60 ch/s	5, 7, 8
NCR 304	1 read	1500 cpm			1 read 1 punch	1800 ch/s	60 ch/s	5, 6, 7, 8 read 5, 7 punch
RCA 502	3 read 3 punch	400 cpm	150 cpm	Yes	2	1000 ch/s	10, 60, 300 ch/s	5, 6, 7, 8
RCA 503	3 read 3 punch	400 cpm	150 cpm	Yes	2	1000 ch/s	10, 60, 300 ch/s	5, 6, 7, 8
RCA 504	3 read 3 punch	400 cpm	150 cpm	Yes	2	1000 ch/s	10, 60, 300 ch/s	5, 6, 7, 8
Transac S-2000	To 20	2000 cpm	250 cpm	Yes	To 21	1000 ch/s	60 ch/s	5, 7, 8
Univac File Computer Model 1	To 10	150 cpm	150 cpm	Yes	To 10	200 ch/s	60 ch/s	5, 6, 7, 8
Univac II	None on line	N.A.	N.A.	N.A.	None	N.A.	N.A.	N.A.
Univac 1105	120 cpm	120 cpm	120 cpm	No		200 ch/s	60 ch/s	5, 7
USS 80/90 Tape	2	150 cpm 450 cpm	150 cpm	No	None	N.A.	N.A.	N.A.

Card and Tape Devices

The important features of card and tape devices, as shown by Table 7-11, are the operating speeds and the number of devices that can be connected.

Card-reading speeds range from 150 to 2,000 cards a minute. Punching speeds are typically 100 cards a minute, although some equipment punches 150 or 250 cards a minute. The number of card devices that can be connected to the computer ranges from 1 reader only to 63 possible devices. Plugboard format control is included for most computers.

Punched-paper-tape reading speeds range from 200 to 1,800 characters a second, whereas punching speeds are commonly 60 characters a second. From 1 to 63 paper-tape devices can be connected to some computers, although many make no provision whatever for paper-tape input and output. Those computers that do handle punched paper tape usually work with 5, 6, 7, or 8 channels.

FEATURES FOR EQUIPMENT APPRAISAL

Seven features of data-processing equipment—internal storage, secondary storage, operating speed, instruction repertoire, magnetic tape, buffers and printers, and card and tape devices—have been discussed. They were covered in some detail because all equipment has these features and concrete facts about them are available.

Nevertheless, other ways of describing equipment in order to appraise it are highly desirable. Management does not buy equipment because of computation, storage, and printing components, as such. Equipment is obtained because of its ability to meet application requirements. A single "index" to measure equipment and application requirements would be valuable. Selection might then be reduced to simple rules: one could find the index for the application, then find the indexes for the equipment available, and finally, select that set of equipment with an index closest to the application index.

Regrettably, no such index exists. A single index for equipment and problem appraisal is difficult to devise, for many features must be considered when trying to get the best match of equipment and application. Three features are discussed here—storage, speed, and versatility—at the risk of omitting some.

Storage and speed were discussed earlier from the viewpoint of equipment alone; here they are considered in terms that are common to both the equipment and the applications.

Storage

Computer storage was classified as internal and secondary storage, which was described in terms of size, transfer mode, and word content in Tables 7-1, -2, and -3.

Internal Storage.   High-speed, internal storage costs more per unit than secondary storage. Internal storage may be only a fraction of the total machine storage. One objective in computer design is to balance the cost of designing and building high-speed storage against the cost saved with its superior performance. Limited internal storage requires segmenting the data or the program, or both, to fit into storage. System efficiency may be reduced because other segments of the program and data must be transferred from secondary or external storage in order to continue computations.

Many medium-scale computers have only a few hundred or a thousand words of internal storage. Some large systems have only a few thousand words.

In recent years it has seemed that the demand for internal storage capacity would always outrun the available storage. Such large internal storage is now being designed and built that a programmer may have a large program completely at his command. But the size and complexity of business problems will continue to grow, so that even with extremely large storage, ingenious programming will be required for efficient operation.

Buffer Storage.   Buffer storage is a synchronizing element between two different forms, usually internal and external storage.

Buffer storage increases the effective operating speed by reducing the time required for data transfer between external and internal storage. So far as the computer is concerned, this time is merely what is required to read in or out of the high-speed buffer. Computation continues during the transfers between buffer storage and either secondary or external storage in some, but not in all, machines. Complete buffering for computer input and output permits concurrent operations of read, compute, and write. Some computers, as listed in Table 7-8, can obtain data from several input sources concurrently without interfering with other computer operations.

Record Length.   Record length affects the effective rate of data transfer to and from secondary and external storage. File records may be simple multiples or fractions of computer record length. If not, clever programming is required to avoid waste. Records on tape are separated by an inter-block gap of constant length for tape starting and stopping. The inter-block gap fraction of tape for systems using a fixed record length is determined by the manufacturer.

Variable-length records on tape have a constant-length inter-block gap, which will occupy a high fraction of tape if records are short. Long records have only a small fraction of tape for gaps. Effective data transfer rates are, therefore, affected by the fraction of tape occupied by gaps.

Storage capacity is related to the speed in each area of the over-all system. Furthermore, the capacity also determines the ultimate power of the equipment. Limited capacity may be more confining than the input and output speed limitations. To some extent, storage and speed can be traded for each other. Small storage may reduce effective operating speed, whereas large storage may fully utilize computer speed.

Speed

Perhaps the most significant feature of electronic equipment is its speed. High-speed operations make possible entirely new approaches to business-data processing. The central computer sets the pace for the entire system, but no single index of speed is wholly satisfactory. An effective balance of operating speeds is more important than an extreme speed for one component that leaves the system unbalanced. Internal processing may, for example, be fast and tape input slow, in relation to each other, so that effective processing speed is limited by the ability to read tapes.

In one early application, tape speed limited effective processing, but rewriting the program to do complete processing in one tape pass completely changed the balance of factors. Operations became limited by the computer because of intensive processing for one reading. Overall efficiency improved and computer use was increased as tape handling was reduced.

This example brings out three points concerning speed. First, equipment has slow as well as fast components. Second, any particular application may point up a weakness of the equipment. Third, program revision may exploit strong points of the equipment and improve efficiency.

Access.   Operating speeds, as shown earlier in Table 7-4, permit a rough rating of computers. Storage access is the time required to read the contents of a given location. Access time to data in core storage is ordinarily constant regardless of the location involved. But access for serial storage devices varies with the location involved and can be decreased by minimum latency (optimum) programming. Automatic routines are useful for optimizing manually written programs, although it is easy to overstress the time saving. An optimum program for 10,000 instructions may cut only a few minutes off the non-optimized program operating time. But if a program is used repeatedly, as in many business applications, a few minutes per cycle may become consequential.

A medium-scale computer using mass secondary storage may benefit little from optimum programming. Mechanical problems of moving the read-write heads from one data track to another may outweigh programming savings. Large-scale computers may have enough high-speed storage to hold a large segment of instructions and data. Other instructions and data need to be suitably stored for efficient transfer for processing.

Computing. Computing speeds for different computers need to be put into comparable terms both for the length of operands and for the number of addresses per instruction. The precise speed for an operation may depend on the number and size of digits in the operands. Memory access time, which may have an important effect on computing speed, is included by some manufacturers, but omitted by others, in the specification of computing speed.

A single figure for computing speed might be obtained, but it would be necessary to spell out in detail the ratio of various operations, length of numbers, range of digits, and access and storage requirements. One index to speed is the time required for performing $(A + B) \times C / D = E$ with all values in storage and E to be stored. The number of digits in each operand also needs to be specified.

Another operating speed index covers three additions, one multiplication, and three storage operations, which is thought to give a fair measure of speed, allowing for different instructions used in each machine. In short, an index is based on the time required to find the value of:

$$A + B = C; \; C + D + E = F; \; G \times H = I$$

Such a speed index takes no account of index registers, special logical operations, tape handling, or input-output. Furthermore, it is aimed at engineering and scientific problems so that it is not intended as a measure of over-all data-processing speed.

Another proposal for a speed index involves the time required for nine addition operations and one multiplication. It is considered more nearly typical of business processing requirements. Emphasis on addition and multiplication speed is warranted, not because these operations are important in business applications, but because the speed of these operations is indicative of computer operating speeds in general.

Effective speed of a particular application depends on many factors. Important factors that the user may be able to control are how many operations of each type are involved, the nature of operands, and whether the strong features of the equipment are emphasized.

Data-transfer Speed. System speed depends on more than computation speed. Transfer rates between internal and secondary storage determine, to some degree, the usefulness of such storage. The need for speed in either part or all of the equipment is related to each application. Early computers had limited and slow input-output facilities.

Emphasis was on intensive computation for a small amount of data to get a small output.

The severe lack of balance between internal speed and input-output ability of early scientific computers no longer exists. Data-transfer rates often exceed computational ability.

Versatility

"Versatility," the ability to turn easily from one task to another, is difficult to appraise. This is true even though general-purpose equipment can usually be switched quickly from one problem to another. A general-purpose computer deals with a new application by reading in another program and related data. Several factors bear on versatility, but it is difficult to combine these factors in one index of versatility.

Internal Storage Allocation. Storage can be allocated between instructions and data in any way desired in most computers, although a few have fixed storage space allocated to instructions and data, which may restrict programming and operating freedom.

Instructions stored in the data section must be transferred to the instruction section before execution. If high-speed storage is relatively limited, operating speed may be increased by reserving most of it for instruction storage.

Word-length. "Word-length" is the number of characters stored in one addressable location and transferred with a single instruction. As pointed out earlier, the length of a word may be either fixed (typically, ten or twelve characters) or variable. Long data words may take two or more computer words. Separate storage of short data words wastes space; but if short data words are put into one computer word, packing and unpacking are necessary.

If word-length is variable, one or more characters can be transferred at a time. Transfer is restricted only by the capacity of buffers, storage, arithmetic registers, and any other devices. Variable-length-word equipment is more flexible than fixed-length equipment, records are more compact, and programming may be simpler. Words can be kept separate and treated individually. Variable-length words avoid the need to pack short data words into one computer word and later extract the desired parts. But, the variable-length mode involves more computer circuitry than the fixed-length mode. It also usually involves a relatively slow serial mode of operation rather than a parallel mode.

Address Mode. The merits of single- and multiple-address modes must be appraised in relation to a particular application. Some new business processors have instruction commands designed especially to cope with problems that occur frequently in business.

Input-output Media. Versatility is also reflected in the ability to handle several types of input and output. They may be handled directly or through conversion equipment. The range of equipment handled may be narrow or broad. The merit of input-output flexibility must be considered in terms of specific applications; factors pertinent to this consideration are the methods of generating data, the work load involved, and the requirements for speed.

Multiplexing involves the simultaneous use of two or more input-output units. Nearly simultaneous operations are obtained by time sharing. Interrogation units, for example, either directly connected to the computer or operating independently, may facilitate operations.

PROBLEMS IN EQUIPMENT DESIGN

The factors necessary to yield balanced, efficient equipment deserve discussion. Efficiency involves compromises between the value of perfectly suited equipment and the cost of its design and construction.

The precise specification of equipment requirements is difficult because no application is typical. Furthermore, general-purpose equipment is used for a wide range of problems so that the requirements of many different applications must be considered. Available design and construction techniques limit some features of proposed equipment.

If computing speed is treated as fixed, the task is to make equipment with that particular speed handle a proposed application. Sufficient internal storage to supply instructions and data to arithmetic and control units may be of central importance. On the other hand, the use of slower-access storage devices has some bearing on the speed designed into arithmetic and control units.

The quantity of internal storage capacity required depends on the class of applications. In general, high-speed storage cost limits the quantity that is efficient for each situation. Some practical compromise must be made between (1) the "ideal" equipment that might have an infinite operating speed and storage capacity and (2) the available, economical equipment that has a limited speed and capacity.

Huge internal capacity may be emphasized. Large storage is considered ideal for holding all data and instructions for problems involving intensive computations. If internal storage will not hold all instructions and data, they must be brought in, processed, and put out.

Secondary storage, at some sacrifice in speed, augments internal storage. Data in secondary storage must be transferred to internal storage for processing. Magnetic-drum secondary storage is popular in large systems, because it provides quick access and high transfer rates to and from internal storage. Disks are popular for similar reasons.

Limited internal storage need not hinder computing speeds. Rapid data transfers between secondary and internal storage greatly facilitate processing. Many business applications—file maintenance for each item in inventory, for example—involve limited calculations repeated on new sets of data.

The labels, "scientific computer" or "business-data processor," are somewhat arbitrary and not always accurate. Business problems, contrary to popular opinion, often involve more complex programs and calculations than engineering and scientific problems. The ratio of computation to data input-output varies greatly for business problems. Interestingly, one medium-scale system designed for scientific work is the one most widely used for business problems.

Costs limit the size of internal and secondary storage. External storage—magnetic tape or punched cards—is used to keep costs down yet provide large storage. Auxiliary storage media are varied and data-transfer rates differ. It is often desirable to use off-line peripheral equipment to increase efficiency. Such equipment is economical for data transfer and conversion.

Medium-scale equipment compromises on over-all speed. Costs are reduced by using lower-speed storage and computational elements. Operating efficiency for many applications is not affected by the reduction in speed.

Medium-scale equipment design involves the same decisions that were discussed earlier for large-scale equipment. The term, "medium scale," is not entirely accurate. Such equipment may have as much flexibility, input-output facilities, and over-all storage capacity as more expensive equipment; but in one or more ways it has less capability than large-scale equipment.

SUMMARY

Components of electronic equipment are "assembled" into data processors. Lists of specifications do not make an acceptance-rejection table, for some important features may not fit into tabulations.

An "index" to measure application requirements and equipment capabilities would be highly desirable. Equipment selection might then be reduced to matching its index to the index for the application. An index that included enough features to make it realistic and useful would be complex. Regrettably, no such index, either simple or complex, exists. Equipment features have to be studied in order to match them with particular application requirements.

Internal storage consists of a magnetic core or a drum. The data code system is binary, binary-coded alphanumerical, binary-coded decimal, decimal, and bi-quinary; but alphabetic capacity is often smaller than numerical capacity. Storage capacity ranges from a few thousand to a couple of hundred thousand characters.

Word-length is often fixed at ten or twelve digits or letters, but is shorter in some equipment. Variable-length-field equipment treats each item of data, whether long or short, as a field in storage. Each approach—fixed- and variable-length field—has certain implications for equipment cost, data storage, and programming.

Input and output may be on-line or off-line. Magnetic tape and cards are used for on-line input and output, and tape and card content can be printed off-line to get readable copy. Consoles and direct-connected keyboards can be used for small volume on-line input. Printers, either low or high speed, may be used for on-line output.

Equipment speed can be appraised for a particular application in terms of computation, access, and data storage. Features of storage are addressability, speed, and quantity. Other aspects are record length and the use of buffer storage to permit concurrent operations.

Versatility is the ability to turn easily from one task to another. Factors in versatility are storage allocation, word-length, address mode, and input-output methods and speeds.

Efficient design is a compromise between the features that are desirable without regard to cost and the features that can be afforded even though less than ideal. The use of high-cost and low-cost components and the quantity of each are balanced to give the best processing facilities for the money. "Best processing facilities" must, of course, be defined in terms of the applications involved.

REFERENCES AND SUPPLEMENTAL READINGS

Adams, Charles W. "Automatic Data Processing Equipment: A Survey," pp. 125-139 in *Electronic Data Processing in Industry: A Casebook of Management Experience*, New York, American Management Association, 1955. This article contains a comprehensive survey of commercially available equipment as of 1955, together with a discussion of some of the problems in evaluating different systems. The basic data-processing operations are defined, and equipment for the mechanization of such operations is categorized as: (a) aids to manual data processing, e.g., adding machines; (b) semi-automatic punched-card equipment, e.g., key punch, tabulator, sorter; (c) small drum-type digital systems, e.g., Electro Data Datatron; and (d) large, general-purpose digital systems, e.g., Remington Rand Univac. Various types of magnetic storage devices, and the difficulties of obtaining large-capacity, random access storage are also discussed.

Berkeley, Edmund Callis, and Lawrence Wainwright. *Computers: Their Operation and Application*, New York, Reinhold Publishing Corp., 1956, 366 pp. This book is in many ways a sequel to *Giant Brains* by Berkeley. Sections one and two deal with automatic digital computing machines. Components and operation are covered in five chapters. Individual chapters cover reliability, advantages, and disadvantages of an automatic computer, and a check list of characteristics. Section three covers automatic analog computing machines, and section four deals with other types. A small relay computer (SIMON) built by Berkeley, is described in section six. Three chapters describe large-scale computers—Univac, IBM 700 series, and ERA type 1103. Applications are covered at some length. A section of miscellaneous chapters includes references, roster of manufacturers and computing services, and glossary of terms and expressions.

Eckert, W. J., and Rebecca Jones. *Faster Faster*, New York, McGraw-Hill Book Co., Inc., 1955, 160 pp. This brief book is subtitled, "A simple description of a giant electronic computer and the problems it solves." The IBM NORC (Naval Ordnance Research Calculator), built as a research and development computer, is described, rather than computers in general. One chapter each covers computer components. Other chapters cover operation, card and tape conversion, checking, maintenance, and problems to calculate. Appendices give NORC characteristics, operations, timing, flow charts, and examples of programming.

Weik, Martin H. *A Second Survey of Domestic Electronic Digital Computing Systems*, Washington, D.C., U. S. Department of Commerce, Office of Technical Services, 1957, 439 pp. This book presents a survey of commercially available and existing operational electronic digital computing and data-processing systems manufactured or operated in the United States. Large, intermediate, and small-scale complete systems are included, including both general and special-purpose equipment. The engineering and programming characteristics of 103 different systems are given, along with photos or sketches of representative installations. For each system presented, data are supplied under the following headings: application; numerical system; arithmetic unit; storage; input; output; circuit elements; entire system; checking features; power, space, and weight; production record; cost, price, and rental rate; personnel requirements; reliability and operating experience; future plans (of the manufacturer); installations; and additional features and remarks.

PART THREE

PROGRAMMING AND PROCESSING PROCEDURES

CHAPTER EIGHT

ADDITIONAL PROGRAMMING TECHNIQUES

The instruction repertoire for a hypothetical computer and the basic features of programming were covered in Chapter 3, which you may wish to review before studying this chapter to refresh your memory on the fundamentals.

The time and skill required to plan and prepare simple routines for a computer give some hint of the costs of preparing lengthy programs for actual business applications. Actual program preparation requires consideration of the nature and condition of input data, processing time, utilization of equipment, output requirements, and treatment of unusual situations. The cost of programming in an actual business environment is several dollars per program step (Gottlieb, 1954). The total cost of preparing a program for one business application is usually enormous because thousands of program steps are required. In fact, initial program preparation costs run to an appreciable fraction of the cost of equipment. Programming costs continue year after year since programs are never quite perfected and conditions change, as when management adopts new rules for managing the inventory or a state legislature enacts a withholding tax.

Any scheme that reduces the cost of programming, and thereby increases computer efficiency, is worth considering. Equipment manufacturers are continuously at work designing equipment better suited to customers' needs and devising more efficient plans for program preparation and operation. This chapter discusses some techniques that facilitate program preparation. Other areas to be covered are input and output format; programming to minimize machine running time; and errors, mistakes, and malfunctions that are likely to occur in data systems operations.

INPUT

The basic discussion of input and output programming in Chapter 3 assumed that the computer unit reads and stores data words of 7 characters exactly as they appeared on the input media, such as punched cards. Although any reasonable-size card is possible, and they do range from about twenty-two- to one hundred and thirty-five-column capacity, commonly used cards hold either 80 or 90 columns. Standardized cards are desirable to gain compatibility with punched-card systems and equipment already in use. Many computers rely heavily on punched cards for input and output.

Many computers are designed to store words longer than 7 characters—8, 10 or 12—or to handle variable-length fields. A one-to-one correspondence between the word-length for data input and for computer storage is not imperative.

Card Editing

Compatibility between the computer and peripheral card equipment is achieved either by editing devices associated with the peripheral units or by editing techniques programmed for the computer. In the case of punched-card equipment, editing is done after reading the card and before transferring the data to the storage buffers in the computer. Data from several fields on a card—columns designated for a particular purpose—can be combined into one computer word. Data from card fields containing fewer than the number of characters specified for a word in computer storage can be filled out with zeros or blanks to form full computer words. Of course, variable-field computers can deal directly with fields of any length on cards since there is no need to fit characters into words. It is also possible to shift, transpose, or suppress digits within a field or rearrange fields with devices for editing input. Blanks or zeros and plus or minus signs can be supplied where wanted in a word by the editing unit during input. Any vacant positions in a numerical word that are not wanted must be filled with zeros (not blanks) during read-in so that the word can be manipulated arithmetically.

Some input, especially key instruction words, must adhere to a specified format. You will recall that Chapter 3 described how the first word—the word-count and location word—on a program load card has a format different from other instructions, for it is numerical with a minus sign. The two cards that load the routine and the transfer card both start with an instruction word and a plus sign. Since the first word on a card may be used in any one of several different ways, it must be punched explicitly and cannot be filled in by editing during read-in.

The arrangement of instructions on a card may be such that there are some spare columns. The spare columns can be used to hold identifying data or remarks. For example, if there are six remaining columns after punching as many instructions as possible in a card, they might be used to identify the program deck, such as LOAD 1 and LOAD 2 for the load-routine cards and SEQCHK for each card in a sequence check routine. Furthermore, two columns might be reserved (if available) for sequence numbering the cards (0 through 99) to help keep them in order for input. The total of these sequence numbers can be punched into the transfer card to allow a check on peripheral equipment during read-in to assure that all cards are loaded. Similar schemes can be used for identifying and sequence numbering input data cards to guard against loss of cards or mixups between decks.

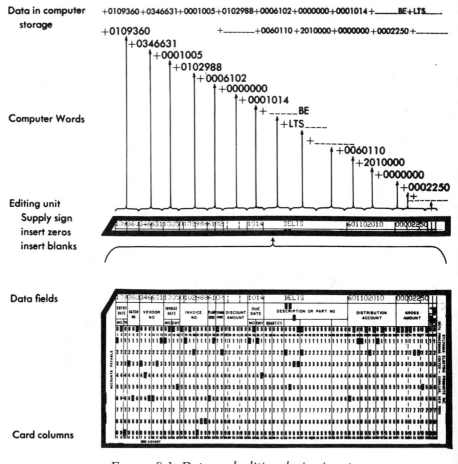

FIGURE 8-1. *Data card editing during input*

Card Format

Figure 8-1 shows how a data card is edited during read-in to store individual fields in separate words inside the computer, or, in some cases, to store two short data fields in one word.

Wired plugboards are commonly used for editing card input. A wire in the reading device connects each card column with the desired character position in the buffer storage; characters can be transposed or shifted by arranging the wires in appropriate fashion. The wires may also be used to connect certain stored characters (blanks, plus, minus, and zero) with desired positions in buffer storage. Card characters not to be read into storage are simply not wired.

A plugboard wired for a particular card format is retained for re-use to save the trouble of rewiring the board each time. Clever editing saves card-reading time, as well as computer time for packing or unpacking characters that need to be rearranged for efficient computer processing. Similar plugboard devices are used for editing data for card-punching units.

Units for handling magnetic tape may not have editing facilities. Instead, editing and rearranging data may be done in separate stages by peripheral equipment, such as card to tape converters, or by off-line printers operating from magnetic tape. Computer programs are also used for further editing, and for rearranging data during input and results during output operations.

TIMING AND MINIMUM LATENCY

Efficient use of a computer is an important criterion of good programming. The amount of time required to handle an application depends on the time the computer takes for a complete operation, the number of operations in a loop, and the number of times each loop is performed.

The complete operation time for an instruction includes the time to obtain the instruction, obtain the operand(s), and execute the instruction. Representative times required for a medium-scale computer to execute some instructions and to obtain or store a word in memory are as follows:

Time to obtain and execute an instruction

Add	2 milliseconds
Subtract	2 milliseconds
Clear and add	2 milliseconds
Compare	2 milliseconds
Multiply	7 + (0.5 x sum of digits in multiplier)
Divide	7 + (0.5 x sum of digits in quotient)
Shift	2.5 + (0.1 x number of positions shifted)
Conditional jump	3 milliseconds
Unconditional jump	2.5 milliseconds

Time to obtain or store a word in drum storage

Average   2.5 milliseconds
Maximum   5 milliseconds

Instruction execution and storage access times are useful guides in writing programs to minimize running time. For example, in a multiplication operation less time is required if the operand with the digits having the smaller sum is used as the multiplier. The sum of digits in the operand 121212 is 9, whereas in the number 898989 it is 51. Multiplying these two operands takes 11.5 milliseconds—7 + (.5 x 9)—with 121212 as the multiplier, but 32.5 milliseconds—7 + (.5 x 51)—with 898989 as the multiplier.

Minimum Latency

Another facet of timing is the choice of locations for storing data and instructions. The access time for a word in a drum location about to come under the reading head may be about 0.1 milliseconds. Access time to a location that has just passed the heads is about 5 milliseconds in high speed drums. Program running time can vary greatly according to the care used in assigning storage locations.

Access time consists of latency and word time. Latency is the waiting time before the reading heads locate the first bit or character in a particular storage location on a drum or disk. Latency can be reduced by clever assignment of storage locations so that the next word wanted comes under the reading heads when it is wanted. Word time is the time required to read or write one word. Word time is fixed by the manufacturer during computer design when he decides on the drum or disk speed and the spacing of data along a track. A program consisting of instructions spaced in adjoining word locations around a drum or disk will take a long time to execute because the next instruction will go by while the prior instruction is being executed. Latency time for instructions stored in serial-access memories can increase program running time enough to warrant using other arrangements for storing instructions. Minimum latency programming, often called "optimum programming," involves the arrangement of data and instructions in storage in a way that reduces waiting time. There are several approaches to achieving minimal latency. The instructions in a routine can be spaced just far enough apart (in terms of time) in storage that the next instruction becomes available after the preceding instruction is executed. Since a drum or disk rotates at a constant speed, the time allotted to the execution of one instruction is proportional to the distance along a track to the next instruction to be executed. For simplicity, the distance along a track in serial storage can be measured as the number of words of data that can be stored in that space. Spacing instructions a constant number of words apart along a track,

8 words apart, for instance, instead of in adjoining locations, is one approach to getting minimal latency. This constant spacing of instructions shortens latency for all instructions that can be executed while the 8 intervening words pass under the reading head. Some computers are designed to apply automatically the constant spacing scheme to instructions that the programmer writes with addresses that would seem to place them in consecutive storage locations. For example, instructions written with addresses 000 through 015 might be placed as follows around a track that stores 100 words:

Address Used by Programmer	Actual Storage Address	
000	000)	Spacing instructions with 8 locations
001	009)	between instruction words
002	018	
003	027	
004	036	
005	045	
006	054	
007	063	
008	072	
009	081	
010	090	
011	099	
012	008	$(108 - 100 = 008)$
013	017	
014	026	
015	035	

Another way to achieve the same result is to spread addresses around the drum so that neighboring storage spaces on the drum have addresses like 000, 012, 024, 036, 048, 060, 072, 084, 096, 001, 013, 025, and so forth.

Some computers are designed with an instruction word to hold two addresses: one for the operand in the instruction being executed, and the other designating the location of the next instruction to be executed. For example, the instruction STA 077   005 might mean: "Store the accumulator content in location 077 and get the next instruction from location 005." Location 005 is 28 words beyond location 077, if there are 100 words around a track. The next instruction can be located a variable distance away to minimize latency. A computer using an instruction format in which every instruction includes the location of the next instruction is sometimes called a "one and one-half address" computer, although some people prefer to call it a "two address" computer.

There are several methods for actually placing data around a drum or disk to minimize latency. The programmer can manually lay out the instructions with suitable spacing; but there are also special routines, which are discussed later in this chapter, to have the computer space the instructions automatically. In this way, a program for handling the clerical tasks of storing location assignments actually aids the programmer in writing more efficient programs. The idea of programs being used to prepare other programs is also discussed later in this chapter.

ERRORS, MISTAKES, AND MALFUNCTIONS

Errors, mistakes, and malfunctions are different factors in giving incorrect results. An error is the difference between the accurate quantity and its calculated value that arises because of the numerical methods used. A mistake is a human blunder that occurs in program preparation, coding, data transcription, and computer operations. A malfunction is a failure in equipment operation.

Errors

Rounding errors, such as treating the average unit cost of a stock item as $467.38 instead of $467.375, are often caused by the finite lengths of computer operating elements. Often numbers must be rounded to fit into storage locations that can hold only 10 or 12 digits. The error from rounding is relatively more important for short numbers, say of 1 or 2 digits, than it is for long numbers, say of 6 or 8 digits. The most commonly used rounding scheme—add 5 to the right of the last digit to be retained, make any carry, and drop unwanted digits—may introduce a large error. For example, workers in a factory may report job time to the nearest half hour. Reported times of 0.5, 1.5, and 2.5 hours are rounded to 1, 2, and 3 hours by following the usual rule for rounding. Either more sophisticated rules are required for rounding or the rounding should be postponed by retaining more digits throughout the operations than are wanted in the answer.

Addition of two numbers may yield a total that exceeds the capacity of a word in storage. One remedy is to test for the occurrence of overflow after performing the addition and, if it occurs, to shift both numbers one position to the right before repeating the operation. The net effect of overflow correction, as described in Chapter 3, is to discard the right-hand digit.

Sometimes it is necessary to use double precision arithmetic to obtain more digits in the answer than seems possible with fixed-length storage locations and arithmetic registers. Operands longer than a computer word are split into two parts to place them in adjoining storage locations and treat them as semi-independent operands. The results of calculations are first stored in separate words and then joined together to yield a precise answer. For example, the numbers 42,864 and 75,793 are to be added in a computer with fixed word-length that, for simplicity, is assumed to be *three* characters. Double precision arithmetic involves splitting each data word into two words for storage: 42,864 becomes 42 and 864; 75,793 becomes 75 and 793. First, add the 864 and 793 to get 1657. Store the 657 and retain the 1, which appears as an overflow digit. The sum of 42 and 75 is 117 plus the overflow 1 giving 118. An overflow occurring when adding the left-hand parts requires the usual remedy of shifting all operands one position to the right and repeating the operation. The two parts of the sum are then put together to get 118,657. In tabular form, double precision addition is as follows:

Numbers	Split into two parts		
42,864	42	864	
75,793	75	793	
	117	1657	Separate sums
	1		Attach right part over-
	118	657	flow to left-hand part
	118,657		Join parts to get total

Double precision operations are also used for subtraction, multiplication, and division. The fact that significant digits disappear when taking the difference of two numbers that are about the same size, for example, $123,479 - 123,456 = 23$, demands care in order to keep the desired degree of precision in the remainder. It is easy to treat the remainder as zero, if enough left-hand digits disappear so that rounding may destroy whatever precision the answer had.

The sequence of performing arithmetical operations affects the precision of an answer. Multiplication should be done before division, where possible, to retain precision.

The numbers encountered in accounting applications seldom exceed the length of computing elements or storage. On the other hand, in statistical or operations-research calculations, long numbers frequently arise that require caution to obtain suitable precision in the answers. The loss of precision in business processing due to the computing methods used may be important only where numbers are shortened in order to pack several items into one computer word so that the rounding off of too many digits results.

When deciding how many digits to use for an item, the programmer should first check the degree of accuracy necessary in the results as specified, preferably, by the user of the output, or, as a second choice, by the systems analyst. The effect of a certain error can be determined by tracing through the numerical operations, which may indicate that it is sometimes imperative to increase the precision of both input data and numerical computing methods. In other cases, less precision is needed so that fewer digits in the data and some short cuts in computing are permissible.

Mistakes

Mistakes are human blunders that result in incorrect data, computer instructions, or manual operations.

Mistakes in transcribing input data and instructions into machine-readable form may be detected by verifying key-punching or tape-writing operations. Totals developed in an earlier stage of processing are often useful for checking the accuracy of input data. Mistakes in punching a program are sometimes detected on printed copies of the card data.

The original programmer or another programmer may study a program and trace through test cases to isolate mistakes; desk-checking can disclose many programming mistakes. Mistakes can be divided into two classes. Some cause the computer to stop before completing the program, while others do not stop operations, but yield a wrong answer or no answer at all.

Examples of mistakes that halt program execution are:

1. Invalid operation codes
2. Incorrect instruction addresses
3. Arithmetical operations on alphabetic characters
4. Unexpected overflow
5. Wiring mistakes in program plugboards

Other types of mistakes may not halt the program, but allow the program to continue beyond the instruction containing the mistake. For example, a jump instruction with an incorrect address may transfer program control to a fragment of some previous program left in the machine or to an unexpected part of the present program. Many instructions may be executed before the computer encounters an instruction or data word that halts operations.

Mistakes that may yield the wrong answer without halting program execution are:

1. Input data inaccuracies
2. Incorrect operation codes or addresses in instructions
3. Misalignment of decimal points in numbers operated on arithmetically
4. Logical mistakes in the program because of incorrect solution method

Built-in checks and program testing are necessary to detect mistakes that give wrong answers without halting operations. A typical

built-in check is a special operation to determine whether an intermediate result is within specified limits. For example, weekly gross pay
can be computed and then tested to check whether it is a positive
amount, but less than $200. Amounts outside the limits of 0 and $200
may point to a mistake in decimal point (450 hours instead of 45.0)
or in logic. Where a check number, such as a total, is available from a
prior operation, it is useful to program a zero-balance check to find
whether the newly computed total minus the prior total equals zero.
If the difference between the check numbers is zero, the program continues; otherwise, a segment of the program can be repeated, the
occurrence of the check failure printed on the supervisory console,
and computer operations halted, as desired.

Testing a computer program for a business application involves
using data for which the solution is known. One fairly common test is to
run the computer program in parallel with an existing system long
enough to detect and eliminate discrepancies. In some cases only part
of the data need be processed in parallel; but in others all data should
be handled both ways for an extended period. Devising a thorough test
for all parts of the program is sometimes a major task; but since program testing serves as a training and testing ground for personnel, the
time spent on it may be justified.

Malfunctions

A malfunction is a failure in equipment operation. Some malfunctions are detected automatically by the computer and will either transfer control to a special routine or halt operations. Other malfunctions
can be detected only through checks included in the program.

Malfunctions are rare in properly operating equipment, but a high
fraction of those that do occur plague input and output operations.
The gain or loss of a pulse results in an invalid character code being
transmitted. A parity-code scheme, as discussed in Chapter 2, is often
used to detect invalid characters. The machine is stopped and an indicator light turned on to show where the malfunction occurred. Some
computers use the parity-bit scheme with data on cards or tape but
drop it in internal storage because of the small risk of losing a bit in
internal storage. Other computers are designed with the opposite approach of using parity-bits internally but not on cards or tape.

Tape-reading malfunctions are often transient, so that a second or
third attempt at reading is satisfactory. Some computers provide for
automatic rereading of tape, if the first attempt does not pass the parity
test. Input cards are read at two stations in the card reader and the
data rejected if there is any discrepancy. Editing devices on input-
output units may also perform special checks to determine whether a
numerical field has any alphabetic data in it or if a sign is missing.

Malfunctions that occur during output have more serious implications than input malfunctions. Faulty tape or card output may not be discovered until the tape is used in the next processing cycle—which may be an hour, day, or week later. To guard against malfunctions during output operations, another reading station may be used to read the actual content of cards or tape and compare with the content of storage or buffer for identity. This proofreading test must be passed for each card punched or tape block written, or operations are halted. A simpler scheme, called "echo-checking," merely determines whether the data just written will pass the parity test.

Some computers check the parity of characters each time a word is handled inside the machine. Others have data checks at key points in a program. Further, at short intervals of five seconds, for instance, contents of all storage locations may be parity tested. If the test is failed, the program is returned to a prior checkpoint where the contents were stored for use in case of subsequent malfunction.

Selected types of operations can be tested by two kinds of schemes designed into the computer:

1. Parallel testing involves simultaneous execution of an instruction along two paths in the equipment and an equality test.
2. Serial testing involves one set of circuits used to repeat an operation and perform an equality test. For example, the product of 345 x 987 can be compared with the product of 987 x 345 by subtracting one product from the other and testing for zero.

Parallel tests that are built into the equipment for selected operations are outside a programmer's control. Serial tests may be included in the equipment or devised by programmers when writing programs.

Special checking programs, also called "engineering decks," are commonly used to check the operation of all instructions and computer units just after the power is turned on. These tests are executed to detect malfunctions when they are most likely to occur and before computations are started.

Malfunctions are rare and may occur once in several million or billion operations. Built-in checks are best suited to detecting malfunctions in business-data processing. Frequently, the correct results for a business application are not known before processing is completed, although results for limited sample cases may be obtained by other means. Programming business applications may be so intricate that devising alternate checking programs (in effect, preparing two programs) to guard against malfunctions is inefficient. From the user's viewpoint, it is desirable to have the manufacturer design checking features into the equipment. Built-in checks increase effective computer speed by performing checking operations while a single program is being executed.

The alternate scheme of detecting malfunctions by programming—to perform the essential features of an operation in two different ways—increases programming work and computer running time. As an example of a programmed check, it is suggested that the accuracy of multiplication be verified by a second multiplication involving slightly different numbers. Assume that the problem is to compute inventory value for the following quantities and prices:

Stock Number	Quantity	Price	Value
1234	4	2	8
8765	8	7	56
2391	3	19	57
	15		121

A "proof figure" scheme for programmed checking of multiplication uses an artificial basis for either the price or quantity so that different numbers are involved in the multiplication; correction is then made to eliminate the effect of the artificial base (Price Waterhouse, n.d.). By introducing an artificial price base of 20, the calculation would become:

Stock Number	Quantity	Artificial Basis		Price	Proof Cost	Quantity Proof Cost
1234	4	20	–	2 =	18	72
8765	8	20	–	7 =	13	104
2391	3	20	–	19 =	1	3
	15					179

The quantity 15 multiplied by the artificial base of 20 gives a product of 300. The original value of 121 plus the proof cost of 179 gives a total of 300, which proves the coincidence of the answer by two different program routes.

More important than the occasional incorrect results from malfunction of equipment is the risk that it may be out of operation for several hours during testing and repair. "Down-time" is likely to be high at first because of injury to equipment during shipping and the early breakdown of defective components. After the initial break-in period, most automatic data-processing equipment is extremely reliable. The availability of similar equipment nearby for emergency use on a reciprocal basis furnishes some protection against protracted down-time. Scheduling operations at 80 to 90 per cent of capacity, after allowing for preventive maintenance, permits making up most down-time. Priority applications can be kept on schedule, despite excessive down-time, by rearranging schedules to postpone less urgent jobs and checking out new programs.

Errors, mistakes, and malfunctions are usually far less troublesome in automatic systems than in manual systems. Accuracy and reliability are higher in automatic systems because systems design receives more emphasis, "special-case" treatment is minimized, "rush" handling is reduced, and people are less directly involved.

SPECIAL OPERATIONS

The repertoire of instructions included for the hypothetical computer described in Chapter 3 was purposely kept short for illustrative purposes. Some computers have command lists as short as 8 instructions. Other computers decode as many as 100 or 200 instructions, although a large fraction of such a large repertoire may be devoted to special features of input-output operations. Each new instruction designed into the computer by the manufacturer increases program versatility and power; but a bigger instruction repertoire has certain costs associated with it. Computer design and construction costs increase because of additional circuits. The cost of training programmers increases because they must master all the skills involved in handling a longer list of instructions. Programming costs are reduced to the extent that one comprehensive instruction can do the work of several simpler ones. There is some risk, however, that more complicated instructions may lead to more programming mistakes.

At the other extreme, a computer can be designed to operate with minimal instructions: subtract, store, conditional jump, and shift. Operating programs can be built from these four instructions, plus input and output instructions; but such programs will be extremely long and appear to be inefficient. For example, the operation of clear accumulator and add can be accomplished by means of two store and four subtract orders, as follows:

STA 100 Store content of accumulator—no matter what the content happens to be—in location 100.

SUB 100 Subtract content of location 100 from accumulator to get 0 in accumulator.

SUB 267 Subtract the operand in location 267, which puts the operand in the accumulator but with the opposite sign (– for +, and + for –).

STA 100 Store the operand, now with an opposite sign, in location 100.

SUB 100 Subtract the operand (with opposite sign) to get 0 in the accumulator.

SUB 100 Repeat the subtraction of the operand (with opposite sign) which yields the operand with correct sign in the accumulator.

The point involved here is an important one for computer designers and users: the added cost of designing and building more instructions must be balanced against the cost of doing programming with either too few or too many instructions. The problem is similar to choosing between basic and standard English: either one might serve, but each has characteristics that make it preferable under certain conditions.

Jump Instructions

Most medium- and large-scale computers have more instructions for transferring control or jumping to another part of the program than were described in Chapter 3 for the hypothetical computer. The jump-if-negative instruction distinguishes between the negative and positive outcomes, but it may be ambiguous about how to treat a zero outcome unless zero is defined as either plus zero or minus zero.

Inclusion of a jump-if-zero instruction in the computer repertoire, along with a jump-if-negative one, eliminates the ambiguity of distinguishing between the negative, zero, and positive conditions. If both the negative and zero tests fail, then the item being tested must be positive.

A jump-if-positive instruction is often included in the repertoire in addition to the jumps for negative and zero conditions. Having these three tests available permits arranging them in any sequence desired without being restricted to using two and detecting the third outcome by elimination.

The instruction to set an index and jump is an entirely different kind of jump instruction. The number in the instruction counter, which keeps track of the instruction to be executed, is stored in an index register as an exit point for later use as an entry point to the main program at the following instruction. When a set-index-and-jump instruction is executed, control is transferred to the location specified in the jump instruction in order to carry out a subroutine that was stored starting at that point. A subroutine is a computer routine already prepared and tested to perform some desired operation. It can be placed wherever desired in storage and used when wanted in conjunction with the main program. After a subroutine is executed, it provides for returning program control to the main program at the instruction following the exit point which is stored in the index. Subroutines can be used repeatedly by means of suitable initializing operations, which set up conditions for jumps from the main routine to the subroutine and for returns from the subroutine to the main routine.

Use of the set-index-and-jump instructions to jump from the main routine to a subroutine and back to the main routine can be illustrated as follows:

Main Program		Subroutine	
Location	Content	Location	Content
060	Any		
061	instructions		
062	desired		
063	. . .		
064	SIJ A980 ⟶	980	Subroutine
065	Continuation ◄	981	instructions
066	of main	982	. . .
067	routine	983	. . .
. . .		984	JMP A001
. . .			
113	SIJ A980 ⟶		

When used the first time, the SIJ A980 instruction sets index register A to 064, which is where the instruction is located in the main program, and jumps to location 980. The subroutine starting at location 980 is then executed. At the end of the subroutine is a JMP A001 instruction to return control to the main program at the location following the exit from the main routine, which is 065 in the first case. Later, at location 113, another SIJ A980 transfers control to the subroutine to execute it on different data and then return control to the main routine. The nature and use of subroutines is described more fully later in this chapter.

Table Look-up

A table look-up instruction is designed into some computers to perform the same operation that a person does to find a desired item in a table. A table consists of reference factors, called "arguments," and entries in the body of the table, called values of a "function." Or, in everyday terms, you look for what you know in order to find what you want. Tables arranged with arguments in ascending order in storage can be searched starting from a certain location, such as 100, when an address between 100 and 199 is used in the table look-up order. The look-up operation ends when it finds the argument that is equal to or just higher than the known argument. The function corresponding to the argument looked up in the table is the desired value. Computerwise, table look-up starts by placing the known argument in a specified location, such as the M-Q register. Upon completion of the table look-up instruction, the *address* of the desired function is copied into a specific location, such as the accumulator. The address of the desired function can be incorporated into instructions so that the function itself can be used.

An example will show how a table look-up instruction might operate. The problem is to update the costs for each department where departmental numbers are stored in locations 100 to 148 and the corresponding departmental costs are stored in locations 150 to 198. A high value ZZZZZZ is stored in location 149 to terminate the table.

Location	Department Number (Argument)	Location	Department Costs (Function)
100	16	150	$ 4,259.67
101	17	151	2,683.45
102	23	152	10,200.00
103	27	153	1,449.58
.	.	.	.
.	.	.	.
.	.	.	.
.	.	.	.
148	85	198	9,295.73
149	ZZZZZZ		

Cost transactions consist of two words: department number and dollar amount. The following program will update the cost table for a transaction that involves department 23, in the amount of $350.00, assuming that the table and program are already in storage.

Location	Content		Explanation
. . .	. . .		Read a transaction into storage: department number in location 001 and cost in location 002.
010	CAM	001	Clear accumulator and M-Q registers and add the number of the department for next transaction into M-Q.
011	TLU	150	The table look-up operation starts with the argument stored in location 100 since the address in the TLU order is between 100 and 199. The look-up operation ends with the number 152 in the accumulator, when the argument stored in location 102—which is 023— equals the new department number—23—stored in the M-Q.
012	STD	015	Store the address portion of the accumulator (right-hand three digits only) in locations 015 and 016.
013	STD	016	
014	CAA	002	Clear the accumulator and add the transaction amount—$350.00.
015	ADD ( )		The addresses of these "dummy" instructions are filled in by the instructions in locations 012 and 013. Add contents of location 152—10,200.00—to get a total of 10,550.00, and store the total in location 152.
016	STO ( )		

017   . . .   Other instructions to test for the end of updating
. . .   . . .   operation, or to return to read in the next transaction.

The table look-up routine for updating account balances involves the use of a new type of instruction—a store-address instruction, STD y x. This instruction stores the right-hand three digits of the accumulator in the address part of the location specified without changing the operation part of the instruction. The store-address instruction stores only part of the content of the accumulator, whereas the STA y x instruction stores the whole content of it. The effect of a store-address instruction can be achieved by adding together the dummy instruction and the word containing the desired address.

"Dummy" instructions—those originally written without addresses—to be filled in as part of the program are an interesting feature of program preparation. Situations also arise on rare occasions in which the *operation* part of the instruction (which is usually expressed as a number inside the computer) is either constructed or modified during the execution of a program.

Scaling. The location of the decimal point within operands must be considered in all arithmetical operations. Decimal (or binary or octal) points must be aligned before addition or subtraction in order to get a correct result. Multiplication and division do not require alignment but do involve keeping track of the decimal point in the result. Overflow arises when numbers are too large to fit into storage. One method for coping with these problems is to scale the operands before calculations are made.

Scaling involves altering units in which variables are expressed to bring all magnitudes within the capacity of the computer or the routine in use. Units are selected so that the largest resulting number can be calculated in registers and stored in memory. It is the programmer's responsibility to keep track of how many digits will occur in a result. If capacity is about to be exceeded, the operands can be shifted to the right and the operation repeated. A loss of digits at the right of the operands is preferable to losing digits on the left of a result. Scaling operands is troublesome for a programmer and increases the computer operating time over that required, if the numbers can be handled by ordinary arithmetic.

Floating Point Arithmetic

The programmer can keep track of decimal points in arithmetical operations for numbers that are within the range of the computer's word capacity, say, .0000001 to 9999999. Shift instructions are used to line up numbers for addition and subtraction operations and to bring products and quotients into "bounds" for further operations. The programmer must anticipate the location of decimal points in the original data, the intermediate result, and the final answer; doing this requires extra programming, and anticipating decimal points is often difficult. One group of special instructions available in many computers deals with floating point arithmetic, which automatically handles decimal points in arithmetical operations.

Extending the example of the hypothetical computer, it would handle floating point numbers as fractions between .10000 and .99999, with an exponent to keep track of the number of places the decimal points were shifted in order to make the numbers fit within this range. To avoid negative exponents in the computer word, an exponent of zero is often considered equal to 50, an exponent of 1 is 51, an exponent of 7 is 57, an exponent of −4 is 46, and so forth. Examples of numbers are:

Ordinary Number	Floating Point		Computer Word	
	Fraction	Exponent	Fraction	Exponent
+ 5327.	+.5327	+4	+ 5 3 2 7 0	5 4
− 368592.	+.368592	+6	− 3 6 8 5 9	5 6
+ 0.4375	+.4375	0	+ 4 3 7 5 0	5 0
− 0.00298	+.298	−2	− 2 9 8 0 0	4 8

A computer equipped with circuitry for floating point operations lines up floating point numbers (so that exponents are equal) before addition or subtraction. In multiplication, the exponents are added and adjustment is made for the extra 50 that results in the exponent. In division, the exponent of the divisor is subtracted from the exponent of the dividend. The product or quotient is adjusted to a fraction and the appropriate exponent.

Computers with a built-in floating point feature also perform arithmetical operations in fixed point or ordinary arithmetic, as described earlier. Floating point operations, if provided for the hypothetical computer considered here, could be defined as follows:

Code	Explanation
FAD y x	Floating point *add* the content of location x, indexable, to the content of the accumulator. Content of storage location x is unchanged. *Both* numbers must be in the floating point mode.

Floating point subtraction, multiplication, and division could be similarly defined and given the codes FSU y x, FMU y x, and FDI y x. Floating point arithmetic is more convenient than fixed point arithmetic for handling numbers with varying decimal points, but there are several objections to its use. Floating point operations are slower than fixed point arithmetical operations. The exponent takes up two digit positions in the computer word, which limits the number of digits available for data. Furthermore, there is usually some difficulty in handling both input and output data. If data are put into the computer in the fixed point mode, it is necessary to use extra operations to convert them to the floating point mode; and reconversion before output may be necessary. On the other hand, original preparation in the floating point mode increases the risk of clerical mistakes. Fixed point arithmetic is usually preferable in most business systems that have a high volume of input and output. Arithmetical operations are unimportant enough in most business-data processing that the added input and output problems and slower computer speeds associated with floating point arithmetic are not justified. Operations research calculations may, on the other hand, be facilitated by floating point arithmetic features of the computer because of the range of size of numbers and the difficulty of anticipating decimal point location after every calculation.

When using the floating point mode, it is necessary to arrange operations in a suitable sequence so that precision is not lost through subtractions resulting in loss of significant digits. Apparent precision in a result may be spurious because some meaningless digits may arise. The occurrence of meaningless digits is detrimental to floating point arithmetic because the programmer often neglects to think about the size of numbers when programming in this mode and overlooks the possibility of spurious accuracy.

PSEUDO-CODES AND RELATIVE ADDRESSES

Programming techniques have been discussed in terms of alphabetic abbreviations for instructions and numerical designations for storage locations. This scheme was chosen for simplicity. Other possible schemes—numerals to identify instructions and letters for storage locations or some combination of numerals and letters—are preferable in some ways.

Pseudo-codes

The name "pseudo-code" is used for an arbitrary code designed to aid a programmer in writing programs. Each pseudo-code instruction must be translated into computer code in order to run the program in the computer.

The instruction codes described for the hypothetical computer in Chapter 3 consisted of two or three letters for each instruction. Some examples are ADD (add), SHL (shift left), STA (store accumulator), and RC (read a card). To make the instructions easy to remember, the code letters were selected from the description of the operation— SHL is the abbreviation for *shift left*. When the pseudo-code is devised so that people can remember it easily, it is called a "mnemonic" code.

Only a limited number of instructions were developed for the hypothetical computer—so few, in fact, that each could be identified by a single letter of the alphabet. Using three letters to identify an instruction when one letter would serve is wasteful, for more characters must be written into the program, prepared for input, and stored in the computer, all of which increase program execution cost. The three instructions of add, shift left, and store accumulator might be abbreviated A, L, and S, and still retain some of their mnemonic value. If the number of instructions designed into the computer exceeds 26, some odd codes arise if each code is restricted to one of the 64 characters that can be represented by 6 bits. For example, Univac II codes for the three operations, add, shift left, and store are: AO, ;, and HO.

Computer designers prefer to use numbers for instruction codes. Two-digit numbers permit representation of 100 instructions—00 through 99. Numerals can be manipulated more readily than letters if one wishes to modify an instruction by, say, addition or multiplication operations performed on the code part itself. The programmer's interest in a mnemonic code for writing programs must be balanced against the computer designer's demands for a numerical code to simplify internal circuitry. As often happens, a difference of interest is compromised by giving each group at least part of what it wants— mnemonic codes for the programmer and numerical codes for the computer designer. For example, both types of codes are used with the IBM 650, as follows:

Operation	Mnemonic	Numerical
Add (to upper accumulator)	AU	10
Shift left	SLT	35
Store (upper) accumulator	STU	21

A programmer can write in a mnemonic code, which is also called "symbolic" code, and then convert to the numerical code by writing the corresponding numerical instruction code before the program is read into the computer. Since the one-for-one conversion of letters to numerals is basically a clerical task, it can be done by the computer. A special program called a "symbolic assembly program" can be used to perform the conversion. But assembly programs, as is pointed out later in this chapter, usually do much more than merely convert instruction codes from alphabetic to numerical equivalents.

Symbolic Addresses

Programming examples given thus far have used absolute addresses—the actual locations in storage of particular units of data— that can be interpreted directly by the control unit of the computer.

Programs written with absolute addresses appear simple and efficient for short programs. The computer assigns the same address as the programmer, which facilitates comparing the contents of storage with the original program at any time. Consider, for example, a three-instruction loop in locations 067 to 069 for modifying the address part of the instruction CAA x in location 070 just before it is executed.

Location	Content		Explanation
067	CAA	070	Clear accumulator and add instruction to be modified.
068	ADD	010	Add the content of location 010, which is the constant 006.
069	STA	070	Store modified instruction in location 070.
070	CAA	( )	Initial value 200 to be increased by 006 each loop.

The simplicity of absolute addresses has its price. If a mistake is found and correction requires inserting another instruction between 067 and 068, unless adequate care is used the instructions in locations 068 to 070 may be shifted up by one to give the following programs:

Location	Content		Explanation
067	CAA	070	
068			New instruction inserted here.
069	ADD	010	
070	STA	070	This instruction will be modified by this revised routine.
071	CAA	( )	This instruction is not changed at all.

The changed program does not do anything that was originally intended. The STA 070 instruction in location 070 will be modified by instructions 067 and 069. Modification of the instruction in location 070 is diabolical because it stores *itself* in location 076 when the loop is executed the first time, in 082 in the second loop, and so forth. Chaos may result if the programmer fails to change the address parts of some instructions when the instructions to which they refer are shifted about in storage. Incredible havoc can occur in a long program because the number of addresses to be corrected mushrooms.

Absolute addresses also hinder the use of a subroutine in more than one main program because the addresses must be changed to fit each particular program. Furthermore, the use of absolute addresses makes it difficult for two or more programmers to work on one program. Each programmer is unsure which location the other is using for certain data, and it is difficult to combine the segments of the program.

Symbolic addresses are one remedy for some of the deficiencies growing out of absolute addresses. A "symbolic address" is a label assigned to a certain word in a routine for convenience of the programmer, and is independent of the location of a word within a routine. A symbolic address consists merely of some unique characters—letters, numerals, or both—assigned as the address of a selected word in a routine. Only those addresses that are referred to in the program have to be identified by a symbolic address. These include the first words in blocks of data or of instructions and other specified words. Words that follow are stored in sequence following the selected word. Symbolic addresses must be converted to absolute addresses for running the program; but this conversion can be done by the computer, as explained later in this chapter under "Automatic Programming."

The fragment of a program given earlier for address modification can be rewritten with symbolic addresses to illustrate the ideas involved.

Location	Content		Explanation
START	CAA	MODIFY	START identifies first location. MODIFY in the address part refers to the location identified by "MODIFY."
	ADD	PLUS SIX	PLUS SIX refers to the location identified by "PLUS SIX" which contains +006.
	STA	MODIFY	
MODIFY	CAA	FILE1	MODIFY identifies location of instruction to be modified. FILE1 refers to the location identified by "FILE1."

Only the fourth instruction is referred to by the instructions shown here so that only the "MODIFY" need be used to identify a location. The "START" is not needed except, perhaps, to enter this part of the program. One or more instructions can be inserted at any point within the four instructions without requiring any changes in the addresses since "MODIFY" is a suitable address wherever located in the program. The symbolic addresses START, MODIFY, PLUS SIX, and FILE1 can be used repeatedly as addresses in instructions, but they *must* be defined in one and only one way to avoid ambiguities. You are accustomed to the fact that absolute addresses must be defined and must be unique so there is little new about these stipulations.

Relative Addresses

Relative addressing is an extension of the concept of symbolic addressing. A relative address is a label used to identify a word in a routine or subroutine with respect to its position in that routine or subroutine. The fragment of a program given above can be written with relative addresses as follows:

Location	Content		Explanation
START	CAA	START + 3	This location is identified by "START"; "START +3" identifies the third location after this one.
	ADD	PLUS SIX	
	STA	START + 3	
	CAA	FILE1	

Inserting another instruction into this routine requires changing the relative address START +3 to START +4. This job is comparable to the task of changing the absolute addresses to permit insertions, as in the example for absolute addressing as first given. Relative addresses do have an important advantage for programming subroutines. After a subroutine written with relative addresses is checked out, it can be used whenever desired in the main program. The four instructions listed above can be used with the instruction identified by START, when it is given an absolute address of 067, 167, 503, or any other location. The programmer has some control over the conversion by the computer of the symbolic address to an absolute address; but it is necessary to avoid interfering with absolute addresses previously assigned.

Symbolic and relative addresses can be converted to absolute addresses either by manual methods or by the computer's using an assembly program, as described later in this chapter. A symbol table, such as the following, may be used for assigning absolute addresses for two selected symbols.

Symbol	Absolute Address Assigned	Explanation
START	067	The program will be stored in locations 067 and following.
FILE1	200	File #1 will be stored in locations 200 and following.

Storage locations will be assigned in turn to each succeeding instruction with a symbolic address that is not assigned an absolute address. If only the first symbolic address is assigned an absolute address, then each succeeding instruction will be assigned to storage with no intervening locations.

By convention, the symbols used to identify storage locations during programming may be restricted to at least one letter and one or more numerals. The letters I and O may be prohibited in symbolic addresses to avoid confusion with the numerals 1 and 0.

SUBROUTINES

Much programming time and effort may be used to program a particular type of calculation or operation that is used in many different programs. A large fraction of the programming time may be wasted because only slight variations exist each time the particular calculation is made. With so much similarity, it is possible to develop subroutines to handle the common elements of many programs (Hopper and Mauchly, 1953).

A "subroutine" can be defined as the set of instructions necessary to direct the computer to carry out a well-defined operation. In short, a subroutine is a sub-unit of a routine. After a subroutine is written and checked, it can be used in any program that requires the operations that it will perform. An example of a subroutine is the program load routine described for the hypothetical computer in Chapter 3. The load routine is useful for loading any program written for that computer.

Open Subroutine

Subroutines are classified as open or closed, depending on how they are fitted into the main program. An open subroutine is fitted directly into the operational sequence of the main program each time it is needed. The relationship between instructions written expressly for the main routine and the subroutines merely included in the main program can be illustrated as follows, although each line may represent dozens of instructions:

$$
\left.
\begin{array}{l}
\text{———} \\
\text{———}
\end{array}
\right\}
\text{Subroutine to load remainder of program}
$$

Program prepared expressly for the application
$$
\left\{
\begin{array}{l}
\text{———} \\
\text{———} \\
\text{———}
\end{array}
\right.
$$

$$
\left.
\begin{array}{l}
\text{———} \\
\text{———} \\
\text{———} \\
\text{———}
\end{array}
\right\}
\text{Subroutine to perform a desired operation—perhaps read in files, records, unpack, and place in suitable storage locations}
$$

Program prepared expressly for the application
$$
\left\{
\begin{array}{l}
\text{———} \\
\text{———} \\
\text{———}
\end{array}
\right.
$$

$$
\left.
\begin{array}{l}
\text{———} \\
\text{———} \\
\text{———}
\end{array}
\right\}
\text{Subroutine to read instructions— edit for accuracy of data, rearrange for efficient processing, and so forth}
$$

———
———
———

(Continued)

The open subroutine scheme is straightforward because each subroutine is included where it is wanted in the main program. Entry to and exit from the subroutine is simple because the whole program—both the hand-tailored parts and the subroutines—is located in consecutive storage locations. Each subroutine must be written with symbolic or relative addresses so that it will operate satisfactorily wherever placed in the main program. The open subroutine has the drawback that it is repeated each time it is used in the main program.

Closed Subroutines

A closed subroutine is stored somewhere away from the main program sequence. The main program jumps to a subroutine when it is wanted and, after executing the subroutine, returns to continue executing the main program. Entering and leaving the subroutine involves knowing where the subroutine is stored, arranging to have the desired operations in correct locations to be handled by the subroutine, and returning to the correct point in the main program. Furthermore, the contents of some registers and indexes may have to be saved so that they are available upon returning to the main program.

The concept of closed subroutines can be illustrated as follows, using a line to indicate one or more lines of coding:

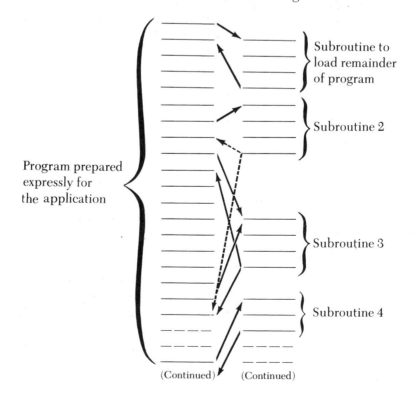

The arrows show jumps to a subroutine and returns to the main program. Solid lines indicate unconditional jumps and broken lines conditional jumps. Several points are worth noting from the illustration. The subroutines can be stored in any sequence desired and need not be in contiguous locations. After a subroutine is executed, program control may return to one of several points in the main program—subroutine 2 has alternate returns—depending upon conditions that arise during execution of the program. A subroutine may be used several times—subroutine 3 in this case—with a return to a different point in the main program each time. Pushed to the extreme, the main program is reduced to little more than a calling sequence which is a series of jump instructions that guide the program from one subroutine to another.

Use of subroutines is common in scientific and engineering work that involves computing square roots, cube roots, sines, cosines, and tangents. Computer running time may be longer for a program built of subroutines than for a program especially prepared for the problem. Nevertheless, the cost of longer running time on the computer may be outweighed by reduced programming costs and shorter elapsed time to prepare programs, especially where each program is used only a few times; but subroutines prepared by the computer manufacturer or other users are readily available.

Business processing programs are used repeatedly; and it is more important to arrange for efficient input, output, and machine utilization than to minimize the cost of programming. Some parts of programs—input, editing, sorting, and output—may be handled by subroutines even though the programs themselves are basically different. This is true despite the fact that it is rare for two organizations to have the same scheme for computing their payrolls or for controlling their inventories.

AUTOMATIC PROGRAMMING

Programming, as it first developed, required that a programmer work with a set of instruction codes aimed more at making the computer function than at solving problems. Instructions, such as ADD y x, CMP y x, and JIN y x, are pseudo-codes that are very similar to the instruction codes actually executed by the computer. It is a simple task to translate this machine-oriented language to actual machine code—as in changing "ADD y x" to "10 y x" on a one-to-one basis.

People with business problems to solve do not really want to bother with ADD, CMP, and JIN instructions. Users would much prefer to write short, simple programs—COMPUTE PAYROLL, BILL

CUSTOMERS, or DETERMINE WHETHER TO BUILD A NEW FACTORY AND, IF SO, WHERE—even though these might force the computer to use a long, intricate program in order to do the required processing. Clearly, a problem-oriented language at the level of COMPUTE, BILL, and DETERMINE is aimed at solving problems rather than running the computer. The ideal problem-oriented language would be independent of the machine language and of any particular computer.

The present state of the programming art lies somewhere between the two limits of either pure machine language or problem language. There are many schemes for blending the problem and machine-oriented languages to produce, by way of a computer, the program required to handle business applications and engineering problems. These schemes, which make up "automatic programming," consist of a problem-oriented language and an executive routine for translating the problem-oriented language into machine language. No longer is a one-to-one translation enough, because the verbs—COMPUTE, BILL, and DETERMINE—are extremely powerful; one such verb may require expansion into 10, 100, or more machine instructions. The ratio of expansion of verbs into instruction steps is a measure of the power of the problem language.

Automatic programming involves master or executive routines to process and control other routines (Automatic Coding, 1957; Hopper, 1958; Laden, 1959). There are two major types of executive routines—interpretive and compiler routines.

Interpretive Routines

An interpretive routine translates a pseudo-code program into a machine code and at once performs the indicated operations by means of subroutines. Thus, two things are happening in quick succession. First, each step written in pseudo-code by the programmer is translated into machine code to perform the desired operations; immediately after this, the machine instructions are executed on the data. The machine program is then discarded so that the interpretation must be repeated to run the program again.

Post-mortem Routines. Post-mortem and trace routines are special kinds of interpretive routine. Either automatically or on demand, a post-mortem routine or examination will print data concerning contents of registers and storage locations; this is done when the routine is stopped in order to assist in locating mistakes in coding. A post-mortem routine gives a static listing of computer storage, register, and index contents after the program "dies." This listing enables a clever programmer to perform an autopsy to determine why death occurred and to find the fatal instruction or instructions. For example, the exit jumps following a compare instruction may have been set up wrong. Indexing may have been erroneous because of mistakes in setting an index register, counting during each loop, or testing for exit from the loop. It is invaluable to know the content of the instruction counter, each index register, and several indexed instructions—both operation code and effective address—that were executed before the program halted. A skilled programmer can, with a thorough post-mortem routine, answer the question: "Who done it?"

Post-mortem routines are used in debugging programs during testing to find why they do not perform as planned. Most programs of any length contain mistakes that may require more time to test and debug than was initially spent preparing the program. With some post-mortem routines, it is possible to try to run test data through the computer without providing for any post-mortem output. If the computer stops, the post-mortem routine will restart the program at the beginning and produce the post-mortem output. But if the computer does not stop, there is no output.

Some simplified forms of post-mortem routines give only a "storage dump," which is a complete copy of all storage locations at the time the computer stopped. A storage dump routine usually lists the instruction that caused the program to stop and the current contents of arithmetic units and indexes.

A program can be debugged by executing it one step at a time from the console. Usually, when a computer stops, lights on the console indicate what caused the stop—overflow or an invalid operation code. It is also possible to find where the instruction being executed was stored. Debugging from the console is slower and harder to follow than a post-mortem routine. In some computers the post-mortem program is merely a subroutine, and console switches are used to provide the actual executive control of the routine. The console switches may provide for a jump to the subroutine after each operation.

Trace Routines.   A trace routine is used to observe how the object program (the program to be run) operates while it is being executed. The instructions in the object program are fed to the control unit one at a time while the executive trace routine actually controls the program. After each instruction in the program is executed, the executive routine keeps track of the following:

1. Location of the object program instruction
2. The instruction itself
3. Contents of the accumulator, M-Q, and index registers

The object program may be traced through its difficult or new, untested parts only. The simpler parts and those checked out earlier need not be traced. Instructions can be included in the object program for entering and leaving the trace routine at any point desired when testing the object program. In a sense, a trace routine permits reconstructing the patient's chart—temperature, blood pressure, and pulse—while healthy, ill, and dead. Of course, executing the trace routine may be wasted, if the object program runs to the end without stopping. A trace routine applied to a healthy program is similar to a medical examination for a person who proves to be healthy. A post-mortem routine may be incorporated into a trace routine to get a dump of storage and selected registers, if the program halts.

Simulator Program. One clever use for interpretive routines arises in computer simulation, whereby one computer operates with instructions and coding designed for another computer. It would be possible, for instance, for a real computer designed to execute one instruction repertoire to operate with a program written in the instructions described for the hypothetical computer in Chapter 3.

A simulator program is essentially a group of subroutines. For each instruction to be executed—ADD A137, CMP B290—the executive program would jump to a subroutine that would perform, in the real machine's codes, the indicated operation. After completing the subroutine for one instruction, the simulator would return to execute the next instruction in the object program.

A simulator is useful when changing from one computer to another; the user can, by means of a simulator, run existing, tested programs until he can rewrite his programs and test them for the new machine. Seldom-used programs may be run by means of the simulator for an indefinite period, despite some loss in machine efficiency. Reprogramming effort can be concentrated on major programs that are constantly used where the extra running time of simulation is too costly.

If a similar computer is not available for emergency use, a simulator may be used to permit running urgent programs on any available computer that has enough capacity and speed. Simulation is also used to test programs when a new computer is to replace one already in use. The existing computer can, by means of a simulation routine, test the new programs. A medium-sized computer may be used economically to test and debug programs for a large computer. The concept of computer simulation bridges some of the lack of compatibility between one computer and another.

In general, a computer operates best with programs written in its code. A large computer interpreting a program written for a medium computer will act essentially as a medium machine. Contrariwise, a medium computer may not be able to efficiently simulate a large machine. Limited storage or complete lack of certain features—tape units, index registers, or ability to handle alphabetic characters—limits the simulation ability of medium computers.

Compiling Routines

A compiler is an executive routine that translates into machine code a program originally written in pseudo-code. The translation may yield another pseudo-code for further translation by an interpreter.

Translator. A compiler can translate the operations specified in the main program before they are executed. In this way the whole object program is set up in the desired language before any of the translated program is carried out.

The output from compiling a program is a translated program that can be executed as such, run by means of an interpretive routine, or used in a secondary compiling step.

A simple compiler might be used to translate a mnemonic pseudo-code into the actual code used by the computer and assign storage locations. Translation from mnemonic to numerical code may complicate debugging because the programmer is not familiar with the machine's numerical code. One way out of the dilemma is to let the programmer use a pseudo-code that he likes and keep his program in the original language during debugging. This can be done by using an interpretive routine to run the object program during debugging. After check-out, the final version of the program (still in pseudo-code) can be compiled into the numerical code of the machine. The program in numerical machine code is then used alone.

Minimum-latency Programs. One common compiling routine is used to produce programs with instruction and data-storage locations allocated for minimum latency. For example, a programmer writes a program with symbolic addresses. The programmer's routine is first run under the guidance of a compiling routine that assigns absolute storage locations to instructions and yields the finished program that will run with the least time spent waiting for instructions and data to become available, which is what "minimum latency" means. For computers that run programs faster if instructions are stored in non-consecutive locations, the assignment of storage locations to get minimum latency can be a major programming job in itself. Some compilers that produce minimum-latency programs require that the programmer provide a program with symbolic addresses and also a table to serve as a guide for assigning absolute addresses. Other compilers work from a statement of the total number of words in each data block and compute the address table, if the programmer merely specifies where he wishes the first instruction to be stored. A compiler may reserve for instructions a portion of storage that cannot be exceeded and cannot be used to store data regardless of the size of the program. This scheme may waste storage locations assigned to instructions; on the other hand, it may require that the data be handled in several passes through the computer because of insufficient storage for instructions.

Simple compiling routines are useful in many types of programs. A program written in machine code with absolute addresses may be preferable in some cases, although the fact that a non-trivial fraction of storage must be reserved for an interpretive or compiling routine deters its use. The extra running time, since a computer is slowed by the execution of non-machine programs, may exceed the number of hours available each day. Quick-running programs are important for big applications that are used repeatedly. An experienced programmer may beat the compiler at achieving minimum latency since he will notice special short cuts. If lack of storage precludes minimum latency for all instructions, the programmer can use optimum locations for the important ones, placing others wherever there is room.

Generating Routines

Advanced compiling routines will automatically select subroutines from a file of routines stored on tape or will generate special subroutines as needed. It is suitable to have the computer compile the necessary subroutines for simple situations. The programmer may specify, for example, that a square-root routine is needed at a certain point in his program. The compiler will search the file, select the subroutine, assign storage locations, and provide for jumps to and from the main section of the program. Minimum latency programming is also sometimes involved.

It may be necessary to devise a routine better suited to the application than any subroutine in the library. A "generator" routine creates a subroutine to handle problems when the parameters—values of factors—encountered in the problem are variable and the compiling routine is to be used for different cases. Facts about the application to be handled are used by the generator routine to generate a tailored subroutine. For example, the following parameters or facts would be needed to generate a routine for checking the sequence of records in a file:

1. Input media used—cards or tape
2. Code used in file—alphabetic, numerical, or alphanumerical
3. Number of records per block and their repeat pattern, if tape is used as input
4. Length of items to be sequence checked—two or more words, one full word, or a part of one word
5. Position in the record—first, second, last, or other word—of the items to be sequence checked
6. End-of-file tag
7. The output desired

A generating routine can, by using a skeleton sequence-checking routine and these parameters, compile a sequence-checking program for the specific application. In a series of steps, compiling routines can be run on the computer to construct complex programs.

Conversion Routines

Special compiling routines are sometimes used to convert data from one mode to another—decimal to binary and fixed point to floating point, or vice versa. In simplest form, such conversion routines do little more than handle the data before the main program takes over. Conversion routines, on the other hand, are often used in conjunction with a more extensive compiling program. A computer that represents numbers in the binary mode requires conversion of input data from decimal to binary form. New computers used for business processing will handle decimal numbers with automatic conversion to machine code as part of the input process. The fact that most business-data processing can be done with alphanumerical data in the fixed decimal-point mode limits the need to use data-conversion routines.

EXAMPLES OF AUTOMATIC PROGRAMMING

Two examples will indicate how compilers are used to prepare programs. One example evaluates a simple formula, and the other example calculates a payroll.

Formula Translation

Intricate compiling routines are used to translate formulas from the way that people write them to a program for the computer to use. The programmer must observe some conventions by writing in a specified format for a formula-translation routine—abbreviated FOR TRANSIT by its designers—to generate a program to evaluate the formula. (*FOR TRANSIT*, 1957.)

For a trivial example, the formula for the area of a circle is $A = \frac{\pi D^2}{4}$, where A is the area, D is the diameter, and π is a constant, 3.1416. A programmer can write a program to find the area of a circle by writing merely:

$$A = (3.1416 \text{ x } D \text{ xx } 2)/4$$

The "x" means multiply, the "xx" means that the following number "2" is an exponent in order to square D, and the "/" means divide. Using the formula as written, the compiling routine will generate a program—that is, translate the formula into a program—to do the following:

1. Square D to get D^2.
2. Multiply D^2 by 3.1416.
3. Divide the product by 4.
4. Store the resulting area in some storage location from which it can be taken later for use in the program or for output.

If the programmer simply wants to find areas of circles for many different diameters, the complete manual program that he writes would:

1. Specify how many values for D will be used, or, if the computer is to find areas for all values between 0.000 and .999 in steps of 0.001, specify this fact.
2. Instruct the computer to READ D, if the values of D are to be obtained from input.
3. Write the formula.
4. Instruct the computer to PUNCH A or WRITE A (or WRITE A, D, if both area and diameter are wanted together as output).

The programmer writes in a simple, set format, as suggested by the operation READ D. The formula-translation compiling routine may include both the generation of a program and the assignment of addresses for minimum latency, if that will cut program running time.

Formula-translation routines work by generating programs from the skeleton subroutines and parameters given in the programmer's instructions. For instance, to generate the part of the program needed to find the area, the compiling routine would use the = sign as an indication that something called A in symbolic language was to be stored in some location for further use. In addition, it would evaluate the (3.1416 x D xx 2)/4 part of the formula. The xx would cause it to generate a routine to multiply D by itself. Then the x would indicate that it should generate a routine to multiply the first answer by 3.1416. Finally, the / will cause it to generate a routine to divide the product by 4. The routines to do these simple things would be skeleton subroutines of a few instructions previously prepared.

Formula-translating routines are, of course, designed primarily for engineering and scientific programming, although they may be useful in some types of business processing.

Business Compiler

Several computer manufacturers have developed compiling routines for business applications. The programming of a simple payroll problem in the FLOW-MATIC system developed for use with the Remington Rand Univac computers will illustrate the use of a business compiler (*FLOW-MATIC*, 1958).

The basic process is extremely simple. The master file and data on hours worked are processed to produce a payroll and a tape to handle erroneous input. Input consists of two files—a personnel master file, and a file of hours worked during a certain period, say, one week.

The programmer provides the facts necessary for the compiling routine by filling in preprinted sheets. The English name of the file "master" is given along with data that the routine will need to handle the file—file design, label, location of label, and other details. These names are spelled out in ordinary English words to provide a cross reference to the program which will simply call for them by their names. The programmer's work in filling in the data design forms is simpler than it first appears because much of it is preprinted, and explanations are listed on the form itself.

Figure 8-2 is a flow chart of the payroll program with the program steps indicated in parentheses. The program starts with the input operation (0) and then in operation (1) compares an employee's badge number in the master file with numbers in the file of hours worked. If there is a record of hours worked for an employee but no master record, represented by the condition A > B, the (e) exit from the comparison is followed to operation (17) to type the badge number error, operation (18) to read another item, and operation (19) to jump to operation (1) to repeat the loop for the next employee.

If the badge numbers match in operation (1), the program continues to operation (2) for testing the badge number against the end-of-file sentinel of Z's. When the end of the file is reached, path (g) is followed to the close-out and stop in operations (22) and (23). Otherwise, the program computes the gross pay in operations (3) and (4) and then makes appropriate deductions in operations (5) and (6) and (11) through (16). The completed item is written out by operation (7) and the next item is read from each field by operations (8) and (9) to start processing for the next employee at (a).

The payroll program itself is given in FLOW-MATIC code in Figure 8-3. The coding is written in English call words and functions, although it must adhere to conventions set by the designers of FLOW-MATIC. A "call word" is a set of characters identifying a subroutine and containing data about parameters that are to be inserted in the subroutine or data about the operands. Some of the 30 call words and functions included in FLOW-MATIC, which can be expanded to include other words through the freedom offered by the X-1 call word, are defined as follows:

Call Word	Function
ADD	Adds two or more fields and places the result in a specified field.
CLOSE-OUT	Terminates the output file.
COMPARE	Examines two fields for magnitude and equality and branches accordingly.

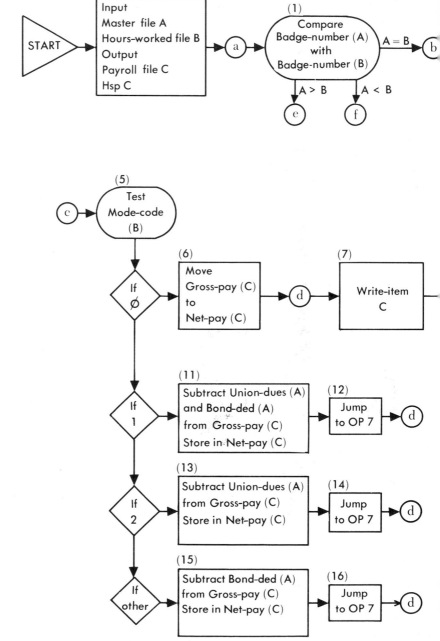

FIGURE 8-2. *Flow chart for payroll program*

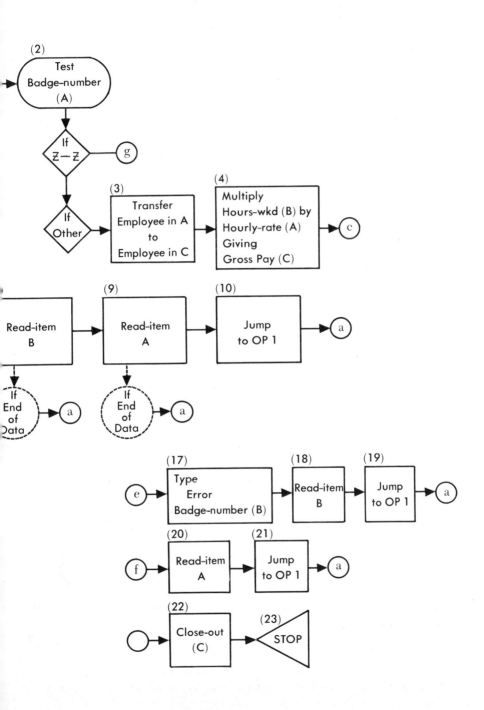

COUNT   Adds an increment to the field specified and, if desired, branches upon reaching a limit.

INSERT   Places a specified constant into one or more fields.

READ-ITEM   Supplies the next item of an input file and branches to a designated operation when the file is exhausted.

X-1   Provides the facility for performing functions not previously described.

These call words and functions, which are oriented toward business problems, should be contrasted with the instruction codes given in Chapter 3, which are machine-oriented. You should quickly get a feeling for the demands that each type of language places on programmers.

As an example of the call words and functions, operation number (1) is written "(1) Compare Badge-number (A) with Badge-number (B); if greater, go to operation (17); if equal, go to operation (2); otherwise, go to operation (20)." The programmer, by writing in this fashion, is actually following the set format:

> (h) Δ COMPARE Δ field-name Δ (f$_1$) Δ WITH Δ field-name Δ (f$_2$) Δ
> ; Δ IF Δ GREATER Δ GO Δ TO Δ OPERATION Δ h$_1$ Δ
> ; Δ IF Δ EQUAL Δ GO Δ TO Δ OPERATION Δ h$_2$ Δ
> ; Δ OTHERWISE Δ GO Δ TO Δ OPERATION Δ h$_3$ Δ .

Operation numbers are indicated by h for the present operation and h$_1$, h$_2$, h$_3$ for others. The field-name is the name assigned to the data field by the programmer; for example, Badge-number, and file letters are f$_1$ and f$_2$. A blank space between words is indicated by a delta Δ. A punctuation mark is also separated from a word by a delta. A line under O indicates the letter, to distinguish it from the numeral zero.

This example of a business compiler applied to payroll processing should be studied carefully to understand the relationship between file and item design, the flow chart, and the program coded in a business-oriented language.

Automatic programming schemes can reduce programming time and cost. The programmer can work with a problem-oriented language and have the computer use executive routines to prepare the machine-language program. The price of using executive routines, apart from the fact that they are expensive to prepare, may be reduced flexibility and increased computing time both to compile the desired program and to run it. An executive routine that could do everything would probably be as difficult to use as a basic machine program. Where particular problems are fairly common, the cost of developing and using an executive routine can be justified. But unusual types of problems that would

(0) Input Master file — A
      Hours-worked file — B
  ; Output Payroll file — C
  ; HSPC.

(1) Compare Badge-number (A) with
Badge-number (B); if greater go to
operation 17; if equal go to operation 2;
otherwise go to operation 20.

(2) Test Badge-number (A) against Z — Z
  ; if equal go to operation 22
  ; otherwise to operation 3.

(3) Transfer employee in A to employee in C

(4) Multiply hours-worked (B) by hourly-rate (A)
giving gross-pay (C).

(5) Test mode-code (B) against 0
  ; if equal go to operation 6; against 1
  ; if equal go to operation 11; against 2
  ; if equal go to operation 13; otherwise
     go to operation 15.

(6) Move gross-pay (C) to net-pay (C).

(7) Write - item C.

(8) Read - item B; if end of data go to operation 1.

(9) Read - item A; if end of data go to operation 1.

(10) Jump to operation 1.

(11) Subtract union-dues (A) and
bond-ded (A) from gross-pay (C)
  ; store the remainder in net-pay (C).

(12) Jump to operation 7.

(13) Subtract union-dues (A) from
gross-pay (C); store the remainder
in net-pay (C).

(14) Jump to operation 7.

(15) Subtract bond-ded (A) from gross-pay (C);
store the remainder in net-pay (C).

(16) Jump to operation 7.

(17) Type error, badge-number (B).

(18) Read - item B.

(19) Jump to operation 1.

(20) Read - item A.

(21) Jump to operation 1.

(22) Close - out file C.

(23) Stop. (End)

FIGURE 8-3. *FLOW-MATIC code for payroll program*

require special executive routines are probably handled more economically by programs written in near-basic machine language so that simple executive routines are adequate. The crux of the matter of manual versus automatic programming is an economic one: Is it more efficient to use a computer to prepare programs than to rely upon programmers? Executive routines are expensive to prepare, and their costs may outweigh many of their other advantages.

SUMMARY

The total amount of money involved in analyzing and programming business applications for computer use is big enough to warrant the use of any programming method that promises to reduce the total cost. Advanced methods are aimed at improving program preparation for business and engineering problems. The broader questions of the economics of data-processing systems are treated at length in Chapters 10 through 12.

Data can be stored differently outside and inside a computer. During the input and output operations, data fields can be rearranged, packed, unpacked, filled in, shortened, or dropped. Constant data can be introduced automatically. Checking and editing during input serve to increase the reliability of the data.

The amount of processing time required depends, among other things, on the latency—the waiting time to get an instruction or operand from storage. Latency is uniformly short, and in the microsecond range, for any address in magnetic-core storage. For magnetic drums latency depends on drum circumference, speed, and storage pattern. Many ingenious schemes are used for reducing latency either by arranging data in suitable locations or by placing several read-write heads around a track.

A programmer can use longhand methods to arrange instructions and data in storage to get minimum latency. Optimum assembly programs are available for a programmer to use in conjunction with his program to arrange it for minimum latency.

Errors, mistakes, and malfunctions have different causes and, of course, different remedies. An *error* is the loss in precision in a quantity because of rounding, inheritance, or overflow. A *mistake* is a human blunder that results in an incorrect instruction in a program or in coding. A mistake may either stop the computer or let operations continue and give a wrong answer. Post-mortem routines aid a programmer in detecting mistakes in a program. A *malfunction* is a failure in computer operation that may arise because of an invalid code, an incorrect code, or a transient condition that causes a pulse to be gained or lost (such transient conditions occur once in a million or billion operations for electronic equipment in good operating condition). In machine design, systems analysis, program preparation, and in computer operation, precautions are necessary to detect the occurrence of and to minimize the consequences of errors, mistakes, and malfunctions.

Computer instruction repertoires range from about a dozen to several hundred orders. Some computers provide for variations on orders so that, effectively, many hundred orders are available to the programmer. Each additional order provided for a computer costs money to design and build. On the other hand, it is easier to prepare programs as the instruction repertoire is increased—but only up to some point. A broader instruction repertoire may be partially wasted because it is difficult to exploit the subtle differences in instructions. The suitability of an instruction repertoire is akin to the choice of using either basic English or the King's English: neither vocabulary is entirely suitable for everyday communication so that most people prefer an intermediate vocabulary. A reasonable range of instructions is considered easy to learn and efficient for both program preparation and computer operations.

Jump instructions may be designed into the computer to handle every possible outcome from a comparison—greater, less, equal, positive, and negative. This avoids any ambiguity that might arise if some of the outcomes were handled explicitly and some were handled as the only logically remaining case. For example, if a test is made for negative or zero and that test is not fulfilled, then the outcome under consideration must be positive. An instruction to set a value in an index register and to jump is invaluable for keeping track of the point of departure from the main program in order to go to a subroutine and later return to the main program at the appropriate point.

Table look-up instructions use an argument—the entry value—to find the function—the desired value, with arguments arranged in an orderly fashion. For example, a table consisting of an orderly arrangement of department numbers and overhead costs can be updated by handling cost transactions in any departmental sequence desired. Otherwise, transactions might be sorted by department number and processed against the file.

Floating decimal point arithmetic is built into some computers to facilitate keeping track of the decimal point. Such operations are similar to logarithms because each number is treated as a mantissa and characteristic. The number 92784.71, for example, becomes a mantissa of .92784 and characteristic of 55—a power of 5, for 10^5 and an artificial base of 50—and is stored in a seven-digit word as .9278455. Instruction execution time may be increased and precision unexpectedly lost by use of floating point. Joint use of both floating and fixed point modes may be desirable in some applications.

Pseudo-codes are widely used to facilitate programming. A programmer writes in mnemonic code and then uses a ready-made program for converting pseudo-codes into machine codes to be run on the computer. The symbolic address scheme is, in some ways, similar to the pseudo-code idea, for it enables the programmer to use alphanumerical names or abbreviations to refer to storage locations. He can postpone the assignment of numerical or absolute addresses to a later stage. The assignment of absolute for symbolic addresses can, of course, be handled by the computer by means of a suitable program. The relative address scheme, which is an extension of symbolic addressing, relates the address of one storage location to another that is nearby. This scheme makes the segment of a program independent of absolute locations so that it can be placed anywhere in storage.

Subroutines to instruct the computer to carry out a well-defined operation are used in programs in either the open or closed mode. The open mode repeats the subroutine at each point where it is wanted in the main program. In the closed mode, a subroutine is placed outside the main program and a transfer to the subroutine is required each time it is used. A transfer is required, of course, to return from a closed subroutine to the main program.

Automatic programming attempts to bridge the gap between a computer-oriented language—add, compare, jump—and a problem-oriented language that a business user would much prefer—update files, prepare payrolls. One approach is to use interpretive routines that translate pseudo-code programs into machine codes and immediately perform the indicated operations by means of subroutines. Postmortems, traces, and simulators are examples of interpretive routines developed for testing and debugging programs.

The compiler approach to automatic programming is a two-phase process: (1) translating a pseudo-code program into a machine-language program, and (2) executing the compiled program. Once compiled, the program can be run whenever desired. Generator routines are used to compile programs that are better tailored to a particular application when the parameters involved are variable.

Two examples of automatic programming for entirely different kinds of problems are formula translation and payroll calculation. These two examples point up some of the differences, and also some of the complexities, occurring in mathematical and business problems. Much hope is held out that automatic programming will bridge the gap between the capacity of electronic computers to solve any problem and the practical implementation of the ability to solve particular problems. The efficient use of computers hinges on resolving the wide gulf between their capability to do anything in general and the abilities of people to make them accomplish a specific task.

REFERENCES AND SUPPLEMENTAL READINGS

Automatic Coding, Monograph No. 3, *Journal of The Franklin Institute*, Philadelphia, 1957, 118 pp. This monograph consists of the proceedings of a symposium held in early 1957 at The Franklin Institute in Philadelphia to discuss the development and use of automatic coding schemes. It includes papers on systems of debugging automatic coding, PRINT 1 (for the IBM 705), the procedure translator, OMNICODE, a matrix compiler (for Univac), a mathematical language compiler, and a mechanized approach to automatic coding.

FLOW-MATIC Programming System, New York, Remington Rand Univac, 1958, 115 pp. This booklet (and the 1959 edition, called *FLOW-MATIC Programming for the UNIVAC I and UNIVAC II Data Automation System*, 103 pp.) describes the FLOW-MATIC method for using an English language description of application requirements as the instruction code. The computer is directed to translate the businessman's vocabulary automatically into detailed coded instructions. The FLOW-MATIC method, charting and program writing, file-data layout and design, storage utilization, relative machine coding, and compiling routine are described.

Gottlieb, C. C. "The Cost of Programming and Coding," *Computers and Automation*, vol. 3: 14-15+ (September 1954). This article discusses the factors that make the cost of programming $2 to $10 per single address order for manually written programs. These estimates of programming costs at the University of Toronto were low because of the omission of overhead, low machine rate, and relationship of Canadian prices to those in the United States. Gottlieb's quoted costs were, on the other hand, high because of concentration on writing library routines, emphasis on developing special aids for writing and verifying programs, and the high salary element in formulating and programming problems.

Hopper, Grace M. "Automatic Programming for Business Applications," pp. 45-50 in *Proceedings of the Fourth Annual Computer Applications Symposium*, Chicago, Armour Research Foundation of Illinois Institute of Technology, 1958. This paper describes the chain of events leading from coding in machine language through interpreters and compilers using pseudo-codes and relative notation. Two requirements exist for business problems: first, a method for describing business data; and, second, a means for writing, for a particular operation, the subroutine to execute that operation on the corresponding data. The concept takes shape as a compiling system with an associated library of generators, service routines, and data descriptions. English language coding has been developed and tested. The next steps are to produce a compiler to make compilers and to advance into the area of programming itself.

Hopper, Grace M., and J. W. Mauchly. "Influence of Programming Techniques on the Design of Computers," *Proceedings of the Institute of Radio Engineers*, vol. 41: 1250-1254 (October 1953). One of the primary problems in the use of computers is the time and skill required for programming. This article describes the early approaches to this problem. It treats the design and use of stored subprograms. Using this method, simple programs are put into the calculator, which can then select from its library of subprograms to produce the final working program. The article discusses the significance of this development to small installations where cost influences preclude having a large programming staff. It also discusses the necessary interplay between design engineers and programmers in the design of a machine for both low initial cost and subsequent low programming time and cost.

Laden, H. N. "Automatic Programming—Fact or Fancy?", *Management and Business Automation*, vol. 1: 29-35 (February 1959). This article is a thorough exposition of automatic programming chiefly through an orderly arrangement of its principal vocabulary and suitable definitions. Advantages, practical applications, and limitations are considered. The current state of development and future prospects are reviewed to show the effect on get-ready costs in applying computers to business problems.

Price Waterhouse & Co. *The Auditor Encounters Electronic Data Processing*, New York, International Business Machines Corporation, n.d., 23 pp. This monograph, prepared by a large firm of auditors for a computer manufacturer, deals with the effect of these systems on internal control procedures and the auditability of such records by internal audit staffs and independent accountants. Processing accuracy is treated in detail under the following topics: record count, hash totals, proof figures, reverse multiplication, limit checks, cross footing balance checks, checkpoints, self-checking numbers, sequence checks, labels, and built-in checks. Optimism is expressed about the ability of the auditor to adapt to evolutionary changes in conditions without sacrificing his basic standards, although a revolutionary change in clerical work is expected.

Programmer's Reference Manual: FOR TRANSIT—Automatic Coding System for the IBM 650, New York, International Business Machines Corporation, 1957, 67 pp. This manual is the basic reference material for FOR TRANSIT, an automatic coding system for the IBM 650. The FOR TRANSIT system makes available to 650 users a language called FORTRAN closely resembling the language of mathematics and designed for scientific and engineering computations. A chief purpose is to provide the scientist with an efficient means of writing programs that require no knowledge of the computer and only a short period of training.

CHAPTER NINE

PROCESSING PROCEDURES

This chapter deals with the basic factors that determine how data are processed. These factors include: how the enterprise is organized and managed, the reports it wants, and the data available to it. Methods already in use or available in the near future also affect the processing techniques that are used. Certain aspects of these techniques are covered in more detail, to show more precisely how the various factors determine the nature of a system; these aspects are fragmentary and consolidated processing, input-output, data flow, sorting, and integrated data processing.

TECHNIQUES AVAILABLE

Processing procedures do not reflect immediately the latest available equipment and techniques. Procedures in use at any one time are based on equipment and techniques developed over a long period of time. One insurance company expert has said, off the record, that an important system change should be made no more than once every three to five years because more frequent changes lead to chaos. Two aspects of available processing techniques that deserve discussion are the degree of automation of the system and the method of organizing and keeping files.

Degree of Automation

Systems range from being solely manual to almost fully automatic. Rarely is a system at one extreme or the other. The ratio of equipment to labor is a quick guide to the degree of automation.

Systems have different characteristics, which correspond to varying ratios of capital to labor. In manual systems, based on loosely defined procedures and rules that are not rigidly followed, operations are flexible and exceptions are handled by supervisors. Arithmetical operations are expensive and inaccurate because people are poor at arithmetic, even when using calculators. Many people are required in even the most automatic systems developed to date, but automatic systems reflect a high ratio of capital to labor. An automatic system relies on carefully defined procedures, and operating routines are followed to the letter. The cost of arithmetical operations is trivial compared to their cost in a manual system. Exceptions and new situations involve program modification or reprogramming; and sometimes rewriting a program by hand may be too slow to meet requirements. Automatic programming promises to increase the flexibility of automatic systems by shortening program revision.

Scale of Equipment.   The scale of equipment can be measured in terms of its capacity for processing data. Any processor, whether manual or highly automatic, must be large enough to handle a program and the data related to it. A segment of an over-all program can partially process the data and then call in and use other segments of the program as required. The results are written out and the cycle repeated on additional data.

Specialization.   Specialization occurs in data-processing systems if facilities are not powerful enough to hold the programs required for processing all types of transactions. Specialization takes many forms. A common plan is to deal with one type of transaction at a time. One class of transactions involves the use of certain procedures for processing these transactions against a part of the over-all files of the organization.

Some kind of specialization—by transaction, procedure, for processing, or organization of file—occurs in most systems. Manual systems follow the principle of division of labor for efficient processing. Transactions are first classified by type and then given to people who are "programmed," (instructed and experienced) to deal with that type of transaction and related files. Specialization may be carried so far that each person does only a small part of the processing required for even one type of transaction. The people operate like links in an assembly line—pick it up, process it, put it down—with little regard for the origin or destination of the item involved.

Similar specialization may occur in using automatic data-processing equipment. People are unable, in any practical sense, to build equipment and design programs that will handle all types of transactions and related files for business-data processing. Programs for automatic equipment are likely to follow the same general plan of specialization that is used in manual systems. On the other hand, the degree of specialization is reduced somewhat in automatic systems because of the high processing speeds, the use of consolidated instead of fragmentary files, and the high cost of input and output operations.

Files

Methods available for keeping files and processing transactions have an important bearing on how data are processed. All files for a business might be kept in one consolidated master file. The duplication of file contents that occurs if records are maintained in several places throughout the organization would be reduced to a minimum. Any transaction could, assuming an appropriate instruction program, be processed against the files whenever desired. If access to the files were quick enough, transactions could be handled on-line without sorting them by type before handling.

Consolidated files for all the records needed by a large organization would require a huge amount of active storage; but the activity rate for many file items would be small. A composite program for processing any kind of transaction against any record in a consolidated file would be more intricate than programs now in use. Available file-processing methods do not ordinarily have enough capacity to handle one consolidated file for a company. Files, programs, and transactions are, therefore, broken into segments for efficient processing.

FRAGMENTARY AND CONSOLIDATED PROCESSING

The fragmentary and consolidated approaches to data processing, mentioned above, deserve more careful consideration.

Fragmentary Processing

The "fragmentary approach" means that the over-all task of data processing is subdivided into parts for efficient solution. A piecemeal approach is used for several reasons. Various parts of a business may be so complex that composite processing would overtax the ingenuity of people and the capacity of equipment.

The limited capacity of manual and electromechanical systems results in a high degree of specialization. It is expensive to instruct people to process data, follow instructions, and perform calculations. People are rather good at referring to files; but having files nearby leads to a high degree of duplication merely for cross-reference purposes and for availability of common data. People and equipment handling only small segments of a problem are scattered throughout the business. The use of many similar facilities gives reserve capacity against peak loads and breakdowns, but it is not efficient.

Fragmentary processing implies multiple passes of master files. Transactions are classified by type and then sorted into sequence. Each type is, in turn, processed against an appropriate master file. Multiple processing is efficient only if files are small enough to permit repeated handling. The fact that most data processors must rewrite a tape file completely in order to change a few records warrants some kind of specialization of files or batching of transactions to increase the effective work done in each file updating pass.

Consolidated Processing

The "consolidated approach" means that the bits and pieces of the fragmentary approach to data processing are combined into larger units. Consolidated processing is warranted, if various parts of the organization are closely related and if input, processing, files, and output have a common usage (Wiseman, 1954). Consolidated processing requires larger-scale facilities than fragmentary processing. Files are consolidated and duplicate parts eliminated so that any type of transaction can be handled in any sequence desired. A master program calls up the appropriate program for completely processing a transaction. Both kinds of routines are large and complex. Furthermore, exceptional situations involve elaborate programming.

The ultimate in consolidated processing would probably be a single pass of all transactions against a master file. Unless random-access storage is used, transactions are probably sorted into sequence before processing in order to facilitate references to a file kept in the same sequence. Each transaction includes a code to call up the appropriate program for complete processing in a single pass of the files. When consolidated files are kept in active storage, they have a low activity rate because all records would be available to process even though the number of transactions remained the same.

Actual Practices

Actual practices reflect aspects of both the fragmentary and the consolidated approaches to data processing. The fragmentary approach has been used for a long time in large organizations, chiefly because of the low capacity of facilities. Because it is so widely used, many people think of fragmentary processing as the "natural" plan. This is true despite the fact that it was devised to cope with certain limitations in processing ability and might never have developed given other kinds of equipment.

In recent years some progress has been made toward consolidating operations in one or two areas of a business in order to take advantage of the capabilities of new equipment. Scattered files for an employee—recording his earnings, pay history, personnel record, medical history, and so forth—may be consolidated for processing. Similar consolidation occurs for inventory—quantity control, distribution, replenishment, financial control, cataloguing, and related operations. The length of the combined file may be condensed by one-third.

Limited experience indicates that consolidated processing, even in selected areas, raises many new points. Comprehensive processing programs are far more complex to prepare than the individual programs required for fragmentary processing. Exceptional situations are more difficult to handle. Difficulties of moderate consolidation may be caused by the lack of ingenuity of people in devising new processing plans; on the other hand, people may overestimate the capacity of available equipment and try to make changes too rapidly.

Available equipment does not have sufficient capacity—file storage space, processing speed, and adaptability to various programs—to permit complete consolidation of data processing in the near future. In addition, experimenting with consolidated processing schemes is necessary to develop efficient plans. Neither equipment nor people can, without severe disruption, change abruptly from one long-established plan to a radically different plan that affects the whole organization.

INPUT METHODS

Input and output methods are closely related, and they affect the way that data are processed. The output from one stage of processing is usually the input to another stage. This is true even when output goes from one organization to another. Only a small fraction of business data is wholly new in the sense that it did not exist before, and rarely is output at any stage discarded without further processing somewhere. In fact, data output that does not lead to some further action, and therefore processing, is of doubtful value.

Factors of input and output that are worth considering here are accuracy, load, timing, and the ratio of equipment to labor. All of these factors influence processing procedures, although some of them are far easier to change than others.

Equipment-to-labor Ratio

Some input plans rely heavily on manual methods for getting data into processable form, while others make important use of equipment. The ratio of equipment to labor and commonly used input methods can be put briefly as follows:

Ratio of Equipment to Labor	Input Methods
Low	Key-punch for cards
	Tape-producing typewriter
Intermediate	By-product data recorders
	Mark-sensing schemes
	Tags attached to inventory item
	Cards in tub files

Production recorders
Point-o-sale recorders
Transacters

High   Direct input of prior output in
                  suitable form
                Character-reading devices

Low Ratio.   A low ratio of equipment to labor means that manual operations are important for input. Two stages are used to get data into processable form. First, people write or type documents; second, they read documents and operate keyboards that punch cards or paper or write on magnetic tape.

Intermediate Ratio. An intermediate ratio of equipment to labor means that more equipment and less labor is used than in systems that have a low ratio. The separate stages of preparing paper documents and converting them to a processable medium are telescoped into one operation. A single manual operation yields data in machine-processable form. By-product data recorders yield two outputs: a printed record considered essential for people to use and data in a form suitable for automatic processing.

Mark-sensing schemes give visually readable and mechanically processable data in one manual operation; but emphasis is usually placed on the automatic processing feature rather than on readability. Cards attached to inventory items or kept in tub files reduce the manual work of data input. Verified cards are mass produced for attaching to items until they are used, at which time the cards are detached for processing. A tub file is a convenient way to store cards that are mass produced until they are selected for processing. In some cases the cards are kept in "pockets" near the item involved.

Production recorders and point-of-transaction recorders may combine data from several sources: manual entries on keyboards; reproductions from cards, plates, or tags; and data set up automatically by equipment.

High Ratio. A high ratio of equipment to labor means that the system is essentially automatic. Almost no labor is required to use the output of one stage of processing as input at the next stage. Punched-card, punched-tape, and magnetic-tape output can be used as input at the next stage.

The ratio of equipment to labor is also high for character-recognition devices. Such equipment recognizes or reads characters and converts them to a form convenient for further processing.

Accuracy

Different ratios of equipment to labor in input systems have certain implications for the accuracy of input data. Although everyone seems to believe that *his* data-processing system is based on good input data, careful analysis usually shows that input data are far from accurate. People make numerous mistakes when originating input data.

The problem of getting accurate input data can be attacked from two directions. One approach is to increase the manual effort; the other, to increase the use of equipment and minimize the manual work of input preparation. Each approach for reducing the margin of error—the difference between the calculated and the correct result—deserves study.

Increased Manual Effort. The manual operations used in preparing input data may be repeated to detect errors. One approach is to repeat the manual operations involved in going from a readable to a processable form. Mechanical comparison of the results of both manual operations can disclose discrepancies to be eliminated. Data verified in this fashion are far more accurate than those resulting from either manual operation alone. Another way to verify the accuracy of input data is to read the results against the original source. Experience indicates that visual comparison is not so effective for disclosing mistakes as duplicated manual operations.

Accuracy can be greatly improved, some analysts say, by making the originators of input data responsible for their accuracy—people are far more careful about the accuracy of data they originate if they must eliminate mistakes that are discovered later. Still, care is needed to avoid spending more than it is worth to get a higher degree of accuracy. These points are covered in Chapter 10.

Increased Use of Equipment. Input data accuracy can be improved by more intensive use of equipment. Control totals developed in an early stage can be used to guard against mistakes in input operations. Some control totals, as dollar amounts or quantities, are useful as part of the data. Other control totals—"nonsense" or "hash" totals of unit prices or catalogue numbers—may be developed solely to improve processing accuracy. In such schemes, the total is recomputed at the next stage and compared with the prior total solely to detect mistakes.

A variation of the control total scheme is to include a check digit calculated according to certain rules for catalogue numbers, or other identifying numbers. A simple rule is to attach a digit to a number so that all digits, including the check digit, add to a multiple of ten. More elaborate rules are required if digits are likely to be switched. Each alternate digit, starting with the right-hand digit, may be multiplied by two before adding and attaching a check digit.

Equipment can edit input data to detect simple mistakes, such as a double punch or no punch, in any card column. Other input media can be edited in a similar fashion. More elaborate input editing can determine the plausibility of data, and new data can be compared with prior data to disclose unusual changes or variations from past patterns.

Load

Some input loads are controllable. Input data arising inside an organization are, within limits, controllable. The nature, quantity, and time of origination of new data are subject to some manipulation. Controllable loads of input data permit greater use of data-processing facilities, so that less reserve capacity is needed to handle peak loads.

Some of the internal data load and most of the external data load, however, cannot be controlled. One solution is to have facilities large enough to handle peak loads, although this reduces the average utilization rate. Another scheme is to save some of the peak load for processing in low periods; but this may lead to intolerable delays.

DATA FLOW

An important objective of system design is to get an efficient flow of data. Several choices of data flow exist after data are available as input for processing:

1. Data can be processed without delay—on line.
2. Data can be stored temporarily and later processed in the same se-quence—in line.
3. Data can be accumulated, rearranged in some way, perhaps by sort-ing, and processed in batches—off-line.

The data-flow plan selected affects input-output facilities, pro-grams, organization of files, and even the design of the data processor.

On-line Processing

The idea of on-line data flow is simple: data go directly to the processing unit, with no intermediate stages of classification or sorting between the origination of data and completed processing. The ac-curacy of input data is increased because people do not recopy data from original documents. Most of the input data can be developed in a suitable form in an earlier operation for selection and use when wanted. On-line operation is a quick way to get data into and results out of the processing unit.

An on-line system involves a quick and uninterrupted flow of data from the point of origin to the processing unit; similarly, the output from processing is available without delay for control purposes. Auto-matic communication channels that depend as little as possible on people are required for a quick and uninterrupted flow of input and output. Wire circuits are commonly used within one location and be-tween scattered locations of an organization.

Example.   A production control scheme for a job shop illustrates on-line processing. A machinist can report when he finishes a work piece by inserting into a card reader a punched card to identify the work piece and operation. He identifies himself by inserting another card or by operating a keyboard. The card reader-keyboard device sends data about the work piece, operation, and operator directly to the processing unit. The processing unit accepts these facts and searches its storage to find what should be done next and whether material and facilities are available.

The processor prints a card or displays data in some way on the shop recorder to tell the machinist what piece to make next. It also authorizes him to withdraw the necessary material. This process involves both on-line input and on-line output.

Factors in Design.   Design of an on-line data-flow plan involves several factors that affect system efficiency. Two or more input stations may send data at the same time and cause a "waiting line" to develop. Faster processing of the data received from each station reduces the waiting time for other data. The processor may be designed to handle service requests from two or more stations at one time. Either faster processing or multiplexing (which handles several inputs at the same time) involves additional cost. If transactions occur at different rates, reserve capacity is required to handle high volumes. The processor is used at less than capacity when the volume of transactions is low. Low-volume periods may be filled in by applications that require only off-line processing. Time sharing between on-line and off-line applications may give good results for both types.

On-line data flow requires that all files and programs necessary to deal with transactions must be available to the processor. In the job shop example given earlier, the processor must find and adjust the records involved in each transaction. Only a few records throughout the whole file are affected for one transaction. Quick processing of large files requires fast access methods merely to find a desired record. On-line data flow is required for applications that need an immediate answer after each transaction so that operations can be controlled, but it may be a luxury where time schedules are not so tight.

Real-time Processing.   "On-line processing," broadly defined, includes computing results and making changes to improve the outcome of a process or operation while the events themselves are occurring. Real-time processing is defined in a similar way. On-line and real-time processing involves three stages: obtaining data, processing data, and making decisions while events are still in progress. Time lost in any stage postpones the ability to make a decision. If the events being reported on are changing rapidly, quick processing and output are needed to make decisions before too much time is lost. If events change slowly, more time is available for processing data and making decisions.

Of course, some time, at least fractions of a second, elapses between obtaining data and making decisions. A small amount of elapsed time exists in even the most elaborate systems. Designers of elaborate systems sometimes become so hypnotized by the ingenuity or immensity of their systems that they are tempted to believe they can process data in zero time. This, of course, is absurd. Processing delay can be reduced, but never to zero, by using (1) automatic recorders to gather data, (2) automatic processors to calculate results and apply decision-making rules, and (3) automatic control equipment to regulate the process itself. Real-time control techniques utilizing computers are fairly well developed for some physical systems—refineries, chemical plants, and other process industries. Business-system control, on the other hand, is in the early stages of development.

In-line Processing

"In-line processing" is defined as the processing of data without sorting or treating in any way other than temporarily storing them. Transactions are accumulated for processing later, but the original sequence is unchanged, for only temporary storage is involved. At the proper time, transactions are appropriately processed.

In-line processing might be thought of as on-line processing done under relaxed time requirements. Processing delay is increased, of course, if input is stored even temporarily before processing is completed.

Example. Inventory might be controlled by on-line or in-line data flow. The nature of an in-line plan is worth examining. Transactions—orders, receipts, shipments, insertions to and deletions from catalogues, and so forth—are recorded in a form suitable for processing. At suitable intervals, perhaps daily, transactions are handled by the processor in the same sequence in which they arrive.

The processing unit, by means of the program, determines what type of transaction is involved, finds the inventory item record, and handles the transaction and file record. When wanted, a list of all inventory items, or only of those requiring action, can be printed.

Capacity and Load. In-line data flow has several advantages: input data handling is minimized; sorting or other manipulation is not required; data are recorded in a form suitable for temporary storage before processing; and processor capacity is required only for an average rather than for a peak load. Input from busy periods can be stored until later so that the average use of equipment is high.

A computer primarily assigned to on-line operations can also be used for in-line processing, if capacity permits.

Storage Requirements.   Processing equipment for on-line and in-line data flow are similar in many ways. Entire programs and all related data must be available in storage when transactions are processed. If master files are large, quick access to storage is necessary to keep processing time within bounds. The fact that transactions are not classified by type or sorted into sequence puts a heavy premium on quick access to storage.

Even the simplest inventory accounting application involves orders, receipts, shipments, and additions to and deletions from catalogue listings. Five different types of operations are involved for inventory transactions:

1. Add ordered quantity to on-order file.
2. Transfer received quantities from on-order to in-stock.
3. Subtract shipped quantity from in-stock.
4. Insert new item in catalogue.
5. Delete old item from catalogue.

Each type of operation requires its own instruction routine, and a control program can be used to select individual instruction routines. More storage is required for programs than if only one type of inventory transaction is handled at a time. If data for cost accounting, payroll, performance evaluation, and other functions are included, instruction program and file storage requirements may become excessive.

On-line and in-line processing are generally limited to controlling a single function or a few functions with limited record files and programs. Comprehensive on-line and in-line data-flow systems for business are still in the developmental stages. Mass storage drums and disks are used to hold files for on-line processing for selected applications, such as inventory control.

Off-line Processing

"Off-line processing" involves accumulating and rearranging data, perhaps by sorting, before they are processed. The necessity of sorting transactions for off-line processing should be kept in mind. At least one transaction, a corresponding file record, and appropriate instruction routines must be available to the processor at one time. If storage capacity is large enough, all transactions, files, and programs are available at one time. If storage is insufficient, and it generally is, then only a part of the transaction, file, and program can be stored at one time.

The sorting operation involves separating transactions by class or type so that selected programs and files can be used in processing. A class of transactions may be further sorted into sequence for processing against a file that is kept in the same sequence.

Example.   The example of inventory processing given earlier can be used to illustrate off-line data flow. Transactions—orders, receipts, shipments, and catalogue changes—are put in processable form and accumulated over a period of time. The mere fact that only inventory transactions are involved means that one stage of sorting—classification by broad type—is already done.

The inventory transactions can be sorted for processing into the same sequence as the inventory file, by stock number, for instance. The processor needs to have the instruction routine, one or more transactions, and the corresponding file records. A convenient portion of the transactions and file can be processed at one time. After each part of the file is processed, it is put out and a new part brought in.

The scheme used for handling files and transactions depends primarily on the nature and volume of the transactions and the length of each file record. Equipment storage capacity and the ability to operate simultaneously (read, compute, and write at the same time) also influence the scheme.

Storage and Run.   Computer storage for off-line processing need only be large enough to hold the instruction routine, some transactions, and part of the related file. The savings in storage capacity are obvious. Off-line processing of one class of transactions at a time requires using an instruction routine for that class only. However, much of the economy from saving storage capacity may be offset by the fact that the master file must be run once for each class of transaction involving that file.

It was pointed out above that on-line and in-line data flow require that the processor have available an instruction routine for each type of transaction. A control program selects the particular program for the class of transaction involved. The master file is handled only once to process all transactions.

Data-origination methods often classify transactions by type. Facts about orders, receipts, shipments, and catalogue changes may arise in different places throughout an organization. Transactions are classified when received at the processing unit and can be kept separate for processing. Each class of transaction can be sorted into sequence for efficient processing against the file kept in the same sequence. Data can originate on any medium desired because facilities are available for sorting data on most media.

Off-line or batch processing involves the following operations for file processing:

1. Accumulate input data by batches.
2. Sort input data by type of transaction or sequence number, or both.

3. Select the appropriate instruction routine and read into storage.
4. Read in the transaction.
5. Read in the appropriate file, process it, and write it out.

Make-ready operations for off-line processing involve manual handling and may absorb a large amount of processor time. Furthermore, manual operations increase the possibility of mistakes. Off-line processing may not be the first choice among data-flow plans, but it is often the only feasible plan when equipment has limited capacity. Since computer storage requirements for program and file are reduced, equipment cost and operating speeds are efficiently balanced against each other.

Internal storage capacity and computer speed will increase greatly in the future so that the present emphasis on batch flow for business-data processing is likely to shift toward in-line or on-line flow.

File Processor.   Off-line or batch processing of files can be further refined by selecting from the main file only those records that are affected by transactions. The selected records make up a smaller file or subset that is one hundred per cent active. Transactions can be processed against this selected file to update the records. The updated active items are merged into the master file during the next processing cycle.

Special equipment called a file processor is sometimes proposed for selecting active items from the main file and returning the updated items to the main file. The main processor need handle only the smaller file, without having to search through a large file of inactive items; this saves processing time and storage otherwise spent on inactive accounts.

The use of a file processor or some other special unit with limited processing capacity that can select active records from the main file and return them to it seems to have desirable features for batch processing. The scheme may be economical, if the use of a file processor does not leave the main processor idle. In actual fact, however, file processors are likely to be so elaborate, being designed to handle so many situations, that they are almost indistinguishable from the main computer.

SORTING

The obvious, *immediate objective* of sorting is to arrange items according to rules. Items are sorted on the basis of a "key," which is a set of characters usually forming a field to identify or locate an item. An inventory record might contain the following:

Part Number	Description	Size	Quantity
35079	Truck Tire	650-16	12,327

Inventory records are commonly sorted by part number or description. If items are to be sorted by part number, then the key is 5 digits—35079. Sometimes inventory items are sorted on the basis of description, location, size, or quantity on hand. The point is that any part of a record might be used as the key. A file may be sorted in sequence on one key and not rearranged; this is because processing that would seem to require sorting on another key can be done by some method that does not require sorting. The other processing schemes might be searching, extracting, tallying, or summarizing.

Items are generally sorted into *sequences* on their keys so that they form either an ascending or a descending string. Each key in an ascending string is larger than the preceding keys: 1, 2, 5, 12, 27, 28. Each key in a descending string is smaller: 50, 13, 5, 2, 1.

Alphabetic sorting treats "A" as the smallest letter and "Z" as the largest. Assignment of machine codes to numerals and letters determines the sorting sequence, which makes up a collation table, as illustrated in Chapter 2.

Off-line data-flow plans involve sorting transactions by type and sequence to facilitate processing. It is interesting to consider *why* data are sorted. Most data-processing equipment can more efficiently handle one class of transactions that are in a specified sequence than it can handle a mixture of transactions in a jumbled sequence.

Imagine the problem of finding your girl friend's phone number, if you had no idea whether it was near the beginning, middle, or end of the telephone book. Telephone books are in alphabetic sequence in order to eliminate most of the reading and searching necessary to find any name. If people or equipment could read fast enough, telephone books, catalogues, and other lists could be kept in any order and serve satisfactorily.

The *basic idea* is that limited-capacity facilities work more efficiently with one problem or a small variety of problems. Arrangement in some order may be easier to handle than a jumbled mass. Sorting will continue to precede processing until equipment with much larger, low-cost storage capacity is used in business. Classification and sorting are preliminary to efficient specialization in later stages of processing.

Sorting procedures commonly used in manual, punched-card, and electronic data-processing systems are discussed here. Some factors that determine efficient procedures and equipment for a particular situation are indicated.

Block Sorting

The fundamental idea of how to sort items into sequence is quite simple and can be illustrated by manual sorting. Items can be sorted into sequence, if any progress whatever can be made by it—even as little as arranging two items in sequence. Such a small step must be repeated many times, of course, but in the end a long sequence can be obtained. You might refresh your memory on manual sorting methods by practicing with each of the methods described. You can use slips of paper or punched cards with two- or three-digit numbers written on them. Playing cards are useful, if you give the suits values of 100, 200, and so forth. If you are already familiar with sorting methods, you may skip the description of manual and mechanical sorting.

People often use a block sorting scheme. It is probably the one you use to sort your canceled checks each month, unless your bank is thoughtful enough to sort them for you or even to reconcile your account. You also use a rough block sorting scheme to sort your bridge hand by suit and value, if you are willing to run the risk of having your opponents appraise your hand merely by observing how you sort your cards.

Block sorting starts by classifying items on the left-hand digit in the key. In sorting items with decimal digit keys, each of the 10 blocks obtained will contain keys that have the same first digit. Each of the 10 blocks is then classified on the second digit from the left to give 10 blocks. This second operation gives 100 blocks containing keys that are alike on the first two digits. Each of the 100 blocks is then sorted on the third digit from the left, which yields 1,000 blocks. The process is repeated until all digits are used. Finally, each "block" contains only one key. The myriad blocks are assembled to get the sorted sequence.

Table 9-1 shows block sorting for two-digit keys. The thirties block, with keys 30-39 obtained from sorting on the left-hand digit, is further sorted to get the items in sequence. Nine other blocks (00-09, 10-19, and on through 90-99) also need to be sorted a second time. One hundred blocks are possible, if all keys within the 00-99 range are used. Block sorting might be called "major-minor" sorting because it starts at the left-hand or major part of the key and ends up on the right-hand or minor part of the key.

A serious disadvantage of the block-sorting scheme is the number of blocks that must be handled *separately*. The number of blocks is A, A^2, A^3, A^4, and on through A^n, where "A" is the number of entries in each position in the key and "n" is the number of positions. For decimal keys the number of blocks is 1, 10, 100, 1,000, and so forth. For alphabetic keys, the number of blocks is 26, 676, 17,576, and so forth.

TABLE 9-1. *Block Sorting*

Sorting on the left digit for all items:

Input   Output

13
39
35
11
28
04
26
32
30
37
38
60
06
43
19
75
31
36
82
46 →

00-09	10-19	20-29	30-39	40-49	50-59	60-69	70-79	80-89	90-99
			39						
			35						
			32						
			30						
			37						
	13		38						
04	11	28	31	43					
06	19	26	36	46		60	75	82	
00	10	20	30	40	50	60	70	80	90
-09	-19	-29	-39	-49	-59	-69	-79	-89	-99

Sorting on the second digit for the 30-39 block only:

Input   Output

39
35
32
30
37
38
31
36 →

30	31	32			35	36	37	38	39
30	31	32	33	34	35	36	37	38	39

Output for the 30-39 block is 30, 31, 32, 35, 36, 37, 38, 39

Sorting on the second digit is also required for the 00-09 through 90-99 blocks.

Recombining the final blocks, which are only a single card each, gives the ascending sequence.

A limited amount of block sorting is useful where a large number of items is involved. Initial block sorting segregates a huge number of items into smaller blocks for sorting by other schemes. Digital sorting may then be used to sort each block into sequence.

Digital Sorting

Digital sorting starts by sorting items on the right-hand digit in the key and ends up working with the left-hand digit. Digital sorting might be called "minor-major" sorting because it starts with the minor part and ends with the major part of the field. The output for sorting digital keys is 10 classes. Each class contains items with the same right-hand digit, but with different left-hand digits. For two-digit keys the result of the first pass of digital sorting would be ten classes as follows: 00-90, 01-91, 02-92 and so on through 09-99. The classes can be abbreviated as X0 through X9 where X is any digit or digits.

The 10 classes can be combined in ascending sequence and sorted on the second digit from the right. When the 10 classes are stacked, the items are in sequence from 00 to 99 on 2 right-hand digits. The process can be repeated until all digits in the keys are handled and the items will be in sequence on all digits 00...0 to 99...9.

A procedure to sort cards with a three-digit key into ascending sequence, which can be done either by hand or by machine, is:

1. Sort on the right-hand or units digit.
2. Stack in ascending sequence on the units digit—X0 on top of X1 on top of X2, and so forth—and sort on the second digit from the right or tens digit.
3. Stack in ascending sequence on the tens digit—0X on top of 1X on top of 2X—and sort on third from right or hundreds digit.

A point to remember about sorting in some machines is that machines deal cards from the bottom of the stack. If the deck is arranged according to the rules given above, it is inverted before being placed in the feed hopper. Table 9-2 shows how cards are distributed in 10 pockets of a card sorter after each pass by dealing from the bottom each time.

Unless you are a "card sharp" you need to turn the cards over to handle them "fair and square" during each operation, if you want to sort them manually. You can use your imagination to develop the manual methods for the digital sorting scheme. But some practice with cards is likely to be more educational than your imagination. In general, you can (1) invert the whole deck and deal from the bottom, or (2) leave the deck alone and turn over each card as you handle it. Confusing? Try it for fun.

TABLE 9-2. *Digital Sorting of Cards*

First pass: Sort cards from Input-1 stack on "units" digit.

Input-1: 338 250 960 506 287 819 621 208 082 585 451 688 895 263 557 630 789 124 017 392

First Pass—Output

250								287	338	
960	621	082			585		557	208	819
630	451	392	263	124	895	506	017	688	789
0	1	2	3	4	5	6	7	8	9

Pockets

Second pass: Stack cards from first pass in ascending sequence on "units" digit to get Input-2 stack.

Sort cards from Input-2 stack on "tens" digit.

Input-2: 819 789 338 208 688 287 557 017 506 585 895 124 263 082 392 621 451 250 960 630

Second Pass—Output

								789		
								688		
					557			287		
208	819	124	338		451	263		585	895
506	017	621	630		250	960		082	392
0	1	2	3	4	5	6	7	8	9

Pockets

Third pass: Stack cards from second pass in ascending sequence on "tens" digit to get Input-3 stack.

Sort Input-3 stack on "hundreds" digit.

Input-3	895
	392
	789
	688
	287
	585
	082
	263
	960
	557
	451
	250
	338
	630
	124
	621
	819
	017
	208
	506

Third Pass—Output

		287				585	688			
		263				557	630			895
082		250	392			557	630		895	
017	124	208	338	451	506	621	789	819	960	⬅— 506
0	1	2	3	4	5	6	7	8	9

Pockets

Stack in ascending sequence on "hundreds" digit to get Stack-4. The items are now in order.

Ten output pockets are useful for sorting digital keys one digit at a time, if a simple decimal code is used. An eleventh pocket takes rejects—cards not punched in that position. Two more pockets are included to accept cards punched in the "11" and "12" positions (above the 0 to 9 positions) so that alphabetic keys can be sorted. In short, most card sorters have 13 pockets for alphanumerical sorting. If a complex coding scheme such as the qui-binary, described in Chapter 2, is used, then fewer output pockets are needed, but more passes are required.

Any number of output pockets, from 2 upward, can be used for sorting. Having only a few outputs requires more passes to get the items into sequence; more output pockets permit sorting with fewer passes. Sorters have been built with dozens of pockets for checks and even hundreds of output pockets for ordinary letter mail, because having more output pockets available requires fewer passes of items through the sorter.

Physical separation of each item is an important feature of manual and mechanical sorting. A slip of paper, a card, or an ordinary envelope used for letter mail contains the key and record. When sorted on its key, the record itself is also sorted. On the other hand, some records cannot be separated for sorting. High-density storage makes records so small that physical separation for sorting is not feasible. Such records are usually recopied during sorting. However, one approach to sorting data on magnetic tape is to cut the tape into 1 by 3 in. pieces and sort the individual pieces. In equipment using these pieces, ingenious vacuum techniques are used to hold the small pieces of tape on a revolving wheel in order to perform a "two-pocket" sort for alphanumerical keys by repeated passes.

Electronic Sorting

Sorting records in automatic data-processing systems usually involves recopying from one tape to another. The essential feature is the comparison of two or more items to find which one should be placed first to build the sequence. Records on long magnetic tape cannot be sorted by physical rearrangement in the same way that paper, punched cards, or even short pieces of magnetic tape are sorted. Records on long magnetic tape are transferred to the data processor storage for sorting and writing on tape. Internal storage serves the same purpose as the table top in manual sorting or the output pockets in mechanical sorting.

Many schemes exist for sorting records with electronic equipment (Friend, 1956). Three of these—comparison of pairs, merge sorting, and digital sorting—are discussed here.

Comparison of Pairs. There are several ways to sort items by comparing their keys, which usually involves sorting on the whole key at one time. A quick review of manual methods for sorting by comparison of pairs will make electronic sorting easier to follow.

Items on slips of paper or cardboard might be laid out on a table and the smallest key selected by inspection in the following manner: The keys of the first two items can be compared and the smaller key selected. The selected item is picked up and its key compared with the key of the third item. If the key of the third item is smaller, the card is picked up and the prior item is put in its place. Comparison of the keys of two items at a time continues until the smallest is found and removed from the set. The process of two-item comparison is repeated to find the next smallest item in the remaining set. Completing this loop merely puts one item—in this case the one with the smallest key—at the end of the deck. The loop is repeated from the beginning to get the next item in sequence. As the sequence gets longer, the number of cards remaining to be sorted in the next loop gets smaller.

TABLE 9-3. *Sorting by Comparison of Pairs*

First pass:		Comparison				
Input	1	2	3	4		Output
338	338					338
960	960	506				506
506		960	143			143
143			960	819		819
819				960		960

Second pass:		Comparison			Output
Input	1	2	3		Output
338	338				338
506	506	143			143
143		506	506		506
819		-	819		819
960					960

Third pass:		Comparison	Output
Input	1	2	Output
338	143		143
143	338	338	338
506		506	506
819			819
960			960

Fourth pass:		Comparison	Output
Input	1		Output
143	143		143
338	338		338
506			506
819			819
960			960

It is not necessary to lay the cards out on a table to sort them by the comparison scheme. The cards can be kept in one deck all the time by using a slightly different procedure: Compare the keys on the first two cards and put the larger behind the smaller, or vice versa, if desired. Next, compare the key on the second card—the larger of the first two—with the third. Again, put the card with the larger key behind the smaller one and continue through the whole deck. One complete pass puts the item with the largest key at the back of the deck. Notice that the item with the largest key is placed at the back of the deck on the first pass. This loop, if repeated enough times—actually, the maximum number of passes through the data is one less than the number of items—will yield a sorted sequence. The number of passes necessary depends on the number of item positions that an item has to be moved, or "bubbled up," toward the small end of the sequence when the larger item is selected in each comparison.

Sorting by comparison of pairs to get an ascending sequence is shown in Table 9-3. The first pass merely puts the item with the largest key at the back of the deck. The second pass puts the second or next-to-largest key ahead of it, and so on.

The smallest item, which is wanted at the front, may be anywhere in the deck. The process is repeated until all items are in sequence within one deck. A total of 4 passes involving 10 comparisons of pairs— $4 + 3 + 2 + 1$—is necessary to sort 5 items into sequence for the worst case when the item with the smallest key is at the other end of the sequence and must be bubbled all the way through the string. The average "distance" for the first item to bubble up is one-half the length of the sequence. In this case, the smallest item comes to the top in 3 passes because it was initially the third item from the top. Nine comparisons are enough here, except for checking the sequence by one extra pass in which no change should occur.

The scheme for sorting by comparison of pairs, whether (1) the items are laid out on a table and a new deck built, or (2) the items are kept in one deck, obviously involves many comparisons. To sort 100 cards into sequence involves 99 comparisons on the first pass, 98 comparisons on the second pass after one item is selected, and so forth. Only one comparison is needed on the last pass when 2 items remain. If the end of the sorting operation can be recognized immediately— it is reached when no item moves toward the small end of the sequence—the number of passes can be cut in half in the average case.

In general, to sort N items by comparison of pairs, N–1 comparisons are made on the first pass. N–2 comparisons are made on the second pass, and so on down to one comparison on the last or N–1 pass. The average number of comparisons for a pass is the sum of the largest and smallest numbers divided by two: $\dfrac{N - 1 + 1}{2} = \dfrac{N}{2}$. The greatest possible number of comparisons in any one case would be the average number, $\dfrac{N}{2}$, multiplied by the number of passes, N–1. The product of $\dfrac{N}{2} \times (N-1) = \dfrac{N^2 - N}{2}$ becomes a huge number when N is large. For example, if N $=$ 1000, then the maximum number of comparisons required is $\dfrac{(1000)^2 - 1000}{2}$ or 499,500.

Sorting by comparison may be used with automatic equipment when all items are kept in internal storage throughout the process. This is comparable to manual sorting by comparison of pairs when the items are kept in one deck throughout. The location of items can be exchanged after each comparison, if necessary, so that only the original storage occupied by the items is necessary for sorting them. The item selected after each pass can be put into another section of storage, but additional storage is required in such a case.

Sorting by comparison of pairs is limited to the number of items in internal storage at one time. If desired, the sorted items can be read out, the memory reloaded, and the sorting process repeated. The result is to sort into sequence the set of items that just fills the working space available in internal storage. Separate sets of items are not related so that the whole set is not in sequence. A plan is needed to merge individual sequences together into one over-all sequence.

Merge Sorting. Business records usually involve so many items that computer storage capacity is exceeded and the sequences developed in storage must be merged into larger sequences. Most of the time the items must be stored externally during the sorting process. Furthermore, it is highly desirable or even imperative that, if some of the items are in correct sequence, the sequence should be exploited. On the other hand, digital sorting, you will recall, destroys any sequence that existed in the data when first sorting on the right-hand digit in the key. A deck of cards, whether in correct sequence—which requires no sorting whatever—or in an inverted sequence—which is the most difficult case—is handled precisely the same by the digital sort scheme. Obviously, a scheme that is completely insensitive to the initial arrangement of the data is not efficient. Efficiency can be increased by taking advantage of any sequences that exist in the data.

The merge sorting scheme takes advantage of whatever sequence exists in the data when the operation starts. A set of data already in sequence is handled only once, and the sorting operation merely checks the sequence. Data in the worst possible sequence—completely inverted order—are passed through the computer many times to merge into sequence. Most situations actually lie in between these extremes, for there is usually some order in the data. If two or more sequences exist in the data, each sequence should, of course, be saved and then merged into an over-all sequence.

The basic feature of merge sorting is that it produces a single sequence of items from two or more sequences that are already arranged by the same rules. The number of sequences is cut in half in each merge sorting pass until all the data are arranged in one sequence.

The merge sorting scheme is frequently used for sorting data stored on magnetic tape. The mechanics of merge sorting are: read data from two or more input tapes, arrange the data in sequence on the desired key, and write the data on output tapes. Longer sequences, which are not limited by computer storage capacity, are developed in each pass through the computer until all items are in one sequence. Merge sorting is easier to follow in detail if only two input and two output tapes are used, one item at a time being read from and written on a tape as soon as it is determined which tape it should be written on. The computer follows an instruction program to compare the keys of items received from each input tape with the key of the item just written on the output tape.

The procedure for merge sorting can be stated very simply: Build the longest string possible at each stage on an output tape. This requires comparing the preceding item written on that tape and the two items that are available which may be added to the sequence. As each item is written on an output tape, another item is read from the input tape where the item just written originated. If it is not possible to continue building the string on one output tape—because both items available are too small—switch to the other output tape and start a new string. In short, a three-way comparison is made each time between two items in storage and the item just added to the sequence.

Merge sorting into ascending sequence is illustrated here. For simplicity, only the key is shown for each item; but the remainder of the record is assumed to follow the key at every stage. This is not to say that handling the rest of the item is trivial, because considerable detail is involved merely in keeping a record associated with its key.

Four-tape Merge. Merge sorting with four tapes—two input tapes, A and B containing items, and two output tapes, C and D— can be illustrated for the following initial conditions:

> Tape A : 5, 2, 18, 7, 15, 27
> Tape B : 20, 8, 9, 3, 21, 13
> Tape C : blank
> Tape D : blank

The steps involved in the four-tape merge sorting shown in Figure 9-1 can be described as follows:

1. Read in the first key, 27 and 13 from tapes A and B. Compare 13:27 and write the smaller, 13, on tape C. See Figure 9-1, step 1.
2. Read in the next key, 21, from tape B. Compare with 27 already in storage to find the smaller. If the smaller, 21, is larger than the key, 13, just written on tape C, then write 21 on tape C, as shown in Figure 9-1, step 2.
3. Read in the next key, 3, from tape B. Compare with 27 to select the smaller of the two. If the smaller key, 3, is larger than the key, 21, just

written on tape C, then write 3 on tape C. Since 3 is smaller than 21, do not write it but compare 27 with 21 and write 27 on tape C since 27 is larger than 21, as shown in step 3.

4. Read in the next key, 15, from tape A. Compare with 3 to select the smaller. Since 3 and 15 are both smaller than the last number written on C, neither can be used to build that sequence. The smaller, 3, is transferred to tape D to start a new string, as shown in step 4.

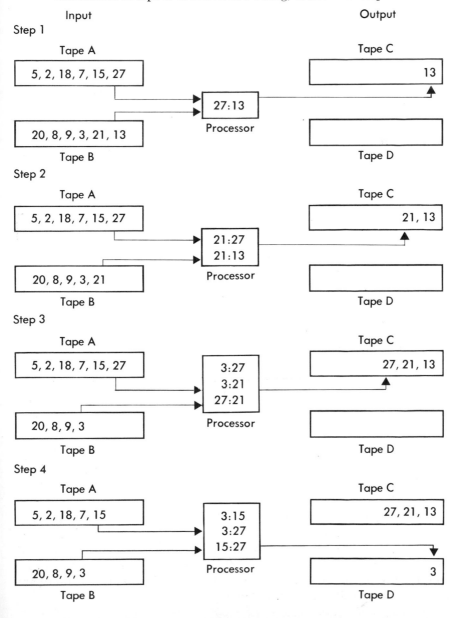

Step 5, conclusion of first pass

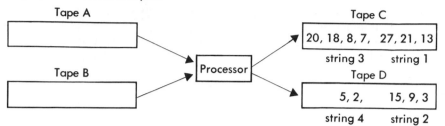

Step 6, conclusion of second pass showing input and output tapes

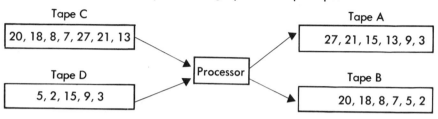

Step 7, conclusion of third pass showing input and output tapes

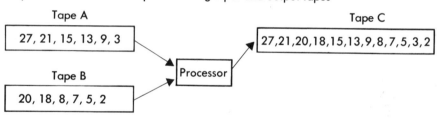

FIGURE 9-1. *Four-tape merge*

The procedure described in steps 2 and 3 is repeated to build the longest possible sequence on tape D. When the available keys will not increase the sequence, a new sequence is started on the other tape. The first pass is completed when all the items on tapes A and B are transferred to tapes C and D. The first pass gives 2 strings on each output tape, as shown in Figure 9-1, step 5.

The output tapes for one pass are input tapes for the next pass. The second pass (notice that tapes C and D are now input) yields one string on each tape as shown in step 6. The third pass, with tapes A and B as input, arranges the items in one sequence, as shown in step 7.

Alternate output is used to get the same number of strings (plus or minus one) on each tape, but it is not necessary to build each sequence on the alternate tape. For a huge number of items, strings can be written on one tape until it is filled. The other tape is then filled. About the same number of sequences is built on each tape, if there are enough items to fill two or more tapes.

Three Tapes on First Pass. The merge sorting example given above assumes that the items are originally stored on two tapes. If items are on one tape, they are separated or dispersed in the first pass. Two items are read in and comparisons are made to build strings as before. The result after one pass is shown below.

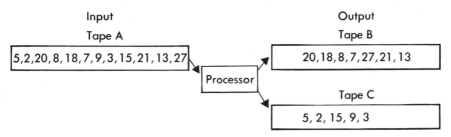

The output of the first dispersion pass starting with one tape corresponds to the result obtained in the illustration involving two tapes, and in this case is identical to it. After the first pass, similar procedures are followed for both cases.

The merge sorting procedure described here uses only one item from each tape. A three-way comparison is made between these two items and the item just added to the sequence on one tape. In a computer with fast internal speeds in relation to input-output speeds, merge sorting is faster; if more items can be compared at one time, longer strings can be built at each stage. The ultimate, for a machine with fast internal operating speed, might be to put all items in storage, arrange them in sequence, and sort them completely in one pass.

Available storage may be filled with the items to be sorted, and later refilled as items are written out in sequence. In this way, the length of each string, counting both key and record, can be about twice as big as the available storage on the first pass. Having longer strings on the first pass reduces the number of passes required, but increases the number of comparisons. The number of items handled simultaneously depends on available storage, record length, number of tape units, input-output speeds, and programming complexities. Input-output speeds become crucial when data are read in and out through many passes.

Number of Passes for Two Inputs. Using more than two input tapes permits building sequences faster and reduces the number of passes required for the case where only two inputs are available. With "n" input tapes (and n is two or more), each pass builds longer strings so that the number of sequences on all the tapes is divided by n. Sorting is complete, of course, when only one string remains. The exact number of passes required depends on the arrangement of data before the sorting operation starts.

The easiest sorting problem occurs when checking the sequence of items already thought to be in sequence. Cards may be sorted into sequences and converted to tape for further processing. The first operation may check the sequence because of the risk that some items may be out of sequence. Each tape starts through the merge sorting procedure, and if the input is in sequence, only one output string is obtained and the sequence is checked. If the input is out of sequence, because cards were not correctly sorted before conversion, two or more output strings are obtained from the first pass. Additional passes are then required to build one sequence.

If items are randomly arranged, some items are already in order. The expected number of sequences is one-half the number of items, because the average string length is 2 items. The general rule for the *expected* number of passes, p, required to sort N randomly arranged items into sequence using n items from the input tapes is stated by the formula:

$$n^p = \frac{N}{2}$$

Comparison of two input items at a time (n = 2) makes it possible to sort N randomly arranged items in an *expected* number of passes, p, according to the formula, N = 2 (n^p) or 2(2^p):

n	p	N
2	1	4
	2	8
	3	16
	5	64
	10	2,048
	11	4,096
	20	2,097,152

The number of complete passes required must be large enough to handle all the items involved. Fractions of a pass are not useful. For example, 11 passes are required to sort any number of randomly arranged items from 2,049 to 4,096 inclusive.

The formula N = 2(n^p) can be written to solve for p:

$$p = \log_n \left(\frac{N}{2} \right)$$

For *randomly arranged* data the actual number of passes required will range between 1 and $\log_n$ N. Only by chance will exactly $\log_n \left(\frac{N}{2} \right)$ passes actually sort N randomly arranged items.

The most undesirable case, as pointed out earlier, is for the original data to be in the reverse of the desired order. Each item is like one sequence, so that the number of sequences and items is equal. The number of items, N, arranged in reverse sequence, that are sortable by p passes is one-half of those shown above. The formula is $n^p = N$ or $p = \log_n N$.

More Inputs, Fewer Passes. The number of passes required in merge sorting can be decreased by using more inputs. Internal sorting of more items to build longer strings on each pass reduces the number of passes. If 8 inputs are handled at one time, the first pass can arrange, say, 65,536 items that are randomly arranged in 32,768 strings into one-eighth as many sequences—4,096. The next pass results in 512 strings. The third pass yields 64 and the fourth, 8 strings. Sorting is complete on the fifth pass, when one sequence is obtained.

Where 8 inputs are used, the number of items in random sequence that are sortable is $N = 2(n^p)$ or $2(8^p)$.

n	p	N
8	1	16
	2	128
	3	1,024
	5	65,536
	10	2,147,483,648
	11	17,179,869,184

Eight input-tape units and 2 output-tape units might be used for merge sorting. A tape on one output unit is first completely filled with sequences; output is then switched to the other output tape and a new tape mounted on the first unit. Output continues at machine speeds without any stop for changing tapes—tape changing is "overlapped" with machine operations. All output tapes are mounted at the same time for the next pass and the operation repeated with 8 inputs and 2 outputs.

Digital Sorting. As described above, punched-card equipment uses the digital or minor-major sorting scheme. Items are sorted on the right-hand digit and re-sorted on the next digit until they are in sequence.

Records on magnetic tape can also be sorted by the digital scheme. One plan is to use a single input tape and 10 output tapes corresponding to the 10 outputs of a punched-card sorter. On the first pass, items with the right-hand digit 0 are put on one tape, with 1 on another tape, and so forth. Outputs are consolidated in order from 0 to 9 and re-sorted on the next digit. When 10 outputs are combined, the sequence is xxx00 to xxx99 where "x" represents any digit from 0 through 9. After three more passes, items with five-digit keys are in sequence from 00000 to 99999. One pass is required for each digit in the key regardless of the number of items, when 11 tapes are used. If the key is short and the number of items is large, digital sorting may be fastest.

Digital sorting with fewer tapes is possible; but more tape passes will be required. With four-tape units, one can be used as input and 3 as output. On the first pass, items with keys ending in 0 or 5 are put on 2 tapes and other items are put on the third tape. Items on the third tape (ending in 1, 2, 3, 4, 6, 7, 8, 9) are transferred to the first tape. They are sorted again with keys ending in 1 and 6 placed after 0 and 5 on the first two tapes, and others (2, 3, 4, 7, 8, 9) on the third tape. Three more passes, a total of 5, put the items in sequence on the right-hand digit. Five more passes are required for each digit in the key. Obviously, a high price is paid in machine time to handle additional passes because of the restricted number of output tapes.

Pre-sorting. One "solution" to the problem of electronic sorting is to arrange items in sequence at an earlier stage. Although this solution does not really solve the sorting problem, the idea of pre-sorting has some merit. Input data might be kept in order as they originate or, perhaps, be sorted before they are put on magnetic tape. Sequence checking might still be desirable, but it might be handled as part of the input editing routine.

On-line and in-line data-flow plans also eliminate the need for internal sorting.

Items on magnetic tape might conceivably be converted to punched cards, sorted by conventional methods, and reconverted to tape for further processing. This scheme involves the cost and time of two conversions. It also increases the possibility of mistakes during sorting, for punched-card sorting is less accurate than electronic sorting. Experience shows that one or more cards may be lost or a stack dropped or misplaced in some fashion when numerous cards are involved. Some people say it is impossible to sort a huge number of cards into perfect sequence because too many things go wrong in the process.

Applications that appear to involve electronic sorting should be examined to determine whether sorting can be eliminated or done elsewhere. Electronic sorting is faster and more accurate than punched-card sorting. Higher-cost equipment may make electronic sorting more expensive, but new equipment and new schemes for use with existing equipment will reduce the costs. The procedures described above represent the current schemes for electronic sorting.

Other Techniques.   Other techniques for sorting may be feasible for some situations. To name them in passing, they are distribution, selection, exchange, and address-calculation schemes.

Some data-processing systems avoid sorting by using random-access storage. Data in the master file are quickly available by means of one of several plans. The key for an item may indicate where the record is located in storage. A table look-up or index may be used to find where a record is stored to obtain it.

Another plan for placing items in storage and later finding them is to use the item number itself as a locator. Some calculations may be performed on the number (square the identification number and select center digits) to get a random-like number. This approach will fit items with ten- or twenty-digit identification numbers into storage for, say, 10,000 records. Only 4 digits (0000 to 9999) are, of course, effective for identifying 10,000 records in storage.

Special Equipment.   Merge sorting schemes involve numerous comparisons. They require comparing one item from each input with the prior item added to the sequence in order to select the next item. These comparisons are made for every item on each pass. The essence of sorting is reading in, comparing, and writing out. The data-processing capacity of a general-purpose computer is only partially used when sorting.

Limited-purpose equipment may sort data at a lower cost than general-purpose equipment. The computer is also free for other tasks that use its capabilities. File processors have been designed that can merge, select, and separate items as well as sort them. Such equipment is similar to and only slightly more complex than sorters.

A file processor is more versatile than a sorter and may be useful even though a sorter is also used. A file maintenance machine is one step more versatile than a file processor. In addition to processing files—by sorting, merging, selecting, and separating—file maintenance equipment makes simple changes, such as additions and subtractions, on items handled. Special-purpose equipment built for sorting, file processing, or file maintenance seems, when built, to be about as complex as general-purpose equipment so that some, but not all, users prefer the general equipment over the special.

System Selection

A system designer may want to minimize either the time or the cost of sorting. An efficient system depends on the equipment available, the sorting scheme employed, and the application involved. Important factors about the application are the number of items, length of record, and number of keys—the items may have to be sorted several times on different keys. Also important are the sequence of the original data, the manner in which data are processed before and after sorting, the speed with which results are wanted, and other functions—editing or checking—that can be combined with sorting.

Sorting data on punched cards is slower, but may be less expensive, than on magnetic tape. Electronic sorting is more nearly automatic than punched-card sorting. Less manual effort is involved, which reduces the risk of mistakes. Punched-card sorting may be preferable if data are already on cards and need be sorted only once.

Sorting data one time merely to count one type of item or re-sorting to accumulate another item is not necessary when a computer is used. Several items can be counted and accumulations made in one pass by the computer with the data arranged in any sequence. The need to sort the items may be eliminated if the computer has enough processing ability to deal with several characteristics of unarranged data.

Merge sorting plans can be programmed to take advantage of any order already in the data, and partially ordered data can be sorted with fewer passes than completely unarranged data. Analysis of the data to devise a more efficient sorting program may be useful. A study might show that a set of items wanted in ascending order is already in descending order. Inverting the sequence would be faster than sorting to rearrange, if it is possible to read the input tape while moving backwards and write the items out in the desired sequence.

Digital sorting, on the other hand, ignores any order in the data. In fact, digital sorting treats every set of items in the same way, for any sequence that does exist is destroyed on the first pass. Digital sorting takes the same number of passes whether items are in the desired, inverse, or random order.

The number of merge sorting passes depends only on the number of items, regardless of the length of the key. The number of digital sorting passes, on the other hand, depends on the length of the key, so that lengthy keys increase the number of digital sorting passes.

An efficient balance is needed between the number of tape units, their arrangement for input and output, programming costs, and computer operating time. Automatic programming methods can "generate" a sorting routine for a set of items. The program provides for computer analysis of the items so that an efficient routine tailored to the application is generated. Having more input units reduces the number of merge sorting passes but increases the number of computer comparisons and other operations on each pass. Each pass takes more machine time, but fewer passes are required.

The above discussion touches factors that a system designer should consider in devising an efficient sorting system: equipment applications, sorting scheme, and system objectives. The point should be kept in mind that a change in equipment or application may eliminate the need for sorting. Frequently, people develop electronic sorting routines following earlier punched-card procedures, but later find that sorting is not required. Increased processing capacity can handle items in any sequence for some purposes—especially counting and tabulating.

FILE MAINTENANCE AND PROCESSING

Business-data processing involves huge files of data on employees, material in stock, customers, production scheduling, and other items. These files must be maintained or updated to reflect non-arithmetical changes in records; this done, the files can be processed to change the contents of individual records by means of arithmetical operations.

File Maintenance

"File maintenance" can be defined as the modification of a file to incorporate additions, deletions, and transfers. More emphasis is placed on the whole record for items than on bits and pieces of a record. Changes in an inventory file, which occur for the following reasons, illustrate the transactions involved in file maintenance:

1. Addition of new stock items to the approved list
2. Deletion of discontinued items
3. Transfers from one section of the file to another because items are reclassified or switched between warehouses
4. Substitution of new facts for old

If the master file is stored on tape in catalogue number sequence, the changes are sorted into the same sequence in order to maintain the file. On the other hand, preliminary sorting of file changes is not required, if the file is kept in random-access storage.

File maintenance inputs, in addition to the computer program, are the master file, new changes, and pending changes left over from the prior maintenance cycle. The outputs are an updated master file, change lists, pending changes, and mismatches. The updated master file will, if everything goes according to plan, reflect addition, deletion, transfer of stock items, and substitution of new facts for stock items that are otherwise unchanged. Change lists are useful for keeping track of the kinds of changes made in the master file and for tracing them, if necessary.

The output called "pending changes" is a peculiarity of maintaining files that are kept in sequence. In one pass of the file, an item can be transferred forward by removing it from its original location and inserting it in the file at a later point. The reverse is not possible because the desired insertion point is passed before the item to be moved is reached. Obviously, the whole record for the item must be obtained in order to insert it at the desired point. In order to move the record for an item upstream in the master file, the record for the item is taken out of the file during one cycle and inserted at an earlier point in the next cycle. The fact that records to be moved upstream are extracted from the master file and kept in a pending change file between two cycles may require that the different types of transactions be handled in a certain order. Otherwise, futile attempts will be made to process the item while it is temporarily "out of pocket."

Mismatches arise in file maintenance whenever the key for an item is incorrect. An attempt to delete, transfer, or substitute an item in the file will end up on an error tape or console print-out, if the input item key does not match the key of a file item. On the other hand, an incorrect key that happens to match the key of another item will result in erroneously changing the wrong record. For an amusing example, a mail order house reported extremely high sales of fur coats because key-punch operators introducing input data tended to transpose the stock number for another item and punch the number for fur coats. Daydreaming and wishful thinking outfoxed the computer; an inventory count and reconciliation was required to correct the record.

Any item can be introduced into a file even though it has an erroneous key. An item with a key 23451 that is erroneously punched as 12345 and added to the file during a file maintenance run will be introduced at the wrong place. The next transaction processed against item 23451 will be rejected as a mismatch (because the earlier item was introduced as 12345) and will be written out on an error tape.

The accuracy of file maintenance operations can be controlled, to some extent, by keeping track of the number of *records* in the file. The initial number plus introductions minus deletions equals the final number of records. Transfers change the number of records in a category, but not in the total. Controls over the modification within individual records require more complicated techniques.

The file maintenance requirements of any application affect the initial selection of equipment, modes of storage, arrangement of master file data, conversion and housekeeping programs, and the amount of computer time that must be devoted to non-production runs. There is a strong tendency for system analysts to concentrate on getting tangible output from production programs without giving careful consideration to the sorting, merging, extracting, editing, and updating programs that must be written and run regularly in order to make a production run possible. A single production run can grow into a half dozen preparatory programs and a like number of one-time file conversion and editing programs.

File Processing

"File processing" can be defined as the modification of a file to incorporate changes that involve arithmetical operations. Examples of inventory transactions handled by file processing are:

1. Purchase and use commitments
2. Receipts
3. Issues
4. Financial accounting

These transactions require arithmetical operations to update the quantity or value of a stock item available or on hand. The transactions are sorted into the same sequence as the master file and processed, by means of suitable programs, against the master files. Many kinds of transactions can be processed in the same run by identifying each type of transaction and having a program to handle that type. The type identifier is used to call up the required subroutine.

The fact that file processing leaves unchanged the number of records in a file facilitates control over a file to guard against erroneous gain or loss of a record. Money amounts can be controlled by keeping control totals—yesterday's balance plus additions and minus deductions equals today's balance—to prove the total of individual account balances. Quantities can be controlled on a unit basis by adding all items, even though dissimilar items are involved.

File processing, at first, seems a simple, straightforward process. Many factors make processing complicated, but one of interest here is the fact that substitution of one stock item for another is possible in some cases. Assume that stock item A is preferable, but if it is not available, then B could be the first alternate, and D the second. Similar patterns of choice may exist for machine assignment in a factory and for a selection of transportation routes. Substitution of an alternate color or a higher priced item for the one ordered may be made. A wag once said that mail order houses try to maximize substitution by sending the alternate, or wrong, item to each and every customer. Ignoring the possible intention of that remark, it is nevertheless possible that every order could be filled "correctly" yet every customer get a substitute.

A matrix can be developed to show how one item can be substituted for another:

Item Wanted	Substitution Choice					
	A	B	C	D	E	F
A		1		2		
B	1				2	
C	No substitutes					
D		1				
E			1			2
F	2				1	

The matrix means that, if A is wanted but is not available, B is the first choice and D is the second choice as a substitute. When processing requests for issues, the decision rules are: (1) try to fill all orders with the item requested, (2) then fill any unfilled orders with first substitutes, if possible, and (3) fill any orders still unfilled with second substitutes, if possible.

In the simple case of 10 units of each item on hand and 10 units demanded, every order can be filled with the item wanted. The situation is more complex if demand for some items exceeds supply. Two or more attempts may be made to fill orders: initially, with the item wanted, next, with the first substitute and, finally, with the second substitute. If the demand for A exceeds the supply, the remaining demand is filled with B and D, *after* the primary demands for those items are filled, and so on.

Another rule for filling orders might be to fill all the orders for A— use A and substitutes B and D, if necessary—then fill orders for B, C, D, and so on. Obviously, the outcome of this scheme depends on whether the order-filling procedure starts with orders for item A and works through to F, or vice versa. More intricate rules might be developed to keep the number of cases of substitution at a minimum or to maximize the quantity ordered that is filled by the item wanted or its first substitute.

Two important points are involved in applying rules to substitute one item for another, if the supply of some items is short. The points are (1) that the allocation cannot be made until a trial run is made involving *all* orders, and (2) some rules are needed to decide how to allocate items in short supply. The allocation rules, once formulated, can be applied as part of the data-processing routine.

File maintenance and file processing have enough in common that they might be handled in the same computer run. Joint treatment may cause some difficulties because control over each kind of operation becomes more difficult. For example, a bank found that checking-account transactions, which were processed in the same run as file changes, often resulted in opening new accounts because of mistakes in account numbers. File maintenance procedures, you will recall, handle insertion of new accounts; and an erroneous transaction account number may either open up a new account or post the transaction to another depositor's account. Erroneously opening a new account causes some difficulty; but posting to the wrong account is at least twice as bad, for it affects two depositors who may be annoyed by the mistake. One remedy is to handle file maintenance and processing in two separate runs so that tighter control can be kept over the opening and closing of accounts.

Maintaining and processing files kept on magnetic tape usually requires rewriting the whole tape each time any part of the file is changed. If only a small percentage of the records in the file change when files are processed on a short cycle, there are several ways to cut down the work of recopying the whole file just to update the small fraction of active records. One way is to update a fraction—one-fifth or one-twentieth—of the master file each day so that the whole file is updated once in a week or a month. The whole file is never really current but, on the other hand, it is almost current, for it averages only 2 days old, if one-fifth is updated each day. On any day one-fifth is current or zero days old, and the other fractions are 1, 2, 3, and 4 business days old, respectively.

A second way to keep files current without rewriting the tape completely is to retain the master tape intact and accumulate the changes on a change tape. Modifications to the master file are accumulated on the change tape until it becomes unwieldy. Finally, the change tape is processed against the master file to update it, the change tape is discarded, and the cycle started afresh. At any time, both the master tape and the change tape must be considered together to get the current status of a record.

There is a third approach to the problem of reducing the waste of rewriting whole tapes just to change a few records. Some computers provide for writing the revised record in the space occupied by the original and leaving the other records unchanged. Precautions are necessary, of course, to keep the new record within the space occupied by the old.

After setting up, maintaining, and processing a file the question arises: "How long should I keep the file and transactions before I discard them?" A commonly used plan is to keep 3 "generations" of files. For example, Monday's output is retained until Wednesday's output is successfully used as input on Thursday. Then Monday's files can be discarded leaving the files for Tuesday and Wednesday for back-up, in case Thursday's output is defective. Certain files—those for the end of each month, for example—may be retained longer to prepare reports and answer unexpected questions. The ability to reconstruct all records from a specified date to the present may be wanted as protection against mishap. If so, copies of the master file for that date and all interim transactions must be kept.

The general rule for deciding when to discard output files, and even raw data, is easy to state: discard the file when the cost of keeping it exceeds the probable value of having the data on hand. Application of the rule is difficult because it is difficult to forecast when and what demands will be made on the files that are saved.

Magnetic-tape files pose problems similar to those of retaining paper records; but some problems are accentuated. The tendency to save data and processed results is stronger for magnetic tape than for other media because of high data density and economical processing. Furthermore, the possibility of selectively rewriting tape files to eliminate some of the detail, while keeping the more consequential facts, is a plus factor in retaining tape files. Selective condensation may be done one or more times before the files are discarded and the tape re-used. Economic analysis alone would cause one to predict that a higher fraction of data in magnetic-tape files will be saved than is the case for paper and card records. This is true even though tape is re-usable. As the cost of an item decreases, the quantity used is likely to increase. For example, the Bureau of the Census reports that many *thousands* of magnetic tapes full of data are being stored for statisticians and others who may want to process them at some future date to answer questions that are not yet formulated. Of course, if all future questions likely to be asked about data in the files could be formulated now, the questions could be answered and the files discarded.

PROCEDURES FOR INTEGRATED DATA PROCESSING

Integrated data processing attempts to improve the flow of data throughout an organization. A brief discussion of the factors that have caused fragmentary data handling will help put the problem into perspective. More extensive discussions of integrated data processing are given by Boardman, 1956; *Establishing an Integrated Data-Processing System*, 1956; and van Gorder, 1954.

Fragmentary Data Handling

Most business organizations are divided into functional departments—as sales, production, accounting, finance, and marketing. Department activities are inter-related, but each is primarily concerned with one function so that no one below the executive vice president has an over-all view of operations. Limited system capacity also contributes to fragmentary data processing. Some limits of people and machines in processing systems are:

1. The number of instructions usable by a processor
2. Speed of a processor
3. Efficient file size, organization, and use

Documents and reports that may vary only slightly in content and timing are often wanted in each department, but these small differences require the preparation of entirely new copies to make slight changes. The documents involved in purchasing a stock item illustrate the degree of repetition that occurs with only minor variations.

1. A purchase request is sent to the purchasing department by the inventory control group.

2. Quotations are requested from several suppliers by the purchasing department.

3. An order is placed with a selected supplier by the purchasing department.

4. The type and number of items actually received is reported by the receiving department.

Some data—the part number, quantity, date wanted, and delivery point—are copied on all forms. Identical data are typed and handled many times and each department involved keeps records and personnel to maintain them. Fragmentary data processing is expensive because of the inefficiency that stems from repetitive operations and file duplication.

Mechanized Duplication

An obvious way to increase the efficiency of fragmentary data processing is to mechanize the operations duplicated at each stage. The concept of mechanizing repetitive operations is one element of "integrated data processing," which is a scheme for mechanically repeating data at each stage of document processing.

Integrated processing minimizes the disturbance of regular office routines. Standard office machines—typewriter, calculator, and posting machine—are used, but are modified to produce and to operate from some low-speed medium. Five-channel paper tape was first used as the common language medium, for it can be sent over wire circuits. Rapid communication is important in order to achieve integrated processing for a geographically scattered organization.

Many office machines operate with five-channel tape; but some operate with six-, seven-, or eight-channel paper tape. New developments in wire communication systems handle these. Punched cards can be punched in regular fashion and also edge punched or end punched with paper-tape codes. If interference between the two styles of punching is avoided, the cards can, of course, be processed with punched-card equipment. Office equipment that handles punched paper tape requires some modification to operate with edge-punched cards.

Either punched cards or punched paper tape can be sent directly over wire circuits; the use of wire circuits, however, may cost more than faster transmission is worth. Some organizations mail punched tape overnight to save money and yet suffer little delay in processing. Others convert punched cards to tape for mailing to avoid the cost of mailing the cards or of sending either the cards or tape by wire.

Basic Rules. The basic procedural rules for integrated data processing are:

1. Record the data initially on office machines that produce tape or cards as a by-product.
2. Process the original data and any additional data on office machines that read and produce punched tape or cards.

Example. Common language data-processing integration can be illustrated by reference to the example of a stock purchase given earlier under the topic of fragmentary data handling. "Common language" means that all the devices involved—typewriters, calculators, transmitters, and others—operate with the same code. The inventory control department initiates a purchase request when available stock falls below the re-order point. The request is prepared on a tape-reading and tape-punching typewriter. A paper-tape strip punched with fixed data—number, name, and re-order quantity—was prepared earlier and attached to each stock record card. This strip is obtained from the stock record card and inserted in the tape reader of the typewriter.

The typewriter copies fixed data from the tape for the item wanted. Variable data—date wanted and request number—are entered on the manual keyboard. Constants, such as the date of the request, might be automatically entered by the machine. Thus, the typewriter produces both a page copy of the request and a punched tape containing either all data or selected parts. The inventory control department keeps a copy of the request and the tape, and sends copies of the request and tape to the purchasing department. The typed copy and punched tape are used in conjunction with files of fixed-data tapes for preparing new documents and tape with minimum manual typing. Copies of documents and new tapes are sent to the next user or filed, whichever is appropriate.

The purchasing department uses a tape reading-punching typewriter to prepare the quotation requests. The tape received from the inventory control group is put in the tape reader to type a bid request. A clerk uses a punched tape from the file or manually enters a bidder's name and address. The typewriter prepares a typed copy and a new tape with the item, quantity, date wanted, and bidder's name and address for each request.

The purchasing department mails the original copy of the request to a bidder and files a copy and the new tape. A purchase order is typed from one bid request tape and sent to a selected bidder. A copy of each purchase order and tape is sent to the receiving department; at this point, bid request tapes are no longer useful and can be destroyed. The receiving department uses the tape from the purchasing department to type a receiving report for single shipments. Clerks enter date and quantity for partial shipment and make reports and tapes to use when the remainder of a shipment is received.

The integrated data-processing scheme for stock control can be used where the inventory control, purchasing, and receiving departments are geographically separated, because punched paper tape can be mailed or transmitted over wire circuits. The example of stock control and supply shows the basic idea of common language between different equipment; but it omits the details. The fundamental point is that manual operations are reduced when duplication of repetitive data is mechanized. Operations are similar to those in a manual system except that they are tied together by five-channel tape or a similar medium. A limited amount of planning and personnel training is required to set up an integrated system.

An integrated data-processing system has a higher capital cost than a manual system. The ratio of capital investment to labor costs is increased and clerical costs are reduced. Data are both more accurate and more timely, as the manual element in processing is reduced.

Functional Integration

Functional integration goes much further than mechanized duplication because it cuts across departmental boundaries in order to consolidate data processing as such. A data-processing department may be set up to use large-scale equipment and specialized personnel. Systems built around large-scale equipment are not limited in the same way that manual or integrated systems built around punched-tape office equipment are limited. Large-scale equipment can be programmed to follow long and complex instructions for processing against huge files. Files that were previously kept separate for people to use can be consolidated into a few files for efficient processing.

Inventory files showing financial value and quantity illustrate the point of separate and consolidated files. These files are kept separate in a manual system because two groups of clerks—those in accounting and production control—maintain them. Each group wants sole control over records for convenience and to avoid mistakes. Automatic processing equipment can process dollar values and quantity transactions against both files. Transactions and files are so closely related that one consolidated file for joint processing of both transactions may be most efficient.

Fundamental changes in the organizational structure may be required for functional integration. Departments may be merged and far-reaching procedural changes made. Large-scale equipment involving a large outlay is at the heart of a functionally integrated system; therefore, the ratio of capital to labor is much higher than in a manual or a common language system. Personnel orientation and training for new equipment and procedures poses many challenges, for intensive planning is required to develop and install a system that integrates functions. Functionally integrated systems save the costs of keeping several sets of processing facilities. Duplicative records are eliminated, clerical tasks are reduced, and office space is freed. Consolidated files permit more efficient processing because transactions can be entered in one pass of the central file, whereas separate files would require individual processing. If you let your imagination range a bit, you will probably conclude that sufficiently comprehensive integration could cut processing loads in half since there are two parties to any bargain and they look at it from opposite viewpoints. A sale by one is a purchase by the other; a transfer of cash is alternately a receipt and a payment.

Common Language and Functional Integration

Common language integration mechanizes the processing of repetitive data. Manual operations are reduced, but everything else remains unchanged. On the other hand, functional integration involves large-scale equipment, consolidated files, and some organizational realignment. The emphasis is on eliminating repetition instead of merely streamlining it.

Common language integration may be useful, if opportunities for functional integration are limited. Some aspects, such as mechanization at the point of origin, are compatible with automatic data processing. Tying several functional areas together with common language media is no panacea; it is not efficient for all situations.

Large scale equipment facilitates merging several functional areas. A common language system may not be an efficient intermediate step between manual and automatic systems. There are drawbacks to an interim system, even though equipment and procedural change costs are modest. Management may postpone further changes until costs of the interim system are recovered, and frequent changes disturb the whole organization and may be resisted by many people. It must be said that both common language and functional integration deserve consideration when an automatic data-processing system is being developed.

SUMMARY

Processing procedures depend on what information is wanted and what data are available. Other factors are the techniques available, the relative advantages of fragmentary or consolidated processing, and time limitations. The points where data originate and their form affect the design of efficient processing procedures. A jumble of transactions requires different schemes for processing than transactions classified by type.

A time lag exists between the development and widespread use of the newest techniques. Some aspects of techniques that are considered are the degree of automation of equipment, and the methods of organizing and keeping files. Equipment must be large enough to deal with an application, although the problem may be partitioned and handled in parts. Specialization arising in this fashion is commonplace.

All files for an organization might be consolidated into one master file; but minimized file duplication, in itself, raises new processing problems because storage requirements are huge and programs extremely complex. Fragmentary processing is a piecemeal approach to the data-processing needs of business. It is useful, if business operations are so independent that there is no reason to combine them.

Input methods depend on where the data originate and where the results go. The form, accuracy, and load of data originating within the organization are more controllable than for data that originate outside. Input methods may make use of low or high ratios of capital to labor. Accurate input data are obtained either by repeating manual operations or by using more equipment. The ultimate is completely automatic input that does not rely on people.

Requirements for equipment capacity—measured in terms of input facilities and processor storage—and processing programs differ with each data-flow plan. The off-line data-flow plan is widely used. On-line flow is used for selected business applications that require quick answers to simple questions, such as how many widgets are in stock at each location. Another question, similar to the one regarding inventory, that is answered by on-line systems is whether airplane seats are available on certain flights between two cities on a particular date.

Data in large files are sorted into an organized sequence because reading or searching through the file to find a desired item is too slow. Facilities with limited capacity work better with one problem or a small variety of problems. Further arrangement of transactions into file sequence is required, if file reference is slow.

Sorting arranges items into sequence on the basis of their keys. A key is a field of characters used to identify or locate an item. An item may have several keys to identify various features—part number, size, location, and so forth. Items may be sorted on one individual key or on two or more keys—one major and one minor. Classification by type of a file item or transaction—as a payroll or stock record and the collection or payment of money—are simple examples of sorting. Arranging items in sequence—ascending or descending—is more complex. The relationship of each key to every other key must be considered in sorting. Commonly used schemes are block, digital, comparison, and merge sorting. People seem to prefer a block-sorting scheme and will balk if forced to use the comparison-of-pairs scheme. Punched-card equipment uses a digital plan, whereas electronic equipment is often programmed to follow the comparison and merge sorting schemes.

Merge sorting with a computer takes items from strings held in external storage, compares them in internal storage, and puts them out in longer strings. The process is repeated in succeeding passes until one continuous string is developed. The number of passes required is related to the number of items sorted, regardless of the length of the key. Merge sorting often uses two-tape input and two-tape output. Sequences are built up in fewer passes by using more input tapes and some applications use as many as eight input tapes. Special equipment—sorters, file processors, and file maintenance machines—are considered useful, if the load on the main processor is heavy and volume of special type of work is high.

The selection of equipment and sorting scheme depends partly on whether the objective is to minimize the cost of sorting or the time required. Important factors in system selection are the number of items, length of key, length of record, sequence of original data, processing required before and after sorting, available time, and other functions that can be combined with sorting. Sorting with electronic equipment is faster and more accurate than punched-card sorting; but it may be more expensive unless the equipment, sorting scheme, and application are closely attuned.

File maintenance covers updating of files not involving arithmetical operations, whereas file processing covers arithmetical operations. Though similar in many respects, these two operations may be kept separate to avoid mistakes from handling both at one time. The use of tape files raises new problems because most computers can update records only by rewriting the whole file. Reduced costs of storing data on magnetic tapes and ease of subsequent processing increase the tendency to keep more data for a longer time than is practical with card or paper records. Partial processing—to allocate stock and make substitutions, for example—is sometimes necessary in order to make operating decisions.

Fragmentary processing of data exists because business is organized by functions and machines have limited capacities. Some limitations of people and machines are storage capacity, number of instructions that can be used, processing speed, efficient file size, and input-output units. Fragmentary processing is expensive because of the file duplication involved. Management information is obtained in bits and pieces from scattered files and unrelated processing.

Integrated data processing mechanizes the duplication of repetitive data. A common language medium, such as punched paper tape, is produced on modified office equipment and thereafter used to operate other similar equipment. Repetitive operations are mechanized; but this approach to integration deals with symptoms instead of with the causes of fragmentary processing.

Functional integration cuts across departmental lines in order to consolidate data processing as such. Fundamental changes in the organizational pattern may be required for functional integration. Departments may be merged and far-reaching procedural changes made. Functionally integrated systems can reduce the cost of equipment, files, and clerical work. Equipment with a large capacity is a prerequisite to functional integration.

REFERENCES AND SUPPLEMENTAL READINGS

Boardman, Lansdale. "What It Means to Integrate Data Processing," *N.A. C.A. Bulletin*, vol. 37: 1191-1198 (June 1956). This article distinguishes integrated data processing as a concept and method from the equipment through which it may be applied. The several data-processing sequences most adaptable to integration are identified, and the steps involved in evaluating a company's needs are listed. An example not involving electronic equipment is described.

Establishing an Integrated Data-Processing System: Blueprint for a Company (Special Report No. 11), New York, American Management Association, 1956, 183 pp. This report was adapted from material originally prepared by Ralph H. Eidem and others for an A.M.A. orientation seminar with the same title held in 1956. The five sections cover the preliminaries, tailoring the program, the installation process, IDP and the worker, and the long view. Three case studies describe the experience of companies in planning for and using integrated data processing.

Friend, E. H. "Sorting on Electronic Computer Systems," *Journal of the Association for Computing Machinery*, vol. 3: 139-68 (July 1956). Sorting is a basic operation in most business and scientific data-processing procedures. Since larger volumes of data are handled with electronic data processing, it is important to use the optimum sorting technique. The form and arrangement of the input data determines the best method or combination of methods that should be utilized. The seven techniques of high-speed internal sorting discussed, compared, and evaluated in detail are internal merging, inserting, exchanging, internal digital sorting, counting, selecting, and radix sorting.

van Gorder, H. F., and others. *A New Approach to Office Mechanization: Integrated Data Processing Through Common Language Machines*, New York, American Management Association, 1954, 62 pp. Describes a concept of integrated data processing by making all office machines operate from a five-channel punched tape, and tells the way in which U. S. Steel originally developed the idea and put it into practice. The fundamentals of the idea, origination of data, calculation and distribution of data, conversion and high-speed processing, and communication of data are covered in detail.

Wiseman, R. T. "Life Insurance Premium Billing and Combined Operations by Electronic Equipment," *Journal of the Association for Computing Machinery*, vol. 1: 7-12 (January 1954). Mechanical processing of insurance company data has been a fractured operation with many files due to the relatively low cost of filing as compared to computation, the limited data capacity, and the limited processing ability of the equipment. Electronics has altered these conditions and led to a "combined operations" approach with one large policy record and longer mathematical processes. The consolidated record on magnetic tape can be stored in 1 per cent of the space used previously. The system devised by Sun Life Assurance Company of Canada has been tested successfully on a Univac. The combined operations result in greater accuracy and will allow many of the inventory jobs now causing a peak year-end load to be spread out over the year. Installation of a computer makes necessary a major, and perhaps painful, reorganization of supervisory responsibilities. The staff reduction, which is one of the justifications for buying an expensive machine, can be handled by a reduced hiring rate without resorting to layoffs. A supplement compares existing and proposed formulas for reserve and dividend determinations.

PART FOUR

PRINCIPLES OF PROCESSING SYSTEMS

CHAPTER TEN

DATA AND
INFORMATION:
COST AND VALUE

Few general principles or even rules exist to serve as guides for designing data-processing systems. This lack of general principles, which stems from several causes, will be examined briefly. Most of this chapter deals with factors that should be considered in searching for fundamental ideas about business data-processing systems. An example shows the formulation of some of the concepts into analytic expressions that describe a simple business situation.

The first reason for lack of general principles is that operating systems are *difficult to describe* in simple terms. This is true whether the system uses manual, punched card, or electronic methods. Analysis is expensive and time consuming. Systems do not remain in a "steady state" but continue to change even during analysis. In fact, the rate of change may outrun the analysts who must keep abreast of the old system while designing a new one.

Second, the operating *environment* and the *problems* to be handled differ from one case to the next. People, data inputs, and reports wanted from the system are all different even though equipment and operations are similar. Such differences limit the value of comparing data-processing operations in two different environments. Comparison of the proposed system with a system that does not change or with an extrapolation of the present system may be valuable for drawing valid conclusions about the effect of new proposals. Laboratory models or controlled experiments are valuable for showing the effect of certain changes. But it is difficult to use a business as a laboratory for testing new ideas about data processing because of the unsettling effect of experimentation and the risk that untested initial operations may fail.

A third reason for the lack of any general rules pertaining to the use of electronic equipment is the fact that its use is still quite *new*. Experience now available covers only a short period of time and not a complete cycle from installation to introduction of still newer equipment. Imagine the problem of an insurance actuary if he were asked to predict average life expectancy on the basis of the life histories of a few children. Important changes in both equipment and the systems built around the equipment occur frequently, and they will continue to occur indefinitely.

Fourth, data-processing systems are *complex*. The equipment is a maze of electronic, electric, and mechanical parts. The system built around the equipment in order to handle the origination of data and distribution of results reaches throughout all parts of a business organization.

These four factors—difficulties of description, lack of laboratory conditions, newness of electronic equipment, and complexity of equipment and systems—impede the development of exact rules for system design and operation.

A formula would be useful for determining system and equipment needs and ways of using them. Such a formula may be developed, but one does not exist now. Lacking a formula, one approach to solving the problem is to search for some of the basic ideas involved. An understanding of the concepts or general principles is useful in any field (Hitch, 1955). It is doubly important in a new and developing field such as automatic data processing. General principles must be developed before useful, specific rules can be devised. A search for general principles reveals new facets of a subject, puts various features into perspective, and discloses new relationships.

This chapter marks out areas that deserve analysis and suggests avenues leading toward general principles about data-processing systems. The two broad areas considered here are (1) the distinction between data and information and (2) the cost of processing data and the value of the information obtained.

CONCEPTS

Some attention must be given to a critical but neglected feature of data-processing systems. A distinction needs to be drawn between the words "data" and "information," which are often used interchangeably.

Data

"Data" can be defined as any facts that are a matter of direct observation. As used in business-data processing, "data" means collections of signs or characters generally arranged in some orderly way to make up facts and figures. Numbers, words, charts, tables, and reports are examples of data which represent the *syntactic* level of an information system—the patterns of formation of messages from words in a particular language.

Data-processing systems are designed to handle data that describe various situations and to produce information, the latter point being developed below. Viewed in this sense, data are essentially the input or raw materials for a system designed to process data and produce some desired output. In order to be useful in subsequent stages of processing, data must be new, accurate, and timely. The output obtained from processing data can, of course, exceed in both quantity and quality the original input. For a simple example, given the quantity of an inventory item on hand and the rate of usage, reports can show these two facts and the projected quantity on hand at any date in the future, including run out.

Information

"Information" is the significance derived from the data, which are vehicles for conveying certain potentially meaningful facts. The meaning of "information" is at the *semantic* level—the relationship between a sign and the actual object or condition represented by the sign. For our purposes, we further give to "information" a significance at the *pragmatic* level—the impact of the objects or conditions on the receiver. In this case, the impact is in terms of (1) the degree to which the receiver knows or has already guessed, based on his knowledge about the situation, the picture presented, and (2) the degree to which he can correctly utilize the picture presented. (The information theorist's view of information is given by Rosenstein, 1955.)

The recipient of a message—a report or document, for example—receives information if he understands the relationship between the symbols and actual conditions (*semantic* level) without already knowing or guessing the content of the message, and can act on the basis of the message (*pragmatic* level). "Information" implies understandability, relevance, ability to act, novelty, timeliness, and accuracy. Discussion and some examples will give meaning to these ideas.

In order for information to be useful, the reader must correctly understand the meaning of the facts and have some use for what he learns. Otherwise he gets misinformation or no information that *he* can use even though correct information is available.

Excessive quantities of information are available. Care is needed to keep it focused on a manager's needs and restricted to his ability to use it. Business-data systems, instead of emphasizing production of all information, should focus on producing information relevant to and useful in decision making. A manager should be able to use the information in making his decisions, which are usually restricted to a limited area of an organization. There are usually more decisions to be made than a manager can make, and he does not have complete freedom to make any decision he wishes. The point is that information must be related to areas that the manager controls, in which he has freedom or "elbow room" to take action. Furthermore, he needs information on any problem while his decisions can still affect its solution.

A report that merely confirms what a person already knows does not provide him with new information, although it may reinforce his knowledge. Newness or novelty is basic to the definition of information content. Novelty depends on the reader's knowledge about the situation described; the more he knows, the less information a report contains for him, although it may contain information for someone else.

Status or condition information pertains to a point in time—the number of widgets in stock on June 30, for instance. Operating or dynamic information, on the other hand, covers a period of time—the number of widgets used during the month or quarter ending June 30. The timeliness necessary for status and operating information depends upon the use made of it. For learning what *did* happen during the period ending June 30, a report by July 25 would be suitable for some purposes, whereas reports by July 5 would be necessary for other purposes. In order to plan operations and manage them before the event so that desired results can be achieved, forecasts of what *will* happen are necessary. Thus, after-the-fact reports are suitable in some cases, but other cases require before-the-fact forecasts in order for the information to be timely.

The degree of accuracy required for information to be useful may vary from being highly precise to being only a rough approximation of the facts. A person expects a bank to keep his account to the precise penny although he may have trouble keeping track of the simple fact of whether the balance is overdrawn. Accurate results can be obtained, in many cases, by devoting enough skill and effort to record keeping, although the cost of the desired degree of accuracy may outrun the value obtained from having it, as pointed out later in this chapter. On the other hand, forecasts, which are more often the basis for operating decisions than are cold, hard facts, are likely to be accurate only within fairly broad limits. For its intended use, each degree of accuracy is suitable, everything considered.

Within a data-processing system, most verification procedures are aimed at detecting syntactical mistakes, such as incorrect numerals or letters. For input data, syntactical mistakes are important; but semantic mistakes probably occur just as often because the characters of the input message do not truly represent the object of the situation in question. A processing system may include procedures to detect some semantic mistakes—a weekly time card showing 99 hours worked can be rejected as semantically incorrect even though it represents an accurate transcription of legitimate characters. Pragmatic mistakes—a wrong decision given the right picture—can occur at the point of information use. A pragmatic mistake arises because the decision rule is incorrect; the rule, for example, might be to decrease production as the stock is depleted. Then too, the correct rule could be incorrectly applied. Correction of pragmatic mistakes may be made through a second look or a review (perhaps by calculating the results of a proposed decision) before implementing the decision.

Improvements in processing data may not, contrary to general belief, always improve the information system. In fact, the two objectives may be in conflict. Modern equipment prepares reports so cheaply that a manager may be literally buried under a mountain of paper. He may react by spending his time searching for information or by merely throwing away reports without glancing at them. Desks and files may become temporary wastebaskets until reports are discarded. In such a case the system may process data, but it does not provide useful information in an efficient fashion.

DATA AND INFORMATION SYSTEMS

The data-processing unit is an element of a much larger system, namely the "management information system." The main purpose of a data-processing unit is to provide information, not merely to marshal facts. Data serve as the carriers for relaying information to management. Managers obtain information from many sources other than the data-processing unit: they look at operations, talk with people, and observe conditions.

Sources of Information

A manager has many ways to learn how many widgets are in stock. He may read an available report, telephone the head widget-keeper, or just guess. If he arrives at the right number of widgets in stock, within a margin of error suitable for the problem under consideration, an additional report contains little information for him. A complete study of a management information system should consider all methods of originating and communicating data.

The design of any information system is influenced by the system already in use within the organization. The system changes because new equipment or concepts become available or because new requirements arise. The mere fact that automatic equipment is being introduced warrants some fundamental changes in procedures. Some changes will be really new, while others will be old ideas that could not be put into effect with the equipment then in use. Flexible, high-speed equipment allows both new and old ideas to be exploited more effectively.

Selection of Information From Data

An important feature of system design is how to select informa-tion useful for decision making from all the facts that are available. The problem is not new and is present in all systems. One approach is to appraise each situation individually. People may develop rules to select information from the facts and apply them to a number of situations. But the introduction of automatic processing equipment warrants, for two reasons, more attention to the problem of efficient selection of information.

First, output reports will increase in both volume and number as data processing and high-speed printing become cheaper. Second, versatile instruction programs for automatic processors can relieve management of some of the task of selecting information from data.

An initial step in making a decision is to obtain information that bears on the problem. Automatic selection of relevant and consequen-tial information permits management to concentrate on decision making without worrying about the mechanics of data gathering and report preparation. A simple way to prepare reports is to develop a list of related items that should be included in the reports prepared each and every period. All items are included in every report without regard to their information content. The procedure is simply to collect data, process them, and print reports. Managers study the reports to find significant facts for decision making.

Figure 10-1 is a block diagram of an elementary system for pro-ducing reports for management. The processing unit produces reports. Management's function is to analyze reports, select information, and make decisions.

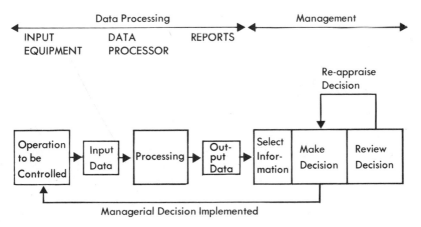

FIGURE 10-1. *Data processing to produce reports*

Exception Principle

The selection of informative data can be accomplished by equipment, instead of by people, in one of several ways. The exception principle is a first step beyond merely processing the data. The exceptions isolated by the processing system are reported in one of two ways. (This section on the exception principle follows Gregory, 1959.)

One method is to have readers scan complete reports to find significant differences. Complete reports can show actual results, planned or expected results, and differences. The differences may be in the same units—dollars, hours, or tons—as the individual items. Percentage variations from expected results are often shown and readers scan reports to find significant differences for action. Complete reports are widely used because their preparation is simple: every item is reported in a fixed format regardless of the amount of the item or its variation. Management's selection task may be difficult because significant items get buried in a mass of data.

A second method for using the exception principle scheme is to report only those items that vary significantly from the planned results (Gregory and Trust, 1959). The processing system examines each variation to find whether it is worth managerial attention. If so, the item is reported. If not, it is omitted. Data must, of course, be collected and processed in order to be available for possible inclusion in reports. But only those items that have significant variations are included in managerial reports. A complete report with all items can, if desired, be prepared for reference purposes.

Figure 10-2 is a block diagram of the scheme for data processing and report preparation by the exception principle. It shows that selected output goes to management. Complete reports are available as back-up and for further analysis to select other items as necessary. Management still makes all decisions.

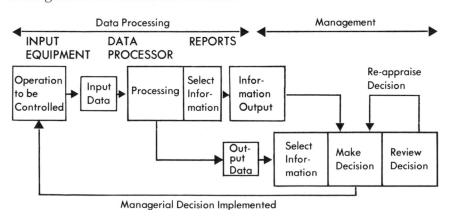

FIGURE 10-2. *Data processing to produce information*

Normal Range.   Several steps are involved in setting up and using an exception principle system. The fact that exceptions can be determined and reported presumes the existence of a target or expected result. A normal range of actual value above or below the expected result is established for each item in a report. The normal or natural range is fixed, so that if actual results are within the range, a single plan of action gives good results. An item that falls inside the normal range is omitted from reports because no new action is required. If an item falls outside the normal range, it can be reported in detail—name of item, planned amount, actual amount, and variation. The manager responsible for its control can take whatever action he thinks best.

The exception reporting plan strives to increase the information content—understandability, relevance, novelty, and timeliness—of reports. The normal range selected for each item to be reported is critical to the success of the plan.

Setting the Normal Range.   The reason for setting up a normal range of expected value is that one course of action is suitable for items within the normal range of value while items outside it require a different kind of action. The normal range should be wide enough to cover all items that do not require new action so that such items are not reported to managers. The width of the normal range is limited by the fact that a plan of action for a particular item should give good results. If the range is too wide, an action plan that is suitable when the actual result is near the top of the range is unsuitable when the actual result is near the bottom of the range. Use of the normal range implies a control plan. The process is assumed to be in control if actual results fall anywhere within the normal range; but the process is considered out of control and new action is required when the actual result falls outside this range. Upper and lower control limits are the boundaries of the normal range.

The control limits to be used are obvious when action rules already exist. For example, re-order points are used as lower control limits for inventory management. Stock items that have smaller balances are reported. A manager can learn which items must be ordered without examining all items and without making any calculations. On the other hand, the normal range may be difficult to set if no action rules exist. A lack of explicit action rules implies that decisions are based on "judgment," which is, in reality, a rather amorphous decision rule. Many factors affect an item and actual amounts may appear erratic. Normal range for an erratic item can be developed by starting with the planned amount and considering the degree of variability or fluctuation in the item. Management may be able to set the planned or expected values for some items but not for others. For example, the planned amount of direct labor is controllable within narrow limits, but the amount of sales generally is not.

The planned or expected values may be based on:

1. Actual amount in the past month, quarter, or year
2. Average, either fixed or moving, of amounts in several past periods
3. Forecast of future results, if the future is expected to be much different from the past

The amount of variation from the expected value depends on operations and is less subject to management control. The permissible amount or degree of variation might be measured in one of several ways. Useful methods are the absolute variation from the expected amount, the percentage variation from the expected amount, or the average or standard deviation from the expected amount.

The use of a normal range for screening items that are out of control is not limited to the final stages of report preparation but can be applied at any stage of data processing. The expected value and variation must, of course, be adjusted to the particular level of operations being considered.

Example. An example will show how the idea of expected value and normal range is applied in the preparation of reports. Part X is manufactured for stock, and inventory is reviewed weekly. The action rules are as follows: no action is taken if 21,000 to 30,000 of these parts are in stock; manufacturing is started if less than 21,000 are in stock; and manufacturing is stopped for an inventory over 30,000.

Three values that might be used for reporting by the exception principle are:

1. Less than 21,000—start manufacturing
2. Between 21,000 and 30,000—take no action
3. More than 30,000—stop manufacturing

Any of these three ranges can be used as normal. Each implies a single plan of action. The range may be selected after examining operating experience for a representative period of time.

On Hand	Number of Weeks
0 to 21,000	Twelve
21,000 to 30,000	Twenty-eight
30,001 and more	Ten

If future experience follows past experience, inventory balance will be between 21,000 and 30,000 most of the time. This is the best range to use as normal for reporting by the exception principle. It is "best" in the sense that it keeps Part X off most of the weekly reports for management. Part X is reported only when its balance is outside of normal—less than 21,000 or more than 30,000. The person responsible for inventory control then observes whether the quantity is below 21,000 or above 30,000 and takes appropriate action.

Some waste motion may occur in reporting and decision making with this plan. A second weekly report is made if inventory stays below 21,000. Since a production order was supposed to be issued after the first report, duplication of the production order must be avoided. The inventory might be defined as "available supply"—the quantity on hand and on order—so that Part X would be reported only when the available supply goes below 21,000. The plan used should, of course, be tailored to the situation.

Appraisal. A system relying on the exception principle increases the information content of reports for management. Reductions in reports can save printing and distribution time. Management time is saved by dealing with shorter reports that pinpoint the needs for action. Items that are reported only rarely can be analyzed to see if they should be dropped. The level of management receiving a report may not be able to take appropriate action; a certain manager may be too high or too low in an organization to rectify a situation, or it may be outside his area of responsibility. Still, the problem of reporting only relevant information to a manager is probably no worse in this scheme than in any other. Managers postpone action on some items outside normal range because action on other items will have more effect on the over-all results.

Internal Decision Plan

An internal decision plan does more than merely report situations outside an established normal range. "Internal decision" means that the data-processing system is programmed to take appropriate action. The action may include issuing instructions to a clerk or to a manager, or it may involve preparing documents—purchase or production orders—for distribution. Even physical action—starting, changing, or shutting off a production line—can be taken if both the data processing and factory operations are automatic.

Figure 10-3 is a block diagram of an internal decision plan. The area labeled "data processing" includes three functions: processing data, selecting information, and making decisions. Management gets data and information about only those items to which no decision rules apply. Management deals with situations that are not handled by the processor; but management's main task is to review decisions. The processor handles tasks that are reduced to rules while a manager sets up and reviews objectives, policies, and decision rules.

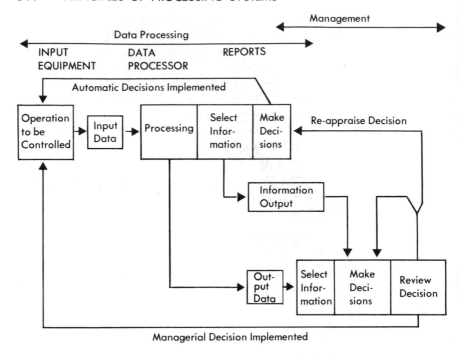

FIGURE 10-3. *Data processing to make a decision*

The formulation of decision rules for various conditions is fundamental to an internal decision plan. These problems are similar to those involved in setting normal ranges, but they are more complex. Management decisions based on available data may follow explicit rules that can be programmed for the data processor to apply during report preparation. Control of many operations may be well suited to using an internal decision system, for automatic equipment is more efficient than people at applying rules in order to reach decisions.

Variable Processing Plan

A variable processing plan examines selected items at key points when it first handles the data. Any key points that do not fall within the normal range of expected values are examined in more detail by processing the supporting data on a second run. This process is repeated until the original data, if necessary, are examined in detail. Limited processing may show that some areas are inside the normal range for control purposes. Data for such areas need not be processed further. Attention can then be concentrated on areas where results are outside the normal range.

Consider a report of total operating cost covering several manufacturing plants. On the first pass, only data on the total cost for each plant is computed. If the total cost for a plant is outside the normal range, the costs for each major function can be computed. If any of these costs is out of range, a detailed analysis is made and printed out.

Processing can be extended to any desired degree of detail, although highly detailed information is seldom worth its cost for managerial purposes. By concentrating on areas that need attention, management can examine them more thoroughly than would be worth while if standardized reports for all plants had to be examined.

Manual Intervention Plan

One plan for designing an automatic system is to provide for every situation that may arise. This scheme requires that computer programs cover both common and rare cases. Such an ambitious scheme may be expensive because of the high programming costs, large internal storage for extra programs, and delays in getting the system into operation.

A second plan is to have the computer handle high-volume transactions. When a rare case arises, the processor notifies the operator and either puts the case aside or waits for instructions. Manual intervention, either later or immediately, assists the processor to cope with the unusual situation.

All automatic systems require manual assistance for data preparation, problem analysis, and programming; but they attempt to minimize manual intervention during computer operations. The chief point is that manual effort is applied in advance of processing. But in the manual intervention scheme, some manual effort is also applied during processing to cover situations that were not programmed for the processor to handle alone.

COST OF DATA AND INFORMATION

Data and information for management purposes were defined above and schemes were suggested for increasing the information content of reports. The cost of obtaining and processing data to get information, as well as the value of the information itself, deserves study, for final system design is usually governed by economic considerations.

Cost Measurement Schemes

Cost is the price paid for obtaining and processing data to produce reports. Two widely used methods for assigning cost to data are worth discussion: the average and marginal cost methods. Developed over a period of several centuries for factory cost accounting, these methods are applicable to data-processing costs today.

Average Cost. Some costs can be identified with a particular project or job for obtaining and processing data. These costs are like direct material costs and direct labor costs of production in a factory. Other costs of processing data are not easily identified with a particular project but are distributed over all the work done. These costs correspond to indirect factory costs—equipment depreciation, supervision, space, supplies, and so forth; they are distributed by overhead rates which supplement the direct costs.

Data-processing costs for large operations may be identified readily with major areas—purchasing, inventory control, production control, payroll, and others. But a detailed job costing within each major area may be difficult because data-processing operations are interrelated within the areas. One set of data may be used for several different purposes, and data from different sources may be combined for one purpose.

Job cost accounting gives useful answers for guiding management, if costs vary with the amount of work done. Factory material costs and labor costs may be closely related to the volume of work; but overhead costs may be essentially fixed and change little or not at all with changes in production volume.

People often use the average cost scheme to distribute costs so that the total costs are distributed to users and the books balance. The arithmetical niceties of the average cost scheme seem to give it stature beyond its merits. Highly automatic operations, whether in a factory or office, have a high fraction of fixed costs that change little with the volume of data that is processed. Job cost accounting loses much of its meaning in such cases, for which another method for assigning costs is more useful.

Marginal Cost.   Marginal cost, popularly called "out-of-pocket cost," is the amount that costs change as volume changes. The operating cost of an automatic data-processing system is constant for large changes in volume of data processed or reports produced; accordingly, marginal cost is small. Marginal cost schemes charge a job with only the additional cost incurred because of that job. For example, preparation of a report might start with data already collected for other purposes and be completed within the basic operating schedule for both equipment and people at a marginal cost of zero.

Marginal costing is often used when considering the installation of a data-processing system. People talk of starting equipment on important "bread-and-butter" applications to absorb the total cost of the system. Afterwards, "gravy" applications that benefit by not having to absorb any costs are started. No charge is made against the additional applications because the marginal cost is zero. This approach to selecting applications follows the slogan, "Anything worth while is worth doing—for money."

The use of either the average or the marginal cost scheme has certain consequences as data-processing volume changes. For an automatic system with large fixed costs, the average cost per unit is high, if volume is low. Such costs discourage use of the equipment when the system is idle. The opposite is also true. Average costing may lead to either too little or too much work. It is probably wise to encourage use of an idle system and discourage use of an overloaded system.

Marginal costing is sensitive to the system load. If equipment is idle, marginal cost is small and encourages use. If equipment is fully loaded, marginal cost is high and discourages use. Marginal cost is the full increase in costs for equipment, personnel, and supplies. Such cost is high for the first application and the application that requires more equipment or that takes a second shift. To overcome this feature of marginal costs, basic system costs may be lumped and not allocated to individual jobs. Decisions either to tolerate idle capacity of equipment or to use it to full capacity are usually made on the basis of marginal costs.

Factors Determining Cost

The cost of data and information obtained from a data-processing system depends on many factors. The more important factors are discussed here: accuracy, timeliness, capacity, and load; selective or standardized processing; and the reporting plan.

Accuracy. "Accuracy" is, in simple terms, the condition of being accurate. Accuracy may mean the precision or amount of detail in a datum. The number 10 may mean exactly (precisely) 10 if integers are used, or any number between 9.50 and 10.49 if fractions are permitted. Details may be dropped by expressing items in large units—tons instead of pounds—or by dropping digits in order to round to the nearest dollar or nearest thousand dollars. "Precision" exactly defines limits beyond which an item cannot fall. "Accuracy," on the other hand, defines limits beyond which an item probably will not fall—the degree of dependability in a datum—or statistically speaking, the standard deviation of a datum. Although your bank statement and your checkbook stubs are kept with the same degree of detail and precision, there is usually less confidence in the latter. An organization usually knows the total amount of accounts receivable with more accuracy than it knows the value of inventory. The costs involved in determining inventory value may force one to stop short of the absolute in pursuing accuracy. The retail inventory scheme, for example, uses the ratio of cost to selling price for merchandise bought to convert inventory taken at selling price back to cost. The use of ratios is an admission that the loss of accuracy in finding the cost of inventory might be more than balanced by the reduction in the expense of keeping detailed cost.

Results may differ from true values because of human blunders, errors in the calculation plan, or malfunctions in equipment. Inaccuracies can arise at any stage from data origination to report preparation. People can misunderstand or misread original data and make mistakes in operating typewriters and key-punches to prepare data for input. Instruction routines may have errors in logic which make all results erroneous. Even when most cases are being handled correctly, others that are not anticipated may give erroneous results. Equipment malfunction can be either repetitive or intermittent.

Many schemes based on partial or complete duplication of operations are used to increase the accuracy of results. Data origination is commonly verified by repetition. A parity-bit associated with each character guards against the accidental gain or loss of a bit that would change a character. Instruction routines are checked for logic and test-checked with simulated or real data to debug them. Duplicate circuitry or programmed checks, or even both, are used to detect malfunctions in automatic processors. Double-entry, balancing, and proof schemes are commonly used to insure accuracy in manual or mechanical accounting systems; more elaborate plans are used with automatic processing systems.

These plans for increasing accuracy (decreasing the difference between results and the true value) also increase the cost of processing data. Additional precautions are required to decrease the margin of inaccuracy from 10 per cent (calculated result within only 10 per cent of the accurate result) to 1 per cent, .1 per cent, and so forth. The precautions required grow rapidly as the margin of permissible error is narrowed.

Another approach to the problem of accuracy is to look at the incidence or frequency of inaccurate answers (Gregory, 1953). The error frequency rate deals with whether one answer in a hundred, a thousand, or a million is wrong, without considering the degree of precision. Manual systems using office equipment may result in one inaccurate answer in a thousand or so arithmetical operations. That is, 999 answers out of 1,000 are correct and one is incorrect. Error frequency rates are smaller within the electronic parts of automatic systems—perhaps one in a million, billion, or more operations.

The important point here is that increasing the accuracy of results—measured in terms of either their precision or their reliability—adds to the cost of originating and processing data. Figure 10-4 suggests the relationship between the cost of data processing and the precision of results. Costs increase sharply as the margin of error is decreased from one part per 1,000 to one part per 10,000, and so forth. Much of the cost increase arises from the trouble involved in organizing and policing data origination and transcription methods. Data that are precise to 8 digits may be more costly to obtain than data with two-digit precision. Step functions or breaks may occur in the cost curve. For example, a number correct to one part in one million requires handling 7 digits, but to get an answer with eight-digit precision would require double precision arithmetic in a computer with a seven-digit word length.

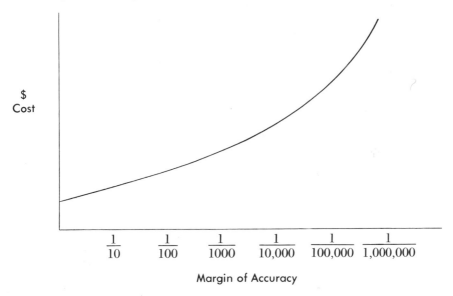

FIGURE 10-4. *Cost and accuracy of results*

Timeliness.   Information may be timely in the sense of being available at a suitable time or being well-timed. Timeliness, or the age of information, has two components: interval and delay (Gregory and Atwater, 1957). "Interval" is the period of time—week, month, quarter, or year—between the preparation of successive reports. "Delay" is the length of time after the close of an interval before information is available for use. The delay covers the time required to process data and to prepare and distribute reports.

A distinction needs to be made between the interval and the reporting period. "Interval" is the frequency of report preparation, whereas "reporting period" means the length of time that is covered by the report. For example, a report covering a period of one day may be prepared only once a week. A fireworks retailer might prepare a statement at yearly intervals to cover the two-week reporting period from June 21 through July 4. On the other hand, for moving or running totals or averages—for example, shipments during the most recent 13 periods of 4 weeks each—the reporting period is 52 weeks but the reports are prepared at four-week intervals. In short, the reporting period may coincide with the interval used, or be either shorter or longer.

People often say that they must have immediate or up-to-the-minute information in order to operate effectively. "Immediate" literally means anything pertaining to the present time or moment. Both the interval and the delay would have to be extremely short or even zero in order to get immediate information. The cost implications of timeliness are treated here, while the values obtained from timely information are covered later in this chapter.

Interval.   There are at least three classes of operations worth considering here. Some operations involved in processing data are carried on throughout a reporting interval without regard for the length of the interval. Data origination and some processing operations may be continuous. Other operations, such as file maintenance and processing, may be flexible; but they must be done at least once before reports are prepared.

The use of short reporting intervals involves additional processing cycles during any period of time. For example, a high fraction of the total magnetic-tape file processing cost is incurred merely by passing tape through the processor. The tape read-write time may be essentially the same whether file activity is low or high. In such "tape-limited" processing, costs are more closely related to the number of file-processing cycles than to the number of transactions handled. Short intervals involve frequent preparation of reports. The cost of summarizing files and preparing reports is related to the number of reports prepared. The point is that some costs of processing—updating files and preparing reports—may double if the reporting interval is cut in half.

The relationship between the cost of data processing and the length of interval is shown in Figure 10-5. Interval length is shown

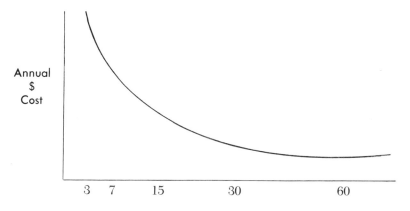

Length of Interval, Days or Any Other Unit

Figure 10-5. *Cost of processing and length of interval*

in calendar days, but business days or any unit of time that you wish may be used. It indicates that costs nearly double each time the interval is cut in half. The ultimate, as the interval approaches zero, is for costs to become infinite. It is, of course, impossible to process data when the interval is zero, for no data are available for an infinitesimally short period.

Going in the other direction, as the interval becomes longer, the costs of processing data will also increase. Extremely long intervals require that more data be held in active storage until reports are prepared and a new interval starts. The preparation of reports serves the useful, but little noticed, purpose of permitting a purge of active files and the adoption of a new starting point.

The cost implications of extremely short intervals are of practical importance for systems that utilize magnetic-tape files. System analysts in one company reported that, over a long period, weekly processing of a policyholder's file was about four times as expensive as monthly processing (Davis, 1955). Similarly, a manufacturing company reported that daily inventory processing would cost about four times as much as weekly processing. Both operations were tape limited. To the extent that processing is computer limited to handle new transactions against the file, processing at shorter intervals may be obtained at little or no cost, if computer running time is not increased. This discussion of the effect of changing the length of the processing interval presumes, of course, that the processing technique remains constant so that only one change in the system is considered at a time.

Now consider the effect of changing the technique of processing from magnetic-tape files to random-access disk or drum storage for files. It appears that the cost of random-access file processing would still be "U"-shaped (high costs for extremely short and long intervals, but lower costs for intermediate length intervals), but would be less than the cost for tape file processing for short intervals because the random-access file would take less search time. On the other hand, a long interval would, it seems, precipitously increase processing costs because of the large number of disks or drums required. Large-capacity ram "boxes" holding even 100 million characters equal the contents of only a limited number of magnetic tapes. Protracted intervals mean that data must be carried forward for a long time before reports are prepared and files can be purged.

Report preparation may cost as much or even more for random-access equipment than for magnetic-tape files because the data-transfer rate of unorganized data from disks and drums is slower than it is for sequential data on magnetic tapes. In summary: data-origination costs may be the same for both magnetic-tape and random-access systems; short-interval processing may be less for a random-access system; and report preparation may be less for a tape system.

Delay. "Delay" is defined as the length of time after the close of a reporting interval before processing is complete and information is available for use. The chief element of delay is the time required to process data; small amounts of time are required to prepare reports and distribute them.

A basic difference in the nature of forecasts and reports of actual results, and therefore the delays involved in issuing each of these, deserves consideration at the outset. Forecasts for the next period are, by definition, available before the period starts. On the other hand, actual results covering a period cannot be obtained before the close of the period. This is true no matter how quickly the data are processed. Accountants are often chided for dealing with history, but they are not alone in this. All facts are history. People who want advance information must be content with forecasts because actual results are not available.

For any particular system using certain methods—manual, electromechanical, or electronic—there is some processing delay that has the lowest operating costs. System and equipment capacity are used at a high fraction of capacity throughout the interval and neither an overload nor idleness occurs.

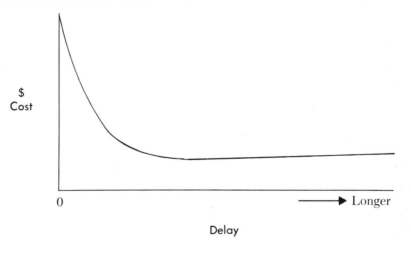

FIGURE 10-6. *Cost of processing and length of delay*

Shortening the processing delay, when the same type of system and equipment are used, increases costs. The relationship between the cost of processing and the length of delay is suggested in Figure 10-6. Costs are at a minimum for some particular delay. Shorter delays increase costs because additional capacity is required, scheduling is more difficult, and average usage is lower. As the delay is decreased toward zero, costs skyrocket because no system, even a "blue-sky" one, produces results with zero delay. Moving in the other direction, longer delays also increase processing costs. The system may bog down because it must store and deal with a great quantity of data before processing can be completed.

These comments on the cost of processing and length of delay are not restricted to any particular system and type of equipment. They apply to all. Changes in system or equipment alter the cost-delay relationship, but do not destroy it. The "U"-shaped cost curve is generally true for all processing schemes in use.

System Capacity.   The capacity of a system must be large enough to handle peak loads. For a steady work load, the use of either faster equipment or more equipment can reduce delay. If work loads are uneven, some trade-off of increased system capacity against longer processing delays is necessary. The fixed costs of a system—equipment, space, basic personnel, and programming—are determined chiefly by the maximum capacity of the system. Operating costs—media, overtime, and others—are more sensitive to total volume. When the peak load is much greater than the average processing load, either more capacity must be provided to handle the peak or the elapsed time required for processing will grow. Such added capacity may then be idle until the next peak load occurs.

Staggering or overlapping intervals so that peak loads occur at different times may smooth out system loads. This approach has merit although it does not deal with the basic problem of short delays and the high cost of processing. It deals with a symptom, not a cause. But cycled work loads can increase processing efficiency. The relation-

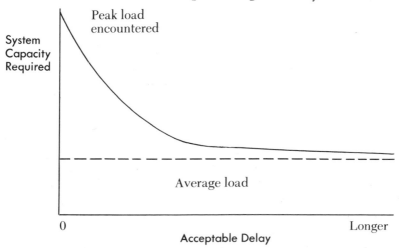

FIGURE 10-7. *Required capacity and acceptable average delay*

ship between system capacity and acceptable delay is suggested by Figure 10-7. As the acceptable delay is increased, the maximum capacity required drops off from peak load size, for short delays, and levels off near the average load.

Interval, delay, and capacity are probably the three most important factors that determine the cost of data processing and information production.

Other Factors.   Several other factors influence data-processing costs: degree of automation, extra capacity, flexibility, communications, processing schemes, and rate of transition.

A higher fraction of total costs is fixed for automatic systems than is the case for manual systems. Total costs change slowly with an increase or decrease in volume.

A system must, obviously, have enough capacity to handle present applications, and additional capacity may have to be obtained ahead of need because available equipment comes in only a few sizes. Extra capacity provides for expansion. The central computer is restricted to one or two sizes although much more freedom exists to add relatively small units of peripheral equipment later when needed.

Flexibility costs money. A system limited to one or a few specific applications that do not change has a minimum cost. At the other extreme, a system may be flexible enough to deal with any application. In such a case, more capacity, systems analysis, and programming are required to handle an application.

Communications methods used may range from regular or air mail to wire and radio transmission. Each, of course, has different cost functions that vary with the volume of data transmitted.

Processing schemes may be standardized or selective. The exception principle, internal decision, and variable processing plans described earlier in this chapter are examples of selective processing schemes. Analysis and programming costs for a selective processing scheme are higher than for standardized processing. Once set up, however, operating costs for a selective scheme may be low because attention is focused on situations that demand it; and situations that are in control are ignored, if that is feasible.

The rate of transition from the old to the new system also affects costs. Rapid changes from one system to another result in confusion and lost motion. Some people, in fact, say that important changes in a system cannot be made more frequently than once every three to five years.

VALUE OF INFORMATION

The concept of the value of information is basic to a study of data processing and information production. The usual definition of "value" is that property of a thing which makes it esteemed, desirable, or useful, or the degree to which this property is possessed. Theories of the value of information fall into three categories: intangibles, cost outlay, and managerial use of information. The first two are only mentioned here; the third is discussed in detail.

Intangibles

It is frequently said, "A proposed system is worth while because it will provide *better* information for operations and for management decisions." "Better" is seldom defined in terms that are measurable so that it can be included in system feasibility or application studies. Improvements are merely treated as plus factors, or intangibles, and no value is assigned. Intangibles that do exist serve to reinforce a decision to adopt a new system.

Treating intangibles as unvalued factors may result in a wrong decision. A change that is not made when the value of intangibles is omitted might be warranted if their value is counted. This point is considered later under the managerial use of information.

Cost Outlay

Many systems analysts adhere to the theory that the value of information is equal to the money cost of obtaining it. When considering changes for an existing system, analysts may insist that the same information or even more information be obtained than before, without any increase in cost. They are, in effect, satisfied with the results obtained by the present outlay for processing data. That is to say, the value of information is considered equal to the money cost involved.

An extremely simple change, such as a 50 per cent decline in processing costs, poses an interesting test case of the cost outlay theory of value. One choice is to save the reduction in cost and spend only half as much for processing. The other choice is to spend as much as before and obtain better information—more accurate, timely, complete, and so forth. A cost outlay theory of value cannot answer the simple question of whether to save the cost reduction or spend the savings to get more information. Any conclusion is suitable, if the same or more information is obtained at no increase in cost.

Managerial Use

A more useful concept is that the value of information should be studied in terms of its relationship to operating performance of the organization or to the revenue obtained. Assume that all factors influencing operating performance can be held constant. If some report or portion of a report is dropped or changed, the resulting decrease in performance would be an indicator of the value of information supplied by that report. If no decrease occurred, the report might be considered valueless.

In real life, the effect of a single report on an over-all result is difficult or impossible to measure. Within a large organization many departments do not sell their products in the market but merely transfer them to other departments at arbitrary values. Changes in revenue associated with any particular reports are difficult to estimate.

Six aspects of information used for business operation and management that deserve study in formulating a theory of value are:

1. Accuracy
2. Age of status information
3. Age of operating information
4. Predictability
5. Relevance
6. Consequences

Some of these factors were discussed under the cost of data processing; they will be considered here from the viewpoint of their information value.

Accuracy. The useful margin of accuracy, as defined earlier, depends on the user and the situation. More accuracy is warranted if a larger margin of inaccuracy might cause the user to make a different decision. Frequently, inaccurate information leads to incorrect decisions. In some cases the margin of inaccuracy may have little or no bearing on the outcome. Assume a simple case in which an item is re-ordered when only 1,000 are on hand. If 2,000 are actually on hand, the decision to re-order is the same whether 1,001 or 1,000,000 are

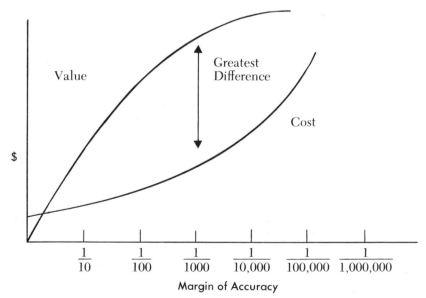

FIGURE 10-8. *Value, cost, and accuracy of results*

reported to be on hand. In such a case a large margin of inaccuracy—ranging from minus 50 per cent to plus hundreds—makes no difference to the decision. On the other hand, when the true quantity is 1,010, an inaccuracy of even 1 per cent may lead to an incorrect decision.

Figure 10-8 suggests the relationship between the accuracy of information, its value for management, and cost of processing. Value is low or negative when the margin of inaccuracy is high. Such inaccuracy frequently leads to incorrect decisions. The value of information increases rapidly as the margin of accuracy is increased or, to put it differently, as the difference between reported and actual results is decreased. Information that is more nearly accurate facilitates correct decisions.

Carried to the extreme, the accuracy of information may be increased beyond the point where it aids decision making; additional accuracy may then be ignored or discarded. Throughout most of the range of accuracy, the value exceeds the cost of achieving that degree of accuracy. The most desirable margin of accuracy is reached when value exceeds cost by the greatest difference.

Age of Status Information. For status or point-of-time information, the minimum age of the newest information available is equal to the delay involved. If processing data to prepare and distribute reports takes 10 days, a report of inventory on December 31 is first available on January 10. The information in the report is 10 days old when it becomes available.

If an inventory report is prepared for the end of each month, new information will next become available on February 10. Just before new information becomes available the most recent inventory, that for December 31, reaches a maximum age of 40 days. The age of the newest information available ranges from 10 to 40 days, so that its average age is 25 days: $\frac{10 + 40}{2} = 25$.

A slightly different way to look at the average age of status information is to start with the minimum age and add half the interval: $10 + \frac{30}{2} = 25$. The average age is, of course, the same calculated by either plan. The age of *status* information relating to a point in time can be summarized as follows:

1. The minimum age for the newest information available is equal to the processing delay.
2. The average age is equal to the processing delay plus one-half of the reporting interval.
3. The maximum age of information on hand before new information becomes available is equal to the processing delay plus the reporting interval.

In systems design work, more emphasis is usually put on reducing the processing delay than on changing the reporting interval. An important advantage of an automatic system is that it can cut down the processing time and reduce the minimum age of information.

Any delay that occurs in processing is the primary determinant of age for information that is used as soon as it becomes available. In such a case the minimum age deserves emphasis. Information may not be exhausted immediately after it becomes available but may be used several times until the next report becomes available one interval later. Both the average and the maximum age are relevant in systems design where the results are used throughout the interval. This is an important point. If the interval is large in relation to the delay, reduction in delay has little effect on the average and maximum age of information available. On the other hand, information may be fully exploited immediately after it becomes available and then discarded so that the minimum age counts for more than the others. Fire departments, for example, answer calls and are soon through; whereas investigators and insurance underwriters may worry about fires for months or years.

The time that a manager spends reading reports and making his decisions must be counted as part of the processing delay for operational purposes. Reports may come so thick and fast that the receiver cannot make full use of one before other reports, or even the next issue of the same report, are delivered to him. His choices are to plow through all the reports and try to get on a current basis or to skip some and start afresh. The timing of reports must be matched with the user's ability. Rarely is the north country sourdough's approach to reading newspapers correct for managers to follow in using reports for controlling operations. The sourdough may get all the newspapers for a whole year at one time and spend the next year reading them at the rate of one a day. The world unfolds for him day by day just as it does for everyone else, except that it is a year or so later.

To return to the example given above, assume that the delay in preparing monthly reports is reduced from 10 days to 5. The average age of information is then reduced from 25, $10 + \dfrac{30}{2}$, to 20 days, $5 + \dfrac{30}{2}$. A change from a monthly to a weekly reporting interval, even though the delay remained 10 days, would reduce the average age to $13\frac{1}{2}$ days, $10 + \dfrac{7}{2}$. Whenever more timely information is required, the possibility of making changes in both the delay and the reporting interval deserves consideration. The problem of selecting an interval of suitable length in order to obtain information that correctly reflects operations is covered later in this chapter.

Age of Operating Information.   The age of information that relates to a reporting period is different from the age of status information. A report of the amount of material used in production refers to events occurring throughout the period. Facts about sales on the first day of a month are a month old by the end of the month. Information about operations throughout a month has an inherent age of one-half a month merely because it covers a reporting period of one month. The processing delay involved before information becomes available must be added to this inherent age before the information is available for use. You will recall that the reporting period can be the same as or different from the interval between reports.

The maximum age of operating information is reached one interval later just before new information becomes available. The age of operating information can be summarized as follows:

1. The minimum age is equal to the inherent age of half a reporting period plus the processing delay.
2. The average age is equal to one-half an interval plus half a reporting period plus the processing delay.
3. The maximum age is equal to one interval plus half a reporting period plus the processing delay.

The age of operating information, it should be noted, is one-half a reporting period more than the corresponding age of status information. This difference arises from the fact that operating information has an inherent age of one-half a reporting period, no matter how long or short the period is. As a result, the age of operating data is more dependent on the length of the reporting period and the interval than is the case for condition data. Delay is less important as a determinant of age of operating data.

Optimum Age.   The best-length interval, reporting period, and delay to select for report preparation are problematical; but some basic guides can be developed. The value of information declines as the delay increases. It may be so out-of-date when first obtained that it does not reflect the situation and is not useful for management. Necessary action can be taken sooner by obtaining information more quickly. The increase in the value of information as the delay decreases might be measured in terms of the additional benefits obtained through earlier action than would otherwise be possible.

The effect of the length of the interval and reporting periods on the value of information poses a more difficult problem. There is no clear-cut relationship between the frequency of processing, the period covered, and the value of results. Extremely short reporting periods that may be associated with short intervals—a high "sampling rate"—

may permit unusual or superficial events to outweigh the real developments. Conversely, long intervals submerge unusual events in longer-term averages. Some intermediate-length reporting period and interval permits optimum sampling to obtain information that represents what is actually happening.

Examples of Age of Information. Some examples will give more meaning to the concept of the age of information. Each "buyer," or merchandise manager, in a department store may want reports by 10 o'clock that show inventory for the previous day, daily sales for the past week, and weekly sales for the month or season. Adequate detail—style, size, color, and maker—is needed for him to decide which items are selling well and need to be re-ordered or which items are selling slowly and must be pushed. Here, reports at daily intervals emphasize yesterday's activity but also cover a longer period to put each day in perspective.

A fire department has different problems regarding the age of information. The first few minutes after a fire starts are so critical that elaborate communication networks are used. The messages are so simple that merely pulling the handle of a fire alarm box transmits the message and the firemen roar out of the station whether the call is real or false. A fire call gets a standard response without delay and with little regard for the interval since the last call, although the interval between calls does count for something. Too-frequent alarms, because of severe fires or numerous fires, will overtax the whole system, for they cannot be handled. For example, fire wardens in heavily bombed cities would merely reply, "So?" when someone rushed up to report that another building was on fire. Fire-alarm and similar systems might be called "event-triggered" because the occurrence of a certain event puts the whole operation in motion. More elaborate defense warning systems are called "real-time" systems for they are supposed to obtain, process, and report on developments with so little delay that proper counter-measures can be taken.

The concept of delay has been discussed as though it were always positive, with processing following the occurrence of an event and preceding decision making. Actually, what is described as a single series of operations is more nearly continuous or circular, for each operation follows the other—gather facts, process, decide, gather facts, process—indefinitely. Furthermore, these operations occur in parallel, for decisions are made today about yesterday's facts while today's facts are gathered for processing tomorrow and for making decisions after that.

Preparation of life insurance premium notices illustrates a different problem that might be called "negative" or "anticipatory delay." To keep work loads level, about 1/240 of all premium notices for the year may be prepared each work day. Well in advance of the due date, say forty days, preparation of notices is started to allow time for preparing and mailing so that policyholders get them in ample time for payment. During the time scheduled for processing, mailing, and collection, changes occur that invalidate some premium notices. Some changes— death, loans, and conversions—are so consequential that corrections must be made before the premium is settled. Other changes—new addresses or beneficiaries—may not require correction before collection of the premium; but quick correction would facilitate operations. The number of changes that must be made after premium notices are prepared can be reduced by telescoping the processing period. Every organization is faced with the problem of handling changes that occur during the processing period, for the output (bills, reports, or whatever) no longer reflects the real situation. The incidence and severity of changes can be reduced by waiting until just before the target date to begin processing, or by completing processing soon after the events involved occur.

Decision Making and More Information. Reports are prepared to supply facts for better management decisions. "Better" can mean that more efficiency, larger revenue, smaller inventory, or some other objective is obtained. The benefits of having more information for use in better decision making are shown in Figure 10-9. The lower line of the shaded area indicates the amount of benefits obtained without a particular report. When reports are obtained at times A, B, and C, management can make better decisions and improve operating results.

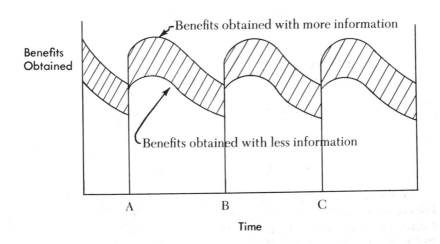

FIGURE 10-9. *Benefits of additional information*

Decision Making and Delay.   Time spent making decisions and putting them into effect will postpone improvements in operations. As information grows older, it has less value for decision making, so that revenue declines toward the level that would exist if less information were available. The cycle of improved decision making is repeated when new facts are obtained. The shaded area represents the increase in revenue arising from a better decision, which indicates the value of report contents.

Figure 10-10 shows the benefits of reduced delay in preparing and circulating reports. A report may be available earlier—at A_1 instead of A, B_1 instead of B. Increased benefits obtained by decreasing the delay are reflected by the shaded area. Two important changes occur when the processing delay is decreased: first, decisions can be made earlier than before; second, decisions can be better because the age is less. As before, when the age of information increases, the benefits obtained from using it, whether it is used throughout the whole interval or only selected portions of it, decrease toward what they would be with less information.

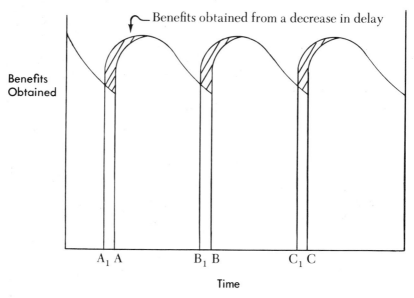

FIGURE 10-10. *Benefits of decreased delay*

Decision Making and Interval.   As pointed out above, the age of information can be decreased by shortening the reporting period. Figure 10-11 shows the benefits obtained by cutting the period in half so that reports are available at A_1, A_2, B_1, B_2, and so forth, instead of merely at A_1, B_1, and C_1. The shaded area represents the increase in value from having information available more frequently.

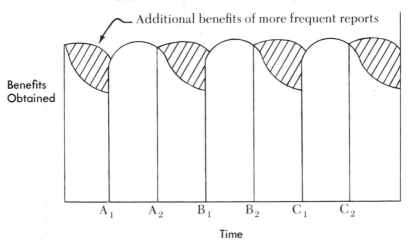

Time

FIGURE 10-11. *Benefits of more frequent reports*

There are limits to the amount of benefits to be obtained from shortening the reporting period to get newer information for decision making. Too-frequent reporting may result in erratic information and lead to erroneous decisions. Several causes are at work: first, unusual events in short intervals can outweigh basic developments, and second, results for short intervals may not be suitable for projecting into the future.

Reports for short intervals may be too close together for consequential changes to occur. Managers wait and consolidate several reports for a real indicator of developments. Systems analysts sometimes find that daily reports, which they have labored over to prepare quickly, are merely saved by the recipients and summarized into a weekly report to be meaningful. Two losses involved are the cost of too-frequent report preparation by professionals and the cost of report summarization by amateurs.

Shorter intervals result in more reports. Managers may become so burdened with reports that they cannot read them or take appropriate action. The other side of the coin should be studied, for short intervals place higher demands for file processing and report preparation on the data-processing system. Any combination of interval and delay is theoretically possible, and each combination gives information with a different age for management purposes and has some influence on the total revenue obtained by basing decisions on such information.

Continued shortening of either interval or delay, or both, for a particular method of processing, will increase costs. The optimal arrangement is the combination of interval and delay with the largest difference between benefits and costs.

Predictability. The value of information is related to the difficulty of predicting what is going to happen next. If it is possible to predict events with certainty, there is no need to have an elaborate data-processing system. Predictable events are similar to the cowboy movies in which the good guys always beat the bad guys: there is no need to watch the movie to know the outcome (nor any need to make the movie at all). Similar comments apply to data processing and reporting when the outcome is essentially certain.

Unpredictability—as reflected in the possible number of alternatives and variations—has an important bearing on the value of information and the design and implementation of business-data systems. A system to handle the number of hours worked on individual jobs needs to be more elaborate than a system to keep track of the number of people on the payroll. Variations in the number of hours worked is much greater than variations in the number of people employed. A job order production shop demands a more complex data-processing system than a factory operating an asssembly line. The most standardized factory operations can be adequately served by relatively simple data-processing systems. Careful observation of the alternatives and variations that may arise will help determine the nature of an information control system.

Use of the exception principle is based on the idea that most results are predictable within fairly close limits. Exception reports need to show only those items that are outside some specified range. A manager may be able to assume that everything is within range unless advised otherwise. In such a case, a report that an actual result is within normal range has no information value.

Relevance. Information must be related to the problem under consideration in order to be useful. Having only relevant information enables a manager to make either better or more decisions because he spends no time hunting for relevant facts among irrelevant ones that do not bear on his problem. If available information is not related to the decision to be made, it has no value. The problem of information relevance is intimately related to the managerial organization pattern. The quantities and location of truck tires in inventory may be valuable information for a motor pool commander but useless for a tank company commander. The old phrase, "Tell it to the Marines," reflects the fact that while an intended message might have value for someone, it might be useless for someone else.

Consequence. Another determinant of the value of information is the consequence of knowing it. One useful yardstick for measuring the consequences of having certain information is the benefit obtained over a period of time. An inventory control procedure that saves a penny per part is consequential if millions of parts are involved.

In some cases there is no freedom to act because the decision is made at a different level of management. Past decisions may limit present action because "sunk costs" carry over to the future. Limitations that will occur in the future but which are already foreseeable restrict the freedom to act now. In such cases, the consequences of more information are nil.

The possible range of consequences should be considered, for perfect information can, at most, increase efficiency by only 15 points if operations are already 85 per cent efficient. Information is more valuable when the possibility of improvement is larger than that. Despite this feature, some areas of business-data processing that are easy to understand and change are favorite targets for improvement. Since much attention has been focused on improving such areas in the past, it is unlikely that further studies and attempts to make improvements have the greatest pay-off. Payroll preparation seems to be an area of data processing with little room for improvement, unless radical improvements occur in processing methods. More can be gained by focusing attention on applications that have been neglected in the past because processing methods were not at all suitable.

The fact that the consequences are a final link in determining the value of information must be kept in mind. The effect of a manager's knowing or not knowing some piece of information and the action that follows such knowledge are important determinants of its value. New developments in systems analysis are given by Hitch (1955).

FORMULATION OF COST AND VALUE MODELS

Although numerous difficulties may arise in giving practical application to the concepts of the cost and value of information, these concepts can be used to formulate analytic expressions which describe simple business problems. The following example illustrates their use in one such problem and shows several possible analyses.

Consider a manager who must make yes-no decisions in problems that arise during each of many time periods. These decisions may be whether or not to continue processing, place orders, dispatch repair crews, or take other similar actions. There is a best or correct alternative for each of the decisions, depending on the real situation. A decision on placing an order, for example, might have the following form:

	Real Situation	
Decision Alternatives	Condition 1 (order needed)	Condition 2 (order not needed)
1. Yes (place order)	Correct	Wrong
2. No (do not place order)	Wrong	Correct

Over a period of time, the real situation is assumed to change in some random fashion; consequently, if the manager lacks information on the current situation, he will not know which decision alternative is correct.

Assume that each correct decision the manager makes results in a profit, but incorrect decisions do not incur losses. He may occasionally decide correctly by mere guesswork; if he has the right type of information, however, he should be able to make correct decisions more often. Information can therefore produce a revenue, but it also has a cost which may depend on such factors as accuracy and the delay necessary for processing. We may thus define the best policy for the manager as being that which increases the value of information or increases the excess of revenue produced by information over the cost of acquiring it. In essence, the general problem thus defined is similar to many common ones in the real world.

To derive an analytical expression for this problem, let V be the value per period of using a given set of information (dollars per period of use). Then V is a function of: A, the accuracy of the information (ratio of correct answers to the total number of answers); T, the delay time required to obtain information (periods); F, the interval over which the information is used (periods per report); P, the probability of making a correct decision without information; Y, the number of decisions made each period; and K, the profit in dollars from making a correct decision. The general form of this function is:

$$V = K\left[\frac{1}{F}\sum_{n=1}^{n=F} f(A, T, Y, n) - g(P, Y)\right] - h(A, F, T) \qquad (1)$$

where $h(A, F, T)$ is the average cost per period of obtaining the information, $g(P, Y)$ is the expected number of correct decisions per period without information, and $f(A, T, Y, n)$ is the expected number of correct answers during each of the periods the information is used. To get total correct answers, $f(A, T, Y, n)$ is summed over the F periods the information is used and is then divided by F to get average correct answers per period. The average correct answers per period with information minus the average without information, $g(P, Y)$, when multiplied by K (the profit per correct answer) gives the average increase in revenue per period that results from using information.

To explore a more specific problem, assume that four situations require decisions during each time period $(Y = 4)$. One of these decisions may undergo a random change at the end of each period, so the subsequent period embraces three former situations and one that may be either changed or the same. The opportunity for change proceeds in a known sequential fashion from situation to situation. At the end of any four periods, all four situations have therefore had an opportunity to change. Although the outcome of a given change opportunity is not predictable, the long-run outcomes are still such that selecting the "yes alternative is a correct decision 60 per cent of the time. In the absence of specific information, the best policy is always to choose the "yes" alternative. Consequently, the probability of a correct decision without information, P, is 0.6, and the expected number of correct answers per period without information, $g(P, Y)$, is 4×0.6 or 2.4.

If completely accurate information is obtained on the real situation in period X, its use during that period will then yield four correct answers. Its use during the next period will yield correct answers for the three decisions that remain unchanged. For the one decision that may have changed, the "yes" alternative is the best decision and results in an expected 0.6 correct answers, making the expected total for period $X + 1$ equal to 3.6. Similarly, the expected total of correct answers for period $X + 2$ is 3.2; for period $X + 3$ is 2.8; and for period $X + 4$ is 2.4. At the end of four periods, all four real situations in the example have had an opportunity to change; so information four periods old or more is worthless. The figure of 2.4 correct answers obtained in period $X + 4$ is identical to the 2.4 obtained with no information.

The collection and processing of information requires time, here referred to as processing delay, T. No delay $(T = 0)$ means that information can be used during the period in which it was collected and will produce four correct answers.

Similarly, delays of 1, 2, 3, and 4 periods correspond to usage in periods $X + 1$, $X + 2$, $X + 3$, and $X + 4$.

The following table summarizes the above behavior and the gain in correct answers produced by using information pertaining to the real situation in period X.

Processing Delay T	Information Used During Period	Correct Answers $f(A, T, Y, n)$			Correct Answers $g(Y, P)$	Gain in Correct Answers
		Unchanged Situations	Changed Situations	Total		
0	X	4	0	4	2.4	1.6
1	X + 1	3	.6	3.6	2.4	1.2
2	X + 2	2	1.2	3.2	2.4	.8
3	X + 3	1	1.8	2.8	2.4	.4
4	X + 4	0	2.4	2.4	2.4	0

Changes in the interval over which information is used have an effect similar to that of delay. If a completely accurate set of information is obtained in alternating periods with no delay and then used for two periods, its use during the initial period results in four correct answers, but during the following period in only 3.6 correct answers. Since the total of correct answers for the two periods is 7.6, using a report for two periods $(F=2)$ results in an average of 3.8 correct answers per period.

A lack of accuracy will degrade the gain produced by a set of information. Accuracy (A) is defined here as the long-run ratio of correct answers to total answers that comprise information—in short, the reliability of information. For example, information which one time out of ten reports the real situation as Condition 1 when in fact it is Condition 2, or as Condition 2 when in fact it is Condition 1, has an accuracy of 0.9.

The preceding discussion of accuracy, interval, and delay can now be combined to produce a specific form of equation (1). Given the assumptions that $Y=4$ and $P=0.6$, and that one known situation has the opportunity to change in random fashion each period, then

$$f(A, T, Y, n) = A \left[4 - (T + n - 1) \right] + 0.6 (T + n - 1)$$
$$\text{for } T + n - 1 \leqq 4,$$

and

$$f(A, T, Y, n) = 2.4 \qquad \text{for } T + n - 1 > 4.$$

where $A [4-(T+n-1)]$ represents the number of correct answers to unchanged situations and $0.6 (T+n-1)$ the number of correct answers to changed situations that will result from using information on period X to make decisions in the period $X + (T+n-1)$.

If specific expressions for $f(A, T, Y, n)$ and $g(P, Y)$ are inserted in equation (1), the new expression for V is then

$$V = K \left\{ \frac{1}{F} \sum_{n=1}^{n=F} \left[A(5 - T - n) + 0.6 (T + n - 1) \right] - 2.4 \right. \tag{2}$$
$$\left. - h(A, F, T), \right.$$

for $T + n - 1 \leqq 4$.

To consider a particular case, assume that $K=\$5.00$ per correct answer, information is perfectly accurate $(A=1)$, one report is generated each period $(F=1)$, and information has no cost $[h(AFT)=0]$. Equation (2) then gives the value of information (V) as follows:

Processing Delay (T)	Correct Answers f(A, F, T, n)	Value V
T = 0	4.0	5(4 − 2.4) − 0 =· $8.00
T = 1	3.6	5(3.6 − 2.4) − 0 = 6.00
T = 2	3.2	5(3.2 − 2.4) − 0 = 4.00
T = 3	2.8	5(2.8 − 2.4) − 0 = 2.00
T = 4	2.4	5(2.4 − 2.4) − 0 = 0.00

Figure 10-12 shows the effect of accuracy on the revenue produced under varying delay conditions. Note that as accuracy decreases, the differences between revenues obtained by using information with different delays also decrease. For this situation, information of less than 60 per cent accuracy produces negative revenue and is, therefore, undesirable even at zero cost. If revenue only is considered, the best choice is to select information with T=0, A=1, and F=1, since this combination produces a revenue of $8.00 per period.

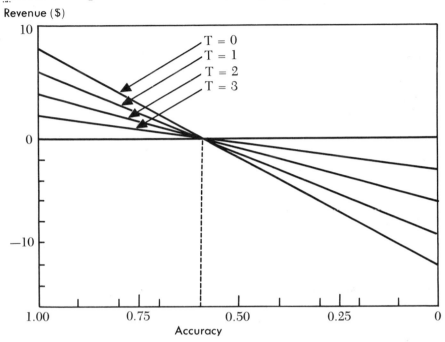

FIGURE 10-12. *Revenue as a function of accuracy and delay*

Costs are incurred in obtaining information, of course. Costs for various delays and accuracies are assumed to be as follows:

Cost of Delay		Cost of Accuracy	
Delay	Cost	Accuracy	Cost
T = 0	C_T = $5.00	A = .99	C_A = $4.00
T = 1	C_T = 3.00	A = .95	C_A = 1.00
T = 2	C_T = 1.75	A = .90	C_A = 0.40
T = 3	C_T = 1.00	A = .80	C_A = 0.10

In this example, the total cost for a set of information is assumed to be $C_T + C_A$, and the cost per period $h(A, T, F) = \dfrac{C_T + C_A}{F}$

When both cost and revenue are considered, the specific expression for the value of information V is

$$V = 5 \left\{ \frac{1}{F} \sum_{n=1}^{n=F} [A(5 - T - n) + .6(T + n - 1) - 2.4] \right\} - \frac{C_T + C_A}{F} \qquad (3)$$

for $T + n - 1 \leq 4$.

The cost and revenue as derived from Equation (3) are plotted in Figure 10-13 for $F = 1$ period per report. The optimal policy is to choose

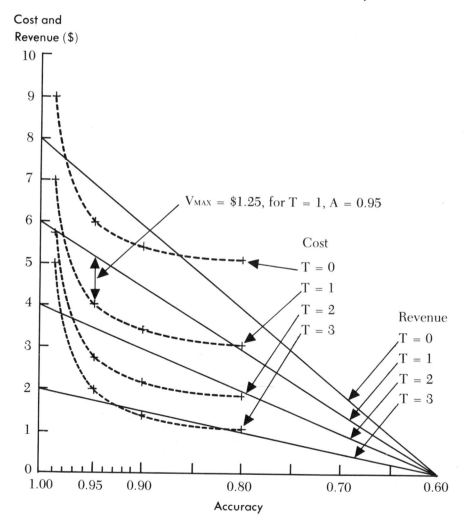

FIGURE 10-13. *Cost and revenue as functions of accuracy and delay for one report each period* $(F = 1)$

A=0.95 and T=1, which gives the information a value of $1.25 per period as shown below:

When F = 1, A = 0.95, T = 1, then from Equation (3):
$$V = 5 [0.95 (5 - 1 - 1) + 0.6 (1 + 1 - 1) - 2.4] - (3.00 + 1.00)$$
$$V = 5 [2.85 + 0.6 - 2.4] - 4.00$$
$$V = 5.25 - 4.00 = \$1.25$$

If a delay of two periods is necessary for some reason, then the best choice for accuracy is A=0.90, giving a per-period information value of $0.85.

Since the cost of information in this example is high, a less frequent reporting cycle has merit. Figure 10-14 shows the cost and value

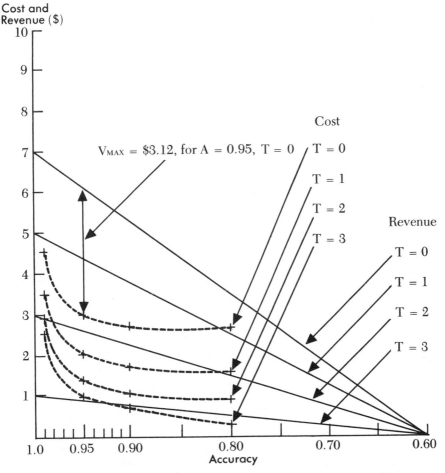

FIGURE 10-14. *Cost and revenue as functions of accuracy and delay for one report each two periods (F=2)*

when a report is obtained every other period ($F=2$ periods per report). For $F=2$ the maximum value of information per period is \$3.12 and occurs when $T=0$ and $A=0.95$. The highest possible value per period for the situation described is \$3.25 and occurs when $F=3$, $T=0$, and $A=0.95$. Once an analytic expression such as Equation (3) is developed for a situation, then the optimal policy for many different sets of conditions can be computed.

Real-world problems are generally more complex than the simple example developed here. Numerous decisions other than a mere "yes" or "no" are possible for many problem situations. Moreover, the accuracy of the data used may have effects on the size and kind of errors which far outweigh the mere knowledge that errors have occurred. The revenue resulting from a correct answer may vary widely under different circumstances, and wrong decisions may have a tremendous cost. For most real situations, these factors complicate the formulation of useful analytical models. Testing and using analytical models is hindered further by the lack of data. Insufficient knowledge of the potential effects of accuracy, delay, and various reporting frequencies is, in fact, a major handicap in analyzing systems.

The fact remains, however, that much data-system design and analysis proceeds without sufficient realization or understanding of the economic consequences. Whether or not it is possible to formulate analytical models for all specific situations, the concepts underlying such formulation are important to effective data system design. In order to build a firm foundation for their work, data system analysts need to develop the knowledge and desire to utilize these cost and value concepts.

SUMMARY

For several reasons, few general principles or rules exist for guiding a person in designing a data-processing system: analysis is expensive and time consuming; systems are unique to an environment; too little experience with new equipment is available to permit long-run conclusions; and data-processing and information-production systems are complex because they pervade an entire organization.

Lacking general principles, basic ideas should be searched for and developed. Two broad areas to explore are the characteristics and the economics of data and information.

At the *syntactic* level, "data" are collections of signs or characters arranged in some orderly way to serve as the vehicle for information. "Information" is the meaning derived from data and represents the *semantic* level—the relationship between a sign and the actual object or condition symbolized by the sign. The impact of the objects or conditions on the receiver represents the *pragmatic* level of information.

Complete, detailed reports may show the variations between actual and forecasted results; this is a first step toward reporting by the exception principle. Exception principle reporting can be extended to omit items that do not have significant variations. Using a "normal range" is one way to set limits for reporting exceptional values. Items falling within the normal range can be handled by one decision rule. Items falling outside that range require different action. Normal ranges for screening out-of-control items can be used at all stages of report preparation.

Expected values may be based on the actual or average amount from the past or upon a forecast of future results. Variations from expected values can be measured in terms of absolute amounts and percentage, average, or standard deviations. The exception principle scheme improves the content of reports by increasing their impact on the receiver. Infrequently reported items can be dropped from "action" reports; but complete reports can be prepared for reference purposes.

An internal decision-processing plan applies management's decision making rules during the main stream of data processing. Managers can still review the results of applying the rules before putting the decisions into effect. A variable processing plan matches the amount of processing to the requirements for information. Situations out of control are analyzed in detail. A manual intervention plan provides for equipment to follow rules where suitable; but situations not covered by rules are turned over to people in order to combine the best abilities of man and machine.

The concepts of average cost and marginal cost are pertinent to the volume of data handled and to decisions for changing procedures. Factors that have an important bearing on the cost of processing data are accuracy, timeliness, and the degree to which the system is automatic. The cost of increasing the degree of accuracy of information—in terms of precision and dependability—may rise faster than its value for decision-making purposes.

Short intervals and frequent reports go together; they are two sides of the same coin. The costs of reporting double each time the interval is cut in half. On the other hand, the value of reports first increases and then may decrease as intervals are made shorter. In extremely short intervals, unusual events may outweigh and mask the basic developments. The delay—the length of time before a report about a single event or a series of events is available—can be shortened to get up-to-date reports. Costs may increase rapidly, if large facilities are used to meet peak demands for quick processing because such facilities are under-utilized most of the time. The increase in the value of results known an hour or minutes earlier depends on the circumstances of the situation.

The value of information is often treated as an *intangible* that is not amenable to analysis. Another approach is to treat its value as being just equal to the *cost* of processing. A better approach to studying the value of information is to examine its *managerial implications.* The crucial question is: What does it contribute to managerial decisions and over-all operations? Factors that affect the value of information are accuracy, age, predictability, relevance, and consequence. Information age depends on the length of the interval, the reporting period, and the processing delay. Minimum, average, and maximum ages suitable for the situation must be considered during system design.

Operations that are predictable require little or no information for effective control. Information needs to be relevant to the problems that the receiver of a report can handle. The consequences arising from knowing something depend on how much change in operations that knowledge will lead to in actual fact.

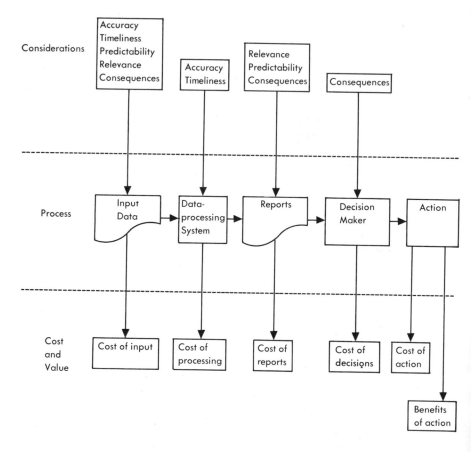

FIGURE 10-15. *Cost and value in a data-processing system*

The basic ideas in this chapter are summarized in Figure 10-15. The *process* row shows the operation of an information system from input data to the action flowing from decisions.

The *considerations* row shows the factors that are important at each stage of processing. The nature of the input data is fundamental to the design and operation of the whole system. All five factors are considered for selection of input data. The data-processing system has some measure of control over timeliness and accuracy, at least at the syntactic level.

Report makeup is determined by relevance, predictability, and consequences. A decision maker gets reports with some degree of accuracy, timeliness, relevance, and predictability. The primary considerations for a report user are the meaning and impact of reports— their semantic aspect. Following these, he must consider the practical consequences of his action.

The *cost and value* row emphasizes the point that costs are incurred at every stage of processing while benefits result only from managerial action. The *raison d'être* of an information system is to improve the operation of the organization. Even good decisions are valueless unless they lead to action.

REFERENCES AND SUPPLEMENTAL READINGS

Davis, M. E. "The Possible Use of Magnetic-Tape Policy Files in a Life Insurance Office," pp. 217-229 in *Electronic Data Processing in Industry: a Casebook of Management Experience*, New York, American Management Association, 1955. This article grew out of the Society of Actuaries' early study of the use of magnetic-tape files in life insurance offices. Three record plans were evaluated: card file, tape file with history card, and tape file without history card. Some estimates of the time required to process tape files on a daily, weekly, and monthly cycle are of particular interest here.

Gregory, Robert H. "The Frequency and Importance of Errors in Invoices Received for Payment," *The Controller*, vol. 21: 11-13 (January 1953). This article deals with the proposition that uniform 100 per cent examination and verification of all invoices in conventional accounting practice is uneconomical; the suggested alternative is the processing of selected samples of invoices. The results of a study of inaccuracies discovered in 35,000 invoices received at the factory of an automobile manufacturer are analyzed.

Gregory, Robert H. "Present and Prospective Use of Computers in Management Control," pp. 21-24 in *Computer Techniques in Chemical Engineering*, New York, American Institute of Chemical Engineers, 1959. In simplest systems, data processing is aimed at producing complete, detailed reports for managers to examine and take appropriate action. The next level of improvement is to have the processing system generate *information* that managers can use to control operations. A further improvement is to have the data-processing system apply the decision-making rules and specify appropriate action. Closed loop control of operations is achieved in some process operations whereas people are usually required within the control loop for batch operations. The value of better information and improved decisions is difficult to determine because (1) the information produced is predictable only with probability and not with certainty, (2) decision-making rules are not well formulated, and (3) decisions have interactions and uncertain consequences.

Gregory, Robert H., and Thomas V. V. Atwater, Jr. "Cost and Value of Management Information as Functions of Age," *Accounting Research*, vol. 8: 42-70 (January 1957). The economics of the age of information is explored in terms of its two components: (a) interval or length of reporting period used, and (b) delay or time elapsed after the end of the period before information is available. The cost of data processing depends partly upon how frequently reports are prepared (length of interval) and how quickly they are available after a period closes (length of delay). Cost of processing may increase sharply as both interval and delay are reduced toward zero in an attempt to get "immediate information."

Gregory, Robert H., and Martin Trust. "Data Processing and Information Production," pp. 65-71 in *Proceedings of the Eastern Joint Computer Conference*, New York, Institute of Radio Engineers, 1959. This paper presents the theory that the function of information selection can be successfully delegated to mechanized elements in the system so that the output is automatically screened for management significance. Rather than generating fixed volumes of reports each period covering all items under consideration, the idea is that the report volumes will fluctuate to cover only those items requiring management action. In short, the system output becomes a function of the information content of the data being processed.

Hitch, Charles. "An Appreciation of Systems Analysis," *Journal of the Operations Research Society of America*, vol. 3: 466-81 (November 1955). This article gives a critical examination of the processes for problem analysis and decision making. Although the article is concerned primarily with military strategy and tactics, many of the points made appear to be of general usefulness. The essential elements of systems analysis are given and some recent developments are discussed, such as (a) the great increase in the number of interdependent factors considered, and (b) the explicit treatment of uncertainty and time phasing. Analysis and intuition are examined, compared, and illustrated by situations for which the two give different answers.

Rosenstein, Allen B. "The Industrial Engineering Application of Communications-Information Theory," *The Journal of Industrial Engineering*, vol. 6:10-21 (September-October 1955). Rosenstein attempts to fit the industrial organization into patterns that are established by communication theory. The operational communications concept is employed and the practical results of the mathematical theory of communication are discussed without developing detailed proofs. The theory is extended to recognize the human elements of the industrial system and, finally, a number of industrial and organizational situations are examined in the light of the generalized theory. Rosenstein includes a lengthy bibliography to the literature on information theory, and he gives special attention to the early work by Claude Shannon and Warren Weaver, *The Mathematical Theory of Communication*, Urbana, Illinois, The University of Illinois Press, 1949.

CHAPTER ELEVEN

SYSTEMS ANALYSIS AND DESIGN

The purpose of systems analysis and design is to develop a data-processing structure that will efficiently meet the information needs of a business.

"Systems analysis" is an orderly study of the detailed procedures for collecting, organizing, and evaluating information within an organization, with the objective of improving control of the operations of the organization.

In planning a data-information system, a systems analyst collects, organizes, and evaluates the facts which will have a managerial use. He studies the information requirements of a business in terms of its objectives, output reports, time requirements, work loads, available input data, the relative importance of problem areas, and the available facilities—equipment, personnel, and procedures.

"Systems design," on the other hand, is the creative stage in devising a new system; it includes the dreaming, inventing, planning, and hard work necessary to fulfill business objectives—which are often expressed in terms of the quantity and quality of output reports, documents, and files. The design phase must also take account of the processing methods, facilities, and data needed to fill the requirements of a given business for both management and operating information.

The basic principles underlying systems analysis and design are discussed in this chapter. The actual methods and procedures for analysis and design are covered more fully in later chapters.

OBJECTIVES OF ANALYSIS AND DESIGN

Fundamentally, systems analysis and design undertakes to determine what information is required for operating and controlling a business and the procedures necessary for obtaining that information. The analysis phase concentrates on taking a system apart to find its elements, while the design phase puts old and new elements together to devise a new system.

The objectives to be accomplished by systems analysis and design should be stated explicitly at the outset in order to keep the work in focus and to measure progress toward the goals established. The objectives should represent a balanced statement of what is to be accomplished both technically and economically.

The level of design work may be so mundane as merely to copy a similar system which has been tested elsewhere and to modify it to the user's environment. An intermediate level of systems design involves devising a new system that makes use of existing equipment. A still higher level of systems design involves the invention of an entirely new system that may require equipment not yet built. The term "equipment" is restricted to the computer, input-output devices, and storage units—the "hardware"—purchased from the manufacturer. "System" covers the broad processing structure built up around the equipment in order to use it. Of course, systems design can be done without introducing new equipment.

Sometimes there is a lack of balance between systems changes and the related economics. Operating problems often seem paramount and changes are demanded at any cost. Often, although not universally, it is thought that a proposed system can be superior and yet operate at no increase in cost; but the direct outlay for data processing may be willingly increased to improve the quality of information obtained.

REASONS FOR ANALYSIS

The first question to ask might well be the somewhat philosophical one, "Why analyze a data-processing system?" Merely asking the question in an operating environment implies that a system exists and that it may not be entirely satisfactory. The basic reason for analyzing business-data systems is to select the areas where system design will yield the greatest improvement. A wholly new organization or operation needs, of course, a system designed from the ground up.

Management problems change from year to year and even from month to month. A system that filled information requests yesterday may be only partly satisfactory today and unsuitable tomorrow. Dissatisfaction usually arises because the system does not fulfill certain business requirements or because it costs too much to operate. Equipment and systems also change over time. Engineers can design and construct better (more reliable, faster, and more economical) equipment, but it is often higher priced. Management analysts can devise and install better systems for collecting and processing data and reporting information to management; but these systems often require new equipment.

Organizational Requirements

There are many ways to answer the question, "What does management really need to know to run the business?" Some analysts with an accounting and systems-design background suggest the straightforward approach—simply asking management people what they must have to control operations (Toan, 1952). Having the consumer specify what he wants has some merit, but is only partly satisfactory. The consumer may have a good notion of the value of the information he receives, but he is likely to have little or no idea of the cost of gathering and processing data. Since the net advantage of knowing something depends on both the cost of learning it and the benefits of using it, any determination of what information is useful involves cooperation by data originators, processors, and users.

Operations researchers have observed that business-data systems, especially those developed and used by accountants, seem to lack focus and operate with unspecified objectives (Churchman and Ackoff, 1955). As a precautionary measure, traditional data systems gather and store huge quantities of facts in order to answer any questions that may arise. According to operations researchers, the remedy for such open-endedness in data origination and storage is to determine what questions will be asked in the future and to retain data to answer these questions alone. If all questions are specified in advance, then unnecessary data can be discarded; in fact, superfluous data need not even be gathered, for they will only be discarded. Of course, the success of a policy of obtaining and storing minimal data rests on successful prediction of future questions. But no one, not even a good operations researcher, feels confident enough to predict what these questions will be.

The problems of determining short-run and long-run data and information requirements are not easily solved. The high cost of reconstructing past facts favors the gathering of data when first available and retaining them on the prospect that they may be used in the future. Collecting and storing numerous facts to have one fact available when wanted may be cheaper than trying to reconstruct one fact after the event. Certain past events (as weather, sales, or factory production) may be impossible to reconstruct; unless recorded as they occur, they will be lost.

Decision Making

In the absence of any efficient way for determining future needs for information, the usual approach is to start with the existing information structure and modify it to remedy known deficiencies and to meet foreseeable new requirements. The management organization deserves examination to find where decisions are made, what facts they are based on, and environmental restrictions on decision making.

It has been argued that studying the details of managerial organization involves a risk of becoming confused by the political strengths and weaknesses of people currently occupying certain positions (Chapin, 1957). As a matter of fact, political situations within a company do have an important bearing on systems design and equipment selection. More narrowly, systems analysis tries to find whether decisions are based on internally produced facts, externally available facts, or merely on hunches; whether decisions follow explicit or implicit rules; what concessions in information requirements are made to adapt to the existing system and available information; and the durability of policy objectives. For example, a shoe manufacturer's specification for same-day shipment of complete orders—absolutely no back orders—to all retailers, and an airline's demand for answers within one minute to most questions about reservations may be fundamental business policies and must, therefore, be complied with by any data system worthy of serious consideration.

Changing the policies of a business, so that a problem easier than the one originally posed can be solved, may simplify systems analysis and design; but it should be undertaken only with full realization of the consequences of solving a different problem. Occasionally, systems analysis is insufficient or misdirected so that design proposals deal with unimportant side issues while leaving main problems untouched.

Limiting Factors

Another reason for analyzing an existing system is to find whether deficiencies can be attributed to people—managers, supervisors, and clerks—or to the equipment in use and the system that has been devised.

At one extreme, the equipment on hand may be suitable but not properly utilized because of limitations in the organization itself, in personnel, or in operating procedures. At the other extreme, an organization capable of developing and applying efficient methods to achieve suitable objectives may not be able to do so because the necessary equipment is not on hand, or perhaps not even available.

The question of suitability of equipment and procedures is illustrated by the enumeration aspect of any census. People may use tally sheets to classify and count the number of people in each age bracket. If punched-card equipment with limited classification and accumulation capacity is used, the cards may be sorted into categories and counted. Given equipment with sufficient classification and accumulation capacity, such as sorters with accumulating features or electronic computers with enough internal storage, the need for sorting before counting may be eliminated. Enumeration may be completed with one pass of the data. What is a sorting and counting operation on one type of equipment may require only a tally, with no sorting whatever, when done on equipment with different capabilities.

The basic point here is that it is necessary to distinguish between fundamental objectives and the methods for achieving them, which may employ various kinds of equipment with different strong and weak points. Important technical changes may lead to entirely new concepts of what information can be supplied economically. Early in any systems study it is desirable to determine whether greater potential benefits lie in improving operations through better use of present equipment or by obtaining new equipment. Effort can then be spent in devising the most profitable improvements.

Amount of Improvement

A data-processing system is analyzed for the same reason that any other system is analyzed: to improve it. In general, improvement takes one of two forms: (1) either reducing the costs of obtaining and processing data, or (2) improving the information obtainable so it will be more useful for management. In either case, net benefits are achieved. In those cases where system output is not improvable (a correct pay-check is only a pay-check), cost reduction is primary. Where the information being produced is deficient, the emphasis in systems redesign is on getting better information.

Cost Reduction. Systems analysis is often undertaken to reduce the cost of processing measured in dollars, man-hours, and processing time. The future costs of operating a system can be reduced by providing adequate expansion capacity for meeting future operational needs without making proportional increases in financial outlay and personnel. A net reduction in either present costs or probable future costs will produce smaller total costs in the long run. The ability to reduce costs depends, in good part, on the ability of engineers to design more efficient equipment and on that of analysts to devise better systems.

Opportunities for systems improvement are greater when more powerful equipment is available and system analysts understand how to use it to meet management needs. The final test of the desirability of more powerful equipment is whether its additional capacity justifies its higher cost.

Information Improvement. Improving the quality of information can be done in several ways:

1. Accelerate the reporting of results over what is obtainable by other means.
2. Improve the accuracy of results.
3. Screen out important from unimportant results to increase the information content of reports.
4. Obtain new kinds of information to meet changing management control needs and eliminate duplication in processing.

Whether improved information leads to any net benefits for an organization depends on several factors. Important benefits may be obtained from large improvements in the quality of information. Comparison of the quality and quantity of information available before and after a system change is an indication of the amount of improvement.

Prospects of Obtaining Benefits

The benefits described above—reduced cost or improved information—cannot be guaranteed by systems analysis and design, however. While managers may have the potential ability to use improved information for decision making, they may have to be retrained before they can use new and improved kinds of information.

The actual operations of an organization—purchasing, manufacturing, selling and whatever—must be responsive to decisions in order to get the full benefits from improved information and decisions. If the quantity and quality of information previously available hampers managers trying to control operations, information improvements will have far-reaching and beneficial results. On the other hand, the operating processes may be hedged about by so many restrictions that few changes are possible; in such cases, better decisions based on improved information have little ultimate effect, and information systems analysis is unlikely to be profitable.

The amount of possible benefit must be considered in terms of the prospects of achieving any particular degree of success—and these prospects range from the almost certain to the extremely doubtful. The problem of making reasonable estimates of future benefits will be discussed further in Chapter 12.

AMOUNT OF ANALYSIS

The question, "How much systems analysis?" is most perplexing. The amount of analysis that is worth while depends on the prospects for improving the situation. Some analysis is required for the sole purpose of appraising a situation, and some exploratory analysis is required before detailed analysis can be started. Beyond this, the merits of continuing the analysis must be constantly reappraised.

There are two extreme situations that may deserve little or no preliminary analysis. Well-known opportunities for effective improvements already exist; in which case it may be better to make changes in the system or equipment which exploit such opportunities, rather than pursuing further analysis. Observation of the experience of others may disclose such opportunities. At the other extreme, the opportunities for improvement may be nil. If that is known to be the case, then analytic effort should be spent elsewhere. In most cases, the situation will lie somewhere between these two extremes—opportunities for improvement will exist, but their precise nature and amount will not be known in advance.

Scope of Analysis

The scope of systems analysis may be either narrow or broad. A data-processing system is always an inter-related whole, but the degree of interdependence between its functions may vary greatly in different organizations. Since some data-information problems of an organization are apart from and outside the main stream, isolated areas can be studied individually, with little regard for how they impinge on other areas. Individual steps in larger processes may bear on only the preceding and following processing steps. The initial step—data origination methods—may bear on data input only. More often, data-information problems are in the main stream of processing and must be studied in relation to their over-all effect. Inventory control, for instance, is closely related to purchasing, production scheduling, cataloguing, financial administration, and other functions.

The selection of either a narrow area or a broad one for systems analysis and design is basic to sound, efficient work. One factor in making this choice is the degree of satisfaction with existing methods. The whole system may fail to meet demands for information so that full-scale analysis on a broad front and complete redesign are required. Another factor is that isolated operations may be handled in an unsatisfactory fashion; when this is so, narrow or sharply focused analysis is an efficient way to deal with the particular problem areas.

Another factor bearing on the desirable extent of analysis is the nature of changes in equipment. New gadgets and even important developments of individual pieces of equipment may be best dealt with by narrow analysis. New input devices may affect the way that data are originated but nothing more. On the other hand, important equipment developments bear on the whole data-information system for an organization. Broad analysis is imperative for efficiently matching the equipment and the system. Anything less may force them together without realizing the potential benefits of broader analysis in depth.

Inquiry. Many situations deserve some inquiry merely to find whether further analysis seems worth while. This is analagous to the initial step in the traditional recipe for making rabbit stew: catch a rabbit. Countless situations may deserve initial examination. From all the possibilities that exist, some can be selected for study. Analysts and management may use various criteria for selecting areas for inquiry. Problem areas that are plagued by high costs or unsatisfactory results deserve reconsideration from time to time, for there is always some prospect of a breakthrough that will lead to big improvements.

New equipment developments promise reductions in the cost of processing, improvements in information, or both. Important developments in equipment and systems should be studied by both staff and operating personnel to take full advantage of improvements as they become available. Applications considered troublesome, and others that are borderline cases, deserve another "look" when equipment and systems change. High-volume, complex, or urgent requirements deserve prime consideration.

The leader in any field must conduct his own initial inquiry, even though exploration is expensive because many paths of inquiry turn out to be blind alleys. The study of some areas may be discarded because initial inquiry overlooks opportunities not disclosed by the first round of study. The firsthand experience gained by initial study is valuable for later guidance, if it is possible to avoid having each mistake become an albatross. The follower has a simpler problem. Observation of the initial studies made by others may permit skipping the inquiry stage and going directly to analysis in depth. Merely to know that something works, even though the precise method is not known, eliminates much of the uncertainty from the early stages of inquiry.

Analysis in Depth. Systems analysis in depth is worth while if initial inquiry indicates that there are good opportunities for improvement. The logical, tentative conclusion is to continue the study in more detail. This discussion, remember, deals with *why analyze* a system and, if so, *how much.* The *how* of systems analysis is considered later in this chapter, and the tools for systems analysis are covered in Chapter 14.

The perplexing problem of how much analysis is worth while continues throughout the analysis-in-depth stage. The value of more analysis is not entirely clear until after it is done, at which time it is too late to modify the course of the study already finished.

Analysis in depth is a sequential process. The findings at any stage may influence the future course of study. At any time it is possible to cut off further study, if it does not appear to be beneficial. Continued analysis is useful if the cost of additional study is likely to be covered by prospective improvements. Costs continue to pile up at controllable rates over time so that the total amount is predictable, if schedules are maintained; but estimating the margin of improvement is more difficult. At any stage a new breakthrough may occur so that possible improvements are much larger. Additional study may merely narrow the margin of inaccuracy in estimates and not otherwise change the results of a study, or additional study may show that earlier estimates of improvement were over-optimistic. Prospective improvements must then be scaled down because of mistaken estimates or subsequent changes in the equipment or the system.

Further analysis in depth is most valuable when prospective improvements are still changing rapidly, and especially when improvements are increasing faster than the costs of analysis. Analysis needs to be carried far enough to reduce the margin of inaccuracy in the estimates of benefits obtainable. Furthermore, the prospects for realizing any particular amount of benefit need to be estimated with some certainty. Continued analysis is no longer warranted when the estimated improvements are not increasing as fast as the cost of study.

Other methods of processing data should be compared, if feasible, with the method under analysis. The most fruitful area or areas should be selected for action.

Cost of Analysis. The outlay made for analysis, both initial and intensive, should be related to the effective improvements likely to be obtained. Costs are controllable, in some sense. A certain number of people can be assigned to systems analysis so that the outlay per period is fixed. If the work stays on schedule, total costs meet the budget. Routine systems analysis can be scheduled because most of the factors involved are known.

Research and development to devise radically different systems or to use new equipment is more difficult to plan and keep on schedule. There is a tendency for work to progress smoothly almost to the point of completion and then bog down. Specific tasks seem difficult to complete. Furthermore, there is always a tantalizing prospect that by a little more work analysts will discover or invent a vastly superior system. These two factors—the inability to complete analysis on schedule and the prospect of new discoveries—may cause systems analysis costs to exceed the budget by huge amounts.

Detailed analysis of systems is expensive in both manpower and elapsed time. Mammoth projects can result from ambitious plans to make detailed studies preparatory to introducing automatic systems. Such projects may be discontinued because of the huge expense and time involved, doubt as to any carry-over value after introduction of new techniques, and personality or jurisdictional disputes between systems analysts and people throughout the company. The costs of analysis and prospective improvements are so closely inter-related that careful estimation of results is required to get optimum results.

Duration of Analysis. Systems analysis should be done over an appropriate period of time in order to gain by the efficient introduction of changes.

Big improvements should be exploited as early as possible; but a long time is required to devise and introduce important changes. On the other hand, trivial improvements can be made quickly, but there is no pressing reason to do so. A paradox results: slow, deliberate analysis is suitable, if improvements are likely to be trivial. Unimportant changes can be installed "tomorrow" with no great loss from postponement.

Analysis takes less time if analysts know the present system and are familiar with the equipment that will be used. A cooperative spirit throughout the organization also speeds analysis. No system, data processing or otherwise, is static, although the rate of change may be fast or slow. Quick analysis is imperative, if the rate of change is high, for studies need to be completed and recommendations put into effect before further changes occur. Analysis and recommendations that take so long to implement that the conditions on which they are based no longer exist are obviously not suitable for installation.

Similar remarks can be applied to the rate of equipment change. Rapid changes in equipment demand quick analysis in order to use a particular model. It is possible to skip from one model of equipment to another, if models change before analysis is complete. Furthermore, it may be easier to switch to newer equipment than to revise an out-of-date systems study because of changes in the structure of the system.

Experience.   Current business literature describes the "on-the-record" experience of many companies in installing data processors. "Off-the-record" conclusions are, of course, not published, although they may be discussed privately. Company representatives often say that the advance planning was neither complete nor sound. Some computers stand partially or even completely idle for months while suitable instruction routines are developed, operating people trained, and many other problems solved. Wrong equipment is obtained in some cases and poor applications are made in others. Complete and careful advance planning would avoid many of these problems or at least improve the solution obtained.

Careful planning is conceded to be important, but it may get boring after a while, for the hustle and bustle of installing and using new equipment is more fascinating than hard thinking, despite the admonition of the placards on every wall. During the early stages of installation, troubles may snowball and the pressure of immediate problems force aside long-range planning. Here, as elsewhere, a series of short-range solutions does not necessarily make a good long-range plan. When troubles pyramid, the value of systems analysis and planning are clearer than ever.

Analysis of Present Methods

Great emphasis is often placed on analyzing and appraising the present methods. Detailed flow charts may be prepared to study the existing system, isolate checking procedures, and eliminate unnecessary duplication. The cautious approach, which is to study the present system carefully before proposing changes, has value if existing methods are not to be altered greatly. The value of detailed study of the present mechanized system declines if radically new techniques and structures will be introduced.

The notion is widely held that substantial benefits can be derived solely from the analysis of existing methods in the light of new techniques, even though they are rejected later. On the other hand, there is reason to believe that greater benefits are obtainable from formulating and appraising the future system in terms of future techniques than from dwelling on the system that is likely to be discarded. You don't learn how to make rockets by studying airplanes.

Analysis of present methods has several well-known characteristics. A data-processing system changes continuously under the influence of new demands for information, the experimental urge to improve, and the difficulty of keeping a widespread system under absolute control. It is difficult to determine, at any one time, both the status and direction of change for a business-data system. Systems involving people are likely to change just because they are examined; merely asking a person why he does something in a particular way may cause him to change his method.

Limits to Analysis

Some warnings concerning the extent and intensity of systems analysis must be raised here. A quick analysis is warranted in areas where important changes are to be made: (first) because the available benefits should be obtained sooner rather than later; and (second) because the new system will be sufficiently different from the old one (which will be largely discarded) that detailed examination is of little value in designing the new system. Systems studies involving many man-years of work have, on several occasions, been halted before completion because of the cost involved, the postponement of any changes until after completion of the study, and the subsequent inapplicability of detailed knowledge when radical changes were in prospect.

There are other reasons for limiting analytic work on the present system. Such analysis focuses attention on what is being done now, even though poorly, instead of concentrating on what should be done but is not being attempted because it is more difficult. Parallel to this, analysts may develop a limited-range view and narrow breadth of vision because today's problems seem overwhelming.

A further reason for limiting analysis of the existing procedures is that systems in use for a long time reach their limits of improvement with the existing combination of manpower, equipment, and mode of operation. For example, analysts of post office operations have concluded that manual sorting methods offer so little opportunity for improvement that effort should be directed toward devising entirely new schemes (Rotkin, 1958). More improvement is thought possible by discarding elements of the old system and starting afresh.

AREAS TO STUDY

The questions, "Why analyze," and "How much analysis," were considered above. The questions to be asked if prospective improvements warrant further analysis are listed here. These questions relate to both the data-information system and its equipment.

Operations and System

Systems improvements may be quite narrow and affect data-processing activities alone. On the other hand, they may be so broad as to impinge on all operations of the organization. Pertinent questions to ask about operations are:

1. What improvements in information are useful?
2. Are cost reductions possible in data processing?
3. Are improvements possible in the over-all operations of the organization?
4. How much analysis—in terms of cost, manpower, and time—is suitable for present and proposed systems?
5. What is the effect—disruption, retraining, and adjustment—of the new system on people?
6. Which applications have priority for analysis?

Equipment

An entirely different set of questions is pertinent for analyzing equipment that is available or may be designed to meet requirements:

1. How much study is needed to understand equipment for both selection and application purposes?
2. What improvements are possible as a result of introducing the newest equipment?
3. What varieties of equipment and what scale—large, medium, or small—are most suitable?
4. Should equipment be able to handle any application or merely specific applications?

5. What is the cost to obtain, install, apply, and operate selected equipment?

6. What non-hardware support will the equipment manufacturer furnish in the way of training, analysis, design, and programming?

Comments made earlier about the initial inquiry and analysis in depth apply to questions about data-processing operations and equipment. A cursory examination or screening is useful as a first step in answering any questions. The results of such an initial inquiry into the prospects for improvement and the probable costs of analysis should determine whether a particular area deserves analysis in depth.

SYSTEMS APPROACH

Many procedures exist for answering questions about data-processing operations and equipment. An orderly plan for analysis is preferable to haphazard action. Facts, numbers, and quantities are preferable to opinions, words, and qualitative statements. Good systems analysis must, at some stage, use a broad approach to avoid the difficulty of confusing discrete points and over-all patterns—the age-old problem of the trees and the forest.

The systems approach views each problem as a whole rather than as bits and pieces. An automatic data-processing system derived by careful systems analysis can achieve many economies, for it can virtually eliminate duplicate files, parallel processing work, and redundant reports.

Structure and Technique

Any system can be examined in terms of structure and technique. The term "structure" is used to cover the nature of managerial organization, the origin and type of data collected, the form and destination of results, and the procedures used to control operations. The structure depends on:

1. The organization and nature of the decision-making process
2. The flow plan—on-line, in-line, off-line—used for processing data
3. The frequency of reporting, length of reporting period, and delay in report preparation
4. The type of processing scheme—consolidated or fragmentary
5. The methods for handling exceptional situations
6. The degree of centralization of data-processing operations

The "technique" of a data-processing system refers to the technical aspects of the method used to originate and process data in order to furnish information in some useful form. Features of a system covered by the word "techniques" are:

1. The amount and type of data-processing equipment used
2. The methods of programming equipment and instructing people to perform operations
3. The number of record files
4. The arrangement of data within files

The introduction of automatic data processing may change techniques drastically because new and entirely different equipment is used. Changes in the structure of processing may, within broad limits, be either important or trivial, according to the user's vision and courage.

Combined Changes.   A change in either the structural or the technical aspects alone seldom results in the best system achievable. More efficient systems can be obtained at less cost by changing both factors. Whether to change the structure or the technique first is usually not important if system changes occur slowly. When equipment changes rapidly, new techniques tend to be adopted faster than changes in the structure; this is due to the rush to obtain new equipment, reluctance to disturb the existing structure for fear of slowing the introduction of new techniques, and the ease of introducing new techniques.

Important structural changes in a system without corresponding changes in technique are probably uneconomical, if not impossible. For example, a business using many individual files for record keeping would be foolish to try to combine all files into one file (or even a few files) unless the technique for file processing were greatly altered. Minor changes in structure may be made in preparation for a change in techniques, although such changes may seem uneconomical when first made. Making them may speed and simplify transition to the new system when the technique is later changed. There are many ways to change from the existing combination to a new combination of structure and technique. One possibility is to change both at one time and move directly from the present to the proposed system. It may be possible to try to change either the structure or the technique alone without changing the other, but any important change in one will probably be accompanied or followed by some change in the other.

Another possible transition is to keep fixed, or nearly fixed, either the structure or the technique and change the other to a position somewhere between the existing and the desired arrangements. The other factor is then modified in a second step to achieve the finally desired arrangement. The first factor can be changed from its intermediate to its final position.

At the risk of oversimplification, Figure 11-1 shows two paths for changing from the present to the proposed system. Representing the structure and technique along individual axes is an oversimplification. Each consists of many factors so that more than two dimensions are required to cover all factors. Two dimensions merely hint at the basic idea.

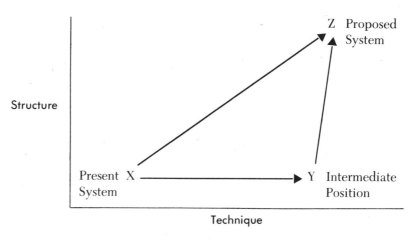

FIGURE 11-1. *Structure and technique change routes*

The diagonal line from X to Z indicates simultaneous change. One or more stopping points along this route are possible, to consolidate the benefit of changes already made. The two-stage change route stops at an intermediate position Y, after changing the technique of processing data, until the results of the first change are consolidated. The structural arrangement is then changed to the desired objective. An alternate path, not shown in Figure 11-1 and seldom followed in practice, is to change the structure first to reach an intermediate position and then move to the proposed system.

Postponement of Structural Changes. An alternative to making combined changes is to adopt the new techniques first, making only the minimum structural changes required. This approach can telescope the time required to get new equipment into operation. Little time is spent initially to develop new procedures or organizational structures. After new techniques are in use, attention can be turned to structural alterations.

There are advantages to introducing equipment first and postponing structural analysis and change until later. The work and confusion of simultaneously installing equipment and changing the technique are minimized. Many jobs performed by people in the old system will be performed by equipment after it is installed. A system reduced to instruction routines for equipment is easier to define and examine than a manual system. Equipment instructions can provide for gathering data about transactions, which can be used in analyzing and modifying the structure. In short, the computer can be used to analyze the system for the purpose of planning structural changes.

Present Tendency. System developments now occurring reflect large, rapid changes in techniques and only gradual changes in the structure of data processing. It is not yet clear whether new systems will stabilize and become rigid or will remain flexible enough to permit further changes. There is a widespread tendency to consolidate an intermediate position and resist further changes. Even revolutionary groups demand a *status quo* as soon as the first revolution is over—"one revolution and no more."

Some organizations undertake a basic re-engineering of existing operating procedures that may result in important structural changes; some of these structural changes, however, are often unplanned, and occasionally unwanted.

Centralization of data processing may increase in the future. The degree of centralization used at any time reflects a balance between the costs of transmitting the mass of raw data for centralized processing and the costs of decentralized processing with transmission of summarized results. Improvements now occurring in communications will facilitate centralization of processing. Improvements in decision making are expected to result from new developments in data processing and management science. The remaining question is whether, and how rapidly, the new opportunities will be exploited by business.

System Selection

The precise criteria employed for selecting one system and rejecting others are seldom stated. It is often difficult to find what reasons caused people to follow a certain course of action. The factors that determine the design of a future system are:

1. Information and data requirements
2. Nature of the existing system
3. Current technology of equipment

Information and data requirements are the most important determinants of system design. The system should be designed to meet information requirements, although this objective may be difficult to achieve in practice. Systems analysis and design often concentrates on studying the existing system rather than establishing data and information requirements for the future without regard for prior limitations. There is a strong tendency for a new system to resemble the existing system to a greater degree than it fulfills future requirements. In short, it is probably easier to solve yesterday's problems than it is to formulate tomorrow's problems, apart from considering how to solve them.

More emphasis is often put on document processing—payroll, billing, and accounting—than on information generation for management control—what to produce, where to sell, and what price to charge. The structural arrangement of systems that emphasize document processing has remained basically the same for a century or so (Gregory, 1956). During that time, processing techniques have changed from manual to electromechanical to electronic.

The current state of technology is a severe restriction on equipment selection. The cost of major design changes to meet particular requirements is so high that such changes are seldom made by manufacturers, though often requested by users. Occasionally, a manufacturer and customer jointly develop special equipment, but special equipment often contains mostly standard components. As a general rule, the user is restricted to equipment that is commercially available now or within the next few years, unless he is willing to pay for equipment research and development.

Structure and Equipment. Changes in data-processing techniques may require large structural changes in the system. Processing schemes designed for manual or punched-card systems may be unsuitable for automatic systems. The delay involved in getting control information and the high cost of calculation and logic are two features of present systems that should not limit future systems.

Daily operating information is often obtained by informal methods aimed at meeting day-to-day needs. The formal reports that follow later may be limited to after-the-fact control and to showing long-term trends. Examination of the present structure may reflect only the information that can be supplied under the restrictions imposed by the old technique instead of what would be required to meet the basic demands for information. In view of the inherent limitations, improved techniques also call for structural changes in order to develop an efficient system.

Inventory control procedures, for example, may require knowledge about the quantity on hand when decisions are made. One-fourth of all items might be reviewed each week when the records are kept by hand; stock clerks make these reviews by studying the records, staggering the reviews to keep down the workload. Automatic procedures might reduce the review time from a week to an hour, so that a cycled review plan is no longer necessary. Complete inventory review might be made at some desired interval—daily, weekly, or monthly—and new re-order points, based on current usage, computed during the review.

An ideal system would give management all useful information at the exact time it is needed. As processing techniques improve, the resulting structures will come closer to giving ideal information. The value of information produced should increase with improved accuracy and timeliness, while processing costs should decrease.

Optimal System. An optimal system is the best that can be designed under any circumstances; but this is not a working definition because people interpret "best" in different ways. It is more useful to define an "optimal system" as the one that comes closest to fulfilling the selected system objectives that are the real yardstick for evaluation.

A wide variety of objectives exists. A common objective is to maximize the excess of value over cost, that is, to *maximize profit*. The system output may be specified and fixed so that the objective is to operate as inexpensively as possible, that is, to *minimize costs*. When both the task and the method are specified, the value is fixed and minimum cost is identical with maximum profit. If there is any freedom for performing the task, minimizing costs may lead to different results from those of maximizing profit; that is, the least expensive procedures may not result in the greatest excess of value over cost.

A common short-range goal is to reduce the cost and time for processing. Improvements are first applied at points where volume, complexity, or urgency presents opportunities for substantial savings. Initial applications will develop knowledge and skills essential to an eventual integration of systems. The long-range goal may be to apply advanced data-processing techniques throughout the system from origination of data to their ultimate use at all levels. More specific objectives used for data-processing system design are these: more accurate, timely, or complete reports; experience in using a new technique; increased job satisfaction; and reduced paper work. Immediate benefits may be difficult to measure, but these objectives maximize profit in the long run.

If no objective is agreed on and each individual involved develops his own, conflicts, cross-purposes, and confusion result. Selection of and agreement on a common objective increase the efficiency of systems analysis and design.

Sub-optimization. Many managers say that their objective is to maximize profits, although profit maximization is a policy objective rather than an operating objective. The value, as described in Chapter 10, is often an intangible that is difficult to measure; and costs are complex because of average, joint, and marginal aspects. The cost of processing and the value of information may be affected by too many factors to permit complete evaluation in a reasonable time.

A practical approach is to select and pursue an operating objective that goes in the same direction as the over-all policy objective. Operating objectives are the concrete plans for action; they are made despite the risk that they may fulfill only a part of the policy objective, or may even go in the wrong direction and result in a condition called "sub-optimization." For example, a policy objective might be to reduce the monthly telephone bill. One operating objective might be to limit the time for each call. This course may reduce costs only slightly, since the minimum time charge is fixed and brief calls may lead to extra calls. A better operating objective might be to reduce the number of calls by transacting more business on each call, or by writing more letters.

The selection of operating objectives is important and should be examined carefully to see that they lead in the same direction as the policy objectives. Efficiency will be greater if every member of a project group knows the group's policy and operating objectives.

SYSTEMS DESIGN

Design of a new system depends on sound work, but more than mere fact gathering is involved; a certain amount of creativity, ingenuity, or inventiveness is essential for devising an efficient system. Entirely new schemes may be necessary to match management's requirements with the available equipment and the capabilities of personnel.

System design is discussed here in terms of fact finding, developing specifications, meeting specifications, and matching equipment with the system. The closely related areas of system installation and follow-up are important enough to deserve separate coverage: analytic tools and methods are covered in Chapter 14, and system installation and review are discussed in Chapter 17.

There are many ways to study the operation of a system. Reading the operating manual and discussing objectives with top-level people will help one discover how a system is supposed to operate. Discussing methods and procedures with operating personnel and observing firsthand what actually happens will bring one much closer to understanding how a system actually works.

Systems Objectives

Systems objectives are established by upper-level management with advice from the people directly involved at all operating levels. Realistically, such objectives are tempered by the ability of the organization to fulfill them. The long-run, fundamental objectives, not just short-run goals, should be spelled out. A change in either the problems encountered or the capability of the system may sometimes alter the short-run goal without changing the long-run objectives.

Some objectives of a data-processing system may be stated explicitly, whereas others are implicit and can be ascertained only by discussions with management and operating personnel or by observing how the system operates. System objectives are reflected by the reports prepared, time schedules followed, data stored for future use, and areas receiving the most emphasis.

Sources of Facts

The rules can be learned by studying operating manuals, which tell what is supposed to be done, and by observing the procedures in operation to find what is actually done; the actual mode is often different from the prescribed mode. Discrepancies arise because some improvements developed in practice are not yet formalized in the operating manuals. Many procedural variations occur unobtrusively, as if by erosion, so that people are unaware of the need to change the written procedures to conform with their practice.

The starting point for fact finding about a manual system might well be the final reports prepared for management and the documents issued to operating personnel; these reflect, in the simplest terms, what outputs are being demanded from the system. Operations involved in processing can be traced back to initial transactions by way of summaries, working sheets, files, calculations, and intermediate papers. Specimen blanks and completed copies of all documents can be obtained to indicate the nature and origin of the source data. The proportion of ordinary and unusual transactions is an important determinant of data conversion and processing loads. Any planned systems analysis should consider similar work still current enough to have validity; surveying the experience of other companies can provide the benefits derived from understanding their successes and failures in similar areas.

Systems Specifications

The starting point in developing systems specifications is the set of requirements imposed by management. The initial list of information requirements may describe what is wanted with little or no regard for the feasibility of supplying such information or the costs involved in gathering and processing the requisite data. Initial proposals for information to be supplied may, upon examination, prove to be so vague that analysts must reduce them to operating terms. On the other hand, initial proposals may be unrealistic because the value of the information obtained will not exceed the processing costs. Realistic targets are established by first weighing the costs and values for many possible systems and then selecting the one with the largest excess of value over cost.

Stating the objective of system design as the maximization of net benefits (excess of value over cost) serves as a fundamental specification for system design, if the value of information output can be measured in monetary terms against the corresponding costs of proc-essing. Some valid concepts exist, but, lacking any general theory of the value of information, it is customary to describe a number of minor objectives for a system—despite the risk that focusing attention on the minor design criteria may result in a sub-optimal system. Sub-sidiary specifications commonly used for system design can be classified as follows:

1. *Information output*—report content, timeliness, frequency, format, focus, and distribution; ability to answer preplanned and unantici-pated random interrogations; and mode and language for commu-nicating with company management, operating personnel, and outsiders.

2. *Organization*—who receives the output; who is responsible for origi-nating and processing data, personnel required, and changes involved.

3. *Equipment and costs*—nature and performance of equipment; invest-ment in equipment, facilities, and preparation (analyzing, designing, programming, and testing); installation and conversion; new relation-ship of fixed and variable costs; work loads and expandability to cover an increased volume of work; and flexibility to handle new applications.

4. *Safety features*—quality of input data; detection and correction of mistakes and errors; safeguards against manipulation of data and processing operations; ability to trace operations and reconstruct results; and the length of time and method of keeping transactions and files.

Since there is no easy way to combine these specifications into a single number, it is difficult to balance or trade off one against another. Consider, for example, the problem of whether an improvement in the ability to interrogate files is worth having at the risk of, say, an in-creased opportunity for manipulation of data in files.

Meeting Specifications

Specifications developed for a proposed system may require com-puters and related equipment, new schemes for getting data into processable form, consolidation of files, and revision of reporting and question-answering services. More often, however, many features of an existing system carry over with only limited changes.

Areas of Freedom. One approach to systems design is to start with output requirements and then determine what processing proce-dures and input data are required for preparing that output. The op-posite approach is to determine what input data will be available and devise processing procedures to fulfill the output requirements. These two approaches may appear to be in conflict, but they are reconcilable in being applicable to different levels of system design. The general formulation of a system may focus on the output to be obtained, with little regard for the methods involved and data required. Filling in system details, however, requires equal care for all stages from the origination of data to the final output.

A different approach to fulfilling systems specifications is to start with the areas where freedom to change is restricted. Areas that have a wide latitude for redesign are handled later when the difficulties of fitting all loose ends together will be much greater. Working from constrained areas toward free areas reduces the number of complete revisions of plans that may be required to make the system meet the conditions imposed.

An example is useful to illustrate the idea of the degree of freedom in system design. A company that issues travelers' checks may want to mechanize the handling of checks that clear through banks for payment. The appearance of travelers' checks—their color, size, style, and paper—is so important to their widespread acceptance that the company may specify that no changes in check appearance will be permitted. Given this constraint, one plan used for mechanization is to pre-print small dots in metallic ink to indicate amount, check serial number, and identification of the issuing agent. The dots blend into the pattern printed on the check and do not change it perceptibly. This approach requires special equipment to handle the paper and "read" the dots for automatic processing. On the other hand, bank customers—and, to some extent, banks themselves—feel free to use paper documents, including checks, in a wide variety of styles, sizes, and papers. Since banks accept the right of depositors to use non-standard checks (although upper and lower size limits are suggested), they are unwilling or unable to impose a high degree of standardization. This policy has led to the development of equipment to print magnetizable ink characters on non-standard-size commercial checks for both machines and people to read and use. The point concerning system constraints is that they must be observed in order to solve the problem as originally posed. Relaxation of the constraints may make solution much easier; but improper relaxations may result in solving an unintended problem.

In general, more stringent limitations are likely to exist on the freedom to change the input and output than on the freedom to modify processing methods. Furthermore, constraints are likely to be tighter for intercompany than for intracompany input and output. Constraints on the freedom to change the system are relative, in the sense that they may be removed quickly if the benefits of a change clearly outweigh the costs involved. In any event, systems change slowly over time even though they are considered immutable. At the risk of seeming obvious, it should be pointed out that some freedom must exist in designing a new system in order for it to be at all different from the old. Lacking any freedom to change, the new system becomes identical with the old.

Form Flow.   The myriad facts gathered about systems operations must be structured in order to be comprehensible. One method for organizing facts is to trace the flow of data for a transaction from origin to final destination. This method is commonly used in analyzing manual systems to show where papers originate, where each copy is sent, briefly what operations occur in each department, and final disposition of each copy. Large sheets with a column for each department and a row for each form can show the flow of documents by means of brief narratives or symbols to represent the movement of documents between and within departments. Form flow analysis furnishes a quick over-all view of how forms are handled without covering the details of each operation. Flow analysis tends to focus on the usual or typical case because graphs become too complex if many variations are handled. In analyzing the flow of forms it is necessary to cover a period that is long enough, such as a year, to encounter forms used only intermittently. In fact, the content and preparation of infrequently used forms will control, to some extent, shorter-term processing. If no flow chart is available, "dummy documents" may be prepared and traced through operations for fact-finding purposes.

Analysis of clerical work is complementary to a study of form flow for observing what happens in processing data. Work analysis is an intensive study of (for example) the processing involved in checking a customer's credit before accepting his order, and it is more likely to uncover unusual operations than is a study of form flow.

Process Charts.   A process chart, which is a pictorial representation of a selected area of data processing, specifies the output results wanted, the input data required to produce the output, and the general processing steps needed.

The set of symbols used for preparing process charts is related, in a general way at least, to the equipment proposed. A symbol for each of the following is commonly used:

1. *File*—magnetic tape, punched card, or punched tape
2. *Run*—rectangle containing a brief explanation of the operations involved to process files or transactions
3. *Output*—report from line printer, character printer, punched card, or punched tape
4. *System flow*—solid line for flow of data from one run to the next
5. *System cycle*—dashed line for output of current run to use as input in the next cycle of the same run

6. *Conversion*—card to tape, paper tape to magnetic tape, and vice versa

7. *Data origination*—key-punch operation, by-product of other manual operations, or automatic character readers

The size of each record item, number of items, number of reels in file, file identification name, and cycle frequency can be indicated on each process chart.

A process chart showing the basic operations in *file maintenance*, whereby changes (such as transfers, new hirings, terminations, and new data) affecting employees are first sorted and then introduced into the main file, is given in Figure 11-2 (Univac II, 1957).

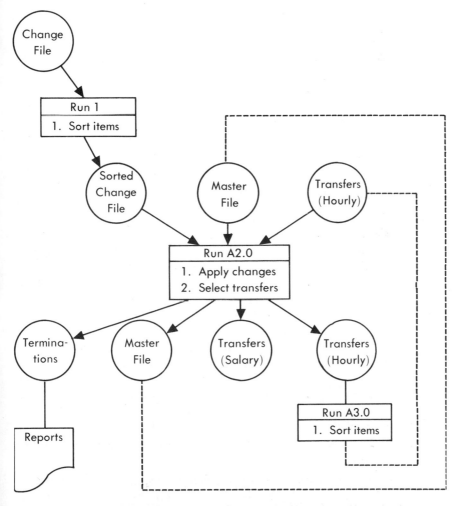

FIGURE 11-2. *File maintenance, basic operations*

The chart for maintenance of the employee data file is representative of the general class of file maintenance. Changes are sorted into the same sequence as items kept in the master file. One or more types of changes and the master file are handled together to prepare lists of deletions, to update the master file, and to carry forward any items that require further processing in the next file maintenance run. Transfers of records within a file pose an interesting problem. Forward transfers—an employee moved from department 14 to 36, for example—can be handled completely in one run by deleting the employee's record from the file for department 14 and inserting it into the file for department 36. A backward transfer, from department 40 to 8, however, would involve selecting the employee's record from the file for department 40 in one run, placing it in temporary storage for sorting, and then introducing his file into the records for department 8 on the next maintenance run. The master file resulting from one maintenance run is, of course, used as input in the next run. The problems arising from trying to keep a file in departmental sequence can be avoided by organizing the file without regard to departments. File maintenance is characterized by additions, deletions, transfers, and other changes in file records that involve few, if any, computations.

Processing runs are similar to file maintenance runs except that transactions (hours worked, for instance) are processed with the master file to compute pay and labor distribution, which may be processed for further computations and output in a subsequent run during the same cycle. Unmatched items that arise because of incorrect identification numbers are listed for follow-up.

An important factor in designing file maintenance and processing runs, which are handled together in some systems, is the frequency of updating the master file. Some applications—as weekly payroll—have an upper limit of processing. In other cases—inventory control, for example—more freedom exists to choose the frequency of processing, and a fraction of the file may be cycled each day in order to handle the whole file within a week. Cycled processing smooths the work load over the week and reduces master file handling from five times to once a week for inventory control. Selecting the optimum processing scheme in terms of frequency and cycling requires matching the increased work load of more frequent processing against the added value of obtaining more current results. Since processing costs may increase rapidly as more timely information is demanded, it is necessary to guard against allowing them to outrun increases in the value of information obtained.

Flow Charts.   Flow charts use conventions, symbols, and abbreviations to outline the elementary logical steps of processing operations. They are an intermediate stage in developing the detail required

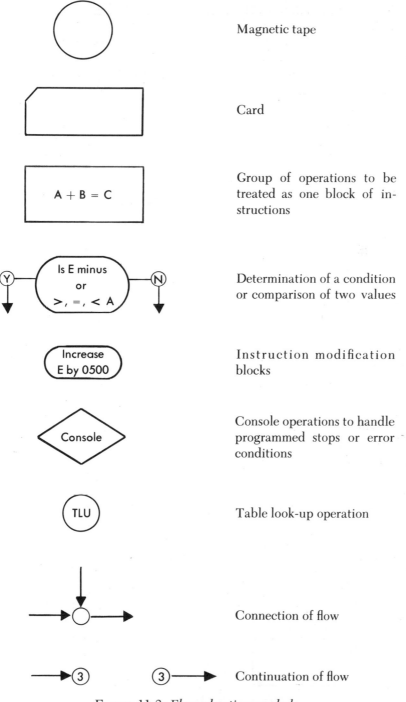

Magnetic tape

Card

Group of operations to be treated as one block of instructions

Determination of a condition or comparison of two values

Instruction modification blocks

Console operations to handle programmed stops or error conditions

Table look-up operation

Connection of flow

Continuation of flow

FIGURE 11-3. *Flow-charting symbols*

to reduce processing plans to operating reality. Widely used flow-charting symbols are shown in Figure 11-3.

An example of an over-all flow chart or block diagram prepared for the calculation of pay using magnetic-tape input and output is shown in Figure 11-4 and following (*Problem Planning Aids*, 1956). The over-all block diagram represents the major components of the problem. The scheme employed here uses a closed loop for all parts

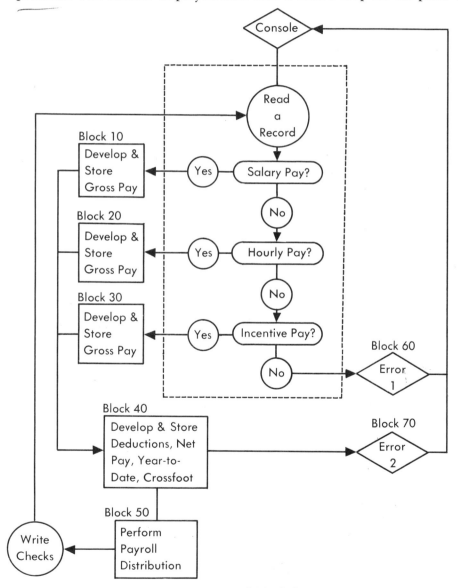

FIGURE 11-4. *Over-all block diagram*

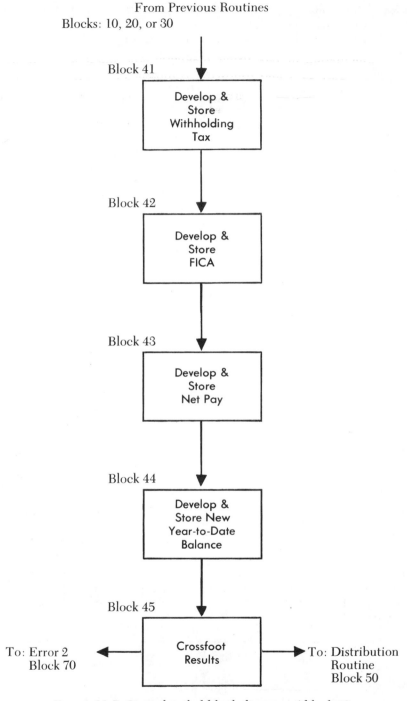

FIGURE 11-5. *Semi-detailed block diagram of block 40*

of the diagram, except for clerical functions, to assure continuous machine operations.

Two more levels of detail are useful in laying out the flow of operations. A semi-detailed block diagram like Figure 11-5 can show an expanded view of a major problem block, breaking the block into smaller components numbered for reference purposes. (Figure 11-5 shows block 40, with components 41, 42, etc.) This intermediate level of charting should disclose any serious errors or omissions arising in developing the run structure.

A detailed block diagram, Figure 11-6, expands semi-detailed block 41 into a series of logical operations numbered 41.1, 41.2, and so forth. This level of detail is a guide for quick preparation of computer instructions.

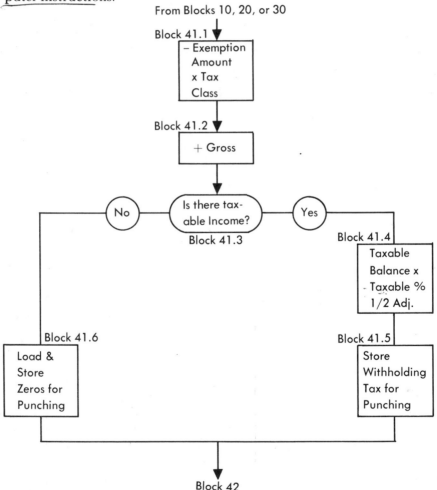

FIGURE 11-6. *Detailed block diagram of block 41*

Each semi-detailed block diagram deals with a separate part of the problem that can be programmed readily with the aid of corresponding detailed block diagrams. Detailed analysis of an application in this fashion simplifies program preparation.

The degree of detail depends upon the problem itself and the desires of the programmer. A programmer dealing with a problem that is small enough for him to handle alone may prefer to skip all flow charting and go directly to computer coding. This direct attack on a problem is advocated by programmers experienced in engineering and scientific problems that can be handled completely by one person. Business applications of computers may not appear to be as difficult as scientific problems, although some people consider them to be more intricate (Bowden, 1953). Complexities arise because of the relationship of each part of an application to another—for example, calculated gross pay must be available for calculating net—and the need to maintain operations without interruption cycle after cycle. The usefulness of flow charts grows as applications increase in scope and complexity. The standardization of flow-charting practices—symbols, arrangement, and degree of detail—simplifies design work and facilitates communication among programmers.

Programming. Flow charts, which are invaluable for understanding and designing programs, are translated into instructions for the computer and some of the supporting equipment. Since programming, in the narrow sense, is covered in Chapters 3 and 8 and depends on the particular computer to be used, it is not treated here.

Records and Files. Development of process charts, flow charts, and instruction codes presumes that records are designed for efficient storage as files, as well as for compatible processing with other input items. Numerous points must be resolved in designing records. Some of the more important of these are: (1) standardization of records for all types of data; (2) length and placement of key or keys for efficient sorting; (3) number of items (one or several) to a computer word; (4) variable- or fixed-length records, and disposition of residue; (5) maintenance of files before cut-over to new system and afterwards; (6) control and audit of file changes; and (7) the most efficient file media—paper, punched card, paper tape, magnetic tape, drum, or disk.

Some features of records and files are independent of the features of the equipment selected, but many others are dependent on such features. Computers that store records as fixed fields and blocks on tape, for example, process records faster if they are arranged one item per field and one record per block or in simple integrals or multiples thereof. Computers that handle variable-length fields have more, but not unlimited, freedom in record design.

Input. The origination of input data may lie outside the scope of operations covered by the process charts. The widespread belief that accurate, timely, and well-organized data will be available for processing as required is frequently not fulfilled in practice. The quality of data rarely matches expectations. The desired and actual nature of data available deserve analysis in order to get an efficient compromise between theory and practice. Briefly, the questions to consider in designing input schemes are: (1) where do data originate; (2) who is responsible for origination; (3) what format, volume, and media are used; (4) what non-trivial mistakes are inherently present; (5) how to detect and correct consequential mistakes before or during computer processing; and (6) what possibility exists for getting automatic or by-product generation of data.

Matching System and Facilities

The steps for meeting system specifications range from finding the degrees of freedom permissible for redesign to establishing input procedures; these steps constitute a first approximation of system design. It is necessary to find whether the proposed system appears feasible before deciding to install it. Modification of the proposed system design may be necessary to simplify its introduction and to keep costs within bounds. Matching the system and facilities involves careful appraisal of equipment, procedures, and personnel.

Equipment. Data-processing includes data origination, communication, and conversion; it requires input devices, the computer proper, file storage units, and output printers. Operating equipment requires support in the form of building space, utility services, and a communications network. Factors for appraising equipment are its capacity for handling present and near-future requirements, cost, compatibility of operations throughout the system, ability to fulfill report and interrogation requirements, flexibility to meet changing conditions, reliability for trouble-free operations, and protection against catastrophe.

The variety of equipment available can be screened to eliminate items that are either too large or too small for requirements or incompatible with other equipment. Enough difficulties arise in integrating equipment offered by different manufacturers to warrant assigning responsibility to one manufacturer for furnishing and coordinating all equipment, whether he manufactures it or purchases it from others.

Procedures. Detailed procedural instructions are needed to guide people in the same way that programs are required for computers. Operating procedures cover steps in the origination and conversion of input data, data transmission, computer operation, treatment of unusual cases, control and safeguards over data and files, system testing, and preparation and distribution of reports.

Difficult problems arise during the period of transition or cut-over to a new system. The fact that important system changes occur only infrequently hinders the preparation of specific, sound procedures and limits their applicability. The ease or difficulty of cut-over depends, in good part, on the care used in systems analysis and design as a whole. Cut-over is only one step, although an important one, in the transition from an old to a new system.

SUMMARY

Systems analysts collect, organize, and evaluate information to enable management to make decisions about a data-processing system. Systems are analyzed because there is some prospect of improving them. Improvements are made either by reducing the cost of operation or by increasing the value of information.

Electronic equipment designed and built in the past few years offers many opportunities for reducing the costs of processing data. Equipment developments have, in some ways, outrun the ability of systems analysts to use such equipment; still, some features of the equipment are not ideally suited to business-data processing and actually compound the user's problems. The quality of information may be improved by accelerating reports, screening important results, increasing accuracy, and obtaining new kinds of output.

The question of whether to analyze a system—and, if so, how extensively and intensively—is most perplexing. Some exploratory analysis is required merely to find areas that deserve analysis in depth. Analysis may be narrow in scope in order to improve isolated parts of the data system or to use limited-purpose equipment. Broad analysis is required for improving the whole system or several parts of it that are closely inter-related. A comprehensive analysis is imperative for the efficient use of large-scale equipment. Troublesome or expensive areas should get first attention; but important advances in equipment and systems often warrant re-evaluating many areas of a data system.

Big improvements in the system or equipment deserve quick introduction in order to exploit them as soon as possible; but the long and careful study required often postpones important changes. The opposite is true for trivial system changes: they can be made quickly, but there is no compelling reason to do so. Efficient systems design must balance the need for important systems changes with the user's ability to make them.

Detailed analysis of present methods is valuable to the extent that it provides learning which applies to the future. The prospective introduction of new equipment and techniques may change everything. In such a case, general analysis to find objectives is more valuable than a detailed analysis. Questions to ask during the analysis stage relate to the operations, system, and equipment. The nature of such questions depends on what ability and experience the analysts have, how rapidly the equipment is being changed, and what new system changes are being considered.

System selection is determined by information and data requirements, the existing system, and the current state of technology. Optimal system design is easier, if the objectives—maximize profit, minimize cost, or something else—are specified. Operating objectives must be consistent with policy objectives in order to achieve optimum results. If conflicts or cross-purposes develop, sub-optimization occurs.

On paper, systems design represents, at best, only a first approximation of an efficient system. Operations often fall below expectations because of requirements that are overlooked or misunderstood during the analysis stage, erroneous conceptions or miscalculations during design, and unplanned-for changes that occur after introduction. At best, the variations from plans that occur may require some minor modifications, and at worst, a complete overhaul of the system.

The question naturally arises whether greater care in analysis and more imagination and vision during design would be more efficient than modification soon after introduction. Two viewpoints are current on how to balance the effort spent on preplanning a system against that spent on overhauling it after installation. At the risk of oversimplification of positions, one school argues that by carefully projecting future requirements, the system will operate efficiently without a major overhaul because long-run needs are essentially met (Canning, 1956). Major changes in data-information requirements will, by careful planning, be made simultaneously with the introduction of new equipment and suitable operating procedures.

In practice, however, systems analysts consider data-information requirements as essentially independent of equipment and related procedures, except to the extent that they are limited by them. The essence of this argument is that changes in information needs or equipment can be made essentially independently of each other, if they are performed in a suitable sequence. New equipment can be introduced with minimal changes in information specifications to be followed by suitable redesign of the system after the equipment is operating. This two-stage approach levels out the work load and permits use of the new system to obtain data and make analyses preparatory to further change and refinement.

The merits of the single and two-stage conversion plan are moot. Some points that have bearing on the superiority of either are the urgency of introducing the new system, the experience and capacity of the systems design group, the availability of equipment suited to short-run and long-run information requirements, and the risk of dissatisfaction arising either from keeping the information system in flux over a long period or of freezing it too soon.

REFERENCES AND SUPPLEMENTAL READINGS

Bowden, B. V., ed. *Faster Than Thought, A Symposium on Digital Computing Machines,* London, Sir Isaac Pitman and Sons Ltd., 1953, 416 pp. Bowden surveys the field of digital computing machines and introduces some of Britain's accomplishments in this field. The subject matter is treated in three basic sections. Part One is concerned with the history and theory of computing machines. Fundamental computer logic, circuit components, organization, and programming are discussed. The historical appendix presents a contemporary account of Babbage's "Analytical Engine," accompanied by extensive notes by the Countess of Lovelace. These early writings reveal great depth of understanding of the concepts and potential usefulness of digital computers. Part Two presents detailed and somewhat technical descriptions of the leading machines in Britain as of 1953, written by the engineers who worked on them. Finally, the book discusses various existing and potential applications for electronic computers. For the most part, these applications are derived from earlier development of scientific and logical calculations, and little emphasis is placed upon applications in business-data processing (one chapter). The applications discussed include the use of computers in crystallography, meteorology, ballistics, engineering, and astronomy.

Canning, Richard G. *Electronic Data Processing for Business and Industry,* New York, John Wiley & Sons, Inc., 1956, 332 pp. In his book, Canning sets forth a comprehensive "systems engineering" approach to be followed by operating personnel in preparing a proposal on electronic data processing for top management. The company is viewed as an integrated operation functioning toward an explicit goal. Control is achieved through: (a) lower level management decisions, (b) paper work that is generated for the instruction of the organization, and (c) actual progress that is measured and fed back to management for further decisions. Electronic data processing can be of assistance in each of these steps. The author's primary emphasis is on the role of systems analysis in clarifying the functions of the data-processing system. Two situations are discussed in considerable detail as illustrations: (a) inventory control in a department store and (b) production control in job shop manufacturing. The significant features of electronic computers are discussed with emphasis on general-purpose digital computers. The advantage of random-access storage for real-time processing is noted; however, the realities of present-day equipment indicate the need for delayed processing systems in most applications during the immediate future.

Chapin, Ned. *An Introduction to Automatic Computers,* New York, D. Van Nostrand Co., Inc., 1957, 525 pp. In this book, (a) the basic operating characteristics of computers and peripheral equipment, (b) their application to business problems, and (c) the fundamental principles of the systems studies and profitability evaluations that should be undertaken to aid management in making an installation decision are discussed. The first three chapters of the book include (a) a very general description of digital computers, (b) a discussion of what computers can and cannot do, and (c) some examples of present business applications. In the following five chapters the author concentrates his attention on (a) the factors that should be considered and (b) the steps that should be taken by management when the installation of a computer is being contemplated. In these chapters, he stresses the need for systems studies and systems changes and describes the procedures that could be used to make such studies. He also outlines a method of evaluating the profitability of computers, and discusses ways of overcoming the personnel problems caused by computer installations.

Churchman, C. West, and Russell L. Ackoff. "Operational Accounting and Operations Research," *Journal of Accountancy,* vol. 99: 33-39 (February 1955). Describes what operations research is and shows how accountants and operations researchers take different approaches to inventory accounting and control. Accountants are criticized for collecting too much data and preparing general-purpose, open-ended reports. On the critical question of what data should be collected for later use, which must be answered if pertinent data alone are to be collected and filed, the only guide is that people should collect now what they will later wish they had collected originally.

Gregory, Robert H. "Document Processing," pp. 56-60 in *Proceedings of the Eastern Joint Computer Conference,* New York, Institute of Radio Engineers, 1956. Gregory outlines the recent and potential improvements in document processing resulting from (a) technical developments, (b) changes in the conceptual framework, and (c) increased recognition of economic considerations involved. The most challenging area for improvement is in the separation of the information from the document on which it is recorded in such a manner that both can be handled efficiently. The document itself might be completely eliminated. The question of improvements within and between business units is considered. Improvements within data-processing systems result from changes in costs of handling data and in the value of information obtained.

Gregory, Robert H. "Present and Prospective Use of Computers in Management Control," pp. 21-24 in *Computer Techniques in Chemical Engineering*, New York, American Institute of Chemical Engineers, 1959. Data-processing systems attempt to meet managerial requirements concerning past history and future prospects by developing both *data*, the mass of facts concerning a business, and *information*, the small number of facts that are useful for decision making. The three schemes for processing data are (1) to produce reports, (2) to generate information, and (3) to make decisions.

Problem Planning Aids, IBM Type 650, New York, International Business Machines Corporation, 1956, 18 pp. This booklet covers block diagramming, planning chart conventions, single instruction loading cards, and preliminary program testing and analysis. Block diagramming is done in three phases: the over-all statement of the problem, the semi-detailed explosion of each major problem block into smaller components, and the detailed block diagram which is a series of logical operations.

Rotkin, I. "The Mechanization of Letter Mail Sorting," pp. 54-57 in *Proceedings of the Eastern Joint Computer Conference: Computers with Deadlines to Meet*, New York, The Institute of Radio Engineers, 1958. Rotkin deals with the background of the letter mail sorting problem—huge volume and little prospect for further improvement of manual methods—and describes several plans in use. He proposes a plan for typing a coded dot pattern on mail during the first handling and using optical-mechanical sorting in the post office at subsequent stages.

Univac II Data Automation System, The, New York, Remington Rand UNIVAC, 1957, 196 pp. This manual, written from the viewpoint of management and managerial problems, offers orientation in the capabilities of computers and also in programming. Chapter 9, "System Design," of interest here, covers types of computer runs, process chart symbols, file maintenance, the processing run, and time estimating procedures.

Toan, Arthur B., Jr. "General Principles of System Work," *The New York Certified Public Accountant*, vol. 22: 599-605 (October 1952). There are three types of general principles, namely (a) those involved in solving any problem, (b) those of handling the human aspect involved in any process of change, and (c) those of acquiring experience essential for doing systems work in the clerical field. Toan's treatment of how to solve a problem clearly distinguishes between objectives and method. He deals also with the problem of fundamental system changes in contrast to merely superficial modifications that do not cope with the basic problem.

CHAPTER TWELVE

SYSTEMS ECONOMICS

The justification for new data-processing equipment and the related system—which includes people, forms, procedures, and so forth—hinges on economic analysis. Economic analysis is aimed at finding out whether revenue obtained will exceed costs during the useful life of the equipment and system (Chapin, 1955). The crucial question is, "Will the new equipment make a profit?"

"Revenue" includes the value of services produced and the salvage value of equipment after it is no longer used. "Cost" includes the outlays for systems analysis, programming, equipment purchase price or rental payments, installation, debugging and conversion, interest on investment, maintenance, materials, labor, and power. Similar revenues and costs are common to the consideration of an investment in any capital goods—whether data processors, milling machines, or automobiles.

The economic analysis of data-information systems has some unique problems, for the value of output—information and reports—is frequently difficult to measure. Since information and reports are rarely bought and sold, "prices" are not available. Some organizations specialize in providing intelligence, as companies that supply credit information. In such cases the commodity is information; in many other companies information may be an important adjunct to the product. At the present time, operating experience with most automatic data-processing equipment is brief, although in some cases it covers the cycle from installation of automatic equipment through satisfactory operation to replacement by still newer equipment. But even longer operating experience is needed to indicate the economic life of any particular type of equipment, for, at any time, a high rate of change in equipment design or users' requirements may result in early replacement. Furthermore, people are an important part of any data-processing system, and they are more difficult to analyze than equipment; but the way they use a system partially determines its value. A systems analyst has only a limited basis for predicting how the people he knows best will react in the face of entirely new developments. He does not know whether a particular manager will or can use a report to help him make better decisions. He is not certain how department heads, supervisors, and clerks will react. He is not sure how the overall operations of the business will respond to system changes.

The objective of cost analysis is to select, from all choices available, that system and required equipment which will provide the greatest excess of value over cost. This objective is basic to the whole scheme of systems analysis. The opportunity to invest in automatic data-processing equipment is only one demand on an organization's funds, and it must live or die in the competitive battle. Since the demand for funds always seems to outrun the supply of funds, some rationing scheme is used to keep demand and supply in balance. One such scheme is to calculate the expected return from each investment and select those investments with returns exceeding a specified cut-off rate. Other less profitable proposals for investment must perish, in a Darwinian sense, in the struggle for survival—unless they are protected by fortuitous circumstances, such as a high official taking an active interest in the proposal. A high cut-off rate is used to ration funds when good investment opportunities are plentiful; and a low cut-off rate is used when funds are plentiful and investment opportunities limited.

Economic aspects are of prime importance to systems analysis, design, and implementation. This chapter deals with theoretical approaches to analysis, decision rules, and application of the rules.

THEORETICAL APPROACH TO COSTS

The primary theoretical question to be answered by economic studies is, "What changes in the cost of data processing and in the value of information can we expect from a proposed course of action?" Some problems of defining and measuring cost and value were covered in Chapter 10.

The objective in proposing new data-processing methods may be either to reduce processing costs while keeping system output constant, or to improve system output, through better management operation, to a greater degree than the related processing costs increase (Wallace, 1956). The first objective appears to be within the province of data-processing specialists, while operations researchers claim pre-emptive rights in the second. Actually, the two viewpoints are probably only two ways of approaching the same problem: how to increase the net value of the system. Stated differently, the first is the "economy" approach, while the second is the "efficiency" approach to system design.

Cost Formulation

An ideal approach to studying costs might be to develop a formula for calculating the cost of operating a data-processing system. The formula would be based on the cost of equipment (including spare parts and test equipment), salaries of personnel, supplies used, facilities (space, utilities, and others), methods and procedures used, and the nature and rate of change from the old to the new system. These basic factors, probably accompanied by others, determine the over-all cost of a data-processing system.

If the cost function for each factor could be established for each system considered, then the cost of each proposed system could be computed mathematically; one system might then be selected because it produces the same information as other systems at a minimum cost. Another selection rule might be to try to increase the value of information obtained over the cost of producing it. Actually, many problems hinder the use of a formula to calculate the costs of processing data. Many of the factors are peculiar either to the business or to the equipment being considered. Given the array of equipment available and the variety of processing patterns that can be developed to meet the needs of a business, a huge number of systems—considering both equipment and processing patterns—deserve cost analysis. The problem involves much more than cost analysis alone, for each possible new system must be "invented" before it can be analyzed.

The expense involved in merely sketching out every possible system, let alone filling in the detail, is so big that some companies try to consider only the "best of all possible systems," without examining other possibilities. There is always a risk, however, that a system selected from a limited number will not be the best obtainable; if all possibilities can be considered at little or no cost, this risk is unwarranted. Regrettably, so little general work has been done to develop cost functions in this field that most economic studies are made by devising a few attractive systems and estimating their costs. Some rough rules do exist for use after an economic evaluation is completed: for instance, "multiply the costs by two and divide the savings by two, to get more realistic estimates." This caveat has some merit in the final stages, but it cannot help in making the original estimates. Furthermore, rules of thumb for adjusting estimates, when made with less than scrupulous care, may lead to erroneous conclusions.

Nature of Costs

Marginal and capital costs are germane to a discussion of data-processing system costs. Covering these types of costs will, by inference at least, raise the concepts of fixed, variable, and average costs. More complete coverage, of course, can be obtained from any economics textbook.

Marginal. "Marginal cost" is the difference in cost associated with any change in the activity, although much attention is given to changes in volume. The change in activity may be reflected in the volume and nature of data processed; the kind, frequency, timing, and number of reports; personnel; and kind of equipment.

Some costs—those for certain supplies, or for messages sent individually—change with variations in volume. Many other costs—such as those of personnel and facilities—may change little or not at all when usable but idle capacity exists. Some analysts say that new equipment should have an unused capacity of at least twenty or thirty per cent when installed, to cover the work load that may arise from mistaken estimates, oversights, and unexpected growth. Until the time that this capacity is required for scheduled operations, it can be used, or sold—on an "if available" basis, as by electric utility companies who offer power at secondary prices—because the cost of providing a modest fraction of unused capacity is small. Large increases in work load may tax the facilities and require more shifts for equipment, although at a lower operating cost than the first shift. Additional time worked by the same personnel may require the payment of premiums. Higher wage rates may have to be paid to attract additional personnel in a tight labor market. In short, the marginal cost may be small for some conditions and large for others.

Actually, the concept of marginal cost is often reflected in pricing unused capacity. Computer users offer data-processing services to others at prices based on marginal costs in order to exploit unused capacity. Incidentally, computer manufacturers who offer regular computing services seem to base prices on average costs, and thus think it unfair for others to price from marginal costs.

Charges for computer services transferred within a company may be based on average cost—total cost divided by total hours either scheduled or operated—so that the applications in use absorb total costs. Such a policy may lead to high rates when the work load is light, and to low rates when the load is heavy. It does not encourage planning to use facilities just up to, but not beyond, the operating volume that has the lowest marginal costs. Applications which cannot cover average cost, although they could cover marginal costs, are rejected when the average-cost rule is followed.

Marginal costs do not seem "right" as a basis for allocating prices to computer users because the amount allocated differs depending upon whether a particular user is the first, second, or later one in a series. The first user would be charged a price covering all initial costs and later users would be charged only for the marginal costs incurred to meet their demands. Actually, however, the essence of this policy of pricing is followed in studies concerning the acquisition of equipment, in which it is often insisted that the first one or more proposed initial applications absorb total initial costs. The treatment of costs to be followed when subsequent applications are started is usually vague, but it is more likely to proceed on the basis of average than it is on marginal costs.

Strange decisions sometimes result from the fact that average and marginal costs are different. One company whose computer designed for business applications was not fully loaded had an opportunity to perform scientific computations for which the computer was slow but adequate. A question arose about the rate that should be charged for computer time in doing scientific calculations. If an average cost rate was used, the total charge would be more than that of obtaining some well-suited equipment.

Computed in this way, the cost for the proposed job was, in fact, so high that it was decided to leave the equipment idle and get scientific equipment. On a marginal basis, however, the cost of using this otherwise idle business equipment for a less well-suited purpose would be nearly zero. Using equipment not wholly suited to an application is reasonable in a case where marginal costs are covered although average costs are not, if no better use is available.

The essence of the point is that large-scale computer capacity is obtainable only from large, complex equipment since the equipment is indivisible (small equipment is not just a small-scale model of large equipment, and building-block construction is only a partial answer); a high fraction of total operating costs is fixed; and the equipment may operate longer and more reliably if operated instead of shut down. Marginal costs for unused time are so small that the use of average costs for pricing may obscure otherwise reasonable decisions about computer utilization.

Capital. Electronic computers involve huge investments in equipment, facilities, and personnel. Such large outlays for systems analysis, equipment surveys, economic studies, equipment, programming, site preparation, and conversion are new to office operations.

Capital invested in data-processing equipment is supposed to serve the same purpose in the office as elsewhere: trading increased present outlays against reduced future operating expenses. To the extent that equipment processes data—calculates, sorts, updates files, prepares reports—more efficiently than people, such an investment is warranted. Investment decisions made today turn on estimates, not facts, about the future, and they hinge on such imponderables as future work load volumes and patterns, capacity of equipment now and in the future, productivity of people, price levels, and interest rates.

A computer and the related equipment required for a data-processing system ranges in cost from a hundred thousand to several million dollars. Systems analysis, equipment selection, and programming costs depend on the complexity and variety of business applications undertaken but may have a range as wide as the cost of equipment. Site preparations, consisting of space and utilities for both equipment and personnel, range from trivial amounts for small equipment to several hundred thousand dollars for large computers. Investments in spare parts and supplies—new paper forms, and especially, magnetic tapes—may be huge.

Equipment cost, on a per-operation basis at least, should decrease as the skill and experience of designers and manufacturers increases and users become better able to utilize more powerful equipment. New equipment that is smaller, faster, or consumes less energy by use of new components will cost less and require smaller facilities for operation—space, power, and air conditioning.

Different Processing Techniques.   The relationship between the marginal and capital cost and the value of information (given differing processing techniques and with the fraction of the data processed as the independent variable) is worth examining. At the risk of oversimplification, the graphs shown in Figures 12-1 and 12-2 are suggestive of the relationship that probably exists. The low and high ratios of capital to labor are indicative of the use of manual and electronic techniques. Techniques with intermediate ratios, such as electromechanical equipment, have cost curves that probably lie between those shown, The cost and value of information are shown along the vertical axis, and the *fraction* of data processed is indicated along the horizontal axis. The "fraction" of data processed can be defined narrowly in terms of the activity within a single application—the proportion of transactions processed against the inventory file, for example. Broadly, "fraction" applies to the number of applications (out of the total) that are handled. The cost curves shown here are similar to the economist's traditional cost curves for two proportions of capital and labor.

The chief differences in these two cost curves are the locations of their starting points and their slopes. As the ratio of capital to labor increases, the basic cost increases and the marginal cost decreases.

The value curves suggest that a small quantity of information has a large value. Thereafter, the value of added information declines to near zero. The value curves may take on different shapes according to changes in the ratio of capital to labor used in data processing, but this difference does not arise solely from the technique employed. Some differences arise from the fact that certain characteristics of the information change whenever the processing technique changes. Furthermore, some companies associate some value with the use of a particular technique apart from the characteristics of the information obtained. The advertising value that may result from processing data by means

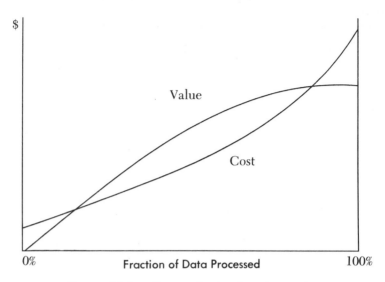

FIGURE 12-1.   *Cost and value for a low ratio of capital to labor*

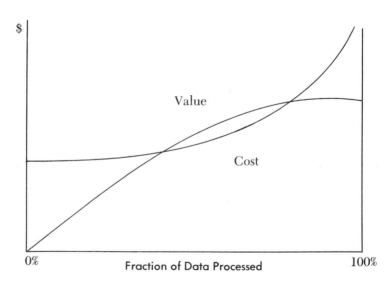

FIGURE 12-2.   *Cost and value for a high ratio of capital to labor*

of certain techniques appears to be a positive factor in adopting a new technique, although it sometimes becomes a negative one because of an excessive number of visitors. The advertising value of using a certain data-processing technique is probably far more difficult to evaluate than the other factors listed earlier, but probably declines rapidly as novelty wears off or, as sometimes happens, the system does not work as well as originally publicized.

The excess of value over cost for the information processed by any given technique is maximized when the value curve is above and parallel to the cost curve. At such a point the marginal value and the cost are equal, and greater or lesser use of that technique, considering that technique alone, would be uneconomical. The different shapes of the cost and value curves (and, therefore, different optimal quantities of information to be processed by each technique) probably help explain why a business uses a mixture of data-processing techniques. The fixed or initial costs associated with another system may preclude its partial use—the price of a different ticket is so high that you have to stick with the same show.

It appears that at any point in time a business probably utilizes a composite of most or even all of the techniques that it has adopted at any time in the past. More specifically, there are numerous indications that yesterday's techniques will be only partially displaced by either today's or tomorrow's techniques. Stone-age techniques, you will recall, are still used to make permanent outdoor markers.

TRANSITION COSTS

Actual operation of the existing data-processing system in a company and introduction of the proposed computer system are separated by the transition costs incurred in making the change-over. Transition costs might be thought of as the price of admission to a real, working demonstration of how useful new computers can be for processing data in a particular business.

A critical question is how much the transition costs will be and how soon they will be absorbed. The reduction in operating costs—measured as present costs minus normal future costs after the operations settle down—must absorb the extra costs incurred during the transition in order to warrant the change. The cumulative break-even point, ignoring the time difference and the effect of interest rates, is reached when the amount of reduction in operating costs matches the total transition costs. More often, people say that they reach the break-even point when the transition period is over and operating costs are down to their prior level. The break-even point, according to this second definition, may be reached in a few months or years, even though the cumulative break-even will not be reached for much longer, if it is ever reached at all. The transition costs discussed here are the costs of systems analysis, facilities, formulation of a proposed system, and conversion to a new system.

Systems Analysis

At the outset, it should be pointed out that operations and analysis are different in nature for any kind of system. Data systems often routinely provide facts to permit analysis of other areas within a company or organization—manufacturing, sales, inventory, and credits; but special investigations seem mandatory in order to analyze the data-processing system itself. Re-orientation of personnel to analyze the data system itself is expensive because it usually involves using personnel divorced from the main stream of data flow and requires their education and training in terms of new techniques that are being considered for adoption (Bagby, 1956). To the extent that a systems analysis or procedures group exists, it may be used for analysis aimed at systems redesign. The cost of initial staffing and background training can thus be saved, although the group will need some education and re-orientation.

The expense of systems analysis raises the question of how thorough an investigation should be. The two extremes of thoroughness seem to be (1) at the minimum, determining the output requirements, and (2) at the maximum, studying in detail all existing operations from data input through processing to information output. Few analysts are brave enough to rely on a minimum analysis for fear of overlooking some requirements that will be disclosed only by studying data input or processing methods. The other extreme—infinitely detailed analysis of data flow—is so expensive that few companies feel they can afford it. Furthermore, it seems doubly expensive because much of what is studied may soon be replaced by new techniques. Extremely detailed analysis poses somewhat the same philosophical problem as whether a person who spends two days writing his personal diary for one day can ever finish it; he could, it is said, if he lived forever. Several highly detailed, comprehensive systems studies have run aground because of the cost and time involved and the doubt as to their ultimate usefulness in system redesign.

A middle ground between minimum and maximum analytic detail is commonly used, first, to reduce the risk of omitting important requirements discernible only by studying existing procedures (because instruction manuals and output requirements are not current or sufficiently descriptive) and, second, to keep the costs and elapsed time for investigation within bounds. The general conclusion one can draw from marginal analysis is that systems analysis should be continued as long as the probable improvement in the design of a new system outweighs the cost of analysis. Benefits and costs, however, are difficult to match for several reasons: benefits are obtainable only in the future, they are fortuitous in that they may arise or even disappear at any time, and they are not readily measurable in monetary terms. The costs of systems analysis are, on the other hand, incurred now or in the near future at controllable rates. But the total amount of these, too, is difficult to control because discontinuance is unlikely. There is usually some prospect, although often small, that continued analysis will lead to added improvements. One big reason for undertaking a systems analysis is to gain an understanding of the managerial organization and to find the political problems which will be involved in the design and use of a new system. It is more often important to understand who is involved than to know what is done or how it is done.

Facilities

The facilities for a computer system serving a business include, in broad terms, equipment, space, and utilities.

Equipment costs include the invoice or rental price of the items selected and, in some sense, the cost of selecting equipment to match the system needs—which involves a risk that the equipment obtained will not be suitable. The specified price of each piece of equipment already available is quoted by the manufacturer. But the aggregate bill may be ambiguous because of uncertainty over precisely which units and how many units are required and the tendency of manufacturers to quote prices for basic or stripped-down units. A complete set of equipment may cost several times as much as the computer alone. The price for equipment not yet available because it is still in the prototype or design stage is even more ambiguous. Experience indicates a strong tendency for prices to increase as equipment progresses from its initial conception through design and prototype stages to the production model. On the basis of price alone, one might be well advised to contract for equipment at the earliest possible moment after its introduction on the market when manufacturers are likely to quote low prices.

Space and utility investments for computer installation are related. The number of electronic and electric components is a rough indicator of the weight and volume of the equipment and of the energy required both to operate the components and to cool all the equipment externally. Costs of building reconstruction to get suitable floor loads, space, power sources, and air conditioning run from trivial amounts for small equipment to important fractions of cost for large equipment. The use of smaller components—transistors or otherwise—that consume less power will reduce space and utility costs in several ways. Components that consume less power can be packaged more closely because they pose smaller heat dissipation problems and will decrease the need for air conditioning equipment.

System Formulation

The second most important computer system cost (after facilities) is for personnel. In most cases, equipment is designed and built by manufacturers without regard for the requirements of a particular business, although with some consideration for business needs in general. Skilled, experienced personnel are the link between equipment as such and a successfully operating data system. Many say that the system is no stronger than the people responsible for system design, installation, and operation.

During periods of rapid technical change, as in the initial years of computer use in business, the user has to rely primarily on his own employees as a source of personnel because the demand for skilled people far exceeds the supply. Aided by equipment manufacturers, consultants, and educational institutions, each company undertakes to select and train employees who appear to have the ability to develop and operate entirely new systems. In selecting personnel, much stress is put on the business environment and system as being difficult to comprehend. It takes people longer to gain sufficient skill and *savoir faire* than to acquire a comparable degree of equipment expertise. A compromise approach that is often used is to obtain one or a few people experienced with computers from either the manufacturer or another computer user. The hiatus between the vastly different backgrounds of newly employed computer specialists and long-term employees skilled in company operations is partly closed by assigning both types to developing the computer systems.

The time and cost spent by each user for building minimum skills in computer methods for its systems people will be smaller in the future as the number of people skilled in computer usage increases. The educational system, in the broadest sense, from high school onward, will bear much of the burden of education and training. Furthermore, the cost of educating, or at least orienting, company managers, officials, and interested third parties, which is high now, will become much smaller as general knowledge spreads and the use of computers becomes commonplace.

Following the initial cost of developing computer and methods skills in an adequate group of employees, there is the continuing cost of systems analysis and programming to develop the proposed system. A bulge in personnel costs starts when people are first assigned to study new methods and equipment and continues until the new system replaces the old one. Some companies minimize the cost bulge by discontinuing methods work on the old system when new system planning begins. Assigning the whole methods group to developing a new system makes sense if only marginal improvements remain to be made and if the existing system will not deteriorate appreciably from neglect during the analysis and transition period.

In the early years of data processing it was often thought that once systems analysis and programming were completed, other areas could be tackled or the programming staff reduced. Several years or even months of experience indicate that programs are never completed in the sense that a solution remains static and further improvements are uneconomical. Business problems change because of managerial decisions and external factors. Furthermore, additional work spent on an operating program seems to follow learning-curve rules in which big reductions in computer running time can be obtained from a small reprogramming effort.

The economics of formulating or designing a new system depend to a marked degree on the amount and rate of change involved in the transition from an old to a new system. Important and quick changes increase the costs of analysis and design because it is difficult to obtain or develop qualified manpower, to schedule changes, to attempt in parallel what should be done in sequence, and to benefit from both internal and external experience.

There seems to be a gestation period of a year or more from initial consideration of computer use to smooth operation in even one major area. The development of a new system to be used with available or proposed new equipment occurs in the early stages, after some familiarity with equipment is gained. General broad design, before all practical limitations are fully realized, is likely to outrun the capabilities of people to make detailed designs and the capacity of the equipment to handle the system. Ambitious systems plans tend to become less far-reaching during the implementation period. The most ambitious system, in terms of breadth and farsightedness, may be designed and put into operation as soon as possible. The more conservative approach is that the burden of formulating a moderately advanced system, in even a limited area, and of introducing it concomitantly with new equipment, is a big enough project to handle initially. Further refinements and extensions to other areas should be made after the initial conversion when operations stabilize. On occasion, users have found the difficulties accompanying equipment installation and initial conversion so great as to require a complete re-orientation of effort to immediate tasks and the postponement of longer-range planning.

Another economic consideration, apart from the cost of actual formulation of a new system, is whether few or many proposed systems should be devised in order to select the best system. Systematic analysis probably requires comparison of at least two alternatives:

(1) the best system if the present equipment is retained, and (2) the best system that can be designed for use with new equipment. The high cost of sketching out general plans, let alone a detailed formulation, is so great as to limit the number of systems that are formulated and examined. Consequently, there is a strong tendency to focus attention on a small number of systems, perhaps only one, and develop it in detail with only limited serious consideration of alternatives.

From the user's viewpoint, the economics of system formulation involve the question of who does the work required and who pays for it—the equipment manufacturer or the user. Systems design either by manufacturers or consultants involves communication and education costs necessary to describe the existing system and its desired objectives. Furthermore, manufacturers' biases strongly influence their findings and proposals, and some consultants seem to operate as adjuncts to equipment manufacturers. Users, as a group at least, pay for the systems work done by manufacturers' representatives and consultants.

Although a complete data-processing system is difficult to test except by actually introducing it, the computer programs involved can be tested under laboratory or clinical conditions on time furnished by the manufacturer, on time rented from other users, or on the user's own equipment when installed. Time supplied by the manufacturer costs least, apart from personal travel and work-scheduling problems, while testing on the user's own equipment may be most expensive in terms of equipment costs but less costly in other ways.

Conversion

The costs of conversion, defined in a narrow sense, cover the period from the final testing of programs to the complete discontinuance of processing by the old scheme. Costs incurred during the conversion period include editing files for accuracy and completeness, converting files from the old to the new storage media, training people to get data of satisfactory quality, operating equipment to process data according to programs already devised, and overcoming the myriad obstacles that arise during the period of dual operation.

Magnetic-tape records obtained by converting paper or punched-card records may be edited for completeness and logical accuracy by means of a computer program. Records not passing the tests can be referred to people for correction. Similar screening programs can be used for new data input after the system is operating. A difficult problem arises in judging a tight screening program that may cause a high fraction of data to be rejected for correction, but that also provides increased accuracy from the substantial amount of manual work required to correct deficiencies. Some computer users find that certain types of editorial corrections (for example, manufacturers using pounds instead of tons as a unit for reporting census data) can be included within the screen-editing program for automatic correction.

After operating the new equipment and system in parallel with the old one long enough to give assurance of satisfactory performance, the old scheme should be discontinued. Some computer users compare the results obtained from both the old and new systems operating in parallel to help isolate errors in the new one. A high frequency of the discrepancies can usually be traced to mistakes occurring in the old and not in the new system. If so, dual operations hinder the conversion rather than facilitate it. Therefore, as soon as the new system appears to be functioning satisfactorily, the old can be dropped completely. Parallel operations on a near-indefinite basis, a situation which occurs occasionally, can hardly lead to more economical operations.

Converting a data-processing system built around one model of a computer to a second model is far less costly than the prior conversion from manual to computer processing. For one electric utility, shifting from one computer to its successor involved paying only the rental on both for less than a month. An interesting and unexpected feature of obtaining an additional computer is the fact that space may not be available economically because it was not provided during original site preparation. When one computer is to replace another, the problem is more difficult because space is required for both computers during the period of installing the second, operating in parallel, and dismantling the first. Furthermore, the second computer may be put, and have to stay, in a less desirable location than the first. One user faced with the problem of outgrowing a large computer located in a new building concluded that only a transistorized replacement computer was suitable, because nothing else would fit into the limited space available while both were in place. Painful problems arise during both the original and subsequent transition periods.

Although capital investments in systems analysis and programming are often thought of as one-time costs, they are more properly considered as recurrent costs, to be faced repeatedly in the future. Changes in policy and new problems require continuing systems analysis and reprogramming. Programmers, being of an analytic, inquiring turn of mind, continually overhaul and improve programs, introduce refinements, and often cut computer running time.

COST ANALYSIS MODELS

The purpose of developing cost analysis models is to establish rules for predicting the future cost and revenues resulting from alternative courses of action. The alternative that appears to have the best future result can be selected. Analysis to devise new systems—procedures, forms, and so forth—and to select new equipment may suggest several alternatives:

1. Adopt the new system and obtain new equipment.
2. Adopt the new system but continue using the existing equipment.
3. Modify the old system and use little or no new equipment.
4. Make no changes in either the system or the equipment.

Any one of these alternatives might be best for a specific situation.

Basic Models

A cost analysis model is a collection of rules, figures, and estimates to represent the behavior of costs and revenue for a system. Such models range from simple forecasts of costs and revenues based on judgment and past experience to large sets of mathematical equations. Mathematical models for cost analysis of data-processing systems would be of great value, except that (1) few people have the necessary knowledge or time to devise and use complex models, and (2) more important, facts for devising and testing a model are frequently not available. Complex cost analysis models may be worth exploration, if someone with mathematical ability is available. Attention is focused here on some principles basic to cost analysis models dealing with data processing.

Short History of a System

The general picture of what happens during the life of an item of equipment is worth examining. Each item has its unique history, but a pattern holds true for many items.

Initial Investment and Salvage Value.   Much money is invested before a new system and the necessary equipment are operating satisfactorily. Introduction of a new data system involves, as described earlier: analyzing the system, training people, preparing programs, installing equipment, and converting from the old to the new system.

"Salvage value" of a system is the sales price of various parts, minus the costs of removing and selling them. It has an important bearing on any acquisition, for a small salvage value restricts your freedom to switch after an initial decision. The salvage value of a brand-new system immediately drops below the initial investment for several reasons. First, the expenditures for training, programming, and conversion are of little value if the system is changed greatly. It is easy to lose sight of changes in the salvage value of training, programming, and conversion. There is a strong tendency to charge programming and conversion costs to expenses during the period in which they are incurred. If the practice of immediate charge-off is followed, it is easy to lose sight of their value in use and how they decline over time. Second, installed equipment, although not used, sells for less than it does when new. Third, it is costly to remove equipment.

After its initial major drop, salvage value continues to decrease slowly over time because of deterioration and increasing obsolescence. The decline in salvage value is a major cost of a new system. It is large in the first year and smaller in succeeding years, and year-by-year changes may be vastly different from the long-term average, so that estimates of annual decreases in salvage value are preferable to an average depreciation figure. Figure 12-3(a) *suggests* the decrease in

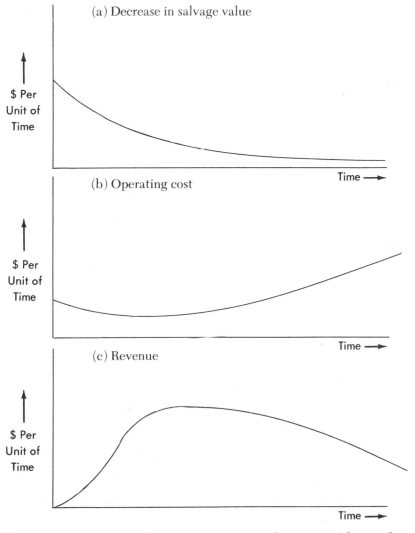

FIGURE 12-3.   *Salvage value, operating cost, and revenue each period*

system salvage value over a period of time, which represents the capital cost of having the system available.

Operating Costs. Operating costs include supervision, reprogramming to meet changing requirements, operating and maintenance labor, power, supplies, replacement parts, and test equipment.

Operating costs rise over time because maintenance costs grow as equipment ages after its initial "shakedown." The information required and the data available both change over time. Continuing analysis, reprogramming, and new procedures are required. Figure 12-3(b) suggests the yearly outlay for operations.

Revenue. The value of data and information produced by a system also changes over time, as shown in Figure 12-3(c). The bugs, confusion, and inexperience typical of a new system limit the amount of revenue during the transition stage and thereafter. Revenues tend to rise to a plateau where they stay for some time, until equipment malfunctions, changes in applications, and unscheduled down-time begin to reduce annual revenue.

Value of System

The value of a system equals its revenue minus its cost. The value can be determined for each individual time period. Figure 12-4 combines the three factors considered separately above—salvage value, operating cost, and revenue. At first, revenue is small and the decrease in salvage is large, so the system operates at a loss. As time goes on, the amount of revenue rises and the decline in salvage value is smaller. The break-even point, where the revenue just covers the cost, is reached at the point marked A. The system then operates at a profit. Eventually, revenue drops and operating costs increase so that losses arise after the point marked C, when the revenue for the period falls below cost.

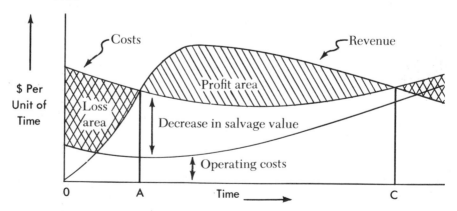

FIGURE 12-4.   *Cost and revenue each period*

Net value can be cumulated from the start to any desired date to get the over-all effect. Figure 12-5 shows the value of the system over time. It accumulates the value for each time period shown above. The value is negative at first because of the immediate drop from the initial investment to the salvage value when the system is introduced. The accumulated value declines further because costs exceed revenue. At the point marked A, the system starts operating at a profit each period. The loss incurred from the start to point A is recovered by point B. The economic behavior described here for a data-processing system is only one possibility; but it appears to be representative of business experience. It is possible for revenue to be less than cost indefinitely, so that the system continues to operate at a loss. On the other hand, the revenue may be greater than the cost from the start.

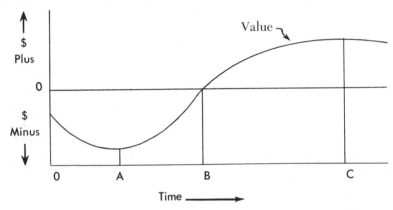

FIGURE 12-5.   *Value of system over time*

The decline in salvage value, operating costs, and revenue is shown in terms of current dollars in each period. The net revenue in each period can be discounted at an appropriate rate to the present date to facilitate comparison. The methods for equating present and future dollars are covered later in this chapter.

Decision Rules for Capital Investment

Rough-and-ready solutions are commonplace: "Buy newer and better equipment that is economically attractive whenever funds are available." "Obtain new equipment when old equipment breaks down frequently or works poorly." "Attractive models," "frequent breakdown," and "poor operations" are ambiguous terms, and decision rules using them are correspondingly vague.

Pay-off.   An arbitrary "pay-off" period, which is the number of years required for net revenue to add up to initial cost, may be used to compare opportunities and select the best alternative. Unless the estimated accumulated revenue exceeds the total estimated cost by the end of the pay-off period, the equipment will not be obtained. But equipment may be used beyond the pay-off period, so that the rule is hard to interpret. On the other hand, the equipment may not last as long as the pay-off period so that a loss will result. Insisting on a pay-off period that is shorter than equipment life is considered to be a conservative approach. A short life restricts investment to equipment that is profitable enough to reach a positive net value in a short time. One- or two-year pay-off periods are sometimes used and three- to five-year pay-offs are often demanded. The pay-off period rule may eliminate equipment that would be profitable over a longer period; furthermore, it weights near-term and long-term revenues in the same way and does not give any consideration to the number of years that the specified return will be obtained.

Rate of Return. The rate of return rule uses compound interest to compensate for time differences and the fact that the amount of revenue may change from year to year. Distant revenues are worth less than near-term revenues. Of course, the initial investment counts for most since it is made at the beginning.

As explained later in this chapter, a series of future revenues can be related, through the present worth of an annuity, to the investment that must be made now. The present worth of an annuity of $1 for 10 periods at a 10 per cent interest rate is $6.14; but it is only $4.19 at a 20 per cent rate. That is to say, if $1 is to be obtained for each of the next 10 periods and a return of 20 per cent is demanded, then the outlay must be limited to $4.19. If the number of periods is shorter or the revenue per period is smaller, then the permissible investment will be reduced.

If the investment to be made today and future revenues can be estimated, then a rate of return can be calculated. Since the calculation is halfway involved, it may be preferable to select a trial rate, use a table to find the present worth of an annuity (if revenues vary over time, several calculations are required), and compare the amount from the table with the required investment. This approximation procedure can be repeated until the rate of return is found or interpolated between two rates that are fairly close.

The rate of return for all investment opportunities for an organization—automatic data processing, manufacturing plant, new product development, or whatever—can be calculated and used to select those with higher rates of return. A proposed investment in new data-processing equipment and systems competes, of course, with all other investment opportunities. A cut-off or minimal rate of return may be used to restrict investment in any opportunity that will not yield a specified rate.

Rental or Purchase of Equipment

Whenever a decision to acquire a computer and related equipment is reached, the question arises whether it should be purchased, rented, or rented with an option to apply some rental against possible purchases in the future. At various times manufacturers have followed policies of renting only, selling only, either renting or selling, and renting with a sales option. Factors involved in choosing a course of action are the ratio of rental price to sales price, availability of funds, interest rates, uncertainty about equipment meeting its specifications, uncertainty about how much and when data-processing system requirements will change, maintenance requirements and merits of either the manufacturer or the user furnishing service, purchasing as a hedge against rent increases or other changes in lease conditions, and management policies toward ownership.

No general statement can be made as to whether renting or buying is more advantageous. Some writers view the problem as being essentially an exercise in determining whether the interest rate required to equate the rental annuity with the purchase price exceeds the rate of return demanded on investments (Anthony and Schwartz, 1957). Actually, the "best" plan depends on system requirements, equipment available, purchase price, funds for investment and operations, rental rates, maintenance costs, obsolescence, and other factors. The advantages of rental, in general, are the disadvantages of purchase, and vice versa.

Rental arrangements have several advantages. Cost is known and is fixed for the term of the contract. Monthly rental rates for electronic equipment are about two or three per cent of the purchase price. The owner supplies maintenance service and parts so that the user avoids the cost of training and keeping maintenance men and of stocking parts. Ownership may involve unexpected costs for maintenance or for major repair.

Lease contracts partially protect the user against the loss arising from deterioration, obsolescence, and reduced work load. Short-term or cancellable rental contracts enable the user to return unprofitable or unsuitable equipment with a limited loss. Newer and better equipment may be obtained by exchange without the capital loss involved in ownership, although users pay for both development and obsolescence whether they buy or rent equipment. The cost of obsolescence is, of course, included in rental rates. On the other hand, any loss is apparent when purchased equipment is sold. A reluctance to absorb a loss on the disposition of purchased equipment may lead to postponing decisions to acquire new equipment.

Rental becomes less desirable as equipment usage increases. Basic lease rental covers one shift a day or 40 hours a week. Preventive maintenance done while the machine is turned on may be included in or excluded from the 40 hours. If equipment is used for more than one work shift of regularly scheduled personnel, additional rental is to be paid. Purchase may be less expensive than rental for two-shift or three-shift operation.

Purchase may be cheaper under normal conditions, but it involves many unpredictable factors, some of which may be very expensive. Purchase offers some protection against price increases that may occur in the future, for purchase prices are in current dollars. Lease rentals start in present dollars, but eventually reflect price increases. Conditions are favorable for purchase when new equipment works satisfactorily and will be fully loaded during its economic life. Radically new equipment or special-purpose equipment may be available by purchase only, for a manufacturer may be either unwilling or unable to bear the financing costs. It is not entirely suitable for a user to adopt a rigid policy either to buy or to rent; the merits of both rental and purchase of equipment should be examined before a decision is made.

A compromise solution to this problem is sometimes possible. Certain manufacturers allow equipment rental for a year or more with an option to purchase, so that part of the rental already paid may be deducted from the purchase price if the option is exercised. An option plan has the advantage of postponing capital outlay until some of the initial uncertainty is removed. Some purchase options require an initial option deposit that is forfeited if the option to purchase is not exercised.

Life of Equipment

Equipment investment analysis requires an estimate of how long each item will be used before it is scrapped or sold. A period of use of some particular length yields the highest net value for an equipment item, and any other period, shorter or longer, results in a lower net value. The economic life of equipment is the period with the maximum net value. Equipment should be used for its economic life and comparisons should be made on that basis, whenever possible. Economic life is not the time at which equipment collapses in a heap from old age—generally, it ends long before that stage.

Single Machine. The economic life of a single machine that will not be replaced is easy to determine, at least in theory. Calculate the net value for periods of one, two, three, and more years. Accumulated net value reaches a maximum and then decreases, as described above, and the economic life ends when the net value is largest. Equipment used for a longer term operates at a loss, but its use for a shorter term precludes potential profits.

Replacement Chain. Most real-life situations involve replacement of one set of equipment by other equipment. New equipment replaces old equipment to make a replacement chain over a long period of time. The long-term objective is to increase the net value of the entire replacement chain, not merely the net value of each item. The problem of increasing the value of a replacement chain is different from the problem of increasing the net value of a single item. The differences arise in two ways: (1) present equipment may operate at a profit, but new equipment may yield more profit; and (2) future new equipment may be superior to both (a) equipment currently in use and (b) new equipment currently available.

The economic life of equipment in a replacement chain is easy to determine in theory. Equipment may first operate at a loss, later operate at a profit, and eventually operate at a loss again. The end of its economic life is reached when the marginal profit from existing equipment is equal to the average profit that can be earned during the economic life of replacement equipment. Note that the *marginal* cost of using the present equipment is compared with the *average* cost of using the proposed equipment. Table 12-1 shows the annual profits from using various sets of equipment—A, A', B, and C. The loss in the first year represents the costs of introducing each set of equipment.

TABLE 12-1. *Annual Profit or (Loss) from Four Sets of Equipment*

Year	Annual Profit for Equipment $000 Omitted			
	A	A'	B	C
1	(400)			
2	100	(90)		
3	120	110		
4	117	130	(60)	
5	115	127	143	(200)
6	105	125	160	150
7	85	115	180	175
8	45	95	200	250
9	(10)	55	160	300
10		0	130	300
11			100	300
12				200
13				100

The conditions are as follows: equipment A is available now and A' will be available in one year. Later introduction of A' for $90,000 hinges on using A for one year; otherwise, there will be a total transition cost for A' of $490,000. Equipment B and C will be available for use in the fourth and fifth years. Equipment can be introduced when first available or, of course, later.

Assume that equipment A is adopted and used one year before A', B, and C are known to be available. The question is, "Should A', B, or C be obtained to replace A?" Furthermore, "When should A be replaced?" Table 12-2 organizes the facts about each set of equipment to answer the question of whether to keep or replace equipment, with the annual profit for equipment A shown as before. Average profits for A', B, and C are shown on a cumulative basis from the beginning through each specified year. The average profit for A' for the first year is, of course, the first-year transition loss of $90,000. The two-year average profit for A' is $10,000, [($90,000 loss + $110,000 profit) ÷ 2]. The average cumulative profit for any number of years is figured in the same way.

TABLE 12-2. *Annual Profit or (Loss) for Equipment A and Cumulated Average Profit for A', B, and C*

	Annual Profit for Equipment $000 Omitted	Average Profit From Date Available to Any Year for Equipment $000 Omitted		
Year	A	A'	B	C
1	(400)			
2	100	(90)		
3	120	10		
4	117	50	(60)	
5	115	69	42	(200)
6	105	80	81	(25)
7	85	86	106	41
8	45	87	125	94
9	(10)	85	130	135
10			130	162
11			127	182
12				184
13				175

The rule given above for determining the economic life of existing equipment can be restated: introduce new equipment when its *average* profit for some period exceeds the *marginal* profit of equipment in use. The average profit of A' is −$90,000, +$10,000, +$50,000, and so forth. The average profit for A' when used for six years is $86,000. This exceeds the annual profit of $85,000 for equipment A in its seventh year. Equipment A′ should replace A at the beginning of its seventh year.

The average profit from B is $130,000 if used six years. B′s average profit for six years exceeds A′s annual profit for each and every year. Equipment B should replace A when it is three years old. This is true despite the fact that A still has five years of profitable life. Greater profit will be obtained from immediate replacement of A′ by B as soon as it becomes available.

The average profit from equipment C is $135,000 if C is used for five years, but it is more if C is used longer. Equipment C should be adopted as soon as available, for its average profits for four years or more exceed A′s annual profit.

Assume that equipment B is obtained immediately after it becomes available to replace A. One year later C becomes available. A new question arises, "Should C replace B and, if so, when?" The *average* profit from C is $162,000 for six years′ use, which exceeds B′s *annual* profit of $143,000 for the second year; therefore, C should immediately replace B.

A different question arises if C becomes available before B is obtained. The question is, "Should we adopt B and then go to C or go directly from A to C?" Equipment C, as pointed out above, is superior enough to replace B immediately even though B is used for only one year.

The choice available for the fourth year is to use A for a profit of $117,000 or adopt B for a loss of $60,000. Clearly, A should be retained one more year. When C is available, it should be obtained so that B is skipped. In future years, assuming that no superior equipment is available, new C should replace existing equipment C after it is eight years old. The average profit of new C for eight years, assuming the same experience as for the original C, is $184,000, which exceeds the marginal profit of $100,000 in the ninth year. When superior equipment—model D, E, or F—becomes available, its average profit for some period of use can be compared with the annual profit of C to decide on either immediate or postponed replacement.

This type of analysis shows the merits of knowing what will be available in the future so that intermediate equipment can be skipped. It also helps explain why equipment manufacturers often announce big improvements long before the equipment is ready. The prospects of further improvements may forestall adoption of available models, especially those made by manufacturers who pursue a policy of build first and announce when ready to deliver.

Practical Problems

The economic life of equipment in use depends on the cost, uses, and speed of equipment (Clippinger, 1955). These factors determine the average profit that can be earned during the economic life of its replacement. Therefore, the economic life of present equipment depends on forecasting the history of the first and all subsequent replacements.

Investment analysis, although difficult, is valuable, and large potential savings are available from good analysis. Understanding the basic principles is vital, despite the fact that complete facts about the future are not available. Educated guesses about facts often serve a useful purpose in solving difficult problems, and, as a last resort, the judgment of people who thoroughly understand the basic principles will be better than anyone else's.

Equipment investment analysis requires, as a minimum, the ability to predict the future cost and revenue for the first item and its replacement. Predictions of the future are difficult and risky, for complete facts about operations are not a sufficient guide to the future, which is frequently different from the past. Available data, information requirements, prices, jobs, and equipment technology all change. Technical improvement may be faster or slower than expected; and systems designed to use new equipment may work differently than planned. System loads may either increase unexpectedly or not materialize. And accurate predictions about the distant future are even more difficult than for the near future. Fortunately, the time value feature of money reduces the present importance of distant future events.

RELATION OF TIME TO MONEY

Future events need to be compared with present events in making investment decisions, and time differences must be compensated for in order to make valid comparisons. The basic fact is that money in the future is worth less than money now. This difference in favor of present money is an important factor in the cost of capital and influences decisions to make present outlays that will yield future revenues. Any investment is expected to yield an amount equal to the present outlay plus a return on the investment. This section describes the time relationship of money in terms of the future amount of a dollar, present worth of a dollar, and the corresponding annuities.

Future Amount of a Dollar.   Money presently available can be invested to obtain both the original sum and interest in the future. The future amount is equal to the total of the present sum and the interest to some future date. The present sum and future amount are equivalent, considering the interest rate.

A dollar invested now at 10 per cent is worth $1.10 at the end of one year and $1.21 at the end of two years [(1.10 x .10) + 1.10]. It grows to $2.59 at the end of ten years, as follows:

Time	Future Amount of $1
Now 1.00
End of Period 1 ....1.10
2 ....1.21
3 ....1.33
4 ....1.46
5 ....1.61
6 ....1.77
7 ....1.95
8 ....2.14
9 ....2.35
10 ....2.59

Figure 12-6 shows the way that $1 now grows at compound interest rates of 5, 10, and 20 per cent over a period of ten years. The general rule is that the amount is equal to $(1 + i)^n$, where i is the interest rate per period and n is the number of periods.

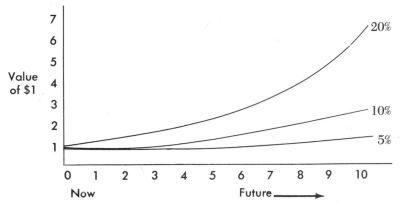

FIGURE 12-6. *Future amount of $1 now*

Future Amount of Annuity.   An investment of $1 may be made now and repeated at the end of each period to make an annuity. The accumulated value at the end of the first year is $2.10—$1.10 from the first investment plus $1 from the second. At the end of the second year it is $3.31—$1.21 plus $1.10 and $1.00.

Annuities often omit the immediate payment, so that the first payment is made one period from now and at the end of each period thereafter. The column for the amount of an annuity should be shifted down one period to adjust for this difference in starting date. The amount of an ordinary annuity is $1.00 at the end of the first period and $15.93 at the end of the tenth period. The formula for the amount

of an annuity is $\dfrac{(1 + i)^n - 1}{i}$ where i and n have the same meanings
as before. The future amount of a single payment or a series of payments is useful for accumulating them into a single amount in the
future.

Present Worth of $1.   Decisions about the future must, of course,
be made in advance, so that the present worth of future payments is
required for comparing future events with present ones. The present worth of a single payment is the reciprocal of (1 divided by) the
corresponding future amount of a single payment, as described earlier.
The present worth, at a discount rate of 10 per cent, of $1 payable
two periods from now is $0.826 (1 ÷ 1.21). A dollar payable ten pe-
riods from now has a present value of $0.385 (1 ÷ 2.59).

Graphs for the present value of $1 at compound discount rates
of 5, 10, and 20 per cent have the same general *shape* as those shown
earlier for the future amount of $1, except that they are equal to $1
at a specified date in the future and have smaller values now. Using the
graph, merely go out the desired number of years, find the amount of
$1 on a selected interest rate curve, and trace it back to the present.
The ratio of future amount to present worth can be applied to any
future amount to find its present worth.

Present Worth of Annuity.   Investment analysis usually involves
the question, "What is the present worth of a series of future payments?" A series of future payments is an annuity and the present

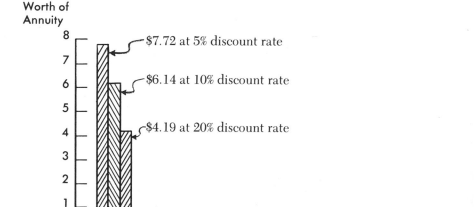

FIGURE 12-7. *Present worths of ten-period annuities*
at 5, 10, and 20 per cent discount

worth of an annuity is easily found for the specified number of periods at a selected discount rate.

The present worth of an annuity of $1 at the end of each of five periods at a discount rate of 10 per cent is $3.79 (total of .909, .826, .751, .683, and .621) using the present worths of $1 for each individual term, as shown earlier.

The present worths of ten-period annuities at discount rates of 5, 10, and 20 per cent are shown in Figure 12-7. Different rates and periods can be used, of course. The formula for the present worth of an annuity is:

$$\frac{i}{1 - \dfrac{1}{(1 + i)^n}}$$

The difference between future payments and the present worth of an annuity is important in equipment investment analysis. It means that future dollars are less important than dollars today. Predictions of revenue and cost are usually more accurate for the near future than for the distant future. The discount relationship between time and money, as described above, heavily weights near future costs and revenues. Fortunately, they are easier to estimate. The discount relation reduces the effect of future events which are more difficult to estimate.

SUMMARY

Economic analysis deals with the determination of revenue and costs. "Revenue" includes the value of services produced and the salvage value of equipment after it is no longer used. Revenue is hard to measure because "market prices" are seldom put on the information produced by a system. "Cost" includes outlays for systems analysis, programming, equipment purchase price or rental payments, installation, debugging and conversion, interest on investment, maintenance, materials, labor, and power.

Different types of costs must be considered for various decisions. Marginal cost is the amount of change with variations in activity. Marginal costs are germane to the question, "Should we do more or less of this or that?" Capital cost arises from investment in equipment. Interest on capital costs for waiting and risk of loss—deterioration, obsolescence, and reduced demand for equipment services—are involved.

Initial investment includes the cost of analyzing the system, training people, preparing programs, installing equipment, and converting from an old to a new system and equipment. Salvage value declines sharply at first and then tapers off slowly. Operating costs include supervision, reprogramming, operation and maintenance labor, power, and supplies. They decline after system shakedown and then increase. Benefits from a new system are small at first because of the transition problems, then increase for a while, and then finally decrease. The net value of a new system is negative at first, then increases, and later tapers off.

Economic life may be determined by judgment, the pay-off rule, or by rate of return analysis. The economic life of a single machine that is not to be replaced ends when its net value is largest. Equipment continued in service after that point operates at a loss.

A replacement chain of equipment poses a different problem. Economic life ends when the *annual* profit from the present equipment falls below the *average* profit expected from replacement equipment. Superior new equipment may displace existing equipment which is still quite new and profitable. Available models should not be procured if vast improvements are expected in the near future. But announced improvements may not be as big as promised or available when expected, and, in fact, they may never materialize. Postponing the procurement of improved equipment that is available to wait for still better equipment may have large rewards, but it also has some risks attached.

Present and future events can be compared at one point in time by compensating for the time difference. The difference in favor of present dollars reflects the cost of capital. A present dollar grows at compound interest to become a future amount. A series of future payments accumulates as the amount of an annuity.

A single future amount can be discounted to get its present worth and a series of future payments can be discounted as the present worth of an annuity. To decide whether an investment is worth while, future revenues can be related to the initial investment in terms of the present worth of an annuity.

Rental and purchase plans have advantages that must be appraised for a particular situation. Some advantages of both plans are available through a lease with an option to purchase equipment.

REFERENCES AND SUPPLEMENTAL READINGS

Anthony, Robert N., and Samuel Schwartz. *Office Equipment: Buy or Rent?*, Boston, Management Analysis Center, Inc., 1957, 92 pp. This monograph presumes that the decision to acquire a piece of office equipment has been made, so that the book deals with the narrower question, "Should you acquire it by outright purchase or by rental?" The problem is one of investment policy and the basic issue is whether the rental and other costs saved when funds are invested in equipment will be a large enough amount to yield an adequate return on the investment. Present worth tables that assume an income tax rate of 50 per cent, straight-line depreciation over equipment life, and a salvage value of 15 per cent simplify calculating the rate of return on a proposed investment. Chapters are devoted to required earning rate, future useful life of equipment, kinds of costs, income tax, and a short-cut method of analysis.

Bagby, W. S. "Deciding Upon an Electronic Data-Processing System," *The Controller*, vol. 24: 216-221 (May 1956). Bagby presents the steps followed by a large insurance company in appraising, installing, and converting to an electronic data system. The questions asked at various stages plus the analysis, plans, adjustments, and training necessary for developing an effective system are outlined. The basic decision turned on a nine-month, 10,000 man-hour study that produced a cost comparison indicating a total outlay of two million for a large-scale system capable of paying for itself in five or six years on one ordinary insurance application. Selection of a particular system was based on less quantitative data. One company's experience is useful in aiding others in selecting a specific system and, more important, in deciding whether any system is economically feasible.

Chapin, Ned. "Justifying the Use of an Automatic Computer," *Computers and Automation*, vol. 4: 17-19 (August 1955). The question of whether or not to use an automatic computer is approached on a cost and benefit basis. Dollars and cents data can be obtained for some costs and benefits, but other factors—management dependence upon the new system and effect of equipment on company operations—are "irreducible" because precise dollars and cents answers are not possible. Costs that will change in the future, rather than those that will continue, must be estimated and compared with the cost of the new equipment to find whether it is justified.

Clippinger, Richard F. "Economics of the Digital Computer," *Harvard Business Review*, vol. 33: 77-88 (January-February 1955). The questions of "costs-uses-speed scale" are faced by the business man contemplating use of data-processing equipment. Clippinger discusses the record-keeping, management decision, and industrial research classes of data-handling problems. Exhibits deal with cost, speed, and peripheral equipment. Two case examples illustrate the economics, and especially the net savings, involved in computer use by a retail chain and a casualty insurance company. The article deals also with the implications of a computer for an individual company in terms of (a) opportunities for savings, (b) availability of a central computing laboratory, and (c) size of the company. Clippinger appraises seven computer systems which are in existence or which he envisions for the near future.

Wallace, Frank. *Appraising the Economics of Electronic Computers*, New York, Controllership Foundation, Inc., 1956, 104 pp. The purpose of this research report prepared by Wallace, a partner in a public accounting firm, is to develop a "common-sense, business appraisal of computers." It does not attempt to give answers, but develops a point of view and an approach helpful in planning action. Emphasis is placed on introducing computers to reduce clerical costs with little consideration for developing better information for management or making operations research studies. Appraisal of a computer as another piece of capital equipment involves determining whether new costs to be incurred are less than costs to be eliminated. A thorough study requires forming a computer team of several people to analyze procedural areas—for example, (a) inventory and production records and (b) costs and budgets—selected on the basis of clerical costs, simplicity for programming, intangible benefits, and effect of centralization upon data transmission costs. Detailed analysis of a system involves (a) flow charts, (b) volume studies, and (c) cost determination to define activities for introduction of new equipment. Improvements can, it is said, be derived from systems study even though existing equipment is retained. The computer feasibility study requires filling in detail (hardware, personnel, operating loads, and programs) to develop projected costs for comparison with present costs. The most economical system should be selected, although the intangible benefits obtainable may be decisive if costs are not greatly different. Wallace also deals with the problems of installation and operating costs.

PART FIVE

SYSTEMS DESIGN

CHAPTER THIRTEEN

ORGANIZATIONAL
STRUCTURE FOR
DATA PROCESSING

The organizational structure of a business depends on many factors. These deserve brief coverage in order to put the method of data processing, whether by computers or otherwise, into a proper perspective, for data-processing methods are only one factor influencing the way a business is organized. Then too, there is a strong interrelation between organizational patterns and data-processing methods, so that changes in either one may induce or even cause changes in the other.

Organizational patterns can be examined broadly and narrowly. In broad terms, the organizational pattern of the company as a whole and any changes that occur in response to new methods of data processing should be considered. More narrowly, changes in the composition and organizational pattern of the group directly responsible for data processing, which deserve examination because dramatic changes occur here before the company at large is affected, are covered in Chapter 17.

FACTORS RELATED TO THE ENTERPRISE

The structure appropriate for any organization depends on the nature of its operations, its managerial organization, its processing system, legal restrictions, and other factors. These factors are closely related and each affects the others.

Operations

The relationships, dynamics, and location of operations to be controlled deserve examination.

Relationships. An important determinant of the organizational pattern of a company as a whole is the relationship between its various parts. Operations of the various parts—whether divisions, plants, warehouses, offices, or subsidiary corporations—may be closely inter-related. As an example of highly related operations, raw material produced at one plant may be finished at another, stocked at all warehouses, and sold to customers by any one of many sales offices. In such a case, a fairly high degree of management centralization is required to coordinate operations. Some data will originate locally: stock receipts, issues, returns, and quantity of inventory on hand. Other data—replenishment plans, availability of substitute items, and future requirements—will originate centrally. The data originating at separate points must converge at some stage during processing in order to relate all factors.

On the other hand, divisions of a company may have unrelated activities which there is little need to coordinate—one division may manufacture refrigerators, and another electric generators. Also, some operations are completely independent of the main stream of activities. The inventory and use of widgets, for instance, may have little or no relation to the payroll at the same plant or warehouse, and inventory and payroll at two different locations may be totally unrelated. Data-processing streams can also be entirely independent. A close relation between operations is likely to be associated with a concentration of decision-making authority within a business. Some uniformity in data processing to simplify interpretation and comparison is a concomitant of centralized management.

Dynamics of Operations. "Static" and "dynamic" are good words to cover the degree of predictability or unpredictability of business operations. Static operations are predictable, for changes follow certain rules or occur slowly. The existence of static conditions reduces the requirements for information and simplifies data-processing procedures. The system load, the input, and the output vary slowly. Only a small degree of flexibility is required because system demands change little, and known loads can be scheduled for efficient processing and reporting with equipment that has little excess capacity. Processing is rarely interrupted to answer unexpected questions or to cope with drastic changes in operations.

Conditions are dynamic when operations are unpredictable and changes occur quickly without following any known rules. Dynamic conditions make data processing difficult, for system load, input data, and output requirements change radically. Changing conditions impose new information requirements that require flexibility in order to meet new conditions. Capacity must be reserved to cover new loads, and smooth scheduling is often interrupted by entirely new processing requirements. Interrogations to get quick answers also disrupt routine operations.

At one extreme, conditions might be as static as the legendary salt mill at the bottom of the ocean. The owner, you will recall, who started the mill grinding, did not know how to stop it so he threw it overboard to get rid of it. Since the mill produces salt at a constant rate without change of any kind, there are no more facts to learn about it. A data-processing system for the salt mill would be trivial, for one report on the product and the output rate would be correct forever.

Static operations—those characterized by small and infrequent changes—may be handled equally well by local or centralized processing. Information requirements are small enough that summary output from local processing is suitable for centralized processing. Original raw data need not be transmitted. At the other extreme, highly dynamic operations might be so completely unpredictable that events one day in the future might have no relation to any present or past events. Even an elaborate processing system cannot cope with this difficult situation. In such a case, reports about past events would be useless in helping management predict future events.

Business operations are always somewhere between the two extremes, however, for neither perfect predictability nor complete unpredictability exists.

Geographical Dispersion.   Operations may be either at one location or scattered geographically. Single location operations, those under one "roof" or nearby, simplify the problem of finding a physical location for data-processing facilities. Even so, the organizational structure within a business at one location poses processing problems which can be solved in various ways. Processing within each administrative unit throughout the organization may be feasible if operations are not closely related, for processing can then be kept responsive to the individual needs of the location; but fragmentary processing may be inefficient because of the limited scale.

Centralized processing facilities may be located in one administrative unit. If a unit with heavy data-information requirements takes responsibility for all processing, there is some risk that its needs will be met and the needs of other users will be neglected, although such neglect may be wholly unintended. Heavy loads may get priority while others are scheduled later. Emphasis on developing some applications may force others into the background. On the other hand, a separate department might be set up to provide data-processing services for the whole organization. Centralized processing can gain from the use of larger-scale equipment than is practical for scattered facilities.

Widespread physical operations—manufacturing, warehousing, and so forth—pose entirely different problems of the physical location and organizational structure of data processing. Data originate at many points, and some centralization is required to bring together facts about inter-related operations so that information is available at the appropriate level for decision-making purposes.

High-cost transportation of material and products acts as an "umbrella," in the economist's terms, and aids the geographical dispersion of operations. Efficient communication networks, on the other hand, help tie together widespread operations, and centralized processing is further facilitated by the availability of large-scale equipment.

An interesting point arises concerning data handling for temporary operations, such as plant, bridge, or highway construction, at an isolated location. Temporary operations may not warrant setting up complete data-processing facilities. In such cases, data may be sent to a central point for processing with the necessary documents and information being returned for local use.

These brief comments about the nature of operations—their relationship, dynamics, and geographical dispersion—indicate their bearing on the organizational structure of data-processing facilities. A more important point is that these factors have some effect on the way that basic operations—manufacturing, warehousing, and marketing—themselves are organized.

Managerial Organization

The chain of command and the schemes used to control operations influence how much data processing there will be and where it will be done. Broader treatment of computers and management control is given in Kozmetsky and Kircher (1956).

Decentralized Management.   Decisions are made at the lowest appropriate level in the chain of command when management is decentralized. Decisions can be made locally, if only a small segment of operations is involved; but decisions with a widespread effect are made at a higher level. The type and number of decisions made by each level of management differ, of course. Top management may delegate only a small part of its decision-making power to lower levels of management. Or, management may delegate many problems for local decision and hold each decentralized unit responsible for results. Where local management makes operating decisions, it needs detailed information at short intervals. The required information may, in many cases, be obtained by either local or centralized processing; but the processing operations and communication patterns are likely to be greatly different for each arrangement.

The over-all performance of decentralized management is usually evaluated by top management at longer intervals, which means that top management's needs for information are less detailed and less frequent than those of the original decision maker. Or, to put it differently, the Monday morning second-guesser needs less detail and needs it less quickly than the Saturday afternoon quarterback. Summaries and digested conclusions prepared under flexible time schedules are suitable for top management.

The word "decentralization" is often used to mean physical separation or geographical dispersion. But geographical dispersion is compatible with centralized decision making because widely scattered plants or units can be controlled from one central location. Geographical dispersion and management decentralization are not synonymous.

Centralized Management.   Decisions are made at one or a few central points under a plan of centralized management. Centralized data processing has some desirable features for centralized management and control. Information is accumulated rapidly at one point for the control of operations that are centrally managed, whether they are at one or several locations. The results of centralized processing can be used to schedule and balance work loads, if several manufacturing plants have similar or complementary facilities. Consolidated purchasing, for example, can reduce buying costs and prices.

The degree of management centralization depends not only on the nature of operations, discussed earlier, but also on the management planning and control techniques that are suitable.

Managerial Control Plan.   Management control plans may range from being carefully specified in advance to being developed as problems arise.

Control plans that are carefully specified by management at one level can be put into effect at other levels and produce the desired results. Data-processing plans are developed in advance and used to get the desired information from the data. The data can be discarded after being fully exhausted. The location of data-processing operations is determined by technical considerations of equipment and communications. Management requirements for information can be met regardless of where the processing is done.

On the other hand, control plans may not be specified in advance but may be developed for each situation as it arises. *Ad hoc* management requires flexible processing of raw data to get information related to each problem to be solved, and processing procedures must be flexible enough to deal with the circumstances. In such a case, management information requirements are best met by having easy access to the data-processing operations—and access is easier if processing operations are under the manager's jurisdiction.

Information produced at a central installation is available for top management planning. Staff personnel located near the control facilities can analyze results for long-range forecasting, as well as comparing different segments of the business with each other and with any performance standards that are used (Kruse, 1954). The work of performance analysis is simplified by standardizing data, operations, and results even when management personnel are not near the central processing facilities.

Operations analysis may require detailed data covering all or a few selected phases in order to develop control plans from a long-term analysis of results. The development of "models" to explain operations in the past and to project them into the future is an important part of improving forecasting and control methods, but it lies outside the main stream of operations. Day-to-day activities continue while operations analysts are at work. Analysts should be located high enough in the management organization to keep an over-all viewpoint and have access to all data in order to develop sound models.

The essential point here is that the organizational structure of data-processing activities is related to existing management control plans—whether they are carefully formulated or *ad hoc*. Operations analysis aimed at improving future management control plans lies outside the main stream of data processing, even though it is essential to sound management.

Analysts' Approach. When designing systems, analysts should consider, first, the data and information requirements of the business and, second, the conditions imposed by various organizational structures. Understanding these features provides an insight into the strengths that can be exploited and the weaknesses that must be rectified.

Small organizations may have complex data-processing problems. For example, production scheduling in a job shop involves many alternatives that are individually simple, but operating conditions may change rapidly so that simple problems compound themselves and become complex. Information requirements may be big enough to justify large-scale processing equipment for small-scale operations.

Large organizations may have simple information requirements because alternatives are few and operating conditions change slowly. Modest information requirements may justify large processing equipment that is centrally located, but not equipment that is dispersed at various locations. The work of systems analysts is covered at length in Chapter 14.

Nature of Processing

Some features of processing systems themselves bear on the organizational structure of data processing; among these are data origination, communication, and information consumption. They can be summarized in a single question: "Should there be centralized or decentralized data processing?"

Data Origination. Data, the raw material of processing systems, originate at the points where events occur. Two choices exist for placing the responsibility for data origination. Decentralization makes local people responsible for data origination that is in keeping with organization-wide plans to assure compatibility of media, form, and schedules for later processing. They are responsible for the initial quality—accuracy and completeness—and the correction of any mistakes that are discovered. Data origination may be a by-product of local needs for facts to control operations.

Responsibility for data origination might be centralized. In such a case, a control group takes the initiative for getting data into processable form, and the quality of the data is a major problem. Centralized responsibility involves a data-gathering organization—people and equipment—that parallels the management organization. The people who originate and process the data are primarily responsible to the comptroller or whoever is in charge of data processing. They must, of course, cooperate closely with local managers to furnish operating information.

Both plans—decentralized and centralized—for data origination are used in business. Establishing a local responsibility for data origination has merit, and it is imperative for decentralized processing. Furthermore, local responsibility is useful for getting high-quality data from geographically separated operations even though management is centralized.

Communication.   Communication among data originators, processors, and users poses important problems for operations at one location. Office-to-plant communication often uses messenger service, telephone, or telegraph channels. Communication problems increase rapidly when operations are geographically scattered. Quick transmission of large volumes of data over telephone or telegraph lines may cost as much as the remaining stages of processing.

Mail and messenger services may be slower than wire transmission for individual messages, but they have high effective speeds because huge volumes of data can be handled at one time. Surprisingly, surface mail or air mail has a high transmission speed—measured in the number of characters and how far they go in a second—when the message load is heavy and distances are moderate.

Combinations of wire and mail services may be used to get low-cost, efficient transmission. In some cases, the bulk of messages may be sent by mail for economy, but messages originating near the end of the reporting period or at other critical times may be sent by wire to reduce the processing delay. In other cases, wire transmission from outlying locations is imperative in order to reduce the delay in central processing.

The point here is that transmission cost and time affect the location of processing facilities. Huge volumes of data originating at each of many widely scattered locations may demand local processing in order to condense the data for efficient transmission. If the transmission of data is expensive, local processing becomes more desirable.

The costs of decentralized processing may be reduced by using efficient communication methods and some centralized data processing. Administrative information—messages involving no processing—may be handled by the communication network used for the operating data. A company operating in many states with decentralized management made substantial cost savings merely by designing one communication network to handle both administrative messages and operating data. In fact, the difficulty in distinguishing between administrative and data-processing messages forced the company to transmit them over the same circuits, by uniform procedures (Gallagher, 1956; Guest, 1956).

Distribution. The distribution of information for management purposes bears on the problem of selecting the appropriate structure for efficient processing. Centralized processing is more attractive if output is used by central management alone. On the other hand, intensive use of results by local managers may be easier with local processing, since transmitting data to the central processing facility and returning the results are unnecessary.

The volume of reports is usually smaller than the volume of original data. The practice of processing data at the lower level and transmitting results to higher management reduces communication costs by avoiding the higher costs incurred for transmitting all raw data to a central processing unit.

Uniform Procedures. Different units throughout the organization may originate and process data by various methods and procedures. Uniform procedures are often consciously modified to meet local conditions, and further variations are often made to meet situations within each unit. Differences in materials, product terminology, and classification may result in such diverse codes as to make over-all report consolidation difficult. Both managerial decentralization and geographical dispersion increase the difficulty of enforcing adherence to uniform procedures.

Centralized data processing is facilitated by uniform procedures, and eliminating company-wide discrepancies can lead to substantial savings. Unit operations are not substantially affected by uniformity, whereas inter-unit communication is made easier. A thorough study of the types of data involved, their ultimate use, and the best way to handle them is required to develop efficient, uniform procedures.

Capacity. Each type of data can be accumulated and processed at one time if processing is centralized. There is no need to duplicate the analysis, programming, and operations that would be required for local processing. Large-scale equipment may have more data-processing capacity per dollar outlay—both invested and operating—than several sets of small equipment. Less space and fewer operating and maintenance personnel may be required at one central facility than would be necessary for several local facilities.

The advantage of large equipment for complex routines is important when scientific or operations-research computations are planned.

The need for stand-by capacity and the risk of equipment failure influence any decision toward centralization. Operations will halt if the only available set of equipment is not usable. If several sets of equipment are needed, two sets of the same type may be obtained; then even though one set fails, schedules can be revised so that remaining capacity can handle high-priority work. Parallel equipment need not be at a particular location for stand-by service—time on similar equipment used by other organizations can usually be "borrowed" in emergencies and repaid when wanted by the lender.

Flexibility. Centralized processing requires some compromise between the uniform procedures necessary for efficient operations and the flexibility needed to meet variable information requirements. Individual needs may be callously submerged in standardization to make central operations efficient, but an individual operating unit loses some flexibility if it must depend on centralized processing. No difficulty arises if individual units perform similar or related activities; their operation and management must be closely coordinated no matter what processing schemes are preferred.

The varied information requirements of independent units are not readily met by uniform processing. Standardized procedures, forms, and data flow may create operating problems at the local level. One division may need daily information, but another may find that a weekly reporting cycle is adequate. An emphasis on central processing efficiency may conflict with local needs. Weekly batch processing for central operating efficiency would not fill local needs for daily information, and if weekly processing were used exclusively, local operations would be hampered.

Compatibility

"Compatibility" can be defined as the ability to exist together in harmony. Every system has problems of compatibility, but they need not be any greater for a decentralized system than a centralized one.

Perfect compatibility would seem to require identical equipment and procedures throughout an organization. Usually, many incompatibilities exist, for various methods are used for representing, carrying, and processing data. Data may be numerical or alphanumerical. Common number bases, as described earlier, are decimal, binary, and octal. Decimal numerals are represented in many ways: decimal; binary-coded decimal; binary-coded excess 3; and five-, six-, seven-, and eight-level schemes. Needless to say, each character is represented differently in each code scheme.

Media to carry data include paper, punched cards, mark-sensed cards, paper tape, magnetic tape, magnetic drums, and other storage devices. Data are originated by manual, mechanical, photographic, electric, and electronic methods. Many structural plans exist for processing data and reporting results. The number of possible input-output schemes, file arrangements, and data-flow plans is almost limitless. In fact, the inability to use the output from one stage of processing as direct input at the next stage is so commonplace it is almost assumed to be natural.

Data Conversion.   Converters solve most of the problems of differences in data representation and media. A common but not efficient plan for data conversion is to assign the task to people. Clerks, stenographers, and key-punch operators spend their time reading visual data and converting them by operating keyboards. The key-punch operator alone produces data in machine-processable form, for the others must repeat the operation at the next stage. Mechanical, electric, or electronic equipment converts machine-processable data from one form to another.

Common data-conversion routes are:

1. Punched cards to magnetic tape or vice versa
2. Five-, six-, seven-, and eight-channel paper tape to punched cards or vice versa
3. One form—card or tape—to wire circuits and back to the original form
4. Printed characters to punched tape, magnetic tape, or punched cards

Data are converted from one number system to another (decimal to binary-coded decimal, for instance) within one piece of equipment. Such conversion is handled automatically by the processor and is a problem for the equipment designer. When designing an over-all system, systems analysts must carefully consider the effect, but not the method of automatic conversion.

Efficient conversion devices shrink the problem of equipment incompatibility. In fact, efficient system design seems to require incompatibility at one or more points. People want to read alphabetic and numerical characters, whereas equipment generally uses some version of the binary scheme to represent data.

Data-processing equipment may be considered compatible for operational purposes if automatic devices exist for converting machine-processable data to media that can be used by all major equipment.

System Conversion. System incompatibility poses far more difficult problems than does data incompatibility. Different data-processing systems have different classifications, files, and programs. Even identical equipment does not erase the incompatibility of structurally different systems. In short, differences in data representation, media, and equipment are handled by automatic converters; but structural differences may take complete system redesign to overcome inconsistencies.

STRUCTURAL SCHEMES

Business operations and the managerial organization reflect a rough balance between several opposing forces, some of which are favorable to centralization and others to decentralization. The data-processing system itself, of course, is one factor influencing the degree of centralization, and changes in the data-processing system eventually have some effect on the managerial organization.

There are four possible combinations of centralization-decentralization for managerial organization and location of data-processing operations. The most controversial combination—centralized processing and decentralized control—is discussed here.

Centralized Processing and Decentralized Control

A necessary condition of decentralized control is that individual managers have the authority and the responsibility to make operating decisions; this is necessary in order to evaluate results by analyzing the profit or the adherence to standards. On the other hand, if top management makes operating decisions, it must share the responsibility for results because complete decentralization no longer exists.

Managers need some control over the system used to enable them to report, measure, and control their operations. Local managers may feel that they are being undermined unless they have some latitude in developing information control systems. From the local manager's viewpoint, data processing may be divided broadly into document preparation and control information.

Document Preparation. The origination of data, which commonly takes the form of document preparation, is an important element of data processing in most businesses. The precise method used to prepare payroll records, orders, bills, and so forth, has little bearing on managerial authority and control. Their preparation is vital, but it is a service function, not a control function.

Document-preparation techniques can either be standardized throughout an organization, or reflect local preferences. Neither approach needs to interfere with decentralized management. Operations that lead primarily to document preparation appear well suited for centralization.

Operating Information.   Finding a proper "home" for producing information for the decentralized manager's control system poses difficult problems.

The information system used to evaluate the over-all performance of several decentralized units might be partially consolidated. But some conflict may arise if top management standardizes systems that individual managers have developed to meet individual needs. The need for reports on production control or daily activity may differ greatly from one location to another, for the abilities of each local manager and his staff influence information requirements.

Freedom From Interference.   It is possible for centralized processing to develop satisfactory information for the control of local operations, but several rules must be followed for harmonious operations. First, the central processing group must limit its operations to data processing alone. Control schemes are developed by managers, both locally and centrally, and are completely outside the province of the data-processing group. Local management's information requirements must, within reason, be filled. Second, top management must not obtain access to information still in the processing stream before it is available to local managers. Premature questions about unusual developments may upset the whole scheme of centralized processing and decentralized management. Local managers may react to having the data pipeline "tapped" and keep unofficial records for furnishing quick answers to top management questions. If so, the economic advantages of centralized processing are lost through some duplication of records.

Geographical separation of a data-processing center from all other operations, as practiced by some companies, has merit. The processing center can be isolated from interference by both local and central management. Isolation reduces the temptation of top management to intercept control reports before they go to local managers. A local manager gains peace of mind and a stronger tactical position by knowing that his detailed control information is not intercepted by top management. A manager does not need to spend time trying to develop excuses for unfavorable short-run results that have little bearing on his unit's long-run performance. Top management should restrict its attention to longer-range information for evaluation and control purposes.

System Flexibility.   Another condition must be filled in order to keep centralized processing of control information compatible with decentralized management. A local manager needs "elbow-room" to develop and modify his information control system. Such freedom is more important if local operations are diverse, because important differences will be reflected in the manager's information requirements. He usually feels that he should be able to tailor his system to his needs. In fact, he may treat his information system as one factor of production similar to labor and material. He increases or decreases each factor of production depending on its costs, how much of it is useful for him, and what he is trying to accomplish.

A manager's information needs change continually, so he must be able to modify the system. A particular report may serve for most purposes, but more frequent or entirely different reports may be needed because local conditions change. The dynamic nature of operations is a factor in determining the appropriate degree of local freedom. Retaining flexibility to meet the needs of individual managers avoids any conflict in devising and adopting uniform schemes.

Centralized data processing can complement decentralized management if both freedom from interference and system flexibility are retained. An organization may use centralized processing when it can not economically justify efficient systems at various locations.

Degree of Centralization

Economic as well as management considerations determine the degree to which a data-processing system should be centralized within a business. Before deciding how a system should serve and be controlled by management, and from what locations and at what levels of management it should do this, the following factors should be considered:

1. The dollar cost of processing data at one or more levels of management
2. Communication costs to transmit either the data or the results
3. The ability to schedule work at a high fraction of system capacity
4. Duplication of programming and coding work involved for people who know the local system but are not familiar with equipment
5. Increased time required for central equipment experts to become oriented and study local problems to design a system
6. Uniformity of classification and report practices and the difficulty of reconciling differences and correcting errors
7. The degree of development of informal systems, if local management concludes that its information requirements are not met

SUMMARY

In theory, the two extremes of wholly decentralized or completely centralized processing are both possible. Factors that affect the organizational structure of data processing are the nature of operations to be controlled, the managerial organization, and the processing system.

The scope of data processing must be matched to the dynamics of the operations for which information is wanted. In order to control dynamic operations, management requires current information. Information needs for static operations can be met by local or centralized processing. Operations that are concentrated at only one location pose little or no problem in the physical location of data-processing facilities, but the problems of organizational structure persist. Centralized processing for all operations offers some economies through the use of larger-scale equipment, although problems of communication and scheduling may offset some of the advantages.

Geographically dispersed operations pose problems of physical location as well as of organizational structure of data processing. The facts about scattered operations must be assembled. Centralized processing is invaluable for dealing with operations at widespread temporary locations. Efficient, quick communication is a prerequisite to control of widespread business operations.

Local managers need detailed information at short intervals in order to plan and control local operations. The over-all results of a unit are evaluated at longer intervals by higher management. Centralized processing is probably mandatory for centralized management and control, and the appropriate degree of centralized control depends on the nature of operations and management planning and control techniques.

Carefully specified control plans make it possible to process data at any level that has the necessary facts available. On the other hand, *ad hoc* management plans developed for each situation require flexible processing in order to get pertinent information. Centrally processed information is available most quickly for top management analysis and planning. Standard or uniform data gathering, processing, and reporting can simplify analysis.

Operations analysis to develop models and new operating plans may require detailed data covering long periods of time. Such analysis is related to but outside the main stream of data-processing activities. Systems analysts must live with the existing over-all philosophy of management when designing systems. Small organizations may have huge information requirements because of the variability of operations, while large, mass production organizations may have simple information needs. Information demands are important determinants of both the location and the scale of processing facilities.

The minor problems of developing an efficient communication system for a single location become complex when the communication system must link many locations. Combinations of wire and mail may give efficient, low-cost data transmission. The communication cost and time to transmit both data and results bear on the optimum location of processing facilities. Centralized processing is facilitated by uniform procedures, but variations arise for local situations. The flexibility needed to meet local information requirements must be balanced against the economies of uniform processing. Timing, processing, and reporting may be sources of conflict on both the local and the central levels.

Compatibility has two facets—equipment and systems. Equipment incompatibility is "solved" by devices that convert between different data-representation schemes and media. Equipment can be considered compatible, if efficient converters are available, although the conversion operation may add to the processing time. System incompatibility poses knotty problems. Structural differences—classifications, file, and procedures—may require complete redesign to overcome inconsistencies.

The possibilities of centralized processing and decentralized managerial control pose interesting questions. Document preparation—payroll records, orders, and bills—has little relation to managerial control. Such operations can be standardized and done centrally without infringing on local management. Data processing to get operating and control information should be responsive to local management needs in order to avoid conflicts that may arise from standardizing systems that were originally developed to meet each individual manager's needs.

Experience indicates that there are two important rules for keeping harmonious relations when centralized processing is used with decentralized management: first, limit the central operations to data processing *per se;* second, prevent top management from intercepting information and prematurely interfering before local managers get their reports. Isolation of the processing center, a practice followed by several companies, may help insulate it from interference by both local and top management.

The appropriate degree of centralization in data processing depends on several economic and managerial considerations. Processing and communication costs, work scheduling, standardization, and planned and "bootleg" duplication of work are important factors.

REFERENCES AND SUPPLEMENTAL READINGS

Gallagher, James D. "Administrative Automation at Sylvania: A Case Study —III. The Program in Operation," pp. 47-67 in *Administrative Automation Through IDP and EDP*, Office Management Series No. 144, New York, American Management Association, 1956. The communication system designed for Sylvania's Data Processing Center was built to serve both administrative and data-processing requirements. Serving primarily as an extension of input and output of the data-processing system, the communication system also functions as a separate unit to handle administrative traffic requirements. A unique communication system was planned to meet several criteria: automatic routing and classification of data, expandability for increasing volume, preliminary processing and routing, minimal decision making at reporting locations, compatibility of equipment, uniformity of reporting and data coding, and automatic reconstruction of messages. Systems analysis work was based on the flow of information, and organization of the Data Processing Center was developed around it. Early projects were payroll and customer order entry. Future planning (as of early 1957) covered the development of automatic cross-office switching of messages, a shift in emphasis from reports for review to reports for management action, and the integration of operational activities of the Center with operations throughout the company.

Guest, Leon C. "Administrative Automation at Sylvania: A Case Study—I. Centralized Data Processing—Decentralized Management," pp. 28-37 in *Administrative Automation Through IDP and EDP*, Office Management Series No. 144, New York, American Management Association, 1956. Predicting that in 1971 there may be one clerical worker for four factory workers and that recruiting costs will be excessive, Guest shows that this situation can be averted by mechanizing the record-keeping function. Sylvania, a highly decentralized but vertically integrated company, devised a communication network, built a data-processing center, and installed an electronic computer that would centralize data processing yet retain the advantages of decentralized management. Much, he says, remains to be done to develop a fully automatic data-processing system and reverse the upward trend in the ratio of clerical workers to factory workers.

Kozmetsky, George, and Paul Kircher. *Electronic Computers and Management Control*, New York, McGraw-Hill Book Co., 1956, 296 pp. This book provides coverage of the managerial and administrative problems involved in study and introduction of electronic computers to a firm. It was written to acquaint the business executive with the many facets of electronic calculation. Fundamental characteristics of electronic systems and basic concepts of the scientific method of analysis are described. The influence that electronic data-processing machinery will have on management planning and control is demonstrated with numerous examples of current installations. A brief explanation of an electronic computer and a survey of electronic methods of data processing are given. Primary emphasis is on the type of administrative problems experienced when introducing computer systems. Four chapters are devoted to the aspects of management planning: (a) management and the scientific approach, (b) management planning and control, (c) programming, (d) scheduling and feedback, and (e) integrated business systems. Present status and expected future development of automation and scientific computation are discussed. The final chapters are concerned with management approach toward (a) selection of an optimum electronic system to meet desired objectives, (b) the responsibility of the executive for new developments, and (c) the effect of automatic systems on our society. An appendix discusses technical problems and presents a mathematical model for an integrated business system, discussing it in terms of matrix algebra.

Kruse, Benedict. "Electronic Brain Keeps Tabs on 11,500 Rexall Stores," *American Business*, vol. 24: 41-44 (December 1954). Considerable differences of work time now exist between Rexall's present computer and previous methods, for example: single payroll, seven minutes' time versus four hours for tabulating-machine operation; and total detailed weekly sales analysis, ten minutes' time versus three man-days for calculations. Use of the computer for analysis of the results of the semi-annual one-cent sale for a selected sample of stores is more fully described. Inventory and sales are analyzed by product and compared with nation-wide and county-by-county standards to determine how much more should be sold to reach standard. Results of the study are used to govern items to be featured in future one-cent sales. Rexall expects to broaden the study to include 5,000 products in the Rexall manufacturing line.

CHAPTER FOURTEEN

TOOLS FOR
SYSTEMS ANALYSIS

Systems analysis involves collecting, organizing, and evaluating the facts about a system; its broad purpose is to determine the information requirements of an organization and develop efficient methods for filling them.

A successful system depends on many factors, some of which are fixed, others of which are modifiable. Input and output (data and information) are often considered to be fixed, although they can be changed in the long run. The ability to process data, which links the input and output together, depends on skilled people, equipment and instructions for processing, and the procedures required to make the system function.

Useful background for systems analysis are Hitch (1955); Kircher (1956); Laubach (1957); and Wooldridge (1954). Some paper forms manufacturers and pamphlets from computer manufacturers are valuable guides to systems-analysis tools.

FACTORS TO CONSIDER

Systems analysis is the basis for building a successful system. Without it, the benefits of automatic data-processing systems would probably disappear completely. Systems analysis should consider the following facets of the system:

1. Data-information applications that demand improvement

2. Management information requirements

3. Data available and their form

4. The kind of data-processing system that will fill information needs from the available data

5. The type, kind, and cost of equipment best suited to system needs

6. Preparations required to introduce the system and equipment

7. Location and uses of equipment

Data-information systems are so large and complex that a systems analyst can remember only a small part of the total picture at one time. Even with all the important factors written on paper, an analyst can become hopelessly muddled trying to relate all the facts. He needs, therefore, an orderly plan for keeping the facts and figures straight before he can deal with the data-processing system as a whole.

Measuring systems operations is difficult and changes are so expensive that an analyst finds it impossible to try all the proposed improvements he would like to evaluate. Experimental testing takes months, costs a great deal of money, disrupts operations, and confuses people throughout the organization.

In lieu of experimentation, analytic tools can be used to create a "model" of the data-processing system. Proposed changes are tested on the model before they are tried on the real system. Testing proposed system changes on a model avoids interfering with day-to-day operations. The use of models is risky, however, because they may give incorrect answers. A proposed change that looks promising in flow-chart form may be inefficient in a real system. Models are useful only if they resemble the real system closely enough to permit predicting the results of proposed changes. On the other hand, models that are too close to the real system become excessively complex for practical use.

ANALYTIC TOOLS

Systems analysts use various tools or techniques in making surveys, gathering facts, and analyzing data and operations in order to develop solutions to data-processing problems.

The tools most commonly used by analysts are:

1. Management, organization, and procedures surveys
2. Analysis of forms and reports
3. Work measurement and performance standards
4. Work improvement or simplification programs
5. Space and layout surveys

These tools are covered only briefly here, for they are discussed in other books in more detail. See, for example, *Workshop for Management* (1956).

Surveys

There are three kinds of surveys useful for systems analysis; these are directed at management, organization, and procedures.

Management.   The foundation of a systems analysis program may be a management survey to locate and define problems. A management survey thoroughly examines objectives, programs, operating methods, practices, organization, and policies. The question, "How can we do better?" is answered by on-the-spot observations, study, research, and testing.

Surveys originate in one of several ways. Each element of an organization may be surveyed on schedule once in a year or so. The head of an operating unit may request a survey for independent appraisal of his operations. The manager or the comptroller may initiate a survey in anticipation of a request from superiors or after a review indicates the need for improvement.

Organization.   An organization survey is a special type of management survey. Its purpose is to appraise the organization and propose improvements in the division of work and in the nature of relationships among individuals and units carrying out related objectives.

An organization survey defines and analyzes who does what, to whom each individual reports, and the relationships among individuals and units in an organization. Good organization principles should be followed to develop the ideal plan, but modifications of the ideal will always be necessary in the light of available personnel, equipment, and material. Organization plans are developed to solve selected problems or to carry out specific objectives. Continual review and modification are required because changes in problems and objectives are endless.

Intensive study of the organization itself is required before attempting to apply a set of principles. Three sets of relationships that must be probed are (1) the formal organization chart, (2) the actual prestige and authority of various positions and individuals who hold them, and (3) the actual lines of person-to-person contact that arise to get things done.

Organization surveys are a major technique in developing sound plans to produce benefits at all levels of an enterprise: they promote better communications among people (which insures coverage of all important activities), clarify the functions of executives and supervisors, strengthen personnel initiative, furnish a valuable basis for training, and improve the morale of employees.

Procedures.   A procedures survey is a critical review of the way a job is done, the tools used, and the physical location of operations. The objective is to eliminate unessential activities, coordinate the methods of conducting essential activities, improve the physical location of work, and determine staff needs.

A management analyst uses many tools in a procedures survey. He may examine the organization structure, interview employees and supervisors, prepare flow charts of work, and analyze the design and use of forms and reports. An analyst needs a clear understanding of the theory, application, and use of each tool. A proper combination of these should be used for solving procedural problems.

Analysis of Forms and Reports

The analysis and control of forms, records, and reports is closely related to procedures surveys. Forms, records, and reports are integral parts of administrative operations. They are the basis of most clerical and much executive action, and they also serve for communicating such action and for maintaining reference files.

Forms reflect administrative activity and contain data used to compile reports. Unnecessary or duplicate forms and reports reflect inefficient work patterns. Poorly designed forms and reports, even though required, also lead to extra work.

The analysis of present and proposed procedures bears on the improvement of forms and reports. Systems analysts have a big stake in the effective control of such documents. Analysts should understand the place and importance of reports and forms in designing and improving procedures. They should, of course, work closely with the people primarily responsible for controlling operations.

Work Measurement and Performance

Performance analysis or work measurement relates the units of work produced to the man-hours spent and other costs involved.

Costs measured in tangible units, such as man-hours and equipment-hours, are easier for first-line supervisors to understand and use. A supervisor can control only the quantity of labor and equipment applied to his operations. Labor costs are so important that effective control of labor is essential to total cost control. The task of developing a work measurement or performance analysis system involves the following steps:

1. Selecting a work area to obtain performance data
2. Establishing a work unit to measure output of an area
3. Developing a fair standard for each work area measured
4. Providing for accurate records of work units produced, man-hours spent, and equipment-hours used
5. Calculating the output per man-hour and per equipment-hour
6. Finding areas with high or low output and determining the cause
7. Taking appropriate action to improve performance

The management analysis staff provides leadership and assistance in developing a work measurement or performance analysis system.

The most profitable work areas can be isolated and operating personnel assisted in developing units of measurements and reasonable performance standards. Such standards are developed either by statistical or engineering techniques.

Performance analysis data should normally flow to operating officials on a scheduled basis in a form which will enable them to evaluate the performance of their units. Work measurement data often flow to the data-processing unit for summarization and then back to the operating officials concerned. Management analysis personnel may intermittently use such data in analyzing a specific problem or making a management survey.

Work Simplification

Work simplification undertakes to increase the efficiency of operations by discovering and introducing improved procedures. Work simplification places in the hands of personnel at all levels some easily understood and applied techniques that they can apply to their own assigned tasks.

People fairly high in the organization, perhaps the comptroller and his staff, initiate the program or act as teachers to perform the following functions in installing a work simplification program:

1. Orient top and middle management supervisors in the over-all purpose
2. Train operating officials and supervisors in the techniques and follow up on the use of such techniques
3. Evaluate and report progress of the work simplification program
4. Provide assistance to staff operating units for solving complex management problems that are identified

Work simplification programs stress four techniques. First, work distribution charting and analysis shows how well work is divided among the individuals in a unit. Second, process charting and analysis provides a simple method for recording and analyzing the steps in a procedure, process, or method. It helps to answer the questions: "What steps are taken? Is each step necessary? Are steps in the right sequence? Where is the step taken? Is the right person taking it?" Third, work counts determine how much work is being done. Fourth, motion economy analysis is done for specific steps or operations to make sure that they are efficient.

Space and Layout Surveys

Space and layout surveys deal with problems of layout at two levels. The first level is the placement of organizational units, and the second level is the physical location of personnel and equipment within a unit.

A space survey conserves the use of space, energy, time, and transportation by eliminating detours, paper shuttling, and poor utilization of equipment. It also improves the working conditions of employees, minimizes physical transportation, and refines methods of handling materials. Space and layout surveys trace the flow of work among people, desks, and files. Who takes what action and where it is taken are recorded on a layout chart to show whether the flow is direct or roundabout. Such facts are used to frame new procedures or to recommend improved layouts.

In brief, organization surveys and work measurement and improvement studies serve a dual purpose. They are useful as a benchmark for later measuring the amount of change that occurs. They are also useful for making limited improvements in the system even though no drastic changes are made by introducing entirely new equipment and procedures.

RUN DIAGRAMS

Run diagrams are used to develop the general plan for processing data. A highly simplified version of a weekly run to update the payroll master file is in Figure 14-1. It shows that the file and changes are processed together to produce an updated master file.

A more realistic example is useful to show the nature and use of run diagrams, although you should search for the general ideas involved and avoid being overwhelmed by the details. A supply and distribution organization handles about ten thousand items. With a central office in Philadelphia and four warehouses in the eastern United States, multiple stocking increases the number of items warehoused to twenty-six thousand. There are three principal functions: stores operations, inventory and financial accounting, and inventory management. These functions are closely related and must be considered together in order to design an efficient system. For our purposes, we will look at stores accounting alone.

The stores accounting processing system is designed to maintain a set of bookkeeping accounts that will reflect the general stock position as well as individual warehouse conditions throughout the organization. Automatic daily transaction posting is wanted, and several management reports generated as a by-product of the system are desired. On each work day, the major system will be run to maintain the master files for invoices, bookkeeping accounts, and accounts payable. Weekly and monthly, a summary billing routine will be processed to yield an analysis of invoices in an accounts receivable status.

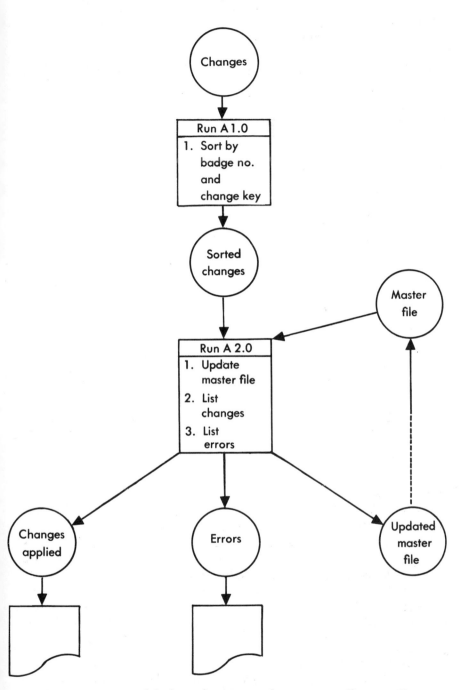

FIGURE 14-1. *Simplified run diagram: updating a payroll master file*

The symbols which are used in the daily stores accounting run diagram (Figure 14-2) are as follows:

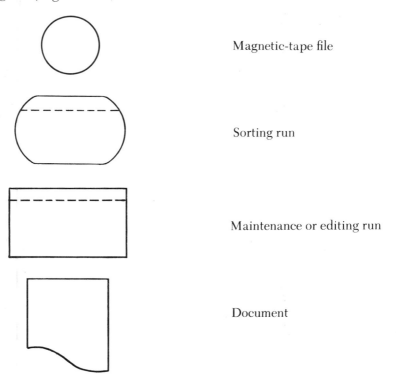

Magnetic-tape file

Sorting run

Maintenance or editing run

Document

Two of the runs, number 200 and number 205, are worth describing briefly to indicate the input, output, processing, and running time.

Run 200

The initial input transaction sorting of the daily stores accounting system is handled by run 200. Each day the daily stores document record, which is a magnetic-tape output of the stores processing run 130 (not shown), is read as the primary input. It contains the requisition line items and their associated headers for the current day, warehouse shipment notices, and additional transactions that result in bookkeeping entries to accomplish system file maintenance. Once each week this input is supplemented by a tape output of the billing routine run 245 (not shown) containing transactions to adjust the billed and unbilled accounts receivable.

This sorting run yields a single output tape in two separate sections. The first section of the tape contains all transactions to be processed against the invoice master file in run 205. These are written in invoice (document control) number order within warehouse sequence. All remaining transactions are dispersed to a holding tape during the input pass of the sort and written on a second section on the output tape at the close of the final output pass.

The processing, based upon the available input and desired output, requires an internal table look-up in the sorting routine to distinguish the items to be sorted from those that are dispersed and added to the output tape during the final pass. The daily stores document record is in document control number sequence; therefore, the input pass disperses by stores warehouse onto four tapes, and a second pass merges these tapes and adds the holding tape to create the final sorted output. Total average processing time for this run, including set-up and take-down, for a computer with a basic operation time of 16μ and tape read-write speeds of 45,000 characters a second is 11.5 minutes.

Run 205

Three functions are performed by run 205: (1) maintenance of the invoice master file, (2) conversion of input transactions to bookkeeping entries, and (3) extraction of data pertaining to materials receivable and accounts payable.

The two inputs to this run, both in invoice number order within warehouse sequence, are the sorted transaction output of run 200 and the invoice master file. The four outputs from this run are: (1) an updated invoice master file with the invoices for the current day added and collected invoices deleted; (2) a tape of internally created bookkeeping entries; (3) an edited-for-printing tape record of the daily cash receipts journal; and (4) a tape containing extracted materials receipts and accounts payable data.

Transactions in the first section of the tape from run 200 are processed against the input invoice master file, and the action indicated by the transaction input code is performed. Collected invoices are deleted and a record for the cash receipts journal is produced. Invoices for the current day are added to the file. These input transactions, as well as those in the second section of the tape from run 200, are examined by input code to determine whether bookkeeping entries should be created. If wanted, the correct entries are already generated; if no entries are wanted, the processing cycle is repeated. The transaction input tape is also scanned for material receipts and accounts payable data which are written on a separate tape to be used as input to run 225 in the accounts payable processing routine. The average time for set-up, take-down, and processing of run 205, with the same computer described above, is 8.6 minutes.

It would be possible to continue the description of each run for daily stores accounting and for accounting and inventory management

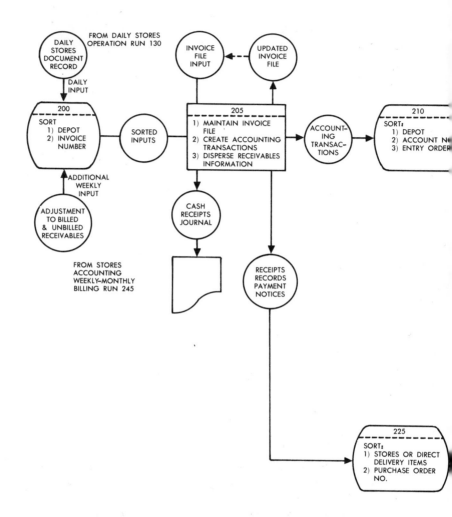

FIGURE 14-2. *Daily stores accounting*

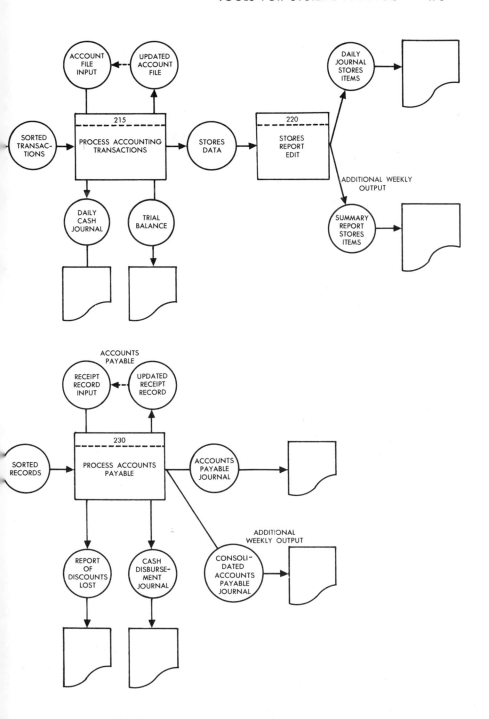

in order to summarize the processing times and find the machine loads. But the two runs described here indicate the general layout for computer runs. Much work remains, of course, to fill in the detail by flow charting and coding the runs in order to reduce them to actual operations.

FLOW CHARTS

Flow charts, data collection sheets, and additional tools are used for studying data-processing systems. They are covered in detail here because of their importance. In case you wish either to refresh your memory or to study flow charts for manual systems as a foundation for studying flow charts for an automatic data-processing system, a brief description is given near the end of this chapter.

Flow charts show the documents, machines, areas, and actions that make up a given data-processing system. Unique symbols used for each major class of items are connected with lines and arrows to represent the flow of documents, data, information, and action. Flow charts covering three major areas are discussed here, the three areas being:

1. Structure of a data-processing system
2. Structure and technique of a data-processing system
3. Instruction routine

Structure Flow Charts

Structure flow charts are used in the general design of a system. They deal with the types, times, and quantities of input, processing, files, and output without indicating how jobs are performed.

A flow chart of the system structure might show that inventory on hand is needed as an input, but without specifying whether it should be on a typed list, punched cards, or magnetic tape. The chart represents the information and data needs of an organization.

Only a few simple symbols are needed, as shown and described in Figure 14-3. Figure 14-4 is a sample of a flow chart dealing with the structure of a system. It shows the scheme for checking inventory to find items that are below the re-order point. File F-1 contains the number of pieces on hand and on order for each inventory item. File F-2 contains the re-order level for each item. The quantity and re-order files can, of course, be combined into one.

Main Flow. The flow in the main path of action is represented by arrows entering at the top of a symbol and leaving at the bottom. Lines to represent data entering or leaving the files are shown at the sides of the symbols. Action lines may leave the sides of a decision symbol to show that the line of action branches into two choices. These conventions make the main path of action easier to follow.

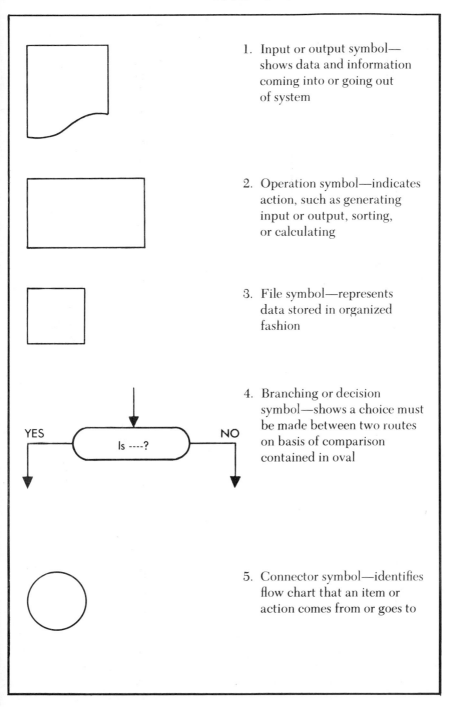

1. Input or output symbol— shows data and information coming into or going out of system

2. Operation symbol—indicates action, such as generating input or output, sorting, or calculating

3. File symbol—represents data stored in organized fashion

4. Branching or decision symbol—shows a choice must be made between two routes on basis of comparison contained in oval

5. Connector symbol—identifies flow chart that an item or action comes from or goes to

FIGURE 14-3. *Symbols for flow charting structure*

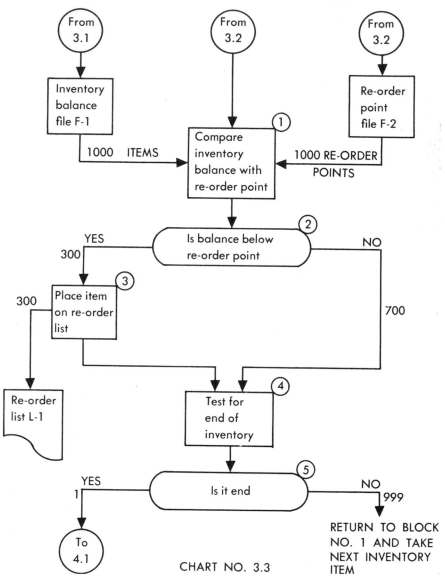

FIGURE 14-4. *Flow chart of structure for inventory re-order procedure*

Identification.   Major blocks, documents, and files are given identification numbers. The same numbers should be used on all flow charts and work load sheets to identify the same item. Inventory-on-hand file "F-1" should appear as "F-1" on the flow chart that shows posting of receipts and withdrawals, and also on the sheet that describes the makeup of the file for inventory on hand.

Quantities.   Flow charts should show the number of times that each path is followed. The two 1000's beside the arrows going into block 1 mean that the inventory contains 1,000 items. Of course, 1,000 re-order points are needed.

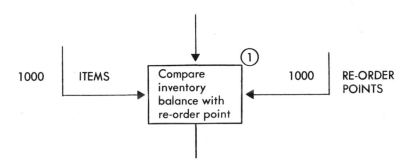

The numbers 700 and 300 by the decision symbol, block 2, indicate that, on average, 700 items are above the re-order point and follow the "no" path because no further action is required. The other 300 items are below the re-order point and follow the "yes" path to the re-order action. Volume figures are valuable later for figuring work load, file size, and processing times.

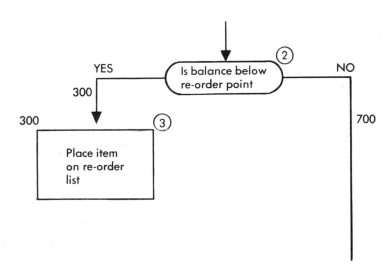

Repetitive Loops.   Repetition of a loop may be indicated by a note, "Return to block 1 and take next item." This loop is repeated 999 times for 1,000 items.

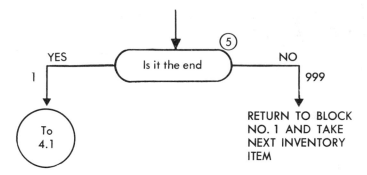

A line can be drawn from the decision point to the desired operations or connector symbols, which can be used to indicate the return points.

Branching and Merging.   Action lines split in two directions at blocks 2 and 5, dependent upon the results of prior processing. One line of action may branch into three, four, or many lines. If the branching scheme involves the three choices of positive, negative, or zero, the diagram is as follows:

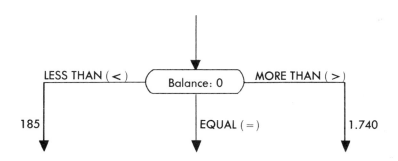

Merging, the opposite of branching, occurs at block 4. Here, the two lines of action that branched at block 2 come back together. The "no" branch of block 2 goes directly to block 4. The "yes" branch passes through operation 3.

Each branch may pass through many, several, or no operations and then merge. The two branches of block 5, on the other hand, do not merge again.

Common Elements.   Flow charting discloses common elements that otherwise might be overlooked. The first chart drawn for the inventory re-order procedure might have one end-of-inventory test and decision block on the "no" branch of block 2. A second test may be

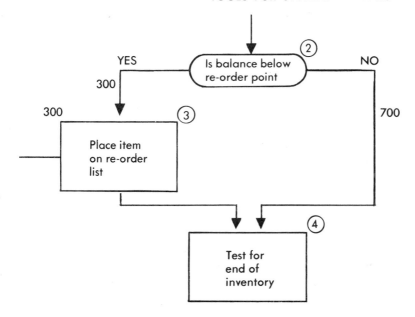

made after block 3. A flow chart discloses that tests for the end-of-inventory condition are common elements in two lines of action. The analyst can merge the two lines of action in the next draft of his chart so that only one test for the end of inventory is required, as shown here.

A flow chart, being only tentative when first drawn, is a tool for discovering and developing improvements. Each new draft may reveal simplifications and improvements.

Connectors.   Connector symbols above files F-1 and F-2 identify the charts that show how these files originated or were previously processed. Symbols below the re-order list developed from operation block 3 mean that its next use is described on chart 4.1. Similarly, the connector at block 5 means that this procedure continues on chart 4.1.

The precise method used to perform a job is irrelevant at this stage. The file of re-order points may be in a book, on punched cards, on magnetic tape, or in a random-access storage unit of a data processor. Comparison of the balance on hand and the re-order point may be made by a clerk, a punched-card collator, or a computer. For this reason, a flow chart of the structure is useful to sketch the general design of a system.

Structure and Technique Flow Charts

Flow charts showing structure and technique represent data and information requirements and the particular methods of fulfilling them. Flow charts of the desired system structure are used often as the basis for charts of structure and technique. These flow charts show the media

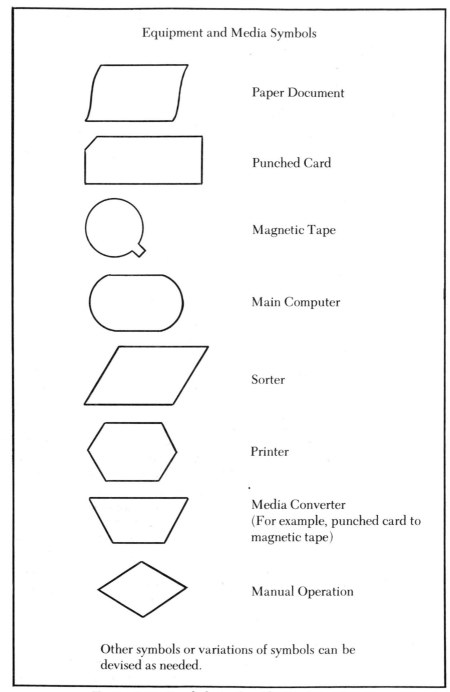

Figure 14-5. *Symbols for flow charts of structure and technique*

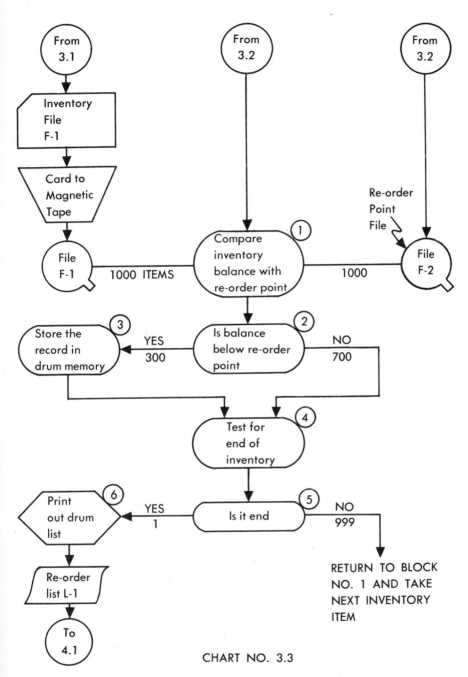

CHART NO. 3.3

FIGURE 14-6. *Flow chart of technique for inventory re-order procedure*

used for input and output, and the files and types of processing equipment are indicated. A separate set of flow charts is required for each set of equipment considered. Flow charts of structure and technique differ in several important ways from the charts for structure discussed above:

1. The media and equipment are specified for the input, output, and operations.
2. A particular technique often requires modifying the structure already developed.
3. More varied symbols are used to represent many aspects of technique.

Additional symbols that may be useful for flow charting structure and technique are shown in Figure 14-5. This list is not complete and other symbols should be added as needed, although numerous detailed symbols may increase confusion rather than simplify systems analysis. A few words of explanation on a flow chart often replace the need for a special symbol.

Manufacturers supply plastic templates containing symbols useful for drawing flow charts for systems designed around their equipment. A template permits drawing symbols quickly and neatly and, not incidentally, it probably orients the user to that manufacturer.

The structure for the inventory ordering procedure shown earlier is reduced to one particular technique in Figure 14-6. The technique shown assumes that file F-1 is originally on punched cards, and F-2 is on magnetic tape. The re-order point test is made by an electronic computer that takes only magnetic tape as input. Of course, several other techniques might be used to handle inventory re-order procedure.

A chart of instruction routine shows each separate machine step needed to solve a problem and is used as a guide for detailed programming. It generally is an expansion of the flow chart of structure and technique. A systems analyst is more interested in instruction routine flow charts if he follows through to the coding stage. Flow charts of instruction routines were treated in Chapters 3 and 8.

Levels of Detail

Flow charts can contain different levels of detail. A general outline of operations may be prepared first to help plan and control further analysis of large operations. A general outline concentrates on the major divisions of the operation and contains little detail. More detail is required in flow charts as system design progresses. Many levels of detail are required for flow charting large-scale operations, whereas one set of flow charts with only one level of detail may serve for small-scale operations.

General flow charts showing few details are useful for summary purposes. Summary charts that show major steps in order to keep overall relationships clear may cover many pages for a large application.

They help guide the preparation of detailed flow charts. Three levels of detail are illustrated here. Figure 14-7 is a sample procedure for weekly inventory processing. The chart contains only three major operations and the associated files, input, and output. Each block contains a reference to a more detailed flow chart, since the degree of detail possible here is inadequate for system design work.

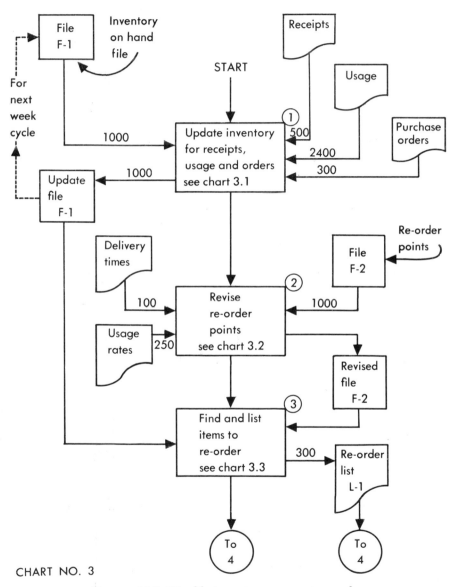

CHART NO. 3

FIGURE 14-7. *Weekly inventory processing cycle*

Figure 14-8 is a more detailed flow chart of operations contained in block 1 of the prior exhibit and is labeled "Chart 3.1." Connector symbols on this chart refer to Charts 3.2 and 3.3 which give details for

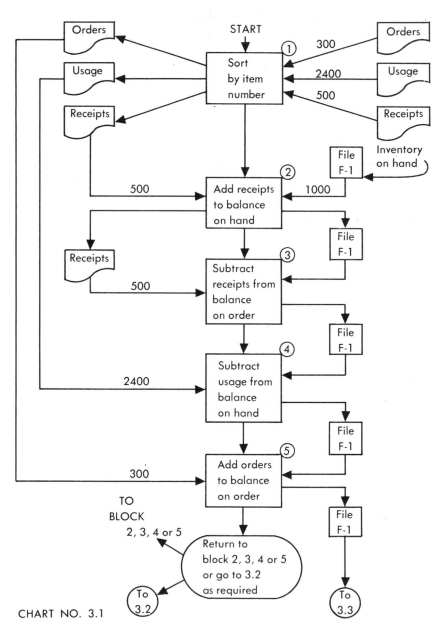

FIGURE 14-8. *Posting weekly transactions to inventory balance*

blocks 2 and 3. More detail is needed for some design work. Figure 14-9 is a further level of detail for block 2 of Chart 3.1. Twenty or thirty charts with this degree of detail may be needed to cover the operations contained on Chart 3. The person preparing the machine instructions routine might draw up a chart with even more detail than Chart 3.1-2 reflects.

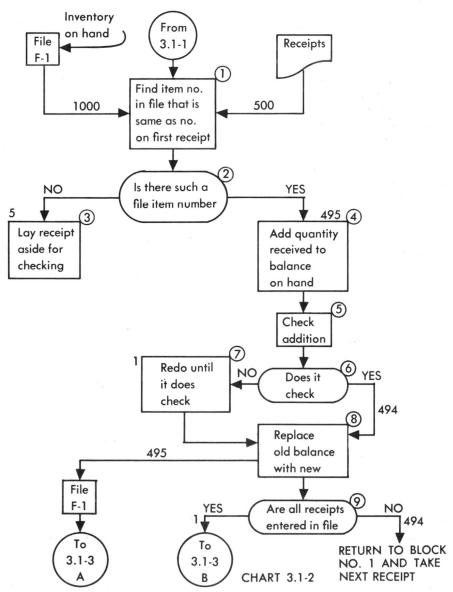

FIGURE 14-9. *Addition of receipts to balance on hand*

Considerations for Flow Charting

Accuracy, simplicity, and understandability are prime considerations in preparing flow charts. "Simplicity" means all relevant facts are presented as clearly as possible.

Frequent explanatory comments, even brief ones, are helpful in following a flow chart. Files, input, output, and operations should be labeled. Skeletal flow charts showing only lines, numbers, and symbols are frequently used for scientific problems; but more detail is desirable for charting business problems.

The flow-chart symbols used in this chapter are merely illustrative. A study team should select the set or sets of symbols best suited to its use. Some flow-charting instructions recommend different sets of symbols for charting the present system, the general plan of the proposed system, and the detail for the proposed system.

As a result of using different sets of symbols, one symbol may have two or three meanings. Equally confusing, several symbols may have the same meaning. Such complexity should be avoided and only a limited number of symbols used, each with a unique meaning.

Conflicting sets of symbols, however, are hard to avoid. An equipment manufacturer's symbols are used to simplify discussion with his representatives alone, at the risk of confusing the study team. On the other hand, the use of a single set of symbols for all systems designed for various equipment might confuse equipment representatives. The adoption of a uniform set of symbols for use within an organization simplifies systems analysis and internal communication problems.

Identification of all the inputs, outputs, operations, flow charts, and documents is useful in systems analysis and design. Documents and files should have a number or some other non-ambiguous identification for use for all references to them. Actions, files, or other items dealt with on two or more flow charts should be cross referenced. Charts at various levels of detail for the same operation should be cross referenced to each other. Extreme care is necessary to keep all the relations and details straight.

Other Flow-chart Forms

Many variations of flow charts exist. A "routine sequence diagram," for example, has a column for each organizational unit. The path of a document and action on it are shown in appropriate columns. Departmental files are also indicated. Action taken in each department is listed on the diagram or separately. Routine sequence diagrams show each action's over-all effect and define the relationships among departments.

Block diagrams are another common type of flow chart. A "block diagram," in the strict sense, is a chart containing square or rectangular blocks connected with lines. Each block is labeled with the name of a unit or component. Block diagrams are used to provide simple descriptions of complex electric and electronic equipment.

DATA SHEETS

A first step in system design is to determine the basic structure. Next, the characteristics of input, output, reference, and transfer data should be recorded in an orderly and complete manner.

Transfer data are the output of one machine process that is used as input at another stage. The essentials of input, output, and files important for systems analysis are:

1. Description of type and arrangement of data

2. Source, use, and destination of an item

3. Media—manual or typed, punched-card, or other medium

4. Average and peak volumes

Facts about these features are useful for estimating file size and work loads, for timing machine operations, and for preparing general flow charts.

Machine operating time for a job is an important factor in selecting efficient equipment. Programmers need information on data arrangement, volume, and requirements to prepare a program so that they can develop operating time estimates.

Data sheets useful for collecting and organizing facts about input, output, reference, and transfer data are illustrated and described here. Other versions of data sheets may be more suitable for a particular use, but the principles are the same.

Input Data Sheets

Input data sheets often are concerned with two or more types of media. Input operations, as pointed out in Chapter 4, consist of two stages. The pre-input stage includes the conversion of written and printed data into some processable form. The input stage includes the read-in of data to the processor. Most business data are written or typed and must be converted to cards or tape. In some cases cards are first punched and then converted to magnetic tape for input.

INPUT DATA SHEET

1. Name: WEEKLY PARTS USAGE REPORT

2. Obtained from: __STOCK CONTROL__   Chart No. ___37___

3. Sequence: ASCENDING BY PART NUMBER

4. Type of media: 80 COL. PUNCHED CARDS

5. Use: _TO UPDATE INVENTORY FILE_   Chart No. 3 AND 71
        AND ALLOCATE COST

6. Schedule: _CUT OFF SAT. NITE -- PROCESSED EACH TUESDAY_

7. Number of transactions: Maximum __4100__ Average __2400__

8.   Transaction Description

Field No.	Field Description	No. of Char. Max.	Ave.	Ave. Use	Wtd. Ave.	Comments
1.	PART NUMBER	10	6	100%	6	
2.	STOCKROOM NUMBER	3	3	100%	3	
3.	QUANTITY WITHDRAWN	5	2	100%	2	
4.	CHARGE NUMBER	4	4	100%	4	
5.	CAPITAL ACC'T. NO.	4	4	10%	0.4	USED ONLY FOR NON-EXPENDABLE ITEMS

9. Total Data Characters	26		15.4
10. Field and Transaction symbols	5		5.
11. Total	31		20.4

12. New Media Type __MAG. TAPE__   Amount Req. _____

FIGURE 14-10.   *Input data sheet*

Figure 14-10 is a sample input data sheet. The items are explained briefly, although many are self-explanatory.

1. *Name*: Title, label, or some identification of input.

2. *Obtained from*: Area or person originating or last handling the data. Usage cards were filled out in the stock room, key punched, and sorted. *Chart No.* describes data origination.

3. *Sequence*: Order of input—ascending, descending, or unordered.

4. *Types of Media*: Forms in which data are obtained.

5. *Use*: Processing procedure that will use input.
   Chart No. is a flow chart of the processing procedure.

6. *Schedule*: How often and when input arrives and is processed.

7. *No. of Transactions:* Maximum—largest number of transactions that will arrive in one peak-volume cycle. Average—typical number of transactions expected in an operating cycle. The maximum may be several times as large as average, if the volume fluctuates greatly.

8. *Transaction Description*
   Record—a set of one or more related fields. An inventory record contains fields for the part number, part name, quantity on hand, and quantity on order.
   Field—a set of one or more characters in a unit of data, such as part number.
   No. of Characters—maximum and average number of characters to represent data contained in a field.
   Average Use—percentage of time that a particular field contains any data. Some fields may be restricted to exceptional cases.
   Weighted Character—average number of characters multiplied by the average use. Represents the average amount of data in a field.

9. *Total Data Characters*: Totals of the maximum and weighted average number of characters in the record description.

10. *Field and Transaction Symbols*: The number of special characters used by some equipment as symbols to indicate end of field and end of record should be counted.

11. *Total*: Over-all total for data and symbols.

12. *New Media Type and Amount*: Type and amount of media used for input to the next processing stage.

Reference Data Sheets

Reference data sheets describe the contents of files. Most of the headings are similar to those used for input data. The requirement for updating, which is new, explains the procedure for keeping the file up-to-date.

Output Data Sheets

Output data sheets, like others, involve a conversion from one medium to another. Some points must be specified to get output in the desired format:

(a) *Media*—printed reports, paper tape or magnetic tape, and punched cards

(b) *Form*—continuous standard page, special document, or variable-length groups

(c) *Size*—page size or width of continuous output

(d) *Pages*—number of pages, if any, in report

(e) *Lines per page*—number of lines per page

(f) *Copies*—number of copies required

(g) *Pre-printed form no.*—reference to form pre-printed with heading and other standard data

FLOW CHARTS FOR MANUAL SYSTEMS

The remainder of this chapter is devoted to a case study of the manual procedures actually used by a successful shoe manufacturer for filling customers' orders. This case should show the relationship between systems analysis of manual and automatic processing methods. Since this case constitutes a separate unit in the chapter, it can be omitted without loss of continuity.

The Brown Shoe Company manufactures 150 styles of children's shoes in widths AA to EEE and sizes 2 to 13 and 1 to 3; but not all widths are made in all sizes. In total, about 5,000 shoes in six price lines are involved. Shoes are manufactured on production orders for cases of 24 pairs of shoes of one style, width, and size at the rate of 667 cases per day throughout the year. Peak sales to retailers occur around Easter and in September. The difference between production and sales rates goes into (or comes out of) inventory, which is now (May) about 500,000 pairs. The inventory of each shoe style is supposed to be about one month's sales. The manufacturing cycle is about seven days for selecting shoes to be produced, preparing production orders, calculating leather requirements and costs, and selecting and cutting leather. The manufacturing cycle is ordinarily about four weeks. Small numbers of cases or individual shoes can be "expressed" through the factory in about one week from the initial planning to completion of the shoes.

Sales range from about 3,000 to 36,000 pairs of shoes a day with Monday (including Saturday) sales about six times as great as Friday sales. It is a long-established policy to ship shoes on the same day that an order is received, except that Saturday's orders are filled Monday because of the five-day work week. It is equally well established that *no* order will be shipped incomplete. To facilitate prompt, complete

THE BROWN SHOE COMPANY
Boston, Maine

Conf. No. **236**

Ship to **Sleyof's Shoes**

City **406 Main, Manchester, Texas**

When Ship **1/3/--**

Dept. No. **25**

Mail

Invoice to **Same**

Date **12/28/--**

How Ship **Express**

Stock No.	Pairs Ordered	Pairs Shipped	√	Width	2	3	4	5	6	7	8	9	10	11	12	13	1	2	3	Price	Amount
0876	1	1		C			1														
	1	1		D			1														
	2	2		E			1		1												
8626	3	3		B						2	1										
	8	8		C						1 1 1 1	1										
	1	1		D						1											
4220	10	10		B								1 1 1 1		1 1						
	14	14		C								1 1 1 1		1 1 1						
	4	4		D								1		1 1	1					
	6	6		A												1 1 1 1		1			

Figure 14-11. *Order form filled in by customer*

order filling, customers have been educated to retain one copy of an order form supplied by Brown and send two copies. A typical order is shown in Figure 14-11. Some facts about the volume of orders are: (1) 100 to 300 sales per day, (2) 60 lines per sales order, and (3) 2.5 pairs of shoes per line on a sales order.

Processing a customer's order, an investigation discloses, involves the following departments and operations:

Sales Department:

1. Scan orders from customer for special requests for catalogues, order books, or other items.
2. Check customer's credit rating and mark "O.K." and continue processing, or "Refused" and return to the customer.
3. Count tally marks for pairs of shoes on order and list the total number of pairs on the original copy.
4. Post the number of pairs ordered and date to a memo card for the customer and store the card.
5. Deliver both copies of the customer's order to stock control.
6. After shipment, use original customer order to find memo card to show the number of pairs of shoes shipped.
7. File original customer order.

Stock Control:

1. Recopy onto Brown's forms any orders not on Brown's form, or a facsimile, or in duplicate.
2. Edit the original copy and carbon of an order for similarity and legibility.
3. Add the totals shown by customer on style-width lines to find the total number of shoes on order and list on carbon copy of order.
4. Reconcile differences in two counts of shoes on order, if original and carbon are different.
5. Separate the two copies and send carbon to order-filling department.
6. Time stamp the original copy.
7. Tally readers read the original copy of the order (style, width, and size) and tally clerks mark the tally sheet—two girls (reader and tally marker) deal with about one-fourth of the shoes.
8. Send original copy of each order to the billing department.
9. Tally sheets are summarized at end of the day for sales summary report by style (which is expected by 5 p.m.) and posted to inventory sheets in detail for each individual shoe.
10. Post production reports to inventory sheets.
11. Use sales report, inventory on hand and shoes in process, at end of day (expected by 6 p.m.), as basis for selecting shoes for issuing new production orders the next morning.
12. Adjust inventory records to count supplied by order-filling department. Substantial discrepancies are re-counted and reconciled.

Production Control:
1. Use sales report and inventory status to prepare production orders and release to factory.
2. Prepare production reports and send to stock control department.

Order Filling:
1. Pick shoes against the duplicate copy of a customer's order and place in a device like a bookcase on wheels that holds about 72 boxes. (Shoes are arranged on shelves made of packing boxes stacked three high and four long that each hold shoe boxes stacked 2 deep, 6 high, and 12 wide. Shoes are arranged by style with smaller and lower-priced shoes at one end of the room. Ordinarily about 12 to 48 boxes of one shoe are placed on these active shelves and additional boxes are placed in inactive storage).
2. One person reads the style, size, and width from box while a listener reads the order and checks for accurate order-filling.
3. Report inventory of shoes (style, width, and size) each six months to stock control.

Shipping Department:
1. Use duplicate copy of each order as the basis for making two copies of a packing sheet which shows the quantity of each style of shoe in each price line (no identification of width and size). Packing sheet clerks stop work at 6 p.m. so that sheets are not prepared for shoes delivered to shipping room after that time.
2. Count the number of boxes and pack them into cartons; place a duplicate copy of the packing sheet in the carton; and ship to customers.
3. Send original copy of packing sheet to the billing department.

Billing Department:
1. Price each order-line on the original copy of customer's order, extend, and total.
2. Price each block (number of shoes in each style-price) on the original copy of packing sheet, extend, and total.
3. Reconcile discrepancies between totals in 1 and 2.
4. Prepare bills on billing machines.
5. Mail original copies of bills; file the copies.
6. Send the original copies of customers' orders to the sales department.
7. File packing sheet duplicate.

Personnel Involved:
1. Sales department—4 girls and supervisor
2. Stock control—8 girls and supervisor
3. Order filling—25 to 35 men and two supervisors
4. Shipping—8 men, 2 girls, and supervisor
5. Billing—4 girls

The set of symbols used here for drawing flow charts is as follows:

Symbols

◯   Handling operation

◎   Origination of document

⬗   Adding to a record

⇨   Transportation

▭   Inspection

▽   Storage

▣   Combined activity

Figure 14-12 shows the flow chart of manual-mechanical procedures for the Brown Shoe Company with the department involved. It gives a quick overview of the processing required for filling customers' orders.

The verbal description of Brown's procedures can be traced to the flow chart to see how raw facts are organized. The flow chart is useful as the foundation for designing a more intricate system involving automatic processing methods.

SUMMARY

The art of systems analysis involves collecting, organizing, and evaluating the facts about a system. Systems analysis considers the available data, management information requirements, the data-processing system, types of equipment, preparation required, and applications.

Analysts use various tools to keep straight the facts and figures for the complex relationships involved in a system. A "model" of a system can be created on paper for testing new ideas. Model building is not equivalent to experiments, but it can be less expensive and more fruitful than experiments on the real system.

A management survey examines the unit's objectives, programs, operating methods, practices, organization, and policies. An organization survey appraises the organization and proposes improvements in the division of work and relationships among individuals and units carrying out related objectives. A procedures survey reviews the way a job is done, the tools used, and the location of operations. It involves interviewing employees and supervisors, charting the organization and work flow, and analyzing forms and reports.

Most clerical and administrative action is based on forms and reports. They are analyzed to insure that they are prepared and used efficiently with minimum duplication of effort.

Performance analysis relates the units of work produced to the man-hours spent. This involves fixing a work unit, setting standards, gathering data on man-hours and output, computing productivity, and finding the areas that are below standard. If done well, performance analysis serves as the basis for administrative action.

Space and layout surveys deal with the placement of organizational units and the physical location of personnel and equipment within a unit. Work is traced from people to desks to files to find how much space, time, and transportation can be saved by eliminating detours, backtracking, and the poor use of equipment.

Flow charts and data sheets are important tools for analyzing data-processing systems. Flow charts show the documents, machines, areas, and action that compose a data-processing system. A unique symbol is used for each major class of items. Lines and arrows connect symbols to represent the flow of documents, data, information, and action.

Structure flow charts cover the types, times, and quantities of input, processing, files, and output for general design of a system. Lines show the main flow path from the top to the bottom of a page. Choices based on a comparison or a remainder exit from the sides of operation boxes. Unique identification is used throughout each file, operation, and elsewhere.

Facts on the volumes of data handled at each stage are used later to calculate work loads. Repetitive loops are indicated by a note, connector symbol, or line returning to the desired operation. Branching follows a course of action depending on the outcome of a comparison or a subtraction operation, whereas merging brings together separate paths that require the same operation. Common elements are disclosed by flow charting so that duplicate operations can be eliminated. Connector symbols identify charts that show how files originated or were last processed.

Structure and technique flow charts represent both data and information requirements and a particular method for fulfilling them so that a separate set of charts is required for each layout of equipment considered. The media and equipment are specified, and the structure developed earlier may be modified when charting structure and technique. The symbols are, of course, more detailed than those used in structural flow charting.

An instruction routine flow chart, which shows each distinct,

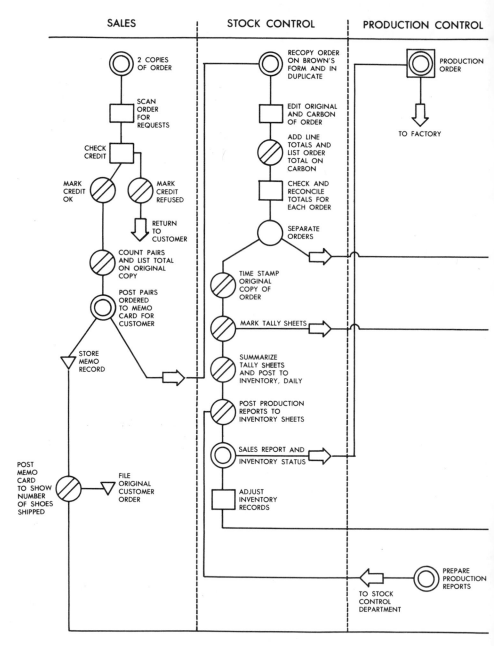

FIGURE 14-12. *Flow chart of manual-machine*
procedure showing departments

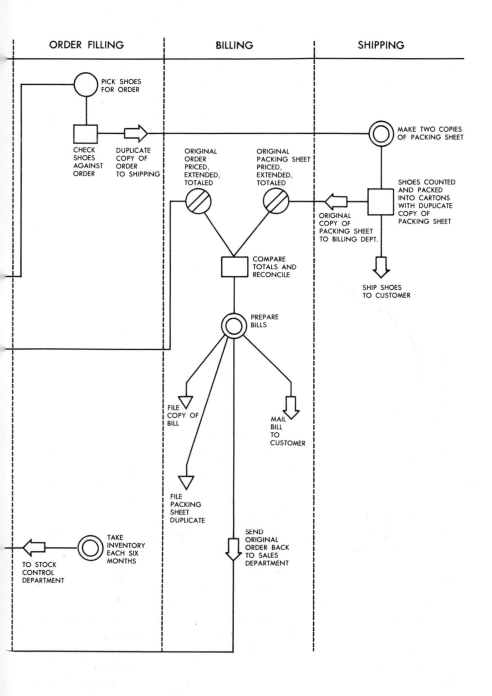

separate machine step needed to solve a problem, may be a direct expansion of a structure and technique flow chart.

The initial charts concentrate on the major divisions of an organization. Both the level of detail and the number of charts increase at each stage. Eventually, hundreds of detailed flow charts are prepared. Unique symbols, each with a single meaning, are imperative for the preparation of simple, useful flow charts. Conflicts may develop from using each manufacturer's set of symbols in flow charting for his equipment, but identification, explanatory comment, and cross references help keep relations straight.

Routine sequence diagrams are also useful for studying the flow of documents and data and the relationships among departments. Block diagrams are simple, basic flow charts.

Data sheets collect facts about input, reference, transfer, and output data. The necessary facts are type and arrangement of data, source and destination of item, media, and peak and average volume. Such facts are useful for programming, when they are later used for timing and balancing machine operations. Data sheets are invaluable for gathering facts about input, reference, and output for a system.

REFERENCES AND SUPPLEMENTAL READINGS

Hitch, Charles. "An Appreciation of Systems Analysis," *Journal of the Operations Research Society of America*, vol. 8: 466-81 (November 1955). (See the annotation for this reference at the end of Chapter 10.)

Kircher, Paul. "Integration of Data-Processing Requirements and the Design of Electronic Equipment," *The Controller*, vol. 24: 107-110 (March 1956). In the past, electronic devices were developed before the accounting systems that were designed to be used with the devices. Today, the emphasis has shifted to the study of business requirements in order to provide a basis for the development of electronic systems. The author suggests the need for a scientific approach to the design of management information systems. Business data are traditionally classified by function, such as financing, purchasing, and personnel administration. An approach is offered in which decision-making requirements provide the basis for classification. The categories would be: (1) strategical programming (determination of long-range plans), (2) tactical programming (determination of short-range plans), (3) scheduling (assigning of duties: personnel, machine), and (4) operating (on-the-spot decisions relating to particular situations).

Laubach, Peter B. *Company Investigations of Automatic Data Processing*, Boston, Graduate School of Business Administration, Harvard University, 1957, 258 pp. A case study of approaches taken by various companies in investigating data-processing needs to determine what equipment, if any, they should get. A brief introduction touches on computers, their operation, and use. Three chapters deal with the Lee Company's preparation for automatic data processing, training of personnel, and equipment survey and installation planning. Experience of many other companies is sketched out in two long chapters. Part Three gives some aspects of the survey and an evaluation of automatic data-processing methods. Individual chapters deal with project organization; use of committees, consultants, and manufacturers' representatives; selection of an application; cost and savings estimates; equipment selection and acquisition, management, and operating support. The concluding chapter deals with benefits of automatic processing methods and discusses survey and evaluation methods.

Toan, Arthur B., Jr. "General Principles of System Work," *The New York Certified Public Accountant*, vol. 22: 599-605 (October 1952). (See the annotation for this reference at the end of Chapter 11.)

Wooldridge, Dean E. "Trends in Electronic Business Data Systems Development," pp. 16-22 in *Proceedings of the Western Computer Conference: Trends in Computers—Automatic Control and Data Processing*, New York, American Institute of Radio Engineers, 1954. Wooldridge treats "systems analysis" from the point of view of the processes involved in order to perform a suitable marriage between (a) the requirements of business establishments and (b) the techniques of the electronics engineer. The procedure and equipment devised should solve the problems of business rather than imaginary problems the engineer thinks the business should solve. Engineers and scientists use an analytic approach at first but divert their attention to developing new components and devices. Hindsight often shows that more analysis is needed before building "hardware." Business systems are subject to more mistakes resulting from insufficient analysis than are military systems. This is because (a) objectives are more difficult to specify, (b) businesses have long histories and many people with fixed notions, prejudices, and traditions, and (c) scientists and engineers generally have had little experience in business and are misled by the language of business. Several important examples of mistakes in systems analysis are given.

Workshop for Management. *Proceedings of the Eighth Annual Systems Meeting*, Systems and Procedures Association of America, New York, Management Magazines, Inc., Book Division, 1956, 499 pp. This conference dealt with three major topics: (a) general management techniques, such as work simplification and procedures analysis, (b) electronic data processing, and (c) operations research. In the area of electronic data processing, speeches or seminars covered such subjects as: (a) information handling with modern communication facilities, (b) organizing for an electronic study, (c) a survey of general-purpose computers, (d) personnel training, and (e) integrated data processing. Case studies were included that discuss (a) IBM 702, IBM 705, and UNIVAC installations, (b) production planning and inventory control applications, and (c) accounting and billing applications.

PART SIX

EQUIPMENT
ACQUISITION
AND UTILIZATION

CHAPTER FIFTEEN

FEASIBILITY STUDY

Earlier discussion has made it clear that setting up an effective automatic data-processing system is a complex and lengthy job. A detailed and carefully organized plan for examining and weighing both facts and opinions is necessary. Many policy and operating decisions that involve large amounts of money must be made, for long-run commitments are involved: the indirect long-run commitments are likely to exceed the direct, immediate outlay for equipment.

The steps involved in any important change in a system can be considered in the following order:

1. Feasibility study—preliminary process of determining the over-all suitability of applying data processors to specific operations
2. Applications study—detailed process of designing a system or set of procedures for using data processors for a selected function or operation and establishing the specifications for equipment suitable to the needs
3. Equipment acquisition proposal—recommendation for management action supported by feasibility and applications studies and other facts
4. Procurement—arrangements necessary to buy or rent equipment and supporting facilities
5. Preparation for installation—site preparation, training, programming, organization adjustments, testing, debugging, and communications arrangements
6. Parallel operations and conversion—a period during which the old system (if one was in use) and the new system are operated concurrently until adequacy of the new is proved

The feasibility study involves analysis of the data-processing requirements of an organization and the equipment that is available to determine whether the new equipment and related system for data processing appear to be more efficient than the system in use.

Starting with a period of orientation and training and then pursuing the over-all and detailed investigation, the study group will reach one of two conclusions at the end of the feasibility study. One possible conclusion is that the present system seems better than any new system studied. The study group has two choices following this conclusion. First, additional systems may be examined in case any were overlooked originally or any new developments occurred during the study period. Second, if all available systems were studied with care and none found superior to the existing system, the feasibility study should be discontinued pending new developments that merit consideration.

The other conclusion possible as a result of the feasibility study is that one or more new systems appear to be better than the present system. If the feasibility study group reaches the second conclusion, it may proceed to the next phase by starting the applications study.

The feasibility study is important to the success of a prospective system, for initial decisions affect all future actions. A decision that an automatic system is not suitable is all-important because it may be the only one ever made. An early conclusion that a proposed system will be highly profitable may cause important factors to be overlooked later. In any case, the outcome of the feasibility study should not be taken lightly. The feasibility study is an extremely important step in a time-consuming and complicated process. One valuable by-product of such a study derives from the discipline required of analysts in making it.

The inter-relationships of the many systems that make up the data-information structure must be examined. An integrated approach requires the highest and most thorough effort by the systems analysts and management conducting the study. In fact, the terms "automatic" and "integrated" data-processing systems are often used interchangeably. A sound feasibility study cannot be approached on a piecemeal basis, but all systems that are included in the operation must be considered.

Other improvements that can and should be made may obviate the need for an automatic system. The feasibility of installing an automatic system should be determined only after taking into consideration all reasonably practicable improvements in procedures and systems that can be made without going to an automatic system.

ORIENTATION

The first few weeks or months spent considering a new data-processing system will generally be confusing. Initially, little or nothing may be known about either the desired features of the new system or the available equipment and procedures.

Management may be unable to decide how extensive the change should be or how much to spend on a new system. As a result, early phases focus on bringing order into an uncertain situation. The initial task is to obtain an understanding of unsolved problems and how to deal with them, rather than to make system changes or merely buy equipment.

Obtaining Support

One of the most vital preliminary steps for the people who are planning a feasibility study, as in the case of any significant undertaking, is to obtain management support and establish good employee relations.

Support of top management can be obtained by suitable presentations, orientations, and briefings. Top management support is vital because of long periods of time involved in the fact gathering and detailed systems analysis that follow a feasibility study. Support is also required to bring about the organizational and procedural adjustments necessary to improve the system. The point should be made crystal clear to all concerned that top management wants effective results from the study.

The initiation of feasibility studies may alarm the staff and working force because of the traditional belief that machines replace people. Employees should be completely informed in order to obtain their full cooperation. They can be reassured by a policy that any resultant personnel adjustments will be absorbed by attrition or minimized by reassignment in preference to any reduction in force. Experience indicates that some employees will be retrained and reassigned within the organization to higher-paying jobs; others may be shifted sideways or downward.

Preliminary Study Group

The first step in starting a feasibility study should be to determine the objectives of the study; then people can be assigned to the project. An accountant from the comptroller's department, a systems or industrial engineer, and an operating department head might work together. One person should be given primary responsibility to keep the study going, while others may serve on a part-time or full-time basis. A group with diverse interests can establish close liaison throughout the organization, understand the problems, and compensate for the biases of individual members.

One or more members of the feasibility study group should become familiar with operations and gain an understanding of the major problems faced by each section. If practical, at least one member should have gained several years' experience at the location being studied.

One member of the group should become familiar with data-processing equipment and modern business control procedures, if there is no one already familiar with them. He can read books and articles dealing with equipment and its application to similar situations. First-hand discussion with more experienced users is invaluable; they often can describe good and bad features of equipment under operating conditions. Classes, conferences, and seminars on data-processing equipment, programming, and methods should be attended. Every member of the feasibility study group will want a good comprehension of the data-information requirements of the organization and of data-processing techniques. At this stage, group members need not be expert programmers or specialists in company organization and operation. But they do need to understand the abilities and limitations of data-processing problems, equipment, and methods. At least one member should have detailed knowledge about each area.

Preliminary Investigation.   Preliminary investigation in a feasibility study should be completed within a few months. The study group should determine the following:

1. Requirements for data processing and information now and in the near future
2. Available equipment and methods
3. Estimated costs in personnel, time, and money to complete the feasibility study
4. Estimates of costs and benefits for a complete study and installation—supported, if possible, by the experience of other organizations

The study group should keep management informed by means of oral and written reports. Management ordinarily is not very familiar with the technical aspects of data-processing systems; but management should be able to make a decision, based on the feasibility study preliminary report, as to whether it is interested in a project having costs and benefits as indicated. If management is not willing to undertake the project, then the feasibility study should be terminated or shelved awaiting further developments. The expense of further study alone, however, will seldom be sufficient cause for shelving a project.

The risk of loss from over-extending a study is often small compared with the gains obtainable from important system improvements. If the study is continued but leads to the decision that change is not feasible, only the cost of the study is lost. On the other hand, large potential benefits may be lost from stopping the study prematurely.

OVER-ALL INVESTIGATION

Over-all investigation requires setting the objectives, defining the problem, and organizing the feasibility study. Personnel must be obtained and educated. A proper balance is needed between experience with the operations under study, knowledge of the new kinds of equipment to be used, and the experience of others in tackling similar problems. The long-range study undertaken by one company is described by Woellner (1956).

Selection of Objectives

Management may reach the conclusion, based on the preliminary study, that an extended feasibility study should be made. In such a case, the study group's preliminary report may help to select the objectives. As the study progresses, it may be desirable to modify the objectives or even to change them completely.

Careful selection of objectives for the extended feasibility study is important. The objectives selected influence the nature of the end-product; and the advantages and disadvantages of each possible objective should be determined. The probable results of each objective are examined to see if they are desirable. For example, an emphasis on up-to-the-minute information may result in a very high-cost system. Unless very timely information has a high value, it is not a good primary objective for the systems study.

Objectives should become real working guides for the detailed feasibility study. The comprehensive objective of increasing company profits makes relevant for study any and all operations that affect the cost of processing data and the value obtained from information. This creates a problem: although a broad approach is desirable for obtaining the best system, it may introduce complexities beyond the time and money budgeted for the feasibility study group.

One simple way to identify areas for further analysis is to list important users, processors, and suppliers of data in the organization. For each unit, consider the following items:

1. Reports and documents produced by or for the unit
2. Data collected within the unit or obtained by it
3. Processing done by the unit or for it
4. Volume, cost, and time requirements for items 1 through 3
5. Requirements imposed by external conditions that are easy or difficult to change
6. Internal changes desirable for this organizational unit, such as a larger quantity of information, more current or cheaper information

Study of these factors can be recorded in simple block diagrams, flow charts, and data sheets. The object is merely to identify areas that are worth further consideration. Excessive detail is neither necessary nor desirable.

Another approach to selecting areas for study is to start with the obvious targets for improvements. Such operations may, by themselves, justify new equipment and a new system. Other areas should be included in the study because of the large capacity of equipment. Obvious target areas are characterized by a high volume or by repetitive operations with high clerical costs.

Within the U.S. Army Ordnance Corps, computer applications for business-type operations include the following activities by functional area:

1. *Supply activities*
   (a) Stock accounting (maintenance of stock record accounts at depots)
   (b) Financial inventory accounting
   (c) Stock fund
   (d) Maintenance of national availability (daily availability and processing demands)
   (e) Requirement studies
   (f) Supply cataloguing
   (g) Parts consumption and rebuild
   (h) Ordnance supply analysis
   (i) Technical materials and equipment (materials for testing and/or manufacturing, station property, etc.)
2. *Command management and accounting activities*
   (a) Command management reporting
   (b) Production control and scheduling
   (c) Cost accounting (labor and matériel distribution)
   (d) Budget and financial accounting
   (e) Personnel management
   (f) Payroll
3. *Industrial activities*
   (a) Procurement and contract status
   (b) Product-contractor evaluation
   (c) Packaging
   (d) Standardization
   (e) Mobilization planning
4. *Engineering drawings activities*
   (a) Parts list
   (b) Generation breakdown
   (c) Cross-reference files
   (d) Data for standardization

Definition of Problem

The object and scope of the feasibility study should be defined in writing in the form of a charter. Careful definition is important because of the fact that the study will cut across organizational lines as well as require authority for suggesting possible changes in procedures, forms, reports, or organization. It is also important to insure a constancy of direction in view of the lengthy, time-consuming process involved and intervening changes in management and supervisory personnel; the charter reduces the probability of branching off on tangents.

A time-phased plan is necessary to provide goals and priorities in order to bring the study to a satisfactory conclusion. A charter also permits review of the progress achieved. In any event, responsibility for the study should be fixed firmly and adequate authority, staff, and resources assigned.

Organization of Study

Organizing to make the study involves decisions about the composition, ability, and education of the working group, and whether to use consultants.

Working Group. The group that made the initial feasibility study and report may continue work to complete the study as a working group. Additional people will be needed, but the original group members should be retained, if possible, because of their initial study experience.

The conduct of the feasibility study requires full-time effort by those selected to carry it out. It is preferable to select carefully the individuals who will logically be assigned to later applications studies. Electric accounting machine specialists are useful to the effort. It is desirable to assign people who plan to remain with the organization, for continuity is highly important in view of the extensive preliminary training requirements.

The chairman of such a group should be extremely well qualified, on a broad scale, in the functions and operations of the entire organization. He should be able personally to plan and carry out this major effort. The following special personal qualifications are desirable:

1. Ability to communicate convincingly and persuasively
2. High degree of ability to reason and think logically
3. Ability to work with varied groups that represent diverse functions and processes
4. Knowledge and experience in the functional areas involved

Working members should be in the supervisory or executive category. Management engineers or analysts, as well as people experienced in various functional fields, are excellent for such working groups.

Education of Working Group. Briefly, the working group should be trained in the fundamentals of electronic data-processing so that they can understand the capabilities and limitations of electronic equipment. Certain members should be trained in computer programming techniques. Members should study the technical literature of the field and keep informed on new and possible future developments in methods and machines. Each level of management should receive appropriate education or orientation from one or more of the following: equipment manufacturers, other equipment users, systems specialists, and the working group.

Courses given by manufacturers, universities, and service schools should be taken by some members of the group. Various members of the group should attend programming courses given by a number of manufacturers so that they may learn the abilities, limitations, and complexities of equipment to be considered. Attendance at professional society meetings should be encouraged. By obtaining a broad perspective, the group will be able to appraise equipment and be less biased toward one particular kind. Reference to the periodical literature on business-data processing (*Data Processing Digest*; Klingman, 1955) and on equipment and applications (Brown; Diebold) is useful for keeping working groups informed.

Scope of Training. The minimum preliminary training for the working group should cover the following subjects:

1. Capabilities, limitations, and characteristics of electronic computers, punched-card equipment, communication devices, and conventional office machines
2. Method of conducting a feasibility study

Use of Consultants. Industry frequently employs specialized consulting firms to carry out feasibility studies and later to do systems analysis. The use of consultants has advantages because of their greater objectivity and experience, which enables them to avoid mistakes they have previously encountered either firsthand or by observation. The principal disadvantage is that consultants must be trained in the client's operations. They leave after the equipment is installed, taking with them much of the knowledge required for successful and continuing operation of the system. Generally, organization personnel are qualified and, with some assistance from consultants or specialists, are capable of doing the system analysis.

DETAILED STUDY AREA

After developing the over-all picture of an organization's data-processing requirements, the feasibility study team should select areas in which the largest benefits would seem to result from using new techniques and procedures. These areas are then studied in detail to determine the merits of using automatic data-processing methods. The ideal approach is to study the largest possible area at one time, so that problems can be handled no matter where they are located; functions can then be integrated to work smoothly without duplication of effort.

Many functions operate jointly with other functions and receive data from or send data to them. If all are studied together, consideration can be given to their common problems as well as to individual ones. This is the "systems" approach to examining the whole operation rather than its parts. Because analysis of large areas raises many problems that must be dealt with simultaneously, there are resultant increases in cost and confusion that may outweigh some of the benefits. A limited-scope study is probably more suitable if prompt results are wanted or if personnel and funds are limited.

Factors to consider when choosing for detailed study an area of data processing that has already been identified are the history of an operation, experience with similar applications, expected benefits, costs, personnel, resources, flexibility, and relationships of the areas. These factors are pertinent for many data-processing situations and, in fact, for most cases where any innovation is considered.

History of an Operation

The history of a particular operation, both locally and elsewhere, often will help to determine whether the operation should be considered for detailed study. Two important facets of this history are (1) the previous efforts to improve similar operations, and (2) the prior systems work on the operation in question.

Similar Applications. Data-processing operations that may be handled by automatic means fall into three classes:

1. Operations already successfully handled automatically elsewhere
2. Untried operations
3. Automatic methods tried, but not yet successfully used

An operation deserves detailed study, if others have succeeded in converting a similar operation to automatic methods. The experience of other companies is valuable for pointing out fruitful areas, typical costs, and efficient system design. The risk and uncertainty are reduced when new techniques are applied to areas where successful applications already exist.

Untried areas, despite the risk and uncertainty, are good areas for detailed studies if potential benefits seem large. But proven areas are preferable to untried areas, if the benefits are roughly equal. Unexplored areas have the important drawback that there is little or no experience for guidance. But this has some rewards, for the lack of experience of others may encourage someone to find an excellent method rather than accept a mediocre one that is already available.

Automatic processing methods are new enough that many fruitful applications are still untried. Some worthwhile applications are untried because they exist in only one or a few organizations. Untried areas probably involve higher conversion costs than areas with a successful history of conversion and application, and the risks of complete or partial failure are higher in new areas. Clearly, new applications must be made, if full benefits are to be realized.

The third class—operations tried by others but not yet successful—should be examined afresh. If the proper analysis is made and a scientific approach is taken, specific areas for improvement can be determined, regardless of the past history or the degree of mechanization through punched-card equipment or other methods. The issue is not what *other* people have failed to do in the past, but what positive steps can be taken in a particular case to develop improved systems.

Prior Systems Work. Varying amounts of systems work have usually been performed in the past on each area under consideration. Some areas are studied almost continually and have gone through several cycles of improvement using manual methods, bookkeeping machines, or punched-card equipment. But other operations may have been improved little, if at all, over long periods of time.

Thorough procedural analysis and a high degree of mechanization for an area have several implications. First, the cost and time required to convert from an operation previously analyzed or mechanized to a new technique are smaller than for a similar operation not so advanced. Second, the potential improvements in either cost savings or additional benefits are fewer than for a similar operation now being handled by less efficient methods. These two points about cost and benefit of change are important. Areas that are incompletely analyzed or applications that are performed by inefficient methods have higher conversion costs; but they also have bigger prospective benefits.

The study group should not conclude, however, that unstudied areas will always produce big benefits. Similarly, areas previously analyzed are not always easy to convert to new methods. General rules apply to many but not to all cases.

Expected Benefits

Automatic data-processing methods are introduced to reduce costs or to obtain new benefits.

Costs. The present costs for data processing serve as a first indicator of new equipment feasibility. Such costs are either (1) replaceable and can be saved if new methods are used, or (2) non-replaceable and will continue even though new methods are adopted. Some kinds of data-processing work will have to be continued even under new methods, and the cost of these cannot be completely avoided—the work of preparing input data and handling exceptions, for instance, may remain essentially unchanged.

If the plans are to replace the existing system without gaining any important new benefits, the area chosen should have replaceable costs at least equal to the costs of the proposed equipment and related system. An area with small replaceable costs is a dubious prospect for conversion if no additional benefits are either desired or expected.

Improved Results. Areas that have limited replaceable costs but good prospects for large additional benefits should be considered for conversion. In addition to lower costs, advanced data-processing methods offer several major benefits not found in manual or punched-card systems:

1. Accuracy in following instructions and handling data
2. High-speed operations that process more data per unit of time and per dollar of cost than other systems
3. The ability to modify the processing program as required by data and output requirements

Accuracy, speed, and flexibility are the major benefits of using automatic equipment, but others are derived from them (Perry, 1953). Some of these derived benefits spring from the ability of automatic equipment to do the following things:

1. Report results faster by decreasing the processing time. Frequent reporting may permit real-time control of rapidly changing operations.
2. Solve complex mathematical and logical problems that involve sequences of calculations too elaborate for punched-card or manual solution.
3. Solve in a reasonable time problems that would involve many man-years of calculation and are consequently fraught with possible errors.

A further benefit is the small marginal cost of handling more data, for an electronic processor is more economical when dealing with large volumes. Data that cannot be processed economically by other means may be worth processing electronically. An electronic system may be feasible for broad applications with a high volume because of the low marginal cost, although it may not be justified for applications with a limited volume.

Personnel. Many office jobs are uninteresting. Several months or a year may be required for training, but thereafter adherence to rote instructions leads to discontent and increased turnover. Hiring and training costs are high and operations are inefficient.

Electronic systems offer advantages because they are impersonal. They do not become bored by routine jobs, have personal prejudices, or object to change of any type. When properly used, they permit the promotion of people to interesting and more productive work; thus, office personnel may benefit from automatic systems that reduce routine tasks.

Space.   Space reductions may be a benefit derived from automatic data processing. In some organizations, the data-processing facilities occupy all the available space. Management wants increased and more useful information, but no room may exist for more clerks, desks, and files. The choices are either to acquire more space or to use the existing space more intensively. Existing methods may be continued and a new office building obtained; or an automatic system may replace enough filing cabinets and desks to allow operations to continue within the existing space.

Experience.   Another benefit obtainable from an automatic system is training and practical experience. If an organization is convinced that it will eventually use automatic methods on a large scale, an early venture can be justified partly on the basis of the experience that can be gained. A well-trained group is valuable in view of the general scarcity of experienced people.

Relationship of Operations

The operating areas of an organization may be either independent or interdependent—inventory control, for example, is independent of personnel records, but it is vitally dependent on production control methods. Operating relationships have an important bearing on the plans for data processing. Both must have the same scope and boundaries to achieve efficient operation.

System-wide Approach.   Assume that a plan is being developed for the exclusive use of punched paper tape by a certain part of a business for the purpose of communicating with other parts of the business. An intensive study of the area's operations might show the plan to be worth while; but such a study would be too narrow in scope. Data and reports are sent to and received from all other parts of the organization so that punched paper-tape equipment would be needed everywhere. The appropriate area to study for such a proposal is the entire organization, not just one segment of it. The basic problem is intra-company communications, for it involves communications between the first department selected and all others that deal with it.

Closely knit or interdependent operations warrant analysis by functional areas in preference to organizational areas. More can be gained by analyzing inventory or intra-company communications than by concentrating on organizational areas such as cost accounting or the production control department.

All related areas must be included when a function is chosen for study. The inventory function includes inventory control and the stock room operations. It is closely related to purchasing, production, shipping, receiving, cataloguing, and cost accounting. All these organizational areas, which make inter-related decisions on inventory, may use similar forms and common or duplicative reference files.

Minimum-area Approach.   If, on the other hand, it is desirable to keep the study within modest limits, it is mandatory to pick an area that is independent of other areas or isolated from them. One plan for selecting a problem area for study is to find the smallest area that could justify the proposed system. A single function should be considered first. If it does not justify the proposed system, two choices are available. Either several functions may be considered, or the size of the proposed system may be reduced until the problem areas and the proposed system are in balance.

As an example, the U.S. Army Finance Center carefully studied many areas susceptible to automatic data processing, but it was decided to limit the initial application to the processing of soldiers' deposits—a savings bank operation. Accordingly, a medium-scale computer was rented. Its use would yield training and experience to provide a stepping stone for future acquisition of large-scale equipment covering the entire range of activities.

A large industrial company found that the money saved by processing the payroll at one plant on a large computer working ten hours a week would cover the total cost of renting, installing, and operating the computer. Concentrating all systems work in one area permitted operations to start months sooner than if a broad approach had been used. The system team converted other areas after the payroll analysis was complete. The company had more than a year's experience in computer operation when the major system study work was finished so that early study mistakes were quickly discovered during actual operations and could be avoided later. A smaller systems study group was able to handle one area at a time. The limited-area approach has merit if management desires to start new operations with a minimum delay, if personnel are not available for a large study, or if no reasonable basis exists for enlarging the study area.

Some objections arise to the minimum-area approach because any equipment obtained may be too small for future use. As further studies are made, it may be necessary either to obtain additional units or replace the original units by larger-scale equipment. Renting initial equipment instead of purchasing it reduces the cost of switching from small to big equipment; but important costs are nevertheless involved in reprogramming, conversion, and installation.

A serious problem exists in a system developed around small equipment because procedures that are developed individually may be difficult to integrate later. The common tendency is to convert individual applications to electronic processing with minimum changes in structure. If individual areas are inter-related, as is the usual case, a change in one area is difficult without changes in others. A piece-by-piece approach discourages viewing the system as a whole. Two functions that have produced almost identical reports under the old system will probably continue to duplicate each other's efforts with the new system. If system analysts are aware of this problem, they can reduce its severity, but it will persist.

Redefinition. The area chosen for a feasibility study should not be thought of as rigidly defined. The study of problems in one area almost always leads into other areas, and large potential benefits may be discovered for an area not originally included in the study. On the other hand, the area first selected may turn out to be too large to handle effectively. If important new factors are discovered, the study team should consider redefining the selected area.

Resources

An automatic data-processing system requires the following resources:

1. *Manpower to*
   (a) Study system and equipment feasibility and application
   (b) Conduct systems analysis and design
   (c) Program and code instruction routines
   (d) Operate and maintain equipment
   (e) Prepare input data
   (f) Use output reports
2. *Money for*
   (a) Personnel
   (b) Equipment acquisition and maintenance
   (c) Installation of equipment
   (d) Conversion from the old to the new system
3. *Space for*
   (a) People
   (b) Equipment
   (c) Supplies
   (d) Files
4. *Time to*
   (a) Conduct studies
   (b) Obtain and install equipment
   (c) Get the new system functioning properly

The scope of the problem areas selected for study should be consistent with the available resources. Studying a problem area that will require vast equipment is worth while only if resources are available for such equipment. A profitable system is valueless if the resources are not available to implement it. Management may restrict the funds allotted regardless of how profitable a system is likely to be. An upper limit may be quite sensible because of the risks involved and the difficulties in securing funds. Limits on resources, whatever the reason, must be considered in setting the scope of the feasibility study.

CONDUCT OF FEASIBILITY STUDY

Actual execution of a feasibility study requires careful planning, thorough analysis, and constant supervision to tie together the many related facets. The most common error is to underestimate the time and personnel needed for a substantive study. A study of a possible conversion to electronic processors should be more thorough than most management studies because it covers a broader area, requires more systems improvements, and presages large expenditures.

Systems design conducted later, during the final applications or engineering study, is considered one of the highest forms of management engineering. The feasibility study is equally important because it establishes the direction and intensity of later systems analysis. Feasibility studies should seldom be considered too extensive, for even a simple study of one operation may take several months to complete.

Framework of Operations

Procedures that proved effective for one actual feasibility study are outlined here. Such procedures are intended as a guide only and would, of course, require adaptation to a particular situation. The logical initial step is to determine the frame of reference for the operating activities.

Frame of Reference. Legal limitations, policy directives, and managerial restrictions have an important bearing on the frame of reference, and these should be examined to determine the organization's goals. Examination is important for several reasons: it promotes early recognition of important problems, it encourages considering the system in the light of its limitations, and it provides criteria for checking the area studied.

Organizational Area. The second step is to define the organizational area being studied to serve as a frame of reference for the data-processing system. The organization should be charted in detail. A simple code scheme can be constructed after the organization and its components are defined. Major elements may be identified by a two-digit number to the left of the decimal point, with sub-elements represented by assigned digits placed on the right of the decimal point, one place to the right for each successive level in the organization, as follows:

00.	Company or Service
00.0	Division
00.00	Branch
00.000	Unit
00.0000	Sub-unit

The preliminary analysis of the organization may, of course, require later correction. A chart may be prepared showing the grade or rank of all personnel in order to keep new operations within the estimated personnel costs of the current authorized distribution of work.

Procedures for Analysis

The next step is to make a detailed analysis of the specific system or systems under consideration. This step has two objectives: to orient the analysis and to define it.

Orientation. In the orientation phase, the analysts obtain as much information as possible, from both internal and external sources, about the existing operation. Questions to ask at this point are:

1. What does the system do?
2. How does this fit into the operations of the over-all organization?
3. How well does it fulfill its intended mission?
4. What integral links exist between this and other operations?

The purpose is to see this operation as a link in the productive or administrative chain, and exactly where it fits in relation to the whole chain. With these questions answered, the next phase can be started.

Catalogue of Internal Functions. The second phase entails collecting and cataloguing facts about the internal functioning of the system. Fact finding can start by having the supervisor of each major organizational element describe the data-processing or paper-work activities that take place in his bailiwick. The supervisor should collect all the working documents, including local forms, used in his activity.

Collected documents can be catalogued in two major classifications. They are (1) source documents on which transactions are originally recorded and (2) end-products resulting from processing these source documents. For purposes of a feasibility study, the documents can be coded as follows:

Description	Code
Source documents	0
End-products	
Basic records	1
Intermediate records	2
Reports or final results	3

Facts contained in source documents are manipulated to get end-products. For example, a journal is a basic record between a source document and an intermediate record. Documents should be coded before the desk interview or other analysis is completed.

Flow Charting. The next step analyzes the routines to be converted. A step-by-step analysis of operations will naturally suggest alternatives. The possibility of eliminating basic and intermediate records is considered because an electronic processor requires fewer intermediate records than a manual or mechanical system. Such records have a doubtful future value and should be examined critically. Analysis may show that data no longer needed are still being compiled or, conversely, that vital facts are not available.

Useful aids for analysis are flow charts, data on work loads, time schedules, and manuals or memoranda of procedures. The objective is to get a "blow-by-blow" description of what happens. Startling facts may be revealed and real benefits come from this careful analysis, no matter what the final decision is regarding new equipment.

Example of Analysis

A department of the Army Task Force studying the use of automatic data-processing systems at large military installations developed an interesting analysis procedure involving grid charts, validity checks, document cards, and cost summaries (Cole, 1958).

Grid Chart. Figure 15-1 is a preliminary grid chart based on the catalogue of documents prepared earlier for a particular data-processing function. Source documents, coded zero, are listed in the first column of the chart. End-products, properly coded 1, 2, 3, for basic, intermediate, or final, are shown across the top. The chart is also identified by functional area—financial inventory accounting, consolidated. Complete control of relationships—on an input-output basis—for a particular data-processing area is established.

Desk interviews are used to find the links between source documents and end-products, which are then marked X in the appropriate cell. The completed chart is referred to the job supervisor for review in order to insure completeness and accuracy. The grid chart provides a control mechanism for conducting the feasibility study by requiring that both the origin and destination of every fact be considered.

Validity Check. Facts obtained on the preliminary grid chart are summarized on a validity check sheet, or its equivalent, and the estimated volumes or work loads are added. The number of line entries or items may be used later as a common denominator for fixing the cost of the operation. Each document may have few or many items to fill. Organizational elements and strengths, both civilian and military, in the functional area being studied are listed in the left-hand stub. Various reports, records, or accounts previously recognized in the

FUNCTION: FINANCIAL INVENTORY ACCOUNTING S-4-FIA SECTION (CONSOLIDATED)

SOURCE DOCUMENTS	Set of Data Code	No.	FGGM-293	FGGM-292 Cat.	FGGM-294 Cat.	FGGM-292 Cont.	FGGM-294 Cont.	FGGM-296	FGGM-297	FGGM-291 Cat.	FGGM-291 Cont.	FGGM-157 SF	FGGM-157 Non-SF	FGGM-160	DA-1257	DA-1887
FREQUENCY			D	D	D	D	D	D	D	M	M	M	M	D	Q	Q
Set of Data Code			1	1	1	2	2	2	2	2	2	2	2	2	3	3
DA-446	O	1	X					X	X							
DA-447	O	2	X					X	X							
DA-5-103	O	3	X					X	X							
DD-1155	O	4	X					X	X							
SF-44	O	5	X					X	X							
DD-250	O	6	X					X	X							
DA-445	O	7	X					X	X							
SF-1165	O	8	X					X	X							
DA-581	O	9	X					X	X							
FGGM-297	2	10	X					X	X							
FGGM-160	2	11	X					X	X							
FGGM-294 Cont.	2	12	X					X	X							
FGGM-293	1	13		X	X	X	X							X		
FGGM-292 Cat.	1	14								X						
FGGM-292 Cont.	2	15									X					
FGGM-296	2	16											X			
FGGM-291 Cat.	2	17										X			X	X
FGGM-291 Cont.	2	18										X			X	X
FGGM-157 SF	2	19													X	
FGGM-157 Non-SF	2	20													X	

FIGURE 15-1. *Preliminary grid chart*

analysis are listed across the top in order to show the number of copies prepared; the frequency of preparation as day, month, or quarter; and the estimated man-hours spent each year on this activity.

The validity check or summary sheet shows the burden attributed to each record and provides a validity check against the total manpower for each organizational element. Total man-hours per year should correspond with the total manpower available. If not, either some data-processing activities have been omitted or some extraneous activities have been included. Any such discrepancies should, of course, be investigated and reconciled.

Document Card.   A separate card to summarize facts is prepared for each source document and for each end-product. The card is given to the appropriate supervisor for review. Work load data (in man-hours per year) derived earlier for each source document and each end-product are converted to an annual cost and listed on the document card. The annual cost is based on the annual average of 2,000 hours multiplied by the average hourly rate. Work-sampling techniques may be used when suitable for the circumstances under study.

Cost Summary.   Costs determined above are summarized by major organization on a cost summary sheet. All source documents and end-products are listed. The organizational sub-elements involved are also shown, and the total costs, based on earlier estimates, are entered. The cost summary is the basis for determining whether mechanization would be economical.

Comparison of Personnel Costs.   The cost summary form shows the total annual cost by present operating methods. Next, the costs are studied to see whether they are big enough to absorb the costs of various sizes of data processors. If the operation does not justify the cost of a full-time processor, the part-time use of service-center equipment can be considered.

The study group decides which equipment has the least cost and is best suited to the data-processing system required. Equipment, as such, is not selected at this stage; the objective is to determine comparative costs for analytic purposes. Estimated costs should cover site preparation, air conditioning, parallel operations, conversion, and supplies. Accumulated cost data are analyzed to find the economic soundness of introducing automatic data-processing methods.

Concluding Feasibility Study

The feasibility study group can develop a tentative design for one or more proposed new systems. Several new systems that offer different combinations of costs and benefits may be considered. The study group should prepare, for each area selected and for each system considered, a summary of:

1. Cost, by functional area, for operating the present system
2. Cost of the proposed system
   (a) Non-replaceable costs that carry over from the present system
   (b) Additional costs for the new system
3. Cost differential for the present and the proposed system
4. Additional benefits, if any, expected from the proposed system
5. Resources—capital expenditures, time, space, and personnel—for the proposed system
6. Adjustment problems—personnel relocation, equipment disposition, and others
7. Future plans for additional work, new procedures, and operations analysis

System Evaluation. A proposed system may be evaluated by comparing its costs and benefits with the present system as it now stands or with improved versions of the present system.

Some analysts say that the most efficient proposed system should be compared with the present system alone. Other analysts argue that both the existing system and any possible improved version of it should be used as yardsticks for measuring the efficiency of a wholly new system—this because the efficiency of the present system might be increased by minor changes, at a small cost.

Considering the present system and some variations—whether minor or major—as a yardstick is more likely to result in the most efficient system. The time and cost required to study every possible system warrants focusing attention on one or two with the most promise. But the haunting question always persists whether any particular system has been studied thoroughly enough to disclose its merits before it is dropped.

Added Benefits. A new system may be justified only by the additional benefits that can be obtained from it. A report should list the benefits, explain their desirability, and show the costs that will be increased or decreased. The costs that will remain constant can be omitted since they should not affect the decision. Management may decide whether the benefits justify the costs. This procedure is an intuitive approach—a sort of educated guessing.

It may be possible to evaluate the extra benefits in dollars. The factors discussed in an earlier chapter that help determine the value of information are accuracy, timeliness, predictability, relevance, and consequence. Even a rough estimate of the value of information is preferable to labeling it an "intangible benefit." More careful study is required if the intangible benefits seem large and the determination of value is complex.

Reporting to Management

The feasibility study group should report to management on its activities, findings, and recommendations. These reports should be prepared intelligently and carefully since they are the foundation upon which a future data-processing system will be erected.

Outline for Report.   A standard report format should be used, if one is available. Lacking a prescribed form, the following outline can serve as a useful guide.

1. Concise statement of conclusions and recommendations, including:
   (a) Cost differences between the present and the proposed systems
   (b) Major resource requirements of the proposed systems
   (c) Extra benefits of the proposed systems
   (d) Major recommendations of the study group
2. Detailed statement of conclusions and recommendations, containing:
   (a) Breakdown of cost figures
   (b) Explanation of extra benefits
   (c) Detailed reasoning supporting the group's recommendations
3. Supporting material for the study, including:
   (a) Group's preliminary report to management
   (b) Outline of how the study was conducted
   (c) Brief description of available electronic equipment
   (d) Copy of the over-all findings of the investigation
   (e) Discussion of why the areas for the proposed system were chosen

Uncertainty.   The degree of uncertainty that is involved in all estimates and forecasts should be remembered, although it is easily overlooked. In the early stages, no one knows with certainty how much the proposed equipment and a new system will cost to obtain, install, and operate. Furthermore, it is uncertain whether the proposed system will work either as well as expected, or even at all. Then too, more than one system has been designed to handle a problem which is soon discovered to be trivial in view of other problems which were previously ignored or unexpected. And even when it is known, the size and scope of the problem may be inaccurately estimated.

Feasibility study reports should make the degree of uncertainty explicit for the reader because the conclusions reached frequently hinge on many conditions. The conclusions are valid, *if* the system works as planned, *if* the equipment meets specifications, *if* people work as expected, *if* the costs are as estimated, and *if* no material mistake was made in fact finding or estimating.

A carefully and intelligently conducted feasibility study is a valuable aid to making a sound decision. Both the study group and management should remember that the study is an attempt to forecast the future. Along with the most probable result, the best and worst outcomes should be considered. If the study shows that the introduction of new processing techniques appears justified, the report should state the elements of cost savings and benefits expected. Sufficient detail should be included to permit the manager to determine whether he will authorize an applications study. In addition, the report should include the plans for initiating an applications or engineering study to develop a system that will achieve the estimated savings and lead to the selection of suitable equipment. The subsequent applications study is, in reality, an extension of the feasibility study.

Looking Ahead

Planning a data-processing system affects the long-term future of an organization. The transition from an existing to a proposed system is time consuming. The actual transition time for a large application is likely to be several years. After the system is in operation, another year or two may be required before it works as efficiently as planned.

The data-processing requirements that deserve primary consideration are not today's problems. More important are the problems that will exist two or more years from now. Present requirements may serve as the only available guides, if nothing is known or can be estimated about future requirements, which may be much different from today's problems.

SUMMARY

A detailed and carefully organized plan is necessary for gathering and weighing both facts and opinions. Steps leading to an important change in a system are the feasibility study, applications study, equipment acquisition proposal, installation preparations, and parallel operations.

The feasibility study analyzes data-processing requirements and equipment to determine whether new equipment and the related system for data processing appear to be more efficient than the system in use. The study is important, for it affects all subsequent action. If the conclusion is to adopt a new system and obtain new equipment, the next stage is the applications study.

The initial step in a feasibility study is to assign several competent people to a preliminary study group. Some study group members should know the data-information environment involved. Some members should know the characteristics of equipment that may be used and the experience of others in using it. Top management support should be enlisted by suitable presentations, orientations, and briefings. Employees should be reassured that personnel dislocations will be minimized.

A preliminary feasibility study, to be completed in a few months, should determine the data-information requirements, available equipment and methods, estimated costs to complete the feasibility study, and the estimated costs and benefits of carrying out the applications study and installing the proposed system. If the outcome of a preliminary study is favorable, the study group should continue work to make a full-scale study.

The objective or objectives—reduced costs, improved information, maximum profit—must be spelled out in order to focus effort on them. Broad or narrow areas may be selected for study. Important users, processors, and suppliers of data should be listed in order to find areas for further analysis. Obvious targets for improvement are areas with high-volume, repetitive operations that have high clerical or manpower costs.

A written charter should define the object and scope of the feasibility study to insure constancy of direction and to serve as the basis for reviewing progress. After the over-all picture of data-information requirements is developed, the most fruitful areas should be studied intensively. Factors to consider when selecting an area are the history of the operation, known experiences with similar applications, expected benefits, costs, personnel, relationship of areas, resources, and flexibility. Expected benefits are reduced costs, improved information, and the ability to handle large volumes without further increases in facilities.

The relationship of operations—independent or interdependent—throughout an organization determines whether one or more small areas can be tackled or if a broad-gauge attack is required on all related problems. The conduct of a feasibility study involves determining the frame of reference in which the system will operate and the organizational structure involved. It is necessary to examine the purpose and function of the system, catalogue internal functions and documents, and make flow charts of operations to get a "blow-by-blow" description of what happens.

An example of a feasibility study shows how a document origination and destination chart, work load summary sheet, and document review card are used to develop a cost summary. Personnel costs are an important factor in absorbing the cost of equipment. The costs, benefits, resources, conversion problems, and future plans for one or more systems should be developed for each data-processing area studied.

Concluding a feasibility study requires reporting to management, by good standard report practices, in order to gain acceptance of recommendations. A concise statement of conclusions and recommendations is usually backed up by a detailed statement and supporting material.

The range of uncertainty involved in estimates should be specified so that conclusions can be tempered by the range of the estimates used.

It is a constant temptation in systems analysis to solve old problems that are still causing trouble. But a long-term viewpoint is vital for coping with future problems that are not yet clearly formulated.

REFERENCES AND SUPPLEMENTAL READINGS

Brown, R. Hunt. *Office Automation: Integrated and Electronic Data Processing* (rev. ed.), New York, Automation Consultants, Inc. This service consists of two parts: (a) a basic reference text in loose-leaf form called *Office Automation* and (b) an updating service. As new developments occur, the updating service supplies additional or replacement material that can be inserted in the basic text. *Office Automation*, according to the foreword, is a non-technical work on office electronics prepared especially for the business man. Intended as a manual for executives, university students, and equipment manufacturers, it deals with (1) commercial aspects of automation, (2) hardware, (3) electronic and automatic accounting, (4) sociological aspects, (5) new scientific techniques, and (6) potential applications. The first section gives some reasons for adopting new equipment and techniques. The pioneering of several years ago is said to be beginning to pay off now, but "pay-off" is never dealt with explicitly. Application examples are drawn from both office and factory. Section two, the longest, deals with new machines for office automation and their use. Half of this section covers machines using native language and common language (producing and using paper tape of five or more channels), communication facilities, and tabulating and computing equipment. The other half of this section covers electronic business computers, available equipment storage, printers, programming, what equipment will and will not do, the rent-buy question, literature available, and conferences and meetings. Section two is replete with illustrations, chiefly photographs or artists' renditions of proposed equipment, and diagrams. Section three spends a few pages on electronic and automatic accounting and its implications. The remaining sections touch briefly on a wide variety of topics: (a) social consequences, (b) operations research, (c) applied cybernetics, and (d) prospective computers and applications. Extensive treatment is given to developmental applications in the banking area. Companion volumes cover applications in selected industries.

Cole, John S. "Electronics for Management: Automatic Data Processing at a Class 1 Installation," *The Armed Forces Comptroller*, vol. 3: 1-8 (June 1958). This article describes the feasibility and engineering study done at Fort Jackson and Fort Meade. The novel feature of the study was the development of a "grid chart" to show the relationship of origin and destination for source documents, basic records, intermediate records, and final reports. The volumes of documents at each point in the sequence of flow are useful for measuring workloads. The fact was recognized that end-product reports determine data-processing requirements. Contents of reports were traced back step-by-step to original data inputs.

Data Processing Digest. Los Angeles, California, Canning, Sisson, and Associates. The main function of *Data Processing Digest*, a monthly periodical, is to review briefly new articles and books in data processing and related fields. Approximately ninety periodicals are scanned for relevant articles. Material is collected on such topics as (a) general information, (b) systems engineering, (c) applications, (d) equipment, (e) management decision-making techniques, and (f) programming. The name and address of each publisher or periodical mentioned in an issue are contained in a reference section. Meetings and training sessions that will occur during the next few months are listed, generally including such information as (a) date, (b) place, and (c) a contact for additional information. Each month, a short comment written by the staff is prepared on such topics as (a) "Developments in Automatic Coding Techniques" or (b) "Notes on Renting versus Buying."

Diebold, John, and Associates. *Automatic Data Processing Service*, Chicago, Cudahy Publishing Company. *Automatic Data Processing Service* is a weekly service consisting of four basic parts: (1) Equipment Reports containing detailed descriptions and appraisals of equipment, (2) Methods Reports that serve as case histories of applications, (3) Policy Reports covering management problems, such as centralization versus decentralization, and (4) Newsletters reporting on current items of interest including scheduled conferences. One type of items is sent out each week in the following order: (a) Newsletter, (b) Policy Report, (c) Newsletter, and (d) Methods Report. Equipment Reports are included in the weekly mailing whenever any new information becomes available. The service also includes orientation materials that are intended to provide a basic background plus an index to all material provided. Loose-leaf binders are supplied for filing the equipment reports and methods reports. The service appears to be one of the most comprehensive available.

Klingman, Herbert F., ed. *Electronics in Business*, New York, Controllership Foundation, 1955, 176 pp. This work is a reference on the application of electronics in business. The first part is an annotated bibliography concerning the business application of electronic machines and is divided into four sections: suggested basic reading, periodicals, pamphlets and reports, and books. A section lists current conferences, seminars, and training programs in the field held in the United States; and, also, educational films about the application of electronics. Descriptions of the characteristics of data-processing machines offered by various manufacturers and location of commercial digital electronic computing centers in the United States are included.

Perry, J. E. "Potentials for Electronics in Banking," *Banking*, vol. 46: 52-3, (October 1953). This article is the first report of the Committee of Electronics of the Savings and Mortgage Division, American Bankers Association. The committee was organized to study the prospects of computer use in dealing with the accounting required to handle greatly increased savings deposits and mortgage activities. Two weaknesses were thought to exist in available equipment: (a) the high initial investment cost, and (b) the fact that all material must be preprocessed. The needs of a banking accounting system are discussed with the point of view that it is the banks' job to serve their customers. The foremost customer requirements are speed and accuracy. The first step in the change-over to accounting machines is simplifying present procedures; however, the committee recommends this step whether a bank is changing to computers or not. Various suggestions for possible applications are mentioned in the article, the most important of which is immediate posting of daily transactions and computation of interest: Another suggestion is an automatic device to notify a teller of a stop-payment order.

Woellner, D. A. "A Computer Development Program," *The Journal of Machine Accounting*, vol. 7: 4-7+ (February 1956). This article gives a step-by-step outline of the electronic systems study made at Convair Division of General Dynamics Corporation. Stage I of this study, which started in 1954, was to develop a planned and integrated program extending to 1960 and beyond. In Stage II, the steps suggested are (a) select the best-suited digital computer, (b) select areas for initial conversion, and (c) establish a schedule of time and cost. Stage III includes (a) training, (b) programming, (c) re-assessing previous work, and (d) determining a firm date for computer acquisition. Woellner presents illustrations of economics, procedures, and activities involved in the program and summarizes Convair's experience to date.

CHAPTER SIXTEEN

APPLICATIONS STUDY AND EQUIPMENT SELECTION

The applications study and selection of equipment are vital stages in bringing a new system one step closer to reality.

SCOPE AND CONTENT OF APPLICATIONS STUDY

The applications study is a more detailed and careful extension of the feasibility study, and it should be conducted within the framework of the general planning and scope of that study. The applications study is more narrowly defined as the detailed process of (1) redesigning a system or set of procedures for the use of electronic data processors, and (2) establishing specifications for selecting equipment suitable for the specific requirements of that system.

Scope of Study

Many alternatives originally considered in the feasibility study are ruled out, since the task of the applications study group is to determine the exact form of the new system. The applications study group makes decisions on many important factors:

1. Methods and procedures to change
2. Files to set up or eliminate
3. Equipment to obtain or discard
4. Organizational changes to make in the area of data processing

An important part of the applications study is to review the economy of the whole proposal. Because the feasibility study group is not able to determine the precise form of the new system, their original cost and value estimates may change greatly. After the system is more carefully designed, it should be reviewed several times to see whether it warrants further study or should be shelved awaiting new developments.

After the new system is basically outlined, the applications group can develop flow charts and data sheets on workloads for the operations that will be covered. Complete flow charts of processes and techniques are drawn so that programs and instruction routines can be devised and processing time estimated. Processing costs and the value of information to be obtained are reappraised. A proposal is then prepared for top management, recommending either that a new system and its required equipment be introduced, or that the *status quo* be maintained.

If management approves, system specifications are developed in order to prepare bid invitations, including functional specifications, which are sent to manufacturers. Prospective systems are evaluated and the most promising one selected.

Content of Study

Techniques used in conducting the applications study should lead to the optimum system design. The use of management analysis techniques, as described in an earlier chapter, is essential. The initial tasks in an applications study are to relate source documents to the end-products and to make schematic and flow-process charts showing the details of current methods. Strong emphasis should be placed on the importance of detailed fact finding about everything that is done, the way in which it is done, the frequency required, man-hour needs, and the complexity of processing.

Detailed analysis uncovers existing areas of duplication and overlap of source documents, data, records, and reports. The need for reduction, addition, or verification of data will be disclosed. Actual system design involves the following steps:

1. Developing source documents and formats to serve as direct input to automatic equipment, when possible
2. Constructing new schematic and flow-process charts
3. Drafting and formalizing plans for integrating data processing, if worth while
4. Redetermining personnel requirements—supervisors, analysts, programmers, operators, and clerks—in view of the new procedures planned
5. Studying equipment in order to identify machine capabilities and limitations within which the system is formulated

The principles of systems analysis are essential to an applications study. The basic components of an applications study are:

1. Fact finding
2. Preliminary evaluation
3. Basic system design
4. Development of systems specifications

The applications study, if approved, leads to the preparation and submission of proposals to equipment manufacturers, followed by the evaluation and selection of equipment. These two points are covered later in this chapter; at this point, each component of an applications study is discussed briefly.

Fact Finding. Fact finding as part of the applications study must be more intensive and extensive than it was during the feasibility study. Fact finding here involves the initial task of assuring that all source documents are collected and related to the end-products and organization elements. Schematic and flow-process charts are prepared which reflect a detailed description of the present system. Facts available from the feasibility study should be used. Here, strong emphasis should be placed on gathering detailed facts about what, where, and how data are processed; uses made of them; frequency required; and the complexity of the process. Development of the current organizational and personnel charts is equally important.

Preliminary Evaluation. Preliminary evaluation is an over-all examination of the facts and flow-process charts. This analytical evaluation establishes the basis for eliminating duplication, combining details, rearranging sequences, validating records, and reporting requirements. Any unnecessary processes can be eliminated; conversely, consideration should be given to adding new processes and essential records, or reports not currently obtainable.

Basic Design. The basic systems design, a continuation of the applications study, consists of a review of data and processes in order to reach the ultimate goal—optimum systems design. It is the first stage in *synthesizing* the system as opposed to *analyzing* it. Three guides leading to optimum design are: (1) achieve multiple use of common source data, (2) organize files for quick reference, and (3) develop procedural instructions that minimize the repetitive use and manipulation of equipment, including basic programming. The new system is constructed in the form of schematic and flow-process charts and source document designs. Organizational requirements, including the need for supervisors and clerks, must be restated for the new procedures. Computer manufacturers and others can help in systems design, but the user is ultimately responsible for success of the system. The need for equipment is dictated by requirements of the over-all system; coordinated functioning of the parts of a system is required to assure proper handling of source documents, records and reports, and to make these fill the needs of auditors as well as the requirements of management. The objective of this stage is to design a system that can make use of any equipment available without becoming "locked" into equipment of one kind. Classes and types of equipment are considered, but particular examples are studied later.

Development of Specifications. The development of systems specifications provides a basis to relate and evaluate the potentials of various equipment. Such criteria are used to solicit manufacturers' proposals, to evaluate manufacturers' offers to furnish equipment, and to select equipment. The following systems specifications represent minimum information for this purpose:

1. *Input.* A description of all known input, including:
    (a) Method or medium by which data will be received or developed
    (b) Format, message length, use of alphanumericals, or other identifying characteristics
    (c) Daily volume, including cyclical peaks
    (d) Hourly rates at which equipment must accept input
2. *Maintenance of files.* A description of the records to be maintained, including:
    (a) Volume of records
    (b) Methods of file maintenance
    (c) Proposed record length
    (d) Alphanumerical requirements
    (e) Requirements for interrogation
3. *Data handling.* To permit proper assessment of the problem, a detailed description of:
    (a) Types of transactions to be handled
    (b) Kinds of computations required
4. *Output.* A description of output needs, including:
    (a) Kind of output and its distribution—printed copy, punched card, magnetic tape, or paper tape
    (b) Daily volume by type of output
    (c) Required formats
    (d) Time after cut-off within which each kind of output report must be produced
5. *Special requirements:*
    (a) Time cycle to accomplish each transaction (e.g., process a requisition)
    (b) Required date for delivery and installation of equipment
    (c) Maintenance of equipment
    (d) Compatibility with other equipment
    (e) Expansibility to accomodate an additional work load
    (f) Other special requirements of the installation
6. *Additional information required:*
    (a) Equipment cost, including make, model, number, and quantity
    (b) Cost of site preparation

(c) Space requirements
(d) Cost of installation
(e) Cost of maintenance and parts
(f) Cost of operation
(g) Cost of training personnel
(h) Manufacturers' assistance in programming
(i) Cost of converting existing operations to proposed system

It is not necessary at this stage of the study to prescribe specifically how each transaction will be processed. Different types of equipment may require varying procedural steps to accomplish the same results.

The applications study places emphasis on specific data-processing jobs, and it can proceed only upon evidence that a complete analysis of the system was performed. It is necessary to have a summary of the present data-processing system covering its scope and the problems encountered—such as inability to obtain information for internal operation and management, time limits for reporting, work load, and maximum cost.

The scope of the proposed data-processing system includes the data currently available and all projects to be mechanized, cost of the system, and benefits expected from it. A work load summary by specific project includes the type and number of documents, line entries, messages for input, and reports to be prepared. The work load is used with tables of machine operating speed to find the required complement of machines.

The scope and content of the applications study have been covered without regard for how the study should be performed. The method of carrying out the applications study is covered below.

CONDUCT OF APPLICATIONS STUDY

An applications study involves designing afresh or redesigning an existing system or set of procedures and establishing specifications for suitable equipment. A comprehensive applications study covers the following points:

1. Schedule for performing and completing the study
2. Organization and personnel
3. Development of the new system

Each of these points is covered in some detail in order to show the relationship among them.

Study Schedule

Making an applications study usually takes much manpower and money expended over a long period of time. Each phase of the applications study should be given definite starting and ending dates. Otherwise, there is a strong tendency for each phase to drag on because people believe that another week or two will permit tying up more loose ends or exploring another interesting possibility. Of course, revisions in the schedule can be made if more time is required for the satisfactory completion of each phase; serious problems should not go unexplored merely to maintain a schedule. On the other hand, consideration should be given to the effect on the schedule of including new areas in the study. Doing this will insure that delays and addition of new areas will be reviewed formally rather than pass unnoticed. Schedules should cover the expected time required for each of the following:

1. Organize, select, and train an applications study group.
2. Flow chart the basic structure for processing data.
3. Tabulate the work load on data sheets.
4. Prepare systems specifications.
5. Evaluate prospective systems (not equipment) and select the most promising one.
6. Complete the flow charting of processes and techniques, perform some coding, calculate the processing time, and estimate the costs and values of the expected results.
7. Prepare the proposal for top management.

Both an over-all schedule and a more detailed schedule for each member of the applications study team may prove helpful.

Organization and Personnel

Participants in the feasibility study can be the nucleus of the applications study group. Additional people are needed because more detailed work is involved and representation of the departments affected by the new system is valuable. Composition of the applications study group might be as follows:

1. Study supervisor
2. Systems analysts
3. Project analysts
4. Programmers
5. Representatives of each operating department
6. Clerks and technicians

Study Supervisor. The study supervisor should be a capable administrator who is respected by and able to work with the organization's executives and group members. Needing to know enough about data processing to lead the study group and to appraise its work, he is responsible for:

1. Keeping the study on schedule and within the budget
2. Making initial contact with operating and staff groups involved in the study
3. Providing training and facilities for the study group
4. Contacting equipment manufacturers
5. Participating in policy determinations that affect data processing
6. Informing management and other people of developments that will affect them

Opinion is divided about the most desirable qualifications for the study supervisor. Some say he should have a thorough knowledge about the organization and its data and information problems. Others say he should have thorough knowledge of and experience with the data-processing equipment that is likely to be used.

In some cases, the problems related to the unit's operations and data processing are more complex, more difficult to understand, than the equipment that will be required. In such a case, the supervisor should have extensive experience with the organization and its requirements. In other cases, operating and data problems are simple and equipment is complex, in relative terms, so that equipment experience is more useful. Supervisors with detailed knowledge of equipment may be recruited from the manufacturer or from other organizations. Study supervisors experienced with both systems and equipment are still rare, but there will be a greater number of them available in the future.

Systems Analysts. Systems or management analysts, being the technical experts for the applications study, should have experience with data-processing equipment and management methods. They should keep informed on new developments, think originally and creatively, and remain open-minded enough to consider any reasonable idea.

A systems analyst is picked for his technical knowledge of accounting, economics, electronics, mathematics, production, or systems design. He should be encouraged to consider unusual opportunities and completely different ways of doing jobs. He should be able to understand problems and limitations of operating areas without being directly involved in systems operations. A person experienced in systems operations may often be able to keep an analyst from devising schemes that look attractive on paper but would fail if put into operation.

Although the study supervisor is in charge, one or more systems analysts are primarily responsible for the methods of approach, the feasibility of various plans, and the over-all system design. A large applications study group requires several systems analysts. One good analyst may be enough; but he should be the best person available, for his work is a critical factor in the success of the study. A systems analyst's duties include the following:

1. Developing a general plan or design for the system
2. Assigning tasks to project analysts
3. Reviewing the work of project analysts and determining what additional work is needed
4. Furnishing advice and guidance to project analysts
5. Reviewing the contents of all study group reports for accuracy and completeness

Project Analysts.   Project analysts do the groundwork for the study. Since they work in specific areas on assigned jobs, they need less skill and background than systems analysts. The success of project analysts depends on their analytic ability, personal initiative, and ability to work harmoniously with operating people. One duty of a project analyst is to determine the following facts for areas assigned to him by a systems analyst:

1. Documents and information wanted
2. Raw data available
3. Processing required to convert the data into desired results
4. Conditions limiting the freedom to make any changes that might be proposed

A project analyst uses data sheets to accumulate facts and flow charts to organize his findings. He may also investigate various items of equipment, prepare cost data, or assist the systems analyst in developing the over-all system.

Programmers.   A programmer plans a computation or process from the first formulation of a question to the final delivery of results, including the integration of operations into the existing system. Programming consists of planning and coding, which includes numerical analysis, specification of printing formats, and other functions necessary to make the system operational.

A programmer's work may be as broad as that of a systems analyst. If so, it covers all or a segment of a whole application, from the initial formulation to the finished program ready to run on equipment. The assignment given to a programmer, especially a beginner, may be limited to coding. If so, he starts with flow charts prepared by analysts and lists in computer code or pseudo-code the computer operations required to solve a given problem. Since analysis and flow charting represent about three-fourths or more of the total task of program preparation, it is rare to have anyone work for long solely as a coder.

Aptitude testing is used, along with interviews and supervisors' ratings, to select personnel for systems analysis and programming work. Selection methods attempt to locate people with the right combinations of managerial skill, imagination, logical reasoning power, perception of details, and persistence. Different abilities and aptitudes are required for each level of personnel ranging from supervisor to clerk.

Some test users claim a high correlation between test scores and long-run success in analysis and programming. Tests are available from computer manufacturers, and many users have devised their own. Some tests are a single question requiring only analytic ability. Two examples of single-question tests, which are actually age-old puzzles, are:

1. At 1:17 p.m. a camper started paddling his canoe upstream at 4 miles an hour against a current of 1.5 miles an hour. At 2:05 p.m. he saw a bottle floating downstream, but continued upstream. Later, overcome by curiosity, he turned around and paddled downstream to catch up with the bottle just as it reached camp. How far did he go from camp before he started after the bottle?

2. Given only a set of balance scales (two pans with no weights), determine which *one* of twelve apparently identical balls is heavier than the others by using the scales as few times as possible. Repeat the operation, if you do *not* know whether the odd ball is heavy or light. (The minimum number of weighings in each case is three.)

Longer tests covering ability to read numbers and solve simple problems in algebra, logic, spatial perception, probability, and other fields are often given to prospective analysts and programmers. An example of a multi-part aptitude test, like those used in business, is shown in Figure 16-1. The example shown here is merely a "for instance" and has not been validated; but it is worth taking to exercise your wits, if for no other reason.

Operating Representatives.   Selecting an operating representative from each data-processing area for cooperating in the applications study is useful. An operating representative should be alert and observant, and have a good general picture of all activities in his area. Several years of solid, well-rounded experience in the area that he represents is desirable, provided he is imaginative enough to devise improvements and willing to accept changes proposed by others.

The operating representative can furnish project analysts with facts on information requirements, data available, procedures, and problems. Additional facts can be collected under his supervision.

Since he is familiar with the problems and people involved, the operating department representative can move more effectively and with less friction than the project analyst alone.

Clerks and Technicians.   Clerks and technicians assist the systems analysts. Analysts may make rough drafts of flow charts, data sheets, and other forms; but the time-consuming work of preparing final copy can be handled by others.

Group Balance.   The applications study group will function best if it represents a balance between analysts and operating people. Management may insist that each group member have both qualifications; but such a requirement may limit progress and decrease the effectiveness of systems analysis.

Basic Structure for a New System

The applications study team may start by focusing attention on the kinds of information wanted, the times when it is required, and the data that are available. The analyst also considers the files and the processing procedures needed to convert input data to the desired output. These and other factors make up the structure of the data-processing system.

One method for developing a new data-processing system (where one is already in use) is to introduce equipment for the first time or to replace the present equipment with more advanced equipment. The second is to redesign the whole system to develop new plans for processing data, keeping files, and preparing reports. The two approaches for developing a new system—mechanization and redesign—deserve further consideration.

Mechanization.   The basic structure can be developed by making flow charts of the existing system, if the objective of the applications group is primarily to introduce either new equipment or more equipment. The currently used techniques that will continue unchanged can be shown on the flow charts. Punched-card input and document output should also be shown with appropriate technical symbols, if they will remain in the new system. Areas that will be changed in the process of mechanization, such as files and processing methods, are first represented by symbols of the general structure and later shown in detail.

Data sheets are prepared for all inputs, files, and outputs in the old system since their content presumably will be changed little. New media, if known, can be listed on the data sheets. Volumes and time schedules for the present system should be recorded if they will be useful in developing the new system. Under the increased mechanization approach, data sheets and flow charts for the present system plus

Part I

Read the following problem carefully. List your answers to the
questions in clear, readable form.

A man lives in a small Alaskan town at the point marked "X." Every
street in the town is shown on the map below. A friend from Ohio is
coming to visit the Alaskan and may arrive on highway U.S. 31 (point A),
highway U.S. 42 (point B), or Jones Road (point C). The Alaskan wishes
to telegraph instructions to his friend. At the telegraph company he
finds that he will be charged one dollar for each single instruction,
such as (a) Turn right on Yukon Drive, or (b) Turn left at the end of
the street.

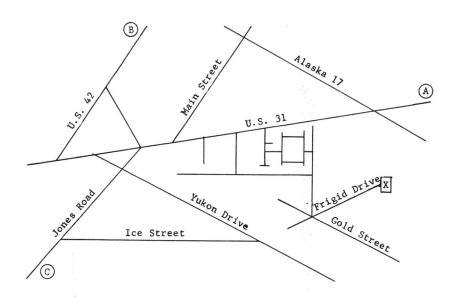

Question 1. Write a complete set of instructions that will (a)
cover the three different arrival points, and (b) minimize the cost
of the telegram. Be very specific, for the friend will do exactly as
he is told and nothing else. Each instruction should be numbered and
must contain only one command as explained in the problem.

Question 2. At each intersection, the friend must make a decision
as to which of the possible alternative routes he will take. For
example, at the intersection of Yukon Drive and Jones Road, he has
three alternatives: (1) turn right, (2) turn left, (3) go straight,
from which to make his decision.

(a) If it takes the friend five minutes to make a decision, what
    route should he follow from point "C" to minimize the
    thinking time required, and what is this minimum time.

(b) If it takes him two minutes to consider each alternative and
    no time to make a decision, what are the answers to part (a)
    above.

Part II

1. Draw a continuous line consisting of four straight segments
   so as to pass once and only once through all nine dots.

. . .

. . .

. . .

2. What number leaves a remainder of 1 when divided by 2, 3, 4,
   5, or 6 and no remainder when divided by 7?

3. A doctor advised a patient that he had no cause to worry about
   his operation because the doctor's last nine patients had
   died from a similar operation and medical statistics
   indicated that one person in ten survived such an operation.
   What were the patient's chances of recovery?

4. A grocer attempts to weigh out identical amounts of sugar to
   two customers, but his scales do not have equal-length arms.
   The first time he puts the weight in one pan and the sugar
   in the other; the second time he reverses the procedure.
   Does he gain or lose? How much?

5. If I were to give 7 cents to each of the beggars at my door, I
   would have 24 cents left. I lack 32 cents of being able to
   give them 9 cents apiece. How many beggars are there, and
   how much money have I?

6. Find the least number of standard weights needed to weigh
   every whole number of pounds from 1 to 40 by placing weights
   in only one pan of an ordinary balance scale.

FIGURE 16-1. *A suggested aptitude test for
analysts and programmers*

facts on minor changes to be made are sufficient to start designing the
new system.

Redesign. The study team's goal may be to redesign the system's
basic structure. If so, the value of flow charting the existing system
decreases, and its merits should be examined carefully before it is
started. The structure of some parts of the system may change little

or not at all. Detailed analysis of the static parts of the present system by means of data sheets and flow charts will be useful. Detailed flow charts and data sheets of the present system are less valuable if the system will be changed appreciably. The approach of the applications study group to detailed analysis is different if the system is to be changed greatly. The existing system should be studied only to get the specifications that will carry over to the new system; beyond that, the group should concentrate on developing the desired system.

Most systems studies fall between the two extremes of mere mechanization and complete redesign. There are several reasons for a middle path. First, it is difficult to introduce radically new equipment without making some changes in the system. Second, complete overhaul of a system may seem too expensive because of the analysis required and the disruption during transition. Third, complete redesign is risky because the new system, while it may provide a few great improvements, may not be as successful in all respects as the system it replaces.

A one-step change involving both mechanization and structural redesign is often said to be more efficient than a two-step change. Since the structure of the system must be redesigned eventually for the best use of new equipment, redesign may as well be done when the equipment is first introduced. This viewpoint will be more acceptable in the future, when analysts are familiar with equipment and can concentrate their attention on system redesign at the same time equipment is being installed.

Input Requirements. Available input data may limit the basic structure of a proposed system. Any form and size of files, type of processing, and set of outputs are theoretically possible if the necessary input is available; but the cost of devising and operating the system is a practical limiting factor. Some facts that are desired and others that are critical may not be available. Sometimes, for instance, the exact quantity of a particular part needed for use in the near future cannot be obtained at any cost.

Many kinds of input data can be obtained in processable form only at a high cost. The job of converting actions and operations into processable data is largely a manual operation. People read numerals and letters on paper and operate key-stroke devices to convert them to processable form. Data origination is costly, time consuming, and subject to mistakes. Automatic recording and direct input devices developed in recent years should continue to reduce the costs and increase the accuracy of input data. Input problems at subsequent stages can be avoided by keeping data in processable form throughout their use in the system.

A system that is otherwise well designed may be unsatisfactory because the necessary input, if available at all, is not accurate enough or not obtainable at a reasonable cost. The analyst should specify exactly what input conditions are required for a proposed system. Efficient system design requires that all input data entering the system be used, that duplication of data input be minimized, and that high-cost manual handling after the first stage be eliminated.

Output Requirements.   Every manager needs some kind of information. Much information is most efficiently obtained from the data-processing system. Some other types of information do not arise in the business-data system as ordinarily defined: a supervisor supplies his secretary with the contents of letters, and a machinist gets operating instructions from a blueprint.

Information available from the existing system may not be entirely satisfactory, so the analyst examines, in cooperation with the users of output from the data system, each separate activity in the study area to find:

1. Decisions made or functions performed by the activity
2. Information useful to the activity
3. Required features of information, such as: accuracy, timeliness, predictability, and consequences of use

The analyst may have firsthand knowledge about decision making and information requirements. He can get additional facts from organization charts, job descriptions, and work procedures. He verifies his findings by checking with operating representatives and with managers. New requirements for data and information can be obtained either by improving the present set or by starting afresh with an examination of managerial decisions and functions. A complete re-examination gives the analyst free range since he does not use the existing scheme as a point of departure; but this entirely fresh approach tends to take more time and money.

Files.   The analyst makes far-reaching decisions about data files while designing a system. Size and arrangement affect the usefulness of files for different processing operations. Various files can be kept separate or consolidated into one compact file by eliminating duplication. Efficient processing, it should be pointed out, requires ingenious schemes to insure that the entire file will not have to be processed in order to handle individual transactions.

Completely consolidated files have some disadvantages, for their huge size often makes them inefficient to use. Congestion can arise during file search because many requests are made on the file at one time.

Record arrangement may be awkward because each use involves scanning unneeded data to find a few desired items. Consolidated files can sometimes be used efficiently in selected areas of data processing—inventory, personnel, payroll, customer accounting, and others. The scheme of a completely consolidated file for a whole organization probably is not practical at the present stage of development because the costs of using such files are too high.

The fact that records are of different lengths raises problems similar to those arising from the use of consolidated files. The record for an inventory item stocked in a hundred warehouses is longer than the record for an item stocked in only a dozen warehouses. Accordingly, equal-length records in files waste file space, whereas using different-length records takes more ingenious file design and processing.

One plan for solving this problem is to classify records by the frequency of their occurrence. The most frequently occurring records can be kept in one file, while infrequently used records are kept separate as trailer records. Both must be handled, of course, for complete processing. Another plan for classifying records within a file is by the frequency of processing: the most frequently processed records can be kept in one file, with the infrequently processed records in a separate file. The optimum number and size of files represents a balance between the costs of establishing, updating, and maintaining the file and the costs of using the file to obtain desired information.

One point should be crystal clear: an orderly arrangement of files is required for their efficient use. An inventory file may be arranged by part number, supplier, user department, end-use, or in other ways. Various uses may require different arrangements of records. Some of these arrangements are obtained by:

1. Sorting records as required for each purpose

2. Maintaining separate files for each arrangement

3. Maintaining cross-reference lists

Each file should be examined during the system-design period to determine the best arrangement for the proposed applications.

Work Load.   Facts about input, files, and output are obtained in order to analyze the system work load. The source and destination of documents can be traced, as described in Chapter 15, to identify data input and output by summarizing the work load for each functional area studied. The summary shows the work attributed to each record and gives a validity check against the total manpower in each organizational element.

Input-load facts, recorded on a separate card for each source document, include all the known inputs; the medium by which they are received or developed; their format, message length, and alphanumerical code requirements; and their daily volume including cyclical peaks and hourly rates.

Facts needed about the files to be maintained include volume, record length, form, codes, serial or random-access storage, method of organization, degree of duplication, rate of change, processing frequency, and complexity of processing.

Output-load facts cover the daily volume of each type of output, format, permissible processing delay, requirements for unscheduled interrogation, and kind of output—tape, paper, or card media.

EQUIPMENT SELECTION

Equipment selection involves obtaining enough facts about equipment and its application to make a reasonable choice of equipment. Facts about equipment can be obtained from manufacturers (brochures, contract schedules, and solicited proposals) from personnel with knowledge or experience, and from other users of equipment. It is vital that an identical specification base be used in analyzing competing equipment, and that all manufacturers' equipment suitable to the application be examined.

Bid Invitation

After discussing application requirements and proposed equipment with manufacturers, their bids or proposals should be solicited. These proposals are necessary in order to reduce discussions and negotiations to concrete terms. The applications study group can request manufacturers' bids after the basic structure of the data-processing system is outlined and the equipment needs are clarified.

One plan for getting bid invitations is to send copies of all flow charts and data sheets to manufacturers, and request submission of bids for equipment necessary to handle the job. If a manufacturer is interested, he will probably send representatives to talk further with the applications study group, in order to gain a clearer understanding of the problems involved. The manufacturer working alone cannot be expected to determine exactly what equipment is needed.

Bid invitations should be sent to all equipment manufacturers who might be able to fulfill the requirements. A new manufacturer may devise novel equipment for a system superior to that devised by the applications study team. Newcomers in a field sometimes develop newer and better equipment and related systems than do established manufacturers. On the other hand, there is a higher risk that radically different equipment and systems may not work out as planned. Both new and established manufacturers occasionally fail in this regard. Prototype equipment put out for field testing often goes "back to the drawing boards."

A well-planned description in the bid invitation is useful because it does the following things:

1. Tells the manufacturer what requirements must be met
2. Reduces the questions asked by manufacturers and thereby saves time for both the applications group and the manufacturers
3. Provides a fair basis for comparing different equipment

Criteria to be used in evaluating equipment should be included in the bid request so that manufacturers will then know both what is desired and what is demanded. *Desires* are merely voiced as the basis for discussion, whereas *demands* are the basis for equipment selection. The equipment storage and processing capacity required should be stated. The adequacy of controls and accuracy of equipment—provided by built-in self-checking or programmed checking—and adaptability to long-range plans are important points. Points to be included in the bid invitation are covered in detail here from the viewpoint of the manufacturer's proposal.

Manufacturer's Proposal

A manufacturer's bid should cover all the details relevant to the proposed equipment that is offered to meet the specifications of the bid request. Features to be covered in the manufacturer's proposal are described here and then summarized in a check-list.

Degree of Automation. An initial point, to be decided jointly by the manufacturer and the user, is what degree of automation the system should have. An automatic system with a high ratio of capital to labor is essential for some applications. Computer operations are often preferable to punched-card and manual operations for purposes of speed and accuracy.

Equipment Items. The manufacturer should specify in detail—make, model, number, and quantity—what items of equipment will be used to meet the problem requirements. Often, several models and makes of one type of equipment are available. The use of an ambiguous term like "magnetic-tape unit" is not precise enough. The media and other operating supplies should be stated.

Operating Requirements. Operating methods—acceptance of numerical or alphanumerical input documents and the processing and output data—that are proposed by the manufacturer should be clearly stated along with machine running time. Different equipment may require varying methods for efficient performance of the same job.

The number of hours of use in relation to potential hours, the ability to achieve processing and interrogation cycles, and the potential for expansion enter into a determination of the time needed to handle required jobs. Random and serial access to storage may be important factors in determining processing time and in meeting short deadlines. Another important feature is the permissible delay in report preparation after either a scheduled or an unscheduled cut-off date. Quick reporting may involve storing current records, updating as each transaction is processed, and printing at high speed when necessary.

The manufacturer and study team together can work out how much flow charting, detailed coding, and timing should be done and who will do it. Manufacturers tend to restrict their attention to the general-level flow charts and do little detailed flow charting and coding unless they get a considerable amount of help from the customer.

Delivery of Equipment.   The manufacturer should give a definite date for equipment delivery and installation. He should also specify any additional time needed to check out the equipment and get it in operation. Penalties may be agreed upon for failure to meet schedules that cause the user to suffer from delay.

The time between the order and the delivery of equipment often runs a year to eighteen months. Check-out may take anywhere from several weeks to a few months. It should be pointed out that manufacturers do a good job of meeting delivery schedules for equipment already in production. Users often have trouble in meeting installation and systems design schedules so that they can put equipment to work when it is released by manufacturers.

Installation Requirements.   Sizes, weights, and recommended floor space for all equipment must be specified in order for the user to prepare housing for the equipment. Arrangements must be made for bringing in necessary electric power and for wiring units together by under-floor, false-floor, or overhead conduits.

A central location, in relation to data origination and use, is desirable. The user will want guidance on the amount of space that he should provide for:

1. Data-processing equipment—input, processor, output, and supporting units
2. Related equipment—air conditioners, water coolers, and motor-generator sets, if required
3. Personnel—supervisors, analysts, programmers, coders, operators, and technicians
4. File and supply storage
5. Maintenance parts, testing equipment, and testing operations
6. Visitors

Air conditioning is required for most electronic equipment to maintain rigidly controlled temperature, dust, and humidity conditions. Equipment operated under unusual conditions—high temperature, corrosive vapor or gas, vibration, dust, or fluctuating power supply—may require additional special precautions.

Manufacturer's Assistance.   The manufacturer generally offers assistance in setting up a new system by furnishing trained analysts and programmers for extended periods. Engineers are usually available for consultation on installation and operation. Equipment manufacturers also offer training courses for programmers and operators. The extent and condition of all assistance should be specified in the contract.

Time is usually furnished by the manufacturer for testing programs on equipment before delivery. Forty hours or so is helpful for debugging programs and speeding up the efficient use of equipment when delivered. The exact period of time available, and where it may be used, should be specified in the bid. Libraries of tested programs and automatic programming techniques facilitate programming and reduce the user's costs. Manual or longhand programming can be extremely expensive and should be minimized.

Rental-purchase Agreement.   A proposed rental arrangement should cover the cost for different levels of usage, length of the rental term, maintenance service, and renewal or cancellation terms. Some agreements may also be made covering the conditions for obtaining an improved model.

Terms should be stated for payment of purchase price, discounts, and guarantees on replacement of parts. Crediting a fraction of the rental payments for one or two years toward a future purchase is sometimes provided for if the option is exercised during a stated period.

Maintenance Contracts.   Any maintenance contract for purchased equipment should specify the parts and supplies included, the number and skills of service personnel, and also the hours reserved for scheduled testing. Scheduled test time should not interfere with regular working hours for the operating staff. A maintenance service contract should specify renewal terms in order to guard against the possibility of large increases in rates after the initial contract expires.

Design Changes.   Occasionally, a unit will not work satisfactorily after it is installed and must be redesigned or replaced by another unit or by a later model. Such work is usually done at the manufacturer's expense.

A manufacturer's bid should cover prospective design changes. A unit that already works satisfactorily may be improved. Another point to be covered is the arrangement for exchanging present equipment for a new model. The trade-in price and priority to owners of present equipment may be specified. Alternatively, used equipment may be sold on the secondhand market at prevailing prices.

Expansion and Integration.   Initially, large units of equipment are seldom used at full capacity. Time is required to develop applications that make full use of additional input-output, storage, computing, and special-purpose devices and thus reach a balance with the central processor's capacity. The manufacturer should specify the possibilities of expanding his equipment. A particular type of equipment may be used with other types by one of two means:

1. Interchangeable media—punched paper tape or magnetic tape that can be used in all equipment
2. Conversion equipment to transfer data from cards or punched paper tape to magnetic tape, or vice versa

The manufacturer may specify conversion equipment available for use with the media handled by his equipment. Also, he can list his other equipment that will accept media used by the equipment being considered.

Check List.   Points to be covered in each manufacturer's bid, as discussed above, can be summarized in a check list:

1. Extent of automation in the system
2. Equipment composition
   (a) Description—make, model, number, and quantity of each unit
   (b) Form of data handled—numerical or alphanumerical, and fixed or variable field
   (c) Storage capacity and method—random or serial access
   (d) Adequacy of controls, method of checking, and length of time between malfunctions
   (e) Operating manual for each major item
   (f) Media and operating supplies needed
3. Operating requirements
   (a) Acceptance of input documents and data
   (b) Time required for each type of equipment to process each major job and the total time available
   (c) Delay after cut-off before reports are available
   (d) Flow charts of jobs showing recommended techniques
   (e) Examples of detailed coding for applications
4. Delivery of equipment
   (a) Delivery date
   (b) Length of time to check equipment and get it in operating condition
   (c) Penalties for late delivery

5. Installation requirements, including both recommended and minimum conditions under which the manufacturer's guarantee applies
   (a) Size, weight, and floor space for each unit including auxiliary equipment
   (b) Electric power—whether public utility or special equipment—and wiring requirements
   (c) Air conditioning—humidity, temperature, dust, and anticorrosion protection
   (d) Space for files, supplies, maintenance parts, test operations, personnel, and visitors

6. Manufacturer's assistance
   (a) Availability of engineers or technicians for analysis, programming, and installation
   (b) Training courses for programmers and operators
   (c) Availability of manufacturer's equipment for use in program debugging
   (d) Program libraries and automatic programming techniques furnished by the manufacturer or available through computer users' associations

7. Rental or purchase or combined agreements
   (a) Rental rate, term of contract—starting and stopping dates—renewal, and cancellation clauses
   (b) Number of hours for one-, two-, and three-shift operation and adjustment for excessive down-time
   (c) Terms of payment, discount, and financing arrangement
   (d) Guarantees on equipment operation, availability of magnetic tape and special supplies, cost of maintenance parts and supplies
   (e) Terms of any purchase option—deposit, fraction of rental payments credited, and expiration date

8. Maintenance contracts
   (a) Maintenance contract cost, service personnel, scheduled maintenance period, availability of a similar machine during extended down-time, and renewal conditions
   (b) Term of contract and renewal rate and term
   (c) Provision for replacement parts, test equipment, and maintenance

9. Design changes
   (a) Replacement of unsatisfactory units
   (b) Arrangements for securing improvements or new models, including trade-in value

10. Expansion and integration
    (a) Additional units that can be added—input, output, storage, computing, interrogation, and sorting

(b) Other equipment that will accept media directly from this equipment

(c) Available equipment for media conversion

Equipment Evaluation

After manufacturers' bids are received, the applications group makes a final evaluation of the proposed data-processing equipment and system. It is sometimes forgotten by people who are evaluating equipment that manufacturers and users of equipment have different interests. Manufacturers sell equipment to make profits. Users want to get information from data, and to do so, they buy equipment. Neither the maker nor the user is primarily interested in the equipment; each deals with it as a means to other goals.

A manufacturer can readily specify what his equipment will and will not do. The user is primarily responsible for determining whether equipment with certain specifications will meet the requirements of his particular applications. This is true even though the manufacturer assists in analyzing applications requirements. An exception arises when a manufacturer guarantees satisfactory performance for an application instead of merely delivering equipment and leaving the customer with the problems of efficiently applying it.

Evaluation and selection of equipment require emphasis on time and cost, but full analysis is required for the following factors:

1. Compliance with terms of bid request
   (a) Equipment composition
   (b) Operating requirements
   (c) Delivery of equipment
   (d) Installation requirements
   (e) Manufacturer's assistance
   (f) Rental-purchase agreement
   (g) Maintenance contracts
   (h) Design changes
   (i) Expansion and integration

2. Capabilities of machine to meet requirements
   (a) Acceptance of input documents and data
   (b) Sufficiency of storage and processing capacity
   (c) Adequacy of data handling
   (d) Production of output in required form
   (e) Adequacy of controls and accuracy
   (f) Reliability of equipment
   (g) Adaptability to long-range plans

3. Time taken to do the job
   (a) Hours of use in relation to potential hours

    (b) Capability to achieve processing and interrogation cycles

    (c) Potential for expansion and mobilization needs

4. Acceptability

    (a) Availability

    (b) Adequacy of maintenance service

5. Advantages of use

    (a) Timeliness of data production

    (b) Production of data desired but previously not available

    (c) Economics

    (d) Other tangible or intangible benefits to be gained

The above points are considered to determine whether the manufacturer's proposal and bid are meaningful. Some further questions are: "Does the manufacturer understand the problem? Has he submitted a proposal in sufficient detail to show that he understands the problems and is in a position to submit appropriate equipment recommendations?" These questions can be answered by evaluating the equipment proposal against the criteria established during the applications study and stated in the invitation to bid. The dollar bid price is only one factor among many.

Selection of the best equipment may proceed along two paths: either identify the equipment that is wanted or reject inferior equipment until only one set remains. The applications study group screens out any bid covering equipment that does not meet the bid request or that falls down on critical points. If only one bid passes initial screening, the group's job may be limited to re-examining it. Re-examination is required to make certain that the equipment offered will operate satisfactorily in the proposed system and result in a specific management improvement. If several bids pass the initial screening, the study group must select the best equipment and related system.

Selection may be difficult because the equipment offered is not wholly suited or is even unsuited for handling the proposed applications. Any manufacturer's equipment usually has both strong and weak points. The decision to select certain equipment may represent a rough judgment about the relative merits of various features that are not easily summarized into an index for comparison. As an example, it is difficult to compare slow sorting and fast interrogation in one set of equipment with the opposite features in another set of equipment.

Equipment Acquisition

The acquisition of equipment involves preparing and submitting proposals to management. Procurement and preparation for installation follow, if the acquisition proposal is approved.

Proposals. The applications study should be summarized and the automatic data-processing proposals submitted to management.

Each proposal should contain the following minimum information:

1. Identification of the organizational element sponsoring the proposal and the location where the equipment is to be installed
2. Description of the scope of the application and objectives to be achieved
3. A sufficiently detailed description of the present method to identify its deficiencies
4. Description of the proposed system in sufficient detail to identify how deficiencies of the present system will be relieved or overcome
5. Reference to other methods of processing data that were investigated and the reasons for rejecting them
6. Pertinent work loads, costs, and other data relating to both the present and the proposed systems and essential to evaluating and justifying the proposal
7. Summary of the makes of equipment evaluated and the method used to select the equipment proposed; name of manufacturer, specific components, and cost of equipment selected; justification for selection in terms of equipment capabilities in relationship to processing time requirements; and justification for the purchase of proposed equipment
8. Personnel and funding implications with a statement concerning the availability of funds
9. Estimated cost of site preparation and proposed installation schedule

Review of Proposals. Equipment proposals should be reviewed by responsible levels of management. Management review will assure that adequate justification for action is documented and will indicate recommendations and comments regarding action.

Preparation for Installation. Upon deciding to introduce the new system, the user should complete all plans and arrangements for installing and using the equipment as soon as it is delivered. Factors which must be considered in planning the installation of equipment include:

1. Space, power, air conditioning, furnishings, and construction
2. Organizational adjustments
3. Recruiting, orienting, training, and retraining personnel
4. Flow charting, programming, and testing procedures
5. Conversion procedures, parallel operations, discarding the old system, rental, and maintenance arrangements
6. Obtaining supplies
7. Communications arrangements

During the period before delivery of the equipment, systems plans should be completed. All initial applications that will require conversion should be programmed and tested on equipment furnished by the manufacturer. Workable and efficient operating instructions must be prepared, and analyses and flow charts reduced to instruction routines for equipment operation.

All remaining personnel required for the automatic data-processing system should be trained and plans adopted for softening the impact of the system on personnel throughout the organization.

SUMMARY

Applications study and equipment selection are vital steps in bringing a proposed data-processing system into reality. The applications study group designs a system or set of procedures and establishes specifications for the equipment required by the system.

The applications study group decides, in cooperation with others, on the methods and procedures to change, the files to set up or eliminate, the equipment to obtain or discard, and the organizational changes to make. This group takes the general proposals developed in the feasibility study and makes them specific; it also reviews the economic aspects of all previous proposals.

Techniques used in the applications study aim at creating the optimum system design. Systems design involves developing inputs, constructing flow-process charts, integrating operations, determining personnel needs, and exploring equipment potentials. Systems analysis and other management engineering techniques are fundamental to the functions of applications study: fact finding, preliminary evaluation, systems design, and specifications development. Designing an efficient system requires providing for multiple use of common source data, minimum repetitive use of identical data elements, and maximum use of automatic facilities. Specifications are developed for input, files, data handling, output, and special requirements.

Conducting an efficient applications study involves advance planning to cover schedules, organization and personnel, systems analysis, system design, new equipment evaluation, and correlation of system and equipment. An applications study schedule should be rigid enough to assure that work progresses; but it should also be flexible enough to permit more intensive coverage of selected areas or exploration of new areas.

Personnel required include the project supervisor, systems and project analysts, programmers, representatives of operating departments, and clerks and technicians. Some of these are recruited from the feasibility study group; others are chosen by aptitude tests, interviews, and supervisors' ratings. A balance of knowledge about both equipment details and system environment is desirable in the applications study group.

System redesign may involve inventing an entirely new processing structure as well as obtaining new equipment. On the other hand, it may be limited to introducing new equipment (mechanization) and little more. The cautious approach is to introduce some new equipment and limit initial changes in the existing system, postponing important systems changes until some later date. The rate and extent of change affect the scope and content of the applications study. Outputs required, inputs available, and files to link them are factors in system design. The work load is determined by tracing inputs through files to outputs. Facts are organized on data sheets and flow charts.

Equipment selection begins with efforts to obtain the facts about equipment and applications that are necessary to make a reasonable choice. Specifications are developed to cover data input, computations, files, and output. Special requirements and features of installation and operation are also specified.

Bid invitations are used to reduce discussions and negotiations to concrete terms. A well-planned bid invitation describes what is wanted, answers questions about applications, and provides a fair basis for equipment comparison.

Manufacturers' proposals should be detailed and explicit enough to show that they understand the problem and are able to deal with it. Proposals should cover the degree of automation, equipment needed, operating requirements, manufacturer's assistance, rental and purchase terms, maintenance, design changes, and expansibility for handling a growing work load. Equipment evaluation determines the extent to which the terms of the bid request are met, the capability of equipment to handle applications, and the operating time required. The price of the lowest bid is only one factor among many to be considered in selecting equipment.

The user relies on the equipment manufacturer for many facts. But the user is responsible for determining the acceptability and advantages of using new equipment and a related system. The margin of error in estimates, which is critical to the final success of the project, must be estimated by the user.

Equipment acquisition hinges on preparing and submitting a proposal that shows a thorough and exhaustive study and justifies acquisition of the desired equipment and system. The proposal is supported by all investigatory work done starting with the initial feasibility study. Proposals are reviewed and, if they are approved, normal procurement procedure is followed. Advance planning for delivery and physical installation is required to assure prompt and efficient use. Applications must be programmed and tested, and personnel obtained and trained in order to start operations when equipment is installed and checked.

REFERENCES AND SUPPLEMENTAL READINGS

Brown, Arthur A., and Leslie G. Peck. "How Electronic Machines Handle Clerical Work," *Journal of Accountancy*, vol. 99: 31-37 (January 1955). The authors attempt to clarify the uses of electronic computers. The payroll operation is used to show manual, electronic, and punched-card systems in the same perspective. Detailed instructions for manual and electronic systems are compared and a flow chart is given for the punched-card operation. An electronic information-handling system is seen to differ from a manual or semi-mechanized system because of its high speed and accuracy and the high proportion of total processing time required for the translation of source documents into machine language. The experience of a large manufacturing corporation in mechanizing its record-keeping system is also discussed. A study team estimated input and output requirements, and the size of the master file through the use of standard sampling techniques. The speed and the capacity of the electronic system needed to satisfy these requirements were then determined. A flow chart was prepared detailing the entire system, and this was reduced to a machine routine by a separate group of coders.

Canning, Richard G., and others. "Business Data Processing: A Case Study," pp. 80-104 in *Proceedings of the Western Joint Computer Conference: Trends in Computers—Automatic Control and Data Processing*, New York, American Institute of Electrical Engineers, 1954. The authors describe a system of unit control wherein all of the conventional functions, such as credit billing and sales slip auditing, are accomplished by one processing. The approach is based on the idea of recording all transactions locally with as little manual effort as possible on some medium which could be periodically collected and processed by a central machine. Alternatively, small, specialized processing machines might be installed in each department. Flow charts are presented, and the operating characteristics of a suitable electronic data-processing machine are outlined. The system is discussed from the programmer's point of view, highlighting the importance of machine characteristics as constraints on programming.

Hattery, Lowell H. "Electronic Computers and Personnel Administration," *Personnel Administration*, vol. 19: 7-13 (March-April 1956). Hattery takes a broad look at the effects of the electronic age on personnel problems. He begins by suggesting that the often-publicized problem of unemployment resulting from the introduction of electronic data-processing equipment has not, to date, been the major problem. The article includes a discussion of each of these problems: (a) job description and evaluation, (b) recruitment, (c) training, (d) career planning, (e) reassignment and layoff, (f) morale and employee relations—resulting from the newness and disruptive effects of mammoth new machines. In concluding, Hattery makes four recommendations for personnel policy in the electronic age: (a) set up a special group to consider the personnel problems associated with electronic computers, (b) provide for a liberal and flexible personnel policy, (c) orient personnel staffs in the fundamentals of electronic systems, and (d) investigate application of electronic computers to personnel functions.

Hattery, Lowell H., and George P. Bush, eds. *Electronics in Management*, Washington, D.C., The University Press, 1956, 207 pp. The articles in this book are adapted from the proceedings of the First Institute on Electronics in Management presented at The American University in November, 1955. Most of the contributors have had considerable experience with electronic data-processing equipment, but the emphasis is on management rather than hardware. The first part contains one article on the management impact of electronic systems. The second part, concerned with equipment, presents no technical details but includes articles of a general nature dealing with: (a) the development of automatic computers, (b) European experience with electronic computers, (c) tailored electronic equipment, and (d) evaluating and selecting equipment. The federal government, which has pioneered in the use of electronic computers, provides the four case examples covered in the third part. Three of the case studies discuss experience with installed equipment, while the fourth outlines a feasibility study. The fourth and last part includes suggestions to management on the key problems faced by any organization installing electronic equipment.

Howell, Frank S. "Using a Computer to Reconcile Inventory Count to Books," *N.A.C.A. Bulletin*, vol. 38: 1223-1233 (June 1956). The reconciliation of inventory counts to books has previously defied economical handling. Howell describes the use of an electronic computer to perform such a job. In the example given, differences between physical inventory count and inventory records continue to appear, even with a careful checking and control system. A detailed description is given of how this problem was analyzed and the electronic processing equipment programmed to decide (a) whether the difference is routine, in which case the computer automatically adjusts the books, and (b) whether the difference is out of the allowable control range, in which case an investigation is made. The allowable control range was based on dollar differences, item differences, and the previous record of accuracy for each item. Howell feels that full utilization of the computer's ability to supply valuable information to management is still hindered by limited vision which sees the electronic computer merely as a means for more rapid performance of established routines.

Lassing, Lawrence P. "Computers in Business," *Scientific American*, vol. 190: 21-25 (January 1954). The author discusses several interesting and important examples concerning the use of large computers to solve industrial problems. Included are Remington Rand's Distributon for inventory control in John Plain Company; IBM's 701 for problems in engineering and aerodynamics in Douglas Aircraft, and for cost distribution in Monsanto

Chemical; and Remington Rand's Univac for factory bookkeeping in General Electric. Each case is examined in some detail, and a final summary is made of the present problems and possible solutions in adapting computers to industrial use.

Martin, William L. "A Merchandise Control System," pp. 184-191 in *Proceedings of the Western Joint Computer Conference: Trends in Computers—Automatic Control and Data Processing*, New York, American Institute of Electrical Engineers, 1954. (See the annotation for this reference at the end of Chapter 1.)

Mitchell, Herbert F., Jr. "Electronic Computers in Inventory Control," pp. 61-67 in *Proceedings of the Conference on Operations Research in Production and Inventory Control*, January 20-22, 1954, Cleveland, Ohio, Case Institute of Technology. Electronic data-processing systems, such as Speed Tally and Univac, can be used effectively in manufacturing stock balances and integrating inventory control in various accounting procedures. Mitchell describes and shows four flow diagrams for inventory systems of increasing complexity: demand meter of John Plain Company; control in assembly plant of an automobile manufacturer; requirements, calculation, and daily scheduling of parts production at several levels in automobile manufacture; and material scheduling and inventory control at General Electric, Louisville, Kentucky.

Occupational Analysis Branch, United States Employment Service. *Occupations in Electronic Data-Processing Systems*, Washington, D.C., United States Government Printing Office, 1959, 44 pp. Following a brief description of the background of data processing, descriptions are given for a wide range of occupations. These include coding clerk, console operator, programmer, systems analyst, and tape librarian. Each description covers job definition; education, training and experience; and special characteristics—aptitude, interests, temperaments, physical demands, and working conditions.

Salveson, M. E., and R. G. Canning. "Automatic Data Processing in Larger Manufacturing Plants," pp. 65-73 in *Proceedings of the Western Computer Conference*, New York, The Institute of Radio Engineers, 1953. This paper offers a clear, detailed working method of using electronic data-processing equipment for a production control system designed for a plant of around 1,000 employees. The machines required for the proposed system are an electronic data-handling machine and a scheduling machine which is similar to a digital differential analyzer. Total equipment cost is estimated at $264,000 to be amortized over two and a half years. Several flow charts illustrate the manner of coding the orders onto paper tape, forming from this tape the various shop requisition forms, and finally printing the production figures and analysis necessary for efficient production control. A general-purpose design philosophy is developed for electronic production control systems which must then be tailored to meet the requirements of a particular plant.

Schmidt, C. W., and R. Bosak. "Production Scheduling and Labor Budgeting with Computers," *Electronic Data Processing in Industry: A Casebook of Management Experience*, New York, American Management Association, 1955, pp. 206-14. Lockheed's Georgia Division is changing over to use computers to develop production schedules and manpower forecasts. The manufacturing operation is divided into four phases, (a) fabrication, (b) structures assembly, (c) final assembly, and (d) production flight operations, each with its own characteristic scheduling problems. A good schedule requires a smooth acceleration of production and build-up of personnel, the lowest peak number of personnel, and an optimum number of units in process. The schedules depend on many management decisions, such as delivery schedule and number of manufacturing line positions. The schedule is planned by working backwards from the contract delivery dates through the four phases, considered as separate operations in series. The restrictions and the principles applied are discussed. Labor analyses are prepared from the schedules. The use of a computer produces a more realistic schedule of activity, a smoother acceleration to peak production, and supplies it faster, allowing a more thorough analysis of its effects. Labor forecasts are an extension of the labor analyses. They take into account production schedules, standard times for operations, and learning curves. The types of forecasts required are described. The advantages of computer preparation are in elapsed time, lower cost, better use of personnel, and accuracy.

Use of Electronic Data-Processing Equipment (Hearings before the Subcommittee on Census and Government Statistics of the Committee on Post Office and Civil Service, House of Representatives, June 5, 1959), Washington, D.C., United States Government Printing Office, 1959, 142 pp. A report of the status of electronic data-processing equipment in the government based in part on the June, 1958 report by the General Accounting Office: *Survey of Progress and Trends of Development in the Use of Automatic Data Processing in Business and Management Control Systems of the Federal Government*. The hearings were wide-ranging and far-reaching for they covered personnel selection and education and equipment selection and application. Much interest was shown in the rent-or-buy question and in the treatment of personnel when work stations were eliminated.

CHAPTER SEVENTEEN

INSTALLATION
AND REVIEW

The group responsible for installation gets the new equipment and related systems into operation. This group, which may include some or all of the members of the applications study group, first sets a schedule for converting from the old to the new system.

Ideas and detailed plans developed in the applications study must be put into actual practice. Equipment is obtained, installed, and put to work. The installation group also deals with physical features, such as space, power, air conditioning, structural clearances, and loading. A major task of the installation group is to orient or train people who will work with the new system in order to achieve a smooth transition from the old to the new.

After the new system operates long enough to settle the initial confusion, the installation group may start reviewing operations. Plans are overhauled to eliminate mistakes, and undesirable departures from valid plans are rectified.

BEFORE DELIVERY OF EQUIPMENT

Problems of installation occur both before and after the delivery of equipment. The decision to obtain a large data processor results from many man-years of intensive feasibility and applications study. Such a decision creates many new problems that must be solved before the new system's full benefits are realized.

The many problems considered during the feasibility and applications studies appear in an entirely new perspective when the time for installation approaches. Problems that must be solved before equipment is delivered involve scheduling, organization, personnel, programming, and physical requirements.

Scheduling

Schedules are used to put installation work in the proper time perspective and insure that all important points are covered.

Lead Time.   A long time usually exists between the making of a contract with a manufacturer and the delivery of electronic equipment; this period is often called "lead time." For equipment that is being developed, a long lead time arises because it may take longer to design, construct, and test the equipment than was planned by the manufacturer. Thereafter, customer demand may create a backlog and a long delivery time may persist.

A long time between ordering and delivery, perhaps with some provision for postponing the delivery date, may be advantageous for the user because it allows additional preparation time. The promised delivery date for equipment is a target for completing all preliminary work. Some customers find that they have insufficient analysis, programming, and debugging time when they try to make their schedule fit the manufacturer's lead time. There is some merit in a different plan whereby equipment delivery is scheduled after the end of programming and testing is in sight. As system analysts and programmers become more skilled, it may be possible to squeeze systems work into a much shorter period than the manufacturer's lead time. Regardless of what plan is used, it is highly desirable to program applications before the equipment is delivered so that it can be used as soon as installed.

Installation work should be scheduled realistically and in detail. Despite the ambiguity and uncertainty of many requirements at this stage, explicit scheduling is imperative. Schedules may be prepared on charts with time marked along the bottom line and horizontal bars showing the starting and finishing date for each operation. Such charts disclose peaks in work loads and aid in sequencing work in the proper order.

Sequence of Work.   Data-processing activities of each application and the steps involved in installation are laid out, taking into consideration records design, data analysis, and the steps necessary to clean up and organize the data. The term "data discipline" is sometimes used to cover the work involved in making incomplete or erroneous data sufficiently complete and accurate for efficient processing. The man-hours required to accomplish the tasks involved are estimated and totaled to arrive at the man-month requirements for each application.

The equipment manufacturer may quote a year or so delay between the date of the contract and delivery of equipment. In addition, several months may be anticipated for installation, debugging, and shakedown.

The work involved during the system development and conversion period can be divided into four parts:

1. Systems analysis and design, involving methods improvement, data discipline, records design, determination of input and output requirements, and development of a functional flow chart of operations.
2. Preliminary programming and conversion, including development of detailed flow charts, writing of detailed operating programs, testing and revising programs, developing procedures for converting present data to automatic equipment codes and media, scheduling operations, and final testing and shakedown of equipment.
3. Extended research of discrepancies, including careful screening of the entire procedure to insure that it is adequate to meet all requirements for efficient operation of the application. Further refinement is made of system methods and data collection and processing, including the pre- and post-automatic processing operations.
4. Operation of both the present system (presuming that one has been in operation) and the proposed procedures during the conversion period. The time required depends on the complexity and diversity of programs and data processing for each application, and the skill with which the new system has been prepared.

Schedules are invaluable for acquainting management with the magnitude of problems to be encountered and assuring that important points are included. But flexibility is needed and care should be taken to revise the schedule as events require.

Organization

The form of any organization reflects its functions. The functions, operating personnel, and equipment are important factors in determining an efficient organizational structure for data processing. Some feeling for why organization changes are made can be derived from looking at the procedures used before and after installing an automatic system.

Before. Data processing at one stock control point involved paper work required to process demands from customers; extracts from the warehouse; shipping orders from the headquarters office; receipts from vendors and other warehouses; returns from customers; and adjustments to stock balances, due-in, due-out, and reserved stocks. This processing required multiple clerical operations involving logical decisions and mathematical computations.

Operations at the stock control point required exhaustive data processing, sorting, calculating, summarizing, transmitting, storing, and recording on a large volume of records in order to maintain detailed records by item stock number. Depot activities of receipt, storage, issue, and maintenance could be accomplished only through the use of detailed records of inventory and financial accounting. This required the maintenance of reference files and the performance of many computations. Much duplication of control information was involved because of mechanical limitations and manual operations. Quantity files were in one location and financial files in another. Separation of the files required duplication in processing transactions affecting property and financial records.

Manual operations inhibited the rapid production of timely information for logical decisions and computations. Limited transaction records required processing in blocks and controlling the blocks from one process to the next. Costs were greater than for an integrated system without any limitation on transaction records or need for block control. Manual operation involved logical decisions that gave rise to multiple errors. Verification of all transactions was required to minimize undiscovered errors.

After.   The application project for this stock control point proposed in-line data flow to provide necessary reports of timely information and management decisions based on what *is* and not what *was* happening.

The new system uses a medium-scale machine for random access to stored data. Automatic transaction editing is used before posting. Logistical data for stock and financial inventory accounting are processed in-line so that the need for block controls, duplicative files, and repetitive operations is reduced. The streamlined organization plan adopted is shown in Figure 17-1. It is reasonably typical of the organization structure used with a medium-scale automatic system, although in some cases the work of systems analysis and of programming is divided between two groups.

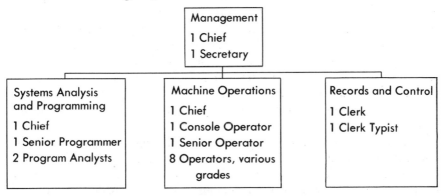

FIGURE 17-1. *Organizational structure for medium-size automatic data-processing system*

Personnel Considerations

The placing of an order for automatic data-processing equipment is the signal for establishing a working organization for the personnel that will be involved. The principles of sound organization apply here as well as elsewhere. It is vital that a qualified individual take over-all responsibility at the outset.

Some centralization of automatic processing is required to get maximum benefits; this suggests that the people involved should report to a higher level of management than the units it serves, although this does not mean that the data-processing organization should be able to impose its will on others. In operating primarily as a service group, as is often the case, it requires enough line support to assure coopera-tion and uniformity for efficient operations.

The introduction of new systems and equipment is received well by most people in an organization, but the necessary changes will cause hardships for some, and some dislocations may occur.

The impact of new systems on personnel tends to be moderate, for the job categories affected usually are in clerical areas that have a high turnover of personnel. Fortuitously, the planning period pre-ceding equipment installation may give enough time for reduction in the work force through normal turnover. Further, the present tendency to increase the volume of data-processing work often requires addi-tional employees in supporting activities. More new jobs may be cre-ated than were eliminated, although these jobs are different from those eliminated, and thus frequently require new people.

Dissemination of Facts.   New systems are adopted because they are expected to produce benefits. The decision to adopt a new system is made after extensive analysis to find what impact the new equipment and system will have on the organization's interests.

By the same token, the employee is anxious to learn what impact the new system may have on his interests. But an important difference exists: the management can obtain independent facts and make deci-sions, whereas employees are dependent on management for facts and decisions. Frank and open discussions by management can reduce rumors that might otherwise present a distorted view of the actual situation.

Secrecy has little advantage after a commitment is made to obtain equipment; but a well-planned information policy throughout the organization has advantages. Introduction of a new system and equip-ment indicates progressive management and confidence in the future. Representations of this nature, when tactfully presented, generate pride and satisfaction in the organization; still, the program should not be oversold or potential difficulties minimized. Dislocated indi-viduals or groups are served best by specific advance notice to permit formulation of individual plans. The important point is the realization by management that all employees need complete and accurate facts.

Selection of Personnel.   One of the first jobs of a data-processing manager is to staff his organization. Members of the applications study group are obvious candidates, for their recent experience is of great value for detailed planning and operations.

An important change in the nature of operations involves a risk at this stage. The data-processing operating organization will be permanent, whereas the feasibility and applications study groups were temporary, having been formed from people with a variety of backgrounds. Some people who willingly served on a temporary basis in the feasibility and applications groups may want to return to their basic career fields. Other people doing feasibility or application study work may not be suited either by training or temperament for a career in systems analysis and data processing. A person may not fulfill a continuing assignment either because he is underqualified or overqualified. Then too, a person who finds preparatory studies interesting because of their variety may not do well when work becomes routine.

Assurances should be given to interested people who are qualified for key positions that the installation and operation requirements are different from those imposed on a study group. These people will be concerned about their prospects for advancement and security. Evidence from top management that the data-processing organization has a long-run future will dispel possible fears. Setting up preliminary job classifications helps orient potential employees to long-range opportunities and will permit revision as experience is gained.

Employees within the existing data-processing group are another source of personnel. Their knowledge of operating procedures may be as valuable as specialized skills that can be acquired in operating assignments. Transferring people from the old to the new data-processing group reduces the future dislocation problem. In general, it is desirable to seek people from within the organization rather than from outside. The effect on employee morale is not to be minimized, for people resent managerial indifference to their plight far more than they do the equipment that appears to have caused it.

Employees within the organization are selected by means of posting job announcements to get expressions of interest, interviews, supervisors' ratings and recommendations, general management ability tests, and analyst-programmer tests. Analyst-programmer tests are designed to test the candidate's ability to think clearly and reach conclusions for problems similar to those he would encounter as an analyst, even though he is not familiar with the equipment and tools for systems analysis.

People with specialized skills for computer programming are apt to be in short supply. Any people trained during the systems analysis and applications projects should be used, if possible. Despite all the arguments for obtaining staff within the organization, a balance of viewpoints and experience is useful. Acquiring people already skilled in using specific equipment can speed up the successful introduction of equipment.

Personnel Required.   The striking change in personnel requirements is the increase in the number of upper-level jobs and the decrease in lower-level jobs. This change is caused by several factors. The new system and equipment is more intricate than the old so that more ability is required on the part of supervisors, analysts, and operators. Problems compound in complexity during the period of analysis, installation, and conversion and demand more skill for satisfactory solution.

Newly created job positions at the upper level must, of course, be approved by management before they are filled. An interesting problem arises in getting new, upper-level job descriptions approved. There is a widespread tendency to think of the importance of upper-level positions in a manual data-processing system as being related to the number of clerks involved. A dilemma arises because more higher-level job classifications are needed for efficient operation of the automatic system even though the total number of people involved is declining. People managing and operating a system with fewer clerks than before still have a critical influence on system efficiency. After the transition period, when operations become normal, the need for top-level skills and management attention declines. Such a reduction in management's attention arises in part from a slower work pace after the often-difficult period of installation and conversion.

The skill of a console operator can, in effect, determine the efficiency of the work that would otherwise require several hundred clerks. Processing time can easily increase 20 per cent or more merely because one operator is not as quick or well versed as others. Similar observations are true for other posts—supervisors, analysts, and programmers. Qualified personnel are critical for system efficiency. New ideas about personnel classifications, as the idea that the mere number of clerical personnel should not determine classification, must be developed when equipment is used for clerical work.

Training.   Much training is usually required, whatever the source of personnel. Key personnel should be educated as well as trained. University courses and association meetings are valuable for learning more than basic computer programming and operating principles; they also furnish background knowledge and permit the exchange of ideas about new equipment and application development.

Equipment manufacturers' training courses and on-the-job training give a practical working knowledge of equipment. Courses in programming and computer operations are offered regularly at central locations by most manufacturers. In addition, most provide resident instruction for specified periods. Government agencies and large companies often conduct their own courses in computer programming and operating principles at both the elementary and the advanced levels.

The classroom, it should be remembered, is not a substitute for experience on the job. Analytic and programming work should be started as soon as some people are trained. Starting actual work provides essential experience and gets the work done. Formal training can be most valuable, if continued with on-the-job training. In this way, advanced techniques can be absorbed and used as soon as the programmer is ready.

A tentative schedule for training and programming used by one organization in conjunction with medium-scale equipment included training sessions for programmers, management, and operators. The training periods were interspersed with periods spent preparing the proposed system, block diagramming and programming, and correcting programs. Training and programming were, in this case, done at the organization's location.

In addition to the training periods, programs were scheduled for testing on equipment at the manufacturer's plant on several different occasions. Program test periods served many purposes. They determined whether the programs would handle test data, and they gave some familiarity with the equipment. Looked at from another viewpoint, program testing also tests the quality of education and training for the programmers.

One approach to work scheduling is to start the first phase of another application before starting the second phase of the initial application. Eventually, a different phase of each application is "in the mill" and being handled concurrently. The workload in any one phase is thus kept nearly constant, although the total elapsed time may be longer than for the parallel-operations approach described above. A compromise between parallel and concurrent scheduling is often used. The way that work is scheduled affects the number of people that must be trained, the timing of their training, and the duration of their assignment to a particular kind of work.

Treatment of Dislocated Personnel.   Careful planning and close cooperation are essential to minimize the possible personal hardship of dislocated workers. Management's self-interest in reducing such hardship is to strengthen the remaining employees' morale and to retain good public relations.

Subsequent lay-offs might be avoided by reduced hiring before the automatic system is installed, although this approach poses difficulties in implementation. Assuming that the present staff is fully loaded, the question arises as to how reductions in force can be accomplished before the automatic system is operating smoothly. Abrupt cutbacks are likely to occur unless staff reductions are made over a long period of time. Unfortunately, no simple answer exists for this and many other personnel problems, although planning and scheduling may help.

In the later stages of systems analysis and equipment installation, extensive overtime can help spread a thinning work force. Temporary reassignment and hiring can be useful. The reaction of employees to such measures is determined in part by whether management has a coordinated plan for conversion. Management's responsibility does not end with reduced hiring and temporary employment, for many transfers may be required because of changes in job structure. Management should handle transfers efficiently and with consideration for employee interests, although some problems will arise in areas that management does not control directly. Disruption of the social structure or changes in status can affect particular individuals severely. By a sincere effort, management can probably retain the support of employees during the transition period.

Some companies find that each level of employees poses different problems. Turnover and reduced hiring may cover clerks and machine operators. Middle-level supervisors may be found young enough in skill, ability, and outlook to retrain for assignment in data processing or in undisturbed areas. Handling upper-level supervisors presents a more difficult problem in view of the limited opportunities for transfer at their level; furthermore, if the number of clerical jobs shrinks, the need for supervisors decreases.

Programming

Workable and efficient instruction routines must be prepared before the new system is installed and operating. Application flow charts and analysis may provide adequate justification for acquiring the equipment, but plans, in order to be useful, must be reduced to specific instructions for the equipment. Idle new equipment is costly and embarrassing, regardless of how well its acquisition was justified.

Instruction Routines. The work involved in preparing detailed instruction routines for electronic equipment was discussed in earlier chapters. The tasks of analyzing a proposed application and preparing instruction routines blend into each other. Together they may cost as much as the purchase price of the equipment involved; analysis runs about three-fourths of this cost, and instruction routine preparation costs make up the remainder. Furthermore, programming costs do not stop with the first successful application, but in most cases seem likely to continue indefinitely. Old programs are revised because the applications change, and new programs prepared as new jobs are undertaken.

Debugging.   Some mistakes are acceptable in many areas of data processing. Manual systems produce several mistakes and errors per thousand operations; but such systems, for two reasons, continue to operate without completely bogging down. First, some clerks specialize—and even take fiendish delight—in locating and correcting mistakes and errors made by others. Second, people can tolerate a modest number of some kinds of mistakes and errors and still function fairly efficiently.

Data-processing instruction routines, when first prepared, are expected to contain human blunders and erroneous computation plans. The equipment will not overlook a typographical mistake, but it may either stop operations or follow such a mistake to absurd conclusions. Elaborate procedures—"desk-checking" and "debugging"—are used to screen out mistakes in preparing instruction routines. Desk-checking is done by having programmers, perhaps even beginners, study each other's programs to try to correct mistakes in logic and calculations. Debugging is done by trying a program on the machine with either test data or real data to find the remaining mistakes.

Locating program mistakes is essentially a refined trial-and-error process. One scheme is to put the program on the computer and trace and correct mistakes as they occur, using several techniques to simplify the chore. The computer is often made to stop at predetermined checkpoints and to indicate the contents of the accumulator, particular registers, and storage locations. A "post mortem" of the routine, as described in Chapter 8, may be arranged if the routine will not function. Another scheme for locating mistakes is to have the computer operate one step at a time so that the routine can be followed as it is executed. The step-by-step approach takes so much computer time that it should be used only as a last resort to find mistakes.

Debugging can take a lot of time, especially in the early stages of processing, before experience is developed in writing routines. Accordingly, routines should be written and substantially debugged before the equipment is installed. Debugging time is usually furnished by the equipment manufacturer, although more than this amount of time is often needed. Additional time may be acquired at a computing center or another installation.

Subroutine Libraries.   Many programming details are common to a wide variety of applications. All programs must include steps that load instructions and data into the processor or edit the output to produce reports. Programming drudgery can be reduced by standardizing these operations and preparing subroutines that can be included in programs written to cover the details of a specific application. A file of subroutines can be kept on magnetic tape for use as required. Part of the programming work is reduced to merely assembling the appropriate subroutines.

One approach to building a subroutine library is to examine all programs for areas that may have general applicability and rewrite them in a generalized form suitable for use as subroutines. This approach is basic, but other methods of automatic programming are available that can reduce the costs for any one user.

Cooperative Associations.   Equipment manufacturers assist in setting up cooperative associations among users for the purpose of pooling their knowledge and experience. Standardization of pseudo-codes and development of basic subroutines are common accomplishments of such groups. In some cases, they have developed highly versatile assembling and compiling routines which can be invaluable to the new user of equipment.

Providing for Physical Requirements

Management is likely to be more familiar with the problems related to the physical installation of large units of production equipment in factories than to the topics discussed immediately above. The new feature, from the viewpoint of the people directly responsible for data-processing operations, is the surprising complexity of large equipment installation, since they are accustomed to dealing with relatively small units of data-processing equipment—office machines and punched-card equipment. A hundred and one points, many of which are individually simple, snowball into an immense task. Complete planning and scheduling are essential in order to avoid last-minute complications and added expense.

General Planning.   The manager of data-processing operations may not be directly responsible for equipment installation, but he must be sure that adequate and complete plans are formulated in order to achieve serviceable operation as scheduled. Factors to consider are space, location, and layout.

Space is necessary for the complete equipment, not merely for the major components. Space for maintenance work, parts storage, and test equipment is also needed; and a reception and visitors' area avoids interference with actual operations. The possibility of short-range and long-range expansion should be kept in mind and space allotted accordingly. The cost of additional space at the beginning may be trivial compared to the expense of alterations or expansion in the future.

Space and facilities comparable to those provided for other office and supervisory employees are required. Some of this may be located

near the processor; but non-operating personnel may be located elsewhere, away from the hurly-burly of the immediate problems of processing operations.

The location of space for equipment and personnel depends on
many factors. Cost is important and is a suitable criterion, if all costs—
intangible as well as tangible—are counted. The impact of a remote
location on communications between the data-processing center and
other parts of the organization is just as important as the cost of installing an air conditioning system.

Other factors in selecting a suitable location are:

1. Adequate floor strength to support weights involved
2. Head room sufficient for largest components
3. Freedom from adjacent machinery—heavy stamping or electroplating
   equipment—that sets up objectionable conditions
4. Electricity, water, and other utilities

The layout of space should be determined early in order to fix the
location of power lines, lighting, and air conditioning. The manufacturer's representatives and the user's own building engineers are best
able to convert equipment specifications into space layouts and facilities plans.

Other important factors in planning space layout are:

1. Location of entrances and exits for convenience of personnel and flow
   of traffic. Ordinarily, one large doorway is enough and helps control
   visitors. Doorways, elevators, and passageways should be checked for
   ability to handle equipment.
2. Adequate operating and maintenance space around each component.
3. "Showroom" window for use by casual visitors. Large processors
   are attractive and have a big publicity value, but they should be in-
   sulated from casual visitors.

Detailed Planning. Engineering and detailed planning of the
area to be used or constructed for data-processing equipment and
people can be handled in the same way as other plant modifications—
by receiving, location, and incoming property groups. A building or
plant engineer can supervise the preparatory work, letting of contracts,
and actual installation. Specific facts about power requirements and
air conditioning loads can be obtained from the equipment manufacturer.

An alternative approach, which is probably best suited to specially
designed equipment, is to contract with the manufacturer for a completed installation. In such a case, a manufacturer's representative
functions quite like a building or plant engineer during the construction and installation phase.

AFTER DELIVERY OF EQUIPMENT

The time required to install equipment can be divided into two phases. The first is physically moving the equipment into place, setting it up electrically and mechanically, and testing it to be sure it meets specifications.

The second phase is to start conversion of operations from the old system to the new. A shakedown period is required to assure that the new system will function as planned or be revised accordingly. Emphasis in this stage is on making the system function properly, since the equipment has already been checked out.

Acceptance Testing

Manufacturer's field service engineers should completely install and test all equipment before turning it over to the user. The manager of data processing is responsible for accepting the equipment when it is functioning reliably. All major features and parts can be checked, although it is almost impossible to test every individual component. One method for testing is to use previously verified data to run a proven program for an extended period. The manufacturer may have a diagnostic routine specifically designed for testing various features.

An alternate test is to run a program prepared by the user. A complex program with real data for testing both the equipment and the data-processing system should use all system components at some point. Verification of the program on other equipment, if available, is useful but not necessary. The test period should be long enough to reveal any weak components. Periods of forty to eighty hours of continuous operation with no more than one or two hours of unscheduled down-time is considered an excellent indicator of reliability.

Off-line equipment is similarly tested, but a word of caution is in order for planning tests. High-speed printers consume not merely reams, but miles of paper during several days of continuous testing. Continuous operation testing becomes practicable only after the printers are installed and in use.

Newly developed equipment may require more thorough testing than established equipment. The engineering design of new equipment requires checking along with the construction—both electric and mechanical—of the product itself. Also useful are specially designed programs for checking out each feature over a range of conditions that simulate unfavorable conditions; this is called marginal checking. Arrangements for developing programs to meet the user's specifications may be made with the manufacturer or with consultants.

Conversion

The pressure to attain maximum use increases quickly after the acceptance of equipment and critically tests the adequacy of all prior planning. An established plan is useful for guiding an orderly conversion to the automatic system. It is also useful for evaluating the progress of conversion.

The procedures themselves are merely a means toward the end of obtaining specific information at certain times and places. A careful check of actual system operations will show how well these ends are met. It is useful to operate the new system on a test basis for a period so that mistakes and errors can be detected without costly impact. One approach is to provide a period of parallel operation where an old system is being displaced. A sample of transactions is handled by the new system and the results checked against the output of the old system, which continues to handle all transactions and is the primary source of information.

When the reliability of the automatic system can be proved by small-scale parallel operations, the responsibility for actual transactions can be transferred. The old system may be operated a short time longer, in order to verify the accuracy of results and serve as a safeguard against system failure during conversion. Users of automatic equipment find that the output from a logically correct and debugged program is extremely accurate, so that little or no parallel operation is needed to verify the accuracy of the new system results. Parallel operations tend to disclose mistakes in the results obtained by manual or electromechanical means rather than by the new system. After the reliability of the new system is proved for both accuracy and the ability to handle proposed applications, the old system can be discontinued.

All people concerned or interested should be advised of what is being done in the way of conversion and when it will be accomplished. Furthermore, every person whose duties will be changed by the conversion should be informed as to what his new responsibilities are and when they start. Publicity about new developments is highly desirable.

Operations

Successful operations require attention to many points. Communications, schedules, operating procedures, and retention of records must be covered.

Communications. Communication channels are set up to get data as required and issue reports when wanted. Efficient channels depend on the form of data, volume, distance, time requirements, and facilities available. Physical delivery of paper or cards may serve in some cases. In others, the information on punched cards is sent by wire circuits. Magnetic tape is physically delivered or may possibly be sent by wire circuits.

Output reports, following similar communication channels, are frequently printed "hard copy" for direct delivery, but some reports may be sent over wire circuits and printed by the user. Communication channels—wire circuits, messenger, or mail—need only have capacity for average message loads, if "waiting lines" are permissible. If any delay is intolerable, then capacity must be large enough to handle peak loads. Some compromise is often reached between the huge capacity required to handle peak loads and the small delay associated with smaller capacity.

Schedules. All operations must be scheduled; but flexibility is obtained by scheduling at less than full capacity in order to avoid chaos if schedules go awry. Scheduled slack time insures that operations can soon get back on schedule. Data origination, conversion, processing, and output must be scheduled for smooth operations. The work must be done on time and in the right sequence. Applications can be assigned priorities in terms of deadlines for output and processing cycles, so that information wanted within fixed, short time limits ranks ahead of information that is wanted merely when convenient. Short-cycle processing can be given a high priority in order to avoid having to combine several cycles to return to schedule if a cycle is lost. Applications having larger cycles—week, month, and quarter—are phased in with daily operations and with each other to get a reasonably level work load.

Testing a new program poses an interesting problem in scheduling. Big daily runs tend to push aside the debugging of new programs because debugging may not seem immediately productive. But clearly, an organization soon has no up-to-date programs or new applications unless it continues to prepare and test new programs. Some engineering and scientific organizations give high priority to debugging new programs. Business users might follow a similar plan to encourage development work.

Daily testing of equipment can be done outside the hours regularly scheduled for the whole processing group. Some users find that maintenance causes the least inconvenience if engineers start work about an hour before the other people each day. Maintenance engineers should be readily available to find and correct equipment malfunctions during operations.

The question often arises whether equipment should be used during one or more shifts. Multi-shift operation costs less per unit of time because many costs increase less than proportionally to the number of shifts operated. On the other hand, employees may dislike working a second shift because it violates traditional "office hours." A similar scheduling problem arises for nation-wide or world-wide operations. Office hours at several places are out of phase merely because of time zone differences. Central operations often grow beyond one shift, when wire circuits are used and kept open to cover the operating hours observed at all locations.

Procedures.   Operating procedures may require many policy decisions in order to achieve uniformity and efficiency. Systems analysis and programming must incorporate such procedures and not merely try to tack them on later. Some programs must provide for checking the accuracy of the work of console operators and tape handlers, while others are needed to guard against mixing programs, inputs, and files—which may cause some loss of data. Console operating logs are included in programs to give instructions to the operator, keep tabs on what he does, and provide for reconstructing files, if severe difficulties occur. Restarting and rerunning procedures are also included in programs.

The duties of the people responsible for originating and processing data and for maintaining custody over the property involved—supplies, inventory, equipment, or money—are separated to meet the internal check and control standards of sound management. Auditors are also interested in a division of duties that safeguards property and records.

Procedures must be set up to deal with intermittent questions about the results of processing. Questions may arise that need an answer more current than that produced in the last regular processing cycle. Answers can be obtained by interrogating the system, if the equipment is able to handle isolated questions. Another plan, used when equipment does not have random interrogation ability, is to get an answer during the next regular processing cycle. Each plan has both good and bad features.

Questions about the long-term history of any record—customer, employee, inventory item—may be handled by occasional, complete print-outs of files. Each individual print-out is non-cumulative and printed-out files may be purged. An index or chain-link scheme is sometimes used to trace the record of a particular item from one print-out to the preceding print-out. In this way it is possible to trace a record as far back as is desired and to assemble the individual print-outs to get the whole story.

Entirely unanticipated questions pose more difficult problems, for new programs and procedures may be needed in order to get answers from files. Some questions may not be answerable because the necessary facts were not obtained or were obtained and then discarded.

Records Retention.   Operating policies must be developed to control the retention of records. The basic question about retention is, "How, where, and how long should original data, interim results of processing, and files be kept?"

Magnetic-tape files are kept for several processing cycles until it is clear that the most recent version is satisfactory for further processing. Current transactions are processed against the previous day's file and, if the output seems satisfactory, preceding tapes can be re-used. In short, keeping files for several cycles guards against having to go back too far to reconstruct files in case of difficulty during the next run. More protection is obtained, of course, by keeping more prior cycles.

Input data may be kept for a longer period of time for any further processing required to answer unexpected questions and to comply with legal and other requirements for historical facts. Data on tape may be retained for economical processing along with the original paper or punched-card data for record and audit purposes. Processing programs and related instructions for operators and tape handlers must be retained after new programs are introduced in order to utilize old files.

Magnetic-tape files are interesting from the record "destruction" viewpoint. Records on magnetic tape can be selectively erased and condensed, if desired. The daily receipts and issues of widgets, for instance, may be useful facts to keep for a month. After a month passes, daily transactions may be summarized by weeks or for the month because the daily activity is no longer useful. This feature permits gradual elimination of each record in keeping with its future value. It differs from the all-or-nothing plan of retaining or destroying paper and card records. Of course, the magnetic tape is not destroyed in this process, and it can be re-used.

Alternative Facilities

A well-designed data-processing system soon becomes a vital part of an organization. The system contains records that will supply a great deal of the information needed to operate, evaluate, and control the organization.

Emergency Systems. Any system may fail either partially or completely. Failure may be temporary, as when caused by an interrupted power supply or equipment malfunction that involves lengthy diagnosis and correction; the failure may be near permanent when caused by fire, explosion, or some other catastrophe. The emergency plan to follow depends on whether operations will be resumed soon or only after a long delay. A complete alternate processing plan for emergency operation should be prepared in advance since the data-processing system is vital to the organization's operations. The plan might be started by the following procedure:

1. List in order of importance all data-processing jobs to be performed and indicate those that can be done without the automatic system.
2. List similar automatic data-processing units and their locations.
3. List duplicate files to be maintained and suitable locations for them.

Priority of Jobs.   The ranking or priority of jobs performed by the data-processing unit varies widely. Some may be needed daily while others can be omitted for a short or long period without seriously hindering daily operations. Priorities might be assigned to jobs somewhat as follows:

1. Absolutely necessary jobs. This group will be small because much information of this type can be handled outside the formal system by telephone, memo, or personal contact.
2. Highly desirable jobs—payroll, accounting, and stock control. Some of these might be done manually in an emergency, despite reduced efficiency.
3. Desirable data-processing jobs, the omission of which for a long time will create much harm.
4. Optional jobs to be done, if conditions are suitable. This group includes applications to improve the level of performance of the organization.

Other Equipment.   If equipment failure is expected to continue for a long time, quick availability of other equipment is valuable. The user may have two or more installations with identical equipment. If equipment at one location is out of service for some reason, part of the load may be handled by the other set of equipment. Equipment may be available in a nearby service bureau.

When the load on one set of equipment is planned, the possibility of performing high-priority jobs from other installations should be considered. Such extra capacity is invaluable in the case of disaster.

Duplicate Files.   A disaster that destroys equipment may also destroy all files; or they can be lost or destroyed during ordinary times. Duplicate files at separate locations are desirable for instruction programs and basic records. Duplicate files will probably be on the same medium as the original files—magnetic tape or punched cards. As such, they are fairly easy to reproduce, transport, and store. Duplicate instruction programs and files can be stored at an installation with similar equipment; if duplicate programs and files are already at the alternate facility, the emergency system can be activated quickly.

Duplicate record files will probably include reference information—lists of items in inventory, part numbers, uses, and suppliers. Maintenance of duplicate record files containing operating data is troublesome because such data are changing constantly. If conditions change fairly slowly, occasional updating may yield duplicate record files sufficiently current for most purposes. If changes are rapid, current duplicate records can be maintained only by frequent updating, which may be costly. The cost of preparing and storing duplicate record files should be related to the probable value of their occasional or infrequent use.

REVIEWING NEW OPERATIONS

Successful conversion of the first major application inaugurates a new period of challenge. Intricate problems remain to be solved in order for management to reap full benefits from the accomplishments to date following conversion to a new system.

Modifications

Preparation of the complete program for an application often is so complex that it is virtually impossible to do it efficiently the first time, and the magnitude of systems analysis and programming is usually underestimated. Lengthy programs written to get operations started can be improved by systematic review during operations. Another source of improvement in operating programs arises from a continuing review of the basic functions of the procedure. The question, "What information is required, when, and by whom?" deserves to be asked, and answered, again and again.

As people throughout the organization become acquainted with the capabilities of the equipment and system, ideas for extension and modification of the information output will arise. The data-processing group may evaluate proposals and implement all changes and improvements thought worth while. The cost of making such changes must be weighed just as it was in the initial installation. But the existence of automatic equipment with excess capacity usable for marginal cost alone will weigh heavily in favor of any application that shows reasonable promise.

Further Applications

Studies for developing additional applications should be exploited and the changeover from manual or semi-automatic to automatic processing accomplished in much the same way as was done for the initial application. Each application profits from the same follow-up approach discussed above. It is worth while, at this point, to recall the course of development that resulted in the new operation program.

First, a feasibility study was made to find key areas susceptible to automatic processing. This was done on the basis of preliminary information and, perhaps, with little detailed working knowledge of electronic equipment. Second, an application study elaborated the key areas and formulated the general plan for data flow through the processing system to reach the desired objectives. Third, the flow charts were reduced to detailed programs and the programs installed. Much experience, both in programming and operating techniques, was accumulated after the early days of the feasibility study.

Experience available at any stage should be used to re-evaluate the foundations of the information system as it exists. Reappraisal involves determining:

1. Where is a greater degree of integration of data, files, and processing suitable?
2. What data-information requirements should be added or eliminated?
3. What new areas can be incorporated in the automatic system?

These questions, and others, should be raised periodically on a systematic basis to assure that maximum benefit is gained from the experience. The system should reflect changes in information requirements, and all the data economically processable should be handled.

Special Studies

Most users have emphasized electronic equipment for mass volume data processing. Such emphasis is suitable because routine data processing is the staple diet for processors in business. In general, routine problems (like keeping up with the number of widgets in stock) that need frequent solution are the primary and immediate justification for equipment use.

Some striking benefits can be derived from using electronic computers for non-routine operations or for special studies. Organized approaches conducted by specialists to satisfy management's immediate need for specific information are more efficient than haphazard approaches and occasional studies. A systematic approach is often indicated because of the following factors:

1. Development of operations-research techniques holds promise of improved quantitative analysis for business operations.
2. Machine-processable data obtained as a by-product of routine data processing are the basis for many studies and eliminate the need for costly collection and manual handling of data.
3. High fixed costs of electronic processors permit additional calculations at small costs after the equipment is installed and operating. Hence, in deciding whether a special study should be undertaken, only the marginal costs of operation are important. Any allocation of fixed charges—computer rental and overhead—is purely for accounting purposes and need not enter into the decision to use a computer.

The electronic digital computer is a remarkably powerful and versatile tool. It is worth remembering that, as with any tool, much skill, practice, imagination, and hard work are required to create a useful product. The product in this case may be a level of control and efficiency not otherwise obtainable in a large, complex organization.

SUMMARY

The installation group is responsible for getting the new equipment and related system into operation. Ideas and plans are made operational, equipment installed, people educated and trained, operations converted to new procedures, old procedures and equipment discontinued, and personnel transferred. Large costs are involved in operating a big data-processing system; the economic stakes are high.

Before equipment is delivered it is necessary to plan for the installation schedule, the operating organization, analytical and programming work, and site requirements. Equipment delivery schedules of a year or so enable the user to do pre-delivery work. Experience indicates that work typically takes longer than planned so that a last-minute rush and even a delay in beginning operations sometimes occurs.

Development and conversion may be divided into four broad phases: systems analysis and design; flow charting, programming, and testing; elimination of discrepancies to get smooth operations; and dual operations of both the new and the old schemes during final testing.

Data-processing organizational structures are revised to reflect changes in operating methods, manpower involved, and concentration of responsibility. Personnel considerations involve keeping all people informed, selecting and training required personnel, and dealing with dislocated personnel. Competent, enthusiastic personnel are just as important as new equipment to the success of the system.

Programming in the broad sense—systems analysis and preparation of instruction routines—is likely to cost as much as the equipment itself and takes many man-years for an important application. Automatic programming and cooperative work by users and manufacturers can reduce the programming costs for each user.

Alternative facilities are valuable safeguards against long downtime or complete disability. Jobs are given priority, use of other equipment is planned, and duplicate record files and programs are stored for safety and convenience.

Continuing review and improvement should follow successful installation. Here, as elsewhere, hindsight is better than foresight for seeing how something should be done. Additional applications make full use of the skilled manpower and equipment capacities. Operations research studies offer a systematic approach to improving data processing and getting more valuable information for management.

REFERENCES AND SUPPLEMENTAL READINGS

Bell, William D. *A Management Guide to Electronic Computers*, New York, McGraw-Hill Book Co., Inc., 1957, 391 pp. Bell's work consists of two independent sections "written for the non-engineering layman." The first half is devoted to a basic introduction to electronic data-processing machines. Each of the major components of a processor—(a) input, (b) storage,

(c) arithmetic and logic, (d) output, and (e) control—is described in elementary terms; and the principles of programming are discussed. The section concludes with (a) a brief look at present and prospective computer developments, and (b) a fairly extensive discussion of management's approach to evaluating and selecting automatic processing equipment. The second half of the book is a compilation of eleven case studies of successful installations, prepared with the co-operation of the users. A variety of systems and applications are included and each is discussed in considerable detail. Problems of selection, installation, and operation are all emphasized, and the results accomplished are noted. The studies included are: (1) Inventory Control at John Plain, (2) Reservation Control at American Airlines, (3) Actuarial Operation at Metropolitan Life, (4) Integrated Accounting at General Electric, (5) Production Control at Lockheed, (6) Air Traffic Control by the C.A.A., (7) Management Reporting at Allstate Insurance, (8) Production Scheduling at General Electric, (9) Installation Problems at Pacific Mutual, (10) Integrated Accounting at International Harvester, and (11) Unit Inventory Control at Chrysler.

Canning, Richard G. *Installing Electronic Data Processing Systems*, New York, John Wiley & Sons, Inc., 1957, 193 pp. This book is a sequel to *Electronic Data Processing for Business and Industry*. Canning discusses plans for installing, programming, and operating equipment. This is a "case" study of the AAA Company, a fictional manufacturer of aircraft components. It introduces a new system to improve work standards, scheduling, and material inventory control. Chapters deal with organization of the over-all program, personnel selection, systems planning, general programming, re-programming after a year, equipment facilities, conversion, reliability, and equipment loads. Chapter 9 points out that reliability is a prime criterion for accepting a new program. Thus, the schedule of machine time for daily, weekly, and monthly jobs must be carefully and realistically planned. A list of eleven "loss factors" for planning the daily workload is included. The second major consideration is accuracy. Four major costs must be carefully budgeted: equipment, personnel, "do-over," and miscellaneous. Experience after four years is summarized in retrospect. Appendices deal with status of systems of plans at the end of the second year and personnel selection-administration throughout the whole program.

Canning, Richard G. and Roger L. Sisson. *Cutting the Cost of Your EDP Installation*, Los Angeles, Canning, Sisson, and Associates, 1958, 173 pp. and appendices. This special report is restricted to the single but important problem of planning and preparing the computer site. The objective is to provide an efficient, economical, tested solution to most of the problems of physically installing a computer. The authors say that they aimed "to pull together all pertinent information on EDP installation problems, combine it with our own experience as EDP consultants, and to present it in a form which can be most useful to you." Written as a report to management that has just ordered an electronic data-processing system, this report is said to be useful for anyone who has reached the feasibility study stage.

Craig, Harold F. *Administering a Conversion to Electronic Accounting*, Graduate School of Business Administration, Cambridge, Mass., Harvard University Press, 1955, 224 pp. Personnel reaction during the installation of an IBM tabulating system in the Commercial Department of the Amalgamated Insurance Company, New York, is the subject of this case study. Conditions are described before and after the change, including (a) the departmental functions, (b) job descriptions, and (c) employee attitudes and inter-relationships. Administrative problems occurring during the conversion period are explained, and the impact on social groupings is analyzed. A second section of the book deals with (a) the planning team, (b) its approach, and (c) changes in key personnel. Considerable space is devoted to a review of conferences among officials and interviews held by the author throughout the planning and installation period. The personnel-oriented approach used by the company resulted in a minimum of friction during the changeover, and in a general acceptance of the new system.

PART SEVEN

SYSTEM
RE-EXAMINATION
AND PROSPECTIVE
DEVELOPMENTS

CHAPTER EIGHTEEN

SCIENTIFIC DECISION PROCESSES

Seeking more effective means of making decisions is an important area of management research. Decision making is the prime consideration and the biggest problem in the design and operation of business systems. It is usually simpler to collect, manipulate, and present huge masses of facts than it is to devise methods of selecting and organizing those facts into useful answers to specific questions. Data-system studies (containing accurate and detailed flow charts, load diagrams, machine characteristics, and cost breakdowns) are often of little use to the manager who must choose a system design, because he cannot use such facts as the basis for selection.

Scientific decision processes are, in essence, systematic means of developing and using explicitly identified data, rules, and criteria in making decisions. These processes appear in many forms and emerge from many disciplines. In the past decade, there has been a tremendous surge of new ideas and methods useful to the business manager or analyst; these emerged not only from operations research and management science, but also from many related fields, such as econometrics and mathematical statistics. Each one of these areas has its own particular emphasis, but they share a number of similar concepts and methods. Earlier, many of these concepts and methods were in use; but widespread understanding and acceptance of them in relation to managerial problems is a recent phenomenon.

This chapter discusses scientific decision-making processes as they apply to management information systems and gives brief descriptions of some of them that appear most relevant to such systems. No attempt is made to explain these processes in complete detail. The reader interested in the actual use of these techniques may refer to one of the several general texts or to the numerous journal articles on specific techniques (Bowman and Fetter, 1957; Churchman, Ackoff, and Arnoff, 1957; and A Comprehensive Bibliography on Operations Research, 1958).

FUNDAMENTALS

In essence, the scientific decision process takes a set of data (either measurements or estimates), manipulates it into the desired form, and compares it against certain criteria in order to enable management to reach a decision.

A very simple example would be a rule that employees may leave work if the sum of the temperature and relative humidity exceeds 150. The data required for this rule are measurements of temperature and humidity; the criterion is a sum of 150 for the two; and the manipulation involved is adding the two measurements and subtracting the sum from 150. A positive number would result in a decision to keep employees at work, while a negative number would cause dismissal for the afternoon. This decision—sum of temperature and humidity compared to 150—is illogical mathematically, for it adds different units—degrees and per cent. The sum of temperature and humidity may be quite suitable for physiological purposes. The "discomfort index," you may recall, is obtained as follows: $(\text{Temperature} + \text{Humidity}) \times .40 + 15$. Most people are supposed to be comfortable when the index is 70 but uncomfortable at 80. Some of the more significant decision processes in use today are almost as simple as the temperature-humidity illustration, although many, of course, are far more complex.

A Program for Solving Problems

The development and application of a decision process requires a careful plan involving the following steps:

1. Define the problem and objectives.
2. Select the decision criteria.
3. Develop the decision-making technique.
4. Determine the data requirements.
5. Establish rules to appraise the results.

A valid plan is essential. Determination of data requirements along with development of a decision technique is necessary to get a workable process. Unless data requirements are considered at an early stage, a researcher may belatedly discover that critical data are not available. Furthermore, it is equally easy to solve the wrong problem or work toward the wrong objective unless all five of the above-mentioned considerations are carefully developed in the original plan.

Define the Problem.   The how, when, why, where, and what of decisions to be made and objectives to be realized are all-important elements in defining the problem. The real problem and the governing objectives are not usually obvious; their definition requires careful thought. The work involved in defining the problem and objectives is circular. Initially, the problem is defined, an objective chosen, and the essentials of the situation studied. Preliminary results of the study are then used to improve the definition of the problem. On the basis of these results, the problem can be redefined to direct more attention to elements that appear important.

Select Criteria.   A careful statement of objectives, although vital to defining the problem, is seldom directly useful for decision making. The goal is to find criteria that can be used for making decisions that lead to the desired objective. The objectives of the temperature-humidity rule discussed earlier might be to prevent costly mistakes, poor-quality workmanship, and a decline in employee morale because of excess heat or humidity. The objectives—reduced costs and improved product—are greatly different from the decision criterion which compares temperature plus humidity to 150. Since the objectives and criteria may not have a simple cause-and-effect relationship, care is necessary to insure that they are compatible. Given two events, A and B, examination may show that A causes B, that B causes A, that something else "C" causes both, or that A and B have only a chance relationship. In the temperature-humidity example, it may be easy to show that some relationships have no bearing on the matter: excess costs and poor workmanship do not cause high temperature and humidity. But it may be far more difficult to find which of the other possible relationships is both valid and useful to indicate actual events. Huge costs may result from use of the wrong decision criteria.

Develop Decision-making Techniques.   An executive can often make good decisions by intuitively weighing all relevant facts in a manner that he cannot explicitly describe. Scientific decision processes, however, rely on explicit statements of all relevant facts and relationships. These processes may employ mathematics, deductive logic, statistical inference, and probability theory—all to operate on some data and produce either a decision or information to guide decision making.

Decision techniques operate in several different ways. Analytic techniques arrive directly at a solution by applying mathematical tools such as algebra and calculus. Numerical techniques can be used to gain a solution by trying different values for the variables until a satisfactory answer is found—basically a trial-and-error process. Iterative techniques, a variation of numerical procedures, use the answer of the previous trial as the starting point for each new one. Some iterative techniques assure that each successive trial will yield a better answer and identify the best answer when it is found.

Another class of techniques deals with problems involving complex interactions among variables whose behavior can be described by probability distributions. Although a few forms of this problem class are soluble by analytic techniques, the majority require a special numerical technique known as "Monte Carlo." The Monte Carlo method uses random sampling procedures and a large number of numerical trials to predict operating experience from the data and rules relevant to the original problem.

The solution of many business problems may utilize a combination of both intuitive and scientific techniques. Scientific techniques might, for example, be used to generate the direct results of a number of different policies and to eliminate those not meeting some general criteria; a manager could then use intuition to assess the results of the remaining policies against a larger environment and to decide upon the best one. As both the level of understanding and the availability of scientific techniques for decision making continue to grow, a much wider range of problems will become amenable to direct solution.

Determine Data Requirements. The set of data required for making a decision is seldom one simple quantity. A shop foreman with 40 years of experience and a digital computer may require drastically different data to do the same job. The data required are determined by the decision process that is used. Take, for example, the problem of deciding upon the re-order level for an item in inventory. Applying one policy may require data only on average demand during an average resupply period, whereas using another policy will require probability distributions of demand and resupply time plus the costs involved in holding inventory, running out of stock, and making expedited orders. The researcher must, therefore, plan to collect different data depending upon which decision criteria he chooses. Or alternatively, after he settles on a data-collection scheme, he has limited the number of decision criteria available to him. The data systems designer can influence the type and extent of research that can be conducted within an organization because he may be able to anticipate future requirements for data (Stoller and Van Horn, 1959).

Establish Appraisal Rules. Insuring *correct* answers is of major concern in business decision making. A first-line supervisor directly observes some results of his decisions and can compensate for changes or try new policies if current ones are not successful. The researcher should examine the whole decision-making process to find whether it produces the desired results. He can make a careful, logical examination of the process and, in some cases, test it under actual or simulated conditions. Appraisal of results is a continuing task, since decision methods that are effective at first may subsequently fail: the original problem may change or the variables may shift to ranges not originally contemplated. Many situations change continuously over time. As new data, rules, and even objectives arise in these situations, the decision technique will produce poor answers. Results must be monitored and changes introduced in order to keep the decision-making process valid. Dynamic organizations—those experiencing rapid growth or encountering new sales and production conditions—must pay especial attention to the possibility of decision techniques becoming invalid.

Regardless of precautions, there is some risk that mistakes will arise in the best designed systems. When a reasonable range of answers is known and provided for in initial design, the decision method can produce a warning flag when conditions are outside this range. A manager or analyst can then examine the flagged answers to determine whether an answer indicates a true departure from normal behavior or a mistake in the processing system. For the most difficult case—plausible but incorrect answers—one remedy is to try to design a system that restricts the number of such answers.

Models

For our purposes, a "model" is a representation of a decision process, a system, or an organization. When properly used, models can describe complicated situations, predict the effects of various sets of conditions, or arrive directly at the single set of conditions that satisfies the criteria imposed on the model. A knowledge of the principles of models is important since models are commonly used for objective decision making.

Models of airplanes or ships are familiar; a model of a business system or decision process is more difficult to visualize. A miniature scale model of a decision process would be a strange sight, but models come in many forms.

The rules for determining the amount of money in a checking account is a simple example of a mathematical model to answer the question, "How much money can I spend?" Present balance = previous balance + deposits − (withdrawals + service charges).

Provided the model truly represents facts, the bank-book balance should exactly determine, or, if applied to the future, predict the amount of money in an account. The model will predict the results of a wide variety of possible actions without necessitating calls, visits, or any other interruption of the bank's operations. If instead, the balance were determined by intuition or experimentation, banking would be chaotic. Because a bank book is so familiar, it may not be recognized as containing a model; yet it illustrates most of the features that make models so useful in business.

There are many forms of models; the three basic forms are iconic, analogic, and symbolic. An iconic model or *replica* simply reproduces all or some of the properties of the original object. The reproduction may be identical; changed by a proportional reduction or enlargement in size; restricted to one dimension, such as in drawings or pictures; or simplified by elimination of unneeded properties, as in an accurate facsimile of the outside of a machine, with the internal mechanism absent. When used for solving problems, as a scale model might be used for layout of the computer room, a replica yields only trial-and-error solutions and provides no means of recognizing a best solution, if and when one is found. If the goal is only to find a workable or acceptable solution, or if other models are unavailable, replicas can be quite useful. They are better suited for describing problems than for solving them.

Analogue models represent original properties by another set of properties easier to illustrate or use. A flow chart, for example, is an analogue model for some properties of a data-processing system. Combinations of lines, squares, circles, and other shapes represent the flows of various media to and from different operations. In similar fashion, small tags on different hooks of a scheduling board stand for jobs at different locations in a shop. Given the complexity of many business systems, the low cost and simplicity of analogue models make them preferable to replicas. Analogue models, like replicas, involve trial-and-error solutions and are unable to identify the best solution.

Symbolic models are important for management decision making because they use mathematical and logical symbols to define a system. A simple mathematical model can solve the following problem: Can a sorter perform a given job within a specified time? If a sorter will handle 1500 cards a minute, then

$$\text{Time required} = \frac{(\text{Number of cards}) \times \binom{\text{Number of digits}}{\text{in sorting key}}}{1500}$$

Given some criterion—such as the job's being worth doing if it takes less than X minutes—the model can quickly and simply show whether the job should be run. A more realistic model might account for time to load and unload the cards plus a safety allowance to re-sort cards that are dropped or mixed up.

Symbolic models are often easy to manipulate. Furthermore, if changes occur in the relevant costs, times, or quantities, simply changing a number will update the model. Computing and data-processing systems already deal with symbols and, hence, are readily compatible with many symbolic models. For symbolic models requiring trial-and-error solutions, computers can make and evaluate the trials if that is warranted by the size of the problem. In addition, answers that meet the criteria can be obtained directly for symbolic models with analytic solutions. Of all types, symbolic models involve the highest degree of abstraction from the real world. Symbolic model building is a formidable task because of the large number of variables that may affect a business system and the vaguely defined nature of management decision processes, environments, and organizations.

One approach to large business problems uses a combination of all three types of models. The RAND Corporation's Logistics Simulation Laboratory illustrates the joint use of several kinds of models (Geisler, 1959). RAND duplicates such items as key people, telephone circuits, reports, and monitor equipment consoles to investigate preferred policies for maintaining and operating a strategic missile force. Punched cards labeled as maintenance men, repair equipment, and spare parts move from place to place as analogues of real counterparts. The behavior of the missiles and of their support equipment—considering failure, repair, and travel time—are generated from mathematical models by a computer. Here a variety of models approximates the behavior of a large, complex organization. Furthermore, the structure of this model changes over time. After the nature of a part of the model represented by an analogue or replica is discovered and understood, that part is replaced with a symbolic model.

Certainty and Uncertainty

In models that deal with certainty—deterministic models—each quantity involved has a clearly defined value at any one time. The number of rows and columns in a punched card, the speed of a sorter, and the monthly rental of a computer are known with certainty. The number of transactions that will need processing tomorrow, however, is frequently not known with certainty. During the past month, the number might have varied from 3500 to 6300 per day. Deterministic models may be used to find the best policy for a low, a high, and an average volume. But the best over-all policy is ambiguous since the model does not provide for random variation or uncertainty. A deterministic model may work satisfactorily if the best policy for an average workload is close to the best over-all policy; however, the policy that is best for the average load may prove to be unsatisfactory in practice.

Systems designers in a department store might plan for the on-line sales processing system to handle the average transaction rate. Sales volume may vary greatly and in a random fashion, so that the system is overloaded during busy periods, causing inconvenience and delay to customers, but is hardly used at all during slack periods. By considering the load variation, the systems designers can predict the long-run amount of customer delay and idle machine time for systems of different sizes and select the system offering the best balance. Or, if none of the systems seems desirable, then transactions might be stored during peak periods for processing during slack periods. In any case, a deterministic model can easily lead a store's management astray. Many business models do, in fact, go astray because they are designed for average loads and cannot cope with random variation.

Models that deal with uncertainty—*stochastic* models—express fluctuating quantities in terms of probability. "Probability," in the simplest sense, is the chance that something will or will not occur and is generally expressed either as a fractional part of one or as a percentage (Schlaifer, 1959). Past experience may be studied to find the probability of an event occurring. Analysis of sales for the past 100 days may show that for 10 days no items were sold, for 60 days one item was sold, and for 30 days two items were sold. The estimated probability of no sale is 10 per cent, of one sale is 60 per cent, and of two sales is 30 per cent. Variations in the real world are often approximated by known mathematical patterns such as the exponential, the Poisson, and normal probability distributions; in each of these patterns a mathematical expression can be substituted for the tabulation of past experience. It is important to note that uncertainty is greatly different from complete ignorance. Probability models deal with variations that have a known or assumed long-term behavior pattern even though their value at a given future time is unknown. Game theory models go one step further by dealing with problems where the probability of occurrence of events is not known (Churchman, Ackoff, and Arnoff, 1957, Chapter 18). In extreme cases, where possible alternatives, costs, and profits are completely unknown, models can provide little help.

Uncertainty is a universally present phenomenon in business processes. Processing times, work loads, sales, costs, delivery times, and quality of product constantly vary over time and among themselves. The ability to understand the nature of uncertainty and to deal effectively with it is a perennial management problem. Models that deal with uncertainty are one of the major contributions of operations research and management science to business decision-making techniques.

Models and the Real World

Since building and using a model costs money, effort, and time, the question will arise, "Why bother—why not merely experiment in the real world?" Models possess many advantages. First, the process of building models encourages the researcher or manager to seek out the important facets of a problem and to organize them systematically. Second, models can be manipulated more conveniently, more economically, and faster than actual objects. A computer and a model can be used to evaluate thousands of situations in a short time, but an equal amount of experimentation might take many years, involving high costs, interrupted operations, increased training, and other problems arising from changes in methods or procedures. Furthermore, the researcher can control changes and analyze them without regard for the confusing clatter and rush of reality. Experimentation is out of the question when a particular policy might result in modest profits or huge losses. Finally, analytic models may arrive directly at the best solution, a result not obtainable from actual experiments.

Models themselves pose some problems. Since a model is an abstraction used to simplify manipulation, it compromises ease of manipulation and strict realism. Models, by definition, cannot be identical to the objects or facts being represented. A model builder disregards many features; he omits some as being irrelevant, and he omits still others because their inclusion would make the model too difficult to use. The important measures of the suitability of a model are:

1. Does it provide the desired answers within an allowable expenditure of resources?
2. Does it accurately predict the relevant aspects of actual behavior?

MATHEMATICAL MODELS

Mathematical models are a particular type of symbolic model used to explore management decision problems. They deal with all kinds of subjects, from stock market speculation to machine maintenance. In complexity, they range from near trivial to near incomprehensible. This section illustrates the construction of a simple model and brief discussions of three specific model families: mathematical programming, waiting lines, and simulation. These three families are selected as being of major interest to designers of data systems. The references listed at the end of this chapter present other areas of interest and also give more complete coverage of the points raised here.

Construction of a Mathematical Model

To illustrate the construction of a model, consider two of the problems that a data-processing system designer faces. The data system must (1) perform routine processing activities and (2) answer interrogations that arise throughout the day. Interrupting the computer program to answer a question costs money, but delaying the answer also involves a cost. One way to reduce the cost of interruptions is to wait until several inquiries arrive and to answer all of them during one interruption. Batching inquiries, however, increases the cost associated with delayed answers. The system design problem is, "How many interrogations should be answered at one time in order to minimize the total costs of interrupting the computer and delaying interrogations?"

The behavior of the system is shown in Figure 18-1. As new interrogations arrive, the number awaiting processing grows until processing is done. At this point, the number of questions waiting to be answered drops to zero and the cycle begins anew.

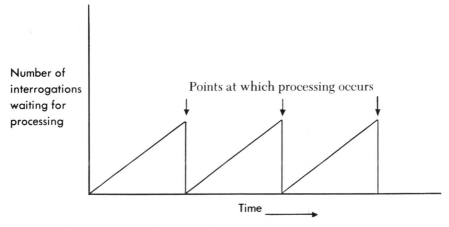

FIGURE 18-1. *Behavior of the interrogative system over time*

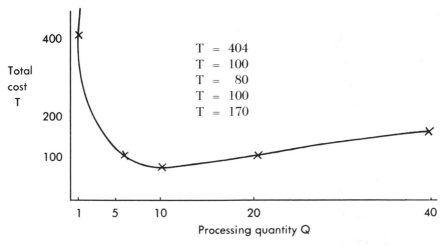

FIGURE 18-2. *Total cost as a function of processing quantity Q*

Assume that D interrogations arrive each hour and that each inter-ruption of the computer costs C dollars; the cost per hour of delaying an interrogation is I, and the number of interrogations processed at one time is Q. If Q items are processed at one time, then D/Q interrup-tions occur each hour and cost a total of DC/Q. The number of in-terrogations awaiting processing varies from zero to Q with an average of Q/2 so delay costs are QI/2. The total relevant cost, T, is the sum of delay cost and per-hour processing cost, expressed as follows:

$$T = \frac{DC}{Q} + \frac{QI}{2}$$

This algebraic expression gives the total cost for any Q, but the object is to find the best Q. For a *particular* set of numbers, Q can be found by trial and error. Using the values D equals 40 interrogations per hour, C equals $10 per computer interruption, and I equals $8 per hour of delay, the total costs which are plotted in Figure 18-2 are as follows:

Processing Quantity Q	Total Cost T
1	$404
5	100
10	80
20	100
40	170

From the general shape of the cost curve, it appears that the best Q is somewhere near ten. If values near ten are used for Q in the total cost expressions, then the values for T are:

$$Q= \; 9 \,; \; T=80.44$$
$$Q=10 \,; \; T=80.00$$
$$Q=11 \,; \; T=80.36$$

Since $Q=10$ has the lowest total cost of interruption and delay, it is the best quantity to process at one time.

For some problems, use of the differencing techniques leads to a specific expression for a maximum or minimum and eliminates the need for trial-and-error solutions. Notice that in Figure 18-2 each additional unit of Q decreases total cost until Q reaches ten. After ten, each additional unit increases total cost. Instead of expressing total cost directly, differencing techniques examine the gain (or loss) that results from adding or subtracting individual units.

In the problem involving file interruption, the addition of one unit to the processing quantity adds one-half a unit to the average number of interrogations waiting and costs $I/2$ per hour. If one more item is held and processed each time, fewer computer interruptions occur so that interruption costs are reduced an amount equal to

$$C\left(\frac{D}{Q-1} - \frac{D}{Q} \right)$$

where Q is the processing quantity after adding the unit, $D/Q-1$ the old number of interruptions, and D/Q the new. The net gain from adding the $Q th$ unit is the savings in computer interruption costs minus the increase in interrogation delay costs or

$$C\left(\frac{D}{Q-1} - \frac{D}{Q} \right) - \frac{I}{2}$$

Unit costs are added to the batch awaiting processing until no net gain occurs or until

$$C\left(\frac{D}{Q-1} - \frac{D}{Q}\right) - \frac{I}{2} = 0$$

Solving the above expression for Q yields

$$Q' = \sqrt{\frac{2DC}{I}}$$

where Q' is the processing quantity that will result in the lowest total cost. Substituting the numbers for the previous example into the expression for Q' will result in an answer of Q' equal to ten, which is identical to the answer obtained by trial and error.

$$Q' = \sqrt{\frac{2 \times 40 \times 10}{8}}$$
$$Q' = 10$$

The essential point here is that specific expressions for a maximum or minimum can be derived for certain problems.

Mathematical models, in common with all models, involve numerous assumptions about a problem. The interrogation problem described here assumes a deterministic situation in which:

1. Interrogations arrive regularly during the day.
2. The cost of a computer interruption is the same regardless of how many interruptions occur and how long each one lasts.
3. All interrogations are of equal urgency and the cost of delay increases linearly with time.

A model is likely to give incorrect results if the underlying assumptions are incorrect. For this reason, the assumptions implied by a mathematical model must be examined carefully.

A Simple Model with Uncertainty

The incremental or differencing approach used to find the least-cost answer for the previous example can also be used to illustrate the solution of a simple problem involving uncertainty. Assume that an organization plans to obtain a new computer and must decide how much random-access storage to rent for the next year. Each unit of storage to handle the records of one customer costs $4 per year. If insufficient storage is available, special records must be set up at a cost of $12 per customer. One unit of storage is needed for each of the firm's customers, but the firm is not sure how many customers it will have. The estimated probability of serving different numbers of customers is shown in Figure 18-3.

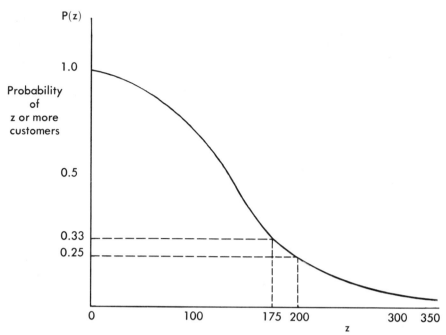

FIGURE 18-3. *The probability that the firm will have z or more customers during the year*

P(z) is the probability that the firm will have z *or more* customers. If z is 200, then from Figure 18-3, P(z) is .25, which means that during 25 per cent of the years the firm will have 200 or more customers. P(z) is also the probability that the *zth* unit of storage will be needed since it is needed if there are z or more customers. If the *zth* unit of storage is not available and the *zth* customer is obtained, then a special account must be set up for him at a cost of $12. The saving, therefore, from adding the *zth* unit of storage is the cost of a special record for the customer ($12) multiplied by the fraction of times the special record is needed, P(z), or 12 P(z). The cost of the *zth* unit is $4, so net savings equals 12 P(z)– 4. The firm wants to add storage until the net savings produced by an additional unit is zero or until:

$$12\ P(z) - 4 = 0$$
$$P(z) = .333$$

From Figure 18-3, a P(z) of .333 corresponds to z = 175. The firm should stop increasing the amount of random-access storage at 175 units since any unit beyond that has a probability of use of less than .333 and will result in a loss instead of a net gain.

Mathematical Programming Techniques

Mathematical programming is used to solve several basic types of problems (Bowman and Fetter, 1957, Chapters 4 and 5; and Churchman, Ackoff, and Arnoff, 1957). In one type, the available resources are stated and the objective is to find the most desirable set of outputs. The management of an existing factory can, for example, decide within certain limits how much and what kind of products it will make to obtain the maximum profit. In the second type of problem, management wants to choose the best combination of resources to produce specified products. For example, many different mixes of materials will produce a certain grade of paint and the objective is to find the lowest-cost mix. In a third type of problem, supplies are available at certain locations and given demands exist at other points. The objective is to match supply and demand in the best way. For example, an electric company has several generating plants and a number of distribution centers hooked together. The objective is to find the least expensive means of supplying the required power to each distribution center.

Linear programming is useful for solving problems where the factors involved behave in a certain way. "Linear" means that the costs, processing time, profits, and other factors are the same for each and every unit. The time required to produce 100 units, for example, or the profit resulting from producing 100 units, is exactly 100 times that for one unit.

The facts required to solve a problem by linear programming methods are:

1. An objective funtion expressing the costs or profits from any process
2. The capacity, quality, and other restrictions on each process
3. Linear, symbolic expressions of costs, revenues, and other relationships

Consider a data-processing organization that has three sections: pre-input, to prepare input data in machine language; computation, to do machine processing; and output, to do off-line printing. On a monthly basis, 40 hours of input preparation, 10 hours of computing time, and 15 hours of output time are still available. Management wants to control inventory on Class 1, 2, and 3 items, but control of all items will require more time than is available so that management must decide which items to control on the computer. The weekly benefit from controlling each item is $.90 for Class 1, $.80 for Class 2, and $.60 for Class 3. The weekly processing times per item are as follows:

Processing Time (Hours/Item/Week)

Class	Input	Compute	Print
1	.050	.025	.020
2	.063	.027	.010
3	.100	.010	.007

If x is the number of Class 1 items processed, y the number of Class 2 items, and z the Class 3 items, then the linear programming problem can be stated:

Maximize: $.90x + .80y + .60z$ subject to:
Input time restriction: $.050x + .063y + .100z \leq 40$ hours
Compute time restriction: $.025x + .027y + .010z \leq 10$ hours
Print time restriction: $.020x + .010y + .007z \leq 15$ hours

This problem is now stated in a symbolic form suitable for the simplex method of linear programming (Bowman and Fetter, 1957; and Churchman, Ackoff, and Arnoff, 1957). The method of solution is routine, although often laborious. This problem is a typical example of linear programming when resources are given, and the objective is to find the best output. The resulting answer, total gain = $420 per week, when $x = 300$, $y = 0$, $z = 250$, is a higher net gain than is produced by any other use of the data-processing system to control the inventory.

The Transportation Method. Problems that possess certain special properties can be solved by a scheme called the "transportation method" (Bowman and Fetter, 1957; and Churchman, Ackoff, and Arnoff, 1957). Such problems involve resources at some locations and demands for resources at other locations. The objective is to match supply and demand in an optimum manner.

The requirements for a problem to be solved by the transportation method are as follows:

1. During one time period, each origin has a specified capacity and each destination a specified requirement.
2. All units flowing from origins to destinations are identical or completely interchangeable for the problem considered.
3. The transportation cost from each source to each destination is fixed.

As an example, an organization that has several data-processing centers to serve a number of geographically dispersed branches has transportation problems. Each branch transmits by teletype data about its operations to one of the processing centers. The quantity of data generated by each branch and the processing capacity available at the centers change so that the company must occasionally reapportion the total work load between centers. Since teletype transmission is relatively expensive, the company would like to reassign branches to centers to minimize data-transmission costs.

In Table 18-1, Part (a), the numbers in the bottom row are the quantity (in thousands of units) of data generated by each branch. The numbers in the capacity column are the quantity of data that each processing center can handle. The number in each box is the cost per unit of transmitting data from a branch to a center. For example, it costs $12 to transmit one unit from branch 3 to center B. The numbers in Table 18-1, Part (b), show the communication pattern to use to get the lowest-cost solution according to the transportation method. For example, the 8 for processing center C branch 1 means that branch 1 should transmit 8,000 units of data to center C.

TABLE 18-1. *Branch Office and Processing Center Assignment by Transportation Methods*

Part (a)

Data generated, processing capacity, and communication cost

Branch Offices

Processing Centers	1	2	3	4	5	Processing center capacity (in thousands of units)
A	$13	$11	$ 9	$8	$ 7	12
B	$15	$10	$12	$6	$10	15
C	$10	$15	$ 9	$9	$11	21
Units of data generated at each branch (in thousands of units)	8	10	9	15		

Part (b)

Communication pattern resulting in minimum cost

Branch Offices

Processing Centers	1	2	3	4	5	Processing center capacity (in thousands of units)
A					12	12
B		10		5		15
C	8		9	1	3	21
Units of data generated at each branch (in thousands of units)	8	10	9	6	15	

The total capacity and total requirements need not be equal in order to use the transportation method, although they are in this illustration. Many other problems—such as the electric power distribution problem discussed earlier and certain scheduling and assignment problems—can be fitted into the format of the transportation method.

Modified Linear Programming. Many problems possess the general form of a linear programming problem, but will not fit into the usual framework. The relationship between costs and quantity is frequently non-linear; for example, set-up costs are likely to be independent of the number of units produced. Because linear programming treats all variables as deterministic, another difficulty arises when the variables are stochastic. Since the length of time to produce a product, the quantity needed, and the cost or profit that results may all be uncertain, stochastic variables exist in many potential programming problems. Still another difficulty arises when the answer must be an integer. Men and machines, for example, are only available in integer numbers. Since these three problems are commonly encountered, much effort is devoted to developing non-linear programming, stochastic programming, and integer programming methods.

Dynamic Programming. Dynamic programming is an approach to understanding and solving a wide variety of multi-stage decision problems (Bowman and Fetter, 1957, Chapter 5). It assumes a system or process whose state at any time is described by data, such as demand, stock on hand, and production rate. To obtain some desired state, management can make decisions: change the production rate, use stock on hand, or simply refuse to fill demands. Decisions made during one period will change or transform the system into a new state; therefore, subsequent decisions must cope with the initial situation and with new problems arising from intervening decisions. The decisions made during a period and the outcome of uncertain parameters, where uncertainty exists, react to produce the new state for the next period. Dynamic programming provides a conceptual framework for analyzing many multi-stage decision problems and a technique for solving certain types. Dynamic programming can produce integer answers and handle situations involving both non-linear relationships and uncertainty.

Decision stages are commonly thought of as time periods, but dynamic programming can also handle other kinds of multi-stage decision problems not involving time. Examples are the best design for a multi-stage air compressor or the optimal loading of different sizes of cargo into a transport vehicle.

Computing Solutions to Programming Problems. The solution of most programming problems requires a medium- or large-scale computer. Dynamic programming techniques were designed with computers in mind and only the simplest problems can be solved by hand. Simplex solutions to small linear programming problems are easy to obtain without a computer; but increases in problem size soon make a computer indispensable. Small transportation problems are best solved by hand; but the use of computers to solve large problems is highly desirable.

Waiting-line Models

The name "waiting line" covers a large class of industrial problems in which a customer requires service and a function provides the required service (Churchman, Ackoff, and Arnoff, 1957, Part VI). For example, data-processing jobs arise and require computer time, airplanes require runway time to land, supermarket shoppers require a check-out lane to process their grocery purchases, and machines break down and require maintenance. Jobs, airplanes, shoppers, and machines are customers requiring service; while computers, airports, check-out lanes, and maintenance are facilities providing service.

The demands for service and the time required to provide service may vary so much that a facility is overloaded in one period and idle in another. Service facility costs can be minimized by providing as few facilities as possible. For customers, however, waiting time also involves a cost. An airplane circling over an airport or a broken machine holding up a production line may incur huge costs. The objective for the system as a whole is to match the supply and demand for service to the long-run costs of providing service facilities and keeping customers waiting.

If both the occurrence of demands for service and the length of time to provide service are known with certainty, the amount of customer waiting time, assuming a given set of facilities, can be calculated directly. But, if arrival times or servicing times or both are uncertain, complex interactions develop and a family of probability expressions known as "waiting-line models" are required to predict system behavior. Tables have been prepared that provide answers for certain situations after the appropriate model is established; but solution of most waiting-line models involves long and laborious computations, if tables are unavailable.

Waiting-line Parameters. The basic parameters of a waiting line are of interest for understanding the problems and for selecting the appropriate model. Important parameters are the customer population, arrival and servicing rates, number of service facilities, and waiting-line discipline.

Customer populations are classified as either finite or infinite. "Finite" means that a limited number of customers exists in the system and that customers receiving service or waiting in line cannot generate a new demand until servicing is completed. Consequently, new demands for service decrease as the waiting line increases since fewer customers remain to demand service. Maximum waiting-line length is equal to the number of customers. For example, a data-processing center with ten tape units that may break down and require service is an example of a finite population.

"Infinite" means that there are so many customers that the probability of a call for service is constant, regardless of the length of the waiting line. At a scientific computing center, for example, research staff members *may* turn in new problems at a constant rate regardless of how many problems are already waiting for service. If the number of potential customers is not infinite but is large in relation to the average length of the waiting line, the case is commonly treated as an infinite population. A waiting line of shoppers approximates an infinite population since the number waiting for check-out service at any time is a small fraction of the store's total number of customers.

Arrival rates of calls for service can be stated as the probability of different numbers of calls arriving during a given period or the probability of different lengths of time between calls. In the infinite population case, "arrival rate" refers to the whole population; but in the finite population case arrival rate is stated on a per-customer basis. The over-all arrival rate for a finite population is a product of the per-customer rate times the number of customers neither currently waiting in line nor being serviced, and hence varies over time. Most waiting-line models assume that the arrival of calls is random and is, therefore, described by the Poisson distribution.

Service time is commonly assumed to be either constant or to follow the exponential distribution. For an infinite population, the average servicing rate must exceed the average arrival rate or the length of the waiting line grows indefinitely. In the case of a finite population, however, any relationship between arrival rates and servicing rates might be acceptable since customers are added to the waiting line (and, therefore, cannot make new demands for service) until a stable state is reached.

"Channel" means the number of independent or parallel service elements in the service facility. A supermarket with three check-out lanes, for example, has a three-channel service facility. "Waiting-line discipline" describes the priority of customer service and the conditions under which a customer will leave the waiting line. Most waiting-line models assume a first-come, first-served basis and that a customer calling for service will remain in line until served. These assumptions are often invalid in practice and special models are used to handle other waiting-line disciplines.

The above parameters determine which waiting-line model is appropriate for solving a particular problem. Specific models exist for only a fraction of the many possible combinations of parameters. When only minor differences exist between actuality and one of the standard models, using the standard will often produce acceptable answers to a problem. For waiting-line problems that contain major complications, the simulation procedures described in the next section may offer the best means of solution.

A Waiting-line Illustration.   Many problems related to data-information systems illustrate waiting-line phenomena. Consider, for example, a data-processing system consisting of a file at a central location that is connected on-line to fifty processors located in out-lying plants or offices. At random intervals, the local processing units need access to the central file either to update it or to extract data. When access to the file is desired by a local processor, an interrogation device at the central office recognizes the request, makes the necessary connections, and performs the desired action. Any processor can use any interrogation device that is free; if none is free, the remote processor waits for one to become free. Each processor is currently loaded to its first shift capacity so that any waiting will require an extra shift and incur additional rental, personnel, and other costs. Furthermore, a high value is put on the ability to supply quick answers for questions arising at the local level. Any number up to ten interrogation devices can be used with the central file. Within this restriction, management must decide upon the optimum numbers of interrogation devices to use to service the local processors.

The requirements, costs, and times are as follows: The arrival of requests from outlying processors for file access are approximately Poisson distributed with a mean of 4.21 requests during each hour of processor operation. Interrogation servicing times for requests are exponentially distributed with a mean of 0.75 minutes of service time required to handle each request. Interrogation units cost $30 an hour to operate and the cost (loss from delayed answers to questions and additional expenses incurred) associated with keeping a processor waiting is $40 an hour.

This waiting-line problem can be summarized by the following parameters:

1. Population type: finite
2. Arrival rate per customer: Poisson, with a mean of 4.21 calls an hour of processor operation
3. Number of customers: 50
4. Service time per request: exponential with a mean of 0.75 minutes
5. Cost per service channel (interrogation unit): $30 an hour
6. Waiting cost per customer (processing unit): $40 an hour
7. Line discipline: customers form a single line, are served in order of arrival, and remain in line until served

The objective is to find the number of service facilities that will minimize the total cost of having facilities available and of keeping customers waiting. The long-run average number of customers that will be waiting in line, with the given number of service units, is obtained from published tables (Peck and Hazelwood, 1959) and shown in column (2) of Table 18-2.

TABLE 18-2. *Service Facilities and Waiting-line Costs*

Number of Interrogators at Central Office Col. (1)	Average Number of Remote Processors Waiting For Service Col. (2)	Cost of Interrogators Per Hour $30 x Col. (1) Col. (3)	Average Waiting Cost Per Hour $40 x Col. (2) Col. (4)	Total Cost Col. (3) + Col. (4) Col. (5)
2	10.50	$ 60	$420	$480
3	1.80	90	72	162
4	.40	120	16	136
5	.10	150	4	154
6	.05	180	2	182

Column (5) shows the minimum cost to be $136 an hour when four interrogation units are used with the central file. Waiting-line problems are solved by tabulating the costs of alternative policies— a trial and error process—for the direct use of calculus is not feasible.

One straightforward way to alleviate waiting-line problems, although it is often overlooked, is to have additional capacity available and to find alternative uses when the service facility would otherwise be idle. For example, maintenance men might overhaul spare equipment or do routine upkeep when they are not busy fixing production line machines. Such an arrangement economically provides a larger service facility capacity to handle peak loads by transferring part of the slack period cost to other jobs. But, for many service facilities, such as fire stations or airport runways, alternative non-interfering uses are difficult to find so that idle time is unavoidable.

The behavior of processes that involve randomly arriving demands for service, varying service times, or both, is frequently misunderstood. Some idle time for a service facility arises from randomly varying demands for service. Attempts to eliminate all idle time by decreasing the service facility may force excessive waiting during periods of high demand. The best solution minimizes the sum of the costs of (1) providing service facilities, and (2) keeping customers waiting, regardless of whether the facility is idle 1 per cent of the time, 99 per cent, or something in between. A decision to keep a service facility continuously busy implies that customer waiting cost is zero; on the other hand, a decision that a customer should never wait implies that service facility cost is zero. Actually, the real situation lies between these two extremes.

Simulation

"Simulation" refers to the dynamic operation of a model. In management research, simulation models often deal with problems similar in structure to waiting-line and some dynamic programming problems. Problems involving many complications—numerous inter-related variables, probability distributions, and line disciplines—that do not follow the standard assumptions used in analytic models are best handled by simulation models. The essential requirements for simulation are:

1. Data or guesses on the behavior of variables—for stochastic variables, this behavior can be described by any known probability distribution regardless of whether a mathematical expression for it can be found
2. A statement of the rules which gives the outcome produced by any possible combination of decisions and circumstances
3. A statement of the decision or management policies relevant to the problem

To determine the long-run average behavior of a situation involving stochastic processes, random draws are used to select particular events from the distributions of possible events. The events are combined with decisions and rules applied to figure out the resultant situation. This result is used as the starting point for a new cycle, which is repeated many times. Many cycles of the simulation process will, presumably, approximate the long-run average for a similar real situation. The simulation of a deterministic process follows the same form except that a list or script of events is used in place of random draws.

A simple illustration will help clarify the simulation processes. Assume that a facility exists to serve randomly arriving customers. The facility is a maintenance man and the customers are computer malfunctions. Customers are serviced in the order of their arrival and must remain in line until served. The arrival distribution is such that in 50 per cent of the time periods one customer arrives and in 50 per cent of them none arrives. Providing service to a customer is usually quick, requiring one time period for 5/6 of the malfunctions, but for the remainder (1/6 of the demands) it is much longer, requiring three periods.

The simulation procedure starts with a draw to determine how many new customers arrive. If the head of a coin represents one customer and the tail no customer, then a coin can be flipped to select particular events from the arrival distribution. After a customer arrives or is waiting in line and the service facility is free, a service time is selected. Dice can be rolled to select events from the service distribution provided that one face, such as the six face, represents a long service period and the other five faces represent a short service period. Table 18-3 illustrates what might occur during a few simulation cycles.

TABLE 18-3. *Simulation of Customer Demand and Service*

Period Col. (1)	Customers in Line at Start Col. (2)	Coin Flip Col. (3)	New Customers Col. (4)	Dice Roll Col. (5)	Service Time Col. (6)	Customers Transferred to Service Col. (7)	Customers Left in Line Col. 2 Plus Col. 4 Minus Col. 7 Col. (8)
1	0	T	0	—	—	0	0
2	0	H	1	6	3	1	0
3	0	H	1	—	↓	0	1
4	1	H	1	—		0	2
5	2	T	0	Not 6	1	1	1
6	1	T	0	Not 6	1	1	0

In the first period, no customer was waiting and none arrived. In the next cycle, since no customer is in line, the arrival that occurs in period 2 is immediately transferred to service and a service draw is made which results in a three-period service time. The customer that arrives in periods 3 and 4 is added to the waiting line since the facility is already busy. When, at the start of period 5, the service facility becomes free, the first customer in the waiting line is transferred to service and a new service-time draw is made. Since the service drawn in period 5 requires only one period, the facility is again free at the start of period 6 and the remaining customer in the waiting line is served.

Repeating the simulation process for many periods permits estimates about its long-term behavior. For example, dividing the sum of the customers left in line (column 8) by the number of total periods that the simulation covered (6 in this case) gives an estimate of average waiting-line length. The fractions of customers served immediately or required to wait one, two, or more periods can also be estimated.

The simulation mechanism, which is an essential part of the simulation model, has three jobs: select specific events from distributions of possible events, combine events and decisions to produce an output, and keep track of all the relevant results of each cycle. People with pencil and paper can carry on simple simulation experiments. Actually, simulation is frequently done on large-scale digital computers. The large data-storage capability, high operating speed, and accuracy make computers well suited for the repetitious calculations of simulation.

The simulation process is flexible and easily handles a wide variety of assumptions. If customers refuse to wait, then the number that would be placed in the waiting line is simply discarded. Under this assumption, column 2 would always be zero. The sum of numbers in column 8 divided by the number of periods covered gives the average number of customers that refuse to wait. A further stochastic element, such as an assumption that 50 per cent of the customers will refuse to wait, can be handled by adding in an appropriate random-event selector. Random-number tables can be used to select events from any known probability distribution, so the ability to approximate the distribution found in a problem by common mathematical expressions is not critical.

If the decision rules are too complicated or vague for explicit statement, a person can be used to make decisions as part of the simulation process.

Simulation of problems with stochastic elements has a unique feature. The answer obtained from a simulation run may not truly represent the simulation process itself. This deficiency arises because the simulation process uses a sample of randomly selected events that may not represent the whole. The average length of waiting line for periods, 3, 4, and 5 in Table 18-3 is $1\frac{1}{3}$ but it is only $\frac{1}{3}$ for periods 1, 2, and 3. Using a larger number of cycles tends to yield a better estimate of actual behavior, but the question remains, "How large and how good?" There are statistical methods for determining whether the answers represent the process and for minimizing the number of cycles required to obtain satisfactory answers.

The simulation process can be applied to an automatic data-processing system. Assume that the management of a company, before deciding to introduce a new system and necessary equipment, would like to estimate how well they will work. Data have been collected during the past year on:

1. How many new jobs arrived each day
2. The operations required for each job
3. The time required for each operation

Probability distributions can be made for the number of jobs arriving each day, the operations required for each job, and the time required for each operation. The simulation procedure is as follows:

1. A draw is made from the distribution of job arrivals to determine how many jobs arrived in the first operating period.
2. For each job that arrived, a draw is made to determine what operations are required.
3. Work is then scheduled into the processing center.

4. For each operation used, a draw is made to determine how long it takes.

5. Any work left unfinished at the end of one period is carried over to the next period.

Performance of the new system—elapsed time from arrival to completion for different types of jobs and the delay due to waiting for different operations—can be estimated by repeating the simulation process through many cycles. Different scheduling policies, various kinds and quantities of equipment, and other aspects of the problem can be studied to make a better-informed decision.

Simulation may represent the only possible means of detailed exploration for intricate situations. Actually trying out new policies may take too long and cost too much to be practical. Analytic models are inadequate when several uncertain elements, such as arrivals, types of operations, and times, interact with each other and with complex rules on scheduling policy.

DECISIONS AND DATA SYSTEMS

The techniques and concepts of scientific decision making are applicable to various problems. There appear to be numerous potential uses for these techniques in data-system design and operation, although published reports are rare. Decisions about the best kind and amount of data-processing equipment raise many waiting-line problems. The selection of a particular set of data from all the data that might be processed has many features of the programming models discussed in this chapter. The arrangement of files, the division of operations between the data-collection center and the processing center, choice of on-line versus off-line data flow, and many other data-handling procedures involve trade-offs between different types of costs similar to the interrogation-batching problem discussed earlier in this chapter. Simulation techniques may provide a practical means of performing the cost and value analyses described in Chapter 10. Scientific decision techniques have been studied or applied in other management systems and areas, for example: inventory management, capital investment, production management, and contract bidding.

It is important to realize that not only data-processing operations but all management decisions are of concern to information system analysts. The designer needs to know and understand the methods for making decisions about sales, finance, production, personnel, and other functions in order to build an efficient data system. Similarly, any attempt to optimize operations within a segment of an organization while ignoring the problems associated with obtaining data is risky: unreasonable data requirements may make costs excessive;

failure is certain if data are unavailable. The objective of the designer of a data system is to develop an optimal system to supply the proper information when it is most useful. The design of data-processing systems and the design of management systems are, therefore, interdependent.

The use of electronic computers has increased the direct interaction between data and management systems. The logical ability, speed, and accuracy that make the computer so attractive as a data processor also make it attractive for handling certain problems, such as inventory control or production scheduling. As a result, the designer of a data system becomes involved in designing management techniques for aspects of a business outside of data processing alone.

SUMMARY

The search for an effective means of making management decisions is an important concern of designers of information systems. Because the information system plays a key role in the management of an organization, system designers must give attention to efficient operation of the data-information system and, more broadly, to effective management of the whole organization. Scientific decision processes, as exemplified by operations research and management science, are systematic means of developing and using explicitly identified data, rules, and criteria to make business decisions. The development and effective use of this knowledge requires careful planning to define the problem, develop decision-making techniques, and determine data requirements.

Knowledge of the principles of model design and use is basic to scientific decision processes. Flow charts and floor plans are one type of model. Symbolic models—mathematical expressions and logical notations—are important for management decision making and have many advantages including ease of manipulation. Data-processing systems deal primarily with symbols and are compatible with many symbolic models.

Decision models, as initially developed, were based on exact values for all parameters: future sales, processing times, and costs. Such *deterministic models* did not take account of the fact that exact values for many quantities are difficult or impossible to predict in advance. Subsequently, *stochastic* models were developed using probability distributions of possible outcomes to represent uncertain parameters. Models that deal with uncertainty are a major contribution of operations research and management science to business decision making.

Since a model is an abstraction to simplify manipulation, it represents a compromise between ease of manipulation and strict realism. The important measures of the value of a model are whether it can efficiently and accurately predict the relevant aspects of the situation under study. Size and complexity do not determine the worth of a model.

A mathematical model is a symbolic representation of the relevant parameters of a problem. The trial-and-error method of evaluating possible alternatives is one way to find the best solution to a problem. Differencing techniques can be used to produce, for certain problems, a specific expression for the best solution. Mathematical models can also deal with some types of uncertainty.

Three families of models of especial interest to data systems designers are mathematical programming, waiting lines, and simulation. Mathematical programming considers several basic types of problems. In one type, the objective is to find the best set of outputs with specified available resources. In a second type, the objective is to find the best set of inputs where outputs are stated. In a third type, the objective is to find the best way to match specified supplies and demands that exist at many different locations. Waiting-line concepts deal with the problem of customers requiring service and functions providing service where customer arrival and serving time are uncertain. Simulation models use random sampling techniques to explore problems involving uncertainty or complex sequences of events.

Much work has been concentrated on scientific decision techniques in the areas of inventory and production management. Although published reports on the use of scientific decision techniques for the design of data-information systems are rare, numerous potential applications seem to exist. Systems designers should exploit scientific decision techniques to design data-information systems and related management systems.

REFERENCES AND SUPPLEMENTAL READINGS

Bowman, Edward H., and Robert B. Fetter. *Analysis for Production Management*, Homewood, Illinois, Richard D. Irwin, Inc., 1957, 503 pp. This book discusses scientific decision techniques in a production management context. The first section is a quick review of production management and the general concepts of analysis. Subsequent sections cover most of the standard mathematical decision models: programming, statistical analysis, waiting lines, the Monte Carlo method, and equipment replacement. An elementary knowledge of calculus and mathematical statistics is assumed. The clear explanations and industrial setting of this text make it a useful introduction to scientific decision techniques.

Churchman, C. West, Russell L. Ackoff, and E. Leonard Arnoff. *Introduction to Operations Research*, New York, John Wiley & Sons, Inc., 1957, 645 pp. This book comprehensively treats a wide range of operations research subjects—from finding a problem to managing the research teams. Sections are devoted to inventory, programming, waiting line, equipment replacement, and game models. A section on "Testing, Control, and Implementation" is especially valuable to the designer of data systems. Most of the twenty-two chapters include an extensive list of references. This text might well serve as the basic handbook for operations research practitioners.

A Comprehensive Bibliography on Operations Research. Operations Research Group, Case Institute of Technology, New York, John Wiley & Sons, Inc., 1958, 188 pp. This volume lists articles and books relating to operations research published before January 1957. Entries are arranged alphabetically by author and coded by general classification; type of organization, function, and techniques involved; and aspects of research and practices discussed. The bibliography may also be obtained on IBM cards. Forty subject bibliographies referenced to the main listing appear at the end of this work along with a supplement for 1957.

Geisler, M. A. *The Use of Monte Carlo Models, Man-Machine Simulation, and Analytical Methods for Studying Large Human Organizations*, Santa Monica, California, The RAND Corporation, P-1634, March 1959, 14 pp. This paper describes some techniques developed and used by the RAND Logistics Systems Laboratory for simulating a large military management problem.

Peck, L. G., and R. N. Hazelwood. *Finite Queuing Tables*, New York, John Wiley & Sons, Inc., 1958, 210 pp. After a few pages of explanation, this entire volume is devoted to tables of waiting-line characteristics for varying numbers of service channels and populations ranging from 4 to 250 customers. The model used assumes that arrivals follow a Poisson distribution and service times are exponentially distributed. Customers are assumed to form a single line, wait in line until served, and be served on a first-come, first-served basis.

Schlaifer, Robert. *Probability and Statistics for Business Decisions—An Introduction to Managerial Economics Under Uncertainty*, New York, McGraw-Hill Book Co., 1959, 732 pp. The fundamentals of probability and statistics, with numerous illustrations of their application to business decisions, are contained in this volume. The clear and complete explanations of each topic require a minimum of previous mathematical knowledge. This text should provide a suitable starting point for the reader new to statistics and probability, and a good review for the reader with some previous knowledge.

Stoller, David S., and Richard L. Van Horn. "Design of a Management Information System," in *Management Technology*, ed. C. West Churchman and Rodger Crane. A monograph of The Institute of Management Science, 1959. In this article, three alternative approaches to information system design are explored and the use of design criteria is illustrated.

CHAPTER NINETEEN

PROSPECTIVE
DEVELOPMENTS

Prospective developments in automatic data processing are considered here in three parts—equipment, systems, and personnel.

EQUIPMENT

Great strides have been made in the design and construction of equipment since the Mark I was completed in 1944 and the Eniac shortly afterwards. Interestingly, the Mark I is still in daily operation at the Harvard Computation Laboratory, and Eniac was used at the Ballistics Research Laboratories of the Ordnance Corps from 1947 until 1958, when it was dismantled.

Generally, each year some feature of data-processing equipment is improved enough to result in an over-all improvement of data-processing capability variously estimated as ranging from two to ten times. This improvement has been cumulative, so that the improvement factor has been many thousandfold over a period of fifteen years. There are numerous indications that because of developments in the laboratory stage as well as in existing equipment, equally significant advancements will be made in the foreseeable future.

Input and Output

Since developments occurring in input and output equipment are similar, they can be considered together. Magnetic tape, the universal, high-speed input medium, can be operated at reading and writing speeds of about 50,000 to 100,000 characters a second by a variety of methods. Data-transfer rates can be improved either by increasing the number of channels or by increasing the density, and both of these improvements will continue to take place. Tape, which was originally seven channels wide, in some designs now holds fourteen and even more data channels. Inter-record gaps can be eliminated by recording in both directions so that gaps left when writing in one direction are filled by records when writing in the other direction. Another scheme is to backspace before recording the next block, when recording discontinuously, thereby taking up the gap. Packing rates have increased from the traditional 100 or 200 characters per inch to 500 in some systems. The extremely high density of video recording on magnetic tape may soon be carried over to digital-data recording and thus yield transfer rates ten and more times greater than those presently achieved.

The manual work involved in originating data will be greatly reduced. Character-recognition devices read characters printed in plain, magnetic, phosphorescent, or colored ink and convert them to machine-processable form. Two-dimensional optical scanners developed by Intelligent Machines Research Corporation are in use. Magnetic-ink character scanners, following work by Stanford Research Institute, are scheduled to be in use in a few years for processing commercial checks. Each has a suitable place depending on the degree of control over the origination and subsequent handling of the document. Several companies are building various types of character readers.

Audio-recognition devices for converting voice input to suitable form for processing may well be perfected. Transaction, production, time, and point-of-sale recorders that take data from time-clocks, cash registers, and other machines, or that operate from tokens, tags, and plates, are being used by business and industry. Handwriting that is subject to only modest constraints can now be read automatically with prototype equipment developed at Bell Telephone Laboratories. Handwriting readers may become an input method in the future.

More refined coding schemes that use an extra check digit to guard against the common types of errors will facilitate automatic preparation of accurate input data by guarding against loss or incorrect digits. At the first processing stage, the rules governing the creation of the check digit are applied to determine whether the whole number conforms to the rules. If the number conforms, it is accepted as accurate input; otherwise, it is set aside for special treatment, or it can be examined by the computer, by means of a special program, to try to determine what it should be.

Interfirm data output and input problems may be partially solved by the widespread exchange of mechanically processable data (data on cards or magnetic tape) rather than printed documents. The output of one organization will be the direct input for another. Communication between organizations—as government and business—as well as between scattered parts of one organization, may be handled by physically transmitting punched cards, punched paper tape, and magnetic tape. Higher-speed telephone circuits will be used for direct transmission of data on magnetic tape. The automatic resending of messages disturbed during transmission will insure higher reliability. Radio channels and television circuits may be used for critical, high-speed purposes.

High-speed media conversion is possible through a magnetic-tape language translator developed by Electronic Engineering Company. The unit will translate from the tape of any one of twenty computers to the tape of any other. The translator also accepts input from paper tape, cards, analogue-to-digital converters, electric typewriters, or manual keyboards. It can convert output for magnetic tape, line printers, paper tape, cards, or plotters.

Charactron and Typotron output equipment generate 25,000 and more characters a second on a tube similar to those used in television sets. Several computers already use this type of output. A high-speed electronic printer developed by Stromberg-Carlson Company operates at 5,000 lines per minute (about 65 feet of paper) for an output of 85,000 words a minute. It can be used either on-line directly with the processor or off-line with magnetic tape. A Charactron shaped-beam tube displaying one million characters a minute reproduces 64 characters—alphabet, numerals, and 28 selected symbols. The Xerox Copyflow printer can be used with stock ranging from thin paper to punched cards in rolls or sheets which are cut to the desired size by an electronically controlled cutter.

In short, the problem of converting paper records into processable form or data into suitable output may be solved partly (1) by improving conversion techniques and (2) by using other media so that the paper document is not created. Paper records, though inefficient, will continue to be used in areas where they have some value as evidence, or where tradition demands them.

Storage

Internal storage will become cheaper because of lower-cost methods of making cores and drums, economies arising from larger capacity units, and the development of entirely new types.

Possible internal storage may well increase to more than a million characters. Mass storage may grow to several billion characters—for use at a reasonable cost and in short access time. In the short run, drums and disks will be widely used. Long experience with drums shows that they are a satisfactory medium-speed storage medium. Drums will be packed more densely and may be made much larger. Disks are, in one sense, variations of a drum, but disks have more surface space than a drum circumference. The cost of read-write heads and circuitry can be cut by using a limited number of them, but the mechanical movement of the heads reduces the operating speed. Disks are already widely used to achieve efficient mass data storage for on-line processing in selected applications.

Mass production methods have reduced the cost of each magnetic core installed and ready to operate from several dollars to about fifty cents. Further cost reductions may result from the use of printed circuit techniques of "stringing" cores. Another interesting development, the Twistor, is similar to a magnetic-core storage plane without the cores; it has magnetic and non-magnetic wires woven together to hold a magnetic charge in the wires alone.

Various crystal and chemical schemes hold some future promise for providing low-cost storage. Photosensitive materials for developing low-cost, compact storage are also being studied. National Cash Register Corporation research indicates the possibility of using a "chemical switch" for data storage. It is based on tiny capsules containing a dye coated on paper or other material—somewhat similar to pressure-sensitive carbon paper. A narrow beam of light "writes" on the capsules in coded dots of color. A neutral light reads without erasing. Another type of light erases the data and returns the capsules to their original state.

Another interesting development in storage techniques is the cryotron, which in the early version consisted of a slender, inch-long rod of tantalum wrapped with a single layer of another wire and immersed in liquid helium. The tantalum is superconductive but regains its normal resistance when current is passed through the surrounding wire. Thus, current in the wire controls current through the tantalum rod just as the grid current controls electron flow in a vacuum tube. Easy to make and inexpensive, the cryotron operates in an extremely cold and inert atmosphere so that it should have a long life. A large-capacity storage unit might occupy only one cubic foot and draw no more than a half watt of power, apart from refrigerating equipment. Cryotron storage units have the interesting feature that rapid, parallel search appears possible even though each individual unit is slow.

Cryotrons and transistors use less power and generate less heat than conventional components. Installation costs will decline because less space, power, and air conditioning are required; and liquid helium costs are negligible.

One version of the cryotron, called a Persistor, developed by The Ramo-Wooldridge Corporation, is a miniature bi-metallic printed circuit that operates at near absolute zero. It requires little power for operation and has been designed with a switching time as short as ten millimicroseconds. Such speed is about a hundred times as fast as ferrite-core storage. A miniature printed circuit cryotron of metallic lead developed by International Business Machines Corporation responds at the same speed as the Persistor. It requires only about a third of the current needed to drive ferrite-core storage of the type now used.

Emphasis on making computers smaller—miniature, subminiature, and microminiature—might be carried so far that a microscope would be necessary for a person to see the individual parts. Buck and Shoulders (1959) suggest that computers may become small enough to hold in one hand and so inexpensive that they could be given away as souvenirs to every visitor to a processing installation.

External storage is improving through higher packing density, transfer rates, and reliability of magnetic tape. Tape storage capacity may increase from five million characters a reel to fifty or even five hundred million characters, which would be equal to the content of about six million punched cards. Reliability has improved to the point where successful and consistent writing and reading on magnetic tape has less than one error in 10^8 recorded bits.

Photographic film storage can store data at 1,000 bits per inch of track and 100 tracks an inch. Extremely high reading rates permit scanning the whole file so that serial access and sorting problems are less critical. Photographic storage cannot be updated directly, but changes can be stored in subsequent photographic records and both the old and the new records considered together. Occasionally, the original record and revisions can be merged to prepare one current record. Another scheme is to keep the interim modifications on a magnetic drum or similar medium and merge the old and new into a new photographic record when desired.

Processing Speed

Each new model of a large-scale computer operates at higher speeds than its predecessor. The Mark I operated at a basic rate set by a shaft turning 200 revolutions a minute. Vacuum tube equipment in use now performs up to 40,000 arithmetical operations a second. The use of transistors instead of vacuum tubes in new computer design will increase operating speeds by five and more times. Even higher-speed computers—several *million* operations a second—are already in the planning stage.

Increases in main frame computation speed are more dramatic than for other components. But the effective over-all speed will be increased by the wider use of simultaneous operations, such as read-while-process-while-write, which have long been used in some equipment. Multiplexing, which involves simultaneous, parallel operation of several units, will also increase effective speeds.

As operating speeds increase, the size of equipment also grows, in order to get a better balance of the components involved, so that the operating costs per hour rise; on the other hand, efficient, intensive use permits each operation to be performed at lower costs. One approach to the problem of keeping operations and programs from restricting machine speed is to connect several consoles to one main frame and storage so that several programs can be run at the same time.

In the interests of economy, large-scale equipment may be shared by several organizations. Four insurance companies in one area have undertaken joint operation of a large processor. Airlines have considered the joint use of a reservation system so that seat availability on another airline can be checked directly by interrogating computer storage; this would eliminate the need for a telephone request to an airline agent to interrogate the storage unit and answer the request. Joint use of equipment offers many economies for organizations that do a great deal of business with each other.

Programming

Systems analysis and programming costs run several dollars per instruction for business problems, and may, in total, exceed the cost of the equipment. These costs may be reduced by various schemes that make the computer do much of the clerical work of developing instructions to solve each problem. Equipment manufacturers and others will continue to develop assembler, interpreter, compiler, and generator programs. People can write instructions in comprehensible words and symbols, and the task of developing the instructions can be turned over to the computer under the guidance of the master program. Questions arising after routine reports are issued will be answerable by quick, one-shot programming to reprocess the data. Instruction command lists will undoubtedly become better suited to the users' needs so that operators will require less training. Ultrafast computers may be designed with a limited number of "microinstructions" that can be combined by the computer to produce desired operating routines.

An attempt has been made to develop a problem-oriented language program which will convert the different languages generated by all the automatic compilers currently being used into one common, computer-oriented language, which, in turn, can be automatically translated into the special language needed for any specific machines that may be built. As each new machine is produced, all that will be necessary in the way of system programming is a single translator to convert the common language into the new machine language. Some work is being done toward having the computer start with manually written block diagrams and prepare its own detailed instruction commands.

The problem of converting one language to another commonly occurs in translating natural languages into numerically coded files, in information retrieval, and in machine translation of foreign languages.

These "machine searching" and "translating" applications of computers may initiate a whole new era of language engineering.

SYSTEMS

Achieving efficient use of new equipment within data-processing systems will probably be more difficult in the future than it is today. The general level of knowledge and experience with equipment will increase; but the rate of equipment improvement will continue to challenge the ability of people to use it for business-data processing.

To date, it appears that few business-data systems using electronic equipment represent radical departures from the structural arrangements for processing previously in use. The task of introducing new equipment seems so great that system changes tend to be restricted to the minimum compatible with the use of new equipment. The brave hope is that the structure will be changed after the problems associated with new equipment installations are solved. It is possible, however, to point out some system changes that are expected to occur.

Data-flow Plans

Most everyone looks forward to having up-to-the-minute facts about everything. Only an on-line data-flow plan can, although there is no certainty that it will, meet such demands. The ideas of off-line and in-line processing deserve a brief review in order to keep the notion of on-line processing in proper perspective.

Off-line Processing. Data processing by the off-line or batch scheme involves sorting the input data and processing them against a file under the control of an appropriate program. Similar transactions are either accumulated over a period of time, or sorted out from other types of transactions, if intermingled, so that the central processing unit deals with only one or a few closely related types of transactions and files at one time. Small-scale equipment will serve because it needs to hold only one file and the related program in order to deal with a class of transactions. New answers or reports may not be available until after all the processing cycles are completed.

In-line Processing. If any transaction that occurs can be handled in its original sequence, although not necessarily immediately, the plan is called "in-line." The central processor must have available all programs and all files that are involved for all types of transactions. No sorting of transactions by type is necessary, but transactions are fed to the processor in their original sequence for complete processing.

Transactions are handled at a desired average rate, but the equipment may be used at partial capacity either because a large memory is required for programs and files, or because programs and files involved in a particular transaction must be called in as needed. Answers are available currently, except for any delay before processing that is used to smooth the work load.

On-line Processing.   The principle of on-line processing involves a direct connection between the points where transactions originate and the main processing unit. As each transaction occurs, it is processed with minimum delay. On-line processing requires that all programs and files involved in handling any transaction be continuously available to the central processor. Current results can be obtained after each transaction, if desired.

On-line processing requires large memories to hold all the programs and files. Equipment speed is limited to the rate at which transactions occur, although some improvement is possible by multiplexing schemes that share the processor's time with other types of transactions, if they are handled on an in-line or off-line basis. On-line processing requires alternative equipment to carry on, if the first set fails even for a short period of time.

On-line processing will probably become widely used for inventory applications where "stock outs" are critical. Banks, for example, put a high value on early information about overdrafts—the depositors' lack of an inventory. Transportation companies want to control ticket sales to get full loads without overselling. Supply and stock management, where accurate, timely control is critical, need to be handled on-line.

There is a widespread belief that on-line flow will facilitate processing in some troublesome areas. The systems design and programming problems for a complete, comprehensive on-line system are likely to be so complex and the utilization of equipment so low that development of such systems should not be lightly undertaken.

Management-by-Exception

Development of the notion of management-by-exception may be carried quite far. Reports can indicate which items are off-standard so that management can focus attention on them. The reports might show only the items deserving attention and omit all others. On a complete or constant-length report form containing one hundred lines, only a few lines will be needed if off-standard items alone are reported. The number of exceptional situations reported can be adjusted to the ability of management and the organization to use the results before they grow stale or are replaced by new reports.

To the extent that the essence of management decisions can be stated explicitly, it is possible to have the data-processing system apply the rules and make the decisions. Managers then need only formulate their decision rules and enforce the decisions specified by automatic application of the rules. The use of a refined and subtle plan for management-by-exception might eliminate a great number of low-level or semi-routine managerial decisions.

Coupling the data-processing system directly to the plant is a step in the direction of completely automatic production. Important advances are being made toward controlling oil refineries and chemical plants by digital computers.

Problem Solving

Business-data systems tend to focus attention on repetitive operations that involve large amounts of input data and small amounts of processing. On the other hand, the solution of engineering and scientific problems often involves small amounts of data and large amounts of processing.

Business has many problems—especially those concerning returns on investment, budgeting, forecasting, manufacturing-distribution patterns, production scheduling, and correlation studies—that require occasional solution and involve numerous computations on only small amounts of data. An example of these is the transportation problem of finding the most economical shipping pattern for handling factory shipments to warehouses. A large food manufacturer solved its transportation problem on a computer at relatively small cost and reduced its transportation costs by a half million or so dollars a year.

Another kind of problem, dealt with by linear programming techniques, involves numerous factors that behave in a linear fashion over certain ranges. For example, the problem may be to blend various components into one product which meets certain specifications—this kind of problem arises in producing gasoline, fertilizers, cattle feeds, and in blending metals. In these cases, the objective of linear programming is to minimize costs by keeping the "giveaway" (or quality in excess of specifications) from exceeding a stated amount. Some refineries make linear programming calculations before blending each batch of gasoline.

PERSONNEL IMPLICATIONS

Two personnel problems associated with the introduction of automatic equipment are widely recognized:

1. Obtaining competent personnel to design, operate, and manage new systems
2. Adjusting the clerical labor force to the new ratio of capital to labor in the office

Problems involved in obtaining competent personnel will be less perplexing in five or ten years. Within that time, equipment manufacturers, users, and educational institutions will probably be training enough people to meet business needs. The problem of reassigning clerical workers will not be critical if national income and employment stay at high levels. Frequently, clerical workers will be reassigned within the same organization or absorbed by turnover and by reduced hiring rates.

Increases in the ratio of capital to labor in an office will cause important changes in the distribution of the labor force. Any absolute decline in personnel needs would probably result in shifts to other types of employment, be absorbed in a shorter work week, or result in unemployment. But it appears probable that the growth of office operations will actually be encouraged because they will cost less than they do today; such growth would offer increased opportunities for clerical employment.

Several other personnel implications are barely recognized at this time. If the management-by-exception principle is carried to the point that computers apply decision rules, part of the training ground for top-level managers may disappear. If so, other means must be developed for giving experience to top-level managers. Some work has been done toward developing the skill of managers by having them "play" business games against a computer that is programmed to follow certain rules of business that may not be disclosed to the players. Game playing may be, in some ways, more effective than actual experience as a way of educating top-level managers whose training grounds are taken over by automatic systems.

Changes in the degree of managerial centralization and geographical dispersion can be expected, but it is too early to predict their probable nature.

Where analysis is concentrated on the computer program, a great proportion of program analysis may be done more efficiently by the computer itself than by people. Furthermore, internal and external auditing to assure compliance with policy directives and stewardship requirements can reduce the huge effort often necessary to trace clerical operations.

The education and experience of future management and systems analysts will change as new systems become more widespread. Members of a future generation may never see a paper document or a complete financial statement. If so, the whole art of data processing and management will, of necessity, change greatly; it will be vastly different from what we are accustomed to today.

SUMMARY

Inventions and improvements in equipment over the past ten years seem to be outrunning the ability of people to use them efficiently for data processing. Spectacular improvements in input and output have eliminated a serious bottleneck in early equipment. Manual effort will be reduced and accuracy increased in input preparation through the use of character readers and transaction recorders, as well as by the transfer of data in processable form.

Computer storage techniques have reached a plateau with magnetic cores. Breakthroughs with superconductors, chemicals, or crystals hold promise for the future. Air conditioning, power, and space requirements will dwindle as new circuits and storage techniques are developed.

Programming—in the broad sense, from initial systems analysis to final instruction routines—traditionally costs as much as the equipment itself. Most of this cost goes for studying an operating system, which is not readily amenable to laboratory analysis and improvement in the same way as equipment. Automatic programming and related developments will continue to reduce the cost of analysis and coding.

Automatic data-processing systems are designed for individual applications—cataloguing, stock control, and stock accounting—because of the huge analysis task involved and the finite capacity of even the largest equipment. Wholly comprehensive plans for processing business data are a long way off. People attack the over-all data-information problem and set up on-line flow plans for small bits and pieces. It appears that in-line and off-line flow plans will remain customary despite heroic attempts to get immediate, up-to-the-minute reports. Data-processing costs are higher and information values are lower than is generally realized for absolutely current facts.

The principle of management-by-exception holds promise, with more highly refined processing, of adjusting the volume and content of reports to management needs and abilities. Procedures that are adjustable to the information content of data can give managers exactly what they want to know—presuming, of course, that managers can and will specify what they want. Intensive, scientific analysis of operating problems holds promise for great improvements in business management. The solution of isolated problems, however, is vastly different from the requirements for mass-volume processing.

It appears that the processing of data for systems employing servomechanism principles for constantly adjusting to varying conditions will become increasingly important. Some examples of problems best solved by systems using servomechanism principles are: controlling plant operations, eliminating aircraft collisions, detecting and guiding missiles, and artificially creating environments suitable for human habitation.

Education may be materially advanced in the future by using computers to aid in the rapid interchange of information between students and an "automatic teacher." Computers are not widely employed for this purpose, but there are indications that electronics engineers are about to tackle the problem of student-teacher relationships. Electronic blackboards which enable students to observe complicated problems being solved by a computer may be used widely. It is speculative whether the "solution" will still be education when the engineers decree the problem "solved."

Computer "libraries" may be set up in which information of general value can be placed in storage and made available by interrogations from local or distant points; an answer might consist of an abstract, a selected portion, or a whole document, as desired.

Personnel problems center on obtaining competent staffs for new systems and adjusting clerical forces—both in number and skill—to new equipment. New staff requirements will be solved in the short run by education and experience. Relocation of clerks and would-be clerks will continue indefinitely as the composition of the labor force changes.

Future managers will need entirely different training grounds, for the path from office boy to president may no longer exist. Business games played in a laboratory might permit simulating management training without risking the consequences of actual decision making.

REFERENCES AND SUPPLEMENTAL READINGS

Buck, D. A., and K. R. Shoulders. "An Approach to Microminiature Printed Systems," pp. 55-59 in *Proceedings of The Eastern Joint Computer Conference*, New York, American Institute of Electrical Engineers, 1959. The era of assembling numerous individual parts in a computer is drawing to a close. An alternative is to make part or all of a computer in a single process. One suggested method is vacuum deposition of electrodes onto blocks of pure silicon or germanium and subsequent diffusion into the block to form junctions. A second method is vacuum deposition of magnetic materials and conductors to form magnetic core memory planes. Vacuum deposition of superconductive switching and memory circuits is a third method that will make possible the printing of an entire computer. Vacuum deposition through a mask is expected to make circuit elements as small as 4 millionths of an inch wide. If achieved, cryotrons might be printed so small that 500 billion would occupy only one cubic inch. Much work remains to be done to make a shoebox size computer, but the chemical reactions tested here appear to work and are a step in the direction of microminiature work.

Hurni, M. L. "Some Implications of the Use of Computers in Industry," *The Accounting Review*, vol. 27: 447-55, (July 1954). According to the author, some forward-thinking, current observations indicate that routine sensing and judgment will be increasingly taken over by machines. To accomplish such a goal, industrial complexity must be reduced by thinking through the fundamental concepts of industrial operations, as well as by using a computer. The computer alone is not an answer because (a) attention should be focused on desired requirements rather than on existing problems, and (b) requirements should be formulated in terms suitable for computer solution. The approach used assumes that operational patterns in business data can be discovered and quantified. Hurni recognizes that many problems exist, such as (a) the magnitude of the data, (b) the complexity of operational patterns, and (c) the lack of useful historical data.

Kircher, Paul. "The Gap Between the Electronics Engineer and the Accountant," *The Controller*, vol. 22: 358-60 + (August 1954). A gap exists between the engineer and accountant because early computers were designed for scientific, not business work, and because there is a language and thought-process barrier. The author suggests closing the gap by having engineers study accounting and accountants understand the machines. Mathematicians may serve as a link between the two. Systems analysis is presented as the first step in computer installation and includes consideration of such items as (a) engineering specifications, (b) dependability, (c) accuracy, (d) accessibility, (e) requirements of auditors and the internal revenue service, (f) cost, (g) flexibility, (h) better control, and (i) planning.

Levin, Howard S. *Office Work and Automation*, New York, John Wiley & Sons, Inc., 1956, 203 pp. In discussing ways to get more effective business information, the author points out two basic needs: (1) for more research into office methods of data collection and processing, and (2) for a business language common to both men and machines. Levin deals with possible development in this area and the available commercial types of machines with their three major effects: (a) elimination of manual intervention in data flow, (b) elimination of special handling through possible program flexibility, and (c) integration of related data-processing functions that cut down repetitive operations. Problems may arise between the businessman and the scientist in pursuing these developments because of the difference in outlook and method. The difficulties inherent in reconciliation of the two groups are discussed, and the use of operations research techniques as a means of overcoming the above situation is investigated and approved. The book concludes with (a) the over-all picture of the advantages and problems of the new office set-up, (b) the significant organizational changes, (c) *the social and economic implications*, and (d) the changes in over-all office control necessary to use new procedures and equipment to their best advantage.

APPENDICES

Appendix I

HISTORY OF COMPUTATION AND DATA-PROCESSING DEVICES

Acceptance of equipment indicates whether it fills a widespread need to solve some problem—computing navigation or insurance mortality tables, preparing bills, keeping books, or quickly printing many copies. The rate of acceptance of new devices has ranged from adopting them immediately to ignoring them completely.

There is not necessarily any direct connection between some of the devices discussed here and automatic data processors. There are, however, some interesting conclusions to be drawn about invention and re-invention of solutions to parts of the problems of computing and data processing. Careful study of history puts present-day work in better perspective and sometimes guides one toward better definition and solution of a problem through avoiding unsuccessful attempts made in the past.

The history of equipment is treated under the following topics: calculating machines, typewriters, punched-card machines, and computers. This discussion is necessarily limited in scope, but the references following this appendix give source material for a more thorough study.

Calculating Machines

The history of calculating devices ("Calculating Machines," 1957) can be traced back to the abacus, which is still used in many countries. The first real calculating machine, which was invented by Blaise Pascal in 1642, consisted of figure wheels, each bearing the numerals 0 to 9 mounted on parallel axes to be turned one-tenth to nine-tenths of a complete turn by means of a stylus or peg. A "carrying" device moved the next wheel to the left through one-tenth of a revolution as a figure wheel was turned from 9 to 0. Pascal's device was improved over a period of time in several ways, notably by the introduction of a sequential carry from one position to the next to avoid the force required for simultaneous carry in several positions; thus modified, it is still widely sold today as a pocket-size calculator.

In 1671 Gottfried Leibniz conceived a calculating machine, later manufactured in 1694, which could perform multiplication by repeated addition. The idea of the stepped wheel or drum having on a portion of its outer surface nine teeth of increasing length, from one to nine, was an important element of Liebniz' machine, and it is commonly used today.

The first successful calculating machine was invented by Charles Thomas of Alsace in 1820. The mechanism had three distinct portions concerned with setting, counting, and registering in order to perform all four arithmetical operations. The modern German calculating-machine industry was founded in 1878 by Arthur Burkhardt, who started manufacturing the Thomas-type machine as the Arithmometer. Many others, including Allen in the United States in 1927, constructed machines of this form.

At about the same time in 1875, Frank Stephen and W. T. Odhner each replaced the Leibniz stepped wheel by a wheel from the periphery of which a variable number of teeth (1 to 9) could be protruded. The machine performs multiplication by repeated addition, as in the Thomas type, but the thin Odhner wheel led to a more compact design. A setting lever, which forms part of each wheel, is set against any figure (1 to 9) on its slot in the cover plate, so that a corresponding number of teeth project from its wheel. Turning the operating handle makes these teeth gear with small-toothed wheels of the product register, which is geared with the number wheels in front. A second register carries the multiplier in case of multiplication and the quotient in division. The Odhner-type machine is still made in many countries, notably by Marchant in the United States (starting in 1911) and by Facit in Sweden (from 1918). A model improved by the original German makers in 1927 had a device for instantly transferring the result registered on the product dials into the setting levers. An earlier model had a 20-figure-result register which could be divided into two parts, enabling multiplication of two different numbers by the same multiplier in one operation. Another type consists of two machines coupled together for operation by a single crank.

In 1887 Léon Bollée invented the first machine to perform multiplication successfully by a direct method instead of by repeated addition. A series of tongued plates represented in relief the ordinary multiplication table up to "nine times." In 1899 Egli marketed the Millionaire machine, embodying the Bollée mechanical multiplication table (which required only one turn of the handle for each figure of the multiplier, which was set up by levers) and automatic shift to the next position. The levers have been replaced by a keyboard in present-day machines of this kind.

Many improved machines that multiply by repeated addition and divide by repeated subtraction have appeared since 1900, with gradual development in speed and convenience. The Ensign, made in Boston in 1905, had many present-day features: motor-drive, keyboard set-up, multiplication keys, and self-stepping carriage. The depression of one of nine multiplication keys added the multiplicand set on the keyboard the appropriate number of times.

Machines capable of automatic division were introduced about 1910 by Charles Hamann and Hans Egli. Both followed the Thomas machine, but Egli included a mechanism providing for automatic division after the dividend and divisor had been set. A bell announces completion of a division and the quotient and remainder are recorded.

Jay R. Monroe and Frank S. Baldwin introduced the first successful commercial keyboard rotary machine in 1911. The original model followed Odhner's design, but wheels for adding were made in two parts, one with five equal teeth and the other with four arranged in steps. Keyboard setting for each digit adjusted the two wheels toward each other to enable the desired number of teeth—from 1 to 9—to gear with the counting wheel when the handle was turned. The machine was later motorized and key-controlled features were included for automatic division, motorized carriage, and electric clearing.

In 1850 D. D. Parmalee obtained a United States patent for the first key-driven adding machine, which could add only a single column of digits at a time. Others of limited capacity were subsequently invented, but in 1887 Dorr Eugene Felt patented his Comptometer, which was the first successful key-driven multiple-order calculating machine. At first each key had to be operated serially (one at a time) to insure the proper carry, but in 1903 parallel operation of keys and carry were introduced.

E. D. Barbour incorporated a printing device with an adding machine in 1872, but the first practical adding and listing machines were produced by Felt in 1889 and W. S. Burroughs in 1892. Numerous versions of these machines can be grouped as (a) single-counter adding machines with or without capacity for direct subtraction; (b) multiple-counter adding machines; and (c) billing, accounting, and bookkeeping machines. The first practical billing machine, invented by Hubert Hopkins, included a direct multiplication feature patterned on Bollée's Millionaire machine. Operations are controlled by the keyboard in some machines, but in others they are controlled by elaborate programming devices operated by the position of the movable printing carriage. Some models have an auxiliary keyboard so that new numbers may be set up while previous ones are being processed. Some of the many improvements and variations that have been developed are: a ten-key board with a repeat feature for multiplication; special controls for multiplication and division; and combination of an adding machine with a typewriter or with an addressograph to print from plates while carrying a running total.

Typewriters

Mechanical printers ("Typewriter," 1957), both low and high speed, devices for transmitting data over wire networks, and punched-tape-operated office equipment are derived from the standard typewriter that has evolved over the past hundred years or so.

The British patent office issued a patent in 1714 for a typewriter and in 1784 for a machine for embossing characters for the blind. Xavier Progin received a French patent in 1833 for a device consisting of an assembly of bars with type, each striking downward on a common center.

Charles Thurber of Massachusetts obtained a patent in 1843 for a machine that spaced letters by movement of a platen, a feature that is still used today. At about this time several other patents were issued in the United States and abroad for machines to duplicate handwriting and emboss characters for the blind.

In 1866 John Pratt developed a type wheel machine based on Burt's work of 1829. This machine, in modern versions, has the type mounted on a circle or segment. Operation of the keys brings each type into correct printing position and a trigger action produces an imprint of type on paper.

The first practical typewriter was invented by Sholes, Glidden, and Soule of Milwaukee in 1867. Numerous models were made before offering it for sale in 1874. Early features, which are still standard, were a paper cylinder with a line-spacing and carriage-return mechanism, an escapement for letter spacing, an arrangement of type to print at a common center, key levers and wires to actuate type bars, an inked ribbon, and the QWERTY... keyboard arrangement. Capital letters only were available on early models but two solutions arose. Initially, separate keyboards and type faces for lower-case letters and capitals were offered. The single keyboard with carriage shift to select the upper and lower case first appeared in 1878; it displaced the dual keyboard when touch typing became popular in the nineties.

Visible writing machines, developed in 1883, first employed the down-stroke and later the front-stroke principle so that the operator could see what was typed. Previously, the type bars had been located under the carriage so that the operator had to raise the carriage to see the written line.

James Smathers pioneered the electric typewriter by producing a working model by 1920. Subsequently, the development of automatic controls allowed typing from remote electric signals instead of by manual operation. Different office machines—typewriter, calculator, telegraph, and electronic computer—were tied together by a "common language" of electric signals sent on punched paper tape, which was developed in the mid-1950's.

High-speed printing of from 50,000 to 100,000 characters a minute, con-trasted with 1,000 a minute for single-character typewriters, was developed in the early 1950's by using a continuously rotating drum and solenoid-actuated hammers to strike the paper against the character to be printed.

Punched-card Machines

The development of punched-card machines dates from the late nine-teenth century (Jordan, 1956). Dr. Herman Hollerith, a noted statistician, was engaged in 1880 by the United States government as a special agent for the 1880 census, which took seven and a half years to finish. Hollerith considered barbarous the manual tabulating methods used to survey a population of fifty million and suggested that machines be devised to facilitate tabulation. It appeared that the 1890 census might not be tabulated until its information had become completely worthless. Furthermore, many of the facts obtained on census returns were not compiled at all or were treated in so simple a manner as to be of little use. Yet both raw data and combinations among various categories were of widespread interest—age and occupation at death, for example, could be used for constructing life tables by occupation in addi-tion to life tables for cities and states.

In 1886 Hollerith completed a system including 3" x 5" corner-cut cards divided into ¼" squares, a punch, a "pin-press," electromagnetic counters, and a sorting box. Cards were punched either by an ordinary ticket punch or by a keyboard invented by Hollerith, the movable punch of which could punch a hole in five or six cards containing identical information. Punched cards were read by placing them over a complete card of a different color.

The pin-press for compiling statistics consisted of a hard rubber plate with a cup under each hole position; the cups were partially filled with mer-cury and electrically connected, by a nail through each cup, to a wire leading to an electromagnetic counter with capacity to count from 1 to 10,000. A hinged box above the hard rubber plate contained a spring-activated point corresponding to each mercury cup. Counters were connected to the desired hole positions (either singly or combined by relays) and sorting boxes were connected in the same way. In operation, a card was placed manually in the pin-press and the hinged box lowered to activate a counter and also to open the lid of a sorting slot for manual deposit of the card at a speed of 50 to 80 cards a minute. Hollerith believed that the benefit of obtaining thorough com-pilations was a more compelling reason for adopting the system than was the reduction in cost and time and the increase in accuracy of results.

Early users of Hollerith's equipment were Baltimore, New York City, and New Jersey, for vital statistics, and the United States government, for compiling the 1890 census. An appraisal of the Hollerith system in 1890 mentioned the use of a wire to check sorting accuracy and an electric bell to indicate non-registration during reading. A test retabulation for about 10,000 returns showed enumeration time was three-fourths and tabulating time was one-eighth of that required for other systems. The 1890 census was tabulated in two and a half years. In 1901, Hollerith introduced the basic form of a numerical punch keyboard; before his retirement in 1914, a new sorter, a lever-set gang punch, and an accumulation tabulator were developed.

In planning for the 1910 census, statisticians sought to improve the methods used in the 1900 census by reducing the time and manual effort in punching and verifying cards, by increasing the accuracy of cards, and by eliminating manual handling of each card during sorting operations. James Powers, an engineer engaged by the Census Bureau to develop new machines, devised completely mechanical machines with many desirable features: a keyboard with 240 keys for setting up all desired data, and provision for visual checking and simultaneous punching of all fields. The cards, containing 45 columns with twelve rows per column, were sorted one column at a time by twelve plungers that picked out the value punched in the card and opened the desired shutter to divert the card into the proper slot. As soon as the shutter was set for a card, the plungers were withdrawn, the card moved by rubber rollers to its proper compartment, and another card moved into reading position at a speed of 250 to 270 cards a minute.

Powers formed a company in 1911 to exploit his improved punching machines and two-deck horizontal sorter. A major drawback, manual transcription of totals on counters to a ledger, bill, or statistical analysis, was overcome by the tabulator-printer developed in 1914. Completely mechanical, the tabulator contained the adding mechanism of the Comptograph and a portion of the Dalton adding machine. Shortly afterwards, Powers' company developed a running-total mechanism, an automatic zero device, a seven-unit tabulator, a twelve-key keyboard, and an automatic numbering attachment.

Another punched-card development, the Peirce system, consisting of perforating, distribution, and automatic ledger machines, was widely used in public utility work before 1915. A completely automatic data-processing scheme, this system introduced data by means of a small perforating attachment on each meter activated by a key after insertion of a card. The clerical work of card punching, and the mistakes often found in it, were thereby eliminated. Card contents were printed as well as punched—by the first printing punch—which made them more usable in permanent record files.

Early uses of punched cards were for insurance tables, transportation and commodity statistics, payrolls, cost accounting, electric utility sales tabulations, water utility customer accounting, consumer trend analysis, and inventory control. Accountants accepted punched-card systems reluctantly, because the record produced was not in the usual format desired for statements or reports.

Improvements in punched-card equipment before 1930, made by successors to the Hollerith and Powers patents, included the mechanical verifier and electric key-punch (1917); the single-deck sorter, and the alphabetic printing tabulator (1919); an automatic control for tabulators (1921); an electric duplicating key-punch (1924); a typewriter connected to the key-punch for simultaneous punching and typing, and an 80-column card and general-purpose accounting machine (1928); and devices for remote-control accounting of merchandise inventory, customer credit and receivables, as well as for the accounting of sales clerk commissions on the basis of cards punched to indicate articles sold, customer charge plates, and sales person identification tags (about 1928). Many functional deficiencies existed in punched-card equipment in 1930: the inability to subtract, multiply, or divide through punched-card control and to punch a summary card automatically from a tabulator.

Machine developments from 1930 to 1950 included numerical interpreters: the offset-hole method of verification, and the universal printing-counting sorter (1930); the 90-column card, multiplying punch, and summary punch (1931); an alphabetic printing tabulator (1932); a test-scoring machine and alphabetic printing punch (1933); an automatic carriage for printing tabulators, and small cards $(2'' \times 2\frac{3}{4}'')$ with 21 columns (1934); a collator to merge and separate cards (1936); a transfer posting machine, reproducing gang summary punch, and 130-column cards (two banks of 65 columns) (1938); mark sensing for cards (1939); a tape-controlled card punch and multiple-line printing from a single card (1941); cross-adding punch (1943); the calculating punch, electronic multiplier, cardatype equipment, and document originator (1946); a tape-controlled automatic carriage (1948); the non-listing high-speed punched-card adding machine, alphabetic collator, card-programmed calculator, and electronic statistical machine (1949). Developments since 1950 are better known, so they need not be listed here.

Computers

The history of automatic computation dates from 1812, when Henry P. Babbage, an Englishman, studying a table of logarithms full of mistakes, hit upon the idea of developing a machine to compute tabular functions. The idea underlying Babbage's Difference Engine, of which he built a small model by 1822, was that appropriate level differences between the values computed for a formula are constant, so that the values themselves are obtainable simply by addition. For example, the differences between X^3 in the simple case $Y = X^3$ are as follows:

X	Y	First Difference	Second Difference	Third Difference
1	1			
		7		
2	8		12	
		19		6
3	27		18	
		37		6
4	64		24	
		61		6
5	125		30	
		91		
6	216			

The third-order differences corresponding to the third power of X in $Y = X^3$ are constant. Succeeding values of Y can be computed by addition alone, for example, where $X = 7$, $6 + 30 = 36$; $36 + 91 = 127$; $Y = 127 + 216 = 343$. Equations involving higher powers of X can be solved in similar fashion by means of higher-order differences. Tables prepared by other methods can be checked by means of differences. The small model of 1822 led to a much larger version of the difference engine that was finally completed in 1859 and used in 1863 for calculating life tables for rating insurance.

In 1833 Babbage conceived the idea of an Analytical Engine to perform any type of digital calculation. Babbage's computer was designed for punched-card input (following Jacquard's use of cards for control of weaving looms), an arithmetic unit, storage for 1,000 numbers of 50 decimal digits each, an auxiliary memory of punched cards, a built-in power of judgment to follow a program, and output in the form of either punched cards or type set and ready to print tables. Babbage conceived, but did not complete, a mechanical computer capable of carrying out a sequence of instructions and of modifying them to cope with situations encountered during operations. The essential components of present-day computers were invented well over a hundred years ago, but none was built until the 1940's.

The modern history of computers dates from 1937, when Howard H. Aiken conceived an Automatic Sequence Controlled Calculator capable of following a sequence of steps punched into a tape. Electromechanical in operation at speeds of three-tenths of a second for addition or subtraction, the machine stores numbers consisting of 23 decimal digits. Input requires standard punched cards, hand-set dial switches, and long loops of punched tape. Output is similar, except that an electric typewriter is used instead of switches. Instructions are entered by the use of switches, buttons, wire plugboards, and punched tape. Containing many features to insure reliability and subroutines to facilitate programming, this was the first machine able to perform long sequences of arithmetical and logical operations.

The ENIAC (Electronic Numerical Integrator and Calculator), built between 1942 and 1946 at the University of Pennsylvania, was the first machine to use electronic tubes for calculating. Programmed at first by means of plug-wired instructions, it could execute 5,000 additions a second on numbers stored in 20 registers (at first) each holding 10 decimal digits. Later modifications permitted storing programs internally in three function tables each of which could hold 600 instructions made up from the repertoire of 60 standard instructions. Input of data—either numbers or instructions—was by means of punched cards, switch settings, or function tables. Punched cards and neon tubes on each accumulator were used for output.

Design and construction of new kinds of electronic computers has been phenomenal: since 1949 a total of some 6,000 units of about 100 different models have been built.

These brief comments give some idea of the history of developments to about 1950 resulting in automatic data-processing systems as we know them today. An understanding of the apparently unrelated developments in calculators, typewriters, punched cards, and computers should clarify the basic functions of data processing.

REFERENCES

Berkeley, Edmund Callis. *Giant Brains or Machines That Think*, New York, John Wiley & Sons, Inc., 1949, 270 pp. An early description of mechanical brains and how they work, with emphasis on the M.I.T. differential analyzer, Harvard Mark I, Moore School ENIAC, and Bell Laboratories' relay computers that were completed between 1942 and 1946. Chapters on an extremely simple computer, "Simon," and on punched-card processing are helpful.

Bowden, B. V., ed. *Faster Than Thought, A Symposium on Digital Computing Machines*, London, Sir Isaac Pitman and Sons Ltd., 1953, 416 pp. Bowden surveys the field of digital computing machines and introduces some of Britain's accomplishments in this field. The subject matter is treated in three basic sections. Part One is concerned with the history and theory of computing machines. Fundamental computer logic, circuit components, organization, and programming are discussed. A historical appendix presents a contemporary account of Babbage's "Analytical Engine," Part Two presents detailed and somewhat technical descriptions of the leading machines in Britain as of 1953, written by the engineers who work on them. Finally, the book discusses various existing and potential applications for electronic computers. For the most part, these applications are derived from earlier development of scientific and logical calculations, and little emphasis is placed upon applications in business-data processing (one chapter). The applications discussed include the use of computers in crystallography, meteorology, ballistics, engineering, and astronomy.

"Calculating Machines," *Encyclopaedia Britannica*, vol. 4: 548-554 (1957). Traces the evolution of numerical calculating devices from Napier's bones, Pascal's figure-wheel adder, and Leibnitz' stepped-wheel multiplier through Thomas', Odhner's, Steiger's, Monroe's, Felt's and Burrough's widely used adding and calculating devices.

Jordan, George. *A Survey of Punched Card Development*, unpublished Master's Thesis submitted to the Massachusetts Institute of Technology, School of Industrial Management, 1956. Traces the development and use of punched-card equipment from 1880 to 1950, with emphasis on the period between 1930 and 1940.

"Typewriter," *Encyclopaedia Britannica*, vol. 22: 644-646 (1957). Traces the development of the modern typewriter from 1867 to the present. Describes the origin of single and dual keyboards for upper- and lower-case characters, electric power, punched tape compatible with other machines directly or via wire networks, and high-speed printing by means of rotating print wheels and elaborate control over striking hammers.

Woodruff, L. F. "A System of Electric Remote-Control Accounting," *Electrical Engineering*, vol. 57: 78-87 (February 1938). Describes the first remote-control accounting system devised for a department store (1928) using punched cards for garments, charge plates for customers, and identification tags for clerks to reduce the manual element in data origination and processing.

Appendix II

QUESTIONS AND PROBLEMS

Chapter 1

1. *a.* Why are data processed? *b.* What is the most important reason? *c.* What is the distinction between data and information? *d.* How can this distinction be used in designing and operating a system? *e.* What operations are included in data processing?
2. *a.* Why is it so difficult to solve the problem of deciding precisely what data to gather and store for use in the future? *b.* What is a rational approach toward gathering useful data?
3. *a.* What data-processing capabilities does a trained clerk have? *b.* What arithmetical and logical operations can a clerk perform?
4. What equipment and support are necessary for an automatic data-processing system?
5. The conversion from a punched-card to an automatic data-processing system is said to be easier than the conversion from a manual system, although the latter pair have many similarities, at least in concept. Reconcile, if possible, the difference in ease of conversion with these similarities.
6. What are the three most pressing problems in data-processing system design and operation?
7. *a.* What steps should be taken to evaluate a data-processing system? *b.* What changes in the way business operations are organized and carried out are likely to accompany introduction of automatic data-processing methods?
8. Many runs are required for processing data, whether by manual, punched-card, or automatic means. *a.* Why are so many runs required? *b.* Is the output of one run often used as the input for a succeeding run in, for example, sales analysis and inventory control? *c.* What facilities would be required to handle all processing for one kind of transaction in one run?
9. *a.* Under what circumstances is the division of a company's records into files useful for efficient processing? *b.* When does a division by files reduce processing efficiency?
10. Until the beginning of the twentieth century letterpresses were commonly used to make copies of handwritten or typed letters. A copy was made in a bound book by wetting the copy paper and pressing it against the letter in a way similar to the operation of a hectograph spirit duplicator. What changes in making copies of business documents have followed the invention and widespread use of typewriters and carbon paper?
11. Typewriters were designed in the eighteenth century to type raised characters for the blind to read by touch. What differences would you expect to find in data collection, storage, and output if people could read faster by touch than by sight?
12. One proposal for report preparation is to use the same format every time so that the location of an item does not change in a given report. A second proposal is to include in a report only those items that have a suitable information content and omit all other items. Answer and explain:
    a. Are reports with high information content and fixed format compatible?
    b. Which report-preparation scheme is more efficient to prepare?
    c. Which scheme is more efficient to use?
    d. Which scheme requires least paper to print?
13. The First National Bank of Ipswich handles the introduction of new accounts and deletion of closed or transferred checking accounts in the same cycle as deposits are entered and checks are paid. There are 40,000 checking accounts and average daily activities are 6,000 deposits, 70,000 checks paid, 105 new accounts

opened, and 90 accounts closed. Customers are identified by initial of last name and four digits, alphabetically assigned with initial spacing of four digits for expansion, for example: John Doe   D3275; Johnny Doe   D3280.

The error rate in manually key punching account numbers is about 2 per cent, but only account openings and closings are verified before processing. After key punching, dollar amounts are summarized and proved against a batch total, calculated in the preceding operation, to discover and correct mistakes.

File maintenance and processing are handled together so that mistakes in account numbers may be posted to another customer's account or a new fictitious account may be opened.

Following is a list of remedies proposed to reduce the incidence of mistakes:

Scan account names and numbers after posting and merging with other checks and deposit slips.

Control the number of accounts handled in daily cycle: number of accounts at start + accounts opened – accounts closed = number of accounts at end.

Control the money balances of accounts in daily cycle: beginning balance + deposits – checks paid = ending balance.

Immediately investigate any overdrafts to find mistakes from posting to the wrong account.

Attach a simplified check digit, either 0 or 1, to each number to make the individual digits add to an even amount. For example, D3275 would get a check digit of 1 to become D32751 so that $3 + 2 + 7 + 5 + 1 =$ an even sum; but F 6965 would be F69650. A mistake such as F69660 would be detectable because $6 + 9 + 6 + 6 + 0$ have an odd total.

Verify key punching of account number and money amounts and drop the summary and proof on money total as described above.

   a. Which schemes might be effective?

   b. Which schemes are not likely to give a high degree of accuracy?

   c. Which scheme has lowest costs?

   d. Which scheme is most efficient per unit of effort spent to reduce mistakes?

   (Make any assumptions required that are not inconsistent with the facts given.)

Chapter 2

1. It is possible to punch a hole in any one of 12 positions in each column of a punched card. *a.* How many different symbols can be represented by punching one hole in each column? *b.* How many different symbols can be represented by using combinations of not more than two punches in a column?

2. Packing density is the number of bits or characters in a given unit of media. An 80-column punched card is about 7 in. long and 3 in. wide. A 1 in. wide paper tape holds a character each 1/10 in. *a.* Compare the packing densities of paper tape, magnetic tape, and magnetic drum track in characters per linear inch. *b.* What is the ratio of packing density of punched cards to magnetic tape in characters per square inch?

3. *a.* Why is the binary scheme favored in the design of electronic computing equipment? *b.* Is the decimal number system the only reasonable one for people to use?

4. A base 26 number system contains the symbols A, B, C,...XYZ where A is the zero symbol, B the one symbol, and Z the highest order symbol. Represent the decimal numbers 5, 27, and 676 in the base 26 system.

5. *a.* How many bits are needed to represent a decimal digit? *b.* How many characters can eight bits represent?

6. *a.* Explain the purpose and use of parity-bits. *b.* How does a parity system operate to detect malfunctions? *c.* Could parity-bits be used on ordinary punched cards? How?

7. What is the relationship of characters, words, fields, records, and files in organizing data?

8. *a.* In designing payroll cards that must be sorted into alphabetic order, what are the advantages of using a fixed field as compared to a variable field for names? *b.* Are there any disadvantages?

9. *a.* Construct a block diagram showing the several stages of data flow through a business. *b.* Explain each of these stages.

10. *a.* Why is a buffer unit necessary in an automatic data-processing system? *b.* How can buffering be eliminated in computer read-out?

11. *a.* What kinds of decisions or choices can a computer make? *b.* How can this ability be used to provide automatic error-checking features on the machine?

12. What methods are used for getting data and instructions into a processor?

13. Sort the following characters into ascending sequence by using the code collating sequence illustrated in the chapter: P K End Data # 0 A 9 $ *)

14. How are items separated on tape and in computer storage when the computer is designed to handle variable-length items?

15. *a.* What kind of addressability of storage is required for computers designed to handle fixed-length fields? *b.* Variable-length fields? *c.* Fixed-variable length fields?

16. Various kinds of paper records have features well suited to storing variable, fixed-variable, and fixed-length items. Classify each kind of paper in terms of its item storage characteristics:

    a. Accountant's ruled working paper;
    b. Blank 8½ in. x 11 in. paper;
    c. Ruled square grid paper;
    d. Roll paper of the type used in tabulating machines;
    e. Printed card records for inventory;
    f. Ruled accounting ledger sheets;
    g. Printed bill forms.

17. The address item of a customer's record on magnetic tape using the code illustrated in the chapter is as follows:

Channel number																																				
7	0 0 0 0 1 0 1 1 1 1 1 0 1 1 1 0 1 1 1 1 1 1 1 0 1 0 0 1 0 1 0
6	1 0 1 0 0 0 1 1 1 1 1 1 1 1 0 1 1 1 0 1 1 1 0 1 1 1 1 0 0 0 1
5	1 1 1 1 1 0 1 0 0 1 1 0 1 1 0 0 0 1 0 0 0 0 1 0 1 0 1 0 0 1 1 1
4	1 0 1 1 1 0 0 1 1 0 0 1 0 0 0 0 0 0 1 0 1 1 0 0 1 1 0 1 0 0 1 1
3	1 1 0 0 0 0 1 1 1 0 1 1 0 0 1 0 0 1 1 0 1 1 1 0 0 1 0 0 0 1 0 1
2	0 1 0 1 0 0 1 0 0 1 1 1 0 1 1 0 0 0 0 0 0 1 0 0 1 0 1 0 0 1 0
1	1 0 1 0 0 0 0 0 1 1 0 0 1 1 1 0 0 1 0 0 1 0 0 0 0 0 1 0 0 1 1 1

    There are, for purposes of illustration, five single-bit errors in the recording of this item.

    a. Detect as many errors as you can by means of the column parity rule (row parity is not used here).
    b. Correct as many errors as you can by applying the parity rule.
    c. How many more mistakes could be corrected by means of the row parity-bit rule (in addition to column parity) if it were used?
    d. Correct as many errors as you can by examining the message and applying what you know about the composition of addresses.

18. A utility that bills customers on a bi-monthly cycle basis (assume a twenty-business day-month) wants to identify each day's group of accounts with the shortest possible code.

    a. How many characters are required if the code is either numerical, alphabetic, alphanumerical, or any alphanumerical and special symbol that can be represented by six bits?

   b. How many characters are required for cycle identification if the utility switches to (1) a monthly cycle, (2) a tri-monthly cycle?

19. Five-channel punched paper tape can directly represent thirty-two characters ($2^5 = 32$). Mode shifts are used to represent a wider variety of characters at the expense of using one character to shift from one mode to another. Further, some characters (blank, carriage return, line feed, and space) may be provided in each mode similar to the typewriter arrangement of space, period, and comma in both upper and lower case. The general rule for the number of characters that can be represented in two or more modes by n channels, with M modes shifts, where C characters are common to all modes is $(2^n - M - C)M + C$.

   a. Determine the number of characters representable by five-channel tape when used in 1, 2, 3, 4, 5, 6, and 27 modes.

   b. Repeat for six-channel tape with 1, 2, 3, 4, 5, 6, and 59 modes.

   c. Which is a simpler approach to representing more characters: (1) more channels or (2) more modes? Why?

   d. What would a typewriter that is limited to 40 keys look like if it operated in 1, 2, 5, 10 and 20 modes? How many characters could be represented in each mode? At what point does the number of modes become so high that only one key is used for characters and all others are used for mode shifts?

20. The following numbers have a decimal base:

2	64	.5	64.25
4	260	.25	327.68
9	4096	.375	4935.33
17	32768	.4375	120685.295

   a. Convert the numbers from decimal to binary base.

   b. Convert the numbers from decimal to octal base.

   c. Convert the binary numbers (from Part a) to octal to show that the octal numbers are the same whether obtained directly from decimal or indirectly through binary.

   d. Convert the numbers from decimal base to binary-coded decimal (8421 code).

   e. Convert the numbers from decimal base to the code illustrated in the chapter.

21. Convert the following numbers from binary to decimal:

10	11111	.101
101	10000	.11011
10110	101010011	11.011
101101	1001001001	1101010.01101

Hint: For whole numbers, start with the bit on the extreme left, multiply by 2, *add* the next bit to right, and repeat multiplication until the last bit *before* bit point is reached (merely add it). Example: $101011._2 = 43._{10}$. For fractions, start with the bit on the extreme right, divide by 2, *attach* the next bit to the left and repeat division until bit point is reached. Example: $.1011_2 = .6875_{10}$.

22. Standard cards can be punched in binary fashion with one word of thirty-six bits in columns 1 to 36 and another word in columns 37 to 72 in each row across the card. Nine rows (0 through 8) are used for data and row 9 is used for a parity-bit for each column.

   a. What is the largest binary number that can be represented by thirty-six bits? What is the octal equivalent? Decimal equivalent?

   b. What is the largest decimal number that can be represented in binary-coded alphanumerical form in each word?

   c. How many letters can be represented in binary-coded alphanumerical form in each word?

    d. Appraise the data content of a card punched in binary code with standard alphanumerical punching of one character per column.

    e. If one bit is reserved for sign and another for parity-bit, what are the largest binary, octal, and decimal numbers that can be represented by each 36 bit word?

23. The Travelers National Bank issues its travelers' checks in blocks of 100 numbered xxxx00 to xxxx99 for each amount ($10, $20, $50, $100) to agent banks on consignment and collects for them after they are sold by the agent bank. The Travelers National Bank wants to keep track of the following facts for each check: (a) issued to agent bank on consignment, (b) sold by agent bank, (c) collected proceeds from agent bank, (d) paid check after use by purchaser, and (e) stop-payment order received from purchaser because check reported lost or stolen. Each block of checks requires 40 characters of constant data.

    a. How can each check be represented by one column in a card and how many cards are required to control a block of checks?

    b. The Travelers National Bank's systems department is proposing that one row across four columns be used to store data for one check. Devise a scheme to implement the proposal and show that forty columns will control one hundred checks by using ten rows for ten checks. What savings in punched cards can be achieved by this scheme?

    c. How much more compression of data could be obtained if punched-card equipment worked with three kinds of punches (—, |, and ●) instead of just one?

Chapter 3

1. What does a computer operating cycle accomplish? Describe the operating cycle for the hypothetical computer.
2. Explain the operation of the following instructions:

    a.   ADD y   x

    b.   CAA y   x

    c.   SUB y   x

    d.   STA y   x

    e.   HLT   x

3. Write a program to read in 12 cards containing five words each in the first five positions and punch them into 6 cards containing ten words each.
4. Write a program to read in 4 blocks of data from tape and write out as follows:
    a. 4 blocks on tape
    b. 2 blocks on magnetic tape consisting of words 0 through 29 from each input block after discarding words 30 through 59
    c. Repeat (*b*) but save words 30 through 59 after discarding words 0 through 29 from each input block
    d. Repeat (*c*) but use punched-card output instead of tape
5. The following instructions are supposed to read in 60 words of data from tape and 20 words from cards and then read them out so that the original data are duplicated in the same media:

RT3		PC2	170
BI4	160	PC2	180
RC2	170	WT3	
RC2	180	RW3	
BO4	160		

    a. Point out the mistakes in the program.

    b. Write the program correctly.

6. *a.* How can the number of loop operations be controlled by cycle counting? *b.* What is the function of index registers in cycle counting? *c.* Which instructions enable a programmer to alter the contents of an index register in the hypothetical computer? *d.* How does a program leave a loop operation after the proper number of cycles is completed?

7. A routine using an index has five elements: set up or load index, compare index to a criterion, increase the index count, perform the operations specified in the main program, and jump to the desired location for repeat or exit from the loop.

    a. In what sequence are these elements used in the illustrations involving indexing in the chapter?

    b. If a loop in the main program is supposed to be performed zero times (that is, not at all), what sequence of elements and what criterion value should be used to guard against performing the main program one time before testing the index content?

    c. A program is supposed to add ten numbers. Prepare versions of a program with different sequences for the indexing and operating elements after setting the index, such as: (1) to test, operate, increase count, and jump; (2) to operate, increase count, test, and jump; and (3) to increase count, operate, test, and jump.

8. *a.* What is an effective address? *b.* How is an effective address formed?

9. The problem is to find the total value of inventory for 200 items stored in locations 100 to 299 as five groups of 40 items each.

    a. Program the addition as specified, using index registers, to place subtotals in locations 500 through 504 and the total in 505.

    b. Prepare a trace of program operations showing the contents of index registers and the effective addresses of locations used during the set-up and cycles 1, 39, 40, 41, 199, and 200.

10. For each kind of comparison instruction described in the chapter:

    a. List the conditions necessary for its use.

    b. State the instructions that must follow the compare instruction in order to utilize each branch condition.

11. *a.* What are the two general types of jump instructions? *b.* Give an example of each. *c.* What provision must be made in a program to effect the jump?

12. *a.* Why must a programmer know how many digits are involved in each number when multiplying them? *b.* Suggest a method of multiplication that eliminates the problem of keeping track of the size of numbers.

13. For the multiplication operation described in the chapter:

    a. What set-up operation is required?

    b. Where is the multiplier placed initially and how is it used during multiplication?

    c. How long is the product and where is it located?

    d. If the product contains 6 significant digits that are in both the accumulator and M-Q registers, how can the product be stored?

    e. Same as (*d*) except that the product contains 8 significant digits.

14. *a.* What do shift instructions accomplish? *b.* In what specific programming applications can shift instructions be used?

15. Assume the following values are in storage:

Storage Location	Value
500	12.3
501	200
502	10.01

Write a program to compute x to the nearest one-hundredth (.01) and store the result in location 500.

$$x = 200 + \frac{(10.01 \times 12.3)}{200}$$

16. *a.* What use can be made of the fact that the accumulator, M-Q register, and console can be addressed? *b.* What limitations are there on an operation that addresses the accumulator, M-Q register, or console?

17. How is the decimal point located in the product after a multiplication operation?

18. Illustrate the modification of the address part of ADD   100 to add a series of fifty numbers stored in locations 100 through 149, if index registers are not available. (Hint: Treat the ADD   100 instruction as a number, add +1 to it; store in its old location; test for completion of cycle; and, if not complete, jump to beginning of loop. Try to use the instruction ADD   149 as the criterion because this instruction is required in the last loop.)

19. Write a program to unpack each of the following items stored together in one word:

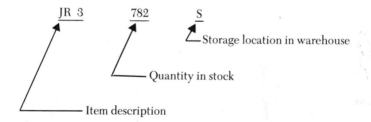

    JR 3   782   S

Storage location in warehouse

Quantity in stock

Item description

20. *a.* What will happen in checking the sequence in a list of names by means of the program illustrated in the chapter if two names halfway through the list are identical and no provision was made for the occurrence of identical names? *b.* Modify the program so that this situation can be handled and output obtained.

21. What changes would be necessary in using the sequence-checking routine illustrated in the chapter if the surname and first name of each person are stored separately in two words instead of jointly in two words?

22. Rewrite the load routine illustrated in the chapter to store it in location 990+. Remember that the next location in storage after 999 is 000. The numbering of storage is circular, so to speak, instead of linear.

23. The following three versions of a piece of a program are supposed to total the quantity of units in stock where the item record contains five words with the quantity in the third word. There are one hundred and ten inventory items and the first is stored in locations 200 and following. Location 099 contains the constant + zero; location 100 contains 550; location 101 contains 110; location 102 contains 445; the main program continues in location 125.

Location	Version 1	Version 2	Version 3
060	SIS A099	SIS A100	SIS C102
061	CAA A200	CAA B204	INC C005
062	ADD A205	ADD B209	CIS C099
063	INC A005	CIS B099	JMP C125
064	CIS A099	INC B004	CAA C203
065	JMP 060	JMP 062	ADD C208
066	JMP 061	JMP 065	

a. Trace through one cycle of each version of the program.
b. Describe the plan in each version for dealing with each item in turn.
c. Revise the nearest correct version of the program so that it is correct.
d. Write a program following a different plan to meet the requirements of the problem.

24. Locations 201 to 252 contain the rainfall at Boston, in hundredths of an inch, recorded in each week of 1959. Put in location 10 the lowest rainfall occurring in any period of four consecutive weeks.

25. Location 2 contains two three-letter English words. Put them into the left-hand halves of locations 3 and 4 in alphabetical order.

26. Location 5 contains an amount of United States money in pennies. Put in locations 10 to 19 inclusive the number of notes or coins of each of the various denominations from 1 cent to $50.00 required to make up this amount.

27. Read twenty cards, each containing an amount of money in dollars and cents (four columns for dollars and two for cents), and punch one card carrying the total.

28. Assuming any convenient punched-card layout, read a card containing:
    a. Two consecutive electricity meter readings of six digits each, in kwh. (Remember that the meter may have overflowed from 999999 to 000000.)
    b. Amount of previous bill in dollars and cents (three digits for dollars and two digits for cents).
    c. Method of charging (1 or 2: see below).
    d. Whether previous bill has been collected (1 = uncollected, 2 = collected).
    e. Name and address (59 characters allowed).
Punch a card containing items (c) and (e) as in the input card, the value 1 for item (d), the later meter reading transferred to the position of the earlier one, and the amount of the new bill computed as follows:
Method 1: fixed charge of $15 plus 9 cents for each kwh over 2000.
Method 2: fixed charge of $3 plus 1.3 cents per kwh.
In either case round to nearest penny and add previous bill if uncollected.

Chapter 4

1. a. What are the merits of verifying data by reading the original copy against the machine-prepared copy? b. What are the merits of having hard (page) copy, as well as machine-readable media, when operating manual keyboard devices? (You can get the feel of *not* having readable copy by starting to type an original and carbon copy but leaving the ribbon in the "off" position so that the original copy is blank. Try it to test your skill and ability to work in the dark. Remember, no peeking at the carbon, because in an actual situation you cannot read a page until

it goes through one or more stages of processing.) *c.* How would you appraise a proposal to send unverified documents (shipping notices, bills, etc.) to customers and rely on them to report mistakes?

2. *a.* What are the advantages of getting data in a form suitable for processing as a by-product of another operation? *b.* What are the disadvantages? *c.* What is the net effect on system efficiency? *d.* What are the audit control features of remote by-product preparation of data when the machine operator is excluded from the tape room and therefore never sees the by-product output?

3. *a.* What is meant by advance preparation of data? *b.* Under what conditions is advance preparation of data input useful? *c.* What effect does this scheme have on the manual preparation of data? *d.* What is the feasibility of advance preparation when your organization has sole control over the data media at all stages (for example, time cards and inventory tags), and when your organization shares control with others (for example, checks and public utility bills)? *e.* What spoilage rate and reconstruction costs are permissible, yet still make advance preparation worth while?

4. *a.* What are the merits of using characters that are readable by both people and machines? *b.* Give examples of character readers for data input. *c.* What are the advantages of character recognition devices to prepare a machine-usable data media? *d.* How are character-readable data verified?

5. *a.* What are the advantages of on-line input? *b.* What problems does on-line data input pose in trying to keep computers operating at capacity?

6. *a.* What types of mechanical printers are used in data-processing systems? *b.* How do they differ in operation from each other? *c.* Why are electronic printers faster than mechanical devices? *d.* Which kind of printer gives characters with the best shape?

7. *a.* What factors should be considered in choosing input and output equipment? *b.* Which factor is most important?

8. *a.* Since equipment is available, or can be developed, for converting data from one medium to almost any other, why should a system designer worry at all about data incompatibility? *b.* What are the merits of direct data conversion—as from punched tape to magnetic tape instead of an indirect scheme of punched tape to punched cards to magnetic tape?

9. *a.* What does multiplexed input mean? *b.* What are the merits of multiplexed input for utilization of both the computer and the input units?

10. Assume that a computer is capable of supplying output at the rate of 100,000 characters a second. The choices offered are to operate output units (cards, paper tape, and magnetic tape) either directly connected or through buffers. If the output units are directly connected, the computer must form characters when they are wanted by the output unit. If a buffer is used, the computer merely loads the buffer and then continues other operations while buffer content is transferred to the output unit.

    a. What fraction of the computer output capability can be absorbed by a card punch, a paper tape punch, or a magnetic tape unit; if a buffer is not used and the computer is able to deal with only that unit?

    b. What fraction of the computer's time will be absorbed in output if a suitable buffer is available for each output unit (80 characters for cards, 1 character for tape and 1000 characters for magnetic tape) which can be filled at computer speeds (and emptied at output unit speeds), but 10 character cycles are required for the computer to test each buffer for readiness to load in the latter part of each output cycle?

11. The printed copy output requirements of one organization are 30,000,000 characters a day, on average. *a.* What printing capacity is required if the output load throughout the week is level and printing deadlines merely require that output be available by the end of the day following processing? *b.* What printing capacity is required if the peak day load in a week is three times the average and

the tight time schedules require completion of printing two hours after process-ing (which takes three hours) is complete? Assume that final data start becoming available for printing halfway through the processing cycle. c. If the conditions in either case (a) or (b) seem too loose or too tight, what changes would you recommend?

12. The following facts are given concerning a tape file that contains 12 million char-acters of data: tape density 200 characters an inch, tape write speed 150 inches a second, rewind speed 300 inches a second, block length not exceeding 511 words of 6 characters each (a block can contain any integral number of records not ex-ceeding 511 words), start-stop time each 10 milliseconds, one inch inter-block gap.

Compute the tape writing time, tape rewind time, and length of tape for each of the following cases:
   a. Records 80 characters long are to be written on tape, in blocked fashion, for use in the next processing cycle.
   b. Records 80 characters long are to be written on tape as individual card records (content of each card separated by a gap) ready for punching.
   c. Records 20 characters long are to be written on tape as individual card records ready for punching.

13. The following facts are available for three cases of data preparation, verification, and correction:

	Case 1	Case 2	Case 3
Ratio of numerical to total characters	.5	.7	.9
Error rate in original preparation of data, per thousand characters	4	2	2
Cost to verify, per thousand characters	$ .20	$ .15	$ .10
Fraction of errors found	.95	.9	.9
Cost to correct a located error	$ .05	$ .05	$ .05
Probability of making satisfactory correction	.7	.8	.9
Penalty for incorrect character going to next stage of processing			
Alphabetic character	$1	$1	$1
Numerical character	$2	$2	$2

For 100,000 characters of data for each case, compute:
   a. The quality of the alphabetic and numerical data after each stage in the verification-correction process.
   b. The cost of the operation, including the penalty for errors remaining in the final data.
   c. Whether more than one verification and correction process appears worth while, if the ratios and costs given above apply to the errors still in the data when the next verification is started.
   d. Whether more verification and correction processes are warranted if the penalties are $3 and $10 for incorrect alphabetic and numerical char-acters, respectively, because of interruptions in later stages of processing.

14. Determine the redundancy ratio (the fraction of non-new data in the total) when each of the following schemes is used:
   a. One check digit per six-character word.
   b. A hash total every 10 messages to list the total of the corresponding char-acters in every message.
   c. One parity-bit per six-bit character and 1 parity-bit per channel after every 5 words of 12 characters each.
   d. Full transponder scheme.
   e. Transmit all numerals twice but alphabetic characters only once.
   f. Spell out all numerals—for example, 351.42 as three hundred fifty-one forty-two—but do not repeat alphabetical characters.
   g. Triplicate the message and accept if two copies agree.

15. Paychecks and stubs are printed on card stock $3\frac{1}{4}$ in. by $7\frac{1}{2}$ in. with a maximum of 50 and 100 characters, respectively. A border of $\frac{1}{4}$ in. on each edge of the check and stub cannot be used for printing and $\frac{1}{4}$ in. must be allowed between successive cards to compensate for the difference between card size and the spacing interval for feeding card stock through the printer. A high-speed printer prints 10 characters an inch along a line and 6 lines per inch at a rate of 1,000 lines a minute. Skips of one to three lines are made at the print rate, but skips of four or more lines are made at the high-speed skip rate of 5,000 lines a minute.
  a. Determine the layout of data for fastest printing of check and stub.
  b. Compute the printing time for 1,000 checks and stubs.
  c. How much faster is side-by-side printing of check and stub instead of serial alternate printing (check, stub, check, stub, etc.)?

Chapter 5

1. a. What would an ideal storage system provide? b. What is the relationship between cost, capacity, and access time of storage media?
2. a. Describe the various schemes used to represent stored data. b. Under what conditions, and why, is the storage capacity for numerical data higher than for alphabetic data?
3. Under what conditions is the fixed-field organization of data superior to variable field?
4. Define: a. stated storage capacity; b. effective storage capacity; c. access time; d. volatility; e. word time.
5. a. What is the principle of random access storage? b. What common storage problem does it try to overcome? c. What is the effect on the usefulness of random access storage if the time required to load or unload the storage is several hours?
6. What effect does a short delay between an event and the need for information about that event have on storage equipment requirements?
7. a. Discuss the value of separating temporary data from permanent data in an external storage system. b. What kind of media would you recommend for each type of data?
8. a. What is an audit trail? b. What changes in auditing methods will accompany the use of automatic equipment? c. Can you visualize auditing procedures that do not use hard copy at all? d. What is the relationship of the audit trail to manual, punched-card, and automatic data-processing methods?
9. a. Why is the ability to interrogate files so important in selecting storage media for automatic data-processing systems? b. How are the requirements met? c. How are similar requirements for other processing systems fulfilled?
10. Appraise these three proposals in terms of printing requirements, ease of finding answers to questions, and economy for printing out files to answer questions:
  a. Print out complete file at short intervals.
  b. Print out complete file at long intervals and supplement the file with a list of transactions (arranged in the proper sequence) since the prior printout.
  c. Rely upon transaction lists only (with a chain linking scheme to help find the prior entry) and never print out the file.
11. a. If a 4 in. diameter magnetic drum rotates at a speed of 5,000 revolutions a minute, what are the maximum and average latency times in milliseconds on a standard band with one read-write head? b. What are the latency times if the drum is 8 in. in diameter? c. What are the latency times for data on a revolver loop if the read and write heads are one-eighth of a drum circumference apart?
12. A programmer facetiously said that his company produced one pint of oil during one word time. The drum involved stored 1,000 words on 20 tracks and revolved at 12,500 revolutions a minute. How much oil did his company produce per month?

13. Storage addresses are often "modulo storage unit size" so that the address after 4096 is 0000 if storage contains 4096 locations. This feature is used in indexing to get effective addresses. What changes would be necessary in programs if memory size were expanded from 8192 to 16,394 locations?

14. *a.* What is the cost, at $.05 each, for magnetic cores alone to make a storage of 1,024 words if each word has a sign and 12 alphanumeric characters each with parity-bit? *b.* What is the cost of a 16,384 word storage if each word has a sign, 36 data bits, and a parity-bit? *c.* What is the most economical configuration for each storage unit considering the cost of read-write circuitry?

15. The proposal is made that punched cards be microfilmed on photographic film so that only the picture and not the card need be stored. What would be the effect of this microfilming on filing equipment, storage space, retrieval equipment, and costs?

16. *a.* What are the merits of magnetic tape, drum, disk, and bin for volume of storage, interrogability, data-transfer speed, and changeability (reloading with new data)? *b.* Would the fact that the data in storage can be arranged in an orderly fashion and used in either (1) the same sequence or (2) in an entirely random sequence affect your answer to (*a*)? How?

17. When using magnetic tapes for data storage it is customary, although not universal, to remove inactive tapes and replace with active tapes. *a.* Could a similar replacement plan be used for magnetic drums, disks, cores, and bins? *b.* How would you appraise the merits of such a replacement scheme?

18. Customarily tape transport units are assigned by pairs for handling multi-reel files so that a "tape swap" can be made from one tape to the other without interrupting processing. *a.* How much processing time is saved by arranging for tape swaps? *b.* What is the effect on the number of tape transports required and their utilization? *c.* Could equipment utilization be improved by having one (or perhaps more) tape transports assigned as "roving spares" to swap with any tape transport on a first-come, first-served basis? *d.* Would a combination of one assigned spare transport for each major tape file and a roving spare for all minor tape files increase equipment utilization without making programming unnecessarily complex?

19. The following estimates are available about the number of tape files and input-output time:

	Number of Tapes	Input-Output Time
Master File	10	8 min. each
Trailer File (contains overflow of each record from master file)	4	20
Transactions	2.7	30
Error Tape (from prior processing cycle)	.2	80
Program	.1	

a. How many tapes are required for the current processing cycle and two complete prior cycles of the file for back-up purposes? *b.* What arrangement of tapes on tape transports will give fastest processing if tape change time (rewind a tape, dismount, and mount a new tape) is 2.5 minutes and 10 tape transports are available? *c.* What arrangement of tapes on tape transports will give fastest processing if tape changing time is the same as (*b*) but 15 tape transports are available? *d.* Draw a line chart (with time shown horizontally) to show the use of each tape transport (running, change, and idle time), if 12 are available. *e.* What is the ideal number of tape transports if they rent for $600 a month, computer time costs $300 an hour, and three jobs similar to this one are being run every business day?

20. An organization specializing in census and statistical work finds that no one is willing to relinquish a tape filled with data, so that more than 10,000 tapes are now in the library. Proposed remedies are (1) to charge the holder $50 for the tape cost, (2) charge $100 to make a profit on each tape, or (3) automatically print out the

contents and re-use each tape that is more than 18 months old. Appraise each of these plans in terms of subsequent usefulness of data, usability of data on tape versus printed lists, and density of tape storage versus printed lists or punched cards.

Chapter 6

1. Draw a block diagram showing the relationship between the following elements of a data-processing system: *a.* input; *b.* internal storage; *c.* arithmetic; *d.* control; *e.* output.
2. Add the following three binary numbers:

$$10110101$$
$$00101101$$
$$11010101$$

3. Describe and compare two methods of performing subtraction operations.
4. What are the advantages of the add-and-shift method of multiplication as compared to the repeated-addition method?
5. *a.* Describe the general procedure used for dividing on a computer, with special emphasis on the formation of the quotient. *b.* Specify the locations of the divisor, dividend, quotient, and remainder before a division operation starts and after it is completed.
6. *a.* Give three examples of logical operations. *b.* How do logical operations differ from arithmetical operations?
7. *a.* Describe one procedure used for multiplying on a computer with emphasis on the use and disappearance of the multiplier. *b.* Specify the locations of the multiplicand, multiplier, and product before a multiplication operation starts and after it is completed.
8. *a.* What are the consequences of mistakenly using an extract even order instead of an extract odd order? *b.* What is the difference between the shift orders described in Chapter 3 and the logical shift or circulate order described in this chapter? *c.* How many circulate orders can you devise taking the accumulator and M-Q register separately and together? *d.* How many of your hypothetical orders in (*c*) would seem to have any usefulness for data processing?
9. *a.* What is the design relationship between the word length, number of addresses per instruction, number of storage locations, use of indexes, number of instructions that the computer can decode, and code scheme? *b.* Given 65,536 storage locations, 16 index registers, 256 decodable instructions and a decimal code scheme, devise minimum length formats for single address and for triple address instructions. *c.* Repeat (*b*) but use a binary code scheme (which you can group into octal, if you wish).
10. What elements in a computer correspond to the keyboard, lower dial, and upper dial of a desk calculator in performing *a.* addition and *b.* multiplication?
11. Form the specified complements for the following numbers:

(a) Nines:	2387, 42591, 9999, 10000, 9876, 6789
(b) Tens:	2387, 42591, 9999, 10000, 9876, 6789
(c) Ones:	1101101, 1000001, 1111111, 0000000, 1000000
(d) Twos:	1101101, 1000001, 1111111, 0000000, 1000000
(e) Binary coded decimal:	0010 0011 1000 0111, 0100 0010 0101 1001 0001, 1001 1001 1001 1001, 0001 0000 0000 0000 0000
(f) Binary coded decimal, excess three:	0101 0110 1011 1010, 0111 0101 1000 1100 0100, 1100 1100 1100 1100, 0100 0011 0011 0011 0011

12. *a.* What methods are available for detecting and correcting computer errors? *b.* Which method is preferable from the viewpoint of minimum equipment? *c.* Which is preferable from the viewpoint of simplest preparation of programs?

13. *a.* What is double-precision addition? *b.* What difficulty does this scheme remedy? *c.* What other remedies are available?

14. *a.* How does the end-around-carry make the nines complement, instead of the tens complement, satisfactory for subtraction operations? *b.* What does the failure of the end-around-carry to occur in an operation signify?

15. It is said that multiple address instruction programs take fewer instructions than single address programs. *a.* How would you evaluate this statement? *b.* How would you determine whether a multiple address program occupies less storage space (considering both the number of words and length of each word) than a single address program?

16. *a.* How can you determine the amount of the remainder following a division operation, if the computer does not make it available? (Consider the relationship of the dividend and the product of the quotient multiplied by the divisor.) *b.* Develop an illustration. *c.* Develop the general rule.

17. The manual and punched-card systems previously in use in an organization sorted incoming documents on double terminal (two right hand) digits in order to divide nearly evenly the workload among 100 clerks. Thus, documents for customers numbered 123456, 123457, 123458 and 123956, would be sorted as though they were numbered 561234, 561239, 571234 and 581234. Clerk number 56 would get the first two, clerk number 57 the next, etc. Since files are arranged in double terminal digit sequence, it is considered desirable to retain the old schemes, at least temporarily. *a.* Why does the double terminal digit scheme give a more nearly even workload than merely sorting on the customer number as such? *b.* How should the customer numbers be manipulated in order to get the desired sequence when sorting on the computer? *c.* What are the merits of retaining the double terminal digit scheme when files are maintained on magnetic tape and processing is done on a computer?

18. *a.* Form the dollar and cents amount of paychecks between 10 00 and 99 99 and insert the "$" before the first digit and the "." before the cents. *b.* Repeat (*a*) to handle any amount from 9 99 to 999 99 and keep the "$" next to the first digit.

19. In one case where a computer has a six-character word, most words have five alphanumerical characters. Devise three schemes, each involving one operation and one test, that will determine whether a word has six characters.

20. One programmer finds that he frequently wishes to add 100 numbers that consist of two or three digits. Since the computer that he is using does not have index registers, he proposes that 01 be placed in the leftmost part of each number and that completion of the summation be determined by an overflow test. *a.* Sketch out the program that he will require. *b.* In how many other situations can he use a similar scheme? *c.* What scheme should he use if index registers were available? *d.* What method would you recommend for loop counting if the computer lacks index registers?

21. Aircraft seat reservation control starts with the number of seats available and subtracts the number of seats sold until zero is reached. It is proposed that initially the number of seats be subtracted and the seats sold added until zero is reached. *a.* Which scheme is faster, if addition and subtraction operations take the same amount of time? *b.* Which is faster if complementing a number takes as much time as adding a number? *c.* Determine the difference between the positive zero that results from the first scheme and negative zero from the second. *d.* If the end-around-carry can be sensed, how can the sold-out condition be most easily determined? *e.* What are two other ways of determining sold-out status? *f.* How can an over-sold condition be detected?

22. Devise a scheme to perform multiplication in a computer that does not have a multiply order. (Hint: set up to multiply 4683 x 275 by means of a multiplication table of 0 and 1 through 9 times 4683 built up by repeated addition and stored in locations 100 to 109 by means of an indexed store order.)

23. The formula for the multiplication operation time in one computer is, in micro-seconds:

$$.017 [N_r (N_d + 4) + 2]$$

where N_r = the number of digits in the multiplier

N_d = the number of digits in the multiplicand

   a. Compute the time required to multiply
>   (1) 1234 x 4567
>   (2) 4567 x 8989
>   (3)   12 x 98765432

   b. Draw a chart with N_r on the horizontal scale and N_d on the vertical and plot the multiplication times for N_r and N_d from 1 through 10. Connect the points that have the same value. *c.* How should the multiplication operation be arranged to minimize the time required for the operation?

24. Given the word 123456 in computer storage, reverse it to 654321 by means of logical shift and extract orders.

Chapter 7

1. *a.* What points should be considered in evaluating computer speed? *b.* Discuss the merits and demerits of using a single index to measure computer performance.
2. What is the effect of business data-processing requirements on equipment design?
3. What factors should be considered in appraising equipment versatility?
4. *a.* Compare the features of an ideal system in relation to an available system. *b.* What steps may be taken to compensate for the lack of ideal conditions?
5. Draw up the specifications for a representative or typical system based on the specifications given for computers in the chapter.
6. *a.* What does the phrase system balance mean? *b.* Is system balance constant for all applications? *c.* How can the lack of balance be corrected short of purchasing new equipment?
7. *a.* What does the phrase tape limited operation mean? *b.* What does computer limited operation mean? *c.* How is it possible for an operation that is tape limited to become computer limited, and vice versa?
8. If you could choose only one feature of a computer to be improved 100 per cent at no cost to you as a user, which feature would you choose?
9. What are the minimum, maximum, and median (middle item in a list arranged in order from smallest to largest) values for the features for automatic processors as listed in the tables in this chapter?
10. Explain how each of the following instructions could be simulated by means of standard instructions in the instruction repertoire: add-to-storage, storage-to-storage transfer, repeat, and table look-up operations.
11. The following choices may be available when a parity-bit error occurs on reading tape: reread one or more times under program control, reread automatically one or more times under computer control, read the faulty record onto a reject tape, or halt all operations. Which one, or more, of these choices would you prefer to have available for use with your computer? Why?
12. It is sometimes said that if a computer has more than four index registers, it should have a hundred. How would you appraise the usefulness of having a hundred index registers in a computer?
13. What factors determine the suitable amount of secondary storage in relation to the amount of internal storage?
14. *a.* Why is the track-to-track access time for magnetic disks shorter than the disk-to-disk access time? *b.* What is the transfer rate for data after the desired disk track is located? *c.* How does the storage capacity of a set of disks compare with the capacity of a magnetic tape and of a tape data file?

15. *a.* What factors determine the optimum number of tape transports? *b.* What is the maximum number of tape transports that can be connected to a computer? *c.* What is the minimum number of tape transports that will serve for a file maintenance operation? For a merge-sort operation?

16. What are the merits of (a) plugboard format control for printers, (b) printers that operate either on-line or off-line, (c) printer buffers?

17. *a.* Calculate the two operating speed indexes as described in the chapter for each one of five computers. *b.* How different is the ranking of computers by operating speed, from the fastest to the slowest, using the two indexes instead of either the addition speed or the multiplication speed alone? *c.* How suitable an index of speed is the following scheme: times required to perform the operations common to all computers under consideration, i.e., the total time for one addition, subtraction, multiplication, comparison, and so on.

18. Some magnetic tape units are designed with a reading head beside the writing head to check-read the data just after it is written on tape.
   a. Why worry about the quality of data written on tape if a parity-bit is used?
   b. About how many characters are there between the write and read head if they are ¾ in. apart?
   c. How should the intervening characters (between the writing and reading heads) be treated in computer storage so that they are available for checking against the data being read from tape?
   d. What are the merits of echo checking to determine that each character merely passes the parity test without comparing it against the corresponding character in storage?

19. How much could the effective data content of tape be increased by each of the following schemes: *a.* eliminating the transverse and longitudinal parity-bits; *b.* doubling the length of tapes; *c.* eliminating the inter-block gap; *d.* making the tape four times as wide.

20. Tape rewinding takes from 1 minute to 10 minutes. What are the merits of the following schemes for effectively cutting rewinding time?
   a. Assign tape units in pairs and swap to a new tape while the filled tape is rewinding.
   b. Dismount wound tapes without rewinding and rewind on a special device.
   c. Dismount wound tapes, do not rewind but mount the reel backwards the next time it is used so that it can be re-used without ever bothering to rewind it.
   d. Process the reel by reading it backwards in the next processing cycle, if the computer has a read-backwards feature.

21. What are the merits of the following features for facilitating operations: *a.* program interrupt; *b.* simultaneous read-compute-write; *c.* simultaneous tape search; *d.* real-time input; *e.* off-line printing?

22. Data are recorded at 100 characters an inch by one computer with an inter-record gap of .75 in. between variable length records on tape.
   a. Draw a chart with record length along the x axis and effective data density (as a percentage of specified density) along the y axis to show the relative tape utilization for records of 25, 50, 75, 100, 200, and so on to 800 characters.
   b. Draw another line for a specified density of 400 characters an inch and .75 in. inter-record gap.
   c. Repeat for 400 characters an inch but assume an inter-record gap of .25 in.
   d. What length of record is necessary in each case to get 25, 50, and 75 per cent effective utilization of the specified density?
   e. What improvement in tape utilization can be gained by blocking several short records into one longer record?
   f. What is the relationship between tape utilization and read-write time for file processing?

23. A computer manufacturer is considering offering a new model computer. His choices are either to offer the same processing capacity as before at a reduced price, or to offer more processing capacity at the same price. Furthermore, the new computer can be designed so that programs for the earlier model computers are compatible. If the new model is lower priced and programs are compatible, users of the prior equipment may insist on either a reduction in rent on the equipment already in use or on its replacement with new equipment.

a. What strategy should the manufacturer adopt for introducing new features and pricing new equipment?

b. How can he protect against users turning in relatively new equipment and demanding newer models?

c. What strategy should a computer manufacturer use to announce a new computer in view of the fact that an announcement causes many prospects to place an order but also causes many switches from orders for other computers including the one that was superseded?

Chapter 8

1. a. What are the merits of editing data on cards during the input operation so that the format in the machine is different from the format on cards? b. How is the data editing operation handled by equipment? c. What character can be usefully inserted or deleted during read-in editing?

2. a. Why is it desirable to achieve minimum latency in computer programming? b. What other schemes are useful for reducing program running time? c. Devise general rules to show how much programming effort can be usefully spent to cut program running time.

3. If computer operating speeds were increased as much as good programmers can cut running time by means of minimum latency, would the emphasis on minimum latency disappear? Explain.

4. Explain the effect on computer running time of each of the following processing plans: a. updating stock balances by adding receipts to prior balances, or vice versa; b. multiplying price (usually 5 to 7 digits) by quantity (usually 2 to 3 digits), or vice versa; c. multiplying whole numbers by decimals (.1000, .2500, .3333, etc.) or dividing by the reciprocal (10, 4, 3, etc.); d. dividing by 10, 100, 1000, etc., by shifting the dividend to the right; e. arranging the program for testing for the most commonly occurring situations first (the frequency of occurrence of certain events is .7, .2, .05, .02, .01, .01, and .01) and less frequently occurring events in sequence, or vice versa.

5. a. Why does the problem of optimum programming arise with the use of drum and disk storage although it does not usually arise with magnetic core storage? b. A manufacturer promising .5 microsecond access time storage when the fastest magnetic cores available had 2 microsecond access hit upon the plan of dividing core storage into four banks and sequentially pulsing each one .5 microseconds later. (1) Is such a magnetic core storage random access? (2) Do optimum programming problems arise with this core storage comparable to those usually associated with drum and disk? Explain.

6. Classify the following as errors, mistakes, or malfunctions:

a. Confusion of the withholding tax and federal insurance contribution rules so that withholding tax is not deducted for gross pay exceeding $4,200.

b. Computer multiplication of gross pay times tax rate gives incorrect amount of withholding tax.

c. Federal insurance contributions rates for the prior period used after the rates were increased.

d. New cards prepared to replace those failing the verification test but not verified before being used as inputs.

7. Show how the proof figure scheme can be used to increase the probability of accurate results in computing inventory value for the following items:

Item	Quantity	Unit Price
1	2,368	$ 4.67
2	5,192	10.11
3	37	59.88
4	14,244	1.23

8. *a.* What factors are involved in determining the ideal number of instructions that a computer should be able to decode? *b.* What are the costs associated with too short an instruction repertoire? Too long an instruction repertoire?

9. One computer user that provides its own maintenance service says that a useful spare time occupation for maintenance personnel is to invent new instructions and modify the computer circuitry to handle such instructions.

    a. What are the merits of having unique instructions in programs that cannot be run on similar equipment elsewhere because of incompatible order codes?

    b. What improvement in the art of designing and building computers might be expected to grow out of users' improvisations?

    c. What effect would customer improvisations have on the salvage value of rented equipment? Purchased equipment?

10. Program the following operations by floating point and fixed point arithmetic given a computer with a word length of 7 characters:

    a. $4321.98 + 26.8756$

    b. $432198. + .268756$

    c. $4321.98 \times .268756$

    d. $4.32198 \div 2687.56$

11. *a.* What is the nature of pseudo-codes, mnemonic codes, and machine codes? *b.* Why is it desirable to have order codes that are not machine codes for a computer?

12. *a.* Why are symbolic addresses preferable to absolute addresses? *b.* What are the disadvantages of absolute addresses? *c.* If computers are designed to operate with absolute addresses only, how can programs that are written with symbolic addresses be used efficiently on a computer?

13. The use of subroutines is sometimes criticized because they are only 85 per cent as efficient as tailor-made programs, they require much study in order to understand them, and they require additional computer storage. The advantages of subroutines are reduced program writing time and debugging time. How would you compare these advantages and disadvantages (plus others) to decide whether it is more efficient to prepare and use subroutines or to write programs for each specific application?

14. What is meant by each of the following terms: *a.* automatic programming; *b.* machine-oriented language; *c.* problem-oriented language; *d.* interpretive routine; *e.* compiler routine?

15. *a.* What is the relationship between a post-mortem and a trace routine? *b.* A trace routine increases computer running time an appreciable amount. Since this additional time is wasted if the program works correctly, explain the conditions under which a trace can be used advantageously.

16. *a.* What function does a translator perform? *b.* Why does the translation of a pseudo-code cause difficulty during the debugging stage? *c.* Why is the value of the minimum-latency feature of compiling routines dependent upon the storage media of the computer used?

17. *a.* What is the purpose of generating routines? *b.* Why are so many parameters required to generate a routine to check the sequence of records in a file?

18. *a.* Why are two entirely different automatic programming schemes, such as FOR TRANSIT and FLOW-MATIC offered to computer users? *b.* How would you appraise the value of an automatic programming scheme?

19. The rules for operating on words containing non-numerals may be stated as follows: In addition or subtraction any digit position that has a non-numeral in either operand, the character in the accumulator is transferred to the result. Normal addition or subtraction occurs for numerals, but carries to or borrows from non-numerals are lost. Multiplication or division of operands containing letters is not allowed and stops the computer.

    a. How can these rules be used to edit alphabetic characters out of a word?

    b. How can these rules be used to edit numerical characters out of a word?

    c. How can the presence of alphabetic characters be determined?

    d. Is it possible to determine the presence of alphabetic characters in one or more specified positions in a word? Explain.

20. Double precision addition can be described as splitting each number into two parts: A + B and C + D (with due regard for digit positions), adding A + C and B + D, and putting the two sums together with due regard for the number of digit positions in each partial number.

    a. Develop a similar scheme for double precision multiplication;

    b. Test your scheme by multiplying 36 x 24; 3060 x 2040; 300600 x 200004;

    c. How much inaccuracy is introduced if the partial product of C x D is dropped?

21. It is sometimes said that high programming costs reflect the fact that automatic processing equipment is not well suited to business application requirements and that equipment manufacturers are not meeting their obligations. *a.* How would you appraise the merits of this statement? *b.* What remedies would you propose in order to reduce the user's programming cost?

22. The usual rule for rounding a number is to add 5 in the extreme left position to be discarded and discard the unwanted digits. An upward bias may result because all numbers ending in 5, 50, 500 in the positions to be discarded, are rounded to the next highest number. A more careful rule for rounding numbers ending in 50 . . . 0 is to make the right hand retained position an even valued digit—odd valued digits are increased by the add-five rule, but even valued digits are left unchanged. *a.* Determine the amount of bias that can arise by applying the usual rule for rounding if only a few digits are rounded; if many digits are rounded. *b.* Devise a computer program to apply the more careful rule for rounding.

23. What factors should the computer user consider in deciding whether to have the computer manufacturer include one additional instruction in the computer's repertoire?

24. Which of the three kinds of inaccuracies—errors, mistakes, and malfunctions—can be minimized by: *a.* verification of data collection; *b.* using more digits in calculations than are required in the final answer; *c.* desk-checking; *d.* using care to perform operations in the correct sequence; *e.* routine test and maintenance of equipment; *f.* built-in program checks; *g.* double precision operations; *h.* testing the program on live data; *i.* designing duplicate circuitry into the computer; *j.* duplicating operations within the computer by programming; *k.* using hash totals and proof figures.

25. *a.* How is a set index and jump instruction used to enter a subroutine? *b.* To return to the main program? *c.* Can it be used repeatedly in a program? *d.* How can the return point in the main program be selected dependent upon conditions encountered in the subroutine?

26. *a.* What is the difference between the store accumulator and the store address instructions? *b.* How is a store address instruction used in conjunction with a dummy instruction?

27. What is the relationship between scaling and floating point operations?

28. One computer user suggested that the exponent be placed to the left of the fraction when forming words in floating point arithmetic so that they could be handled as one word for sorting into numerical sequence. Explain and illustrate how the proposed scheme would work.

29. *a.* Would it be possible to write a program, using symbolic and relative addresses, so that the programmer would make no commitment about where it should be placed in storage? *b.* If not, what is the minimum that he must specify?

30. It is suggested that, in addition to arithmetical and logical shifts to left and right, a figure 8 shift instruction be included. The characters shifted out of the left end of the M-Q register would be introduced into the left end of the accumulator; characters shifted out of the right end of the accumulator would be treated in corresponding fashion. *a.* Assuming the characters ABCDEFGH are stored in the accumulator and M-Q register combined, trace through enough operations to show that continued figure 8 shifting would return to the original condition. *b.* Devise a useful application for the figure 8 shift instruction.

31. Given a list of numbers in no particular order find: (a) how many of them taken in sequence have a sum just under 1000; (b) a sum just over 1000; and (c) a sum closest to 1000. Write the program to compute the sum in each case.

32. The gross sales of branch offices 1-10 are to be accumulated sequentially in storage locations 031-040. Locations 021-030 can, if desired, be used to store the branch office numbers. Fifty sales are stored in locations 100-199 with the office number and the amount of sales in pairs of words: 100-1, 102-3, etc. Write the program to accumulate sales under these conditions: *(a)* if index registers are available; *(b)* if a table look-up instruction is available; *(c)* if neither index registers nor the table look-up instruction is available.

33. Internal storage contains 200 account balances with debits as plus numbers and credits as minus numbers. The identifying account number is stored in one location and the balance in the next location in pairs 001 through 399.

    One hundred and fifty transactions are read into the computer in account number order, with each consisting of identification number and amount (debits plus and credits minus). These transactions are stored in locations 700 through 999.

    Location 401 contains the number 400, which is the total number of accounts times 2 and location 699 contains 300 which is the total number of transactions times 2. Index register A might be used to keep the file count and index register B the transaction count.

    a. Draw a flow diagram of the steps involved in locating an active record, updating the amount balance, and moving to the next transaction.

    b. Write a program to update the account balance using absolute addresses for file records and transactions.

    c. Write a program to update the account balances using symbolic addresses as follows:

FILE	First file record address
TRANS	First transaction address
FCOUNT	Number of records times 2
TCOUNT	Number of transactions times 2
MATCH	Start of processing routine for matches
ERROR	Start of error processing routine

    d. Assign absolute addresses to the symbolic addresses to show that the two programs written in (*b*) and (*c*) can be made identical for purposes of computer operations.

    e. If a computer program is used to assemble the symbolic address program into the minimum storage space, what absolute address will be assigned to the symbolic addresses?

34. An asterisk is sometimes used to indicate the present location when using the relative addressing scheme. Thus * + 3 means 3 storage locations after the present location.

There is a traditional story that a fisherman once suggested that the good fishing spot be marked by an X on the side of the boat; he was farsighted enough to see that even if he did not always use the same boat, he would probably get a boat that someone else had marked with equal care. *a.* What is the relationship between the two relative addressing schemes? *b.* What keeps the * in relative addressing in programming from being as fluid as the X on the boat?

Chapter 9

1. *a.* What is meant by the degree of automation in data processing? *b.* What influence does the degree of automation have on processing procedures and flexibility of operations? *c.* What factors determine the degree of automation that should be achieved by an organization?
2. *a.* Why does specialization of functions and operations occur in data-processing systems? *b.* What are the charactetistics of a system with either minimum or no specialization?
3. *a.* What is the meaning of fragmentary processing? *b.* What is the meaning of consolidated processing? *c.* What factors determine whether an organization will use fragmentary or consolidated processing?
4. *a.* What is the relationship between the cost of data collection and the ratio of equipment to labor used in data origination? *b.* How can the accuracy of input data be improved by changing the ratio of capital to labor used in originating data? *c.* How would you determine what degree of accuracy in input data is most efficient for over-all processing? *d.* What is the relationship between the degree of accuracy and the cost of obtaining that degree of accuracy?
5. How is a processing system influenced by the place and method of data origination?
6. *a.* What is the meaning of the terms proof totals and hash totals? *b.* Develop an example of proof totals and hash totals. *c.* Under what conditions is each type of total suitable? *d.* How is each type of total obtained most efficiently under operating conditions?
7. *a.* Describe and distinguish between the following data-flow plans: (1) on-line processing, (2) in-line processing, (3) off-line processing. *b.* What capacity of equipment is required and what degree of utilization of equipment is achieved by each data-flow plan? *c.* Give an example of a business or industrial situation in which each data-flow plan would be either desirable or mandatory. *d.* How would you relate the benefits of obtaining results more quickly (by on-line processing, perhaps) to the costs involved?
8. *a.* Describe and distinguish between on-line processing, real-time processing, event-triggered processing, and batch processing. *b.* Can an industrial or business system continue to operate satisfactorily without real-time control? Explain. *c.* What are the differences in the processing requirements required to maintain real-time control of (1) a sailing vessel, (2) an elevator, (3) an automobile, (4) an airplane, and (5) a rocket?
9. *a.* Why are data sorted? *b.* How does sorting facilitate the subsequent stages of data processing? *c.* How can data be processed efficiently if they are not sorted? *d.* Some people object to the term sort, since no item is eliminated (unlike sorting bad apples from good) but prefer the term marshall. Evaluate.
10. *a.* Define and distinguish between the following schemes for sorting data: block, digital, comparison of pairs, and merge. *b.* Show how items with the following keys would be sorted by the digital, comparison of pairs, and merge schemes:

   13, 39, 35, 43, 11, 28, 04, 26, 32, 30, 37, 98,
   38, 60, 06, 43, 19, 11, 75, 31, 36, 82, 95, 46.
11. *a.* Why might block sorting be called major-minor and digital sorting minor-major? *b.* What are the differences in the operations involved in the two sorting schemes?

12. You are told that a series of items is sorted into ascending sequence when you receive them. *a*. How can you check their sequence most efficiently? *b*. If you are not aware of the existing sequence, how much work is involved if you try to sort them into ascending sequence by the block, digital, and merge schemes? *c*. What sorting schemes exploit any sequence that already exists? *d*. What scheme is most efficient for sorting these items into descending sequence?

13. *a*. Why is the comparison-of-pairs scheme also called the bubble scheme? *b*. What determines whether the item with the smallest or largest key bubbles up (or settles out) in the comparison-of-pairs scheme? *c*. What is the average distance for an item to bubble up?

14. *a*. What is the general rule for the number of tape passes required for merge sorting randomly arranged items? *b*. How many more passes are required to sort items that are in the reverse sequence than to sort items that are in random sequence when first received? *c*. How is the calculated number of passes rounded to find the actual number of passes required? *d*. How is the number of merge passes required to sort data affected by the number of tape inputs?

15. *a*. What is the difference between file maintenance and file processing? *b*. What are the arguments either for combining or for separating file maintenance and processing? *c*. Why and how do pending changes arise in file maintenance? *d*. How does the quantity of available computer storage affect efficient file maintenance and processing methods?

16. *a*. What are the consequences for file processing of having incorrect keys in (1) input transactions and (2) the main file? *b*. How can each type of mistake be detected and corrected?

17. *a*. Describe the concepts involved in common language data processing and integrated data processing. *b*. What are the objectives of integrated data processing? *c*. Is integrated data processing compatible with automatic processing? *d*. What is the relationship between integrated data processing and consolidated processing?

18. *a*. What is functional integration? *b*. How does functional integration attempt to improve data-processing operations? *c*. Are functional integration and common-language integration compatible?

19. *a*. Why is it either desirable or necessary to process different types of transactions (for example, receipts, shipments, orders, returns, cancellations) in a specified sequence? *b*. What sequence would you suggest for processing inventory transactions?

20. Banks are interested in preventing customers from utilizing float, which can be defined as balances arising from items deposited that will not be collected for a number of days. Items in float may be considered collected either a specified number of days after deposit or when notice of collection is received from the drawee bank. What processing procedures are required to restrict depositors' use of float when float is managed by each of the two schemes?

21. A newspaper controller suspects that there are names included in the subscribers' list from whom no collection has been made. *a*. How might names occur incorrectly in the subscribers' list? *b*. How would you try to find the nature and extent of the mistakes? *c*. What procedures should be used to correct the present situation? To prevent its recurrence?

22. Any change in account numbers or classifications reduces, or eliminates, the comparability of results obtained before and after the change date. Examples are the introduction of account numbers for a bank's depositors, new catalogue numbers and classes for a company's products, and a redefinition of a trade area for collecting census data.

    a. Under what conditions is a proposed change in account numbers of classifications warranted in view of the loss of comparability?

    b. What preparations should be made to facilitate such a change?

    c. What additional processing is necessitated to obtain comparability of the results obtained before and after such a change?

23. How should a file be organized for efficient processing, if any item within a record may need to be used as the sorting key?

24. Prepare charts to show the time required to sort randomly arranged items into sequence with a punched-card sorter and with a large-scale automatic processor that can handle each pass within the time required to pass tapes. Assume that data are already on cards or tapes as desired. (Facts about automatic equipment are given in Chapter 7. Card sorters are available to sort 400, 1,000 or 2,000 cards per minute on one column.)

   a. Cover the range of 1,000 to 100,000 records of 80 characters each with a key of 8 characters.

   b. Cover the range of 10,000 to 500,000 records of 200 characters each with a key of 20 characters.

25. A manufacturing company codes each master file record to indicate its origin (for example, customer or stock number) and its destination(s) (for example, list of delinquent customers or of stock items depleted). In order to prepare reports, each record is repeated once on tape for each report in which the item will be included. One way to arrange the items for report preparation is to segregate the items for each report and then sort each subset into report sequence. Another method is to devise a combined report and item code so that all items can be sorted (without any segregation) into one over-all report and item sequence.

   a. What efficiencies are gained by sorting a large set of items into one over-all sequence instead of into many short sequences?

   b. Devise a combined report and item code classification that will meet the requirements of the second method for arranging items for report preparation.

   c. What are the implications of each method for report editing and printing operations?

Chapter 10

1. a. How are data and information defined in the chapter? b. Why are two different definitions used here when dictionaries use quite similar definitions? c. Why are relevance and freedom of action considered in defining information? d. If the definitions of the two words, data and information, do not satisfy you, develop new meanings for them.

2. The words data and information are sometimes considered to be synonymous with condition and operating results. Should a distinction be drawn? If so, what is the distinction?

3. a. If all facts are necessarily past history, why do people rail at accountants for reporting what has actually happened? b. If accountants stopped dealing with past events, would another group develop to fulfill the same function? Explain. c. If facts about the past are not wanted, how might the data-processing system be redesigned to cut costs?

4. a. What sources of information are available to a manager in an organization? b. How do managers get information outside the formal data-processing system? c. Does the acquisition of information outside the formal channels imply that the formal system should be expanded or scrapped? Explain. d. How would the managerial function change if only formal information channels were available to a manager?

5. a. Describe the nature and operation of a data system that supplies full reports to managers who must select information to make decisions. b. What is the exception principle applied to report preparation? c. What are the implications of the differences between full reporting and exception reporting?

6. a. How is the idea of a normal range related to exception reporting? b. What methods can be used for setting normal ranges? c. Why is it important not to set

the normal range too wide? Too narrow? *d*. What are the advantages and disadvantages of the exception reporting plan?

7. *a*. What is the distinction between internal decisions and information selection? *b*. Why is it easier for a data-processing system to select and report information than it is for it to make internal decisions?

8. *a*. What is the difference between accuracy and precision? *b*. Describe how a system may produce precise but inaccurate results. *c*. How is accuracy measured?

9. *a*. In what ways do inaccuracies arise in the results produced by a data-processing system? *b*. What is the relationship between the cost of processing and the degree of accuracy required as it is increased toward perfect accuracy?

10. *a*. What is the relationship of the length of the processing interval and the cost of processing? *b*. Why do processing costs increase rapidly as the interval approaches zero whereas they increase slowly if the interval is greatly extended? *c*. Could an indefinitely long interval be used to minimize processing costs? Explain.

11. What is the effect of the degree of automation, the type of processing scheme, and the rate of transition on the costs of data processing?

12. *a*. What aspects of information deserve study in formulating a theory of value? *b*. Discuss the relationship between three of these aspects and the value of information. *c*. Under what conditions (considering each aspect) is the value of information the highest?

13. *a*. How is the age of information defined? *b*. Why is the age of status and of operating information defined differently? Explain.

14. If i indicates interval, d delay, and r reporting interval, develop formulas to calculate the minimum, maximum, and average age of status and operating information.

15. *a*. Under what conditions is a data-processing system optimized in terms of accuracy, interval, and delay? *b*. Why not simply push each factor to its limit—perfect accuracy, shortest interval, and least delay—when designing a data-processing system?

16. *a*. How does the degree of predictability affect the value of reports? *b*. What are the factors that determine the relevance of information for management's use? *c*. Why is it important to examine the consequences of having (or not having) information when designing or altering a data-processing system?

17. In the section dealing with the formulation of cost and value models, an illustration indicates that a manager needs to make yes-no decisions. *a*. Why does the manager want information? *b*. Will he always make the wrong decision when he lacks information on the current state of the real world? *c*. Does the manager in this problem ever have zero information? *d*. What is the best policy for the manager to follow in obtaining information?

18. For Equation (1) for the value of V as described in the chapter: *a*. Define accuracy (A), delay (t), use interval (F), and probability (P). *b*. What do each of the terms such as f(A, T, Y, n) in Equation (1) represent in an actual situation? *c*. Why are the correct answers summed for F periods and then divided by F?

19. Based on the situation represented by Equation (2) in the chapter and assuming K = $10: *a*. What is the value per period of a report that is prepared once each five periods with no delay, has perfect accuracy, and costs $12? *b*. What is the value of a report prepared every other period which contains one mistake for every five correct answers? The report is not available until one period after the data originate and it costs $12.50 to prepare.

20. Why are models for determining the cost and value of information not frequently used?

21. Assume that the situation described in the first part of the formulation of cost and value models holds except as follows: there are ten decision alternatives corresponding to ten equally likely actual conditions. A correct answer results in a profit, K, and an incorrect answer results in a loss, L. *a*. For this problem set up an

expression similar to Equation (2) in the chapter. *b.* Find the best information system if K = $10, L = $–5, and

$$H(A, F, T) = \$\frac{5}{F}\left[1 + \frac{1}{(1-A)3^T}\right]$$

22. Forecasting or reporting timely events—elections, security prices, weather, fast- or slow-moving stock items—may place a high premium on getting results quickly. *a.* What is the nature of the reporting period, interval, and delay in each of the examples cited? *b.* What factors determine the value of timely results obtained from data processing in each example? *c.* Why are flash reports for merchandising reports and indexes—Dow Jones and Associated Press for reporting security prices—considered invaluable?

23. *a.* Show what will happen over a period of one year to the time-phasing of trans- actions for a company that plans to bill customers, pay bills, and so forth, on a 28-day month when all others use a calendar month. *b.* What will happen to de- positors' balances at a bank if the delay in clearing checks is suddenly cut from several days to one day? *c.* What are the implications of April 15 instead of March 15 as a tax return filing date if a pay-as-you-go plan is used that withholds too much (or too little) tax?

24. Some insurance companies may start the preparation of notices six weeks before the due date and mail them one month before the due date because of processing time and legal requirements. During this six-week period, the following kinds of changes occur and have certain costs for correction:

Kind of change and example	Frequency per 1000 policies per year	Cost to prepare each correction	Estimated loss associated with each uncorrected mistake
Trivial—change of address	250	$ 1.40	$ .20
Consequential—premium change	140	3.80	5.00
Critical—lapse or death	50	12.00	50.00

Five per cent of the notices that should be changed slip through unchanged or incorrectly changed. *a.* How would you describe the six-week and one-month periods involved here in terms of interval, delay, and reporting period? *b.* What costs can be saved and what benefits obtained by reducing the six-week period to one month? *c.* Is there enough at stake to warrant asking state insurance author- ities to reduce the premium notice period from one month to, say, ten days?

25. Managers in one large organization requiring huge amounts of data say that they are not able to get sufficient precision but that they must rely on daily, weekly, or monthly results instead of hourly data. Untangle the concepts that they have mixed.

Chapter 11

1. *a.* Why are data-processing systems analyzed? *b.* What factors are studied in analyzing a system?

2. *a.* Appraise the statement, "If all questions are specified in advance, then unneces- sary data can be discarded; in fact, superfluous data need not even be gathered, for they will only be discarded." *b.* If you disagree with this statement, formulate a superior statement to express the relationship between the data available and the data stored for possible future use.

3. *a.* What merit is there in the operation researcher's comment that accountants design systems that lack focus and specified objectives? Explain. *b.* What risks are systems designers trying to guard against by designing open-ended data systems?

c. Could operations researchers, or anyone else, design systems that are sharply focused and precisely fulfill completely specified objectives? Explain. *d.* How does the high cost (or even impossibility) of reconstructing facts about the past influence systems design?

4. *a.* Explain the idea of amount of improvement in systems analysis and design. *b.* In what ways can the net effectiveness of a system be improved? *c.* Which area, cost reduction or information improvement, offers greater opportunity for system improvement? Explain.

5. *a.* Why should future expansion requirements be considered in deciding on the present capacity of a system? *b.* How useful is the simple rule, "Install equipment with capacity to absorb an annual increase in work load of 20 per cent during the expected economic life of the equipment." *c.* If the 20 per cent rule is not entirely satisfactory, devise a superior rule.

6. *a.* How is the cost of analysis related to effective improvements? *b.* What causes costs to become excessive when systems analysis is being done?

7. *a.* What is the systems approach to analysis and how does it differ from other approaches? *b.* What are the chief advantages and disadvantages of the systems approach?

8. *a.* Why should the long-run systems objective be spelled out when one starts to design a new system? *b.* What are the sources of information about system objectives? *c.* Who establishes system objectives?

9. How is systems design affected by the concept of available areas of freedom?

10. *a.* What function do process charts fulfill? *b.* In general terms, what symbols are needed to prepare process charts? *c.* Illustrate a particular set of symbols that is useful for preparing process charts.

11. *a.* What is the function of flow charts? *b.* How are flow charts and process charts related? *c.* What set of symbols is useful to prepare flow charts?

12. How are systems and equipment matched for efficient processing?

13. It is commonly said that, "Careful analysis of any non-automatic data-processing system to determine the merits of installing a computer is worth while because of system improvements that will naturally be made." Appraise this statement in view of the comments in the chapter concerning scope and amount of analysis.

14. *a.* Why should systems analysis work be done quickly in most cases? *b.* Under what conditions is a turtle's pace quick enough for analytic work?

15. A firm of data-processing consultants says that there are three reasons why new systems are unprofitable: no reduction in costs, no increase in revenues, and no improvement in the company's market position. Another situation is said to arise, however, in which automatic data processing must be applied regardless of profit in order to fulfill the data-handling requirements of the company because personnel are unavailable or the work load is so great that no reasonable number of people can do a day's work in a day's time. *a.* Are there actually four arguments here, instead of only two (since reductions in cost and increases in revenue should, it seems, cover all specific situations)? *b.* Is the situation involving high volume and high labor costs merely an example of high costs and low revenue that need correction? Explain.

Chapter 12

1. *a.* What are the chief differences between the economy and the efficiency approach to systems design? *b.* Which approach is superior?

2. *a.* How are good investment opportunities cut off when funds are limited? *b.* What is the opposite situation, and how is it treated?

3. *a.* What is meant by inventing a new system before determining its cost? *b.* What are the implications of the fact that systems design and analysis is so expensive that only one or a few systems are usually studied in great detail?

4. *a.* What are the capital costs for data-processing systems? *b.* What factors determine the amount of capital costs and when they are incurred?

5. *a.* How do the fixed or initial costs associated with each system affect decisions to use two or more systems at the same time? *b.* How small must the capital costs be for utilizing a second system to warrant its partial use to supplement the main system? (For example, exceptional cases amounting to 5 per cent of total volume might be handled manually while all others are handled automatically, if the cost of having and operating a manual system is not excessive.)

6. *a.* Why does an operating data-processing system not provide all the facts required for analysis of the system? *b.* Does this lack of analytical facts indicate that the operating system is unsatisfactory? Explain.

7. *a.* Why does a bulge in personnel costs occur during the period of transition from one system to another? *b.* Why do high personnel costs commonly persist longer than first anticipated?

8. *a.* Appraise the statement, "The total cost of a two-stage conversion, equipment introduction first and major redesign second, may not be the most economical approach, but it may have the important merit of leveling the workload over a longer period." *b.* How can a scheme have merit if it is not the most economical one available? *c.* Why must a certain time sequence be observed in making system changes when new equipment is introduced?

9. *a.* What costs are involved in converting from one data-processing system to another? *b.* Why are costs to convert from one automatic processor to another lower than the cost of the original change from a manual or electromechanical system to an automatic system? *c.* What kinds of costs would probably be incurred in returning from an automatic to, say, an electromechanical system?

10. *a.* What is the purpose of a cost analysis model? *b.* How can cost analysis models be useful if they are not identical with reality? *c.* Would models be useful if they were truly realistic? Explain.

11. *a.* What is the meaning of salvage value for a data-processing system? *b.* Why does salvage value decline sharply at first and then taper off? *c.* What are the merits of capitalizing the total initial investment versus immediately charging off all the intangible costs (those not associated with tangible, physical stuff)?

12. *a.* What factors determine and what conditions indicate the end of the economic life of a data-processing system? *b.* Should a system be discontinued as soon as annual revenue declines so that it barely covers the sum of operating costs and the decrease in salvage value, or should a system be continued in use until cumulative costs equal cumulative revenues? Explain.

13. *a.* Should a system be discarded before its economic life is ended? Explain. *b.* Is there any combination of operating cost, decrease in salvage value, and revenue that might cause a data-processing system to have indefinite economic life? Explain.

14. An organization that has a policy of making all investments that have a pay-off period of 4 years or less finds one attractive opportunity with a pay-off of 3.5 years but a service life of only 3.0 years. *a.* How is it possible to have a pay-off period longer than the service life? *b.* Should this particular investment be made? Explain.

15. *a.* What does the rule for rate of return attempt to do that the pay-off rule fails to do? *b.* Does the rate-of-return rule satisfactorily handle the case where service life is shorter than the pay-off period? How? *c.* What is the correct decision rule for selecting investment opportunities when the rate-of-return rule is used?

16. *a.* What factors enter into the rent-or-buy decision? *b.* Why is equipment rental preferable under some conditions? Purchase under others?

17. *a.* What is the economic life of equipment? *b.* What are the rules for finding economic life for the single machine and for the replacement chain cases? *c.* Why are the two cases treated differently?

18. *a.* Why is it necessary to know or to forecast what equipment will become available in the future and what its operating experience is likely to be in order to determine the economic life of present equipment for replacement purposes? *b.* Are such facts or forecasts necessary in calculating the economic life of a single machine considered individually?

19. *a.* Why should compound interest calculations be considered in decisions to acquire equipment? *b.* What is the general scheme for computing the rate of return when outlays are made both today and in the future but revenues are received only in the future? *c.* Why are compound interest calculation refinements worth while, if amount invested, operating cost, and revenue are not known with certainty?

20. Describe how each of the following situations should be treated with compound interest techniques (future amount of 1, present worth of an annuity, etc.) to find the rate of return in each of the following cases:

    a. Investment to be made now with operating expense and revenue to continue at a level rate over a period of five years.

    b. Investment now with level operating expense and revenue for two years, when expense will increase and revenue decrease to new amounts and then continue for four more years.

    c. Investment now with operating expense and revenue following Figure 12-3, parts (*b*) and (*c*).

    d. Equipment rented with option to apply half of rental toward purchase price at any time during the first two years. Operating expense to remain level for two years and then gradually increase. Revenue to remain level for four years and then gradually decrease.

Chapter 13

1. Some organizations are vertically integrated to cover all operations from producing raw material through the final stages of selling to ultimate consumers.

    a. How different are the data requirements of vertically and horizontally integrated organizations?

    b. What opportunities exist for making data processing more efficient in a vertically integrated organization than in a horizontally integrated one?

    c. Are there any operating areas within an organization that are completely unrelated to the main stream of operations? If so, explain how data processing for them can be handled most efficiently.

2. *a.* What is the difference between static and dynamic business operations? *b.* In what ways do the data and information requirements of a dynamic organization differ from the requirements of a static organization? *c.* How are these differences in data and information requirements reflected in efficient systems design?

3. The controller of one corporation said, "We will continue to use decentralized management throughout our widely scattered organization no matter what changes we make in our data-processing system." *a.* Under what conditions is such a strong adherence to decentralized management warranted? *b.* What changes would warrant complete re-examination of the controller's announced position?

4. Managerial control plans are said to range from being carefully specified in advance to being developed as problems arise.

    a. Why do most actual control plans fall somewhere between these two extremes?

    b. What are the data-processing requirements for these two extreme plans of managerial control?

    c. Under what conditions would it be efficient to specify completely detailed control plans in advance for every conceivable problem that is likely to arise?

d. How does the management control plan being used influence data-processing system design?

5. Why should a systems analyst consider, first, the data and information requirements and, second, the organizational structure when designing a data-processing system?

6. *a.* How is it possible for a small organization to have bigger data-processing problems than a large organization? *b.* Can you generalize from this relative simplicity of data and information systems for large organizations that they are likely to have a much faster growth rate than small organizations?

7. *a.* How much freedom does a systems analyst have to separate the actual work of originating data from the responsibility for collecting accurate, timely data? *b.* What are the advantages of making the data originators take responsibility for the quality of data?

8. *a.* How is the geographical location of data processing influenced by the cost of communication in view of the fact that the volume of data usually exceeds the volume of information? *b.* What geographical location scheme would be used if the volume of output from data processing were several times as large as the input?

9. In recent years there has been a strong tendency for communication companies to increase their rates by charging more for services, requiring longer term commitments by users, and restricting the freedom of users to add and drop circuits at will. How should a company modify its extensive communication network if these cost increases are occurring?

10. *a.* How would you reconcile the economies of uniform processing with the desire to have complete freedom at the local level? *b.* What degree of freedom to meet local information requirements is compatible with the need to consolidate reports for an organization as a whole?

11. *a.* What is the relationship between capacity and flexibility for a data-processing system? *b.* If the statement, "Larger systems have lower unit processing costs than smaller systems," is true, should an organization have one completely consolidated data-processing system? Explain. *c.* Why is centralized processing more critical for dynamic operations than for static operations?

12. Compatibility may be defined as "the ability to exist together in harmony."
    a. What kinds of incompatibility exist in data-processing systems?
    b. Why is it possible to reconcile some kinds of incompatibilities but not others?
    c. Describe the nature of a perfectly compatible system, then evaluate this argument: "Compatibility can be achieved for any system because it is possible to convert data from any media to any other media, so that there is no need to worry about compatibility when designing a data-processing system."

13. *a.* What possibilities exist for organizing data-processing operations within a company that operates at a single location? *b.* How would you decide which plan to select?

14. What are the implications of centralized data processing for each of the following areas: *a.* document preparation; *b.* operating information; *c.* freedom of local managers from interference by central management; *d.* system flexibility.

15. What are the merits of using a joint communication network to handle both data-processing and administrative messages? Can you reconcile this joint use of a communication network with this often expressed opinion: "The communication network is merely an extension of the data processor that permits it to operate effectively throughout the organization."

16. How is the origination of data and the consumption of information relevant to the location of processing facilities?

17. A large company is considering adoption of one of the following organization plans for its data-processing activities:

      a. Application—payroll, inventory control, sales, engineering, operations research

      b. Functions—engineering, production, finance, marketing, management, accounting, special analysis

      c. Data Flow—data collection, transmission, processing distribution

      d. Systems—analysis, planning and development, systems design, programming, systems installation, communications, computer operations

      e. Geographical Areas—eastern, mid-western, and western U.S.

      What useful guidance can you give toward selecting the best organization plan?

18. Many precautionary controls are exercised by one company over data sent to the data-processing department. These include message numbering, control totals, hash totals, limit checks, and field editing. Despite these precautions, some mistakes are not discovered until file processing runs are started. The question is whether the data-processing department should take the responsibility for correcting input data or whether they should ask the originators of the data to correct it.

      a. How would you determine which scheme for making corrections is preferable?

      b. Would you recommend a different scheme for making corrections if the data originating locations are several hundred miles from the data-processing center instead of being in the same building?

19. A company that has the manufacturing plants of its five major household appliance divisions located in adjoining buildings is planning to introduce one or more computers for use in forecasting demand, scheduling and controlling production, controlling inventory, analyzing sales, etc. The company has not decided whether to establish one data-processing department in each of the five divisions or to establish one center to serve all divisions.

      a. What factors would bear on the use of five data-processing departments or one data-processing center?

      b. If the idea of a data-processing center is approved, should it be set up within a manufacturing division or set up as a separate service center? Explain.

Chapter 14

1. *a.* What is the purpose of systems analysis? *b.* What does systems analysis work involve?

2. What facets of a system should be considered when analyzing it?

3. *a.* Why is an organized, documented approach to systems analysis necessary? *b.* What are the merits of using models of a system to study the effectiveness of new schemes instead of actually experimenting with each new scheme?

4. *a.* What work is included in management, organization, and procedure surveys? *b.* Why are these surveys useful preludes to systems analysis?

5. *a.* How does work simplification differ from work measurement and performance? *b.* What features of these two analytical methods are useful when the system utilizes manual, electro-mechanical, and automatic means?

6. *a.* What is the purpose of space and layout surveys? *b.* Does space and layout survey work provide for finding the optimum arrangement and identifying it when it is found? (Chapter 18 sheds more light on the general problem of finding and identifying the optimum.)

7. *a.* What is a run diagram? *b.* What is the function of run diagrams? *c.* How much detail does a run diagram include? *d.* What are the basic symbols used in drawing run diagrams?

8. *a.* What are the basic building blocks of a run? *b.* How many times are the basic building blocks repeated in the run diagram for the daily stores accounting illustrated in the chapter?

9. *a.* What is the purpose of structure flow charts? *b.* Draw and explain the symbols used for structure flow charts. *c.* What is the relationship between run diagrams and structure flow charts?

10. How is each of the following shown on structure flow charts: *a.* main flow of data; *b.* identification of blocks, documents and files; *c.* quantity of items handled at each stage; *d.* repetitive loops; *e.* branching and merging; *f.* connectors.

11. *a.* What is the function of a structure and technique flow chart? *b.* What symbols are useful for drawing them?

12. What rules can you devise by studying the flow charts in Figures 14-6, 7, 8, 9 that would serve as a guide for finding bugs in similar flow charts. For example, there must be two branches (or perhaps three, to cover **<**, **=**, **>** cases) following a test.

13. *a.* Why does the number of flow charts required at each successive level of detail increase so much? *b.* How big (or small) a gap should exist between the most detailed flow chart and the program to be prepared from the flow chart?

14. *a.* What is the purpose of input data sheets, reference data sheets, and output data sheets? *b.* In general terms, what does each type of data sheet show? *c.* What general observations can be drawn concerning the purpose, content, and use of these three types of data sheets?

15. *a.* What symbols are used to draw flow charts for manual data-processing systems? *b.* Why is the set of manual system symbols quite different from the symbols used for automatic data-processing systems?

16. What rules can you devise concerning flow charting for manual systems by studying Figure 14-12?

17. *a.* Why is continual review of forms and reports important for efficient operation of a data-processing system? *b.* What recommendations can you suggest for reconciling the conflict that is likely to arise between the desire to standardize the preparation of reports and the need, described in Chapter 10, to keep the information content high in order to make reports useful for management?

18. Prepare a run diagram and suitably detailed flow charts for a simple stock control application. A manufacturer of machine parts wants a daily listing of every stock item and a separate listing of each item falling below its re-order point. The stock file from the previous cycle is available and transactions are classified as follows: items completed, items shipped, returns from customers, returns to the factory, and reworked parts received from the factory.

19. Assume the same conditions as in Question 18 except that management realizes it is able to deal with only a limited number of re-order items each day. Two possibilities exist: One, print a complete list of re-order items for management to use the portion it can and carry over the remainder of the list for the next day. Two, arrange to print a list of re-order items only as long as management can deal with each day and start printing at that point during the next processing cycle.

    a. How should these two schemes be shown on run diagrams?

    b. On flow charts?

    c. What are the merits of these two schemes for simplicity and efficiency of both data processing and management operations?

20. *a.* Design a suitable format for the input data sheet record illustrated in Figure 14-10. *b.* Design a suitable format for the file record described in the chapter.

21. What are the chief differences between the structure flow chart (Figure 14-4) and structure-technique flow chart (Figure 14-6) illustrated in the chapter?

22. Expert programmers of scientific and engineering problems discount the value of detailed and elaborate run diagrams and flow charts. Equally expert programmers of business applications say that good run diagrams and flow charts are invaluable. How would you reconcile these viewpoints?

23. A manager of a programming and analysis staff says that one of his most difficult problems is to get people to document their work so that program maintenance work can be done easily several months later by the same programmer or by another one, in case the original programmer is not available. What suggestions can you offer to solve this almost universal problem?

24. A series of tests are performed on 1,000 items to identify those that fall into certain categories. The initial test yields 800 items (usually) in category (A) and 200 in category (B) which might be abbreviated: Initially 1000 ➤A800, B200. Thereafter: A800 ➤ C750, D50; B200 ➤ E190, F10; C750 ➤ G715, H35; D50 ➤145, J5; E190 ➤ K100, L90; F10 ➤ M6, N4; G715 ➤O650, P65; M6 ➤ Q5, R1.
  - a. Draw a flow chart to show the parallel testing sequence suggested by the nature of the data and the number of items identified by each binary (yes-no) test.
  - b. Calculate the number of tests required for ultimate identification of every item. (H, I, J, and 7 other categories are ultimate.)

25. Assume that the conditions are the same as for question 24 except that the ten ultimate cases can be classified directly by a serial pattern of testing.
  - a. Draw a flow chart to show the testing sequence to classify ultimate cases in alphabetical sequence (H, I, J...) and calculate the number of tests required.
  - b. Draw a flow chart to show the testing sequence if the most frequently occurring item is classified first, then followed by the next most frequent item, etc., and calculate the number of tests required.
  - c. What conclusions can you draw concerning the sequence for performing tests?

26. An electric utility issues bi-monthly bills to residential customers. Follow-up for uncollected bills is taken on the basis of the uncollected balance, number of days overdue, the customer's credit rating, and whether the customer has a deposit. The conditions for issuing a reminder and a warning notice can be summarized as follows:

Uncollected Balance	Days Overdue	Customer Credit Rating	Customer Deposit	Action
$25 or more	30	2	None	Reminder
$75	60	1	Yes	Reminder
$22	30	3	None	Warning
$20	60	2	None	Warning
$50	90	1	Yes	Warning

  - a. Draw a flow chart showing the steps involved to determine whether to issue a reminder, issue a warning, or take no action.
  - b. What changes in the rules followed by the utility can you suggest to simplify processing without upsetting their business practices?

Chapter 15

1. a. What steps are involved in making important changes in a data-processing system? b. Why is it important to keep the steps in the correct sequence?
2. a. What is a feasibility study? b. What are the differences between feasibility studies in the area of data processing and any other area, such as plant machinery and equipment? c. How does a feasibility study differ from a casual or once-over-lightly examination?
3. a. What logical conclusions can be expected from a feasibility study? b. Why is the cost incurred from prematurely making a feasibility study likely to be less than the loss that may be suffered from postponing it too long? c. What by-product benefits can be expected from making a feasibility study?

4. *a.* Why is it necessary to obtain the support of top management before making a feasibility study? *b.* How can top management support be obtained most readily?

5. *a.* What are the advantages of having broad representation from different areas of the organization in the feasibility study group? *b.* Why should a feasibility study group divide its attention between new equipment and the data-processing system? *c.* When and under what conditions would you expect to find a feasibility study group concentrating exclusively on either new equipment or the data system?

6. *a.* What is the distinction between a preliminary feasibility study and an extended or detailed feasibility study? *b.* What is the basis for deciding to extend a feasibility study to the detailed level?

7. *a.* What factors are used to identify areas in order to make a detailed feasibility study? *b.* How does one decide whether to enlarge or limit the number and scope of the areas selected for detailed study? *c.* Why is a careful definition of the object and scope of a feasibility study imperative?

8. *a.* What attributes are necessary for members of the working group assigned to the feasibility study? *b.* How broadly and thoroughly should the working group be trained?

9. What are the merits of accepting an equipment manufacturer's offer to furnish all the training desired by members of the feasibility study group?

10. When planning for a detailed feasibility study, which is preferable: *a.* to accept a consultant's offer to furnish either senior analysts at full rates or junior analysts at half rates; or *b.* to take an equipment manufacturer's offer to make the study at no cost?

11. When selecting areas of data processing for feasibility study, how much consideration should be given to each of the following factors: *a.* length of time since important improvements were last made; *b.* degree of automation already achieved in the area; *c.* potential improvement by using newest equipment and developing the most advanced system; *d.* experience of other organizations in the same area using the techniques that are being considered?

12. *a.* Why must replaceable and non-replaceable costs be treated differently when analyzing proposed changes to a system? *b.* Name some costs that might easily be misclassified as replaceable costs.

13. *a.* Why are reductions in costs much easier to appraise than improvements in the value of information obtained when studying proposed changes to a system? *b.* What general rule can you devise for the introduction of a new system and equipment when cost reductions are in view but it is unlikely that the information obtained from the data system will be improved?

14. *a.* What direct benefits are likely to be obtained from introducing advanced data-processing methods? *b.* What indirect improvements are obtainable from an advanced data system and why are they so difficult to evaluate?

15. How would you decide whether a particular area should be included in a system-wide approach to a feasibility study?

16. There is an old saw about committee inaction: "Individually we can do nothing and collectively nothing can be done." How can the comparable problem of selecting the limited-area or system-wide approach to systems analysis be avoided?

17. *a.* What is the minimum area within a data-processing system that is worth studying? *b.* What are the advantages of and objections to the minimum-area approach to systems analysis?

18. Two plans exist for introducing a new system. One scheme is to select small areas, convert them individually and, finally, integrate them. A second scheme is to start with a small fraction of all areas, convert them at the same time and, finally, expand them to handle all of every area. What are the merits of the two plans both during initial stages of system conversion and later?

19. *a.* What resources are required for an automatic data-processing system? *b.* What is the relationship between available resources and the scope of the area selected for study?

20. What bearing does the frame of reference and the organizational area under consideration have on the scope of the feasibility study?
21. *a.* What is supposed to be accomplished during the orientation phase of a feasibility study? *b.* How are internal functions of an organization catalogued?
22. *a.* What constitutes a blow-by-blow description of a data-processing system? *b.* Why is such a detailed study worth while?
23. *a.* What is a grid chart? *b.* What is the purpose of such a chart? *c.* How is a grid chart prepared?
24. *a.* What is a validity check sheet? *b.* What is the relationship between a grid chart and a validity check sheet?
25. *a.* What is a document summary card? *b.* Why are document summary cards prepared?
26. *a.* What does a cost summary for a feasibility study include? *b.* How are decisions made on the basis of facts in the cost summary?
27. *a.* What should be covered in the feasibility study group's concluding report? *b.* What conclusions should the feasibility study group be expected to draw?
28. *a.* What points should be covered in addition to those included in the outline for the feasibility study report given in the chapter? *b.* How are uncertainties about present and future plans handled in preparing a feasibility study report?

Chapter 16

1. *a.* What is involved in making an applications study and selecting equipment? *b.* What is the purpose of an applications study? *c.* How are the feasibility study and the applications study related?
2. *a.* What kinds of decisions are made during the applications study? *b.* Why should the new system be outlined before flow charts, data sheets, and workloads are determined?
3. *a.* What steps are involved in designing a data-processing system? *b.* What principles of systems analysis are involved? *c.* Why are the steps in design and the principles of analysis entirely different?
4. What is involved in the basic design of a new system?
5. *a.* What is the minimum information for systems specifications? *b.* What additional information is desirable? *c.* How is the information for systems design used?
6. *a.* Why is an applications study focused on specific data-processing jobs? *b.* Is it theoretically possible to make an applications study in general terms or for a hypothetical situation without regard to actual applications? Explain. *c.* What are the practical merits of a hypothetical applications study?
7. *a.* What schedules are useful for conducting an applications study? *b.* How should the uncertainty arising from the possibility of including new areas in the applications study be treated in initial scheduling?
8. *a.* What is a desirable composition of personnel for the applications study group? *b.* Sketch the qualifications—capabilities, experience and background—of each kind of personnel that should be included in the study group.
9. Why is more technical competence in the area of data processing demanded in analysts and programmers than in the study supervisor?
10. *a.* What is the task of the applications study supervisor? *b.* How does the work of a systems analyst differ from that of a project analyst?
11. *a.* Solve, unless you have already done so, the two individual questions that are suggested for selecting analysts and programmers. *b.* Solve the hypothetical multipart aptitude test given in Figure 16-1. *c.* Identify the areas covered by these two tests and appraise them for their usefulness in selecting analysts and programmers.
12. *a.* What steps would you suggest in order to validate the illustrative questions and test given in the chapter? *b.* What information would you want about a person besides scores on either individual questions or tests, in order to select potential analysts and programmers?

13. *a.* How is a satisfactory balance of capabilities, backgrounds, and experience obtained among members of the applications study group? *b.* Why are operating representatives included in the applications study group?

14. *a.* What is covered by the phrase, "basic structure for a new system?" *b.* For developing a new system, what are the merits (and demerits) of (1) mechanization and (2) redesign? *c.* Why do so many people advocate complete redesign of a system and yet restrict their efforts to mechanization of procedures already in use?

15. *a.* What bearing do input and output requirements have on system design? *b.* Do output requirements or available inputs deserve more emphasis in systems design? Explain. *c.* If a system can be described precisely in terms of inputs and outputs, why is any consideration given to the processing operations between input and output?

16. Are the *input* and *output* of a data-processing system synonymous with *data* and *information* as developed in Chapter 10? Explain.

17. Appraise the statement, "Concentration on data inputs when designing a system is incorrect because it is based on the assumption that if enough data enter a system, the desired results are *pushed* out. Instead, concentration on outputs is correct because their careful definition will cause the necessary data to be *pulled* into the system."

18. *a.* What factors must be considered to design an efficient file structure? *b.* How can the following situations be handled when designing files: (1) duplication because partial records for one item are kept in several different files; (2) different length records because some fields are not needed for some items; (3) different length records because some fields are repeated many times for some items.

19. *a.* What facts should be obtained about workloads during an applications study? *b.* How are these facts used in designing a system? *c.* How are the facts about workload obtained in an applications study related to corresponding facts obtained in the feasibility study?

20. *a.* What steps are involved in selecting equipment? *b.* What is a bid invitation and how widely should it be distributed? *c.* Why should both new and long-established manufacturers of equipment be given bid invitations?

21. How are a user's *desires* for certain features in equipment separated from his *demands?*

22. *a.* What should an equipment manufacturer cover in his proposal? *b.* Why should the system processing loads, which were probably supplied by the prospect, be restated in the manufacturer's proposal? *c.* Why is the user interested in a firm, inflexible delivery date for equipment that he orders?

23. *a.* What are the installation requirements for a large-scale data processor? *b.* How much do these requirements change if a fully transistorized processor is obtained instead of a vacuum tube processor? *c.* If a vacuum tube processor is already installed and operating, how much can be gained by replacing it with a transistorized processor?

24. What consideration should be given to each one of the following points in the manufacturer's proposal: *a.* rent or purchase option; *b.* maintenance service; *c.* education and training of user's staff; *d.* equipment design changes before and after installation; *e.* precise units, models, and capacities of equipment proposed; *f.* programming aids—compilers, service subroutines, etc.; *g.* machine time for testing user's programs before and after delivery of equipment.

25. *a.* What factors must be considered in evaluating equipment? *b.* How can various excess capabilities and deficiencies of different equipment be weighed in order to select the equipment best suited to application requirements? *c.* Where does the ultimate responsibility for equipment acquisition rest within an organization?

26. *a.* What steps are involved in preparing for equipment installation? *b.* Since equipment manufacturers have more experience in delivering equipment than users have in installing it, how is it possible to synchronize the work of both parties for prompt, efficient installation?

Chapter 17

1. *a.* What sequence of work should be followed in systems installation planning? *b.* Why is careful, realistic installation scheduling worth while?

2. *a.* What is the relationship between the form and function of an organization? *b.* How does the introduction of automatic data processing affect the structure of the organization responsible for data processing?

3. *a.* How much difference is there among the work involved in the three phases of studying, installing, and operating a data-processing system? *b.* What skills, education, training, and experience are required for personnel working in each phase?

4. *a.* Develop a program for training key personnel and working personnel. *b.* Who has the primary responsibility for educating and training personnel responsible for study, installation, and operation of a data-processing system?

5. *a.* When a new system is introduced, why does the amount of manpower required for a data-processing system grow before it can be reduced? *b.* How is the problem of dislocated personnel handled most effectively? *c.* Why are upper-level personnel sometimes said to pose a bigger relocation problem than do lower-level personnel?

6. Some companies promise employees that no one will lose in any way (reduction in rate or loss of job) upon introduction of automatic processing equipment. *a.* How can such a policy be rationalized if the objective of systems change is to reduce clerical costs? *b.* If smaller manpower requirements are met by reduced hiring rates, what are the future employment implications for white-collar workers?

7. *a.* Why does debugging receive so little attention in manual data-processing? *b.* How are mistakes corrected most effectively for manual systems? For automatic systems?

8. *a.* What benefits can be gained by a computer user's joining a voluntary association of users of similar equipment? *b.* How is it possible for a computer user to contribute its experience to a cooperative association without revealing trade secrets? *c.* What would you recommend to an organization that claims to have unique applications and therefore believes it should not join any cooperative association, for it would neither contribute to nor benefit from membership?

9. False flooring, which costs $5 to $10 a square foot, is recommended by many computer manufacturers as the best way to provide space for connecting cables and power lines. A prospective user is offered two choices: one computer that is usually set up with 3,000 square feet of false flooring or a competitive computer (with equal or higher capacity) that occupies 600 square feet and does not require a false floor.
    a. What consideration should a computer user give to this possible saving when selecting equipment?
    b. Should the computer manufacturer or user (or both jointly) benefit from the savings in space and flooring costs? Explain.

10. How should the reduction in air conditioning costs (estimated to be $60,000 for a large computer with vacuum tubes and $20,000 for a comparable transistorized computer) for transistor versus vacuum tube computers be shared between the equipment manufacturer and the user?

11. What provision should an equipment user make to protect himself against the possibility that equipment will not immediately pass acceptance tests? That it may never pass acceptance tests?

12. One computer manufacturer's time estimates for handling four major applications is 12 hours a day, whereas two other manufacturers estimate 7 and 9 hours a day for the same applications. The first manufacturer proposes (unofficially) to count only the first shift time (8 hours a day) and ignore any additional time in order to retain his price posted, yet be competitive. What reaction would you have to

to such pricing practices if you worked for: *a.* the customer; *b.* the first manufacturer; *c.* the other manufacturer; *d.* some other user who was not offered similar price adjustments; *e.* the Federal Government, which insists that a manufacturer adhere to his price posted with the government procurement agency (General Services Administration) and not offer discounts to anyone.

13. *a.* What is involved in conversion from one set of equipment to another? *b.* How can the optimum amount of parallel operation of the old and the new system be determined?

14. *a.* How should the cost of long-term retention of files be balanced against the benefits obtainable from having the data available? *b.* What are the differences in reconstructing files when (1) the immediately preceding generation of files is still available, and (2) the most recent file available is two generations old?

15. *a.* Why should a review of new operations be started either shortly or immediately after conversion to a new system? *b.* Appraise the statement, "Our system doesn't need to be reviewed because we designed, with the aid of the equipment manufacturer and some consultants, the most efficient system possible before we ordered our equipment."

16. How would you appraise the argument, "All the talk about the value of getting faster, better, more complete data and doing operations research studies is mere rationalization for the fact that the reductions in the cost of data-processing that were originally promised have not been achieved?"

17. *a.* What kinds of personnel problems accompany the introduction of new systems and equipment? *b.* What are the advantages and disadvantages of freely distributing information about the organizational changes that will occur?

18. *a.* Why does feasibility and applications study work differ from career work in systems analysis and data processing? *b.* Where in the company can installation and operations personnel be obtained? *c.* How can management eliminate apprehension about advancement and security among the members of the installation and operations group?

19. When a mechanized system replaces manual operations, what changes occur in: *a.* level of personnel required; *b.* salary structure; *c.* total labor cost.

20. *a.* Why is parallel operation of manual and mechanized systems often used during the conversion period? *b.* How long should parallel operations be continued?

21. *a.* What is the purpose of scheduling computer operations? *b.* What difficulties tend to disrupt schedules?

22. Describe the kinds of procedures that must be established at the data-processing installation.

Chapter 18

1. *a.* Define scientific decision processes. *b.* Where can one find information on these processes? *c.* What other methods can be used to make decisions?

2. *a.* Name and describe three managerial decision rules that you have encountered. *b.* What improvements can you suggest for these decision rules?

3. List and describe two examples of each of the following situations: *a.* solving the wrong (or unintended) problem; *b.* selecting an incorrect objective; *c.* using criteria that do not lead toward the desired objective.

4. *a.* What is the relationship between the data that operations researchers would like to have for their studies and the form and quantity of data that people responsible for processing operations are willing to obtain and keep available? *b.* If there is a conflict of interests, how should it be reconciled?

5. *a.* Define analytical and numerical techniques. *b.* What special features do iterative and Monte Carlo techniques possess? *c.* How would you classify iterative and Monte Carlo techniques—as analytical or numerical?

6. *a.* List four reasons why a decision process may yield incorrect answers. *b.* What precautions are available to minimize incorrect answers?

7. *a.* What does a computer program model or represent? *b.* Is a computer program an iconic, analogic, or symbolic model? *c.* What are the merits of each kind of model?

8. *a.* What is the difference between deterministic and stochastic models? *b.* If *uncertainty* does not mean that nothing is known about a system, what does it mean? *c.* Why is the idea of uncertainty important in the design and operation of business-data systems?

9. Draw a graph (similar to Figure 18-1) showing the number of interrogations awaiting processing if both the arrival rate and the interval between processing operations are subject to wide variation.

10. *a.* For the computer interrogation model described in the chapter, plot total cost versus processing quantity (similar to Figure 18-2) for the following facts: fifty interrogations arrive each hour, each computer interruption costs $12, and delay in answering an interrogation costs $.10 a minute. *b.* What quantity of interrogations processed at one time gives the lowest total cost? *c.* Use the differencing technique to check your answer for the lowest cost arrangement obtained graphically.

11. *a.* What types of problems can be solved by mathematical programming? *b.* Why are certain programming methods called linear programming? Do non-linear programming problems exist? Explain. *c.* What is the meaning of a "best" solution to a programming problem? Why is it best?

12. Explain the nature of a multi-stage decision process and show how it differs from a single-stage decision process.

13. *a.* What is a waiting line problem and how does it differ from a queueing problem? *b.* Why is the smallest number of service facilities not the optimum solution?

14. *a.* Define the parameters of a waiting line problem. *b.* Why is it not possible to give a single arrival rate that applies to an entire finite population? *c.* How can the cost of service facility waiting time be reduced in some situations but not in others?

15. For the remote processor problem described in the chapter, calculate the best number of interrogators for the following conditions: the cost of an interrogator is $20 per hour (instead of $65 per hour) and processor waiting cost is $40 (instead of $150 per hour).

16. What are the merits and demerits of the following policies: *a.* keep service facilities busy all the time; *b.* never make a customer wait.

17. *a.* Simulation is useful for what types of problems? *b.* List the essential requirements for simulation. *c.* Explain briefly the operation of the Monte Carlo type of simulation process.

18. What are the advantages and disadvantages of simulation that are not applicable to waiting line models?

19. Why should data system designers be interested in the over-all management structure of an organization?

20. The inventory manager of the Ready Rocket Company frequently demands a comprehensive report on current stock status. Daily preparation of the report by the data-processing center costs $53.00. Waiting until the manager requests a report involves interruptions and special processing at a cost of $112.00. The manager's requests, which are erratic, have been studied by an inquiring young fellow who obtained the following demand pattern:

Day of the Week	Per Cent of Time Report Requested
Monday	85
Tuesday	26
Wednesday	43
Thursday	21
Friday	49

Special days:

End of month	97
Day before board meeting	99
Day before holiday	10

The inventory manager's demand follows a weekly pattern; but special days override the weekly pattern and the day of the week is irrelevant.

 a. Set up a decision rule showing whether to prepare the report in advance.
 b. Draw a flow chart of the decision rule in a form suitable for machine programming.
 c. What cost and value conditions would make it immaterial whether the report is prepared on a daily schedule or only on demand?

21. Lone Point Bank is about to install an automated accounting system, the PQ-10. One feature is that the central file can be interrogated to determine the current balance of any account. During a six-hour period, the bank receives an average of 120 requests for current balance. The manufacturer says that with the equipment planned, a request can be answered in one minute except that for 25 per cent of the accounts always undergoing updating, a special 6-minute procedure will be required. The bank manager has been told that the PQ-10 is more than adequate for his average needs. He has noticed, however, that requests arrive irregularly. The interval between requests is one minute 25 per cent of the time, 3 minutes 50 per cent of the time, and five minutes the remaining 25 per cent of the time. Even if the system works, the manager feels that some customers may have to wait a long time. He wants, therefore, a thorough investigation of the whole project.

 a. Can the PQ-10 handle the load?
 b. What is the longest time a depositor will ever have to wait?
 c. Can standard queueing models predict the average time a depositor will have to wait?
 d. What kind of model will predict the above information?
 e. Set up such a model.
 f. Determine the average waiting time and the percentage of depositors that will wait 2 minutes or less, 5 minutes or less, and 10 minutes or less to learn their account balance.

22. An alternative set of equipment, the SLO-7, is available at a higher price to the manager of the Lone Point Bank (see Question 21). This equipment can provide the current balance for any account in 2.25 minutes. The bank's directors feel, however, that the SLO-7 is not as good as the PQ-10 and that in addition, it costs more, so they have dismissed it from consideration. a. On average, can a customer's inquiry be answered faster with the PQ-10 or the SLO-7? b. What is the shortest time that a customer will ever have to wait to get a balance from each system? c. Were the directors wise to dismiss the SLO-7 from consideration?

23. At several geographical points the Gaskins Gasket Company has six computing centers; all have large excess capacity on the first shift. A recent operations research project resulted in a decision to handle ten different applications. Because the computing centers have different equipment and operating costs, the time required for an application varies from one center to another as follows:

Center	Operating Cost/Hour	Application									
		1	2	3	4	5	6	7	8	9	10
A	$100.00	1	6	3	2	10	1	6	6	1	12
B	137.00	1.5	6	4	2.5	5	2	3	5	2	12
C	125.00	1	6	7	1	7	1	5	6	2	11
D	113.00	1.7	6	5	1.2	6	1	4	5	1	11
E	205.00	2	6	4	1.2	9	2	5	5	1	12
F	95.00	6	6	4	1	9	1	4	6	1	7

 a. Is this a standard linear programming problem? Explain.
 b. Find a feasible way to perform these ten applications.
 c. Find the lowest cost way to perform these ten jobs.

GLOSSARY OF AUTOMATIC DATA-PROCESSING TERMINOLOGY

This glossary includes definitions for widely used data-processing terms with specialized meanings. Intended for people without special training who are interested in business-data processors, it generally omits highly technical words related to computer design. Primary emphasis is placed on general-purpose, stored-program digital processors, and related equipment.

Cross referencing between entries is minimized to reduce the over-all length of the glossary, but it may be necessary to look under a second entry to find a desired item.

A glossary cannot provide a short course in automatic data processing. Space is not available here to explain and relate satisfactorily the many items included. This glossary attempts only to provide a *standard* meaning for those terms that have some especial significance in business-data processing; its object is to enable people to communicate more effectively with each other.

It is almost needless to say that the Association for Computing Machinery's *First Glossary of Programming Terminology* was frequently utilized for standard definitions.

Access Time—Time required to transfer control to a particular storage location and to read or write a complete word there. Frequently used to mean average access time for all storage locations. *See also* "Search Time."

Accumulator—A register in the arithmetic unit which stores operands and in which arithmetical results are formed. *See also* "Register."

Acoustic Delay Line—A device using regenerated shock waves in a conducting medium (for example, mercury) for storing information.

Address—A label, such as an integer or other set of characters, which identifies a register, location, or device in which data are stored.

    Absolute Address—Actual location in storage of a particular unit of data; address that the control unit can interpret directly. Also, the label assigned by the engineer to a particular storage location in the computer.

    Relative Address—A label used to identify a word in a routine or subroutine with respect to its relative position in that routine or subroutine. A relative address is translated into an absolute address by addition of some specific starting address for the subroutine within the main routine.

    Symbolic Address—A label assigned to a selected word in a routine for the convenience of the programmer. The symbol used is independent of the location of a word within a routine. It identifies the field of data to be operated on or the operation to be used rather than its storage location.

Alphamerical—See "Alphanumerical."

Alphanumerical—A coding system capable of representing alphabetic characters and other symbols as well as numbers.

Analogue Computer—See items under "Computer."

Argument—The known reference factor necessary to find the desired item (function) in a table.

Arithmetic Unit—That portion of the hardware of an automatic digital computer in which arithmetical and logical operations are performed.

Asynchronous (Computer)—A mode of computer operation in which performance of the next command is started by a signal that the previous command has been completed. *Contrast* "Synchronous," characterized by a fixed time cycle for the execution of operations.

Automatic Data-processing System—A system that uses minimum manual operations in processing data.

Automatic Programming—*See* items under "Programming."

Band—*See* "Channel."

Batch Processing—Collection of data over a period of time to be sorted and processed as a group during a particular machine run.

Binary—Pertaining to the number 2; more specifically, a number system whose radix is the quantity 2.

Binary Cell—An element that can assume either of two stable states or positions and is thus able to store a binary digit.

Binary-coded Decimal System—A system for representing decimal numbers in which each digit is expressed by a code written in binary notation. Among the several systems are the 8-4-2-1 and the excess-three schemes.

Binary Notation—A system of notation utilizing only two symbols. These are usually designated 0 and 1.

Bi-quinary System—A binary-coded decimal system in which each decimal digit is represented by one binary bit, having an assigned value of 0 or 5, and one quinary digit having a value of 0, 1, 2, 3, or 4.

Bit—A binary digit; hence, a unit of data in binary notation.

Block—A group of consecutive machine words considered or transferred as a unit, particularly with reference to input and output. *Contrast* "Record."

Block Diagram—A chart setting forth the particular sequence of operations to be performed for handling a particular application. Used as a tool in programming. *See also* "Flow Chart."

Boolean Algebra—A binary system of algebra; hence, a useful tool for logical analysis of binary computers.

Breakpoint—A point in a program at which a computer may be made to stop automatically for a check on the progress of the routine.

Conditional Breakpoint—A breakpoint at which the routine may be continued as coded if desired conditions are satisfied.

Buffer Storage—*See* under "Storage."

Bus—A path over which information is transferred, from any of several sources to any of several destinations.

Call—A set of characters identifying a subroutine and containing data about parameters to be inserted in the subroutine or data about the operands.

Capital-to-labor Ratio—Ratio of the dollar value of data-processing equipment to the number of people performing various functions related to data processing. Expressed in units of dollars per person.

Carry—(1) Digit to be added to the next higher column when the sum of digits in one column equals or exceeds the number base. (2) Process of forwarding the carry digit.

Cathode-ray Output—A cathode-ray tube used to display output information in graphic form or by character representation.

Centralized Data Processing—Processing data at one location for an organization that is decentralized either managerially or geographically. Decentralized data processing involves processing at various managerial levels or geographical points throughout an organization.

Channel—A path along which data, particularly a series of digits or characters, may flow or be stored. In storage which is serial by character and parallel by bit (for example, a magnetic tape or drum in some coded decimal computers), a channel comprises several parallel tracks. In a circulating memory, a channel is one recirculating path containing a fixed number of words stored serially by word. *See also* "Track."

Character—(1) One of a set of elementary symbols, such as those corresponding to the keys on a typewriter. The symbols may include decimal digits 0 through 9, the letters

A through Z, punctuation marks, operation symbols, and any other single symbols which a computer may read, store, or write. (2) A binary representation of such a symbol.

Characteristic—The integral part of a logarithm; the exponent of a normalized number.

Check—A means of verifying the accuracy of data transmitted, manipulated, or stored by any unit or device in a computer.

Built-in Check (Automatic Check)—Any check constructed in hardware.

Duplication Check—A check which requires that the results of two independent performances of the same operation be identical.

Mathematical Check—A check making use of mathematical identities or other properties, frequently with some degree of discrepancy being acceptable; for example, checking multiplication by verifying that $A \cdot B = B \cdot A$, checking a tabulated function by the difference method.

Parity Check—A summation check in which the binary digits, in a character or word, are added (modulo 2) and the sum checked against a single, previously computed parity digit; for example, a check which tests whether the number of ones is odd or even.

Programmed Check—A mathematical check inserted in the operating program.

Redundant Check—A check which attaches one or more extra digits to a word according to rules so that if any digit changes, the malfunction or mistake can be detected.

Summation Check—A redundant check in which groups of digits are summed, usually without regard for overflow, and that sum checked against a previously computed sum to verify accuracy.

Transfer Check—A check on transmitted data by temporarily storing, retransmitting, and comparing.

Twin Check—A continuous duplication check achieved by duplication of hardware.

Clear—To replace information in a storage device by the character zero. *See also* "Erase."

Code (noun)—A system of rules for using a set of symbols to represent data.

Computer Code; Machine Code—The code that the computer hardware was built to interpret and execute.

Instruction Code—The symbols, names, and operation descriptions for all instructions represented by computer code.

Numerical Code—A code in which the symbols used are all numerals.

Pseudo-code—An arbitrary code, independent of the hardware of a computer and designed for convenience in programming, that must be translated into computer code if it is to direct the computer.

Code for computer (verb)—To express a program in a code that a specific computer was built or programmed to interpret and execute.

Collate—To produce a single sequence of items, ordered according to some rule (that is, arranged in some orderly sequence), from two or more ordered sequences. The final sequence need not contain all of the data available in the original sets. If, for example, two sets of items are being matched, items that do not match may be discarded. *See also* "Merge."

Command—A pulse, signal, or set of signals initiating one step in the performance of a computer operation. A command is one part of an instruction. *See also* "Instruction."

Common Language—A single code used by devices—typewriters, calculators, transmitters, and others—manufactured by different companies.

Comparator—A device for comparing two different transcriptions of the same information to verify agreement or determine disagreement; a circuit that compares two signals and indicates agreement or disagreement; a signal may be given indicating whether they are equal or unequal.

Compile; Compiler; Compiling Routine; Compilation—*See* items under "Routine."

Complement—A quantity that is derived from a given quantity, expressed to the base n, by one of the following rules and which is frequently used to represent the negative of the given quantity.

(a) Complement on n: subtract each digit of the given quantity from $n-1$, add unity to the least significant digit, and perform all resultant carries. For example, the twos complement of binary 11010 is 00110; the tens complement of decimal 456 is 544.

(b) Complement on $n-1$: subtract each digit of the given quantity from $n-1$. For example, the ones complement of binary 11010 is 00101; the nines complement of decimal 456 is 543.

Computer—Any device capable of accepting data, applying prescribed processes to them, and supplying the results of these processes. The word "computer" in this glossary usually refers to a stored-program digital computer.

> **Analogue Computer**—A computer which calculates by using physical analogues of the variables. Usually a one-to-one correspondence exists between each numerical variable occurring in the problem and a varying physical measurement in the analogue computer. The physical quantities in an analogue computer are varied continuously instead of in discrete steps as in the digital computer; for example, as in the speedometer on a car.

> **Digital Computer**—A computer capable of accepting and operating on only the representations of real numbers, or other characters coded numerically.

> **Stored-program Computer**—A digital computer capable of performing sequences of internally stored instructions, as opposed to calculators on which the sequence is impressed manually. Such computers usually possess the further ability to operate upon the instructions themselves, and to alter the sequence of instructions in accordance with results already calculated.

Conditional Transfer—See items under "Transfer."

Contents—The data stored at any address or in any register.

Control Counter; Program Counter; Instruction Counter; Control Register—A counter built into the control unit and used for sequencing instructions to be executed. It normally contains the address of the next instruction to be performed.

Control Panel—A device for controlling the functions to be performed in a computer or other data-handling machine. The panel is manually wired, and may usually be removed and changed if other functions within machine capabilities are desired.

Control Sequence—Normal order of selection of instructions for execution. In some computers one of the addresses in each instruction specifies the control sequence. In most computers the sequence is consecutive except where a jump occurs.

Control Unit—Portion of the hardware of an automatic digital computer that directs sequence of operations, interprets coded instructions, and initiates proper commands to computer circuits to execute instructions.

Converter—A device for transferring data from one storage medium to another; for example, a punched-card to magnetic-tape converter.

Cycle (noun)—(1) A set of operations repeated as a unit. (2) A non-arithmetical shift in which digits dropped off at one end of a word are returned at the other end in circular fashion; cycle right and cycle left. (3) Maximum access time to internal storage. In the case of a recirculating serial storage element: time for one rotation, for example, of a magnetic drum or of pulses in an acoustic delay line.

Cycle (verb)—To repeat a set of operations a prescribed number of times including, when required, supplying necessary address changes by arithmetical processes or by means of a hardware device, such as a cycle counter, B-box, or index register.

Data—Figures, words, or charts that refer to or describe some situation. See also "Information."

Data Processing—Rearrangement and refinement of raw data into a form suitable for further use.

Debug—To test a program on a computer to find whether it works properly. If mistakes are revealed, they must be traced to their source and corrected.

Delay—The length of time after the close of a reporting period before data pertaining to that period become available. Delay covers the time to process data, and prepare and distribute reports.

Delay Line—See "Acoustic Delay Line."

*Digit—*One of the n symbols of integral value, ranging from 0 to n – 1 inclusive, in a system of numbering with radix n; for example, the ten digits 0, 1, 2, 3, 4, 5, 6, 7, 8, 9 in the decimal system; 0, 1 in the binary system.

Digital Computer—See items under "Computer."

*Down-time—*Time when a computer is malfunctioning or not operating correctly due to machine failure.

*Dummy—*An artificial address, instruction, or other unit of information inserted solely to fulfill prescribed conditions (such as word length or block length) without affecting operations.

Dump—(1) To withdraw all power accidentally or intentionally from a computer. (2) To record the contents of internal storage at a given instant of time, usually as an aid in detecting program mistakes or errors.

Edit—(1) To arrange or rearrange information for the output unit of the computer to print. Editing may involve deletion of unwanted data, selection of pertinent data, insertion of invariant symbols, such as page numbers and typewriter characters, and application of standard processes, such as zero-suppression. (2) Editing is done on input data to insure their accuracy and relevance prior to key punching.

*Electronic Data-processing System—*A machine system capable of receiving, storing, operating on, and recording data without the intermediate use of tabulating cards, and which also possesses: (1) the ability to store internally at least some instructions for data-processing operations, and (2) the means for locating and controlling access to data stored internally. *See also* "Stored Program" under "Computer."

*End-of-file—*Automatic procedures to handle tapes when the end of an input or output tape is reached. A reflective spot, called a record mark, is placed on the physical end of the tape to signal the end.

*Erase—*To replace all binary digits in a storage device by binary zeros. In a binary computer, *erasing* is equivalent to *clearing*, while in a coded decimal computer where the pulse code for decimal zero may contain binary ones, *clearing* leaves decimal zero while *erasing* leaves all-zero pulse codes.

*Error—*Amount of loss of precision in a quantity; difference between an accurate quantity and its calculated approximation. (*Errors* occur in numerical methods; *mistakes* occur in programs, coding, data transcription, and operating; *malfunctions* occur in computers.)

*Inherited Error—*Error in the initial values; especially, an error inherited from previous steps in a step-by-step integration.

*Rounding Error—*Error resulting from deleting less significant digits of a quantity and applying some rule of correction to the part retained.

*Truncation Error—*Error resulting from the use of only a finite number of terms of an infinite series, or from the approximation of operations in the infinitesimal calculus by operations in the calculus of finite differences.

*Exception-principle System—*An information system or data-processing system which reports on situations only when actual results differ from planned results. When results occur within a "normal range," they are not reported.

*Excess-three Code—*A binary-coded decimal system which represents each decimal digit as the corresponding binary number plus three. For example, the decimal digits 0, 1, 8, 9 are represented as 0011, 0100, 1011, 1100, respectively. The nines complement of the decimal digit corresponds (also in excess-three code) to the ones complement of the four binary digits.

External Storage—See items under "Storage."

*Extract—*To obtain certain digits from a machine word as may be specified. Or, to replace contents of specific columns of another machine word, depending on the instruction. Or, to remove from a set of items of information all those items that meet some arbitrary condition.

Feasibility Study—A study in which a projection of how a proposed system might operate in a particular organization is made to provide the basis for a decision to change the existing system.

Field—A set of one or more characters constituting a unit of data. *Contrast* "Word." (A field need not correspond in length to a word.)

File (noun)—A collection of information or data arranged for convenient reference.

File Maintenance—Modification of a file to incorporate changes that do *not* involve arithmetical operations; for example, insertions, deletions, transfers, and corrections.

File Processing—Modification of a file to incorporate changes that do involve arithmetical operations; for example, receipts, issues, returns, and losses of stock items.

Fixed-point Arithmetic—A method of calculation in which operations take place in an invariant manner, without regard for location of the radix point. This is illustrated by desk calculators or slide rules, with which the operator must keep track of the decimal point. Similarly with many automatic computers, in which the location of the radix point is the programmer's responsibility. *Contrast* "Floating-point Arithmetic."

Flip-flop—An electronic circuit having two stable states, two input lines, and two corresponding output lines such that a signal exists on either one of the output lines if and only if the last pulse received by the flip-flop is on the corresponding input line. A flip-flop can store one binary digit (bit) of information.

Floating Address—*See* "Symbolic Address" under "Address."

Floating-point Arithmetic—A method of calculation which automatically accounts for the location of the radix point. This is usually accomplished by handling the number as a signed mantissa times the radix raised to an integral exponent. For example, the decimal number $+88.3$ might be written as $+.883 \times 10^2$; the binary number $+.0011$ as $+.11 \times 2^{-2}$.

Flow Chart—A systems analysis tool providing a graphical presentation of a procedure. Includes block diagrams, routine sequence diagrams, general flow charts, and so forth.

Gate Circuit—An electronic circuit with one or more inputs and one output, with the property that a pulse goes out on the output line if and only if some specified combination of pulses occurs on the input lines. Gate circuits provide much of the hardware by means of which logical operations are built into a computer.

Hardware—The electric, electronic, and mechanical equipment used for processing data consisting of cabinets, racks, tubes, transistors, wires, motors, and such.

IDP—*See* "Integrated Data Processing."

Index Register—A register to which an arbitrary integer, usually one, is added (or subtracted) upon the execution of each machine instruction. The register may be reset to zero or an arbitrary number. Used with indexable instructions to get "effective" instruction addresses during execution. Also called "cycle counter" and "B-box."

Information—Knowledge which was not previously known to its receiver. Information can be derived from data only to the extent that the data are accurate, timely, unexpected, and relevant to the subject under consideration.

Information System—The network of all communication methods within an organization. Information may be derived from many sources other than a data-processing unit, such as by telephone, by contact with other people, or by looking at an operation.

In-line Processing—The processing of data without sorting or any other prior treatment other than storage.

X *Input*—(1) The process of introducing data into the internal storage of the computer. (2) [not recommended] The process of introducing data into secondary storage.

Instruction—A set of characters which defines an operation together with one or more addresses (or no address) and which, as a unit, causes the computer to operate accordingly on the indicated quantities.

Instruction Code—*See* items under "Code."

X *Integrated Data Processing*—A system designed as a whole so that data are recorded at the point of origin in a form suitable for subsequent processing without any human copying.

Interlace—To assign successive addresses to physically separated storage locations on a magnetic drum or other rotating storage device in such a way as to reduce average access time. *See* "Minimum-access Programming."

Internal Storage—*See* items under "Storage."

Interpret, Interpreter, Interpretive Routine, Interpretation—*See* items under "Routine."

Jump—*See* "Transfer."

Justify—*See* "Normalize."

Key—A field used for identification of a record.

X *Key-punch (noun)*—A typewriter-like machine for recording data on punched cards.

Latency—In a serial storage device: The time required to locate the first bit (or character) in a particular storage location. Access time for such a device includes latency plus the time to read out or write in a complete word.

Logical Design—Computer design from the viewpoint of data flow within the computer without consideration of the hardware.

X *Logical Operation*—(1) An operation in which a decision affecting the future sequence of instructions is automatically made by the computer. The decision is based upon comparisons between all or some of the characters in an arithmetic register and their counterparts in any other register on a less than, equal to, or greater than basis; or between certain characters in arithmetic registers and built-in standards. (2) A shifting operation in which the digits dropped off one end of a word are returned to the other in circular fashion. (3) Operations on a word on a character-by-character basis without regard for other characters as in "logical and" and "logical or" operations.

Loop—*See* "Cycle."

X *Magnetic-core Storage*—A storage device consisting of magnetically permeable binary cells arrayed in a two-dimensional matrix. (A large storage unit contains many such matrices.) Each cell (core) is wire-wound and may be polarized in either of two directions for the storage of one binary digit. The direction of polarization can be sensed by a wire running through the core.

X *Magnetic-disk Storage*—A storage device consisting of magnetically coated disks accessible to a reading and writing arm in much the manner of an automatic record player. Binary data are stored on the surface of each disk as small, magnetized spots arranged in circular tracks around the disk. The arm is moved mechanically to the desired disk and then to the desired track on that disk. Data from a given track are read or written sequentially as the disk rotates.

/ *Magnetic-drum Storage*—A storage device consisting of a rotating cylindrical drum surfaced with a magnetic coating. Binary data are stored as small, magnetized spots arranged in closed tracks around the drum. A magnetic reading and writing head is associated with each track so that the desired track can be selected by electric switching. Data from a given track are read or written sequentially as the drum rotates.

Magnetic Read-write Head—A small electromagnet used for reading, recording, or erasing polarized spots on a magnetic surface.

Magnetic-tape Storage—A storage device consisting of metal or plastic tape coated with magnetic material. Binary data are stored as small, magnetized spots arranged in column form across the width of the tape. A read-write head is usually associated with each row of magnetized spots so that one column can be read or written at a time as the tape is moved relative to the head.

Malfunction—Incorrect function occurring in equipment.

Mantissa—The decimal part of a logarithm; the normalized number.

Masking—An operation that replaces characters in the accumulator with characters from a specified storage location that correspond to the "ones" in the mask which is in a specified storage location or register.

Master Clock—The electronic or electric source of standard timing signals, often called "clock pulses," required for sequencing computer operation. This source usually consists of a timing pulse generator, a cycling unit, and sets of special pulses that occur at given intervals of time. Usually in synchronous computers the basic time frequency employed is the frequency of the clock pulses.

✕ *Matrix*—(1) A rectangular array of numbers, subject to mathematical operations, such as addition, multiplication, and inversion, according to specified rules. Any table is a matrix. (2) An array of circuit elements, such as diodes, wires, magnetic cores, and relays, arranged and designed to perform a specified function; for example, conversion from one number system to another.

Matrix Printing—The printing of alphanumerical characters by means of the appropriate selection of pins contained in a rectangular array on the printing head.

✕ *Memory*—Synonymous with "storage." The term "memory" carries "magic brain" connotations which are considered undesirable; hence, "storage" is preferred.

✕ *Merge*—To produce a single sequence of items, ordered according to some rule (that is, arranged in some orderly sequence), from two or more sequences previously ordered according to the same rule, without changing the items in size, structure, or total number. Merging is a special kind of collating.

Microsecond—A millionth of a second; "μs."

Millisecond—A thousandth of a second; one thousand microseconds; "ms."

Minimum-access Programming—*See* items under "Programming."

Multiplex—The process of transferring data from several storage devices operating at relatively low transfer rates to one storage device operating at a high transfer rate in such a manner that the high-speed device is not obliged to "wait" for the low-speed units.

Normal Range—A range of values with specified limits used so that as long as results of a particular plan of action fall within the range the results are considered satisfactory. This concept is used in "exception-principle systems" for reporting only results which are not within the normal range.

Normalize (in Floating-point Arithmetic)—To adjust the exponent in such a manner that the radix point of the mantissa appears in a prescribed, standard location with respect to the leading non-zero digit.

Octal—Pertaining to the number 8; a number system whose radix is the quantity 8. The octal and binary number systems bear a convenient relationship to one another because each is an integral power of 2.

"On-the-fly" Printing—High-speed printing which makes use of rotating print wheels and fast-acting hammers which press the paper against the wheels at the instant that specified symbols are in position. Each character position in a line has a print wheel containing all symbols.

✕ *On-line Equipment*—Equipment for which the transfer of data to or from the unit is under direction of the control unit of the computer.

Operand—Any one of the quantities entering into or arising from an operation. An operand may be an argument, a result, a parameter, or an indication of the location of the next instruction.

Operation—(1) A defined action. (2) The action specified by a single computer instruction or pseudo-instruction. (3) An arithmetical, logical, or transferral unit of a problem, usually executed under the direction of a subroutine.

Operator's Console—Equipment which provides for manual intervention and for monitoring computer operation.

Optimum Programming—*See* items under "Programming."

Output—Process of transferring data from internal storage of a computer to some other storage device.

Overflow—In an arithmetical operation, the generation of a quantity that is too large for the capacity of the register or location which is to receive the result.

Pack (data)—To combine two or more different fields into one machine word. For example, the fields of an employee's pay number, weekly pay rate, and tax exemptions may be stored together in one word, each of these fields being assigned a different location within the word.

Parallel—The internal handling of data in groups, all elements of a group being handled simultaneously. *Contrast* "Serial."

    Parallel Access—(1) Simultaneous access to all bits in a storage location comprising a character or word. (2) Equal access time for any bit, character, or word in a storage device.

    Parallel Transfer—Simultaneous transfer of all bits in a storage location comprising a character or word.

Parameter—A quantity in a mathematical calculation which may be assigned any arbitrary value.

    Preset Parameter—A parameter incorporated into a subroutine during input.

    Program Parameter—A parameter incorporated into a subroutine during computation. A program parameter frequently comprises a word stored relative to either the subroutine or the entry point and dealt with by the subroutine during each reference. It may be altered by the routine or it may vary from one point of entry to another.

Parity Check—*See* items under "Check."

Patch—A section of coding inserted into a routine (usually by explicitly transferring control from the routine to the patch and back again) to correct a mistake or alter the routine.

Permanent Storage—*See* "Volatility of Storage," under "Storage."

Plugboard—*See* "Control Panel."

Positional Notation—The procedure used in conventional number systems wherein the value assigned to a particular digit is determined by the symbol used (for example, 3 v. 6) and by the position of the symbol relative to the radix point (for example, 300.0 v. 60.0).

Post Mortem—*See* items under "Routine."

Precision—The degree of exactness with which a quantity is stated; a relative term often based on the number of significant digits in a measurement. Contrast with "accuracy," which refers to the absence of error regardless of precision. For example, a two-digit number is accurate if correctly stated; whereas a five-digit number may be inaccurate, despite having greater precision.

Pre-store—(1) To store a quantity in an available or convenient location before it is required in a routine. (2) To set an initial value for the address of an operand or a cycle index.

Program (noun)—A plan for the automatic solution of a problem. A complete program includes plans for the transcription of data, coding for the computer, and plans for the absorption of the results into the system. The list of coded instructions is called a "routine."

Program Tape or Drum—A tape or drum used to store a complete routine for future input. In the event that the length of the routine exceeds the available internal storage capacity, it will be read in and operated upon by the computer one segment at a time.

Programming—The process of creating a program.

Automatic Programming—A way of writing programs based on a problem-oriented language and an executive routine for translating this language to machine language.

Minimum-access Programming; Minimum-latency Programming; Optimum Programming—In reference to serial storage systems: a program which, by judicious arrangement of data and instructions in storage, reduces actual latency to appreciably less than expected (average) random-access latency.

Pulse (Electric)—A momentary and significant rise or fall in voltage level. Pulses provide the primary means for transmission of data into a computer. The presence or absence of a pulse during a particular time period is interpreted as binary information.

Punched Card—A card of standard size and shape upon which data may be stored in the form of punched holes. The hole locations are arranged in columns, a given pattern of holes in a column representing one character. (Cards are usually of 80 or 90 columns but may have more or fewer columns.) The holes may be sensed mechanically, electrically, or photoelectrically.

Punched-card Field—A set of columns fixed as to number and position into which the same item or items of data are regularly entered.

Punched Tape—Tape, usually paper, upon which data may be stored in the form of punched holes. Hole locations are arranged in columns across the width of the tape. There are usually 5 to 8 positions (channels) per column, with data represented by a binary-coded alphanumerical decimal system. All holes in a column are sensed simultaneously in a manner similar to that for punched cards.

Radix—The base of a number system; that is, a quantity that defines a system of representing numbers by positional notation; the number of digit symbols required by a number system. Examples:

System	Radix
decimal	10
octal	8
quinary	5
binary	2

Radix Point—The dot that marks the separation between the integral and fractional parts of a number. In the decimal number system, the decimal point; in the binary number system, the binary point.

Random Access—Access to storage under conditions in which the next location from which data are to be obtained is in no way dependent on the location of the previously obtained data.

Read—(1) To copy, usually from one form of storage to another, particularly from external or secondary storage to internal storage. (2) To sense the meaning of arrangements of hardware.

Real-time Operation—Processing data in synchronism with a physical process in such a fashion that results of data processing are useful to the physical operation.

Record (noun)—A set of one or more consecutive fields on a related subject, as an employee's payroll record. Contrast "Block." A record need not correspond in length to a block, although such correspondence is often useful.

Reference Record—Output of a compiler that lists the operations and their positions in the final specific routine and contains information describing the segmentation and storage allocation of the routine.

Register—A device for the temporary storage of one or more words to facilitate arithmetical, logical, or transferral operations. Examples are the accumulator, address, index, instruction, and M-Q registers.

Register Capacity—The upper and lower limits of the numbers which may be processed in a register.

Re-run Point—One of a set of planned-for points in a program, used so that if an error is detected between two such points, to re-run the problem it is only necessary to go back to the last re-run point Re-run points are often three to five minutes apart so that little time is required for a re-run. All information pertinent to a re-run is available in standby storage during the whole time from one re-run point to the next.

Rounding Error—The error resulting from dropping certain less significant digits of a quantity, and applying some adjustment to the more significant digits retained. Also called "round-off error." A common round-off rule is to take the quantity to the nearest digit. Thus Pi, 3.14159265..., rounded to four decimals is 3.1416.

✕ *Routine*—A set of coded instructions arranged in proper sequence to direct the computer to perform a desired operation or series of operations. *See also* "Subroutine."

Compile; Compiler; Compiling Routine; Compilation—An executive routine that, *before* the desired computation is started, translates a program expressed in pseudo-code into machine code (or into another pseudo-code for further translation by an interpreter). In accomplishing the translation, the compiler may be required to:

Adapt—To specialize performance of the task at hand by means of preset parameters.

Allocate—To assign storage locations to the main routines and subroutines, thereby fixing the absolute values of any symbolic addresses. In some cases allocation may require segmentation. *See* "Segment."

Assemble—To integrate the subroutines (supplied, selected, or generated) into the main routine; that is, to adapt, incorporate, orient.

Convert—To change numerical information from one number base to another (for example, decimal to binary) or from some form of fixed point to some form of floating-point representation, or *vice versa.*

Decode—To ascertain intended meaning of individual characters or groups of characters in the pseudo-coded program.

Generate—To produce a needed subroutine from parameters and skeletal coding.

Incorporate—To place in storage.

Orient—To change relative and symbolic addresses to absolute form.

Select—To choose a needed subroutine from a file of subroutines.

Diagnostic Routine—A specific routine designed to locate either a malfunction in the computer or a mistake in coding.

Executive Routine; Master Routine—A routine designed to process and control other routines. A routine used in realizing "automatic coding."

General Routine—A routine expressed in computer coding designed to solve a class of problems, specializing to a specific problem when appropriate parametric values are supplied.

Generator—A general routine that accepts a set of parameters and causes the computer to compute a specific routine for further use. Among other things, the parameters may specify the input-output devices to use, designate subroutines, or describe the form of a record.

Interpret, Interpreter, Interpretive Routine, Interpretation—An executive routine which, during the course of data-handling operations, translates a stored pseudo-code program into a machine code and at once performs the indicated operations by means of subroutines.

Post-mortem Routine—A routine which, either automatically or on demand, prints data concerning contents of registers and storage locations when the routine is stopped in order to assist in locating a mistake in coding.

Re-run Routine; Rollback Routine—A routine designed to be used in the wake of a computer malfunction or a coding or operating mistake to reconstitute a routine from the last previous re-run point.

Service Routine—A routine designed to assist in actual operation of a computer. Tape comparison, block location, certain post mortems, and correction routines fall in this class.

Simulator Routine—An interpretive routine to enable one computer to operate with instructions and coding designed for another computer.

Specific Routine—A routine expressed in specific computer coding designed to solve a particular mathematical, logical, or data-handling problem.

Test Routine—A routine designed to test whether a computer is functioning properly.

Trace Routine—A routine used to observe how the object program (the program to be run) operates while it is being executed.

Translator Routine—A compiler that converts the operations specified in the main program into the object program before execution.

Search, Binary—A technique for finding a particular item in an ordered set of items by repeatedly dividing in half the portion of the ordered set containing the sought-for item until only the sought-for item remains.

Search Time—Time required to locate a particular field of data in storage. Searching requires a comparison of each field with a predetermined standard until an identity is obtained. *Contrast* "Access Time," which is based upon locating data by means of the address of its storage location.

Secondary Storage—*See* items under "Storage."

Segment (noun)—In a routine too long to fit into internal storage, a part short enough to be stored entirely in the internal storage and containing the coding necessary to call in and jump automatically to other segments. Routines which exceed internal storage capacity may be automatically divided into segments by a compiler.

Sentinel—A symbol marking the beginning or the end of some element of information, such as a field, item, block, tape, or tag.

Sequential Control—The manner of control of a computer in which instructions to it are set up in a sequence and are fed in that sequence to the computer during solution of a problem.

Serial—The internal handling of data in sequential fashion. *Contrast* "Parallel."

Serial Access—Sequential access to elements of data (bits, characters, or words) within all or part of a storage device. For example, storage in which words, within a group of words (as on a track of a magnetic drum), appear one after the other in time sequence is said to be serial by word. Access may still be parallel by character or by bit, despite being serial by word.

Serial Transfer—The transfer of elements of data in sequence over a single path in consecutive time sequence.

Shift—To move the characters of a unit of data columnwise right or left.

Arithmetical Shift; Numerical Shift—To multiply or divide a quantity by a power of the number base.

Cyclic Shift; Logical or Non-arithmetical Shift—A shift in which the digits dropped off at one end of a word are returned at the other in circular fashion.

Simulation—A pseudo-experimental analysis of an operating system by means of mathematical or physical models which operate in a time-sequential manner similar to the system itself.

Skip—An instruction to proceed to the next instruction; a "blank" instruction.

Sorting—The process of arranging data into some desired order according to rules dependent upon a key or field contained by each item.

Digital Sorting—To sort first the keys on the least significant digit, and to re-sort on each higher-order digit until the items are sorted on the most significant digit. A punched-card technique.

Four-tape Sorting—Merge-sorting in which input data are supplied on two tapes and are sorted into incomplete sequences alternately on two output tapes. The output tapes are used for input on the succeeding pass, resulting in longer and longer sequences after each pass until the data are all in one sequence on one output tape.

Merge Sorting—To produce a single sequence of items, ordered according to some rule, from two or more previously unordered sequences, without changing the items in size, structure, or total number. Although more than one pass may be required for a complete sorting, items are selected during each pass on the basis of the entire key.

Storage—A device capable of receiving data, retaining them for an indefinite period of time, and supplying them upon command.

Buffer Storage—(1) Secondary storage used exclusively for assembly and transfer of data between internal and external storage. (2) Storage used to facilitate transfer of data between any two storage devices whose input and output speeds are not synchronized.

Dynamic Storage—Refers to mobility of stored data in time and space. Acoustic delay lines, in which stored data are constantly in motion relative to storage medium and require continuous regeneration, are an example of a *dynamic* storage device. Magnetic-core storage, in which stored data are fixed in time and space, is an example of a *static* storage device.

Erasability of Storage—Ability to erase data that are recorded in a particular location and replace them with new data. Storage media are said to be *erasable* (for example, magnetic tape) or *non-erasable* (for example, punched cards).

External Storage—Storage from which the data to be operated upon are normally obtained. It may be under the control of the computer, but data to be operated upon must be transferred to secondary or internal storage before operations commence, and are returned to external storage only after operations are completed. External storage devices usually have larger capacities and lower access speeds than internal and secondary storage.

Internal Storage—Storage which is directly accessible to the arithmetic and control units of a computer. It is usually used for storage of instructions and for data currently being operated upon.

Secondary Storage—Storage whose primary function is to augment the capacity of internal storage for handling data and instructions. Data from secondary storage must be transferred to internal storage to become operable.

Volatility of Storage—The tendency of a storage device to lose data when the electric power is cut off. Storage media may be classed as *volatile* (for example, electrostatic storage tubes) or *non-volatile* (for example, magnetic tape).

Storage Capacity—Number of units of data that may be stored in a given storage device at one time. It is variously expressed in terms of bits, characters, or words.

Storage Density—The number of characters stored per unit length or area of storage medium (for example, number of characters per inch of magnetic tape).

Storage Location—A storage position holding one machine word and usually having a specific address.

Stored Program—*See* "Stored-program Computer," under "Computer."

Structure (of a system)—Refers to the *nature* of the chain of command, the origin and type of data collected, the form and destination of results, and the procedures used to control operations. *Contrast* "Technique."

Sub-optimization—The process of fulfilling or optimizing some chosen objective which is an integral part of a broader objective. Usually the broad objective and lower-level objective are different.

Subroutine—The set of instructions in machine code to direct the computer to carry out a well-defined mathematical or logical operation; a part of a routine. A subroutine is often written with symbolic relative addresses even when the routine to which it belongs is not.

Closed Subroutine—A subroutine not stored in its proper place in the linear operational sequence, but stored away from the routine which refers to it. Such a subroutine is entered by a jump, and provision is made to return, that is, to jump back to the proper point in the main routine at the end of the subroutine.

Dynamic Subroutine—A subroutine which involves parameters, such as decimal point position or item size, from which a relatively coded subroutine is derived. The computer itself is expected to adjust or generate the subroutine according to the parametric values chosen.

Library Subroutine—A standard and proven subroutine which is kept "on file" for use at any time.

Open Subroutine—A subroutine inserted directly into the linear operational sequence, not entered by a jump. Such a subroutine must be recopied at each point where it is needed in a routine.

Static Subroutine—A subroutine which involves no parameters other than the addresses of the operands.

Summary Punch—A punched-card machine which may be attached by cable to another machine (for example, a tabulator), and which will punch out on a card information produced, calculated, or summarized by the other machine.

Synchronous (Computer)—A mode of computer operation in which performance of individual commands occurs at equally spaced intervals as determined by a "master clock" within the computer. *Contrast* "Asynchronous."

System—Any regular or special method or plan of procedure.

Systems Analysis—An orderly study of the detailed procedure for collecting, organizing, and evaluating information within an organization, with the objective of improving control over operations of the organization.

Table Look-up—Computer operation which consults a stored table directly for desired words, reference factors, or parameter values.

✗   *Tabulating System*—Any group of machines capable of entering, converting, receiving, classifying, computing, and recording data by means of tabulating cards, and in which tabulating cards are used for storing data and communicating them within the system.

✝   *Tabulator*—A punched-card machine which takes in punched cards and instructions and produces lists, totals, and tabulations of the information on separate forms or one continuous paper.

Technique (of a data-processing system)—Refers to the *method* used to collect data inputs, to process them, and to convert processed data into reports or some other usable form. *Contrast* "Structure."

Trace—*See* item under "Routine."

Track—A sequence of binary cells arranged so that data may be read or written from one cell at a time in serial fashion. For example, a track on a magnetic drum is a path one bit wide around the circumference of the drum. *See also* "Channel."

Transceiver—Equipment for card-to-card transmission by way of telephone or telegraph wires.

Transfer—(1) To transfer control by means of an instruction or signal which specifies location of next instruction and directs computer to that instruction; to jump. A transfer is used to alter the normal sequence control of the computer. (2) To transfer data; to copy, exchange, read, record, store, transmit, transport, or write data.

Conditional Transfer—To transfer control only if some specified logical condition is satisfied. If the condition is not satisfied, the next instruction is taken in normal sequence. *See also* "Logical Operation."

Unconditional Transfer—A jump is made to occur under all possible conditions.

Transistor—A small, solid-state, semiconducting device, ordinarily using germanium, that performs nearly all functions of an electron tube, especially amplification.

Trapping Mode—A scheme used mainly in program diagnostic procedures for certain computers. If the trapping mode flip-flop is set and the program includes any one of certain instructions, the instruction is not performed but the next instruction is taken from location 0. Program counter contents are saved in order to resume the program after executing the diagnostic procedure.

Underflow—In an arithmetical operation, the generation of a quantity too small to be stored by the register or location that is to receive the result.

Variable-cycle Operation—Operation of a computer whereby any cycle of operation may be longer or shorter than the average. An asynchronous computer has a variable cycle.

✗   *Verify*—(1) To check, usually with an automatic machine, one typing or recording of data against another in order to minimize the number of human errors or mistakes in the data transcription. (2) In preparing data for a computer, to make certain that data prepared are correct.

Word—A set of characters which occupies one storage location and is treated by the computer circuits as a unit and transported as such. Ordinarily a word is treated by the control unit as an instruction, and by the arithmetic unit as a quantity. Word lengths are fixed or variable depending on the particular computer. *Contrast* "Field."

Write—(1) To copy information usually from internal to external storage. (2) To transfer information to an output medium. (3) To record information in a register, location, or other storage device or medium.

Zero Suppression—Elimination of non-significant zeros to the left of the integral part of a quantity before printing; part of the editing routine.

ILLUSTRATIONS

LIST OF ILLUSTRATIONS

Figures

Tables

ACKNOWLEDGMENTS
OF ILLUSTRATIONS

We are indebted to the following organizations for supplying material for figures and tables, as indicated:

Ampex Corporation: Fig. 4-12

Bendix Computer Division of Bendix of Aviation Corporation:
Entries in Tables 7-1 to 7-11

Burroughs Corporation: Fig 4-2, Fig. 5-2, Fig. 5-3, Fig. 5-5, entries in Tables 7-1 to 7-11

Commercial Controls Corporation: Fig. 4-1

Commonwealth Edison Company: Fig. 6-6

Control Data Corporation: Entries in Tables 7-1 to 7-11

Farrington Manufacturing Company: Fig. 4-9

The First National Bank of Boston: Fig. 4-8

International Business Machines Corporation: Fig. 2-1, Fig. 2-2, Fig. 4-3, Fig. 4-4, Fig. 4-11, Fig. 4-13, Fig. 4-15, Fig. 4-19, Fig. 5-4, Fig. 6-6, entries in Tables 7-1 to 7-11, Fig. 11-4, Fig. 11-5, Fig. 11-6

Minneapolis Honeywell: Entries in Tables 7-1 to 7-11

Monroe Calculating Machine Company: Fig. 4-4

Moore Business Forms Inc., Fig. 2-3

The National Cash Register Company: Fig. 4-2, entries in Tables 7-1 to 7-11

New England Telephone & Telegraph Co., Fig. 2-3

Philco Corporation: Entries in Tables 7-1 to 7-11

Radio Corporation of America: Fig. 2-5, entries in Tables 7-1 to 7-11

Remington Rand Univac, Division of Sperry Rand: Fig. 1-3, Fig. 2-1, Fig. 2-2, Fig. 2-4, Fig. 4-5, Fig. 4-7, Fig. 4-10, Fig. 4-16, Fig. 6-6, entries in Tables 7-1 to 7-11, Fig. 8-2, Fig. 11-2, Fig. 14-1

Royal McBee Corporation: Entries in Tables 7-1 to 7-11

Stromberg-Carlson, a Division of General Dynamics: Fig. 4-17

Sylvania Electric Products Inc.: Fig. 2-4, Fig. 5-1, Fig. 6-6, entries in Tables 7-1 to 7-11, Fig. 14-2

The Teleregister Corporation: Fig. 4-14

Underwood Samas: Fig. 2-1

United Shoe Machinery Corporation: Fig. 4-12

United States Department of the Army, Headquarters: Fig. 14-10, Fig. 15-1, Fig. 17-1

Western Union Telegraph Company: Fig. 4-18

INDEX

INDEX

NOTE: This index covers the material in Chapters 1-19 of this book. It is also suggested that the Glossary and other appendices be consulted as necessary.

A